Counseling and Psychotherapy

Counseling and Psychotherapy

A CHRISTIAN PERSPECTIVE

Siang-Yang Tan

Baker Academic

a division of Baker Publishing Group
Grand Rapids, Michigan

Published by Baker Academic
a division of Baker Publishing Group
P.O. Box 6287, Grand Rapids, MI 49516-6287
www.bakeracademic.com

Printed in the United States of America

Library of Congress Cataloging-in-Publication Data
Tan, Siang-Yang, 1954–
    Counseling and psychotherapy : a Christian perspective / Siang-Yang Tan.
       p.   cm.
    Includes bibliographical references and index.
    ISBN 978-0-8010-2966-0 (pbk.)
       1. Counseling—Religious aspects—Christianity. 2. Counseling. 3. Psychotherapy—Religious aspects—Christianity. 4. Psychotherapy. I. Title.
    BR115.C69T36 2011
    261.8′322—dc22   2010026145

11   12   13   14   15   16   17   7   6   5   4   3   2   1

To Carolyn Li-Jun Tan, my daughter, for her honest and helpful editorial feedback that has made this book a better one, with deep gratitude, love, and prayers.

Contents

Preface

Several good introductory texts on counseling and psychotherapy are available, but they are written mainly from a secular perspective (e.g., Corey 2009; Corsini and Wedding 2008; Prochaska and Norcross 2010; Sharf 2008). However, there is a significant lack of texts written from a distinctively Christian perspective.

Stanton Jones and Richard Butman (1991) wrote a very helpful and comprehensive Christian appraisal and critique of modern psychotherapies over fifteen years ago, but they did not adequately cover counseling techniques. Don Browning and Terry Cooper (2004) have updated their book on religious thought and the modern psychologies or psychotherapies, but it contains mainly theoretical and theological critiques and perspectives. More recently, Mark Yarhouse, Richard Butman, and Barrett McRay (2005) have provided a comprehensive Christian appraisal and critique of modern psychopathologies, but it does not focus on counseling and psychotherapy per se. Neil Anderson, Terry Zuehlke, and Julianne Zuehlke (2000) coauthored a text on Christ-centered therapy, but it is not a comprehensive survey of the major approaches to counseling and psychotherapy. Similarly, several recent books on Christian counseling (including Clinton and Ohlschlager 2002; Clinton, Hart, and Ohlschlager 2005; Collins 2007; Malony and Augsburger 2007; and McMinn and Campbell 2007), although helpful, do not include comprehensive descriptions of the major approaches to counseling and psychotherapy that are usually covered in introductory texts in this area.

The present text has therefore been written to meet a crucial need for a book on counseling and psychotherapy that provides substantial descriptions of ten major approaches to counseling and psychotherapy, with appropriate biblical, Christian critiques and perspectives on each major approach. Hypothetical transcripts of interventions in each major approach are included to give readers and students a better sense of the clinical work involved. The latest research findings are also covered.

In addition to these major features, a unique part of the present text is the final section, which consists of several chapters describing a Christian approach to counseling and psychotherapy that is Christ centered, biblically based, and Spirit filled. This new text on counseling and psychotherapy from a Christian perspective will be useful to professors or teachers and students in Christian undergraduate and graduate programs in counseling and related people-helping fields such as clinical psychology, counseling psychology, professional counseling, marital and family therapy, social work, psychiatry, psychiatric nursing, and pastoral counseling; clinicians, especially Christian counselors and psychotherapists in practice; pastors, chaplains, lay counselors, and other caregivers in churches and parachurch organizations; seminary students; Christians who have graduated from secular graduate programs in counseling-related fields; and anyone else interested in increasing his or her counseling knowledge and skills from a distinctively Christian perspective.

I trust and pray that this new text will be a real blessing to you as you read and use it.

Acknowledgments

I t has taken me a few years to complete the writing of this major textbook on counseling and psychotherapy from a Christian perspective. I could not have done it without the support and prayers of many people—and the grace of God.

First, I want to thank Brian Bolger, managing editor at Baker Academic, who approached me about writing this textbook and helped me in the final process of getting it published, and Jim Kinney, associate publisher and editorial director of Baker Academic and Brazos Press, who patiently supported me during the editorial revision of the book. I am deeply grateful to Jim for his help and understanding when deadlines had to be extended and for his excellent editorial feedback. An anonymous independent reader provided helpful suggestions and comments for which I am grateful.

I also want to thank the many friends and intercessors who provided prayer support for me when I was writing this book, especially the Wednesday night prayer meeting group and the pastoral and church staff at my church, the prayer partners of RENOVARE and the RENOVARE Board/Team, and the members of my small group. I also want to mention, with deep gratitude, two of my special prayer partners at Fuller: Jeffrey Bjorck and John Martin, both professors of psychology.

Special thanks to Fuller Theological Seminary for graciously granting me two one-quarter sabbaticals in the fall of 2007 and 2008, during which I wrote much of the book. I gratefully acknowledge the excellent administrative and word-processing help of Janneke Last and Daniel Groot, as well as of Sharon Nambiar, Katy Riddell, and Marcia Hyde at Fuller and Lynn Mori at my church.

My daughter, Carolyn, provided much honest and helpful editorial feedback, which has made the book a better one. I am very grateful to her for doing this while completing her studies and graduating from Loyola Law School in Los Angeles. I have therefore dedicated this book to her. I am also deeply thankful for the love, patience, support, and prayers of Angela, my wife, and for the interest and support of Andrew, my son.

Above all, I want to humbly thank God for his guidance, wisdom, and strength without which this book could not have been completed. To him be all the glory!

Basic Issues in the Practice of Counseling and Psychotherapy

1

Overview of Counseling and Psychotherapy

Theory, Research, and Practice

Sigmund Freud (1856–1939), the founder of psychoanalysis, is often credited with the birth of psychotherapy, or the "talking cure." However, the deep roots of counseling and psychotherapy go back many centuries before Freud. Today the field of counseling and psychotherapy is large and diverse. There has been a proliferation of major therapies in the past fifty years: from thirty-six systems of psychotherapy identified by R. A. Harper in 1959 to over four hundred today (Prochaska and Norcross 2010, 1). Even the definitions of counseling and psychotherapy differ from author to author and from textbook to textbook. Most people think of counseling and psychotherapy as involving a professional counselor or therapist helping clients to deal with their problems in living. Let us take a closer look at some definitions of counseling and psychotherapy in this introductory overview chapter.

Definitions of Counseling and Psychotherapy

There are many different definitions of psychotherapy, none of which is precise (Corsini and Wedding 2008). James Prochaska and John Norcross (2010) have chosen to use the following working definition of psychotherapy (from Norcross 1990, 218): "Psychotherapy is the informed and intentional application of clinical methods and interpersonal stances derived from established psychological principles for the purpose of assisting people to modify their behaviors, cognitions, emotions, and/or other personal characteristics in directions that the participants deem desirable" (3–4).

Similarly, there are also several possible definitions of counseling. Christian psychologist Gary Collins has defined counseling as "a relationship between two or more persons in which one person (the counselor) seeks to advise, encourage and/or assist another person or persons (the counselee[s]) to deal more effectively with the problems of life" (1972, 13). He further states: "Unlike psychotherapy, counseling rarely aims to radically alter or remold personality" (14). Some authors therefore try to differentiate counseling and psychotherapy on a continuum, with psychotherapy dealing with deeper problems and seeking to significantly change personality. However, most authors in the mental health field today do not differentiate between counseling and psychotherapy (see, e.g., Corey 2009; Day 2004; Fall, Holden, and Marquis 2004; Parrott 2003; J. Sommers-Flanagan and Sommers-Flanagan 2004), agreeing with Charles Truax and Robert Carkhuff (1967), who, years ago, already used the two terms interchangeably. In fact, C. H. Patterson emphatically asserts that no essential differences exist between counseling and psychotherapy (1973, xiv). This is the view I take in this textbook on counseling and psychotherapy from a Christian perspective.

John Sommers-Flanagan and Rita Sommers-Flanagan also use counseling and psychotherapy interchangeably and define it as a process that involves "*a trained person who practices the artful application of scientifically derived principles of establishing professional helping relationships with persons who seek assistance in resolving large or small psychological or relational problems. This is accomplished through ethically defined means and involves, in the broadest sense, some form of learning or human development*" (2004, 9, italics in original).

Psychotherapy and Psychological Treatments

More recently, David Barlow (2004, 2005, 2006) has attempted to differentiate psychotherapy from psychological treatments, which may add more confusion rather than clarity to the already diverse definitions available for counseling and psychotherapy. He suggests that "psychological treatments" should refer to those dealing primarily with pathology, while "psychotherapy" should refer to treatments that address adjustment or growth (2006, 216). Psychological treatments are therefore those that are clearly compatible with the objectives of health-care systems that address pathology. He further stresses that the two activities of psychological treatment (which is more specific) and psychotherapy (which is more generic) would not be distinguished based on theory, technique, or evidence, but only on the problems they deal with. He is aware that these are controversial recommendations. However, I believe Barlow's

(2006) recommendation is not only controversial, but it is also potentially confusing and may not really help to clarify the definition of terms. Examples of psychological treatments provided by Barlow include "*assertive community treatment, cognitive-behavioral therapy, community reinforcement approaches, dialectical behavior therapy, family focused therapy, motivational interviewing, multisystemic interpersonal therapy, parent training* (for externalizing disorders in children), *personal therapy for schizophrenia,* and *stress and pain management procedures*" (2004, 873, italics in original). We can see that many of these examples of psychological treatments are already part and parcel of counseling and psychotherapy.

Overview of Counseling and Psychotherapy: Theory

Although over four hundred varieties of counseling and psychotherapy presently exist, most of them can be subsumed under the major schools of counseling and psychotherapy that are usually covered in textbooks in this field of people-helping. There are ten to twelve major ones, depending on the author and the text. In this book the following ten major theoretical approaches to counseling and psychotherapy will be covered in some detail, based on the theories and techniques developed by their founders and practitioners: psychoanalytic therapy, Adlerian therapy, Jungian therapy, existential therapy, person-centered therapy, Gestalt therapy, reality therapy, behavior therapy, cognitive behavior therapy and rational emotive behavior therapy, and marital and family therapy.

Psychoanalytic Therapy. The key figure of psychoanalysis and psychoanalytic therapy is Sigmund Freud. He originated a theory of personality development focused on experiences in the first six years of life that determine the subsequent development of personality. Freudian or psychoanalytic theory emphasizes unconscious factors, especially sexual and aggressive drives in motivating human behavior. Psychoanalytic therapy employs techniques such as *free association* (allowing the client to say whatever comes to his or her mind without censorship); *dream analysis* (interpreting the latent or hidden meaning of the dream mainly through the use of symbols that have consistent significance for almost every person); and *analysis of transference* (when the client responds to the analyst or therapist as a significant person of authority from his or her life, thereby revealing childhood conflicts he or she has experienced). The goal of psychoanalytic therapy is to help make the unconscious conscious and strengthen the ego. Contemporary versions of psychoanalytic therapy such as object-relations theory focus more on attachment and human relationship needs rather than on sexual and aggressive drives.

Adlerian Therapy. Alfred Adler founded Adlerian therapy, which was originally called individual psychology. Another major figure in this approach is Rudolph Dreikurs, who was responsible for making it better known in the

United States. Adlerian therapy is based on a growth model of the human person. It emphasizes the need for the client to take responsibility in making choices that help determine one's own destiny, and that provide meaning and direction for one's life. Adlerian therapy uses techniques such as *investigating the client's lifestyle* or *basic orientation toward life* by exploring birth order, early recollections from childhood years, and dreams; *asking "The Question"* ("What would be different if you were well?"); and *paradoxical intention* (encouraging clients to do or exaggerate the very behaviors they are attempting to avoid).

Jungian Therapy. The key figure of Jungian therapy, or analytical psychology, is Carl Jung. Jung's interest in mystical traditions led him to conclude that human beings have a significant and mysterious potential within their unconscious. He described both a personal unconscious as well as a collective unconscious. Jungian therapy encourages clients to connect the conscious and unconscious aspects of their mind in constant dialogue, with the goal of individuation or becoming one's own person. Jungian therapy techniques include the extensive use of *dream analysis* and the *interpretation of symbols* in order to help clients recognize their *archetypes* (ordering or organizing patterns in the unconscious). Examples of archetypal images include major ones such as the persona, the shadow, the anima and animus, and the Self, as well as others such as the earth mother, the hero, and the wise old man.

Existential Therapy. The key figures of existential therapy include Vicktor Frankl, the founder of logotherapy; Rollo May; Ludwig Binswanger; Medard Boss; James Bugental; and Irvin Yalom. It focuses on helping clients experience their existence in an authentic, meaningful, and responsible way, encouraging them to freely choose or decide, so that they can create meaning in their lives. Existential therapy therefore emphasizes more the relationship and encounter between therapist and client rather than therapeutic techniques. Core life issues often dealt with in existential therapy include death, freedom, meaninglessness, isolation, and the need to be authentic and real in responsibly choosing one's values and approach to life. Existential therapists can be optimistic or pessimistic to the point of being nihilistic, and they include those who are religious as well as those who are antireligious. Although techniques are not stressed in existential therapy, Frankl has developed several techniques in logotherapy, a particular approach to existential therapy. Some examples are *dereflection* (encouraging the client to ignore the problem and focus attention or awareness on something more pleasant or positive); *paradoxical intention* (asking the client to do or exaggerate the very behavior he or she fears doing); and *modifying the client's attitudes or thinking* (especially about the past, which cannot be changed, so that more meaningful or hopeful ways of looking at things become the focus).

Person-Centered Therapy. Carl Rogers founded person-centered therapy, which was previously called non-directive counseling or client-centered therapy.

Person-centered therapy assumes that each person has a deep capacity for significant and positive growth when provided with the right environment and relationships. The client is trusted to lead in therapy and is free to discuss whatever he or she wishes. Person-centered therapy is therefore not focused on problem solving but aims instead to help clients know who they are authentically and to become what Rogers calls "fully functioning" persons. According to Rogers, three therapeutic conditions are essential for facilitating client change and growth; these are the major person-centered therapy "relationship techniques": *congruence or genuineness*; *unconditional positive regard* (valuing the client with respect); and *accurate empathy* (empathic understanding of the client's perspective or internal frame of reference).

Gestalt Therapy. Frederick (Fritz) Perls and Laura Perls founded Gestalt therapy, an experiential therapy that emphasizes increasing the client's awareness, especially of the here and now, and integration of body and mind. The Gestalt therapist assumes a very active role in helping clients become more aware so that they can solve their problems in their own way and time. Examples of Gestalt therapy techniques that focus on doing include *dream work* that is experiential; *converting questions to statements*; *using personal nouns*; *assuming responsibility*; *the empty chair*; *exaggeration*; and *confrontation*.

Reality Therapy. William Glasser founded reality therapy, which focuses on the present and emphasizes the client's strengths. It is based on choice theory as developed by Glasser, which asserts that people are responsible for choosing their own thinking and actions, which then directly influence their emotional and physiological functioning. Choice theory also posits five basic needs of all human beings: survival, love and belonging, power, freedom, and fun. Reality therapy helps clients to become more responsible and realistic and therefore more successful in achieving their goals. Examples of reality therapy techniques include *structuring*; *confrontation*; *contracts*; *instruction*; *role playing*; *support*; *skillful questioning* (e.g., "Does your present behavior enable you to get what you want now, and will it take you in the direction you want to go?"); and *emphasizing choice* (e.g., by changing nouns and adjectives into verbs).

Behavior Therapy. The key figures of behavior therapy include Joseph Wolpe, Hans Eysenck, Arnold Lazarus, Albert Bandura, B. F. Skinner, and Donald Meichenbaum. Behavior therapy applies not only the principles of learning but also experimental findings from scientific psychology to the treatment of particular behavioral disorders. It is therefore an empirically based approach to therapy that is broadly social learning oriented in theory. Behavior therapists view human beings as products of their environments and learning histories. The behavior therapist plays an active and directive role in therapy. Behavior therapy has developed many techniques that continue to be refined through systematic empirical research. Examples of therapeutic techniques used in behavior therapy include *positive reinforcement* (reward for desirable behavior); *assertiveness training* (role-playing with clients to help them learn to express their thoughts and feelings more freely); *systematic desensitization* (pairing of a neutral or pleasant stimulus with one that has been conditioned to elicit fear or anxiety); and *flooding* (exposing the client to stimuli that elicit maximal anxiety for the purpose of eventually extinguishing the anxiety).

Cognitive Behavior Therapy and Rational Emotive Behavior Therapy. The key figures of cognitive behavior therapy (CBT) and rational emotive behavior therapy (REBT) are Aaron Beck, the founder of cognitive therapy (CT), and Albert Ellis, the founder of REBT. Donald Meichenbaum, already mentioned in the preceding discussion of behavior therapy, is also often noted as an important figure in CBT because he developed cognitive behavior modification (CBM) and stress-inoculation training (SIT), which are incorporated into CBT. Beck's CT approach focuses on how maladaptive and dysfunctional thinking affects feelings and behavior. It attempts to help clients overcome emotional problems such as depression, anxiety, and anger by teaching them to identify, challenge, and modify errors in thinking or cognitive distortions. Similarly, Ellis developed REBT as an active and directive approach to therapy that focuses on changing clients' irrational beliefs that are viewed as the root of emotional problems. CBT and REBT assume that clients have the capacity to change their maladaptive thinking and hence to change problem feelings and behaviors. CBT and REBT employ a wide range of therapeutic techniques, many of which have been empirically supported by documented results or systematic research. Examples of CBT techniques include *coping skills training* (helping clients use cognitive and behavioral skills to cope more effectively with stressful situations); *cognitive restructuring* (helping clients to change or modify maladaptive, dysfunctional thoughts); and *problem solving* (helping clients to explore options and implement particular solutions to specific problems and challenges). Examples of REBT techniques include *use of the A-B-C theory of REBT* (**A** refers to Activating Events, **B** to Irrational Beliefs, and **C** to Consequences—emotional and/or behavioral—of such beliefs) and more specifically *keeping an A-B-C diary* of daily experiences; *disputation* (of irrational beliefs); and *action homework*.

Marital and Family Therapy. Marital and family therapy is an umbrella term referring to over twenty systemic therapies. The important figures in this approach include Salvador Minuchin, the founder of the *structural approach*; Jay Haley and the Milan Group, who developed the *strategic approach*; Murray Bowen, who developed family systems theory and transgenerational (multigenerational) family therapy; and Virginia Satir, who developed conjoint family therapy. More recently, Susan Johnson and Leslie Greenberg have become well known for their development of emotionally focused therapy for couples. Other key figures include Nathan Ackerman, Carl Whittaker, Ivan Boszormenyi-Nagy, Steve de Shazer, Michael White, Neil Jacobsen, John Gottman, and Alan Gurman. Marital and family therapy approaches assume that the crucial factor in helping individuals to change is to understand and work with the interpersonal systems within which they live and function. In other words, the couple and the family must be considered in effective or efficacious therapy for individual problems as well as marital and family issues. Examples of marital and family therapy techniques that seek to modify dysfunctional patterns of interaction in couples and families and effect therapeutic change include *reframing* (seeing problems in a more constructive or positive way); *boundary setting* (either to establish firmer limits or lines of separation or to build more flexible boundaries for deeper connection); *communication skills training; family sculpting* (asking a couple or family members to physically put themselves in particular positions to reflect their family relationships); and constructing *a genogram* (a three-generational family tree or history).

A more detailed discussion including biblical perspectives and critiques appears in the chapter devoted to each of these ten major theoretical approaches to counseling and psychotherapy. Counseling theory is important. It provides a framework of understanding and practice that guides the counselor and psychotherapist in their attempts to help clients (see Truscott 2010). Every one of us has his or her own implicit, if not explicit, theory of counseling. We may, or may not, be aware of our basic assumptions and views of how to best help people with their problems in living. Kevin Fall, Janice Holden, and Andre Marquis have provided the following questions for clarifying and articulating one's theory of counseling, which you may find useful in formulating your own theory, no matter how basic it may be:

1. *Human nature:* Are people essentially good, evil, or neutral? How much of personality is inborn or determined by biological and/or other innate factors? Are there inborn drives, motives, tendencies, or other psychological or behavioral characteristics that all human beings have in common? How much of a person's individuality is determined by heredity or other innate factors?
2. *Role of the environment in personality development*: How influential is one's physical and/or social environment in one's personality development, and how does the environment affect personality development?
3. *Model of functionality*: What constitutes functionality/mental health or dysfunctionality/mental unhealth in an individual? How do innate and environmental factors interact in influencing a person's functioning, be it relatively healthy or unhealthy?
4. *Personality change*: How does personality change after it is to some extent developed? What conditions are necessary but not alone sufficient for personality change to occur, and what conditions are both necessary and sufficient? (see Fall, Holden, and Marquis 2004, 9–10)

These are the kinds of questions we need to ask ourselves in reflecting on our own theory of counseling. We will also ask such questions of the ten major theoretical approaches to counseling and psychotherapy that will be covered in more depth and detail later in this book. Combs (1989) has noted that many counseling theorists value a theory of counseling that is complete, clear, consistent, concrete, current, creative, and conscious, that is, that has the seven Cs (see Fall, Holden, and Marquis 2004, 10–11).

Overview of Counseling and Psychotherapy: Research

Theory plays an important role in guiding the counselor or therapist in helping clients. However, every theory must be subjected to research to determine its truth or validity, as well as the efficacy and effectiveness of its applications in actual practice. Research is therefore another crucial dimension in the field of counseling and psychotherapy. Scientific and systematic research on the processes and outcomes of counseling and psychotherapy only began in the 1940s when Carl Rogers started recording his therapy sessions, which could subsequently be studied and evaluated. Since then, research in this field has mushroomed, although some controversies and issues still remain. See the appendix for a review of research in the field of counseling and psychotherapy, focusing on the question "Is psychotherapy effective?" and why.

Overview of Counseling and Psychotherapy: Practice

In this final section of the overview of counseling and psychotherapy, we will briefly cover the following topics: primary theoretical orientations of counselors and psychotherapists in practice in the United States; major types of therapists or mental health practitioners and the settings in which they practice; several contemporary developments in the practice of counseling and psychotherapy; and examples of major professional organizations and their Web sites for counselors and psychotherapists.

Primary Theoretical Orientations of Counselors and Psychotherapists

Prochaska and Norcross have summarized the major findings from several surveys or studies of the self-identified primary theoretical orientations of clinical psychologists, counseling psychologists, social workers, and counselors in the United States (2010, 3). The most popular theoretical orientation self-reported by most of these mental health professionals has been *eclectic/ integrative therapy* (using theories and techniques from various approaches): 29 percent of clinical psychologists, 34 percent of counseling psychologists, and 26 percent of social workers. However, *cognitive therapy* is self-reported as the primary theoretical orientation by 28 percent of clinical psychologists and 29 percent of counselors (the highest percentage for counselors). Only 23 percent of counselors selected eclectic/integrative therapy as their primary theoretical orientation. Judith Todd and Arthur Bohart (2006) note that while eclecticism is the most popular approach among practicing psychotherapists, cognitive therapies and theories are now the dominant therapeutic orientation in many professional contexts including university clinical psychology programs.

Prochaska and Norcross (2010) have also summarized the main findings of a Delphi Poll they conducted with sixty-two expert panelists; its composite ratings indicate what will happen in the field of psychotherapy over the next ten years. In terms of primary theoretical orientations of the future, *cognitive behavior therapy* was ranked first for the greatest increase over the next decade, followed closely by culture-sensitive/multicultural therapy, cognitive therapy (Beck), interpersonal therapy (IPT), technical eclecticism, theoretical integration, behavior therapy, and systems/family systems therapy. There was also consensus that psychotherapy will become more directive, psychoeducational, technological, problem focused, and brief in the next ten years. One of the major predictions concerns the length of therapy: long-term therapy will significantly decrease, while short-term therapy will become predominant.

Major Types of Mental Health Practitioners and Practice Settings

There are over a dozen major types of mental health practitioners in the United States who may provide counseling and psychotherapy. Les Parrott lists the following (see 2003, 14–16):

1. *Psychiatrists* are medical doctors who have specialized training in the diagnosis and treatment of mental disorders. They are qualified to prescribe psychotropic medications and can practice counseling and psychotherapy. Some psychiatrists have also been trained in psychoanalysis.
2. *Psychoanalysts* have received advanced training of at least three years in Freudian psychoanalysis or some other more contemporary version of psychoanalysis at institutes of psychoanalytic training. Such training institutes often require their psychoanalytic trainees to be licensed psychologists or psychiatrists.
3. *Clinical psychologists* are educated at the doctoral level (PhD, PsyD, or EdD), including internship training in psychological assessment and psychotherapy. They must be licensed in the state in which they practice.
4. *Counseling psychologists* are usually educated at the doctoral level with internship training in helping people deal more effectively with their problems in living. Counseling psychologists also must be licensed to be in independent practice. They function very much like clinical psychologists do, except that counseling psychologists tend to see clients with

less severe psychopathology, although this is less often the case today than in the past.

5. *School psychologists* are usually educated at the doctoral level to closely work with educators and others to facilitate the holistic development of children in school. They often assess and counsel children with different types of problems, as well as consult with teachers, parents, and other school staff.

6. *Industrial/organizational psychologists* are educated at the doctoral level. They are involved in enhancing the effectiveness of organizations and helping to improve productivity and the well-being of employees as well as management staff.

7. *Marriage and family therapists* are trained at the master's or doctoral level in marital and family therapy. In most states they must be licensed to practice as marriage, family, and child counselors (MFCC) or marital and family therapists (MFT).

8. *Social workers* usually have a master's degree in social work. They also must be licensed in many states as clinical social workers in order to do individual as well as family counseling and therapy.

9. *Psychiatric nurses* have an associate's or baccalaureate degree, specializing in psychiatric services. A psychiatric nurse with a master's degree in nursing (MSN) and psychiatric/mental health certification can also do private practice.

10. *Pastoral counselors* are ministers, usually with master's degrees in theology or divinity, who also have had special training and experience in counseling from a spiritual perspective. Many of them have received training from a clinical pastoral education center in the United States, which has over 350 such centers.

11. *Vocational counselors* have a master's degree that prepares them to counsel people in order to help them in their vocational choices and professional development.

12. *Occupational counselors* have a bachelor's or master's degree and internship experience that prepares them to help people with physical challenges to make the best use of their resources.

13. *School counselors* have an advanced degree in counseling psychology and are involved in helping people with career and educational issues.

14. *Substance-abuse counselors* have bachelor's or master's degrees and counsel people with alcohol and/or drug addictions or substance-abuse problems.

15. *Paraprofessional or lay counselors* have limited training in counseling but do not have advanced degrees in counseling and are not licensed mental health professionals. They usually do their counseling work under the supervision of a licensed mental health professional.

Another group of mental health practitioners not mentioned by Parrott (2003) is the category of *professional counselors* or *licensed professional counselors* (LPCs) with master's degrees in counseling who have also been licensed in the state in which they practice.

There are several major practice settings in which mental health professionals do counseling and related work including: private practice, community mental health centers, hospitals, human service agencies, and schools and workplaces (see Parrott 2003, 16).

Some Contemporary Developments in Counseling and Psychotherapy

Several significant contemporary developments in counseling and psychotherapy have occurred in recent years. Not surprisingly, given the computer and Internet revolution in this information age, one such development has been in the area of *technological applications and innovations*. Examples include the use of computer technology in *virtual therapy*, in which virtual reality is used as a therapy intervention for the treatment of anxiety disorders. Psychotherapy can also be provided by telephone, videoconferencing, and videotelephone, in what has been called *telepsychotherapy*. Such therapies, of course, raise serious ethical and logistical issues, but such technological innovations in psychotherapy are here to stay (see Prochaska and Norcross 2010).

Another contemporary development in clinical practice is the *integration of religion or spirituality and psychotherapy* (see Tan 1996c, 2001b). Since Allen E. Bergin (1980) published his seminal article on psychotherapy and religious values over three decades ago (see also S. L. Jones 1994), religiously or spiritually oriented psychotherapy has become an important part of the current practice of counseling and psychotherapy (for more recent examples, see Aten and Leach 2009; Pargament 2007; Plante 2009; Richards 2006; Richards and Bergin 2000, 2004, 2005; Sperry and Shafranske 2005). More specifically, Christian approaches to therapy have further developed in recent years (see, e.g., N. T. Anderson, Zuehlke, and Zuehlke 2000; Clinton, Hart, and Ohlschlager 2005; Clinton and Ohlschlager 2002; Collins 2007; Malony and Augsburger 2007; McMinn and Campbell 2007; see also S. L. Jones and Butman 1991; Yarhouse and Sells 2008), and research findings so far have provided some support for the efficacy (see Worthington and Sandage 2001) and effectiveness in actual clinical settings (see Wade, Worthington, and Vogel 2007) of Christian therapy (see also T. B. Smith, Bartz, and Richards 2007).

Contemporary clinical practice has also been significantly impacted by multicultural perspectives, feminist therapy, and postmodern approaches such as narrative therapy, solution-focused brief therapy, and social constructionism (see Corey 2009).

As a final example of another significant contemporary development in therapeutic practice, let us turn to a major movement in psychology today called *positive psychology*. Martin Seligman and Mihaly Czikszentmihalyi (2000) introduced the emerging science of positive psychology over a decade ago, referring to the study of positive emotion, positive character, and positive institutions and how to nurture them. This movement has really taken off with a mushrooming body of literature as well as recent empirical attempts to validate or support positive psychology interventions (M. E. P. Seligman, Steen, Park, and Peterson 2005; see also Tan 2006a for a review and biblical perspective and critique of applied positive psychology). Martin Seligman, Tayyab Rashid, and A. C. Parks (2006) reported findings from two research studies that provided empirical support for the effectiveness of *positive psychotherapy* (based on positive psychology) employing exercises or interventions explicitly aimed at increasing positive emotion, engagement, and meaning in treating depression. A more recent meta-analysis of 51 positive psychology interventions with a total of 6,018 participants (Sin and Lyubomirsky 2009) showed significant enhancement of well-being (effect size = .29) and significant alleviation of depressive symptoms (effect size = .32). Positive psychology (including positive psychotherapy) focuses more on identifying the character strengths and virtues of clients and less on their psychopathologies or psychological deficits (see Linley and Joseph 2004; C. Peterson and Seligman 2004).

Examples of Major Professional Organizations for Counselors and Psychotherapists

The following list includes examples of major professional organizations and their Web sites that are relevant to counselors and psychotherapists in clinical practice:

- American Counseling Association (ACA), www.counseling.org
- American Psychological Association (APA), www.apa.org
- American Association for Marriage and Family Therapy (AAMFT), www.aamft.org/index_nm.asp
- National Association of Social Workers (NASW), www.naswdc.org

Two examples of specifically Christian professional organizations and their Web sites are

- Christian Association for Psychological Studies (CAPS), www.CAPS.net
- American Association of Christian Counselors (AACC), www.AACC .net

Recommended Readings

Castonguay, L. G., & Beutler, L. E. (Eds.). (2006). *Principles of therapeutic change that work*. New York: Oxford University Press.

Corey, G. (2009). *Theory and practice of counseling and psychotherapy* (8th ed.). Belmont, CA: Brooks/Cole.

Linley, R. A., & Joseph, S. (Eds.). (2004). *Positive psychology in practice*. Hoboken, NJ: Wiley.

Nathan, P. E., & Gorman, J. M. (Eds.). (2007). *A guide to treatments that work* (3rd ed.). New York: Oxford University Press.

Norcross, J. C. (Ed.). (2002). *Psychotherapy relationships that work*. New York: Oxford University Press.

Prochaska, J. O., & Norcross, J. C. (2010). *Systems of psychotherapy: A transtheoretical analysis* (7th ed.). Belmont, CA: Brooks/Cole.

2

The Person of the Counselor

Chapter 1 provided an overview of the field of counseling and psycho-therapy, focusing on theory, research, and practice areas. Research findings have shown that in general, therapeutic change in clients results from client and therapist factors more than from techniques (Lambert and Barley 2002; see also Hubble, Duncan, and Miller 1999). The person of the counselor or therapist is therefore crucial in effective therapy. Although knowledge and skills are important in conducting effective counseling, the person of the counselor is one of the most important determinants and instruments of effective therapeutic work (Corey 2009). Who you are as a person and a professional in the counseling field is therefore the focus of this chapter. In practice, the person and the professional are actually integrated or intertwined entities that cannot be separated (Corey 2009). However, we will consider the counselor with regard to these two intimately connected categories: the counselor as a professional and the counselor as a person.

The Counselor as a Professional: Personal Characteristics of Effective Counselors

The counselor as a professional, or a therapeutic person, is usually described as someone with particular helpful characteristics. Gerald Corey has provided a list of personal characteristics of effective counselors (emphasizing that the crucial quality involves the counselor's willingness to struggle to become a more therapeutic person), including the following: "Effective therapists have an identity; respect and appreciate themselves; are open to change; make choices that are life oriented; are authentic, sincere, and honest; have a sense of humor; make mistakes and are willing to admit them; generally live in the present; appreciate the influence of culture; have a sincere interest in the welfare of others; possess effective interpersonal skills; become deeply involved in their work and derive meaning from it; and are able to maintain healthy boundaries" (2009, 18–19). No one counselor or therapist possesses all these desirable characteristics of an effective counselor. However, every counselor should be willing to develop these traits.

Other personal qualities of effective counselors based on a review of the research literature available on this topic include psychological health, genuine interest in others, empathic abilities, personal warmth, self-awareness, tolerance of ambiguity, and awareness of values (see Parrott 2003, 24–35). Gary Collins (2007) added three other important counselor traits: integrity, courage, and genuine ability to care. While such personal qualities of effective counselors apply to both Christian and secular therapists, there are some unique characteristics of distinctively *Christian* counselors that warrant further description.

Unique Characteristics of Christian Counselors

Christian counseling can be simply defined as counseling or psychotherapy that is Christ centered, biblically based, and Spirit filled (see Tan 2001b, 24). Christian counseling also primarily concerns character, including the personal godliness of the counselor or therapist. This emphasis is consistent with this chapter's focus on the person of the counselor and James Guy's (1987) classic book on the personal life of the psychotherapist.

Personal or intrapersonal integration referring to a person's own appropriation of faith and integration of psychological and spiritual experience is therefore foundational in all integration work (i.e., integration of Christian faith and psychology or counseling) that includes principled (theory and research), professional (practice), and personal integration (Tan 2001b). As I have noted:

> Carter and Narramore (1979) have suggested several essential attitudes and attributes relevant to intrapersonal or personal integration, which cover both psychological and spiritual aspects, including the following: humility and an awareness of finite limitations, tolerance for ambiguity, balanced expression of one's intellect and emotions, openness instead of defensiveness due to personal anxieties and insecurities, and an eternal perspective on our work as part of humanity's God-ordained task of reconciling human beings to God, themselves, and others. Crabb (1977) . . . has emphasized the need for Christian psycholo-

gists to do the following: spend as much time in the regular and systematic study of the Bible as in the study of psychology; have both a general grasp of the structure and overall content of Scripture as well as working knowledge of Bible doctrine; and be involved in the fellowship of a Bible-believing church. (Tan 1987b, 35)

The spirituality or spiritual growth of the Christian counselor is therefore a unique and distinctive aspect of the person of the Christian counselor. In this context, the use of spiritual disciplines in a grace-filled way, empowered by the Holy Spirit, is crucial in facilitating personal and spiritual growth into deeper Christlikeness in both the Christian counselor and the client (Tan 1998; see also Eck 2002). Spiritual disciplines include practices such as solitude and silence, listening and guidance, prayer and intercession, Bible study and meditation, repentance and confession, yielding and submission, fasting, worship, fellowship, simplicity, service, and witness (Tan and Gregg 1997). They should be practiced not in a legalistic way but in dependence on the power and presence of the Holy Spirit and God's grace. They are therefore "disciplines of the Holy Spirit" (Tan and Gregg 1997).

The uniqueness of the Christian counselor can be characterized by at least four distinctives of Christian counseling: (1) *unique assumptions* that are based on the Bible, including beliefs about God's attributes (e.g., God is a compassionate, sovereign God), the nature of human persons, the reality of sin, the authority of the Bible, the forgiveness of sins and salvation through Jesus Christ, and hope for the future; (2) *unique goals* that include not only alleviating symptoms or reducing psychological and emotional suffering but also facilitating spiritual growth when appropriate based on Christian or biblical values; (3) *unique methods* that go beyond standard counseling skills and techniques, for example, avoiding immoral or unbiblical methods such as encouraging extramarital or premarital sex, and using spiritual interventions such as prayer and Scripture ethically and appropriately in counseling sessions; (4) *unique giftedness* from God in the work of counseling or people-helping (including having spiritual gifts from the Holy Spirit such as encouragement or exhortation) (see Collins 2007, 18–21).

A Christian counselor is therefore a counselor who practices in a Christ-centered, biblically based, and Spirit-filled way. Additional elements of such a distinctive or unique approach to counseling from a Christian, biblical perspective will be provided in the latter part of this book.

Issues and Potential Pitfalls Facing Beginning Counselors

Novice counselors or therapists face certain issues and potential pitfalls as they begin their counseling work. It can be helpful for beginning counselors to be aware of these issues and possible pitfalls early, so that unnecessary anxiety or pain can be avoided. I will briefly review two helpful lists of these issues and pitfalls.

Corey has listed and briefly described the following issues that novice counselors usually face as they begin seeing clients in clinical practice (see 2009, 29–35): (1) *dealing with their anxieties and self-doubts*, by talking them over with a supervisor and other beginning counselors; (2) *being themselves and disclosing their experiences*, while maintaining a proper balance between hiding behind a professional facade and sharing too much about themselves and burdening clients as a result; (3) *avoiding perfectionism* or trying to be a perfect counselor, which is impossible; instead being open to making mistakes and learning from them, especially in supervision; (4) *being honest about their limitations*, so that they learn which clients and problems they can or cannot effectively counsel, after sufficient exposure to diverse clients, problems, and settings; (5) *understanding silence* so that they explore its meaning with their clients and are not afraid of silence or react anxiously to it; (6) *dealing with demands from clients*, especially if they are unrealistic or unreasonable demands; setting clear expectations and boundaries in the first session with clients can be helpful; (7) *dealing with clients who lack commitment*, especially involuntary clients, for example, those who have been mandated by a court order to have therapy; it may help to prepare such clients for the process of counseling; (8) *tolerating ambiguity*, for example, when clients do not seem to be improving at all; sometimes clients get worse before they get better, so counselors need to be patient with such ambiguity for a while; (9) *avoiding losing themselves in their clients*, for example, by worrying too much about them or taking on too much responsibility for them; counselors need to engage in their own self-exploration with a supervisor, peer, or even their own therapist; (10) *developing a sense of humor* that is appropriate, so that they do not take themselves and their work too seriously yet do not underrate the pain and suffering of their clients; (11) *sharing responsibility with the client*, so that ultimately the client is empowered to make his or her own decisions, with the counselor's help and support; (12) *declining to give advice* all the time to clients who need to grow in making their own decisions; counselors need to learn to provide guidance and make suggestions only judiciously, with proper respect for the client's decision-making process and responsibility (unless there is a crisis situation when the client is unable to function or make decisions); (13) *defining their role as a counselor*; this may change over time and also in the particular clinical setting with specific types of clients and problems; (14) *learning to use techniques appropriately*, with careful selection of techniques that may best fit and help a particular client with a specific problem; (15) *developing their own counseling style* over time and with enough experience, so that the counselor achieves a unique and distinctive approach to counseling that is congruent with his or her personality and giftedness or strengths; (16) *staying alive as a person and as a professional* to avoid professional burnout;

self-care strategies are crucial, and they will be described and discussed in more detail later in this chapter.

In a similar vein, Parrott has listed and briefly described the following common pitfalls that beginning counselors may face: premature problem solving, setting limits, fear of silence, interrogating (or asking too many questions of clients), impatience, moralizing, and reluctance to refer (see 2003, 35–39).

Novice counselors will benefit from reviewing these two lists and preparing themselves to deal with such potential or common pitfalls before they actually encounter them.

The Counselor as a Person

The counselor as a person, with human strengths and weaknesses, faces several other areas of potential concern. Collins (2007) has listed a few, including the following: the counselor's motivation, the counselor's mistakes, the counselor's burnout, and the counselor's counselors.

With regard to the *counselor's motivation*, the counselor may have several personal needs that are potentially harmful to the client and the counseling process. Examples of such needs include the need to control or rescue; the need for relationships; the need for information based mostly on unhealthy curiosity; the need for affirmation, acceptance, and approval; and the need for assistance with the counselor's own personal problems (see Collins 2007, 31–32).

With regard to the *counselor's mistakes*, it is helpful to bear in mind that all counselors make mistakes. However, the following common mistakes should be avoided as far as possible: visiting or engaging in casual conversations with the client instead of counseling; attempting to solve problems prematurely; asking too many questions too quickly; showing a disrespectful or judgmental attitude; being too emotionally involved; being distant or superficial; being defensive when feeling threatened or challenged (see Collins 2007, 32).

With regard to the *counselor's burnout*, counseling can be emotionally draining work and thus entails a high risk of burnout. Burnout symptoms include exhaustion, a feeling of detachment from clients, and the tendency to withdraw. To prevent or recover from burnout, counselors need spiritual strength, social support from other people, freedom from the drive to achieve, awareness that they cannot do everything, periods of time to be away from people, continued development of their counseling skills, and other people with whom they can share their load or burdens (see Collins 2007, 32). Strategies for self-care, including preventing burnout, will be covered in more detail later in this chapter.

Finally, with regard to the *counselor's counselors*, counselors are encouraged to have other counselor friends who can provide support and perspective and can point them to Jesus Christ, the ultimate Counselor who gives us hope, strength, and direction through the Holy Spirit (see Collins 2007, 32). Christian counselors can cast their cares and clients upon the Lord Jesus through prayer in their own individual lives and walk with God.

In the last section of this chapter, we will examine in more detail the crucial topic of self-care for the counselor.

Self-Care for the Counselor

Self-care is essential for the well-being of the counselor, as well as for the efficient, effective, and ethical practice of counseling and the ultimate benefit of the client (see Norcross and Guy 2007). Some people may misunderstand the term "self-care" to mean "selfish care" or "self-centered care" for oneself. Self-care for the counselor, however, refers to healthy and wise strategies for taking good care of oneself as a counselor in order to manage stress well and prevent burnout. The eventual effect of good self-care, which is an ethical imperative throughout a counselor's professional life, is the ability to function well and effectively as a counselor and therefore to better help clients (Barnett, Baker, Elman, and Schoener 2007). It is thus loving and wise to engage in proper self-care that eventually leads to the helping and healing of others.

The Resilient Practitioner: Burnout Prevention and Self-Care Strategies for Counselors and Others

Thomas Skovholt (2001) has written a very helpful and practical book that comprehensively covers burnout prevention and self-care strategies for counselors, therapists, teachers, and health professionals. Such self-care strategies can help a counselor become a resilient practitioner who has learned to prevent burnout and to grow in balanced wellness in physical, spiritual, emotional/ social, and intellectual areas of health. Skovholt emphasizes the counselor's need to take care of the self just as the opera singer must take care of the voice, the baseball pitcher the arm, the carpenter the tools, the professor the mind, the photographer the eyes, and the ballerina the legs (2001, ix). Before we more closely examine the specific self-care strategies for producing the resilient practitioner, it may be helpful to first consider the poor self-care deadly dozen that Skovholt has listed. These pitfalls should be avoided as far as possible by counselors who want to prevent burnout and grow in balanced wellness:

1. Toxic supervisor and colleague support
2. Little fun in life or work
3. Unclear understanding of one's own needs
4. Lack of professional development process that helps transform experience into greater competence and reduced anxiety
5. Absence of energy-giving personal life

6. Inability to turn down unreasonable requests
7. Accumulated effects of vicarious traumatization
8. Personal relationships that are mainly one-way with self as giver or provider of caring
9. Perfectionism in tasks at work
10. Ambiguous professional losses that remain unresolved
11. Need to be needed that is strong
12. Professional success defined only in terms of client positive change or appreciation (see Skovholt 2001, 210)

Self-Care Strategies: Sustaining the Professional Self

The following are strategies for nurturing and sustaining the professional self of the counselor: avoiding the impulse toward grandiosity; thinking long-term; putting together and actively applying an individual development method or plan; cultivating professional self-understanding; creating a professional greenhouse (environment for growth) at work; having leadership that facilitates balance between self-care and caring for others; drawing on professional social support from peers; getting support from bosses, supervisors, and mentors; being nurtured from work as managers, supervisors, and mentors; learning how to be both playful and professional; releasing emotions of distress through professional venting; learning to be a "good enough practitioner"; understanding the reality of early professional anxiety, which is pervasive; reinventing oneself to increase excitement and reduce boredom; dealing with ambiguous professional loss by minimizing it; learning to refuse unreasonable requests (see Skovholt 2001, 206–7, 130–44).

Self-Care Strategies: Sustaining the Personal Self

In the area of nurturing and sustaining the personal self of the counselor, Skovholt focuses on self-care activities to nurture the emotional self, the financial self, the humorous self, the loving self, the nutritious self, the physical self, the playful self, the priority-setting self, the recreational self, the relaxation and stress-reduction self, the solitary self, and the spiritual or religious self (2001, 208–9, 148–62).

Based on research done with trauma therapists (Pearlman and MacIan 1995), the top ten helpful activities for self-care of trauma therapists are: discussing cases with colleagues; attending workshops; having time with family or friends; enjoying travel, vacations, movies, hobbies; talking with colleagues between sessions; socializing; exercising; controlling case load; developing spiritual life; and receiving supervision in general.

In more recent research on self-care and burnout, several interesting findings have been reported. A study of intern self-care with 363 psychology predoctoral interns found that some of the most frequently used strategies for self-care during the internship year were social support from family and friends, active problem solving, and humor (Turner et al. 2005). The most effective strategies were receiving social support from family and friends, seeking pleasurable experiences, and cultivating humor. Women were more likely to employ self-care strategies and also reported more effectiveness from their use.

Another study, focusing on gender and work-setting difference in career-sustaining behaviors and burnout among professional psychologists, found that the following six strategies were highly important for all 595 psychologists surveyed: maintaining a sense of humor; maintaining self-awareness/self-monitoring; maintaining balance between personal and professional lives; maintaining professional identity/values; engaging in hobbies; and spending time with spouse, partner, or family (Rupert and Kent 2007). Those working in solo or group independent practice reported a greater sense of personal accomplishment, more sources of satisfaction, fewer sources of stress, and more control at work than those working in agency settings. Women working in independent practice reported less emotional exhaustion than women working in agency settings.

Another example of recent research on burnout and coping in human service practitioners is a study in Spain of 211 professionals, either child-protection workers or in-home caregivers, who completed an inventory on coping and an inventory on burnout (Jenaro, Flores, and Arias 2007). Burnout was conceptualized as consisting of emotional exhaustion, depersonalization, and a reduction of personal accomplishment. Coping strategies were classified as problem focused (e.g., planning and active coping, focus on efforts to solve the problem or situation, social support, personal growth, and positive reinterpretation) and emotion focused (e.g., religion, humor, alcohol/drug intake, disengagement, focus on emotions and venting them, acceptance, denial, and restraint coping). This study found that coping strategies by themselves may help prevent worker turnover but do not preclude burnout. It also reported that high job and salary satisfaction, together with active coping strategies, play an important role in enhancing personal accomplishment, whereas low job and salary satisfaction together with passive or emotional coping strategies predict higher emotional exhaustion.

Sidebar 2.1

Ten Activities for Self-Care
(see Skovholt 2001, 212)

1. Being with family
2. Training or education for job skills
3. Pursuing a hobby that is fun
4. Engaging in physical activity
5. Reading
6. Receiving supervision or consultation
7. Socializing at work
8. Having time alone
9. Spending time with friends, partner, spouse
10. Taking a vacation

Self-Care: Some Reflective Questions and Further Suggestions

In bringing this chapter on the person of the counselor to a close, I would like to briefly review the helpful insights provided by Michael J. Mahoney, a well-known psychologist who has more recently developed constructive psychotherapy (2003). In an earlier and significant book on human change processes and the scientific foundations of psychotherapy, he lists twenty-three reflective questions for counselors to ask themselves in order to engage in better and healthier self-care (1991, 370). Some examples of these helpful reflective questions for self-care are "How happy are you most of the time? How do you feel about yourself? Do you seek and accept help or comfort from others? Is your rest usually adequate and satisfying? What are your fears? What gives meaning or purpose to your life? What are your hopes? What could you *do* to be more self-caring? With whom can you talk about your inner life? Do you laugh and cry? What forms of music and movement do you enjoy? What are your spiritual needs and comforts? If you could change three things in your life, what would they be?" (370). Mahoney emphasizes the importance for the counselor to be vigilantly sensitive to his or her own physical, emotional, and psychospiritual needs, all of which are interdependent.

> **Sidebar 2.2**
>
> **Self-Care Strategies for Counselors and Psychotherapists**
> *(Norcross and Guy 2007, xvii)*
>
> 1. Valuing the person of the psychotherapist
> 2. Refocusing on the rewards
> 3. Recognizing the hazards
> 4. Minding the body
> 5. Nurturing relationships
> 6. Setting boundaries
> 7. Restructuring cognitions
> 8. Sustaining healthy escapes
> 9. Creating a flourishing environment
> 10. Undergoing personal therapy
> 11. Cultivating spirituality and mission
> 12. Fostering creativity and growth

More recently, Mahoney has made several helpful recommendations for counselor or therapist self-care in the context of doing constructive psychotherapy (which integrates ideas from constructivist and narrative therapy with insights from cognitive-behavioral, humanistic, systems-based, psychodynamic, and other therapeutic approaches):

1. Be gentle with yourself; honor your own process.
2. Get adequate rest.
3. Make yourself comfortable.
4. Move your body often.
5. Develop a ritual of transition for leaving work at the office.
6. Receive regular professional massages.
7. Cherish your friendship and intimacy with family.

8. Cultivate your commitment to helping; honor the privilege of our profession.
9. Ask for and accept comfort, help, and counsel (including personal therapy).
10. Create a support network among your colleagues.
11. Enjoy yourself.
12. Follow your heart and embrace your spiritual seeking. (2003, 260–61)

From a more distinctively Christian perspective, the regular use or practice of the spiritual disciplines mentioned earlier in this chapter (see Tan and Gregg 1997) can be very helpful in preventing burnout by facilitating spiritual growth and centering in Christ, with the power and presence of the Holy Spirit. Specific means of God's grace to enable the Christian counselor to enter more into God's rest or to experience God's peace in a restless world include Shepherd-centeredness in Christ, Spirit-filled surrender to God, solitude and silence, simplicity, Sabbath-keeping (one day a week ceasing from gainful employment—resting and worshiping God), sleep, spiritual community, servanthood, and stress management from a biblical perspective that emphasizes values such as love, faithfulness, and humility, rather than success, competitiveness, and perfectionism (see Tan 2003d; Tan 2006b). Learning to rest in Christ (Matt. 11:28–30; see also Mark 6:31; Luke 10:38–42) in these ways will help a Christian counselor to better manage stress and prevent burnout (see also Hart 1995, 1999). Self-care for the Christian counselor, like self-care for any counselor, is therefore an essential and biblically sound aspect of the person and experience of the counselor or psychotherapist. This is so because appropriate and healthy counselor self-care eventually leads to more effective and ethical helping and healing of clients (see Norcross and Guy 2007).

Recommended Readings

Guy, J. D. (1987). *The personal life of the psychotherapist*. New York: Wiley.

Mahoney, M. J. (2003). *Constructive psychotherapy: A practical guide*. New York: Guilford Press.

Norcross, J. C., & Guy, J. D. (2007). *Leaving it at the office: A guide to psychotherapist self-care*. New York: Guilford Press.

Skovholt, T. M. (2001). *The resilient practitioner: Burnout prevention and self-care strategies for counselors, therapists, teachers, and health professionals*. Needham Heights, MA: Allyn & Bacon.

Tan, S. Y. (2003). *Rest: Experiencing God's peace in a restless world*. Vancouver, BC: Regent College.

3

Legal and Ethical Issues in Counseling and Psychotherapy

Counseling or psychotherapy is a unique kind of work that places the welfare and well-being of the client above and beyond the needs of the counselor or therapist. However, there are potential pitfalls and dangers in doing such therapeutic work, with the ever-present possibility of harming the client. The therapist therefore must be aware of the major legal and ethical issues involved in conducting therapy in order to avoid certain pitfalls and prevent possible harm to the client.

Legal issues involve the laws of a particular country, state, or province that govern the practice of counseling or psychotherapy in that geographical area or political entity. Legal issues facing therapists are therefore those that relate to "state and federal laws and regulations, binding case law, administrative rules, or court orders" (Knapp, Gottlieb, Berman, and Handelsman 2007, 54). *Ethical issues* are broader and encompass professional standards of right and wrong that guide the work of counselors and therapists, helping them to enhance the well-being and welfare of their clients and avoid harming them. Professional counselors and organizations of counselors and therapists have similar ethical codes governing their practice, such as the American Psychological Association's Ethical Principles of Psychologists and Code of Conduct, or APA Ethics Code (American Psychological Association [APA] 2002) for psychologists. More often than not, the laws that regulate the practice of counselors and therapists are consistent with the ethical principles that govern and guide such counselors in their professional work. For example, Samuel Knapp and his colleagues note that most ethical therapists or practicing psychologists would agree with the following standards: sex with clients is prohibited; information about clients must be kept confidential (with few exceptions); therapists should be competent in the services they provide; and therapists must refrain from insurance fraud (Knapp, Gottlieb, Berman, and Handelsman 2007, 54). However, there are times when laws and ethics may collide or conflict with each other in particular situations with specific clients. At such times, the therapist may choose to follow the law despite the ethical dilemmas he or she may be struggling with, or the therapist may decide that the most ethical position would be that of conscientious objection to a particular law. Knapp and his colleagues provide a helpful review of these difficult situations and issues and make suggestions for a constructive decision-making process at times when laws and ethics may collide (Knapp, Gottlieb, Berman, and Handelsman 2007; see also Knapp and VandeCreek 2006). Usually, however, ethical therapists will follow the laws regulating their practice as well as the ethical codes of their professional organizations. Although what is legal may sometimes not be ethical, and vice versa, most often the ethical choice is the legal one, and vice versa.

Legal Issues in Counseling and Psychotherapy

Counselors and therapists are affected by the law in their practice in various ways. Todd and Bohart (2006, 440–44) note that legislation passed in the United States regarding privacy and security issues can directly or indirectly impact the professional practice of therapists; an example is the Health Insurance Portability and Accountability Act (HIPAA) passed by Congress in 1996. Another example is licensing laws that directly govern the professional practice of therapists or counselors, who must possess the requisite educational degrees and hours of supervised clinical experience and pass specific licensing examinations in a particular state before they are legally qualified to be in independent practice in that state. There are other laws that apply to health care in general but that affect the professional practice of counselors and therapists.

Todd and Bohart (2006) also emphasize another area of law that impacts therapists: litigation or lawsuits filed against counselors and therapists for malpractice or negligence. Court decisions made in such lawsuits become legal precedents that subsequently directly affect professional therapeutic practice. For example, having a sexual relationship with a current client is not only unethical but also illegal in many states in the United States at this time. Mandatory reporting of child, elder, and dependent adult abuse and of clients considered a danger to self or to others has also become law in most states. Counselors and therapists engaged in professional practice therefore must be aware of such legal issues that directly or indirectly affect them (see, e.g., Levicoff 1991; Ohlschlager and Mosgofian 1992).

Ethical Issues in Counseling and Psychotherapy

The APA Ethics Code most recently revised and published in 2002 "is intended to provide specific standards to cover most situations encountered by psychologists. It has as its goals the welfare and protection of the individuals and groups with whom psychologists work and the education of members, students, and the public regarding ethical standards of the discipline" (APA 2002, 1062). The APA Ethics Code can also be used, with some adaptation, by other counselors and therapists who may not be professional psychologists. Other professional organizations in the mental health field, of course, also have their own ethics codes (e.g., American Counseling Association [ACA], American Association of Marriage and Family Therapy [AAMFT], and the National Association of Social Workers [NASW]). The APA Ethics Code begins with a section on five aspirational general principles meant to reflect the very highest ethical ideals of psychologists; the code then delineates specific ethical standards representing the particular obligations of proper professional conduct. Here are the five general principles with some explanatory text (APA 2002, 1062–63).

Principle A: Beneficence and Nonmaleficence

"Psychologists strive to benefit those with whom they work and take care to do no harm. In their professional actions, psychologists seek to safeguard the welfare and rights of those with whom they interact professionally and other affected persons, and the welfare of animal subjects of research. . . . Psychologists strive to be aware of the possible effect of their own physical and mental health on their ability to help those with whom they work" (APA 2002, 1062).

Principle B: Fidelity and Responsibility

"Psychologists establish relationships of trust with those with whom they work. They are aware of their professional and scientific responsibilities to society and to the specific communities in which they work. Psychologists uphold professional standards of conduct, clarify their professional roles and obligations, accept appropriate responsibility for their behavior, and seek to manage conflicts of interest that could lead to exploitation or harm" (APA 2002, 1062).

Principle C: Integrity

"Psychologists seek to promote accuracy, honesty, and truthfulness in the science, teaching, and practice of psychology. In these activities psychologists do not steal, cheat, or engage in fraud, subterfuge, or intentional misrepresentation of fact" (APA 2002, 1062).

Principle D: Justice

"Psychologists recognize that fairness and justice entitle all persons to access to and benefit from the contributions of psychology and to equal quality in the processes, procedures, and services being conducted by psychologists" (APA 2002, 1062).

Principle E: Respect for People's Rights and Dignity

"Psychologists respect the dignity and worth of all people, and the rights of individuals to privacy, confidentiality, and self-determination. . . . Psychologists are aware of and respect cultural, individual, and role differences, including those based on age, gender, gender identity, race, ethnicity, culture, national origin, religion, sexual orientation, disability, language, and socioeconomic status, and consider these factors when working with members of such groups" (APA 2002, 1063). In this context, the need for a multicultural perspective in ethical clinical practice has been emphasized (see Corey 2009).

> **Sidebar 3.1**
>
> **Ethical Standards Contained in the APA Ethics Code**
>
> The more specific ethical standards contained in the APA Ethics Code (APA 2002, 1063–73) cover the following ten areas:
>
> 1. Resolving ethical issues
> 2. Competence
> 3. Human relations
> 4. Privacy and confidentiality
> 5. Advertising and other public statements
> 6. Record keeping and fees
> 7. Education and training
> 8. Research and publication
> 9. Assessment
> 10. Therapy

Ethics therefore are the moral principles and standards that guide a group or a person regarding right behavior. Gerald Corey, Marianne Corey, and Patrick Callanan (2007) differentiate between *principle ethics* and *virtue ethics* in the context of counseling and therapy. Principle ethics are the specific rules for right behavior in particular situations. Virtue ethics are the highest ethical ideals to which counselors or therapists aspire and thus focus more on the character of the counselor or therapist than on specific behavior. The five general principles of the APA Ethics Code can be viewed as virtue ethics, and the more specific Ethical Standards as mainly principle ethics (see also Barnett and Johnson 2008).

Confidentiality, Competence, and Choice

Major ethical issues in counseling and psychotherapy can also be summarized in three major categories, as W. W. Becker (1987) has done (in his application of ethical and legal issues more specifically to the area of paraprofessional or lay counseling): *confidentiality*, *competence*, and *choice*, aimed eventually at maintaining *trust* in the counseling relationship since trust is the essence of such a relationship.

In the category of *confidentiality*, ethical counselors will keep confidential anything a client reveals or discloses to them in the process of counseling. There are exceptions, however. Many states now require by law that professional counselors report situations involving child, elder, or dependent adult abuse or those in which a client may potentially harm himself or others.

In the category of *competence*, professional counselors must receive the requisite academic or educational degrees, supervised clinical training and experience, and licensing (after passing licensing board examinations in particular states) in order to be in independent practice, charging fees for their services (with some pro bono or free work at times). They should also practice within the limits of their professional expertise or competence and refer clients to other, better-qualified or trained professional counselors when such clients present clinical problems beyond their own professional competence to treat. However, clinical competence for practicing psychologists or counselors is not as easy to define as it may seem, and its definition should be viewed more as "a work in progress" (Barnett, Doll, Youngren, and Rubin 2007, 510; see also N. J. Kaslow et al. 2007). Nevertheless, graduate student educators and clinical supervisors, as gatekeepers of the profession of counseling and psychotherapy, need to be ethically responsible and adequately deal with professional competence problems in trainees or supervisees (W. B. Johnson et al. 2008), including those in Christian practitioner training programs (Palmer, White, and Chung 2008; see also W. B. Johnson 2007b; M. L. Nelson, Barnes, Evans, and Triggiano 2007).

Finally, in the category of *choice*, the client's freedom to decide whether to participate in counseling must be protected. Informed consent must be obtained from clients before therapy is started. However, the exact parameters of what a counselor or therapist should share with a client in obtaining his or her informed consent before starting therapy are not always clear cut. Moreover, obtaining informed consent should also apply to other roles that psychologists or counselors may have such as conducting clinical assessment, research, or clinical supervision (see Barnett, Wise, Johnson-Greene, and Bucky 2007). J. E. Barnett has pointed out that for informed consent to be legally valid, the following three conditions must be fulfilled (see Gross 2001): the information presented must be understood by the client, the client must provide the consent voluntarily, and the client must have the competence needed to provide the consent (Barnett 2007a, 181). He also cites from the APA Ethics Code that each informed consent agreement in the therapy context should include information about "the nature and anticipated course of therapy, fees, involvement of third parties, and limits of confidentiality" (APA 2002, 1072) and adds "reasonable alternatives available, their relative risks and benefits, and the right to refuse or withdraw from treatment" (Barnett 2007a, 180). Barnett emphasizes that informed consent should not be viewed as a one-time event that takes place just before therapy is started. Instead, it should be seen as an ongoing process because significant changes in the therapy provided may sometimes be proposed in the course of treatment, and hence further informed consent may be needed.

There are of course many other ethical principles and standards that the APA Ethics Code covers, and it should be read and consulted for more detailed information that will be helpful in ethical decision making (see APA 2002). However, no ethical code is sufficient in and of itself to provide concrete answers to all ethical dilemmas that counselors may face. Counselors and therapists therefore need to learn the steps necessary to engage in a constructive process of ethical decision making.

The Process of Ethical Decision Making

Corey, Corey, and Callanan (2007) have provided a helpful integrated model consisting of the following steps to help a counselor carefully reflect on potential ethical problems in the process of ethical decision making: identify the ethical issue or problem and clarify whether it is primarily moral, legal, ethical, clinical, or professional in nature; identify the various aspects of the ethical dilemma, including the rights, responsibilities, and welfare of every person involved in it; consult appropriate ethics codes for any guidance that may be helpful and relevant to the ethical issue being faced; be aware of laws and regulations that are relevant to the ethical problem; consult various sources, including other professionals, in order to receive different perspectives on the ethical issue at hand; explore all possible options for action, with further discussion of various options with other professionals as well as with the client if appropriate; consider the consequences of each of the options available for action, and especially how it would affect the client; choose what seems to be the most appropriate or best ethical option for action and then execute it, with follow-up evaluation of the results to see if any further action may be needed.

Different counselors may sometimes come up with different solutions for complex and difficult ethical dilemmas (Knapp, Gottlieb, Berman, and Handelsman 2007; see also Pope and Vasquez 2007), including situations where there may be conflict in values of diverse cultures (Knapp and VandeCreek 2007). The crucial task before a counselor is to engage in a process of constructive and mature ethical decision making, keeping in mind always the welfare and well-being of the client, and to do no harm to the client. One particular ethical issue that often comes up for discussion among counselors and therapists concerns boundary issues and dual or multiple relationships with clients, which we will now examine.

Boundary Issues and Dual and Multiple Relationships: A Crucial Ethical Issue in Counseling

Boundaries and multiple relationships (including dual relationships) are among the most commonly discussed and debated ethical issues in the context of clinical practice (see Pope and Wedding 2008). Some authors and counselors will advocate avoiding all dual and multiple relationships with clients as an ethical boundary in order to prevent any possible exploitation of or harm to the client. Others have advised engaging in dual and multiple relationships with clients only when necessary and in clinically helpful situations, such as practicing in certain rural or military situations and culturally diverse contexts (see Barnett, Lazarus, Vasquez, Moorehead-Slaughter, and Johnson 2007).

The APA Ethics Code states the following as part of Standard 3.05 on "Multiple Relationships":

> A multiple relationship occurs when a psychologist is in a professional role with a person and (1) at the same time is in another role with the same person, (2) at the same time is in a relationship with a person closely associated with or related to the person with whom the psychologist has the professional relationship, or (3) promises to enter into another relationship in the future with the person or a person closely associated with or related to the person.
>
> A psychologist refrains from entering into a multiple relationship if the multiple relationship could reasonably be expected to impair the psychologist's objectivity, competence, or effectiveness in performing his or her functions as a psychologist, or otherwise risks exploitation or harm to the person with whom the professional relationship exists.
>
> Multiple relationships that would not reasonably be expected to cause impairment or risk exploitation or harm are not unethical. (APA 2002, 1065)

It is clear from the last sentence quoted that not all multiple and dual relationships with clients are unethical because such relationships do not automatically or always cause impairment or risk exploitation or harm to the client. The APA Ethics Code therefore does not prohibit all dual or multiple relationships. *Boundary crossings* into clinically helpful multiple relationships with clients can therefore be appropriate and ethical, and such crossings should be differentiated from *boundary violations* that cause impairment and harm to clients. An example of a boundary crossing is to touch a client on the shoulder or forearm as an expression of comfort when that client is experiencing deep grief over the loss of a loved one. An example of a boundary violation is to touch a client in a sexually explicit way (see Barnett 2007b). The APA Ethics Code is very clear that psychologists should not get involved in exploitative multiple relationships, such as engaging in sexual intimacies with clients they are still treating (APA 2002, Standard 10.05) or with relatives or significant others of such clients (Standard 7.07). Psychologists also should not provide therapy to former sexual partners (Standard 10.07).

On the other hand, there are other kinds of multiple relationships that do not involve boundary violations and are therefore not unethical (Lazarus and Zur 2002; see also Zur 2007). Arnold Lazarus (2007) has recently emphasized the need to strongly challenge restrictive draconian views such as prohibiting all multiple or dual relationships in clinical practice:

> One of the most contentious issues has revolved around deep concerns in several quarters about dual or multiple relationships. Thus, when I argued that therapeutic benefits accrued when I selectively transcended strict professional boundaries and "partied and socialized with some clients, played tennis with others, took long walks with some, graciously accepted small gifts, and gave presents (usually books) to a fair number" (Lazarus 1994, p. 257), I was assailed by eight critics, who saw me as a dangerous, iconoclastic maverick. . . .
>
> It must be clearly understood that the foregoing boundary crossings were not carried out in a rash or capricious manner without careful consideration. Dual relationships are rarely advisable with borderline, histrionic, violent, antisocial, or other seriously disturbed clients. As was underscored by Lazarus and Zur (2002), "before entering into a dual relationship take into consideration the welfare of the client, . . . avoidance of harm, exploitation and conflict of interest, and the risk of impairment of clinical judgment" (p. 474). The raison d'être behind any boundary crossing is the psychotherapist's confidence that it is likely to prove beneficial to the client. (Lazarus 2007, 405)

Therefore, it is necessary to clarify which dual or multiple relationships should be avoided and which ones are acceptable or even necessary (Barnett 2007b). For example, in certain rural areas with small populations, the counselor or therapist may have to treat someone in the community whom he or she knows quite well, such as the church pastor or the local banker, in a necessary and potentially helpful dual or multiple relationship with the client.

W. B. Johnson emphasizes the need for *virtue ethics* that focus not only on the ethical guidelines and principles for dealing with boundaries and dual and multiple relationships with clients but also on the person or character of the psychologist or therapist and "clear moral virtues such as prudence, integrity, and compassion" (2007a, 440). Counselors and therapists therefore need to personally grow in the process of becoming ethical helping professionals (R. Sommers-Flanagan and Sommers-Flanagan 2007). Christian or biblical perspectives on ethics that emphasize agape love and virtue ethics and ethical practice by Christian counselors or therapists are also crucial (see Browning 2006; Ohlschlager and Clinton 2002; R. K. Sanders 1997; Tjeltveit 1992, 1999). There are distinctively Christian codes of ethics governing the practice of Christian counselors and therapists (see, e.g., American Association of Christian Counselors 2004 for the AACC Code of Ethics). These perspectives and codes will be covered in the last chapter of this book, which focuses on legal and ethical issues in Christian counseling and psychotherapy.

Recommended Readings

American Association of Christian Counselors. (2004). *AACC code of ethics: The Y2004 final code*. Forest, VA: AACC.

American Psychological Association. (2002). Ethical principles of psychologists and code of conduct. *American Psychologist, 57*, 1060–73.

Barnett, J. E., & Johnson, W. B. (2008). *Ethics desk reference for psychologists*. Washington, DC: American Psychological Association.

Corey, G., Corey, M., & Callanan, P. (2007). *Issues and ethics in the helping professions* (7th ed.). Belmont, CA: Brooks/Cole.

Pope, K. S., & Vasquez, M. J. T. (2007). *Ethics in psychotherapy and counseling: A practical guide* (3rd ed.). San Francisco: Jossey-Bass.

PART 2

Major Counseling and Psychotherapy Theories and Techniques

4

Psychoanalytic Therapy

S igmund Freud, the founder of psychoanalysis, is still a towering figure in the field of counseling and psychotherapy. Some authors and textbooks have erroneously credited him for being the founder of psychotherapy, but other important figures such as Paul Dubois (1848–1918) and Pierre Janet (1859–1947) were also influential in the history of modern psychotherapy (see Corsini and Wedding 2008, 11–12). In fact, therapeutic work in the care of souls preceded Freud by many centuries. However, the theories and therapeutic techniques developed by Freud in psychoanalysis are still unique and substantial. Although the Freudian psychoanalytic approach is no longer as popular or widespread today, it is still influential in the development of more recent psychoanalytic or more broadly psychodynamic approaches to therapy that have gone beyond some of Freud's original ideas. Examples of such contemporary psychoanalytic therapies include ego psychology, object relations psychology, self psychology, and relational psychoanalysis, which will be briefly described later in this chapter. Of course, other schools of therapy have been developed in reaction to Freud's psychoanalytic views and even in outright rejection of many of his ideas and techniques.

Biographical Sketch of Sigmund Freud

Sigmund Freud was born to Jewish parents in Freiburg, Moravia (formerly in Austria, now in the Czech Republic), on May 6, 1856, the eldest of eight children (five daughters and three sons). The Freud family moved to Vienna when Sigmund was four years old so that his father, who was a wool merchant, would have better business prospects. In their crowded apartment, Sigmund had his own study and bedroom. His mother favored him and had high expectations for him to excel academically and professionally. His father was very authoritarian, like many fathers in that era and culture (E. Jones 1953).

Freud excelled in his academic work and graduated summa cum laude from secondary school. He was fluent in several languages, including Greek, Latin, and Hebrew, the classical languages, as well as English, Italian, French, and Spanish (Ellenberger 1970). Freud eventually decided on a career in medicine and obtained his medical degree from the University of Vienna in 1881, when he was twenty-five years old. He married Martha Bernays in 1886, and they had six children. Their youngest child, Anna Freud, eventually became a well-known psychoanalyst herself, focusing on the treatment of children and on the development of the ego or that system of personality in Freudian theory that interacts with the reality-based external world.

Freud had been exposed to the work of Josef Breuer on hysterical illness during the six years he worked with Ernst Brucke, a well-known physiologist, while still in medical school. Due to financial reasons, Freud left Brucke and began a residency in surgery. In 1883, he trained in neurology and psychiatry at the Viennese General Hospital. He also spent four months in 1885 in Paris with Jean Charcot, a renowned neurologist who used hypnosis to treat hysterical symptoms. This experience enabled Freud to recognize the significance of the unconscious mind, although he later questioned the usefulness of hypnosis as a therapeutic technique. He also discussed with Josef Breuer how Breuer helped his patient Anna O., who had exhibited hysterical symptoms, by mentioning emotional material while she was under hypnosis. Freud began using this technique with his own patients, and he and Breuer published *Studies on Hysteria* in 1895.

Freud's father died in 1896; around this time his collaboration with Breuer also began to deteriorate. Freud's radical views on how traumatic sexual experiences in childhood can cause hysteria did not sit well with others, including Breuer. In 1897, in his early forties, Freud began a painful three-year process of psychoanalysis on himself, including analyzing his dreams and exploring his own childhood memories. He suffered from significant emotional problems at this time, such as serious worries about his finances and phobias of death and heart disease. He came to realize through his self-analysis that he had strong feelings of hostility toward his father and sexual feelings as a child toward his mother. From his own self-observations and reflections, as well as his treatment of patients, Freud continued to develop his unique psychoanalytic theory and psychoanalysis as a major therapeutic approach. He published his best-known work, *The Interpretation of Dreams*, in 1900, after this intensive three-year period of self-analysis.

In 1902, Freud formed the Wednesday Psychological Society, which met initially at his home to discuss his psychoanalytic ideas. In 1908, this group became the Vienna Psychoanalytic Society, numbering among its members prominent and brilliant colleagues of Freud, such as Alfred Adler, Carl Jung, and Otto Rank. However, Freud's inability to tolerate dissenting views and his insistence on having absolute control of what constituted psychoanalysis, as its founder, alienated many of his colleagues. As a result, key figures such as Adler and Jung eventually left the Vienna Psychoanalytic Society. Adler went on to found his own school of psychotherapy, called individual psychology; Jung likewise founded another school of psychotherapy, called analytical psychology.

Freud thus spent the later part of his professional life in relative isolation, working more on his own while, ironically, becoming more renowned and successful. He continued to keep a grueling schedule, working eighteen-hour days, seeing patients and writing. Freud habitually smoked twenty cigars almost daily, and in 1923 he was diagnosed with bone cancer of his jaw and mouth. He eventually underwent thirty-three operations, but despite his painful struggle with bone cancer for the last almost two decades of his life, he continued to work long hours and produced many significant writings. Freud reluctantly left Vienna for London in 1938, just before World War II. A year later, in September 1939, he died, most probably from physician-assisted suicide, using a lethal dose of morphine (Gay 1988). Freud left behind what many still consider to be the most comprehensive and substantial theory of personality, psychopathology, and psychotherapy in his unique approach of psychoanalysis. His published collected works ultimately include twenty-four volumes (see *Standard Edition of the Complete Works of Sigmund Freud*, published by Hogarth Press, London).

Freud's life and work have been described in more detail by several authors. For further information and details of Freud's life and professional career see E. Jones (1953, 1955, 1957, also 1961), who gives the most complete account, as well as H. F. Ellenberger (1970), Peter Gay (1988), Paul Roazen (2001), and A. Demorest (2005), as recommended by Richard Sharf (2008).

Major Theoretical Ideas of Freudian Psychoanalysis

Perspective on Human Nature

Freud's view of human nature was mainly pessimistic and at best somewhat neutral. It was also a deterministic view, in which human actions or behaviors are understood as caused by irrational forces, mainly unconscious, called *drives* or *instincts*. These innate instincts evolve through several stages of psychosexual development in a person's childhood so that his or her personality is essentially formed by the age of six.

Freud divided such human drives or instincts into two major types: the *life instincts* (*Eros*), or *libido*, originally referring to sexual energy but eventually broadened to include all life energy that seeks to experience pleasure and avoid pain, and the *death instincts* (*Thanatos*), which are associated with death and aggression. Both of these sexual and aggressive drives, or life and death instincts, are crucial motivators of human action or behavior, according to Freud.

The Unconscious and Levels of Consciousness

Freud's concepts of the unconscious and of the different levels of consciousness that exist in a person are often viewed as his most significant contributions to the mental health field. He described three levels of consciousness: the *conscious*, the *preconscious*, and the *unconscious*. The *conscious*, or what one is aware of experiencing at a particular moment, such as holding a pen in one's hand or feeling painful sensations, is actually only a small part of a person's mental life. The *preconscious* includes memories that can be easily recalled, such as remembering what one ate for lunch yesterday or details from a movie seen last weekend. The largest level of consciousness, however, is the *unconscious*, which contains memories and experiences that have been repressed or pushed out of consciousness because they are too threatening, such as feelings of hostility toward a parent or painful childhood memories of sexual abuse. The unconscious also refers to everything that one is unaware of, including hidden needs and motivations. Freud viewed the conscious level as only a small part of the mind, like the proverbial tip of the iceberg. The unconscious, which exists below the level of awareness, is the largest part of the mind and influences or controls most psychological functioning. It cannot be directly observed but can be inferred from phenomena such as dreams, forgetting a well-known fact or name, and slips of the tongue (e.g., saying "nipple" instead of "ripple"). The major goal of psychoanalysis is therefore to make the unconscious conscious, so that a person can have more freedom to choose.

Personality Structure

Freud's psychoanalytic theory postulates three major systems in the personality structure of each person: the *id*, the *ego*, and the *superego*. These psychological systems should not be understood literally as referring to three physically separate parts of a person. However, the three systems are seen as consisting of psychic energy that is limited in its availability. The *id* can be conceptualized as the biological system, the *ego* as the psychological system, and the *superego* as the social system of personality, broadly speaking (Corey 2009), but all three systems function together as a whole. In a nutshell, the id refers to powerful biological forces, the superego to the conscience, and the ego to the rational system of one's personality that interacts with external reality and mediates between the id and the superego.

The Id. The id (or "it") is the original, unconscious system of personality. A person is born with his or her id, and one might say that an infant is all id. The id is full of psychic or instinctual energy waiting to be discharged so that homeostasis can be maintained. It is driven by the *pleasure principle*, seeking always to avoid pain and experience pleasure and satisfaction of its seething needs. The id remains so throughout a person's life, wishing and acting to fulfill desires without rational thinking. The id therefore is characterized by *primary process thinking* that is irrational and primitive, and that seeks self-gratification with no concern for others. The two basic instincts operating in the id are the life (or sexual) and death (or aggressive) instincts or drives. The newborn infant therefore invests energy or *cathects* in objects that will immediately meet or fulfill its demanding needs. The object may be a nipple or a blanket that serves to reduce the infant's needs.

The Ego. The ego (the "I") is the system of personality that interacts with the real world "out there." It can be likened to an executive who provides control and regulation of one's personality. It begins functioning around age six to eight months to help the id fulfill its demanding needs and impulses in a more appropriate and acceptable way in the real world. The ego therefore acts to control consciousness and regulate the primitive drives or instincts of the id. The ego follows the *reality principle*, using rational and realistic thinking, or *secondary process thinking*, that results in action plans for meeting needs that do not impulsively follow the pleasure principle but instead suspend or control it. It therefore censors and restrains the id, a function described as *anticathexis*. The ego, in this context, helps an infant or young child not to act out angrily or cry when his or her wishes are not fulfilled.

The Superego. The superego is the social or judicial system of personality that contains the social and parental values and standards to which a person has been exposed. It follows the *morality principle* and guides a person in deciding whether a particular behavior is right or wrong, good or bad. The superego therefore provides a moral code by *introjection* (the process of incorporating into oneself the values and standards of parents and society). The id impulses are controlled or restrained by the superego, but the ego is also influenced by the superego to aim for perfection and moralistic ideals rather than more realistic and reasonable goals. The superego therefore strives for perfection, not pleasure, and can push a person into an extreme or legalistic submission to perfectionistic and pathological standards that cannot be attained. When this happens, when the superego is functioning against both the id and the ego, neuroses or psychological disorders can develop. *Anxiety* is often experienced by a person when the id, the ego, and the superego are in such conflict.

Anxiety

Anxiety is a central concept in psychoanalytic therapy. It refers to a feeling of dread and tension resulting from previously repressed factors, such as feelings, experiences, and memories, coming to awareness. Anxiety functions as a warning of potential danger that also motivates people to act in particular ways (see Corey 2009, 63).

Freud conceptualized anxiety as consisting of three major types: reality, neurotic, and moral. *Reality anxiety* is the fear of an external situation that is appropriate to the degree of real danger present, such as fear of a nearby poisonous snake about to strike. *Neurotic anxiety* is the fear of being overwhelmed by one's instincts or drives (id) so that one ends up doing something that will be punished. *Moral anxiety* is the fear of violating one's own conscience or internalized parental and societal standards (superego). Neurotic and moral anxieties are therefore related to conflicts or threats within the person. When an individual experiences anxiety, the ego copes or responds by using *defense mechanisms*.

Defense Mechanisms

The ego employs defense mechanisms to deal with the pain of anxiety by distorting or even denying reality. Defense mechanisms operate at the level of the unconscious. When the ego uses them infrequently and appropriately, they can serve a constructive purpose by reducing stress or anxiety and enabling the person to cope more effectively. However, if they are used too often in order to avoid the pain of anxiety by denying or blocking out reality, they can become destructive and pathological, resulting in more-severe psychological disorders. Common defense mechanisms include repression, denial, displacement, sublimation, reaction formation, projection, rationalization, regression, intellectualization, and identification.

Repression. Freud considered repression the most fundamental or important defense mechanism, one on which his psychoanalytic theory was founded. Repression is the unconscious attempt of the ego to block out of consciousness (i.e., repress) negative experiences that are too painful or threatening for a person to acknowledge. Particularly painful experiences or memories of the first five to six years of a person's childhood are repressed, so that they are stored in the unconscious. However, they still affect and motivate the thoughts, feelings, and behaviors of the person later in his or her life. An example of repression would be a man who has feelings of hostility and hatred toward his father, but these feelings are entirely repressed or blocked from conscious awareness because they are too overwhelming for the person to acknowledge. Such repressed feelings are not under the voluntary control of an individual because repression operates at the unconscious level.

Denial. Denial is a defense mechanism that usually functions at more preconscious and even conscious levels, whereby an individual refuses to accept the reality of a given situation or event that is negative, painful, or anxiety provoking. This mechanism therefore denies reality. For example, an individual refuses to accept the news that he or she has cancer and continues to live as if there were no cancer, without getting much-needed medical treatment. Another example is some fanatical fans of Elvis Presley who still deny that he is dead!

Displacement. Displacement is a defense mechanism whereby an individual copes with anxiety by shifting the discharge of his or her impulses from a threatening object or person to a much safer substitute. For example, a very mild-mannered man who has received a strong reprimand from his supervisor at work comes home and kicks his dog (out of frustration and anger actually at his supervisor but now displaced or redirected to his dog).

Sublimation. Sublimation is the defense mechanism that redirects sexual or aggressive drives into more socially acceptable behaviors. Freud viewed sublimation as the healthy way of coping with demanding and often unacceptable impulses or drives, although it will still not completely satisfy such drives or impulses. An example would be someone who has very aggressive drives channeling them into active participation in martial arts and martial arts competitions, in which he wins trophies and the adulation of fans and spectators.

Reaction Formation. In reaction formation, an individual expresses the opposite of the impulse that he or she is really experiencing as a defense against the objectionable impulse. For example, a woman who really hates her husband ends up being extremely nice and kind to him, cooking him his favorite meals and giving him many compliments. Freud viewed reaction formation as an inferior version of sublimation.

Projection. Projection is the defense mechanism of unconsciously attributing to others one's own objectionable impulses and drives, usually sexual or aggressive in nature. In other words, projection occurs when a person blames others for his or her own shortcomings. An example would be a boy who hates his father but asserts and believes that his father hates him.

Rationalization. Rationalization is an individual's attempt to explain away painful experiences with reasons or excuses that are not accurate or true. For example, a man who does not get a much anticipated and desired job promotion believes that he really did not want the promotion because of all the extra stresses and responsibilities that come with it, including much international travel.

Regression. When the ego is threatened, an individual may use the defense mechanism of regression to return to an earlier stage of development that was less stressful but also uses less mature or less appropriate behaviors to cope with the current anxiety. An example can be found in a first-grader who is failing academically and then resorts to infantile behaviors such as crying for her mother and sucking her thumb.

Intellectualization. Intellectualization is a defense mechanism whereby a person detaches from a painful emotional experience by focusing only on his or her thoughts and the minute details involved in trying to analyze and explain the negative emotional experience. For example, a mother who just received news that her two-year-old son was killed by a drunken driver begins a long discussion of the meaning of life and death and how it is all fated and beyond anyone's control, instead of dealing with her feelings of shock, grief, loss, and anger at the drunken driver.

Identification. Identification is a defense mechanism whereby an individual who is threatened by anxiety or other negative feelings assumes the characteristics of others who may be more successful or associates or identifies himself or herself with them. An example would be a male adolescent who struggles with deep feelings of failure and inferiority, but ends up identifying himself with a famous rock band by dressing like the band members and mimicking their speech.

Personality Development: Freud's Psychosexual Stages of Development

Freud was radical in his time when he described the psychoanalytic theory of psychosexual stages of development that every person goes through. He believed that the personality development of an individual is basically completed by around age five or six. His theory is biologically based, focusing on the flow of sexual or libidinal energy through the following psychosexual stages of normal human development: *oral, anal, phallic, latency,* and *genital.* The oral, anal, and phallic stages of psychosexual development occur by age five or six, after which comes the relatively calm latency stage, which lasts for about six years. Then the genital stage in adolescence occurs, around the onset of puberty. Gratification of the sexual drive is central to Freud's theory, but this is experienced in different parts of the body as a person matures, eventually culminating in the genital area. If a person experiences certain traumatic events in early childhood in any of these psychosexual stages of development, *fixation* may then occur at a specific stage, with such abnormal development resulting in an individual being more vulnerable to stress and crisis later in life.

Oral Stage. The oral stage takes place in the first eighteen months of life. It focuses mainly on the mouth for experiencing gratification of the infant's needs and drives, which are virtually all id-driven at this first and earliest stage. The infant initially is unable to differentiate between self and others or the environment. Dependence on the mother for gratification of the infant's needs through sucking and eating is crucial; therefore, the mother-infant relationship is central in the oral stage. The mouth is also involved in other activities such as biting, spitting, holding on to, and closing, besides eating and sucking. The specific experiences of the infant or child in the oral stage will affect his or her adulthood. For example, if the child depends too much on the mother and she overindulges the child, the child may experience fixation at this oral stage and become an overdependent adult later on. However, if the mother underindulges the child and provides irregular or inattentive feeding, the child may become insecure and have trouble trusting others or forming intimate relationships with others as an adult.

Anal Stage. The anal stage occurs between the ages of eighteen months and three years, when the focus of gratification and pleasure is the anal area, involving the holding or releasing of feces or the defecation processes, as well as urination. It is during this anal stage that the ego begins to differentiate from the id. Children are also learning to have more control over their own bodily processes as well as control over others (e.g., by often saying, "No"). Toilet training is a central developmental task in the anal stage. Depending on how strict parents are in toilet training their children, the child may later develop an obsession with cleanliness and orderliness with a fixation on this stage described as being anal-retentive, or the child may become disorderly and even destructive, that is, anal-expulsive.

Phallic Stage. The phallic stage occurs around the age of three to five or six years, when the gratification of sexual needs moves from the anal area to the genital area. Self-stimulation of the penis for boys and the clitoris for girls (masturbation) leads to pleasurable experiences. The realization that boys have penises but girls do not is a crucial part of the phallic stage, leading to what Freud called *penis envy* (or wishing to have a penis of one's own) in girls and *castration anxiety* (or the fear of losing one's own penis) in boys.

Boys also have an unconscious sexual desire for their mothers and wish to get rid of the father as a rival. They resolve this *Oedipus complex* by identifying with the father and channeling their sexual wishes into more acceptable outlets. Girls in a somewhat different way have an unconscious desire for their fathers (who have their desired object, a penis) and a hatred for their mothers; Carl Jung and others have labeled this the *Electra complex*, a term that Freud himself was reluctant to use. Girls also need to resolve this complex by identifying with their mothers so that they can vicariously have the desired object. This aspect of Freudian psychoanalytic theory has received strong criticism from other theorists and feminists. Problems leading to fixation at this phallic stage may result in sexual identity difficulties in adulthood and possible difficulties in relationships with the opposite sex or with the same sex.

Latency Stage. The latency stage occurs from around the age of six to twelve years or puberty. It is a period of relative calm, with sexual drives being more repressed. Children at this latency stage spend more of their energy focusing on school and friends and developing important social and technical skills to prepare them to function well as adults in society. Their personalities have already been formed in the previous stages of psychosexual development, by age five or six, after which Freud believed that significant personality change is almost impossible.

Genital Stage. At puberty, around age twelve, an individual enters the genital stage, when pleasure is experienced more directly through genital stimulation in the context of heterosexual relationships. The focus now is on others rather than on the self, in the experience of genital sexual satisfaction. If a person has gone through the other earlier stages of psychosexual development without significant fixations or traumas, then there is sufficient libidinal energy available for him or her to live a relatively normal life. Such a life means having the ability to love and to work, the ideals of personal maturity that psychoanalysts try to help their patients achieve in successful psychoanalysis.

Freud's theory of psychosexual stages of development has been strongly challenged and criticized by other psychoanalytic theorists. Erik Erikson (1902–94), for example, emphasized much more the *psychosocial stages of development*, focusing not only on child development but also on the entire adult span of human development until death. Briefly, Erikson (1950) delineated and described the following stages of psychosocial development: *infancy* (first year of life) focusing on developing *trust versus mistrust*; *early childhood* (ages one to three) focusing on developing *autonomy versus shame and doubt*; *preschool age* (three to six) focusing on developing *initiative versus guilt*; *school age* (ages six to twelve) focusing on developing *industry versus inferiority*; *adolescence* (ages twelve to eighteen) focusing on developing *identity versus role confusion*; *young adulthood* (ages eighteen to thirty-five) focusing on *intimacy versus isolation*; *middle age* (ages thirty-five to sixty) focusing on developing *generativity versus stagnation*; and *later life* (ages sixty plus) focusing on developing *integrity versus despair*. More recently, in her nineties Joan Erikson, Erikson's wife for sixty-four years, included another stage that she termed "*disgust versus wisdom*" (ages in the eighties and nineties) focusing on developing gerotranscendence (Sharf 2008). This ninth stage of psychosocial development involves moving from a rational and materialistic perspective to a deeper focus on spirituality and experiencing peace of mind (Erikson 1997).

Other challenges and modifications to traditional psychoanalytic theory as originally described by Freud have come from more contemporary approaches to psychoanalytic therapy and, in particular, the four major schools: ego psychology, object relations psychology, self psychology, and relational psychoanalysis.

Ego Psychology

Ego psychology focuses more on the ego and its conscious and adaptive functions rather than on the id and unconscious drives, which seemed to preoccupy Freud. Anna Freud (1895–1982), Sigmund Freud's daughter, made significant contributions to ego psychology by emphasizing the ego in child development in her description of *developmental lines*, an example of which is the gradual evolving of more other-centered behaviors rather than self-centered behaviors as a child matures (A. Freud 1965). She also expanded the notion of defense mechanisms to include normal and constructive ones that enable an individual to deal more effectively with the world (A. Freud 1936). As already mentioned, Erik Erikson is another major theorist in ego psychology, noted especially for his description of the psychosocial stages of human development over the entire lifespan of an individual. Other well-known figures in ego psychology, sometimes labeled as "the American school," include Heinz Hartmann (1958) and David Rapaport (1951).

Object Relations Psychology

The *object relations* perspective focuses more specifically on how past childhood relationships between a child and his or her significant others, especially the mother, or other love objects in the child's life affect personality development and later adult life. It also emphasizes past internalized relationships or object relations rather than internal sexual or aggressive drives in the determination of one's present and future behavioral patterns. A specific process described by object relations theorists as *individuation* refers to how an individual can separate from his or her mother and develop into an independent person. Well-known theorists in object relations psychology, sometimes described as "the British school," include Donald Winnicott (1966), W. R. D. Fairbairn (1954), Melanie Klein (1957, 1975), Margaret Mahler (1968, 1979a, 1979b), and Otto Kernberg (1975, 1976). More detailed descriptions of object relations approaches can be found in St. Clair and Wigren (2004).

Self Psychology

The *self psychology* school is based on the major contributions of Heinz Kohut (1913–81), who wrote several significant books (1971, 1977, 1984) that define and describe his theoretical concept of the self (see also St. Clair and Wigren 2004). He emphasized how relationships with other people, especially parental figures in childhood experiences, have a profound influence on the development of the sense of self in an individual. If such childhood experiences have been nurturing and healthy, a stable sense of self will result so that one is able to develop mature relationships with others as an adult. However, if early childhood experiences have been more negative and emotionally depriving, then a less healthy sense of self will result and the person's ability to relate to others well will be significantly limited. Kohut particularly focused on the treatment of narcissistic and borderline disorders that involve a person's sense of a damaged or inadequate self.

Relational Psychoanalysis

A more recent development in psychoanalytic theory and therapy has been the significant work of Stephen A. Mitchell (1988, 2000) and his colleagues (see J. R. Greenberg 2001; J. R. Greenberg and Mitchell 2003) on *relational psychoanalysis*. This approach emphasizes the mutuality of the therapeutic relationship between the analyst and the client. In other words, *both* the analyst and the client influence each other on the conscious and unconscious levels such that the analytic or therapeutic relationship cannot be viewed as neutral, with the analyst objectively observing and analyzing the client in a unilateral way. This relational perspective has been described as intersubjective (see Orange, Atwood, and Stolorow 1997; Stolorow, Atwood, and Brandchaft 1994; Stolorow, Brandchaft, and Atwood 1997), interpersonal, or relational (see also Wachtel 2008). Mitchell also focused on how culture affects both the analyst and the client, thus critiquing and moving beyond Freud's original idea of unconscious biological drives that affect every individual because they are supposed to be universal in nature.

These four major schools of contemporary psychoanalytic approaches have critiqued and modified traditional Freudian psychoanalysis. Psychoanalytic therapy today is more diverse and less authoritarian, especially regarding how the analytic relationship is viewed and experienced. A greater emphasis on the conscious and adaptive functions of the ego (and less on the unconscious drive of the id), on object relations or internalized relationships with significant others or love objects, on the development of the self, and on a more mutual and reciprocal analytic relationship between the analyst and the client are examples of the newer approaches to psychoanalytic theory and practice. The therapeutic process and relationship as well as the major therapy techniques and interventions of more traditional psychoanalytic therapy will now be discussed.

Therapeutic Process and Relationship

Traditional Freudian psychoanalysis (with the analyst seeing the client usually four times a week, sitting behind the client who lies on a couch) and psychoanalytic therapy (with the analyst seeing the client one to three times a week, usually face-to-face) have two main *goals of therapy*: to help bring the unconscious to conscious awareness and to strengthen the ego so that an individual is less influenced by instinctual drives (sexual and aggressive) of the id or demanding perfectionistic standards of the superego and freer to act in more realistic ways. Psychoanalysis therefore aims at restructuring one's personality and not simply attenuating symptoms or solving problems. Insight or understanding of childhood experiences is achieved by analyzing them through the use of several major psychoanalytic methods of therapy. Such insight is seen as a key curative factor in successful psychoanalysis. However, it is not merely intellectual insight or understanding; it is insight based on working through or experiencing particular memories and feelings, especially from childhood.

Sidebar 4.2
Psychoanalytic Therapy Techniques *(Corey 2009)*
1. Maintaining the analytic framework
2. Free association
3. Dream analysis
4. Interpretation
5. Analysis of transference
6. Analysis of resistance

The *therapist's function or role* in traditional psychoanalysis is a passive one, aimed at maintaining neutrality or anonymity, with almost no self-disclosure at all. The analyst therefore behaves like a "blank screen" to facilitate the development of a *transference relationship* in which the client will project or transfer unconsciously onto the analyst feelings and experiences that originally were associated with past parental figures, especially in early childhood. The analyst does his or her best to achieve a good *working alliance or therapeutic relationship* with the client. Most of the time, the analyst is simply listening to the client, occasionally asking key questions, murmuring the proverbial Freudian "Um-hmm," and judiciously and infrequently interpreting the client's unconscious material as well as resistances.

Psychoanalysis and psychoanalytic therapy are therefore very intensive forms of psychotherapy that require a client to commit himself or herself to a long-term therapeutic relationship that can last for several years. The client must be willing to follow the "fundamental rule" of free association, or saying whatever comes to mind without any evaluation or censorship, in order to reveal unconscious material for the analyst and the client to explore. This is hard work, and the client's motivation or readiness to change is crucial for psychoanalysis and psychoanalytic therapy to be successful. Psychoanalytic therapy is usually considered modestly successful if it has effectively helped the client to be able to love and work in life.

Major Therapeutic Techniques and Interventions

Several major therapeutic techniques or interventions in traditional psychoanalytic therapy have been somewhat modified in more contemporary approaches to such therapy (see McWilliams 2004). However, the primary methods of traditional psychoanalytic therapy are still foundational. At least six of them are basic to psychoanalytic therapy: maintaining the analytic framework, free association, dream analysis, interpretation, analysis of transference, and analysis of resistance (Corey 2009).

Maintaining the Analytic Framework

Traditional psychoanalytic therapy involves several essential elements relating to therapeutic style and procedure that psychoanalytic therapists do their best to preserve in maintaining the analytic framework. Examples of such elements include the analyst being as neutral and anonymous as possible with very little or no self-disclosure, scheduling therapy sessions on a regular and consistent basis, and ensuring that sessions begin and end on time. Being consistent in these ways is itself a crucial therapeutic part of the analytic framework.

Free Association

Free association is the bedrock foundational method of psychoanalytic therapy and has also been called the "fundamental rule." It involves encouraging the client to say whatever comes to mind, without any evaluation or censorship. In this way, unconscious material is supposed to surface for the analyst to explore with the client and to interpret to help the client gain insight into underlying unconscious dynamics. Traditional psychoanalysis requires the client to lie on a couch, with the analyst out of sight behind the client. This physical arrangement is supposed to facilitate more free associations on the client's part.

The analyst listens intently to the client and his or her free associations, paying particular attention to disruptions or blockages in free association, which may indicate the presence of repressed anxiety-provoking material that is beginning to emerge into consciousness. The analyst listens especially for hidden meanings in the client's free associations and notices slips of the tongue, or Freudian slips, that may be due to unconscious conflicts. The analyst therefore does not take whatever the client expresses at face value. The analyst, in using the technique of free association, ultimately identifies and interprets unconscious material and conflicts that may emerge, so that the client can gain deeper insight and understanding.

Dream Analysis

Freud considered dreams "the royal road to the unconscious." Dreams are the raw material of the unconscious. Dream analysis is therefore another crucial technique or method in psychoanalytic therapy. The analyst encourages the client to record and report his or her dreams and free associate to them, saying whatever comes to mind as he or she describes the dreams. The analyst then discusses and interprets the client's dreams and free associations to the dreams or parts of them that can be viewed on two levels: the *manifest content* of a dream, referring to the surface material or details of the dream, and the *latent content* of a dream, referring to its unconscious or hidden meaning. The analyst is particularly involved in pointing out and interpreting the latent content and meaning of a dream.

Freud described several symbols in dreams often reported by clients that seem to have consistent meanings for almost every client. Examples are tree trunks and candles representing the penis, and steps and ladders symbolizing sexual intercourse. However, there is a danger of overgeneralizing such symbolic meanings in dreams, so dreams should still be interpreted in the proper context of a particular client's life.

Interpretation

Interpretation is the psychoanalytic technique whereby the analyst clarifies and explains to the client the meaning of certain unconscious material emerging in the client through dreams, free association, experiences in the therapeutic relationship between the analyst and the client, and resistances or blockages. Through the use of interpretation, the analyst enables the client to gain insight into unconscious material that is surfacing and to help his or her ego deal with such material more effectively and realistically.

Interpretation must be well timed and based on sufficient unconscious material to substantiate the accuracy of a particular interpretation. Otherwise, "wild analysis" or wild interpretation that is off target can occur, to the possible detriment of the therapeutic process and the relationship with the client. The readiness of the client to accept a specific interpretation is also a crucial factor. Interpretations are most helpful if they involve material that is preconscious or beginning to become conscious; if they begin with more surface material and proceed to deeper levels of meaning only as far as the client is ready to go; and if they deal with a defense or resistance first before pointing out the possible deeper meaning of the feeling or conflict underlying the defense or resistance that has been identified (Corey 2009).

Analysis of Transference

Another important technique of psychoanalytic therapy is the analysis and interpretation of transference. *Transference* occurs when the client unconsciously relates to the analyst as if he or she were a parental figure from the client's earlier life, usually childhood. Both positive (e.g., admiration) and negative (e.g., anger) experiences and feelings can occur in transference to the analyst or therapist. The analyst allows the transference to develop and then interprets its meaning to the client. This analysis of the transference helps the client to achieve deeper insight into his or her past experiences and how they may still be affecting and influencing present relationships and experiences.

The traditional Freudian view is that the analysis of transference is an essential part of psychoanalytic therapy. The analyst also needs to be careful of his or her own unconscious responses to the client that actually reflect unresolved issues with significant figures from the analyst's own past relationships, especially in childhood, a phenomenon known as *countertransference*. Analysts are therefore required to have their own personal or training analysis and further consultation or supervision when necessary in order to become more aware of and minimize countertransference to their clients. More-contemporary approaches to psychoanalytic therapy, however, also focus on how to constructively use countertransference to better understand the client, rather than always viewing countertransference as an inappropriate or unhealthy phenomenon requiring constant vigilance and control by the analyst.

Analysis of Resistance

Resistance is a basic psychoanalytic concept that refers to a client's blocking or defending against bringing unconscious and repressed material into conscious awareness, mainly because it is emotionally painful and provokes anxiety to do so. Resistance therefore is a major barrier to therapeutic progress in psychoanalytic therapy. A client can show resistance in a variety of ways such as being consistently late for appointments, not producing much by way of free associations, talking incessantly about superficial topics like the traffic or sports, and, especially, abruptly terminating psychoanalytic therapy early in the therapeutic process.

The analyst will analyze and interpret the client's resistances so that the client can overcome them and become more aware of his or her unconscious issues and repressed feelings, memories, or experiences. It is crucial, however, for the analyst to first interpret resistances that are clear or obvious to the client so that the client will be more accepting of the interpretation rather than further resist the analyst's interpretation. The analysis and interpretation of resistance must be conducted in a deeply empathic and clinically sensitive way so that the client's defenses are not too quickly or harshly confronted. Otherwise, further resistance may result.

Traditional Psychoanalysis and Psychoanalytic Therapy in Practice

A Hypothetical Transcript

Client: I'm feeling anxious again today . . . like I usually feel . . . and for no good reason too. I don't have anything pressing or stressful to do today and yet I'm having this dreadful anxiety almost all the time . . .

Analyst: (does not say anything and remains quiet)

Client: It's really hard for me to deal with these horrible anxious feelings when I don't know why or where they're coming from . . .

Analyst: (continues to be quiet and simply waits)

Client: Sometimes I feel like I'm going to explode or die of a heart attack or something horrible, because of these intense feelings of anxiety and fear . . .

Analyst: Um-hmm . . .

Client: I guess my anxiety may be a bit worse today, especially as I was thinking of coming here for my session with you, and wondering what else will come up in our session together . . .

Analyst: What comes to mind?

Client: Well . . . I know that you've asked me to keep a record of my dreams and to talk about my dreams openly here with you . . . and I did have a horrible dream, almost like a nightmare, just last night, and I'm feeling really anxious already just bringing it up . . .

Analyst: Um-hmm . . .

Client: I guess I should tell you about this dream or nightmare . . .

Analyst: (remains quiet)

Client: Well . . . I had a scary dream last night that I was all alone in this big, huge house, and suddenly it caught on fire . . . and I was inside the house all by myself and panicking seeing the fire and smelling the thick smoke . . . and I tried to get out by trying to find a door or exit . . . but I kept on running in circles with the fire coming closer to me, and I couldn't find an exit! I really felt overwhelming anxiety and fear and was so sure that the flames would engulf me and I would quickly be burned to death, up in smoke for sure . . . but then I woke up, trembling in sweat!

Analyst: What else comes to mind now? What other feelings, thoughts, or experiences?

This hypothetical transcript of a small part of a traditional psychoanalysis or psychoanalytic therapy session illustrates the use of free association and the beginning of dream analysis, two major techniques in traditional psychoanalytic therapy. The analyst also maintains a more traditional analytic framework, in saying very little and remaining neutral and anonymous, with no self-disclosure in this example.

Critique of Psychoanalytic Therapy: Strengths and Weaknesses

Traditional psychoanalysis and psychoanalytic therapy are based on Freud's theories, which many still consider to be the most comprehensive view of personality, psychopathology, and psychotherapy. Several psychoanalytic concepts such as the unconscious, defense mechanisms, transference and countertrans-ference in the therapeutic relationship, and resistance are still helpful ones being used not only by psychoanalysts and psychoanalytic therapists but also by other psychotherapists. Some therapists have found the psychoanalytic ap-proach to be the richest and deepest in theory and practice among the many psychotherapies available today.

However, Freudian psychoanalytic therapy has several significant weaknesses and limitations. First, although Freud's psychoanalytic theory is comprehensive, some of his ideas are not easily translated into testable hypotheses that can be verified by empirical research, for example, the id, the ego, and the superego, or Eros (life instinct) and Thanatos (death instinct).

Second, his theory narrowly focuses on sexual and aggressive drives and emphasizes his conviction that biology is destiny. However, there are other motivational forces or drives that Freud did not consider that may be equally or even more important than sexual and aggressive instincts in influencing human behavior. Other theorists and therapeutic approaches have emphasized other drives or motivations (e.g., social or spiritual), which will be discussed in later chapters of this book.

Third, some of Freud's original ideas have been viewed as sexist, especially by women and feminist therapists. For example, penis envy, the Oedipus com-plex, and the tendency to blame the mother in poor parent-child relationships that supposedly lead to adult psychological disorders have all been criticized for denigrating women and viewing them as inferior to men.

Fourth, traditional psychoanalysis or psychoanalytic therapy is an intensive, long-term, and hence expensive form of psychotherapy that only the relatively wealthy can afford. It is therefore not as suitable for managed care, which emphasizes and covers shorter-term and brief therapies. It also focuses on intrapsychic or personal conflicts and dynamics, often without paying sufficient attention to other real-life concerns such as employment, poverty, and social issues that may be more important and relevant to people from more diverse socioeconomic and cultural backgrounds. From a multicultural perspective, psychoanalysis and psychoanalytic therapy may therefore not be as meaningful or appropriate for some clients from certain ethnic and cultural groups, who may prefer a more direct, problem-solving approach to therapy.

Fifth, the neutral and anonymous therapeutic stance of the analyst in tradi-tional psychoanalysis may be difficult for some clients to tolerate. It may also be experienced by certain clients in a potentially harmful or antitherapeutic way. The traditional analytic approach also requires a minimal level of ego strength on the part of the client, in order to participate in and benefit from such an intensive and demanding form of therapy. Some contemporary ap-proaches to psychoanalytic therapy such as relational psychoanalysis have therefore modified the analytic relationship into one that is more mutual and reciprocal between analyst and client.

Finally, the empirical or research support for the efficacy of traditional psychoanalysis is either nonexistent or scarce. There is some empirical support for the efficacy of short-term psychodynamic therapy, which has modified the traditional psychoanalytic approach (see Chambless and Ollendick 2001; see also Summers and Barber 2009).

A more recent meta-analysis concluded that long-term psychodynamic psychotherapy (similar to psychoanalytic therapy) is an effective treatment for complex mental disorders and significantly better than shorter forms of treatment (Leichsenring and Rabung 2008). However, serious methodological problems with this meta-analysis do not allow more definitive conclusions to be made at this time (see the section on "Research" later in this chapter).

A Biblical Perspective on Psychoanalytic Therapy

Freud's view of human nature was somewhat negative and pessimistic: a person must struggle with the basic aggressive and sexual instincts of the id as well as the perfectionistic standards and demands of the superego, with the ego mediating these extreme forces to realistic compromises so that the person can learn to love and work satisfactorily in life. The biblical view of human nature as sinful and fallen (Rom. 3:23) is somewhat consistent with Freud's description of the human psyche. However, this is only half the story. The Bible also teaches that we are created in the image of God (Gen. 1:26–27) and therefore have the potential to be somewhat like God in our character, especially if we are in Christ, who makes us new creations (2 Cor. 5:17) capable, by the power of the Holy Spirit, to be transformed into deeper Christlikeness (Rom. 8:29). The potential for change through Christ is therefore greater than a purely Freudian view would allow, especially in its deterministic notion that one's personality is already formed by age five or six (see S. L. Jones and Butman 1991).

Second, Freud's emphasis on the unconscious and the need to gain insight that is not only intellectual but also experiential in making the unconscious conscious and resolving intrapsychic conflict points to the need for wisdom and awareness of the darker side and interior part of human nature, a view that can be seen as consistent with biblical teaching (Ps. 57:6; Jer. 17:9). However, his narrow focus on aggressive and sexual instincts in the motivation of human behavior is unbalanced. There are other human motivations such as spiritual longings for God, including agape love for God and for neighbor or the other (cf. Mark 12:30–31), that are real and not illusory or a pathological obsessional neurosis, as Freud (1927) claimed in his antireligious views emphasizing that we created God in our image in wish fulfillment of a longing for a father, rather than that God created us in his image.

Third, the traditional therapeutic stance of the analyst or therapist in staying as neutral and anonymous as possible, with a clinical aloofness that is assumed to facilitate transference, which can then be interpreted by the analyst, can be

viewed as problematic from a biblical perspective that emphasizes the centrality of agape love in all human relationships (1 Cor. 13), including therapeutic
relationships (see Browning and Cooper 2004). Contemporary approaches to
psychoanalytic therapy such as relational psychoanalysis, however, have modified
this traditional analytic stance so that a more mutual and reciprocal relationship between the analyst and the client can be achieved, based more on agape
love from a Christian approach to relational psychoanalysis (see M. Hoffman
2007). Several Christian approaches to contemporary psychoanalytic therapy
have recently been described in a special issue of the *Journal of Psychology and
Theology* (35, no. 1, 2007) devoted to psychoanalytic psychotherapy and religion,
using a case study approach, edited by B. D. Strawn (2007). It was published in
honor of the late Christian psychologist and contemporary psychoanalyst Ran-
dall Lehman Sorenson and his recent major work, *Minding Spirituality* (2004),
which focuses on the integration of spirituality or religion and psychoanalysis.
It should be pointed out, however, that some Christian psychoanalysts will
maintain that the traditional psychoanalytic stance of the analyst is actually a
manifestation of deep agape love and empathy for the client.

Research: Empirical Status of Psychoanalysis and Psychoanalytic Therapy

Most outcome evaluations of the effectiveness of psychoanalysis and psychoanalytic therapy have involved uncontrolled case studies and clinical surveys
over the last several decades or so (see Blomberg, Lazar, and Sandell 2001;
Galatzer-Levy, Bachrach, Skolnikoff, and Waldron 2000; Sandell et al. 2000;
Wallerstein 1986, 1996, 2001). The best-known and most widely published
study reported by Robert S. Wallerstein, called the Menninger project, involved
a thirty-year extensive assessment and follow-up of forty-two patients seen in
traditional psychoanalysis or psychoanalytic therapy. Wallerstein concluded
that traditional psychoanalysis was less successful than expected, whereas
supportive psychoanalytic therapy was more successful than expected, but
both were relatively beneficial. He also noted that therapeutic change is not
contingent on inner conflict resolution, and interior structural change cannot
be clearly differentiated from external behavioral change.

The uncontrolled case studies and clinical surveys conducted so far have
found that psychoanalysis and psychoanalytic therapy produce similar therapeutic or positive benefits (with reported improvement rates of 60 percent
or better). However, controlled outcome data from more-scientific research
studies are still lacking or limited, so a common assertion is that no definitive
statements can presently be made regarding the effectiveness of traditional
psychoanalysis and psychoanalytic therapy (Prochaska and Norcross 2010;
see also Fisher and Greenberg 1996).

A more recent meta-analysis involving 23 studies (11 randomized controlled
trials and 12 observational studies) with a total of 1,053 patients concluded

that long-term psychodynamic psychotherapy (with a minimum of 50 ses-sions or a year of treatment) is an effective treatment for complex mental disorders with significantly better therapeutic outcomes than shorter forms of psychotherapy (Leichsenring and Rabung 2008; see also Glass 2008). There are, however, several serious methodological problems with this meta-analysis that preclude more definitive conclusions about the effectiveness of long-term psychodynamic or psychoanalytic therapy (see Beck and Bhar 2009; Kriston, Holzel, and Harter 2009; Roepke and Renneberg 2009; Thombs, Bassel, and Jewett 2009; see also Leichsenring and Rabung 2009). However, Jonathan Shedler (2010) has more recently reviewed the outcome research on psycho-dynamic or psychoanalytic psychotherapy, whether short term or long term, and concluded that the empirical evidence available supports the efficacy of psychodynamic therapy. Effect sizes for psychodynamic therapy are as large as those found for other empirically supported or evidence based treatments.

Future Directions

Many authors and counselors have predicted the demise of psychoanalysis and psychoanalytic therapy in the last few decades, but it has not happened. In fact, interest in psychoanalysis and psychoanalytic therapy continues to be strong, even among Christian therapists (see Strawn 2007). However, the percentage of psychotherapists in the United States who endorsed psychoanalytic therapy as their primary theoretical orientation is still small, about 3 percent of clini-cal psychologists, 1 percent of counseling psychologists, 5 percent of social workers, and 2 percent of counselors (Prochaska and Norcross 2010, 3).

Several crucial modifications to traditional Freudian theory have been made in recent years. As noted earlier, the therapeutic relationship in psychoanalytic therapy is now more often viewed as mutual and interpersonal. There is also more openness to and integration of other psychotherapy approaches, such as humanistic and cognitive therapies, as well as the integration of neuroscience and psychoanalysis, called neuropsychoanalysis (Prochaska and Norcross 2010; see also E. B. Luborsky, O'Reilly-Landry, and Arlow 2008). Relational theory has been further developed and refined so that relational psychoanalytic con-cepts can be integrated with other psychotherapeutic approaches, including cognitive-behavioral therapies (Wachtel 2008).

Traditional or classical psychoanalysis is being provided to less than 1 percent of all clients receiving counseling or psychotherapy today. It will be-come less important as shorter-term versions of relational psychoanalysis and time-limited psychoanalytic therapy become more widespread and popular, a shift that is already happening (Prochaska and Norcross 2010). A specific development in this context is the use of treatment manuals that provide de-tailed instruction for conducting time-limited or brief psychoanalytic or more broad-based psychodynamic therapy (Sharf 2008). The Core Conflictual Relationship Theme method developed by Lester Luborsky and his colleagues has been described in detail in treatment manuals (Book 1998; L. Luborsky 1984; L. Luborsky and Crits-Christoph 1998). This method is a sixteen-session model for conducting brief psychodynamic or psychoanalytic therapy. The therapist focuses on relationships that the client brings up, clarifying the client's wish, a response from the other, and a response from the self. The therapist makes carefully timed interpretations of client transference, reflecting the client's attitudes and behaviors from past, early relationships that still influence current relationships with others, including the relationship with the therapist (see Sharf 2008, 60).

Despite these current changes and future directions of psychoanalysis and psychoanalytic therapy, several important concepts from Freud still remain today, based on substantial empirical and clinical support. They include the importance of the unconscious; the crucial role of childhood traumas and experiences in the development of behavioral problems; the pervasiveness of inner conflict in the lives of human beings, who must then devise compromise solutions; and the powerful impact that mental representations of self, others, and relationships have on the current functioning of individuals (Westen 1998).

Formal training to be a psychoanalyst usually requires a minimum of four years of coursework, after one obtains a doctoral degree (PhD or PsyD) in clinical psychology or completes a psychiatry residency and is admitted into a psychoanalytic institute of training. Some institutes also admit social workers in clinical practice. The formal training includes the personal analysis of the candidate in training by a senior psychoanalyst, as well as supervised treatment of clients or analysands seen by the candidate three to five times a week for a few years. The American Psychoanalytic Association (www.apsa.org), founded in 1911 and part of the International Psychoanalytical Association, is the largest psychoanalytic society in the United States, with twenty-nine professional training programs and forty-two affiliate societies. Division 39, or the Division of Psychoanalysis of the American Psychological Association, has a list of ninety-two training programs in psychoanalysis. Many psychoanalytic journals are also being published, including the *International Journal of Psychoanalysis* and the *American Journal of Psychoanalysis* (E. B. Luborsky, O'Reilly-Landry, and Arlow 2008, 28–29). Psychoanalysis and psychoanalytic therapy will therefore continue to be a significant part of contemporary counseling and psychotherapy.

Recommended Readings

In addition to Freud's own works (a total of twenty-four volumes of the Standard Edition published by Hogarth Press in London), the following books are recommended for further reading:

Brenner, C. (1974). *An elementary textbook of psychoanalysis* (Rev. ed.). Garden City, NY: Doubleday (Anchor).

Hall, C. S. (1999). *A primer of Freudian psychology*. New York: Meridian.

Jones, E. (1961). *The life and work of Sigmund Freud* (Abridged ed.). New York: Basic Books.

McWilliams, N. (2004). *Psychoanalytic psychotherapy: A practitioner's guide*. New York: Guilford Press.

Mitchell, S. A. (2000). *Relationality: From attachment to intersubjectivity*. Hillsdale, NJ: Analytic Press.

Person, E. S., Cooper, A. M., & Gabbard, G. O. (2005). *Textbook of psychoanalysis*. Washington, DC: American Psychiatric Publishing.

St. Clair, M., & Wigren, J. (2004). *Object relations and self psychology: An introduction* (4th ed.). Belmont, CA: Brooks/Cole.

5

Adlerian Therapy

Alfred Adler, the founder of *individual psychology* (or Adlerian therapy), was originally part of the inner circle of Sigmund Freud's Vienna Psychoanalytic Society and even served as its president and editor of its journal. However, Adler had substantial disagreements with many of Freud's psychoanalytic views, which Freud could not tolerate. Adler therefore parted ways with Freud in 1911, founding his own school of therapy as well as a new society and journal. Individual psychology, or Adlerian therapy, emphasizes social motivation and subjective perception more than sexual drives in human behavior. In particular, Adler was much less deterministic and more optimistic in his view of human nature. He focused more on the significant influence of life goals on behavior, the crucial role of a basic striving for superiority in every individual, the importance of social interest and connecting with the community, the effects of birth order, and especially the substantial influence of a person's core assumptions and beliefs (erroneous or valid) on his or her lifestyle, with some freedom of choice (Corey 2009).

Adler's great impact on contemporary counseling and psychotherapy is not limited to his own individual psychology or Adlerian therapy school. His theoretical ideas and therapeutic techniques have significantly influenced so-called neo-Freudians such as Karen Horney and Erich Fromm, as well as founders of other schools of therapy like Carl Rogers and Albert Ellis, as well as Viktor Frankl and Rollo May. He also helped to popularize his ideas for the general public, who often associate Adler with the concept of the inferiority complex.

Biographical Sketch of Alfred Adler

Alfred Adler was born on February 7, 1870, in a small Austrian village near Vienna. He was the second son (and third child) in a family of six children with Hungarian-Jewish parents. He grew up in an ethnically diverse neighborhood and was more Viennese than Jewish in his identity. He became a Protestant when he was thirty-four years old.

Adler had an unhappy early childhood filled with emotionally painful experiences and various serious illnesses, including a brush with death due to pneumonia when he was five years old. Two years earlier, when Adler was three years old, a younger brother died in a bed next to him. Adler himself was seriously injured in a couple of bad street accidents near his home. His older brother was very successful and talented, and Adler was deeply envious of him and felt inferior to him. Adler did not do well academically as a young child, so much so that his teacher advised his father to apprentice him to a shoemaker so that he could learn a trade rather than continue in school. However, his father ignored this teacher's advice and instead encouraged Adler to pursue further schooling. Adler did so and ultimately did well academically. He chose to study medicine at the University of Vienna and graduated with his medical degree in 1895. His childhood experiences obviously had a strong effect on his subsequent ideas, such as those regarding inferiority and the inferiority complex and the basic striving for superiority or mastery and perfection.

Adler married Raissa Epstein in 1897, and they had four children, two of whom also pursued careers in psychiatry and psychotherapy. His wife, who was from Russia, was seriously committed to socialism and feminism. She had a significant influence on Adler and his emphasis on the equality of women and men.

In 1898 Adler began his private practice as an ophthalmologist but changed to general practice. Later, he specialized in neurology and psychiatry. As a practicing psychiatrist, he took a keen interest in the whole person, paying attention to the psychological, social, and physical aspects of an individual's life.

In 1902 Freud invited Adler to become part of the psychoanalytic group that Freud was forming at the time. Adler was one of the four original members of the group, and in 1910 he succeeded Freud as president of the Vienna Psychoanalytic Society. However, he had serious disagreements with many of Freud's ideas, especially with Freud's emphasis on sexual drives. Adler focused more on social motivations and subjective perceptions in explaining human behavior. He also did not undergo psychoanalysis for himself. Freud was unable to tolerate Adler's significant differences with him, and Adler parted ways with Freud in 1911. Adler founded the Society for Free Psychoanalytic Research or Investigation, which was later renamed the Society for

Individual Psychology, and in 1914 he and a colleague launched the *Journal of Individual Psychology*.

Adler interrupted his theoretical work to serve as a medical officer in the Austrian army during World War I. After the war, he demonstrated his social interest, especially in children, by establishing over thirty child guidance clinics in the Vienna school system. He also began training other professionals to use his ideas and the techniques of individual psychology, which focused on the whole or total individual. Adler advocated for school reforms and better child-rearing practices and spoke out against prejudices that were responsible for conflict.

Adler also wrote for the general public and was able to popularize his ideas and the methods of individual psychology. His book *Understanding Human Nature* (1959) became a widely read best seller in the United States.

Adler first visited the United States in 1926 and subsequently made many trips to lecture in the United States and other countries. In 1935 he and his wife moved to New York, where he held a faculty position at Long Island College of Medicine. Adler kept a very busy, grueling schedule. Although his friends urged him to slow down, Adler ignored their warnings. He died of a heart attack on May 28, 1937, in Aberdeen, Scotland, during a lecture tour. After Adler's death, Rudolph Dreikurs played a major role in the expansion of individual psychology in the United States.

For further information on Adler's life and work, see P. Bottome (1957), H. Orgler (1963), J. Rattner (1983), E. Hoffman (1994), T. J. Sweeney (1998), H. H. Mosak and M. Maniacci (1999), and J. Carlson, R. E. Watts, and M. Maniacci (2006).

Major Theoretical Ideas of Adlerian Therapy

Perspective on Human Nature

Adler's perspective on human nature was much less pessimistic and deterministic and more optimistic than Freud's view. Adler emphasized the individual's freedom to responsibly choose his or her life goals and purpose in life, which will guide one's life and lifestyle. He has therefore been considered a forerunner to the existential school of therapy by existential therapists such as Rollo May and Viktor Frankl, who also emphasized one's freedom to choose and be fully responsible for one's own life. Although Adler acknowledged that a person's basic approach to life is already formed within the first six years of childhood, he focused more on one's interpretation of the meaning of early childhood experiences and a longing for social connectedness as crucial motivations of human behavior. Adler also emphasized the *teleological*, or goal-oriented, nature of human beings, focusing on conscious choice more than the unconscious, in seeking fulfillment and meaning in life.

A major aspect of Adler's theory is his description of *inferiority feelings*, which are seen as normal, occurring in every human person. Every individual has some area of deficiency that will lead to feelings of inferiority. However, in order to compensate for such feelings, a person will be motivated to strive for mastery, competence, or success: a basic striving for "superiority" or perfection, but not necessarily in an arrogant way. Adler was therefore basically optimistic in his view of human beings as capable of positive *compensation* for inferiority with a creative striving for superiority.

Adler also emphasized the whole person or total personality of an individual, with attention to all aspects of functioning, including the social and systemic context and the psychological and physical dimensions. He called his approach to therapy *individual psychology* to emphasize that it focused on the whole person in social context instead of being reductionistic and narrowly attending to only the internal psychological or biological aspects of the individual.

> **Sidebar 5.1**
>
> **Theoretical Ideas of Adlerian Therapy**
> *(see Corey 2009)*
>
> 1. Subjective perception or interpretation of reality
> 2. Unity and holistic development of personality
>   - Goal-oriented and purposeful behavior
>   - Inferiority and striving for superiority
>   - Lifestyle
> 3. Social interest and community feeling
> 4. Birth order

The major theoretical ideas of Adlerian therapy are subjective perception or interpretation of reality; unity and holistic development of personality (including goal-oriented and purposeful behavior, inferiority and a basic striving for superiority, and the lifestyle of an individual); social interest and community feeling; and birth order (Corey 2009).

Subjective Perception or Interpretation of Reality

Adlerians take a *phenomenological* approach to understanding their clients by focusing on how a client perceives or interprets reality and gives meaning to his or her experiences. In other words, the crucial element is a client's subjective experience of reality in terms of his or her own perceptions, interpretations, assumptions, beliefs, values, thoughts, and feelings, not some objective reality out there. This subjective, phenomenological view of the client's experience of reality as a major influence on human behavior is a key concept not only in Adlerian therapy but also in many other contemporary approaches to counseling and therapy, such as person-centered therapy, Gestalt therapy, existential therapy, reality therapy, cognitive-behavioral therapies, and some systemic therapies and postmodern therapies (Corey 2009). Recently, attempts have been made to integrate Adlerian therapy with cognitive and constructive therapies (Watts 2003).

Unity and Holistic Development of Personality

Adler viewed human personality holistically, with the individual developing in a unified way by self-selecting a basic *life goal* formed in the context of his or her unique life experiences as well as particular family, social, and cultural environments. The interpersonal relationships in the social context of an individual are considered in Adlerian therapy much more than the person's internal or psychological dynamics.

Three major concepts in Adlerian therapy relating to human personality development in a holistic way are goal-oriented and purposeful behavior, inferiority and a basic striving for superiority, and lifestyle.

GOAL-ORIENTED AND PURPOSEFUL BEHAVIOR

In addition to Freud, with whom he increasingly disagreed over time, Adler was also influenced by several significant historical figures, including Pierre Janet, who asserted that the general reason for neurosis is an underlying sense of inferiority; Friedrich Nietzsche, who stressed the central significance of the individual as well as the striving for perfection; Karl Marx and his ideas on socialism and social forces as the major influence on human behavior; and especially Hans Vaihinger, a philosopher who wrote *The Psychology of "As If"* (1911), emphasizing that people form their own perceptions of truth or reality and live by their own self-selected purposes and fictional goals (Parrott 2003).

Adlerians therefore view human behavior as being goal oriented and purposeful, motivated more by future goals than past experiences, a *teleological* explanation rather than a deterministic one. *Fictional finalism* is a term often used by Adlerians to refer to a self-selected, imagined life goal that influences an individual's behavior and actions. However, Adler himself eventually replaced this term with others such as "goal of perfection" or "guiding self-ideal" to refer to a person's basic striving for mastery or superiority (Watts and Holden 1994). Clients can choose their own subjective life goal that will help them to act in ways consistent with it and to perceive and interpret their experiences accordingly.

INFERIORITY AND STRIVING FOR SUPERIORITY

Adler assumed that fundamental feelings of *inferiority* and the need for their *compensation* expressed in a basic *striving for superiority* or perfection or completion are innate in all human beings. Earlier he had written about *organ inferiority*, referring to physical defects or personality deficiencies, in the causation of neurosis (1917). However, Adler was optimistic that human beings can compensate for their feelings of inferiority originating in child-hood by striving for superiority or competence and mastery, resulting often in creative and successful achievements in life.

Nevertheless, feelings of inferiority can become abnormal when they form an *inferiority complex*, in which an individual appears to himself and to others as someone who is unable to solve a problem in a socially useful way (Ansbacher and Ansbacher 1956). Abnormal feelings of inferiority can also result in a *superiority complex*, whereby a person appears to herself and to others as someone who is capable and strong, but the external appearance of self-importance and inflated self-confidence actually mask deep and abnormal feelings of inferiority (Sharf 2008).

Lifestyle

A person's *lifestyle* in the Adlerian context refers to a plan for living or a style of life based on one's fundamental beliefs that pulls together reality for the person and lends meaning to life experiences. One's lifestyle is thus the typical way that one lives or moves toward a self-selected life goal. Adlerians view people as proactive participants in life and society. Although they believe that an individual's life goal is mainly set within the first six years of life, he or she can still correct faulty or invalid assumptions and beliefs and consciously choose a more appropriate life goal based on more accurate and valid assumptions and beliefs and hence a new lifestyle guided by the revised life goal (Corey 2009).

Social Interest and Community Feeling

Adler's ideas about social interest and community feeling may be his most unique and important theoretical contributions to individual psychology (Ansbacher 1992). *Social interest* refers to a person's sense of empathy and identification with others and interest in achieving a better future for all humanity. Social interest is usually demonstrated through shared social activities with respect for others. Alder viewed social interest as a crucial characteristic of mental health. *Community feeling* is closely associated with social interest and refers to a sense of belonging and social connectedness with others in the contexts of family and society (Corey 2009).

Adler described the following three life tasks that everyone seeks to successfully accomplish: (1) the social task of building friendships; (2) the love-marriage task of achieving intimacy; and (3) the occupational task of work or making significant contributions to society (see Dreikurs and Mosak 1966). Three other life tasks that Adlerians have added are: (4) the self-acceptance task of learning to get along with oneself (Dreikurs and Mosak 1967); (5) the development of spirituality task, which involves growing in one's life goals, meaning, values, and relationship with the cosmos or universe (Mosak and

Dreikurs 1967); and (6) the parenting and family task (Dinkmeyer, Dinkmeyer, and Sperry 1987).

Birth Order

Adler viewed birth order and sibling relationships as another crucial factor influencing a person's social relationships and lifestyle. He emphasized that the *psychological*, or perceived, birth order of the child is more significant than the actual, or chronological, birth order. He provided possible influences of birth order on the oldest child (who is treated like an only child with some pampering until the next child comes along), the second child (who must share attention with another child, often with some competitive struggle), the middle child (who often feels forgotten or squeezed out and can be a problem child or a peacemaker), the youngest child (who tends to be the most pampered child), and the only child (who is often pampered by parents and may have trouble sharing with others) (see Corey 2009, 103–4). Adlerians often criticize birth-order research that focuses only on actual position or birth order in the family. A good example that illustrates the need to look more at the perceived or psychological birth order rather than simply at actual birth order in a family is provided by Sharf, using the model of a family with three children, in which the first child is one year older than the second (or middle child), who in turn is twelve years older than the youngest (or third child). Adlerian therapists may approach this particular family as consisting of two subsystems: the first as a family with a younger and an older sibling (the first two children), and the second as a family with an only child, with the youngest child viewed more like an only child (2008, 118).

Therapeutic Process and Relationship

In helping their clients, Adlerian therapists use a model that is more psycho-educational than medical. They do not view their clients as mentally ill and in need of a cure. Instead, Adlerian therapists believe that the major problem for their clients is that they are *discouraged* in dealing with problems and struggles in living. *Encouragement* is therefore the most important thera-peutic method employed in Adlerian therapy, which also involves directly providing information, teaching, and guiding clients to help them change their *faulty assumptions* and the *mistaken goals* in their *private logic* or thinking, so that they can be reeducated to live more on the useful rather than the useless side of life. Clients will then experience more social inter-est and community feeling, with greater courage and self-confidence to live this way.

The therapeutic relationship between the Adlerian therapist and the client is a warm and collaborative one in which they can work together to make the changes necessary for the client to live a more meaningful and fulfilling life. The Adlerian therapist focuses on strongly encouraging and affirming the client, in order to counter the significant discouragement that often brings clients into therapy in the first place. The Adlerian therapist is therefore active and directive, but also very empathic, supportive, and encouraging. The client needs to be open and willing to disclose personal and family information. For example, the Adlerian therapist will use a questionnaire to assess the client's *family constellation*, or relationships and experiences with parents, siblings, and others who are living with the client at home. The therapist will also ask the client to provide *early recollections*, or memories of particular events in childhood, that the client is able to reexperience, in order to further assess how the client views himself or herself and others, as well as the future. The Adlerian therapist uses such methods to assess the client's lifestyle, so that clearer goals for therapy can be collaboratively set. Adlerian therapy tends to be relatively short term, usually lasting from several months to a year or so.

Some of Adlerian therapy's main psychoeducational goals for the client include fostering social interest, countering discouragement and reducing feelings of inferiority, and modifying faulty assumptions and mistaken goals— that is, changing a person's lifestyle, changing faulty motivation and values, encouraging an individual to have a sense of equality with others, and helping a person to become a productive member of society (see Mosak and Maniacci 2008, 79).

Major Therapeutic Techniques and Interventions

Adlerian therapy is usually conducted in the following flexible and sometimes overlapping phases (Dreikurs 1967):

1. Establishing a therapeutic relationship
2. Conducting an assessment of the client's dynamics
3. Providing insight and interpretation
4. Facilitating reorientation and reeducation

More-specific therapeutic techniques and interventions in each of these four major phases of Adlerian therapy will now be briefly described. It should be noted that Adlerian therapists are quite pragmatic and eclectic in the particular therapeutic techniques they use to help clients achieve their therapeutic goals.

Establishing a Therapeutic Relationship

The Adlerian therapist works at forming a warm, empathic, and collaborative relationship with the client based on genuine caring, encouragement, and mutual respect and trust. The therapist does not rush in to problem-solve but instead provides much support and understanding to facilitate client exploration and disclosure.

In this first phase of therapy, the Adlerian therapist employs the following therapeutic techniques: listening and attending with deep empathy, sensitively understanding and tracking the client's subjective experiences as far as possible, clarifying and setting goals, and making tentative interpretations of the possible purposes of the client's behaviors and symptoms (Corey 2009).

Conducting an Assessment of the Client's Dynamics

This second phase of Adlerian therapy uses two main types of interview: the subjective interview and the objective interview (Dreikurs 1997). In the *subjective interview*, the Adlerian therapist, through active listening with demonstrated deep interest, supports the client in telling his or her life story as fully as possible. The therapist attempts to identify the purposes and meanings of the client's life experiences. The client is often asked toward the end of this subjective interview whether he or she has anything else to share with the therapist so that the therapist can better understand the client and his or her concerns. In order to further clarify the client's problems and goals, Adlerian therapists often end the subjective interview by asking "The Question": "How would your life be different, and what would you be *doing* differently, if you did not have this symptom or problem?" (Corey 2009, 109). A shorter version of The Question is: "What would be different if you were well?" (Parrott 2003, 135)."

The *objective interview* seeks to obtain information in the following areas: the history of the client's problems; precipitating events, if any; medical history, with past and present medication usage; social history; reasons for the client coming to therapy at this particular time; the client's way of coping and dealing with life tasks; and an assessment of the client's lifestyle (Corey 2009). Adler conceptualized lifestyle as consisting of four major components: the *self-concept*, or one's view of oneself based on reality; the *self-ideal*, or one's view of oneself as one would like to be; the *picture of the world*, or one's view of the reasons for things working the way they do in the external world; and one's *ethical convictions*. This lifestyle, or basic strategy or map for living, influences one's choices and behaviors. There are three major "entrance gates to mental life" that Adlerian therapists explore with clients in order to assess and better understand their lifestyles: birth order and the family constellation, early recollections or memories, and dreams (Parrott 2003).

Birth Order and Family Constellation. Birth order, or perceived psychological birth order, is an important part of the assessment of the client's family background and experiences or family constellation. The Adlerian therapist explores with the client not only his or her birth order, but also experiences with his or her mother and father, siblings, and others in the family; the marital relationship between the client's mother and father, including how they dealt with conflicts; and the disciplinary methods they used with the children. Adler viewed such family-of-origin experiences as having a crucial effect on the personality development of an individual.

Early Recollections or Memories. Adler emphasized the crucial significance of a person's earliest memories or recollections of specific, clear events or experiences, especially in childhood, for understanding his or her present lifestyle or current view of life. The Adlerian therapist will often ask the following question in order to guide a client to recall such early memories or recollections: "I would like to hear about your early memories. Think back to when you were very young, as early as you can remember (before the age of ten), and *tell me something that happened one time*" (Corey 2009, 111). A shorter version of this question would be: "Think as far back as you can and tell me your earliest memory from your childhood years" (Parrott 2003, 126). The therapist will ask for more specific details about a particular recollection and not settle for vague, general memories. Clients often provide several specific early recollections, which the Adlerian therapist will record in order to identify possible themes that may be connected to the client's current lifestyle or view of life.

Dreams. Adler viewed dreams not as wish fulfillments (as Freud did) but as an individual's attempts to deal with future difficulties. The moods or emotions experienced in a dream may also be related to the next day's anticipated events. Adler further interpreted dreams as possible reflections of progress (or the lack of it) in Adlerian therapy. He noted that dreams may become more active as therapy progresses more successfully and the client makes more therapeutic changes in his or her life and lifestyle. Dreams can therefore be used in conjunction with family constellation, including birth order, and early recollections or memories to assess a client's lifestyle in Adlerian therapy.

In addition to these three major ways of lifestyle assessment, Adlerian therapists may also use two others: assessment of *basic mistakes* and assessment of a client's *assets* (Sharf 2008, 124). *Basic mistakes* are based on early recollections and refer to the negative, self-defeating aspects of a client's lifestyle. Harold Mosak and Michael Maniacci (2008, 82) describe five categories of basic mistakes:

1. *Overgeneralizations*, for example, "Life is dangerous."
2. *False or impossible goals of security*, for example, "I have to please everybody."
3. *Misperceptions of life and life's demands*, for example, "Life is so hard."
4. *Minimization or denial of one's worth*, for example, "I am stupid."
5. *Faulty values*, for example, "Be first even if you have to climb over others."

Identifying basic mistakes can be helpful in the assessment of a client's lifestyle, but correcting or modifying such mistakes in thinking or worldview is more difficult because a client may not be consciously aware that he or she is making basic mistakes in thinking.

The assessment of *assets* involves focusing on what is good and positive in a client rather than on what is deficient and negative. In assessing and identifying a client's assets, such as academic skills, athletic abilities, or integrity, Adlerian therapists can provide strong encouragement to a client by giving direct and affirming feedback about his or her particular strengths.

Providing Insight and Interpretation

In this third phase, Adlerian therapists proceed to interpret material collected in the process of lifestyle assessment in order to facilitate the client's self-understanding or insight into his or her behavior. In Adlerian therapy, the therapist makes interpretations only with regard to the client's goals and purposes, and not about his or her internal psychological dynamics (Dreikurs 1967).

Interpretations are provided in a tentative and well-timed manner, so that clients are less likely to react in a defensive way or with resistance. Adlerian therapists often present an interpretation in the form of a tentative suggestion or question, using statements such as, "I wonder if . . . ," "It seems to me that . . . ," and "Could it be that . . ." Clients are more likely to accept interpretations phrased in this sensitive and tentative style and thus develop deeper insight and self-understanding into the purposes and goals of their current functioning as well as dysfunctioning, including symptoms. They may also realize how they can go about changing or correcting their basic mistakes in thinking or in their private logic and in their mistaken goals.

Facilitating Reorientation and Reeducation

The last phase of Adlerian therapy is action oriented and focuses on facilitating the client's reorientation and reeducation or helping the client to translate insights into actions. Adlerian therapists employ several therapeutic techniques to do this, but the crucial intervention is the use of encouragement. Clients are encouraged as well as challenged to take courageous steps and risks in order to bring about constructive and positive changes in their lives.

Some clients may need to make enormous changes, but many clients need only to be reoriented to what is called the *useful side of life*. This term refers to several characteristics such as courage, being valued, having a sense of belonging and connectedness with the community, caring for others and their well-being, embracing imperfection, confidence, a sense of humor, a willingness to contribute, and friendliness that is shown outwardly. In contrast, the *useless side of life* involves self-protection and self-absorption, avoiding engagement in life tasks, and committing negative acts against other people (Corey 2009). Adlerian therapy seeks to help clients move from the useless side of life, which is associated with less functionality and more psychopathology, to the useful side of life.

The following are the main therapeutic techniques used in Adlerian therapy to facilitate reorientation and reeducation in clients: encouragement, immediacy, asking "the question," acting "as if," catching oneself, spitting in the client's soup, avoiding the tar baby, push-button technique, paradoxical intention, task setting and commitment, homework, life tasks and therapy, and terminating and summarizing the interview (see Sharf 2008, 126–30; see also Bitter, Christensen, Hawes, and Nicoll 1998; Bitter and Nicoll 2000; J. Carlson, Watts, and Maniacci 2006; Dinkmeyer and Sperry 2000).

> **Sidebar 5.2**
>
> **Adlerian Therapeutic Techniques**
> *(see Sharf 2008, 126–30)*
>
> 1. Encouragement
> 2. Immediacy
> 3. Asking "The Question"
> 4. Acting "As If"
> 5. Catching oneself
> 6. Spitting in the client's soup
> 7. Avoiding the tar baby
> 8. Push-button technique
> 9. Paradoxical intention
> 10. Task setting and commitment
> 11. Homework
> 12. Life tasks and therapy
> 13. Terminating and summarizing the interview

Encouragement. Encouragement is the most significant and unique therapeutic technique used by Adlerian therapists to support and affirm clients as an antidote to their discouragement in life. Encouragement is especially crucial in helping clients to believe that they can make the changes they want and need to make and to actually take action and even risks toward therapeutic and constructive change. Encouragement does not consist only of comments such as, "Keep on trying; I know that you are capable of doing this." Adlerian therapists use creativity and deep caring, as well as courage, to strongly affirm and support their clients.

Adler himself was once confronted by a young woman suffering from schizophrenia. Even though she physically hit him, he responded with friendliness instead of retaliation. He did this in order to encourage and affirm her, which led to her renewed courage. She then broke his glass window and cut her hand as a result. Instead of locking her in her room, Adler bandaged her hand without reproaching her and again engaged in creatively and courageously encouraging her. She responded well to Adler and these therapeutic interventions (see Ansbacher and Ansbacher 1956, 316–17, cited in Sharf 2008, 126–27).

Immediacy. With this technique, an Adlerian therapist comments on what he or she is presently experiencing with the client in the actual therapy session as it is unfolding. It may involve verbal or nonverbal communication by the client that somehow relates to the therapy goals already agreed upon with the therapist. The therapist will make an immediacy response or comment in a tentative way and will often ask a question at the end of the comment such as, "Is that right?" or "Is this correct?" This process will help the client to be more open and less defensive so that he or she can respond to the therapist's immediacy expression by further exploring what may be blocking the achievement of therapeutic goals.

Asking "The Question." Another Adlerian therapeutic technique is to ask "The Question": "What would be different if you were well?" This crucial question helps clients clarify what and how they really want to change. Adler initially used this question to help him assess whether a client's problems were mainly physiological or psychological. Although it is typically used in earlier phases of therapy as an assessment tool, it can be used at any time in the therapy process. For example, if a client who complains of pain answers "The Question" by saying, "I would be able to sleep better at night without pain," it might indicate a more physiological basis for the complaint. On the other hand, if the client responds by saying, "I would be a better husband and father," it might indicate that the client's pain is a way of avoiding psychological issues. However, the way in which an Adlerian therapist can interpret a client's answer to "The Question" may not be so clear cut. Thus, it may be better to simply use this technique to help clients focus more clearly on what they really want to change and how they can go about doing so.

Acting "As If." In this technique, the Adlerian therapist asks the client to act "as if" he were capable of executing or doing certain actions that he is afraid to try and actually to do them as a homework assignment in the week ahead. For example, a very shy client may be encouraged by the therapist to act "as if" she were a confident person and to try to assert herself at work by asking the boss for a long-overdue pay raise. The therapist may also role-play this behavior in the therapy session with the client, before the client attempts it in real life in the coming week.

Catching Oneself. The technique of "catching oneself" involves instructing a client to catch himself or herself just before engaging in a negative or problematic behavior, and therefore to be aware of it in time to change it before it occurs out of habit. Over time, a client may be able to catch himself or herself just *before* rather than after engaging in a particular self-defeating behavior and to stop just in time to replace it with a more constructive and helpful behavior.

Spitting in the Client's Soup. This technique's name is based on a bad habit that children at boarding schools used to practice in order to get another person's soup by spitting in it. The Adlerian therapist uses this technique by making a comment about a specific client behavior that takes the reward or attraction out of it. For example, a mother may express how much she sacrifices in order to provide for her children. The therapist may then comment on how sad it is that the mother has no time for herself and her own enjoyment of life, thus removing the heroic aspect out of her self-sacrifice.

Avoiding the Tar Baby. Adler used the phrase "tar baby" to refer to an issue that is sticky (tar) or difficult for a client to face. A client may therefore be particularly sensitive to how this issue is addressed and be defensive or resistant if the therapist deals with it in an insensitive or confrontational way. For example, a client may feel that colleagues at work tend to ignore him and now wonders if the therapist may also not be really interested in his problems and thus may be ignoring him. To avoid the tar baby, the Adlerian therapist reassures the client by asking more questions about what is happening in the client's work situation.

Push-Button Technique. This Adlerian technique described by Mosak (1985) involves asking a client to close his eyes and first imagine a very pleasant memory (such as a beautiful sunset or a success experience) and attend to the positive feelings associated with it. The client is next instructed to imagine a horrible memory (such as the death of a loved one or a failure experience) and attend to the negative feelings associated with it. The third and final part of this technique involves asking the client to imagine again another very pleasant memory or go back to the first pleasant memory and experience the positive feelings associated with it. At the end of this three-part imagery technique, the client opens his eyes and realizes that he can have some control over his feelings by the thoughts or memories he chooses. The Adlerian therapist therefore helps the client learn this push-button technique: that one can control one's feelings through the thoughts, memories, or images one chooses, or by the buttons one pushes in one's mind.

Paradoxical Intention. With this technique, the Adlerian therapist encourages clients to actually practice and even exaggerate the very symptoms or problematic behaviors troubling them. Adler has described this intervention as "prescribing the symptom." For example, the therapist will instruct a compulsive hand-washer to wash his or her hands even more frequently. In so doing, the Adlerian therapist expects the client to find the inappropriate behavior, now exaggerated, to be less attractive and therefore be more likely to stop it or change it.

Task Setting and Commitment. This therapeutic technique involves the Adlerian therapist collaboratively working closely with a client to plan specific steps of action to overcome certain problems or achieve particular goals. The client chooses what he or she is willing to do and therefore makes the commitment to perform certain tasks to achieve his or her goals. The therapist then helps the client to plan and implement the steps needed to accomplish a task that has been broken down to a manageable size, with a greater likelihood of success.

For example, a client who has decided to return to work after taking medical leave to have surgery will be asked by the therapist what specific steps he or she would take, such as looking at job ads and postings, applying for relevant job openings, going for job interviews, and finally accepting a job offer if appropriate. The therapist encourages the client to focus more on getting good job leads or possibilities first, rather than on getting a job, as the initial task set before the client.

Homework. Adlerian therapists frequently assign homework for clients to complete between sessions, to help clients accomplish the tasks they have chosen to do. The homework needs to be something that is clear, concrete, and relatively easy. For example, the therapist may suggest to a client who is looking for a job that he or she contact a social worker for possible job leads before their next counseling appointment. They can then discuss the job options and plan the next steps for the client to take.

Life Tasks and Therapy. This technique involves the therapist asking the client to rate his or her level of satisfaction or happiness in particular life-task areas, such as family, work, friends, and community. In doing this, the client may discover issues needing work that were previously unrecognized by the client. This technique can also be helpful in assessing therapeutic change and progress toward achieving the goals of therapy throughout the course of therapy.

Terminating and Summarizing the Interview. This technique involves setting clear time limits for a therapy session so that the therapist ends a session on time with a client (e.g., thirty-minute sessions for a child and forty-five-to-fifty-minute sessions for an adult client). The Adlerian therapist will usually summarize the interview at the end of the session with a client and assign appropriate homework.

It should be clear by now that Adlerian therapists use a variety of therapeutic techniques to help their clients. They also freely give appropriate and well-timed advice, suggestion, and direction in the reorientation phase of Adlerian therapy, which is more action-oriented, after insight and interpretation have already been provided. Helpful advice is therefore seen as an appropriate therapeutic intervention in Adlerian therapy (see J. Sommers-Flanagan and Sommers-Flanagan 2004, 101).

Adlerian Therapy in Practice

A Hypothetical Transcript

Client: I'm feeling tired and lethargic . . . like I have no energy to do anything, and I don't feel like doing anything. . . . I guess I'm feeling depressed again . . . and stuck with no real meaning or direction in my life.

Adlerian Therapist: You're feeling down and fatigued again, as well as somewhat lost and aimless in your life. What would be different if you were well?

Client: If I were well and not so tired out and depressed and aimless? Well . . . I am tired of being so tired and depressed! It would be nice to be well again. . . . I guess if I were well I would of course feel better and want to do more things like I used to . . .

Adlerian Therapist: What things would you do more of, if you were feeling better, if you were well?

Client: I guess I would go bowling more often, something I used to enjoy so much that I belonged to a bowling team and played in bowling leagues. That was years ago . . . I just don't have the interest or energy to do this anymore. If I were well, I would also be more involved in community service such as tutoring inner city kids in math and English, which I did for a couple of months some time ago. I would also take up painting again, as a hobby . . .

Adlerian Therapist: Great! Sounds like you actually do have several enjoyable and fulfilling activities you would like to do if you were well, like bowling, tutoring, and painting. I actually believe that you can begin to take small, baby steps to do some of these things, to act "as if" you were better or almost well again. . . . What do you think?

Client: I'm not sure . . . this constant fatigue really drags me down. My doctor has done all kinds of tests and not found anything physically wrong with me. However, I do feel a little hope and interest as I think of myself being well and doing some of these things such as bowling and painting. . . . The tutoring is a bit more difficult for me at this time. So, are you asking me to act as if I were better or almost well and perhaps start a bit of painting again?

Adlerian Therapist: Yes, you're getting the hang of it, that if you begin to act as if you were better or almost well, you may be able to actually do some of these meaningful and enjoyable activities you mentioned. Your idea of starting to do some simple painting again sounds great, and I'm wondering if you can tell me more how you plan to go about trying to accomplish this in the coming week.

This hypothetical transcript of a small part of an Adlerian therapy session demonstrates the use by the therapist of several Adlerian therapeutic techniques: asking "The Question," acting "as if," and judiciously but clearly providing encouragement, suggestion, and some direction for the client. The therapist is also beginning to formulate homework for the client, in collaborative planning with the client.

Critique of Adlerian Therapy: Strengths and Weaknesses

Adler's theoretical ideas and therapeutic techniques were far ahead of his time and have had a pervasive and significant influence on the entire field of counseling and psychotherapy. His emphases on how one's thinking significantly affects one's feelings and behavior, how one's future goals and current values influence one's life, how one can choose to change one's lifestyle, and how one is motivated by social factors such as social interest and community feeling have all greatly impacted other schools or approaches to counseling and psychotherapy but often without acknowledgment to Adler (Ellenberger 1970). However, Albert Ellis did acknowledge Alder as the "true father of modern psychotherapy" (Ellis 1970, 11).

Adlerian therapy has been used to help clients with a wide range of psychological disorders or problems such as anxiety disorders, some affective disorders, personality disorders, conduct disorders, and antisocial disorders (L. Seligman 1986). It has been applied in various settings and with different age groups, for example, with children, parents, adolescents, families, teacher groups, and other social segments. It is therefore a versatile and broadly applicable approach to therapy (Parrott 2003). It has also been applied to education, parent education, couples counseling, family counseling, and group counseling (Corey 2009).

Adlerian therapy is also a comprehensive approach that deals with the whole or total person—hence the term "individual psychology," which emphasizes treating the individual in a holistic or comprehensive way, focusing on the physical, psychological, social, and even spiritual aspects of human life. The emphasis on social motivation makes Adlerian therapy more open and sensitive to social, cultural, and diversity issues, compared to a more traditional Freudian psychoanalytic approach, which tends to focus too much on internal or intrapsychic conflicts and dynamics.

Adler's emphasis on the equality of women and men has shaped Adlerian therapy to be an egalitarian approach to counseling that can be incorporated more easily within contemporary therapies such as feminist and postmodern approaches.

Adlerian therapy also uses several practical and helpful therapeutic techniques with the clear, overarching therapeutic principle of facilitating *encouragement* of clients. Some of these counseling interventions are simple and straightforward, based on a more commonsense approach to helping clients. Adlerian therapy also views the judicious provision of advice, suggestion, and direction as therapeutically helpful and valuable. Adlerian techniques can therefore be used not only by counselors or therapists but also by teachers, parents, and the clergy, due to their simplicity and wide applicability.

Finally, Adlerian therapy can be practiced within a time-limited, short-term model of helping clients within several months to a year. This is another strength of this approach since effective or efficacious short-term therapies are particularly valued by managed care in the current health-care context in the United States.

Adlerian therapy, however, has several weaknesses. First, Adler was not that systematic and thorough in the development and description of his theoretical ideas and therapeutic techniques. Many of his writings and publications consist of lectures he had given. He emphasized teaching and practice more than careful, systematic theory building and clear operationalization and definition of terms used in individual psychology. In fact, even calling his approach individual psychology may be misleading since his unique emphasis is on social motivation rather than individual dynamics.

Second, some critics regard Adlerian therapy as somewhat superficial and simplistic, since it emphasizes eventual reorientation and reeducation of the client and pays less attention to insight and interpretation, although it does not ignore interpretation and the need to explore early childhood recollections. Adlerian therapy, however, diverges significantly from traditional Freudian psychoanalytic therapy, which focuses mainly on interpretation of unconscious intrapsychic dynamics and conflicts. Thus Adlerian therapy has been criticized by traditional Freudians for not being deep enough.

Third, Adlerian therapy may not be the most appropriate approach for helping clients who need more direct assistance with addressing immediate concerns and stresses, such as poverty, unemployment, and violence. Although Adlerian therapy is more directive and short term than Freudian psychoanalysis, it still requires clients to explore their early recollections and dreams as well as engage in lifestyle assessments.

Finally, Adlerian therapy has not been sufficiently evaluated in well-controlled therapy outcome studies. Most of the evaluations of Adlerian therapy have been uncontrolled case studies, which can be biased and methodologically flawed. Definitive conclusions about the effectiveness of Adlerian therapy therefore cannot be drawn at this time.

A Biblical Perspective on Adlerian Therapy

Adler's view of human nature is more optimistic and less deterministic than that of Freud. Although Adler believed that an individual's basic approach to life is formed within the first six years of life, he allowed for change to occur through a person's freedom to choose new goals and new ways of thinking and perceiving reality. His more positive view of human nature, emphasizing choice and the possibility of change, is somewhat consistent with the biblical view, which also emphasizes the need to choose (cf. Deut. 30:19; Josh. 24:15). However, Adler's view may be too optimistic or positive, paying insufficient attention to the darker side of human nature that is fallen and sinful (Jer. 17:9; Rom. 3:23) and in need of redemption and salvation through Jesus Christ (Rom. 6:23; 2 Cor. 5:17).

Adler's focus on how future goals can motivate and direct a person's behavior is a good corrective to Freud's overemphasis on the deterministic influence of early childhood and past experiences on an individual's personality and current functioning. It is also more consistent with a biblical perspective that is future oriented, viewing Christ's second coming or heaven and eternal realities as crucial motivational goals that Christians look forward to, in a way that purifies and positively affects their present behavior and life (see Titus 2:11–14; 1 John 3:2–3).

Adler's emphasis on the need to identify and correct mistaken goals and basic mistakes in thinking is also consistent with the biblical perspective on the need to be transformed by the renewing of our mind (see Rom. 12:2). One's thinking does greatly affect one's feelings and behavior, and truthful, biblical thinking is especially crucial from a Christian perspective.

Another aspect of Adlerian theory that is consistent with a biblical perspective is its focus on social interest and community feeling. Adler emphasized the need for every person to be connected with his or her community and to contribute to others' welfare by having a genuine social interest in other people. Scripture also emphasizes the need for other people and connection not only interpersonally but also spiritually as members of the body of Christ (1 Cor. 12), serving one another with genuine agape love (1 Cor. 13), which is deeper than social interest. The Adlerian idea of social interest is therefore more in accordance with the Bible's emphasis on body life and community.

The crucial role of encouragement in Adlerian therapy is another aspect that agrees with the Bible's emphasis on encouraging one another (see, e.g., 1 Thess. 5:11, 14; Heb. 3:13; 10:25), especially with the spiritual gift of encouragement if one is blessed with it by the Holy Spirit (Rom. 12:8). The spiritual gift of encouragement may be particularly helpful in counseling and people-helping ministries (Tan 1999b).

The reorientation and reeducation phase of Adlerian therapy, which is action oriented, makes it a more balanced counseling approach that does not narrowly focus on insight and interpretation of personal, internal dynamics. The Bible similarly emphasizes the need to take steps of faith, to have appropriate works of obedience, because faith, without resulting works, is dead or not true faith at all (James 2:17, 26). Such action steps, however, should still be done in dependence on God and the power of the Holy Spirit, and not simply by self-effort.

Finally, the comprehensive assessment of life tasks in an individual's life in Adlerian therapy includes the spiritual dimension as an important and valid part of human life. This is a good corrective to Freud's reductionistic view of religious longings as an obsessional neurosis based on wish fulfillment and longing for a father. However, the Adlerian view of the spiritual dimension is still somewhat vague and generic and does not necessarily refer to God or religious beliefs. The Bible's view of spirituality is more substantial and specific and ultimately Christ centered, emphasizing our goal to become more like Jesus in authentic Christian spirituality (Rom. 8:29).

Other criticisms of Adlerian therapy can be made from a biblical perspective. The emphasis on being action oriented with the use of some simple techniques to encourage change can be somewhat superficial and simplistic. Although Adlerian therapists do use interpretation to help clients gain insight, it may be necessary to focus on this aspect more and deal with the deeper and darker issues of the human heart, which is fallen and sinful (Ps. 57:6; Jer. 17:9). Another emphasis of Adlerian therapy is the phenomenological or subjective view of one's perception of reality. This Adlerian view can conflict with the Bible's view of eternal biblical truth, which is more objective. The Adlerian perspective is actually somewhat contradictory because it does identify mistaken goals and faulty assumptions and delineates several basic mistakes in thinking that assume some objective measure of truth.

Finally, the Adlerian focus on inferiority and the compensatory striving for superiority (perfection or competence) in every individual as a foundational motivation can be problematic from a biblical perspective. Although such compensatory striving for superiority need not be prideful or arrogant, it nevertheless focuses on the human tendency, even if creative, to emphasize strength and mastery in oneself. Pride may very well be present, in subtle, if not obvious, ways. Even if the striving for superiority does not deteriorate into a more pathological and negative superiority complex, it is nevertheless dangerously close to sinful pride because it focuses on self-achievement and strength in oneself. The Bible's emphasis on humility (see, e.g., Phil. 2:3–5; 1 Pet. 5:5–6) and how God's power is made perfect in weakness (2 Cor. 12:9–10) and *not* in strength or superiority is not easily reconciled with Adler's focus on striving for superiority. Ultimately, such striving must be surrendered to the Lord Jesus, who will enable us to experience sufficient grace and strength in weakness so that delightful security and stability in him will replace both feelings of inferiority and the striving for superiority. Our goals will also be directed by God and his will for us, rather than setting our own life goals, which again may be mistaken.

Research: Empirical Status of Adlerian Therapy

While some aspects of Adlerian theory have received attention in research or empirical evaluation, such as the effects of birth order (see Derlega, Winstead, and Jones 2005) and social interest (see Watkins and Guarnaccia 1999), there has been limited empirical evaluation of the effectiveness of Adlerian therapy itself. The few outcome studies of Adlerian therapy (see M. L. Smith, Glass, and Miller 1980) whether with children (see Weisz, Hawley, and Doss 2004) or with adults (see Grawe, Donati, and Bernauer 1998) are not well controlled enough and are too few in number to allow any definitive conclusions about the effectiveness of Adlerian therapy at this time. The best tentative conclusion that can be drawn from the limited empirical evidence available is that Adlerian therapy is better than no treatment and seems to be as effective as client-centered therapy and psychoanalytic therapy in several studies (see Prochaska and Norcross 2010, 84).

Adlerian therapists have preferred the case method, or uncontrolled clinical case studies, over controlled outcome research to evaluate the effectiveness of Adlerian therapy (Mosak and Maniacci 2008). It is hoped that Adlerian therapy will be subjected to more well-controlled outcome studies in the near future, so that the empirical status for its effectiveness can be more solid.

Future Directions

Adler has had a great impact on contemporary counseling and psychotherapy. It is ironic that the success and popularity of many of his ideas and therapeutic techniques have resulted in their incorporation into other approaches to counseling and therapy, so that the distinctiveness of Adlerian therapy has become more diluted as time has gone by (J. Carlson and Englar-Carlson 2008). At the same time, Adlerian therapists are also becoming more eclectic in their views and therapeutic practice, incorporating ideas and techniques from other schools of counseling and therapy. Some authors have therefore concluded that Adlerian therapy may become less distinctive and less important in the future (Prochaska and Norcross 2010). However, Mosak and Maniacci (2008) recently painted a more optimistic picture of the future of Adlerian therapy as that of a respectable, viable, and growing therapeutic system. Individual psychology societies currently exist in over a dozen countries.

There are many loyal practitioners of Adlerian therapy, as well as training institutes and schools, including the Adler School of Professional Psychology in Chicago (www.adler.edu). The *Journal of Individual Psychology* is published by the North American Society of Adlerian Psychology (www.alfredadler.org), which has around twelve hundred members. Although less than 1 percent of psychotherapists surveyed in the United States indicated Adlerian therapy as their primary theoretical orientation (Prochaska and Norcross 2010, 3), the actual number of Adlerian therapists in practice is larger. Adlerians are also better known for their work in educational settings and public schools (Sharf 2008). Adlerian therapy will survive and even flourish if current practitioners preserve its unique approach even with further refinements of Adler's ideas and techniques and if more controlled outcome research is conducted to establish a stronger empirical base.

Recommended Readings

Adler, A. (1958). *What life should mean to you*. New York: Capricorn.

Carlson, J., Watts, R. E., & Maniacci, M. (2006). *Adlerian therapy: Theory and practice*. Washington, DC: American Psychological Association.

Dinkmeyer, D. C., & Sperry, L. (2000). *Counseling and psychotherapy: An integrated individual psychology approach* (3rd ed.). Upper Saddle River, NJ: Merrill/Prentice-Hall.

Mosak, H. H., & Maniacci, M. (1999). *A primer of Adlerian psychology*. Philadelphia: Brunner/Mazel.

Sweeney, T. J. (1998). *Adlerian counseling: A practitioner's approach* (4th ed.). Philadelphia: Accelerated Development.

6

Jungian Therapy

arl Gustav Jung, the founder of *analytical psychology* (Jungian therapy or analytical psychotherapy) was Sigmund Freud's colleague. They first met in 1907 but agreed to end their close relationship in 1913 because of growing differences Jung had with Freud's psychoanalytic views. Jung also resigned then as president of the International Psychoanalytic Association and as editor of the *Psychoanalytic Yearbook*. Freud had earlier treated Jung with deep respect and appreciation and even considered him to be the crown prince of psychoanalysis or Freud's successor in 1909. Both Jung and Adler eventually parted ways with Freud and went on to develop their own approaches to therapy, which differed from Freud's psychoanalysis in significant ways. There were also tensions and differences between Jung and Adler. Although Jung's analytical psychology has some foundation in Freudian and Adlerian views, it goes beyond them.

Jung's unique contribution is his idea of a collective unconscious in addition to a personal unconscious in each person. In Jungian therapy, clients are encouraged to connect the unconscious and the conscious layers of their mind in constant dialogue. Jungian therapists use techniques such as dream analysis and the interpretation of symbols to help clients be more aware of their *archetypes*, that is, the organizing patterns in their unconscious that are more transpersonal or collective. The goals of Jungian therapy include self-knowledge, reintegration, and individuation, all of which can best be achieved in the context of a healing and profound encounter and relationship between the Jungian therapist and the client (Douglas 2008).

Biographical Sketch of Carl Jung

Carl Gustav Jung was born in 1875 in the small village of Kesswil in Switzerland. He was the eldest son in his family and had a sister nine years younger. His father was a clergyman whose own father was a well-known physician and classical scholar. His mother's ancestors included many theologians, including her own father. In fact, eight of Jung's uncles were pastors. He was therefore exposed to Protestant theology and church tradition from an early age. He also received an excellent education that included classical Greek and Latin. Later in his life, Jung struggled with the religious beliefs that he was brought up with.

Jung's childhood was not a happy one. He often felt lonely and had a number of insecurities and fears. He also tended to be an introspective person. When he was three years old, his mother became ill and had to be hospitalized and absent from the home for a significant period of time during which Jung felt abandoned. Jung was close to his mother, but he experienced her in a divided way, involving two sides of her personality: one was the intuitive side, which included an interest in parapsychology and more mysterious things that he feared, and the other was her warm and maternal side, which comforted him. Jung's relationship with his father, however, was less close.

Not surprisingly, Jung developed a particular attraction to intuitive women who were similar to his mother. Many of his patients were women. He especially remembered a nursemaid who attended to him while his mother was recovering from her illness in the hospital for a few months. His cousin Helene Preiswerk, who conducted several parapsychological experiments, also greatly influenced him. He even wrote his medical school dissertation based on her exceptional psychic experiences and experiments with séances that he had witnessed (Douglas 2008).

After earlier considering training in theology and archaeology, Jung enrolled at the University of Basel in 1895 to study medicine. He read widely in diverse disciplines, including philosophy, anthropology, theology, science, and mythology. Jung was influenced by several well-known philosophers such as Immanuel Kant, Carl Gustav Carus, Eduard von Hartmann, Gottfried Leibniz, and Arthur Schopenhauer as well as early cultural anthropologists including Johann Bachofer, Adolf Bastian, and George Creuzer (see Sharf 2008, 76). Familiarity with these thinkers helped him develop his ideas of the collective unconscious and archetypes.

After he completed medical school in 1900 and chose psychiatry as his specialty, Jung also trained with two well-known psychiatrists, Eugen Bleuler in Zurich and Pierre Janet in Paris (in 1902). He worked with Bleuler at the Burgholzli Psychiatric Hospital from 1902 to 1909 and saw many mentally disturbed patients, especially those suffering from schizophrenia. He wrote a major work on schizophrenia, *The Psychology of Dementia Precox*, in 1907. He also developed the well-known word association test and conducted various studies with it that supported the existence of the unconscious. As a result of his studies and work, Jung began to correspond with Sigmund Freud (Douglas 2008).

Freud initially appreciated Jung and respected his significant work. They met in 1907, after writing to each other in 1906. Freud appointed Jung president of the International Psychoanalytic Society and editor of its journal. Jung traveled with Freud in 1909 to the United States to give lectures on their respective perspectives on psychoanalysis at Clark University in Worcester, Massachusetts. Freud even considered Jung to be his successor. However, Jung's theoretical ideas increasingly differed from Freud's psychoanalytic views, and he was quite blunt in his private correspondence with Freud about these differences. Freud eventually wrote to Jung in January 1913, proposing that they abandon their personal relationship completely. Jung agreed in his response to Freud, and they permanently ceased writing to each other.

In 1903, Jung married Emma Rauschenbach, and they had one son and four daughters. After leaving the Burgholzli Hospital in 1909, he eventually entered private practice. Jung began training others in his analytic psychology approach to therapy, including his wife, who was one of the earliest Jungian or analytical therapists.

After parting ways with Freud in 1913, Jung experienced a six-year period of deep introspection and exploration of his own unconscious by analyzing his visions and dreams. It was a time of suffering and what some considered a creative illness for him (Ellenberger 1970). He did not do much writing or research during these six years. However, he emerged from this dark period of his life with greater creativity and published an important work, *Psychological Types*, in 1921.

At this stage of his life, Jung became much more productive in his teaching, writing, and practice, and began traveling widely and frequently. He visited people in primitive cultures to learn more about symbols, myths, and folklore in order to have a better grasp of the collective unconscious and archetypes, crucial aspects of his theory. For example, in 1924, he traveled to New Mexico to meet the Pueblo people there. In 1925, he went to Tanganyika to visit an African tribe. He also visited Asia, and studied Chinese folklore and writings, as well as astrology, alchemy, clairvoyance, fortune-telling, and divination. He accumulated an outstanding library of books and writings on medieval alchemy and used the symbolism found in these works to help develop his ideas of the collective unconscious and archetypal imagery (Sharf 2008).

Jung's productivity was exceptional, and most of his work, totaling twenty-two volumes, has been published by Princeton University Press. He also received many awards and honors, including honorary degrees from Oxford and Harvard. Jung remained busy and productive until his death on June 6, 1961, at the age of eight-five. Jungian therapy and Jung's theoretical views continue to exert significant influence.

For further information on Jung's life and work, see D. Bair (2003), H. F. Ellenberger (1970), B. Hannah (1976), A. S. Harris (1996), Carl Jung (1961), R. Papadopolous (2006), S. Shamdasani (2003), A. Storr (1983), and E. C. Whitmont (1991), as well as Jung's own collected works published by Princeton University Press.

Major Theoretical Ideas of Jungian Therapy

Perspective on Human Nature

Jung's perspective on human nature was more optimistic and positive than Freud's pessimistic and deterministic view emphasizing conflictual sexual and aggressive drives in the unconscious. Jung's view of the unconscious went beyond basic instinctual or biological drives to include the collective unconscious, with transpersonal and universal archetypes based on symbol, folklore, myth, and even mystery. He focused more on the tremendous potential and creativity within people, individually and collectively, in the unconscious, which contained both powerfully positive as well as darker negative aspects (J. Sommers-Flanagan and Sommers-Flanagan 2004).

Jungian therapy, or analytical psychotherapy, emphasizes helping clients to achieve wholeness and self-realization, with the therapeutic goals of self-knowledge, reintegration, and individuation. The deep and healing therapeutic relationship between the Jungian therapist and the client is considered a crucial factor in achieving the therapeutic goals for the client. The therapeutic process involving helping the client to know and understand the archetypes in his or her personal and collective unconscious and to express them in his or her life assumes that a client is capable of such insight and growth and eventual individuation and self-realization (Vitz 1994). The Jungian approach to counseling and therapy therefore is based on an essentially optimistic and positive view of human nature and the human ability for self-realization, although it does acknowledge the darker side of personality.

Personality Theory

Jungian personality theory can be described and summarized under four major areas: levels of consciousness, archetypes, personality attitudes and functions, and personality development (Sharf 2008).

LEVELS OF CONSCIOUSNESS

Jung described three levels of consciousness: the conscious, the personal unconscious, and the collective unconscious.

The *conscious* level of personality is an individual's accessible side, with conscious awareness of thoughts, feelings, senses, desires, and behaviors. It is

Sidebar 6.1

**Main Areas of Jungian
Personality Theory
(Sharf 2008)**

1. Levels of consciousness
2. Archetypes
3. Personality attitudes and
   functions
4. Personality development

that aspect of a person that he or she can know or access directly and be aware of. The conscious level begins at birth and develops in the course of one's life, so that as a deeper level of consciousness is experienced, greater individuation or development of the whole person is achieved.

Jung used the term "psyche" to describe the total personality of an individual. The *ego* is at the center of consciousness and organizes the conscious mind. It selects what an individual will be aware or conscious of and screens out or represses other thoughts, feelings, and memories, which will remain at the unconscious level. The ego, therefore, is the unifying or integrating force in the psyche. It is one aspect of but not identical to the psyche. The ego is actually a *complex*, that is, a constellation of thoughts brought together as a whole, usually by a unifying feeling. A complex of conscious thoughts and memories enables an individual to have a sense of continuity and identity. As a person develops and experiences more individuation or self-realization, integrating all aspects of the psyche in balance, a new center, *the self*, emerges to replace the ego, which still exists, but as only one aspect of the psyche (Ryckman 2008).

The *personal unconscious* is that aspect of personality in which thoughts, feelings, experiences, and perceptions that the ego has screened out of conscious awareness are stored below the level of consciousness. This stored material may be trivial, or it may include unresolved conflicts or concerns or emotionally laden thoughts that the ego has repressed.

Material kept in the personal unconscious often appears in dreams. When related thoughts are unified, typically by a powerful feeling with an obvious emotional effect on the person, a *complex* has developed. Jung's idea of a *complex* focused especially on the *emotional* impact of a group of connected thoughts, feelings, and memories. He also emphasized the archetypal core of complexes, which includes material not only from the personal unconscious but also from the collective unconscious, which is more universal and transcendent. Some examples of complexes with archetypal roots include the father complex, the mother complex, the martyr complex, and the savior complex. Complexes are part of the unconscious, and therefore need to be made conscious, usually with the help of a Jungian therapist. They can have both positive and negative dimensions. When a positive complex becomes a negative one, the *transcendent function* is triggered. This process involves bridging two opposite conditions or attitudes (e.g., an unconscious influence and a conscious thought), which results in a third force that is usually operative in the form of an emerging symbol (Sharf 2008; see also J. C. Miller 2004).

The *collective unconscious* is a unique Jungian concept; it is a deeper level within the psyche that is not conscious and contains materials that are transpersonal and universal to all human beings in their common ancestry. Jung did not propose that particular images or memories are universally inherited by all human beings. Instead, he emphasized that it is the predisposition toward specific ideas, *archetypes*, that is inherited. Archetypes, according to Jung, are particular ways of structuring and perceiving experiences. Jung's idea of archetypes is crucial and foundational to his analytical psychology (Sharf 2008).

ARCHETYPES

Archetypes have form but not content. They provide possible ways of perceiving experiences in particular patterns or themes that are present across cultures and history. Archetypes also connect the collective unconscious to the conscious and therefore can influence behavior in an individual. They can be considered organizing patterns that are unconscious (J. Sommers-Flanagan and Sommers-Flanagan 2004). Jung had a special interest in archetypes that have endured for a long time in the history of humankind, with strong emotional aspects. Examples of such archetypes according to Jung are death, birth, power, the child, the hero, the wise old man, the earth mother, the god, the demon, the snake, and unity. They are manifested as archetypal or primordial images or symbols. However, Jung emphasized that the most crucial archetypes in the make-up of one's personality are the persona, the anima and the animus, the shadow, and the self. The persona is most relevant to daily functioning, while the self is most critical to proper personality functioning (Sharf 2008; see also Shamdasani 2003).

The *persona* ("mask" in Latin) refers to the way one presents himself or herself in public. It is literally the mask we wear in order to interact with people in socially appropriate ways. The persona is an archetype that is universally present in all human beings. It can be helpful in controlling one's thoughts, feelings, and actions in particular contexts and situations. However, the persona can also be overused, blocking deep feelings, and resulting in shallowness and superficiality in an individual.

The *anima* and the *animus* are characteristics of the other sex that an individual has and must integrate within himself or herself in order to experience a healthy and wholesome balance in personality functioning. This idea is partly based on the biological fact that each person has varying levels of male and female hormones. The anima is the feminine archetype in a man's psyche, and the animus is the masculine archetype in a woman's psyche. The anima is associated with feelings and emotional experiencing, while the animus is related more to rational thinking and logic. However, the anima can also have more negative characteristics such as moodiness and vanity, and the animus likewise with manifestations such as social insensitivity and argumentativeness. Although Jung viewed the anima and the animus as universal archetypes, some critics have charged him with being influenced by cultural stereotypes of men and women and therefore of being somewhat sexist and patriarchal (Ryckman 2008).

The *shadow* refers to the dark, potentially evil side of human nature, which exerts a powerful influence on people's lives. The shadow includes repressed or unacceptable sexual and aggressive instincts in the personal unconscious as well as evil tendencies in the collective unconscious. Such negative characteristics of the shadow tend to be projected onto others, which can lead to conflicts and even wars. The persona archetype that tries to maintain socially appropriate behavior helps to keep the shadow under control. As with all archetypes, the shadow has both negative and positive aspects. Although the shadow is described mainly as a negative archetype that is potentially dangerous and evil, it can also be manifested more positively in experiences of creativity, spontaneity, and vitality.

The *self* is the center of personality and includes the conscious and the unconscious levels in an individual. The self integrates conscious and unconscious aspects and organizes one's personality functioning. It encompasses the whole psyche or total personality, whereas the ego is only part of the psyche and is limited to consciousness.

According to Jung, we are all on a path toward self-realization and individuation, that is, to maturing into our unique self (and not to egotism or selfish individualism). Everyone strives for the goal of deeper knowledge and development of the self, which is an archetypal potentiality in each person. This goal is difficult to attain and in fact is never fully achieved. It requires an individual to be in touch with both conscious and unconscious material and to have enough experience in life to deal with conflicts and to integrate opposites in his or her psyche. Striving toward this goal results in more healthy and balanced personality functioning. Jung therefore believed that progress toward self-realization cannot be substantially made until at least middle age (Ryckman 2008). Dreams and religious or spiritual experiences can be very helpful in making the unconscious conscious and in integrating conscious and unconscious processes.

Archetypes do not have content but are expressed through *symbols*, which are the content of archetypal images that only have form. Such symbols appear in dreams, visions, fantasies, myths, art, folklore, fairy tales, and other ways. Jung engaged in extensive study of many symbols across various cultures that he found to be archetypal images containing the accumulated wisdom of human and prehuman history. With such knowledge of the history and meaning of symbols, Jung was able to use *amplification*, or elaboration of the meaning of a dream or some unconscious material, for a particular patient. It is therefore important for Jungian therapists to learn as much as possible about symbols and their meanings in various cultures.

Jung described many symbols that represent particular archetypes. For example, the symbol of the mask for the persona archetype, the symbols of the Mona Lisa or the Virgin Mary for the anima archetype in men, the symbols of King Arthur or Christ for the animus archetype in women, and the symbols of evil such as Hitler and the devil for the shadow archetype. The *mandala* is a very significant symbol for the archetype of the *self*; it usually

has four main sections in a circular shape, representing a search for wholeness (Sharf 2008).

Personality Attitudes and Functions

Jung viewed personality as consisting of two major dimensions, with conscious and unconscious elements: *attitudes* and *functions* that together form
specific *personality types*. *Extraversion* and *introversion* are the *two main
personality attitudes* described by Jung. Extraversion is an orientation to or
preference for the outer world consisting of people, activities, and things,
whereas introversion is an orientation to or preference for the inner world
consisting of ideas, concepts, and inner experience. Extraverts tend to enjoy
social activities and have many friends and are energized by being with people,
whereas introverts tend to enjoy spending time by themselves and have fewer
friends and are usually not comfortable in social situations. Although an
individual may exhibit some characteristics of both an extravert and an introvert, there is usually a preference for one. However, Jung believed that at
midlife an individual may change from one personality attitude to the other
(J. Sommers-Flanagan and Sommers-Flanagan 2004).

Jung also described four main functions of personality: the nonrational or irrational functions of *sensing* and *intuiting* for perceiving the world and oneself,
and the rational functions of *thinking* and *feeling* for judging experiences.

Sensing involves using the senses of taste, smell, touch, sight, and hearing, and responses to sensations one experiences, whereas *intuiting*, or
intuition, involves having a guess or hunch about something or someone
that is difficult to clearly articulate. These two personality functions of
sensing and intuiting are primarily engaged in perceiving and responding
to stimuli. *Thinking* involves using intellectual and rational processes to
understand the world and ideas, whereas *feeling* refers to making evaluations or judgments about one's experiences based on having negative or
positive feelings or values about them. These latter two personality functions of *thinking* and *feeling* are primarily engaged in making judgments
and decisions (Sharf 2008).

Jung developed a *theory of psychological types* based on the two basic
personality attitudes and the four main personality functions. He focused on
eight major personality or psychological types: introverted and extraverted,
thinking, feeling, sensing, and intuitive types (see Ryckman 2008, 91–94). Jung
was very concerned, however, that people would be too quickly and inaccurately
labeled as one of these eight personality types. It is important to be reminded
of Jung's emphasis on the uniqueness of each human person.

Personality Development

Jung's theoretical conceptualization of personality development is not as
systematic or well developed as Freud's stages of psychosexual development.

Jung described four major stages of personality development: childhood, adolescence (or youth and young adulthood), middle age, and old age. He was particularly interested in middle age (see Sharf 2008, 86–87).

According to Jung, children in the *childhood* stage have mainly instinctual psychic energy that is expressed in activities such as eating and sleeping. Jung believed that parents need to help their children channel their energy in more constructive and disciplined ways. He related children's problems to parental conflicts at home. If parental conflicts are reduced or resolved, children's disruptive behavior and other difficulties will also be ameliorated. Children are also in a process of growing in their sense of personal identity and therefore need to separate from their parents in doing so.

In the stage of *adolescence*, the individual must deal with several major decisions in his or her life, including choosing an appropriate education and eventually a career or profession. Adolescents also need to grapple with their sexual drives and learn to relate to members of the opposite sex. They will respond or react differently depending on whether they are more inclined toward introversion or extraversion. However, they all need to develop an appropriate persona that goes beyond their parents' influence in order to cope with the external world and social demands. As they grow into young adulthood, they must continue to be their own unique person.

In the *middle age* stage, Jung believed that crucial questions and issues emerge such as searching for the meaning of life, because a deeper sense of emptiness and meaninglessness is often experienced by people in this stage of life. This experience is sometimes called the midlife crisis. Jung himself went through such a period in his life for six years during which he engaged in deep introspection and analysis of his own dreams and visions, coming to know better his own unconscious. It was a painful and dark time of suffering and struggle for him, but he emerged from it more creative and insightful. Many of Jung's patients were in this stage of life and therefore were similarly dealing with losses, emptiness, and meaninglessness in their lives. Religious and spiritual experiences are often a crucial part of middle age.

In the stage of *old age*, individuals spend even more time connecting with their unconscious, and Jung believed that older people should take time for deeper reflection so that they can grow in wisdom from their experiences and find greater meaning in their lives. Death and mortality are common preoccupations of older people, who can continue to grow and develop psychologically as they allow themselves to reflect more and be in deeper touch with their unconscious.

Therapeutic Process and Relationship

Jungian therapy focuses on helping clients not only to make the unconscious conscious but also to integrate the unconscious with the conscious so that they can become more whole persons in the process of individuation, or becoming one's own unique person. This is the overarching goal of Jungian therapy: the individuation of the client. There can also be secondary goals of therapy relevant to a particular stage of personality development. For example, the goal may be to help clients in midlife develop a deeper meaning in their lives, often with spiritual and religious elements, and therefore to go beyond just pragmatic concerns such as making money and taking care of a family. In pursuing therapeutic goals, Jungian therapists or analysts use a variety of therapeutic techniques or interventions such as dream analysis, active imagination, and dealing with transference and countertransference in the therapeutic relationship.

However, the most important factor in Jungian therapy is the therapeutic or analytic relationship between the Jungian therapist or analyst and the client. Jung placed major emphasis on the therapeutic relationship and believed that the therapist's personality can have therapeutic effects on the client's personality. For this to take place, the Jungian therapist must be a relatively mature and ethical person who is integrating his or her own unconscious and conscious. Therefore, having had one's own training analysis is essential. The Jungian therapist also relates to the client in a more human and egalitarian way that is mutually respectful and relational. Jung did not use the couch as Freud did, but saw his clients face to face instead. Transference and countertransference, including projections that occur in the context of the therapeutic relationship and interaction between the Jungian therapist and client, can be explored and interpreted. The therapeutic relationship is central to Jungian therapy because it can be viewed as providing a *container* for the personality of the client, much like an alchemical vessel in which the different aspects of a client's psyche can be contained and eventually changed in a therapeutic way (Sanford 1999).

Jungian analysis is usually relatively long term and involves meeting several times a week with a *Jungian analyst*, whereas Jungian therapy in general is more flexible. The term "Jungian analyst" applies only to someone who has received formal training and certification by the International Association for Analytical Psychology. Jungian analysts come from various professional backgrounds, and many have completed their official training in pursuit of a second career (Sharf 2008).

Major Therapeutic Techniques and Interventions

Before describing the major therapeutic techniques and interventions of Jungian therapy, we should note that Jung wrote about four main *stages of therapy* in a flexible and not necessarily sequential or even essential way: confession, elucidation, education, and transformation (see Douglas 2008, 122–23).

In the first stage, *confession*, the Jungian therapist listens intently to the client in a warm, accepting, and empathic way so that the client can open up

Sidebar 6.2

Jungian Stages of Therapy
(from Douglas 2008, 122–23)

1. Confession
2. Elucidation
3. Education
4. Transformation

and freely share his or her feelings and secrets as well as basic conscious and unconscious material. It is a time for catharsis and release of emotions that may have been repressed or blocked for some time. The client is therefore helped to feel more human again. However, the client may also come to depend on the Jungian therapist and experience some transference.

In the second stage, *elucidation*, the Jungian therapist interprets the transference relationship between the client and the therapist. The therapist does so in order to help the client gain insight, both intellectual and emotional, into the childhood origins of the client's transference experiences with the therapist; this process is similar to the approach that a Freudian psychoanalyst would use. Dreams and fantasies are also explored and interpreted by the Jungian therapist in collaboration with the client.

In the third stage, *education*, the Jungian therapist helps the client to be more connected to society, dealing more with his or her persona and tasks that are ego related. Following a process similar to that of an Adlerian therapist, the Jungian therapist encourages the client to engage in socially responsible behaviors that are constructive and positive for him or her as well as for the social community.

In the final stage, *transformation*, the Jungian therapist is even more deeply involved in the transference-countertransference relationship with the client, who is motivated to delve more into archetypal material from his or her collective unconscious. Clients in this stage are often in midlife or older. Many clients in Jungian therapy do not progress to this final stage of therapy. The clients who do proceed to the transformation stage usually experience deeper self-actualization or individuation into a more mature, balanced, and whole unique person, valuing both conscious and unconscious experiences. The Jungian therapist's own unconscious experience, especially through his or her own dreams, is often carefully brought into the therapy sessions to help clarify and interpret the transference-countertransference phenomena that usually occur in the therapeutic relationship with the client at this stage of therapy.

Although these four stages of therapy can overlap or even occur concurrently, Jung believed that a complete analysis or therapy will include all four stages. However, the length of each stage and the order in which each stage occurs are not fixed (Douglas 2008).

Jungian therapy uses different therapeutic techniques depending on the particular Jungian therapist and his or her professional background and training. However, the following are the major therapeutic techniques or interventions in Jungian therapy using an analytical psychology approach: *analysis and interpretation of transference and countertransference, dream analysis*, and *active imagination* (Douglas 2008).

Analysis and Interpretation of Transference and Countertransference

Transference refers to the client's unconsciously projecting or transferring aspects of himself or herself or significant others onto the therapist. Countertransference refers to the therapist's projecting, or countertransferring, unconscious feelings onto a client. Both transference and countertransference phenomena that occur in the therapeutic relationship between the Jungian therapist and the client must be identified and analyzed. Doing so benefits the client, who can then acknowledge her own projections or transference and gain insight into her own personal and collective unconscious.

According to Jung, there are four stages of the analysis of the transference. The *first stage* involves pointing out the client's projections of childhood or early relationships and experiences onto the therapist as if the therapist were the problematic figure from the client's past. The client is thus helped to see and acknowledge his own projections, to remove such projections from the therapist, and to integrate them more consciously into his own personality (Douglas 2008). In the *second stage*, the client comes to realize which projections are from his personal unconscious and which are from the collective unconscious and is enabled to stop such projections. In the *third stage*, the unique personality of the Jungian therapist becomes clearer to the client, who can now begin to relate more normally to the therapist as a person. In the *fourth and final stage*, the client continues to connect with the therapist in deeper and healthier ways with an even more accurate perception of the therapist, as the transference is resolved. The client usually experiences more self-realization and greater self-knowledge in this final stage of the analysis of the transference.

The analysis and interpretation of transference and countertransference phenomena in the therapeutic relationship between the Jungian therapist and the client are therefore a crucial therapeutic technique in Jungian therapy.

Dream Analysis

Another major therapeutic technique in Jungian therapy, similar to Freudian psychoanalysis, is the *analysis or interpretation of dreams*. Jung, like Freud, believed that dreams are crucial pathways into the unconscious, but he did not agree with Freud that dreams are usually reflections of repressed unconscious material or wish fulfillments that can be interpreted following standard dream symbols. Instead, Jung felt that dreams should be viewed as significant reminders to an individual of what he or she should be paying attention to. Dreams therefore can have a variety of possible functions. They may reflect fears and wishes, or express hidden, repressed impulses, or lead to solutions to problems in the internal or external world of the individual. They can also serve a *prospective* purpose of helping people anticipate their future and prepare for it, as well as a *compensatory* function in helping people to be more balanced with better integration of opposites in their personalities (see Corey 2009, 80). Dreams and dream analysis are crucial in Jungian therapy for the deeper understanding of the client's unconscious inner life and also for identifying changes in the client's psyche, especially over the course of therapy (Douglas 2008).

Since clients do not all remember or recall their dreams, Jungian therapists usually ask their clients to record their dreams on paper or with a tape recorder as soon as possible after the dreams have occurred. As much detail as possible about the dream should be recorded. Jung differentiated "little" dreams from "big" dreams. Little dreams are more common; they come from the client's personal unconscious and often include elements from the daily activities of the client. Big or significant dreams, however, usually contain images or symbols that may be from the collective unconscious. Such big dreams are usually remembered throughout the lifetime of a particular individual (Sharf 2008).

The *structure of dreams* according to Jung usually includes *four main elements*. The first part of the dream encompasses basic descriptions, such as the place (and time) of the dream, the main characters involved in the dream, and the dreamer's relationship to the situation recurring in the dream. The second part is the dream's plot and its development, often including conflicts and tensions. The third part of the dream usually involves a critical or decisive event that leads to a significant change in the dream. Finally, the last part of the dream concerns a solution or conclusion. Jungian therapists will look for all four parts of a dream, but as noted earlier, clients do not always remember or recall all aspects or parts of their dreams. Dream interpretation of partial or fragmentary dreams should be more cautiously conducted than interpretation of dreams that are more fully recalled (Sharf 2008).

In *dream analysis or interpretation*, the Jungian therapist usually begins by using an *objective* interpretation in which the characters or objects in the dream are viewed as actually representing themselves. However, the therapist can also use a *subjective interpretation* of the dream in which each character or object in the dream is viewed as representing a particular part of the client. Jungian therapists also find it helpful to analyze several dreams together, connecting current or later dreams to earlier ones, for clearer interpretation of the possible meanings of the dreams (Sharf 2008). Jung also believed that dreams contain religious or spiritual meanings and have a transcendent source (J. Sommers-Flanagan and Sommers-Flanagan 2004).

Jungian therapists often find the following *types of dreams* to be particularly helpful and useful: the initial dream at or near the beginning of Jungian therapy; recurrent dreams that occur several times; dreams with material from the client's shadow such as those involving violence, rage, or immoral behavior; and dreams that involve the therapist or the therapy (which may reflect the client's unconscious transference feelings toward the therapist). Dreams can also be a barrier to progress in therapy if the client fills the entire therapy session with an overload of dream material, becomes stuck in his or her dream world rather than dealing with real-life issues, or resists expressing his or her emotional responses to the dreams. The Jungian therapist will point out such defensive behaviors on the part of the client at an appropriate time and help him or her understand what is really happening (Douglas 2008).

Active Imagination

Active imagination is another major Jungian therapeutic technique. It uses meditative imagery in which the client clears his or her mind and then focuses intensely on a particular inner image or figure that may have emerged from a dream or some other unconscious material. The client continues this active imagination until he or she is involved in the scene and becomes part of what is happening in the imagination. A client must have a strong enough ego to engage in such active imagination, which attempts to deal with unconscious images in a direct and intense way (Douglas 2008). This Jungian therapeutic technique of active imagination is therefore an intervention that enables the ego as the center of consciousness to connect with the collective unconscious (Sharf 2008).

Other Techniques

Jungian therapists may also use several other therapeutic techniques to facilitate a client's integration of unconscious processes into consciousness. They include creative interventions or techniques such as painting and drawing, poetry, and dance and movement therapy; the empty-chair technique, often used in Gestalt therapy, in which a client talks to an imagined person in an unoccupied chair; and the sandtray consisting of a sandbox and small forms and figures to which a client (adult or child) can give particular meanings (Sharf 2008).

Jungian therapists also pay attention to a concept that Jung termed *synchronicity*, referring to coincidences or random events occurring close together that nevertheless lead to new knowledge or an answer. The following are examples of synchronicity: premonitions that actually come true, the client having dreams that are very similar to the therapist's dreams, and a solution suddenly appearing to a vexing problem (see J. Sommers-Flanagan and Sommers-Flanagan 2004, 124).

Jungian Therapy in Practice

A Hypothetical Transcript

Client: I've been having a recurrent dream . . . three times already in the last two weeks . . . and so I thought I had better bring it up in our session today.

Jungian Therapist: Tell me more about the dream. It usually has significant meaning for you if it's occurring so often.

Client: OK. In this recurrent dream, there is a priest who is very prim and proper and who commands great respect from his parishioners, who really appreciate him and his eloquent preaching. However, as he is preaching one of his sermons from the pulpit, his head suddenly turns into a monstrous-looking face, full of red-hot anger and rage, as if he were about to burst. He then suddenly stops preaching from the Bible and instead spews out curses and swear words at his congregation, who are shocked by his behavior and horrible words. He then takes out a machine gun and shoots at his parishioners, but only evil and curse words come out of the gun . . . and some of his parishioners actually get killed by the words like bullets coming out in quick succession from his machine gun. It's a horrible and weird dream that I've had three times already.

Jungian Therapist: Um-hmm . . . Who do you think the priest in your dream may represent?

Client: I don't know . . . maybe it could represent me since I'm a prim and proper sort of guy who is very religious and conservative. I am usually very self-controlled and soft-spoken in social situations, and I hold high moral and ethical standards that center on loving God and loving people.

Jungian Therapist: Let's just assume that the priest in your recurrent dream is you, what other parts of the dream may have meaning for you?

Client: Well . . . I'm not sure but I feel like maybe the monstrous part of the priest full of rage and anger, and curses and swear words used like bullets to kill or hurt people in the congregation may mean that there is a darker side to my personality too . . .

Jungian Therapist: A darker side like . . .

Client: Well . . . like a darker, hidden side of me that may have a lot of anger and rage, that wants to strike out at all the nice people out there who want me to always be so prim and proper.

Jungian Therapist: Do you think that you do have this darker or shadow side?

Client: I do get angry once in a while, and I sense the presence of such a darker or shadow side of me at such times. But I'm afraid of what's inside that part of me, so I quickly get over my occasional anger and try to be nice and self-controlled again.

Jungian Therapist: So you've become somewhat aware of this less attractive side of your personality. Do you think you may need to be more connected to it, to be more aware of it, so that you can integrate it into your consciousness in a more constructive way rather than deny it or block it out or run away from it?

Client: You mean I should reflect on this angry side of me more and see what I can learn from it?

Jungian Therapist: It may be helpful for you to do just that. One way is for us to take a little more time to analyze your recurrent dream and see what else it may mean to you. What else comes to mind?

This hypothetical transcript of a small part of a Jungian therapy session demonstrates the use of dream analysis and interpretation and empathic understanding by the therapist, who is helping the client to understand his recurrent dream and come to terms with his shadow, which is expressing rage and anger in the dream.

Critique of Jungian Therapy: Strengths and Weaknesses

Jung's analytical psychology approach to understanding the human personality and conducting therapy with clients is in some ways similar to Freud's psychoanalytic approach, for example, in emphasizing the unconscious and the crucial role of dreams and dream analysis in connecting with the unconscious. However, Jung's unique contribution is his idea of the collective unconscious and the archetypal images contained in it, which are universal and transcend culture. His theory of personality is quite comprehensive, and Jung touched on a wide variety of other areas such as creativity, education, marriage, religion, and even the occult (Ryckman 2008). His contributions have influenced not only the field of psychology but also other disciplines, such as literature, art, history, philosophy, and metaphysics, with perhaps even more significant impact (Todd and Bohart 2006).

Jung made another significant contribution with his description of psychological or personality types, which has been popularized by the widely used Myers-Briggs Type Indicator (MBTI), although there are some methodological problems or limitations with this instrument (see R. B. Johnson 1999). Nevertheless, Jung's delineation of the basic personality attitudes of extraversion and introversion, and of the main personality functions of thinking-feeling and sensing-intuiting, is a helpful way of understanding personality functioning.

A third strength of the Jungian approach is the focus on midlife and the search for meaning in life that acknowledges the importance of religious and spiritual aspects and experiences.

A fourth strength is Jung's emphasis on the tremendous wisdom and potential contained in the unconscious, which enable an individual to continue to grow throughout his or her life by connecting the unconscious, both personal and collective, with the conscious. Jung's view of the unconscious is therefore more hopeful and positive than Freud's (J. Sommers-Flanagan and Sommers-Flanagan 2004).

Another strength is Jung's focus on the need to integrate the darker side of human personality so that an individual can grow into a more mature and balanced person. Jung did not deny the potential for evil and destructive tendencies, especially in the shadow of each person. However, he believed that acknowledging and accepting such a darker, shadow part of one's personality without yielding to it will help a person to be more whole and balanced.

Finally, Jungian therapy also developed several useful therapeutic techniques such as analysis of the transference and countertransference in the context of a more mutually respectful and warm therapeutic relationship, dream analysis in a unique way that included paying attention to both the personal and the collective unconscious and its archetypes, and active imagination and other creative interventions. Some of these techniques are used not only by Jungian therapists but also by other counselors and psychotherapists practicing from other theoretical approaches to therapy.

There are, however, several weaknesses in Jungian theory and therapy. First, Jung's idea of the collective unconscious and his belief that its archetypes are universal and transpersonal have been criticized as somewhat mystical and fuzzy, with confusing descriptions. It is also almost impossible to operationalize the collective unconscious and to subject it to empirical verification. However, recent research in the areas of neurobiology and cognitive science has led some cognitive psychologists to conclude that inborn or innate ways of organizing information may exist, similar to Jung's idea of archetypes that are universal to all human beings (Todd and Bohart 2006; see also Stevens 1982; and Browning and Cooper 2004). His focus on the unconscious, both personal and collective, is nevertheless an intrapsychic one that tends to pay insufficient attention to biological and sociocultural factors that can also affect an individual's psychological functioning and dysfunctioning.

Second, the psychological or personality types described by Jung have been popularized to such an extent that they may be used to erroneously label or categorize individuals as oversimplified personality types. There has therefore been some resistance from the psychological community, including many

Jungian therapists, to the inappropriate uses of measures of personality types, such as the MBTI.

Third, although Jung's focus on midlife and the search for meaning, including religious and spiritual aspects and experiences, is a good corrective to Freud's antireligious stance, Jung is still somewhat biased against dogma and religious beliefs that seem to be more cerebral or cognitive and not experiential in nature. (This may have been partly a reaction to his father's arid and dry form of religious belief.)

Fourth, Jung's emphasis on becoming aware and accepting of the darker, shadow side of one's personality in order to grow in wisdom and mature balance may be somewhat naive. Although he acknowledged the reality of evil, he did not deal adequately with the full nature and meaning of evil and how to overcome it.

Fifth, some of the therapeutic techniques of Jungian therapy must be used with great clinical and ethical caution. For example, the use of active imagination and deeper analysis of dreams, which can be especially frightening or disturbing, may not be appropriate with clients who may have fragile egos or who may be prepsychotic. Jung was aware of this danger, however, and he refrained from using such techniques with more severely disturbed clients. Dreams may also not always be the pathway to the unconscious, and they can sometimes be overinterpreted, with spurious or misleading meanings imposed on them.

Finally, because Jungian therapy is a complex, intense, usually long-term approach to helping clients, there is little empirical evaluation in terms of controlled outcome studies of its therapeutic efficacy or effectiveness.

A Biblical Perspective on Jungian Therapy

Several strengths and weaknesses of Jungian theory and therapy have already been noted. From a biblical perspective, Jung's attempts to understand the depths of a person's psyche or "soul," acknowledging both the tremendous wisdom and the potential residing in one's personal and collective unconscious as well as in the darker, shadow side of human personality, which is capable of evil and destructive tendencies, are more balanced than Freud's. They are also somewhat consistent with the biblical view of humankind as fallen and sinful (Jer. 17:9; Rom. 3:23) yet created in the image of God (Gen. 1:26–27). However, Jung's conceptualization of evil is inadequate, with an ambivalent theory of evil that can be confusing (Browning and Cooper 2004). He does not ultimately see the full extent and substance of evil and the need to overcome it or the need for redemption from sin and evil through the saving work of Christ. Jung emphasized the need to become aware of and to accept the darker, shadow side of one's personality, as if this were enough to deal with evil tendencies. To acknowledge sinful tendencies deep within one's being, however, is only the first step in dealing with evil. Other essential steps include turning to Christ for redemption and cleansing and to the Holy Spirit for power to overcome sin and evil with the goodness and grace of God, in whom there is no evil, contrary to what Jung believed about God being amoral or having potentialities for both good and evil, like a human being (Browning and Cooper 2004; see also S. L. Jones and Butman 1991). The reality of the evil one, the devil as our archenemy, and spiritual warfare (Eph. 6:10–18) also need to be emphasized in a more biblical and fuller perspective on evil. The Jungian perspective can therefore be too optimistic and positive about human nature.

Jung's views on the importance of dreams and how they can be religious messages from a transcendent source beyond the individual have been well received by some Christian therapists and clergy who also see dreams as possible messages from God. There are several examples in Scripture of how God spoke to people through dreams, but dreams can be overinterpreted and are not necessarily the chief way that God speaks to people. Although Jung uses religious and spiritual language and symbols, he does not seem to believe in a personal Triune God and in the historicity of the death and resurrection of Jesus Christ to save and transform sinful human beings (S. L. Jones and Butman 1991). Jung's analytical psychology comes close to being a religion itself, but with a gnostic approach emphasizing the need to know oneself and one's personal and collective unconscious through a mystical archetypal force that guides one to become a unique person. As Paul Vitz has observed: "This goal of self-realization or self-actualization is at heart a Gnostic one, in which the commandment 'know and express thyself' has replaced the Judeo-Christian commandment 'Love God and others.' (In many respects, all modern psychology of whatever theoretical persuasion, because of the emphasis on special, somewhat esoteric knowledge, can be interpreted as part of a vast Gnostic heresy.)" (1994, 3). Implicit in the Jungian idea of self-realization is an optimistic reliance on the individual's ability to engage in such individuation (normally with the help of a Jungian therapist), leading to what Browning and Cooper have called "ethical egoism" (2004, 150), an ethic that falls short of the Christian ethic of loving God and others. Jung can therefore be viewed "as a particularly complex example of . . . the psychological culture of joy" (2004, 151).

Jung's focus on religious and spiritual experience, including mystical experience rather than arid and dry dogmatic beliefs, is another area for concern from a biblical perspective. Jung is well known for a statement he made in 1961, shortly before he died: "Suddenly I understood that God was, for me at least, one of the most certain and immediate experiences. . . . I do not believe; I know. I *know*" (see Kelsey 1972, 119, quoted in Hurding 1985, 80). It is difficult to interpret accurately what Jung really meant by this statement. Experiencing God, based on what we know of him through Scripture, involves encountering a real, personal God who is there. This is not the same as psychological experiences of an idea of God that is in our collective unconscious as an archetypal image. Caution is needed in using some Jungian concepts because they may not be biblically consistent even if they sound familiar.

On the other hand, Roger Hurding (1985, 357) has pointed out that the Jungian approach can challenge Christians to take more seriously the Christian mystical tradition, which emphasizes devotional practice (e.g., contemplation and meditation) and godliness of life. This tradition can help us know God in a more experiential way, but one still based on Scripture, in the inner journey of our lives. Hurding especially reviewed and critiqued the writings of Christopher Bryant, William Johnston, and Morton Kelsey, who attempted to integrate Jungian psychology with the Christian mystical tradition (see Hurding 1985, 334–60).

Jungian therapy, however, does have some noteworthy aspects that Christians and Christian therapists can appreciate: the use of a warm and empathic therapeutic relationship that is mutual and collaborative; the serious focus on dreams and dream analysis in order to connect deeper unconscious material to one's consciousness, including honestly facing one's darker, shadow side; and the exploration of religious and spiritual experiences and the search for meaning in life (especially at midlife and after) that comes close to the process of spiritual direction. However, Jung's delving into the occult and Eastern mysticism can be potentially dangerous because some Christians view this as delving into the demonic and spiritually evil realm.

One conclusion with regard to a biblical Christian perspective on Jungian theory and therapy is the following somewhat critical statement provided by Jones and Butman: "C. G. Jung was a prolific and creative thinker with few equals in this century. . . . But while the issues he raised and questions he asked are vital, the answers Jung generated are of deep concern. . . . And the psychology of Jung, with its deeply flawed understanding of our religious nature and the most fundamental religious truths, would be a poor guide on that inner journey" (1991, 139–40). However, more recently, Ann B. Ulanov and Alvin Dueck (2008) have provided a more nuanced and appreciative perspective on what Christians can learn from Carl Jung.

Research: Empirical Status of Jungian Therapy

Some of Jung's theoretical ideas such as psychological or personality types, especially as measured by the MBTI, and his theory of dreams have received some empirical support (see Ryckman 2008, 94–96; Sharf 2008, 103–4; and Douglas 2008, 127–28, for summaries of the research literature).

However, the evaluation of the effectiveness of Jungian therapy has consisted mostly of clinical case studies, usually single case studies using clinical observation of a client over the course of Jungian therapy (Douglas 2008). Randomized controlled outcome studies evaluating the efficacy of Jungian therapy are lacking at this time. No definitive conclusions can therefore be presently made regarding the effectiveness of Jungian therapy.

It is particularly difficult to conduct controlled outcome studies of Jungian therapy because there are relatively few clinicians who describe themselves as solely Jungian therapists or analysts. However, some outcome research evaluating the efficacy of long-term Jungian therapy is being undertaken at the Jung Institute in Switzerland in a study sponsored by the Swiss Society of Analytical Psychology. Further details of this research project can be obtained at the Jung Institute Web site (www.jung.edu) (see J. Sommers-Flanagan and Sommers-Flanagan 2004, 132).

Future Directions

Some authors of textbooks in the field of counseling and psychotherapy have recently reduced or left out detailed coverage of Jungian theory and therapy because of an apparent decrease in interest in Jungian therapy (see, e.g., Corey 2009; Day 2004; Fall, Holden, and Marquis 2004; Parrott 2003; Prochaska and Norcross 2010). Jung was especially popular in the 1950s and 1960s, but interest in Jung and Jungian therapy seems to have significantly decreased; less than 1 percent of psychotherapists in the United States have identified themselves as Jungians in recent surveys conducted (see Prochaska and Norcross 2010, 61).

However, other authors have reached quite different conclusions concerning the current status and future directions of Jungian therapy. Claire Douglas, who is a Jungian analyst herself in independent practice in Malibu, California, has recently described the growth of Jungian therapy and the apparent increase in interest in Jung's analytical psychology approach. She noted that the International Association for Analytical Psychology (www.iaap.org) had more than 2,860 certified analyst members in 28 countries, 57 professional societies including 19 in the United States, and 19 developing groups, according to 2006 statistics. Several professional journals focus on Jungian theory and therapy, including the well-known British *Journal of Analytical Psychology* (Douglas 2008, 113). There is also the Society of Analytical Psychology (www .Jungian-analysis.org).

Training in Jungian analysis is rigorous, requiring six to eight years on the average before a therapist can be formally certified as a Jungian analyst. An essential and required part of the training is the personal or training analysis of the therapist, which usually lasts many years, often involving work with two different Jungian analysts. Other requirements in the formal training leading to certification as a Jungian analyst in the United States usually include four years of coursework or seminars in clinical theory and practice from Jungian as well as neo-Freudian perspectives, archetypal psychology, and dream analysis; personal interviews; oral and written examinations; and a clinical dissertation (Douglas 2008, 113–14).

Douglas (2008, 114) also describes exciting current and future developments in Jungian theory and therapy, including integrating object relations psychology with Jungian analytical psychology and integrating more multicultural and feminist perspectives with Jungian theory and therapy. However, she also notes that more-conservative Jungians are reacting to some of these contemporary developments with a backlash, asserting that Jung's original views should be preserved and not diluted and reinterpreted in ways that he might not agree with today.

In a similar vein, Sharf (2008, 101–2) notes that in addition to Jung's ideas being popularized with the American public recently through the publication of certain books and the broadcast of television series focusing on myth, Jung's collective unconscious, and archetypes, two other significant influences are impacting the current and future development of Jungian therapy: postmodern perspectives and post-Jungian views.

Jungian theory and therapy, therefore, seem to be doing well enough and may actually be growing in influence. Douglas has noted a growing number of therapists who have not undergone the rigorous training required to become a certified Jungian analyst, but who nevertheless consider themselves to be "Jungian-oriented therapists" (2008, 113), although they are not Jungian analysts. Surveys showing that less than 1 percent of therapists identify themselves as Jungians thus may be somewhat misleading because the therapists participating in the surveys may be interpreting "Jungian" in the strict sense to mean Jungian analysts, rather than more broadly to include Jungian-oriented therapists. The actual number of counselors and clinicians who practice as Jungian-oriented therapists may therefore be greater than these surveys indicate.

The empirical support for the effectiveness of Jungian therapy, however, is still lacking. Additional research is needed before more-definitive conclusions can be reached regarding the therapeutic outcomes and efficacy of Jungian therapy. It is encouraging to know that such research is currently being conducted at the Jung Institute in Switzerland.

Recommended Readings

In addition to Jung's own collected works (a total of twenty-two volumes published by Princeton University Press), the following books are recommended for further reading:

Bair, D. (2003). *Jung: A biography*. Boston: Little, Brown.

Harris, A. S. (1996). *Living with paradox: An introduction to Jungian psychology*. Albany, NY: Brooks/Cole.

Jung, C. G. (1961). *Memories, dreams, reflections*. New York: Random House.

Papadopolous, R. (Ed.). (2006). *The handbook of Jungian psychology*. New York: Routledge.

Storr, A. (1983). *The essential Jung*. Princeton, NJ: Princeton University Press.

7

Existential Therapy

Existential therapy is really more a *philosophical attitude or approach* in counseling rather than a particular school of therapy with specific techniques, although some therapeutic interventions have been developed and used by existential therapists. Existential therapy is therefore not a unitary approach, and it would be more correct to describe this approach as consisting of several *existential psychotherapies* (R. A. Walsh and McElwain 2002). Nevertheless, the term "existential therapy" will be used in this chapter to refer to counseling and therapy approaches that are based on existential philosophy.

Existential therapy focuses on helping clients experience their existence in an authentic, meaningful, and responsible way. It is based on an existential philosophy that views human beings as having freedom as well as responsibility to choose in order to create meaning in their lives. Although people may have some limiting circumstances to deal with in their particular life contexts, they still have the freedom to choose how they want to handle their own life situation. Crucial issues that every human being must ultimately deal with include death and mortality, freedom, meaninglessness or emptiness, isolation, and the need to be real and authentic in choosing one's approach and values in life in a responsible way.

Existential therapy emphasizes the therapeutic relationship and authentic encounter between the existential therapist and the client more than therapeutic techniques. Existential therapists vary in their basic view of human nature, ranging from optimistic to pessimistic, to even nihilistic, and they include religious as well as antireligious adherents. The approach of existential therapy has been strongly influenced by several nineteenth- and twentieth-century philosophers and thinkers, including Søren Kierkegaard (1813–55), a Danish philosopher who wrote about *angst*, or dread and anxiety; Friedrich Nietzsche (1844–1900), a German philosopher who wrote about subjectivity and the "will to power" needed to maximize the human potential for originality and creativity; Martin Heidegger (1889–1976), a philosopher and key figure in the development of phenomenology or phenomenological existentialism, which focuses on authentic living and choosing to live wisely and deeply each day; Jean-Paul Sartre (1905–80), a French

> **Sidebar 7.1**
>
> **Important Figures in Existential Therapy**
>
> 1. Ludwig Binswanger
> 2. Medard Boss
> 3. Viktor Frankl
> 4. Rollo May
> 5. James Bugental
> 6. Irvin Yalom

philosopher and novelist who emphasized even more the radical freedom that each human being has in choosing his or her own values and his or her own person, no matter what one's past may have been; and Martin Buber (1878–1965), a theologian who emphasized dialogical conversation in an "I-Thou" authentic personal relationship with the real presence of the two people involved in such a relationship (see Corey 2009, 134–36).

Other important theological philosophers from an existential perspective besides Buber include Gabriel Marcel (1889–1973), a Catholic theologian who emphasized trust, and Paul Tillich (1886–1965), a Protestant theologian who focused on courage. Edmund Husserl (1859–1938) and Karl Jaspers (1883–1969), two other existential philosophers, and several playwrights and novelists, including Fyodor Dostoyevsky, Albert Camus, and Franz Kafka, also influenced the development of existential therapy. The views of the theological philosophers tend to be more optimistic, whereas the views of the existential writers are generally more pessimistic and sometimes even nihilistic (pointing to the ultimate meaninglessness or nothingness of life) (see Sharf 2008, 147–49; see also Van Duerzen and Kenward 2005).

Biographical Sketches of Originators and Important Figures in Existential Therapy

We will now briefly examine the lives of several originators and important figures in existential therapy: Ludwig Binswanger, Medard Boss, Viktor Frankl, Rollo May, James Bugental, and Irvin Yalom (see Corey 2009, 132–33, 136–39; Sharf 2008, 149–51).

Ludwig Binswanger (1881–1966) was a Swiss psychiatrist who became an existential analyst. Initially exposed to Freud's views on instinctual drives and motives, he was ultimately more influenced by Heidegger's (1962) phenomenological existentialism. Binswanger emphasized the individual's freedom to choose and ability to perceive meaning in his or her own life. According to Binswanger, existential analysis focuses on the spiritual and subjective aspects of human life and existence and regards crises in therapy as significant times for the client to make crucial choices (Binswanger 1963).

Binswanger became the chief medical director of the Sanitarium Bellevue in Kreulinger, Switzerland, in 1911, following in his father's footsteps, and he began using his existential therapy ideas there. He also completed an internship under the well-known psychiatrist Eugen Bleuler and developed a deep, lifelong interest in studying the existential dimensions of patients suffering from significant psychological disorders. He retired in 1956 but continued his work until his death, at the age of eighty-five, in 1966 (see Prochaska and Norcross 2010, 95–96).

Medard Boss (1903–91), another Swiss psychiatrist, was originally trained in psychoanalysis and was analyzed by Freud himself. He also trained under Eugen Bleuler. However, like Binswanger, Boss was eventually greatly influenced by Heidegger's (1962) existential ideas. Boss attempted to integrate existentialism with psychoanalysis when he wrote *Daseinanalysis and Psychoanalysis* (1963).

Boss served for many years as a professor of psychoanalysis in the medical school at the University of Zurich, which is still the center in Europe of Daseinanalysis, the existential analysis that was developed by Boss. He died in 1991, at the age of eighty-eight (see Prochaska and Norcross 2010, 96).

Both Binswanger and Boss were early originators of existential therapy and existential analysis. Two other key figures helped develop existential therapy as we know it today: Viktor Frankl and Rollo May.

Viktor Frankl was the founder of *logotherapy*, an existential therapy that literally means "therapy through meaning," focusing on an individual's will to meaning or search for meaning in life as the most fundamental of human motivations. Frankl was born in 1905 in Vienna and was educated at the University of Vienna, where he earned his medical degree in 1930 and his PhD in philosophy in 1949. He taught at the University of Vienna and was also a visiting professor at several American universities, including Harvard and Stanford.

Frankl is renowned for his best-selling and widely read book *Man's Search for Meaning* (1963). He described his personal experiences during World War II as a prisoner in the Nazi concentration camps at Auschwitz and Dachau from 1942 to 1945. Many of his family members died in the camps, including his wife and children and his parents and brother. Through his own suffering and experiences, he came to his existential conclusions that love is the highest aspiration any human being can have, that freedom to choose one's attitudes and values can never be taken away from an individual even under the worst circumstances, that the search for meaning is the most fundamental of human motivations, and that meaning can be discovered by experiencing values such as love or significant work or by enduring suffering.

Frankl was exposed to Freud and his psychoanalytic views but rejected Freud's deterministic ideas in favor of more-existential perspectives emphasizing freedom, choice, meaning, and responsibility. His writings are now available in over twenty languages, and his logotherapy approach has become a significant part of contemporary existential therapy. His impact on the field of counseling and psychotherapy has been so substantial that he has been called the founder of the "Third School of Viennese Psychoanalysis" (see Corey 2009, 132; and Frankl 1997; see also Gould 1993).

Frankl also developed several therapeutic techniques in logotherapy, such as *dereflection* (encouraging the client to ignore the problem and focus attention on something more pleasant or positive) and *paradoxical intention* (asking the client to do or exaggerate the particular behavior he or she fears doing), although existential therapy on the whole does not emphasize therapy techniques. Frankl died in 1997. Some authors (e.g., Sharf 2008) consider Frankl one of the originators of existential therapy, together with Binswanger and Boss.

Rollo May is usually considered the best-known contemporary author and advocate of existential therapy (Sharf 2008), although he is sometimes also described as an early existential therapist together with Binswanger and Boss (Prochaska and Norcross 2010). May was born in 1909 in Ada, Ohio, but when he was still a young child his parents moved the family to Michigan. May described his childhood as an unhappy one, although his parents favored him, as the oldest child, over his sister and five brothers. The parents were apparently very strict and authoritarian, and there were frequent marital conflicts at home. His father was often away on business trips, and his mother suffered from depression and loneliness. May had his own existential struggles in life and experienced two marriage failures.

May attended Oberlin College, where he majored in English with a minor in Greek history and literature, and graduated with a BA degree in 1930. He then went to Greece to teach for three years. He visited Vienna during the summers and studied under Alfred Adler in seminars that Adler conducted. He came back to the United States after his teaching experience in Greece and entered Union Theological Seminary in New York. After taking a year off to help support his younger siblings following his parents' divorce, he resumed his studies at Union, where he was greatly influenced by Paul Tillich, a Protestant theologian who became a friend and mentor to May. Tillich introduced him to the existential views of Kierkegaard and Heidegger, which had a profound impact on May. In 1938 he graduated cum laude from Union with a bachelor of divinity degree and then spent two years as a pastor in Verona, New Jersey. It was a disappointing experience for him, however, and he eventually entered a doctoral program in clinical psychology at Columbia University (see Parrott 2003, 148–49).

While working on his doctorate, May contracted tuberculosis. During his two-year stay in a sanitarium in upstate New York, he had to face his own existential anxiety over mortality and possible death. He read the writings of Kierkegaard, which influenced his subsequent development of an existential approach to therapy, including writing his well-known book based on his doctoral dissertation, *The Meaning of Anxiety* (1950). He obtained his PhD from Columbia in 1949.

May emphasized that anxiety is crucial to human existence and should not always be viewed as abnormal or pathological. He also focused on helping clients find meaning as they learned to deal with the problems of being and existence rather than simply trying to solve problems and difficulties in their lives. Examples of problems of being include issues such as aging, dealing with death and mortality, and sex and intimacy (Corey 2009, 133). He did not develop a system or school of existential therapy as such, but described an existential perspective or attitude in conducting therapy that would be labeled as existential therapy today.

After his recovery from tuberculosis, May continued writing, teaching, and practicing therapy. He was a visiting professor at several universities, including Harvard, Princeton, and Yale, and published several widely read books on existential psychology and therapy. He also received numerous awards and honors for his significant contributions to psychology. He died in October 1994 of congestive heart failure in his home in Tiburon, California, at the age of eighty-five (see Ryckman 2008, 475–77; see also Abzug 1996; DeCarvalho 1996).

A few other important figures in contemporary existential therapy should be mentioned. *James Bugental* has developed an approach to existential therapy that focuses on the immediate here-and-now experiences during the therapy session itself (Bugental 1999) in order to help clients increase their self-awareness and capacity to self-actualize. Bugental also favors a humanistic emphasis on living with authenticity and integrity for each person according to his or her own chosen answers to life's existential questions (see Bugental 1987). Common existential themes engaged by Bugental include change, contingency, responsibility, and relinquishment (see Sharf 2008, 151).

Irvin Yalom is another key figure in existential therapy today and has described perhaps the most systematic and comprehensive approach to existential therapy to date in his classic text, *Existential Psychotherapy* (1980). He integrates the existential views of several philosophers, theologians, and therapists, such as Kierkegaard, Nietzsche, Heidegger, Sartre, Buber, and Frankl. Yalom's approach to existential therapy specifically focuses on four ultimate human concerns: *death, freedom, isolation,* and *meaninglessness*. He has also published several detailed case studies on his approach to existential therapy (see Yalom 1989, 1999), and coauthored a text on group psychotherapy (Yalom and Leszcz 2005). Most recently, he has written a book on overcoming the terror of death from an existential perspective (Yalom 2008).

Two British existential therapists who have also had an impact on the development of contemporary existential therapy are R. D. Laing (see Laing 1959,

1961), and Emmy Van Duerzen (formerly Van Duerzen-Smith) (see Van Duerzen 2001; Van Duerzen and Kenward 2005; Van Duerzen-Smith 1990, 1997, 1998). Laing created a therapeutic community for very disturbed psychotic patients in England, using an existential approach that showed deep respect for the patients (M. Cooper 2003). Van Duerzen has been instrumental in developing a strong interest in existential therapy in England, fostering what is known as the British School of Existential Psychotherapy (see Sharf 2008, 151). She also founded the Society for Existential Analysis in 1988 in England.

Thus existential therapy is not a unitary school or system of counseling and psychotherapy but rather a philosophical approach to therapy based on existentialism and its different varieties. However, there are still some commonalities across the diverse existential perspectives, which will now be discussed.

Major Theoretical Ideas of Existential Therapy

Perspective on Human Nature

Existential therapists are a diverse group with different perspectives on human nature, depending on their particular version of existentialism. There are religious, atheistic, and antireligious existentialists who may view human nature more positively with some optimism and hope, or more negatively, focusing instead on meaninglessness, emptiness, nothingness, and despair (see Parrott 2003, 152). Nevertheless, the existential approach emphasizes the freedom that every human being has to choose his or her own values and meaning in life. Basic or foundational existential questions that every individual must eventually face and answer include "Where have I come from? Why am I here? Where am I going? What do I value?" (Mendelowitz and Schneider 2008, 299).

Existential therapy does not have a fixed view of human nature. Each individual is constantly changing and evolving in becoming whoever he or she chooses to be. Although experiences and future aspirations and goals have some influence and effect on the person, present awareness is more crucial in choosing freely and responsibly who each individual is being or becoming, according to his or her own values and meaning in life. The existential perspective on human nature is therefore not at all deterministic or fatalistic. It emphasizes instead the capacity of all human beings to freely choose their own person and destiny. Such freedom of choice inevitably leads to the experience of existential anxiety in every person.

Personality Theory

Existential therapy describes several characteristics of human beings as they exist in the world, but they are not the same as particular or fixed traits within a person.

Existential therapists emphasize *existence* first without any fixed or essential personality traits for each human being. Such existence is often described as *being-in-the world*, or *Dasein*, where the being and the world of a human person are not dualistically split but are instead a unity experienced by an individual in the way he subjectively or phenomenologically chooses to perceive or construct it. There are three levels of the world to which each person relates as he exists in the world, designated by the German terms *Umwelt*, *Mitwelt*, and *Eigenwelt* (Binswanger 1963; Boss 1963). *Umwelt* refers to the physical and biological dimensions of the world, including living as well as inanimate objects. The *Mitwelt* is the social world of people. The *Eigenwelt* is one's own inner world of experiences that one can subjectively perceive, evaluate, and reflect on. *Umwelt* can be simply translated as *being-in-nature*, *Mitwelt* as *being-with-others*, and *Eigenwelt* as *being-for-oneself* (Prochaska and Norcross 2010, 97–98).

Every human being is free to choose how he or she relates to these three levels of the world: being-in-nature, being-with-others, and being-for-oneself. The existential perspective emphasizes that the best option is to choose to be *authentic*—transparent, open, and honest without hiding anything from ourselves. An authentic existence is therefore viewed as a healthy existence that has a harmonious and spontaneous relationship with all three levels of being in the world (nature, others, and self). However, it is not easy to live authentically because the level of awareness required inevitably leads to experiencing dread, or *existential anxiety* (Tillich 1952). There are several sources of such existential anxiety: *death or nonbeing* (which each of us will experience sooner or later), *the need to act*, *meaninglessness*, and *isolation* or fundamental *aloneness* in this world. All these sources of existential anxiety really point to the ultimate characteristic that is true of all human beings: our *finiteness*. They have also been described as the basic *contingencies of life* or *existential givens* that are certainties in life for every person. For example, everyone must die, and everyone must act. However, out of the certainty of death can come life, out of meaninglessness can come meaning, and out of isolation and aloneness can come intimacy. In other words, out of nonbeing can come the creation of being. An authentic person therefore does not avoid nonbeing and the inevitable existential anxiety. Instead one embraces the freedom to choose and its accompanying existential anxiety: one chooses to choose because not to choose is already a choice that is inauthentic. An authentic person also realizes that existence itself is an ongoing cycle or flow from nonbeing to being and back to nonbeing again (or ultimately death). Daily life is similarly a cycle or flow from the yesterday that does not exist anymore into the present of conscious experience, and eventually into the tomorrow that does not yet exist and therefore is nonbeing for now. Authentic being thus is an experience that occurs only in the present (Prochaska and Norcross 2010, 99–101).

More recently, Van Duerzen-Smith (1997, 1998) added a fourth way of being-in-the-world called *Überwelt* in German. The *Überwelt* encompasses one's beliefs about the world that are usually spiritual or religious in nature; it refers to one's *ideal world* or the world as one wants it to be (see Sharf 2008, 153).

According to May (1961) there are six major characteristics of an *authentic* person, or an "existing person":

1. Human beings are centered in themselves, and anxiety is only one way that they protect their own center of existence.
2. Human beings usually experience anxiety existentially because they struggle against what would destroy their being.
3. Human beings have a need to preserve their center and therefore use their will to be self-affirming.
4. Human beings are able to move from their centeredness to interaction with other people, although some risk is unavoidable in doing so.
5. Awareness refers to the subjective aspect of centeredness—human beings are capable of being subjectively aware of whatever they are in contact with.
6. Human beings are unique in being able to experience self-consciousness or awareness of themselves in relating to the world, including awareness of external threats and dangers to their existence.

Frankl (1963) has added a seventh characteristic to May's list:

7. The search for meaning is the primary force or motivation in human beings. Each individual needs to use his or her will to find his or her own particular and unique meaning in life (see Parrott 2003, 153–55).

Development of Psychopathology

The existential approach to therapy views the avoidance of existential anxiety and nonbeing by lying to ourselves as well as to others, and thus choosing not to live authentically and truthfully, as the fundamental reason for developing psychological problems. Prochaska and Norcross put it bluntly and succinctly: "Lying is the foundation of psychopathology" (2010, 101). Lying or living inauthentically leads to neurotic anxiety, as existential anxiety is avoided. Neurotic anxiety can then lead to other psychopathological symptoms and behaviors (e.g., obsessive-compulsive checking behaviors).

Psychopathology is usually associated with an overemphasis on one level of being-in-the-world while ignoring the other levels in an imbalanced way. For example, an individual may spend most of his time in social situations with people in order to avoid neurotic anxiety that is a consequence of run-

Sidebar 7.2

Fundamental Dimensions of Being Human

In summarizing the views of existential philosophers and therapists on the basic or fundamental dimensions of being human, Corey (2009, 139) lists and describes the following six propositions:

1. The capacity for self-awareness
2. Freedom and responsibility
3. Creating one's identity and establishing meaningful relationships with others
4. The search for meaning, purpose, values, and goals
5. Anxiety as a condition for living
6. Awareness of death and nonbeing

Such propositions or characteristics of the human condition are often explored and dealt with in existential therapy.

ning away from an inner emptiness when he is alone. This person is overdoing being-with-others and not attending enough to being-in-nature and being-for-oneself. Lying can also occur at the different levels of existence. There can be *lying-in-nature* (as in the case of a hypochondriac who lies to herself about how illnesses can be avoided simply by consulting the doctor quickly and frequently), *lying-to-others* (as in the case of someone doing whatever it takes to fake a good front or appearance to please others, get their approval, or win a business deal), and *lying-for-oneself* (as in the case of a workaholic who erroneously believes the lie that he can perform perfectly and thus avoid rejection or criticism simply by working harder and longer). Such lying is at the root of psychopathology according to the existential perspective (see Prochaska and Norcross 2010, 101–4).

Therapeutic Process and Relationship

Existential therapists help their clients pursue the following therapeutic *goals*: to embrace their freedom to choose and act in responsible ways; to experience as fully as possible their existence and grow in self-awareness; to search for and discover meaning and purpose in their lives; and to be more authentic, real, and truthful, thus letting go of self-deception and lying. Authenticity then is the most fundamental goal of existential therapy (M. Cooper 2003). Core issues often explored and addressed in existential therapy include *anxiety, living and dying, freedom and responsibility, isolation and loving or intimacy*, and *meaning and meaninglessness* (Sharf 2008, 160).

The *therapeutic relationship* between the existential therapist and the client is the crucial factor in helping the client adequately explore and deal with these core existential issues. It should be an authentic, respectful, warm, and personally connecting relationship in which the existential therapist and client can experience a deeply therapeutic encounter (May 1958) and meaningful dialogue—what Martin Buber has described as an "I-Thou" relationship. The existential therapist genuinely cares for the client with what has been called "therapeutic love" (Sharf 2008, 163); he or she develops a profoundly helping relationship with the client, what Yalom has described as a "loving friendship" (1980, 407). It is this therapeutic relationship that heals (Yalom 1980, 401).

The personal authenticity and integrity of the existential therapist are essential if such a therapeutic relationship is to occur and be experienced by the client. The existential therapist as a "wounded healer" (see Mendelowitz and Schneider 2008, 312–13) will therefore be real and transparent and share or disclose himself or herself with the client in appropriate and helpful ways to facilitate the client's own self-awareness and honesty. As May has noted, the goal of existential therapy is not so much to "cure" clients of their symptoms or psychopathology, but rather to help them to become more self-aware and to be free from the role of being victims in their lives (1981, 210). The ultimate therapeutic responsibility in existential therapy lies with the client, who has the freedom to make choices even about therapy.

Existential therapists thus are not particularly focused on using specific therapeutic techniques in helping their clients. The person of the therapist and the therapeutic relationship are more crucial and essential in existential therapy. Some existential therapists even criticize the use of specific therapeutic techniques as a form of objectification of clients and their problems. They fear that clients' phenomenological, subjective experiencing of themselves and their existence, which is the hallmark of existential therapy, may be lost in an overemphasis on techniques and the technology of therapeutic change. The focus in therapy should be more on existential issues rather than problems and problem solving per se. Nevertheless, several therapeutic techniques have been used in existential therapy, most notably in logotherapy as developed by Viktor Frankl, although different existential therapists will use quite different therapeutic techniques or very few specific techniques. Existential therapy is still basically a philosophical approach to therapy rather than a specific school of therapy with a particular set of therapeutic interventions.

Existential therapy is not usually short term. Although it can be more structured and time limited, its goals in such instances may need to be more restricted. Existential analysis, following psychoanalysis but with an existential perspective, can be intense, with several therapy sessions a week, over a relatively long period of time that can last several years. Although issues of transference and resistance may arise and be interpreted, the therapist will not focus much on transference because doing so can interfere with having a truly authentic relationship with the client (Cohn 1997).

Major Therapeutic Techniques and Interventions for Dealing with Core Existential Issues

The person of the therapist or use of the therapist's self and the authentic therapeutic relationship between the therapist and the client are the crucial "methods" in existential therapy. In this context, Van Duerzen-Smith (1997) emphasizes that openness to the creativity and uniqueness of both the therapist and the client is the fundamental ground rule for the use of more specific therapeutic techniques in existential therapy, which basically deemphasizes techniques. Whatever interventions are eventually employed by existential therapists will be adapted to fit the particular needs of each client as well as the unique personality and style of the therapist, to ensure authenticity in the use of therapeutic techniques. The variety of techniques used may include "advocacy, empathy, concern, sincere personal interest, reflection, action, environmental modification, or support" (Parrott 2003, 157). They may also include psychoanalytic interventions such as interpretation and dream analysis, especially when the therapist attempts to integrate psychoanalysis with existentialism.

In dealing with the core existential issues of living and dying; freedom, responsibility, and choice; isolation and loving (or intimacy); and meaning and meaninglessness, the existential therapist may use several different therapeutic interventions (see Sharf 2008, 165–69).

Living and Dying

A central existential issue that every individual must face is the reality of death. Yalom (1980) has described the various ways that people avoid the issue of death, including clinging to unrealistic fantasies of their own invulnerability to sickness or death or believing in a magical rescuer who will somehow prevent them from dying. The denial of death (see E. Becker 1973) is still a very real phenomenon of contemporary American culture and society.

However, having to deal with the death of a loved one such as a parent, child, sibling, spouse, friend, or pet brings one face to face with the reality of one's own mortality and eventual death. It also requires the person to deal with grief over such losses, including associated painful feelings such as anger, guilt, ambivalence, anxiety, sorrow, and depression. The existential therapist will help the client facing the issue of death to choose nonetheless to embrace living life as authentically as possible while realistically accepting mortality and grieving over significant losses. Although some existential therapists such as Yalom (1980) would prefer to focus on discussing issues like death and dying directly with the client rather than use specific techniques, other existential therapists may be open to using techniques such as *guided imagery or fantasy*, in which a client imagines his own death and funeral; *writing an epitaph or obituary for oneself*; and *talking with an elderly person or someone who is terminally ill* (see Sharf 2008, 166).

Freedom, Responsibility, and Choice

Existential therapists believe that their clients have the freedom to choose to live as authentically as possible despite their past histories, which may include much pain, trauma, or abuse. They therefore help clients not to dwell on the past but instead to be more aware of their present experience and especially their freedom to choose their own values and make their own decisions in their life circumstances and thus to discover their own meaning in life.

Existential therapists also emphasize the importance of clients taking responsibility for their own choices and actions. The therapist will use gentle but firm *confrontation* to help clients recognize how they may be running away from accepting personal responsibility for particular actions, including their behavior toward the therapist. Authenticity or honesty is crucial in existential therapy, and the therapist will confront the client with the need for the client to take responsibility for his or her own actions and choices, instead of denying such responsibility or blaming others.

Choice is usually viewed by existential therapists as a process with three aspects, as described by May (1969): wishing, willing, and deciding. Clients are encouraged to be in touch with their feelings so that they are more aware of their inner wishes, desires, and values. They are then helped to reach the point of being willing, that is, when they are ready to choose and make a decision. Finally they make a choice responsibly and are supported in taking action to follow through with their decision. Clients take full responsibility in this process of choice involving their own wishing, willing, and deciding. The existential therapist therefore uses *empathic listening*, *authentic dialogue* with gentle but firm *confrontation* when necessary, *support*, *encouragement*, and *self-disclosure*, or authentic sharing of the therapist's own experiencing of the client during a session, to help the client deal with the core existential issues of freedom, responsibility, and choice.

Isolation and Loving (Intimacy)

The essential isolation or aloneness of each human being as an individual person who came into this world alone and who will die and leave this world alone is an existential reality that everyone must face. The struggle with one's isolation or aloneness and the yearning for loving relationships and intimacy with others are crucial issues that are explored and addressed in existential therapy.

The provision of a deeply caring relationship based on therapeutic love (Yalom 1980) by the existential therapist can help the client to deal more authentically with his or her sense of existential isolation. This may result in the client having enough courage to change and reach out to others in order to develop mutually loving and reciprocally caring relationships with them. However, Bugental (1981) has pointed out the danger of the client becoming so overdependent on the therapist's therapeutic love and genuine caring that he or she does not seek to establish intimacy in relationships with others outside the therapy session. The therapeutic relationship is not reciprocal in nature: the client receives the therapeutic love or genuine caring from the therapist but does not need to reciprocate or give such love and caring back to the therapist. A wise and loving existential therapist will help a client see the need to develop intimate friendships and relationships that are more reciprocal in nature, with other people outside therapy. Such a therapist will also set appropriate boundaries with the client in their therapeutic relationship to prevent the client from developing an unhealthy overdependency on the therapist, for example, by limiting the number of phone calls and meetings each week, except in serious emergencies.

Meaning and Meaninglessness

Some existential philosophers such as Sartre and Camus have a very pessimistic view of existence and being-in-the-world, to the point of being nihilistic about life in emphasizing its ultimate meaninglessness, emptiness, and nothingness. Suicide is even viewed as a rational option to choose in the context of such ultimate meaninglessness. However, other existential theorists and therapists have a more optimistic and affirming perspective on meaninglessness or emptiness in life and emphasize the will to meaning or an authentic search for meaning as the primary force or motivation in human beings. Frankl (1963, 1969, 1978, 1997) developed logotherapy as a specific approach to existential therapy that focuses on *meaning* as the fundamental existential issue and need of every individual, and as the key characteristic of someone who is mentally healthy (see also Wong, Wong, McDonald, and Klaassen 2007). However, Frankl also paradoxically emphasized that one cannot find meaning or happiness in oneself or by simply searching for them. Rather, happiness is a by-product of committing oneself to someone or something that transcends the self. Self-absorption, or focusing too much on oneself, will not lead to a happy life but instead will cause one to lose a meaningful perspective on life. Meaning that comes out of the existential realities of meaninglessness or emptiness in life is often discovered or experienced when one is connected in deeply authentic ways with other people in loving relationships or in creative and significant work such as writing or painting, and even in suffering. Religious and spiritual beliefs and experiences can also help one find ultimate meaning in life in one's *Überwelt*, as Van Duerzen-Smith (1997, 1998) has observed and described as the fourth way of being-in-the-world.

Sidebar 7.3

Four Techniques Used in Logotherapy

1. Socratic dialogue
2. Paradoxical intention
3. Dereflection
4. Attitude modification

Frankl has described more-specific therapeutic techniques in logotherapy than most other existential therapists have in the various approaches to existential therapy. In fact, some existential therapists such as Yalom (1980) have criticized Frankl's logotherapy for focusing too much on techniques rather than on core existential issues. Nevertheless, logotherapy has become a widely known approach to existential therapy that is often appreciated for its more practical therapeutic techniques, which can be used to help clients in concrete ways.

Frankl has developed at least four specific therapeutic techniques that are often used in logotherapy to help clients (Hillmann 2004): Socratic dialogue, paradoxical intention, dereflection, and attitude modification.

Socratic dialogue involves discussing with clients several issues in their lives, including assessment of their present circumstances, discovery of their strengths, and the search for meaning in their lives, using questions that help clarify the clients' basic assumptions and beliefs so that their erroneous notions can be corrected with the therapist's input. Clients are then encouraged to be less self-focused and more concerned about others in order to experience more meaning in their lives. Some authors such as David Guttman (1996) consider Socratic dialogue to be the major therapeutic technique of logotherapy.

Paradoxical intention is a therapeutic technique that requires clients to exaggerate their symptoms or do even more of the very behavior they fear. It is also an Adlerian intervention that has now been incorporated into many other approaches to counseling and psychotherapy. An example of paradoxical intention would be an existential therapist or logotherapist asking a client who is afraid of excessive sweating when talking to a supervisor at work to sweat as profusely as possible when he is facing this supervisor. This process usually helps the client to become less self-focused and to see more clearly the irony and humor of the situation he or she fears, often resulting in a reduction in fear or anxiety.

Dereflection is another technique in logotherapy that involves encouraging clients to turn away from focusing on their own problems and instead to direct their attention or awareness to something else that is more pleasant, positive, or meaningful. For example, a client who has suffered several financial losses in the last year is encouraged to focus more on the spiritual lessons she has learned about being less materialistic and counting her other blessings, such as the birth of a healthy first grandchild. Such dereflection can help clients to put things in better perspective, to be less absorbed with their own problems, and to enjoy other more meaningful and positive experiences in their lives.

Finally, the fourth therapeutic technique in logotherapy involves *attitude modification*, or modifying or changing the client's attitudes or thinking about something that cannot be changed such as a negative past event or memory, so that more meaningful or hopeful perspectives can emerge for the client. A logotherapist using attitude modification will encourage a client who is depressed over the sudden death of a very good friend to see the more positive side of the many good years of a genuinely caring friendship that they had as a real blessing for which he should be thankful. The client can also be helped to face the existential issue of death and dying and the need to develop deeper meaning in his own life. The logotherapist usually conducts attitude modification in a direct way, using other, more general therapeutic interventions such as reasoning, persuasion, interpretation, confrontation, and self-disclosure or sharing on the part of the therapist. Attitude modification is therefore very similar to the technique of cognitive restructuring in cognitive therapy. Logotherapy focuses even more on meaning in therapy than some other existential approaches to therapy and is more similar to short-term psychodynamic therapies, whereas existential analysis is closer in practice to psychoanalysis (see Prochaska and Norcross 2010, 118).

Another existential therapy technique called *embodied meditation* has been recently developed and described by Kirk Schneider, a contemporary existential therapist (1998, 2007). In this therapeutic intervention, the client is introduced to a simple grounding exercise that usually involves progressive relaxation or breathing awareness with eyes closed. The client is then asked to become more aware of bodily experiences and sensations, including specific areas of tensions. The client proceeds to describe as vividly and as clearly as possible the area of tension once it is located and identified. If the client is able to go on, she is asked to place her hand on the area of tension and then to freely associate any experiences such as sensations, feelings, or images that may be connected to contact with this bodily area. Schneider has reported that clients may experience powerful and deep emotions released through this technique, but there is also a danger that some clients may feel overwhelmed by such an experience. An awareness-intensive therapeutic intervention such as embodied meditation should therefore only be practiced cautiously and ethically by an existential therapist who is sensitively attuned to the needs and capacities of particular clients (see Mendelowitz and Schneider 2008, 309).

Existential therapy is most helpful to clients who are facing developmental crises (e.g., dealing with identity issues in adolescence, experiencing disappointments in middle age, coping with children leaving home, facing failures at work or in marriage, or struggling with the challenges and limitations of aging), experiencing grief over losses, encountering death, and having to make important decisions (May and Yalom 2000). It is also particularly appropriate for clients who are experiencing emptiness and alienation in their lives and thus are looking for a more meaningful existence (Van Duerzen-Smith 1990), including clients who are struggling with a lack of a sense of identity (Bugental and Bracke 1992). Edward Mendelowitz and Kirk Schneider have noted that clients who are experiencing an existential crisis are frequently easier to work with compared with those who are preoccupied with everyday neurotic complaints (see 2008, 310–11). Nevertheless, existential therapy has been used with a wide variety of clients and clinical problems (see Schneider 2007) and even in short-term intervention (Lantz and Walsh 2007). It has also been applied not only in individual therapy but also in group therapy and therapy with couples and families.

Existential Therapy in Practice

A Hypothetical Transcript

Client: I don't understand why I'm feeling so empty and almost dead deep inside the core of my being, despite all my success in my business ventures, which have brought me more financial profits this year than ever before. . . . Maybe it's my age. I turned forty this year. . . . Am I having what's called a midlife crisis?

Existential Therapist: (remains silent for a few moments) What do you think? What are you experiencing deep within you?

Client: I don't know for sure whether I'm experiencing a midlife crisis, but I sure have become more aware of this inner sense of emptiness and meaninglessness . . . and the money doesn't mean much anymore.

Existential Therapist: Sounds like you are going through something like a midlife crisis, but the labeling isn't that important. Let's explore more what this emptiness may mean for you, and why money doesn't seem to be that crucial anymore. . . . What do you think?

Client: Well, I guess I'm learning that material things that money can buy such as my big, lovely house, beautiful clothes, and a really nice car don't bring meaningful happiness deep inside my heart. I long for something more meaningful and fulfilling in my life. . . . I'm tired of doing the same old, same old business stuff although I'm really good at it. But I feel kind of stuck . . . and I don't know what to do about this.

Existential Therapist: (remains silent for a few moments) Let's explore this key issue of longing or searching for more meaning and fulfillment in your life. What would bring deeper meaning for you at this time? And remember that you have the freedom to explore your options and to choose or decide.

Client: Well . . . I don't really know . . . but you keep reminding me that it's up to me to choose and decide what would be meaningful or significant to me in my life. . . . I've thought sometimes of being involved in some kind of volunteer work to help disadvantaged children . . . such as the Big Brother program . . . to get outside my own world of business deals and making money . . . to be involved with helping other people more.

Existential Therapist: It looks like you are now really exercising your freedom to choose your values and actions and to be involved in something that is meaningful to you . . . like the Big Brother program. . . . What are you experiencing now and how do you really feel about doing something like this?

Client: I actually feel some energy and inspiration welling up inside . . . like this will actually help me to experience more meaning and fulfillment in my life as I reach out to help others. . . . Perhaps I've been too self-absorbed and even selfish . . . and I am still single at forty! Perhaps I should also explore seriously dating women again to see if I can really find a life partner to love and have a deep relationship with, in marriage . . .

Existential Therapist: So you're thinking not only of helping out with the Big Brother program but also of beginning to seriously date women again with the possibility of settling down in marriage . . . that this also seems potentially meaningful to you, having a loving, committed relationship with a woman?

Client: I guess so . . . but I haven't had much success in my dating experiences before . . . so I haven't seriously dated for a few years now, instead just thrown myself almost completely into my work and business deals. . . . I have to admit that I'm actually quite nervous when I date a woman, and I get sweaty palms and am afraid to shake her hand or hold her hand in case she notices my sweaty palm.

Existential Therapist: I see . . . but you still seem to want to pursue serious dating again except for your fear of your date noticing your sweaty palms . . . right?

Client: Yes, you got it! I'm not sure what to do with this fear I have, that holds me back from initiating dates. . . . Otherwise, I'm a pretty good conversationalist, and people, including women, seem to enjoy talking with me.

Existential Therapist: Let me suggest that you deal with your fear of having sweaty palms by doing something that may sound silly or crazy to you at first but that may actually help you. In your imagination, can you do your best to make your palms sweat even more and as profusely as possible while going on your first date with a woman?

Client: You mean right now . . . in my imagination? I'm willing to try if you'll guide me.

Existential Therapist: All right. Please close your eyes and take a slow, deep breath to clear your mind. . . . Now I want you to imagine going out on your first date with a woman you are interested in and attracted to. . . . As you meet her for the first time and begin to shake hands with her, you feel your palms sweating . . . and sweating . . . and really sweating profusely, with huge drops of sweat. . . . Go on and imagine this happening as vividly and as clearly as possible. . . . What's happening and what are you experiencing now?

Client: I'm trying . . . but it's not working! I'm trying to sweat more and sweat really profusely . . . but the harder I try, the less it seems I am sweating . . . and I'm realizing how funny and silly this all is! And ironically, I don't feel as fearful anymore.

Existential Therapist: Good! I'm glad that you've found this intervention helpful.

This hypothetical transcript of a small part of an existential therapy session that included logotherapy demonstrates the existential therapist's use of Socratic dialogue and attitude modification involving a series of questions, as well as paradoxical intention focusing on the client's fear of having sweaty palms. The existential therapist also engaged in genuine encounter and authentic dialogue with the client using empathic understanding, support, encouragement, and gentle confrontation to help the client find meaning and purpose in his life, as well as accept his responsibility and freedom to choose and decide.

Critique of Existential Therapy: Strengths and Weaknesses

Existential therapy has a number of strengths. First, it focuses on the person with a unique and deep existential perspective, emphasizing the individual's self-awareness, freedom to choose, and responsibility to live an authentic life with meaning. It has a genuine respect for the person and opposes any dehumanizing approach that objectifies a human being as a thing. Second, it directly deals with core human or existential issues such as death, freedom, isolation, and meaninglessness, instead of avoiding them. Third, it views the therapeutic relationship as the central healing factor in therapy for a client. It emphasizes the crucial significance of therapeutic love or genuine caring for the client in a therapeutic relationship that involves authentic encounter and honest, genuine dialogue between the therapist and the client. Fourth, it also views the person of the therapist or the use of the therapist's self as crucial in effective existential therapy and does not subscribe to notions of professional objectivity and distancing often found in more mechanical approaches to therapy that emphasize techniques. The existential therapist therefore is a wounded healer who openly shares his or her own existential struggles with authenticity, honesty, and integrity in walking together with a client on life's journey, which is filled with core existential or ultimate human concerns. Fifth, it is particularly helpful and appropriate for clients who are facing developmental crises or important choice points in life, or who are experiencing emptiness or a lack of a sense of identity and a deep longing for meaning in life.

However, existential therapy also has several weaknesses. First, its major theoretical concepts have been criticized for being vague and unclear and at times even confusing. Terms such as "authenticity," "living in the here and now," and "taking responsibility for oneself" can be interpreted in various ways by different therapists or clients (Todd and Bohart 2006, 240). It is also difficult to conduct empirical research when such concepts or terms cannot be easily operationalized or clearly defined.

Second, in order to be authentic (real or honest) in therapy, some existential therapists may be more confrontational than is appropriate or helpful for certain vulnerable clients who may not be able to handle such confrontations even if they are authentic. Authentic confrontation of the wrong kind can therefore be potentially harmful for some clients (see Todd and Bohart 2006, 240).

Third, while one of existential therapy's strengths is its focus on core existential issues such as death, freedom, isolation, and meaninglessness, and on finding meaning in life, this is also a potential weakness. Some clients are not interested in exploring and dealing with these ultimate human concerns, preferring instead to stick to symptom alleviation of psychological problems like anxiety and depression or marital conflicts. The existential therapist may inadvertently impose an existential agenda on such clients, who may not want to discuss issues like meaninglessness and meaning in life. However, existential therapists do emphasize the client's freedom to choose, so imposing an existential agenda on the client is unlikely though possible.

Fourth, existential therapy does not emphasize therapeutic techniques or clear therapeutic structure and process, so the actual practice of existential therapy is somewhat vague and can vary from one existential therapist to another. Logotherapy as an existential approach to therapy is, however, a bit more structured, time limited, and technique oriented. Nevertheless, existential therapy is more an attitude or philosophical approach to counseling and therapy, and therefore it is difficult to empirically evaluate its effectiveness with clients because its therapeutic techniques and structure are hard to operationalize and standardize. Existential therapists are also often negative about scientific research on the therapeutic outcomes of specific therapeutic approaches or techniques.

Fifth, existential therapy's focus on the experiential aspects of an individual's existence and his or her freedom to choose may not give sufficient attention to biological as well as sociocultural factors in the development of psychological disorders. Some types of psychopathology such as major depressive disorder, bipolar disorder, schizophrenia, obsessive-compulsive disorder, and attention deficit disorder may have biological bases and may need appropriate psychiatric medications (see Day 2004, 188). Also, some problems in living are due to negative environmental and sociocultural factors such as poverty, unemployment, homelessness, discrimination, and racism, which may require social and environmental intervention and not simply choosing one's attitudes and responses or reactions to such adverse circumstances. Although attitude modification or choosing meaningful and hopeful ways of thinking is crucial, environmental or social modification is often also critical. However, when environmental and sociocultural factors cannot be easily modified or changed, clients, including those from culturally diverse backgrounds, may find it particularly helpful to be reminded by existential therapists that they still have the freedom to choose their attitudes and find meaning even in the midst of adverse and horrible circumstances.

Finally, existential therapy, especially if it is practiced as existential analysis, which is more similar to psychoanalysis, is not usually brief and structured, with logotherapy being a possible exception. It focuses not on symptom alleviation but on helping clients live more authentically and find meaning in their lives. Thus medical insurance companies or managed health-care providers may resist paying for existential therapy because they now prefer to pay for shorter term treatments that effectively alleviate the symptoms of clients' psychological problems (see Todd and Bohart 2006, 241). However, short-term existential intervention or therapy has recently been developed (described in Lantz and Walsh 2007).

A Biblical Perspective on Existential Therapy

Existential therapy has a deep respect for the person and the human capacity for freely and responsibly choosing to live an authentic life with meaning. It also directly deals with core existential issues or ultimate human concerns such as death, freedom, isolation, and meaninglessness. These concerns are also found in Scripture, and hence existential therapy can be seen as the therapeutic approach that best mirrors biblical concerns or basic issues of the Christian faith, especially as described in Ecclesiastes (see Haden 1987). The existential questions or concerns raised by existential therapy are right on target, but the answers provided by secular existential therapy are often inadequate, incomplete, misleading, and at times simply unbiblical and wrong (see S. L. Jones and Butman 1991, 289–300, for a helpful Christian critique of existential therapy). Existential therapy emphasizes the individual's freedom to choose and define himself or herself and to do so authentically and honestly. There are no absolute or objectively true ways of being authentic. Any subjective, self-originating answer that is authentic will do. However, from a biblical perspective, such relativism and self-autonomy in an individual's becoming an authentic person are misplaced because the Bible's view is that human beings are meant to center their lives in objective values that are real because God exists and is the source of such eternal, objective values (Tweedie 1961, 165). Subjective self-chosen, arbitrary values may conflict with biblical values and God's will, which ultimately focuses on our spiritual formation and growth into deeper Christlikeness in our being or character as well as lifestyle (Rom. 8:29), including the practice of spiritual disciplines and the cultivation of Christian virtues or the fruit of the Spirit (Gal. 5:22–23).

Existential therapy can also become stoical and even nihilistic if it overemphasizes the ultimate emptiness and meaninglessness of life and the isolation and aloneness of each individual in this world and cosmos, especially in the face of mortality and death. It can be spiritually hopeless without the gospel of Jesus Christ, who died and rose again for fallen, sinful human beings so that they can have eternal life (which is the ultimate answer to death and mortality) and fill their God-shaped vacuum or existential emptiness in their hearts by simple faith in Christ as their personal Lord and Savior. The Christian, biblical perspective is more complete and whole: the core existential emptiness and meaninglessness inside each human being points to the need for meaning in life and salvation that only Jesus Christ can provide because of what he has historically done on the cross in his death and resurrection, so that each fallen, sinful human may be reconciled to God (2 Cor. 5:17–21). Jesus Christ is also the ultimate answer to death, having conquered death by his resurrection (see 1 Cor. 15:50–57), and he offers eternal life now and forever in heaven (see Alcorn 2004) to those who turn to him in simple trust (see John 3:16; see also Lucado 2007). However, existential therapy reminds us of the need to deal deeply and authentically with such core human concerns as inner emptiness and meaninglessness and not give religious answers too quickly or superficially.

Some forms of existential therapy such as Frankl's logotherapy do acknowledge the importance of spiritual or religious values, beliefs, and experiences in helping human beings find deeper meaning and purpose in their lives (see Wong, Wong, McDonald, and Klaassen 2007). However, secular existential therapy such as logotherapy tends to be universalistic in its view of faith and religious and spiritual beliefs. For example, Frankl saw all religions and denominations as equal, and none as superior or more true than others. He also believed that as one's faith grows stronger, one would be less dogmatic (see Tweedie 1961). Again, the universalism and relativism of secular existential therapy in its approach to religious faith are not biblical. The existential emphasis on experience rather than dogma is also problematic from a biblical perspective that emphasizes the importance and need for objective truth and values, especially as revealed in Scripture as inspired revelation from God (2 Tim. 3:16). A Christian approach to existential therapy will therefore deeply and authentically deal with anxiety, emptiness or meaninglessness, and isolation, as well as sin and despair. It will do so in spiritually meaningful and transforming ways that help ground an individual in God as the ultimate and true ground of being, that is, spirit grounded in Spirit, as Kierkegaard put it, or self grounded in Self (Finch and Van Dragt 1999; see also Evans 1990; Finch 1982; Malony 1980).

Existential therapy emphasizes the therapeutic relationship as being the key healing factor in helping clients, as well as the person of the therapist and his or her provision of therapeutic love or genuine caring for the client. These are commendable emphases that are more consistent with the biblical perspective, which considers agape love (1 Cor. 13) that deeply cares for others (Mark 12:31) a crucial value in human relationships, including helping or therapeutic relationships, compared to other therapeutic approaches that may overemphasize technique and the technology of therapeutic change and potentially dehumanize the client. Nevertheless, such therapeutic love and authentic vulnerability on the part of the existential therapist as a wounded healer can also have limitations and dangers. Therapeutic love is not the same as agape love, which is the fruit of the Holy Spirit (Gal. 5:22–23) and comes only from God. As a fallen, imperfect human being, the existential therapist can only go so far with therapeutic love and authentic vulnerability. The darker side of human personality, or the fallen, sinful nature in every human being, is also present in the existential therapist. The danger exists that the existential therapist will try too hard to be therapeutically loving and authentically vulnerable and ultimately do so in ways that are potentially harmful to the client. Examples include genuinely caring for the client but without appropriate boundaries, for instance, allowing too frequent phone calls and sessions that may not be warranted, possibly leading to overdependency on the therapist; and engaging in inappropriate touch to comfort the client, with the therapist being unaware of his or her own countertransference phenomena, which may be sexual in nature. Agape love, which comes from being filled with the Holy Spirit, is pure and deeper than therapeutic love, but even the Christian existential therapist must be careful and prayerfully dependent on the Holy Spirit for his help and guidance in the therapeutic relationship and process of helping clients. Any intimate helping relationship, especially one steeped in therapeutic love as in existential therapy, has its dangers, which must not be overlooked.

The existential therapist also assumes a heavy responsibility in the role of helping clients find meaning in life in the midst of painful existential struggles. Such a therapeutic role comes very close to the role of a priest, pastor, or spiritual director, in being a "midwife" (Evans 1989) to help clients "birth" more authenticity and meaning in their lives. There are potential dangers inherent in such a role because the existential therapist can inadvertently influence the client to embrace certain secular values, such as authentic atheism, that may make temporary sense to them but are ultimately spiritually bankrupt from a biblical perspective. A Christian approach to existential therapy will be careful to direct clients ultimately to God so that they can become a self grounded in Self or a spirit grounded in Spirit (see S. L. Jones and Butman 1991, 299–300), and not just in the autonomous self of the individual. From a biblical perspective the autonomous self will not fill the deep *existential vacuum* in each person, which is ultimately God shaped and which only God can fill. Frankl correctly affirms that human beings are more likely to find fulfillment and meaning in life if they are focused more on something or someone beyond themselves, that is, if they engage in self-transcendence. But he does not go far enough to recognize and affirm that this self-transcendence must be centered ultimately in what the Bible reveals as the transcendent reality of God himself, who objectively and truly exists (see Hurding 1985, 136–37; Tweedie 1961, 175). Furthermore, the emphasis on the client's capacity for active self-healing in existential therapy is another aspect of its focus on the autonomous self, and it can result in too much self-effort and confidence in oneself (cf. Vitz 1994). The biblical perspective emphasizes instead the need to depend on the power of the Holy Spirit and to be filled with the Spirit (Eph. 5:18; Gal. 5:16–25) and not to depend on one's fallen, sinful nature or old, false self. Dependence on God is crucial for healing and wholeness as well as holiness in Christ.

In conclusion, existential therapy is helpful in raising key existential questions and describing how to deal with them in a deep and authentic way, in the context of a therapeutically loving or genuinely caring relationship with the client. However, the ultimate answers to these vexing existential questions centering on meaninglessness, mortality, isolation, and freedom to choose cannot be found in secular existentialism or existential therapy itself. The Bible, as God's inspired revelation, provides ultimate and objectively true answers centered in Jesus Christ and the gospel.

Research: Empirical Status of Existential Therapy

Existential therapists generally do not conduct or appreciate controlled outcome studies evaluating the effectiveness of a particular therapy approach with clients suffering from a specific psychological disorder. They have, however, described several "eloquent case studies" (Schneider 2003, 169). No controlled outcome research seems to have been conducted to date on the effectiveness of existential therapy (see Prochaska and Norcross 2010, 121–22). Some research, however, has been done on the effectiveness of paradoxical interventions in general and includes Frankl's logotherapy technique of paradoxical intention but also other forms of paradoxical interventions. Meta-analyses of such research studies have shown paradoxical interventions in general to be as effective as other typical treatment interventions, but not more effective. Their mean effect size compared to no-treatment controls was 0.99, meaning that a client receiving paradoxical interventions would be more improved than 84 percent of clients receiving no treatment (K. Hill 1987). In one meta-analysis, paradoxical interventions were also found to be more effective than other treatments of more severe cases (Shoham-Salomon and Rosenthal 1987). These research findings, however, do not apply to logotherapy or existential therapy per se.

A little-known study by Loren Mosher (2001) shows evidence that schizophrenia treated with an existentially based growth-oriented approach that provided caring, empathic, supportive relationships without routine psychiatric treatment at Soteria House in the San Francisco Bay area of California had better therapeutic outcomes compared to those who received conventional psychiatric treatment or medication, at two-year follow-up (see also Schneider 2003, 120; and Todd and Bohart 2006, 233, 239). The outcome measures used focused on rehospitalization, psychopathology, independent living, and social and occupational functioning.

Schneider (2003) asserts that there is now a significant though small base of empirical support for existential-humanistic therapy, and especially for some of the major concepts of existential therapy, such as the therapeutic relationship, the therapist's personality or presence, and the client's active self-healing (see Mendelowitz and Schneider 2008, 317). However, Schneider and others (e.g., Todd and Bohart 2006) have lumped together existential therapy with the broader range of experiential and humanistic therapies (such as Carl Rogers's person-centered or client-centered therapy and Fritz Perls's Gestalt therapy plus other experiential therapies) in their review of research studies evaluating the effectiveness of existential therapy. This is confusing because existential therapy is not equivalent to other experiential or humanistic therapies, although it may share similarities with them.

At this time, it is best to conclude with Prochaska and Norcross (2010) that there is still a lack of well-controlled outcome data available. Thus no definitive conclusions can be presently made about the therapeutic effectiveness of existential therapy. However, it is encouraging to see the expansion of empirical work being done on existential concepts and existential therapy (see, e.g., R. A. Walsh and McElwain 2002) as Schneider (2003) has noted. Sharf

(2008, 177–79), in his brief review of research on existential therapy, concluded that there is support for the view that existential themes can be successfully covered and dealt with in existential group therapy. Some research has also investigated existential concepts such as concerns with death, meaninglessness, and finding meaning in life, for example, by using the Purpose in Life Test (PIL) (Crumbaugh 1968; Crumbaugh and Henrion 1988). Much more well-controlled outcome research specifically evaluating the effectiveness of existential therapy for particular psychological disorders is still needed, however.

Future Directions

The percentage of psychotherapists surveyed in the United States who indicate the existential approach to therapy as their primary theoretical orientation is small, around 1 percent of clinical psychologists, 4 percent of social workers, 5 percent of counseling psychologists, and 5 percent of counselors (see Prochaska and Norcross 2010, 3). However, the influence of existential therapy is actually more substantial and pervasive in the field of counseling and psychotherapy, with many schools of therapy incorporating core existential concepts (Prochaska and Norcross 2010, 126–27). As society becomes more technologically oriented, there is a greater tendency for people to be dehumanized and also to feel victimized. More people in the decades ahead may find existential therapy particularly helpful in dealing with emptiness and their search for meaning, with an emphasis again on their freedom to responsibly choose to live an authentic life.

Interest in existential therapy from a professional point of view continues to be alive and is particularly strong in Europe, where several organizations support and further the approach, including the Society for Existential Analysis (www.existentialanalysis.co.uk), founded in 1988 in England; the International Federation for Daseins-analyse; and the Eastern European Association for Existential Psychotherapy in Lithuania. A professional organization based in this hemisphere is the South American Existential Association in Colombia. Training programs in existential therapy are currently available in over a dozen countries, including several European countries and the United States. Earlier existential therapists came mainly from psychoanalytic backgrounds, but today therapists schooled in other orientations such as person-centered therapy, Gestalt therapy, Jungian therapy, feminist therapy, and some cognitive-behavioral therapies (e.g., rational-emotive behavior therapy) have also incorporated existential perspectives into their clinical practice with clients. Logotherapy in particular has grown in many parts of the world, with the Viktor Frankl Institute of Logotherapy still publishing a journal, the *International Forum for Logotherapy*. There are also logotherapy centers in Germany and South America and the International Network on Personal Meaning (www .meaning.ca) with Paul T. P. Wong in Canada as its founding president (see

Wong, Wong, McDonald, and Klaassen 2007). It should be noted that many religious workers and clergy have been interested in logotherapy because of Frankl's emphasis on the spirit in a person and the search for meaning in life as the primary human motivation (see Sharf 2008, 176–77). More recently, the Interpersonal Society for Existential Psychotherapy and Counselling (www .existentialpsychotherapy.net) was established in 2006, in London, England (see Corey 2009, 160).

Existential ideas have also been influential in areas other than therapy, for example, in art, literature, music, film, and religion. Schneider has especially focused on the existential concept of *awe* and the "rediscovery of awe" (Schneider 2004, 2007), referring to how we relate to mystery with wonder, boldness, constraint, and humility.

Due to the predominance of managed health care in the United States and the growing impact of biological and medicalized approaches to the treatment of psychological disorders, clients who undergo existential therapy may have difficulty receiving reimbursement for these therapeutic services; short-term existential intervention, however, is now available (Lantz and Walsh 2007). Nevertheless, some clients will still be interested in receiving existential therapy, whether within or outside the managed-care system, because they want help with their core existential struggles and search for meaning and a more authentic life. The outlook for existential therapy has therefore been described as "guarded yet promising" (Mendelowitz and Schneider 2008, 303). The empirical base supporting the effectiveness of existential therapy is currently lacking and needs to be strengthened if its future is to be even more promising. Christian approaches to existential therapy also need further elaboration and development.

Recommended Readings

Frankl, V. (1963). *Man's search for meaning: An introduction to logotherapy*. Boston: Beacon.

May, R. (1953). *Man's search for himself*. New York: Dell.

Van Duerzen, E. (2001). *Existential counselling and psychotherapy in practice* (2nd ed.). Thousand Oaks, CA: Sage.

Van Duerzen, E., & Kenward, R. (2005). *Dictionary of existential psychotherapy and counselling*. London: Sage.

Yalom, I. D. (1980). *Existential psychotherapy*. New York: Basic Books.

8

Person-Centered Therapy

Person-centered therapy, originally called *nondirective therapy* in the 1940s and then *client-centered therapy* in the 1950s, was founded and developed by Carl Rogers. He began what some have considered a revolution in the counseling and therapy field by emphasizing that certain core therapeutic conditions (i.e., congruence, unconditional positive regard, and empathic understanding) provided by the therapist in the relationship with the client are necessary and sufficient to facilitate client change. Rogers also had an optimistic view of human beings, including therapy clients, believing in their capacity for positive change and growth into fully functioning persons, given appropriate support and safety. Rogers's person-centered approach focuses on the capacity of the client to heal and to grow in the context of a warm, empathic, and genuine therapeutic relationship with the therapist. He deemphasized techniques and diagnoses that tend to dehumanize people. Instead, Rogers placed the client as a person and the therapeutic relationship in the center of effective counseling and therapy. This was revolutionary at a time when more-deterministic views prevailed, such as Freud's psychoanalytic approach and the beginnings of some behavioristic conditioning approaches that emphasized the clinical expertise of the therapist and therapeutic techniques for helping clients change. Rogers used the term "client" rather than "patient" to refer to the person receiving therapy, because he did not perceive the client as someone who is "sick" and in need of a cure.

Rogers eventually expanded his person-centered therapy approach to areas other than counseling and therapy such as marriage, education, business and management, administration, and politics. In his later years, he even became involved in applying his ideas and approach to efforts at reducing international conflicts and enhancing world peace.

Biographical Sketch of Carl Rogers

Carl Ransom Rogers was born on January 8, 1902, in Oak Park, Illinois, a suburb of Chicago. He was the fourth child in a family of six children, five of whom were boys. His father was a contractor and civil engineer who did well professionally and financially. Although his parents were warm and loving, they were also legalistic and controlling, influenced by their fundamentalist Protestant religious background that frowned on activities such as dancing, drinking, card playing, and going to the theater (see C. R. Rogers 1961). When Rogers was twelve years old, he and his family moved to a large farm near Chicago. A sensitive, shy introvert, Rogers was not very sociable and preferred to spend time with his books and in his own world of thought (H. E. Rogers 1965).

Rogers also spent much of his time in the summers using farm equipment and developing his interest in agriculture and scientific methods in farming (Kirschenbaum 1979). He initially pursued scientific agriculture as his major at the University of Wisconsin. Rogers became involved with the YMCA on campus and was selected to be one of the twelve students from the United States who traveled to Peking (now Beijing), China, in 1922 as delegates to the World Student Christian Federation Conference. In meeting other bright and creative students who had religious beliefs that differed from the strict fundamentalistic beliefs of his parents, Rogers experienced a deep transformation of his own religious views, becoming more open and liberal. He also became more of himself (Bankart 1997, 292), with his true personality emerging after being away for six months on this significant trip.

Rogers changed his major from agriculture to history and graduated from the University of Wisconsin in 1924. Two months later he married his childhood sweetheart, Helen Elliott, and they drove to New York City, where he studied at Union Theological Seminary, a school that was more liberal than his parents would have preferred (Thorne 2003). His father had offered to fund his theological studies at Princeton, but Rogers exercised his independence by going to Union instead. After two years at Union, where he took a few psychology courses, he left the seminary and began a PhD program in clinical and educational psychology at neighboring Columbia University. Rogers completed this doctoral program in 1931.

Rogers worked for twelve years in the Child Study Department at the Society for the Prevention of Cruelty to Children in Rochester, New York, where he gained valuable clinical experience working with underprivileged and delinquent children referred by social agencies and the court system (C. R. Rogers 1961).

He also trained and supervised other psychologists and social workers. Rogers eventually went beyond the traditional psychoanalytic approach to therapy and began to develop a more nondirective counseling approach. He wrote *The Clinical Treatment of the Problem Child* (1939) during his time in Rochester.

Rogers moved to Columbus, Ohio, to become a full professor at Ohio State University in 1940. He gave a groundbreaking lecture titled "Newer Concepts in Psychotherapy" at the University of Minnesota on December 11, 1940, and recalled this date as the "day on which client-centered therapy was born" (Kirschenbaum 1979, 112). This significant lecture and his subsequent book, *Counseling and Psychotherapy* (C. R. Rogers 1942), sparked a major response from mental health professionals, with both enthusiastic support for and scathing criticism of his nondirective counseling ideas (Thorne 2003), which deemphasized technique and diagnosis. Rogers therefore became a "quiet revolutionary" (see Farson 1975).

Rogers's early ideas on nondirective counseling, or client-centered therapy, were partly influenced by Otto Rank, who, like Jung and Adler, had broken away from Freud and his psychoanalytic group. Rogers attended a three-day seminar in Rochester conducted by Rank. He was thus exposed to Rank's ideas emphasizing the uniqueness and experience of the client and the need for the therapist to relinquish the role of an authority and instead become more of a nonjudgmental helper (Rank 1945). Rogers's thinking was also influenced by two other people with whom he had contact: Elizabeth Davis, a Rankian-trained social worker at the Rochester clinic, and Jessie Taft, who was one of Rank's students (C. R. Rogers and Haigh 1983).

In 1945, Rogers went to the University of Chicago, where he became a professor of psychology and the director of the university counseling center. He further developed his theoretical ideas and also engaged in research with his colleagues and graduate students to evaluate the effectiveness of his non-directive counseling approach, which eventually was renamed client-centered therapy in the publication of his significant book *Client-Centered Therapy: Its Current Practice, Implications, and Theory* (C. R. Rogers 1951). In 1956, Rogers received the first distinguished Scientific Contribution Award, presented to him by the American Psychological Association, an organization he had served as president in 1946–47. He thus became a well-known figure in the counseling and therapy field, and client-centered therapy established itself as a major approach to therapy.

Rogers left the University of Chicago in 1957 to assume a new position at the University of Wisconsin in the Department of Psychology and then in the Department of Psychiatry. He had a difficult time in the Department of Psychology, disagreeing with how graduate students were treated in a somewhat oppressive educational environment that did not offer them enough freedom and support to develop their own creative ideas and work. As a result, he had frequent conflicts with his colleagues (Thorne 2003; P. Sanders 2004a).

Rogers undertook a large research project that evaluated the impact of the therapeutic relationship on schizophrenics who were hospitalized (C. R. Rogers, Gendlin, Kiesler, and Truax 1967), but the study encountered several problems and yielded few statistically significant findings. However, two conclusions could be made from the results of this research project: clients who experienced the highest level of accurate empathy were the most successful, and clients' evaluation of the therapeutic relationship correlated more highly with therapeutic success or failure than the therapists' evaluation. Rogers managed to write and publish another substantial book, *On Becoming a Person* (1961), which led to even greater renown for him. In 1957, he had also published what is now a classic article on the necessary and sufficient conditions of therapeutic personality change, focusing on congruence, unconditional positive regard, and empathy. He resigned from the University of Wisconsin in 1962.

In 1964, Rogers moved to La Jolla, California, where he became a resident fellow at the Western Behavioral Sciences Institute for four years. After leaving the institute in 1968, he helped form the Center for Studies of the Person in La Jolla, where he also became a resident fellow. The center was the base from which he traveled around the world to deal with international conflicts and to work on peacemaking efforts. He continued to publish significant books on a wider variety of topics covering the application of person-centered ideas to areas such as education (1969, 1983), encounter groups (1970), marriage (1972), and personal power including psychotherapy, family life, administration, education, and politics (1977).

Rogers continued to travel, write, and work on international projects and global issues until the last days of his life. He received many awards and honors in his lifetime, including the Distinguished Professional Contribution Award from the American Psychological Association in 1972. He was even nominated for the Nobel Peace Prize as a result of his tireless efforts in trying to resolve global conflicts in a peaceful way. In 1987, Rogers broke his hip in a fall. He had successful surgery for the broken hip, but died shortly thereafter from a heart attack on February 4, 1987 (Cain 1987a). Rogers has been described as a man who lived his life in a way that was consistent with his person-centered theory, and as an author, therapist, and person he was consistently the same man (Cain 1987b).

Major Theoretical Ideas of Person-Centered Therapy

Perspective on Human Nature

Person-centered therapy as developed by Rogers has a positive and optimistic perspective on human nature. It views the person as basically good and trustworthy, with an inner and innate tendency toward growth and wholeness leading the person to be all they can be. This *actualizing tendency*, which is the major motivation in every human person, moves an individual toward self-actualization or becoming mature and autonomous, under appropriate conditions that are supportive and safe for the person (see C. R. Rogers 1961, 35).

Rogers also described the *organismic valuing process* that guides the actualizing tendency with an innate capacity to choose what will be self-enhancing or self-actualizing rather than what will be self-destructive. He believed that when person-centered therapists provide the therapeutic conditions of congruence (realness or genuineness), unconditional positive regard (warmth and acceptance or respect), and accurate empathic understanding (of the client's inner, subjective world) in a way that the client can experience them, then the right conditions of support and safety enable the client to grow and self-actualize. On the other hand, if negative "conditions of worth" are imposed on a person or a client, usually by society and parental figures or other family members, then the actualizing tendency is alienated, and the individual may then develop defensive and maladaptive reactions to an environment that he or she experiences as oppressive and dangerous. The behavior that eventually results may include evil acts of cruelty and hatred, which Rogers acknowledged can and do occur. However, he was convinced that this is not the innate nature of a human being but rather an acquired aspect of human behavior (see Parrott 2003, 178).

Rogers believed that given appropriate conditions fostering growth, human beings are basically good and trustworthy, capable of choosing their own direction in constructive and insightful ways and able to be productive and effective in their lives (Cain 1987b). Person-centered therapy therefore focuses on the client and his or her capacity for healing, growth, and self-actualization as well as self-determination. It does not view the therapist as an authoritative expert. The ultimate responsibility for healing and growth in therapy lies with the client (see Corey 2009, 169–70), who is capable of becoming a *fully functioning person* when the actualizing tendency is allowed to blossom and be expressed.

Person-Centered Theory of Personality

Rogers has developed and described both a theory of personality as well as a theory of psychotherapy from a person-centered perspective (C. R. Rogers 1959). His theory of personality consists of nineteen propositions that are somewhat complex, and it has therefore attracted much less attention than his theory of psychotherapy (C. R. Rogers 1980, 60).

Rogers's (1959) theory of personality (including a theory of psychopathology) from a person-centered perspective with its nineteen propositions can be condensed into four major features according to J. Sommers-Flanagan and Sommers-Flanagan (2004, 179–82).

The first feature of a person-centered theory of personality is that it is mainly a *self-theory* (Bankart 1997). Rogers described the *organism* as the locus of a person's total psychological experience and the *self* as that part of the organism that is "me," whether conscious or unconscious. Thus a person's experience of self can differ from his or her total psychological experience as an organism. Rogers labeled such a discrepancy as *incongruence*. On the other hand, when a person's self experiences are in line with his or her total experiences as an organism, *congruence* exists between self and organism, a highly positive situation that facilitates the development and growth of the individual into a more mature, autonomous, and fully functioning person.

> **Sidebar 8.1**
>
> **Features of Person-Centered Theory**
> *(see J. Sommers-Flanagan & Sommers-Flanagan 2004, 179–82)*
>
> 1. Self-theory
> 2. Phenomenology and the valuing of experience
> 3. Learning and growth potential
> 4. Conditions of worth

The second feature of Rogers's theory of personality is his emphasis on *phenomenology and the valuing of experience*. It highly values personal, subjective experience that is direct and nonverbal, what has been called "intuitive knowing" (Bohart 1995, 91). Person-centered therapy seeks to help clients be more open to their own wide variety of subjective, personal experiencing and to decide which experiences can help them become more fully functioning persons.

The third feature of a person-centered theory of personality is its focus on *learning and growth potential*. Rogers emphasized that every person has an innate *actualizing tendency* that moves him or her in the positive direction of growth, maturity, and autonomy, becoming more who he or she really is. It is a potential for learning and growth in every moment of one's life and one's experiences. Rogers observed: "There is one central source of energy in the human organism. This source . . . is most simply conceptualized as a tendency toward fulfillment, toward actualization, involving not only the maintenance but also the enhancement of the organism" (1980, 123).

The fourth and final feature of a person-centered theory of personality concerns *conditions of worth*. In addition to an individual's innate actualizing tendency to maintain and enhance himself or herself as an organism, there are also two important learned or acquired needs: the need for *positive regard* and the need for *self-regard*. If the need for positive regard or approval from significant others, especially parents or parental figures in one's life, is not met because disapproval or negative feedback is sometimes given to the person for particular behaviors, then *conditions of worth* are set up for him or her. The individual will then experience positive regard or approval from others for some of his or her behaviors, but negative regard or disapproval for other behaviors. This will result in a similar mix of internalized positive and negative self-regard and an incongruent sense of self, with discrepancies between the *social self* based on others' expectations and the *true self* based on one's actual feelings about one's experiences. Internal genuine values that are unconsciously appreciated organismically by the person often clash with externally imposed and consciously incorporated values from significant others. Under conditions of worth that are not supportive or safe, an individual will usually become increasingly out of touch with his or her *true self*, that is, become more incongruent and therefore ultimately unable to learn or grow from experience, leading to psychopathology. It is therefore crucial for an individual to experience unconditional positive regard in order for him or her to have appropriate self-regard and to recover from psychopathology and grow again as a person. We should also note that Rogers viewed people as capable of perception without awareness, a process called *subception*.

In addition to these four major features of Rogers's person-centered theory of personality, he also provided descriptions of fully functioning persons that individuals are motivated to become as they allow their organismic valuing processes to be more fully utilized. According to Rogers (1961, 187–96, italics as set in original), *"Fully functioning persons are open to experience, are characterized by existential living, trust their organisms, are creative,* and *live richer lives than do other people"* (see Ryckman 2008, 454). He later expanded and elaborated on these characteristics of the fully functioning person to include the following descriptions of what he termed *emerging persons* (e.g., corporate executives who are committed to living a simpler life, countercultural young people, nuns and priests who have overcome dogmatism to live more meaningfully, and ethnically diverse people and women who have overcome passivity to live more assertive and constructive lives): *"They are honest and open; they are indifferent to material comforts and rewards; they are caring persons; they have a deep distrust of cognitive based science and a technology that uses that science to exploit and harm nature and people;* and *they have a trust in their own experience and a profound distrust of all external authority"* (C. R. Rogers 1977, 255–74, italics as set in original; see also Ryckman 2008, 455–56).

Therapeutic Process and Relationship

Rogers's theory of psychotherapy, compared to his theory of personality, is much better known and more widely applied in the practice of counseling and psychotherapy. It focuses on the therapeutic process and the therapeutic relationship between the therapist and the client as the crucial factors in effective therapy. Rogers believed that a client should lead in the process of therapy and be free to choose his or her own specific goals or direction in therapy. The basic aim of person-centered therapy is not to solve problems but to provide the *necessary and sufficient therapeutic conditions of congruence, unconditional positive regard, and empathic understanding* so that the client *can freely grow to become more of a fully functioning person* in a safe and supportive therapeutic environment.

Clients who are becoming more fully functioning or more actualized have been described by Rogers (1961) as being open to experience, trusting in themselves, evaluating themselves more internally than externally, and being willing to continue growing.

More specifically, Rogers described the following *necessary and sufficient conditions of therapeutic personality change* in his theory of psychotherapy: "For constructive personality change to occur, it is necessary that these conditions exist and continue over a period of time:

1. Two persons are in psychological contact.
2. The first, whom we shall term the client, is in a state of incongruence, being vulnerable and anxious.
3. The second person, whom we shall term the therapist, is congruent or integrated in the relationship.
4. The therapist experiences unconditional positive regard for the client.
5. The therapist experiences an empathic understanding of the client's internal frame of reference and endeavors to communicate this experience to the client.
6. The communication to the client of the therapist's empathic understanding and unconditional positive regard is to a minimal degree achieved." (1957, 95)

Rogers was firmly convinced that these core conditions alone are sufficient and necessary for therapeutic or positive personality change to occur in any client. He believed that no other conditions or therapeutic methods are necessary for therapeutic personality change to take place in a client. Such a person-centered approach places major emphasis on the equality and mutuality of the therapist-client relationship in which the therapist is a fellow traveler with the client on the client's journey through life. The therapist is not viewed as an expert with specialized knowledge for accurate diagnosis of the client and techniques for solving the problems of the client. Instead the therapist is a guide who provides and communicates congruence or genuineness, unconditional positive regard or acceptance, and accurate empathic understanding to the client to facilitate the client's growth into a more fully functioning person. However, this therapeutic process is not as easy to achieve as one might think. The therapist must trust the client and provide this special kind of therapeutic relationship with the client (see J. Sommers-Flanagan and Sommers-Flanagan 2004, 182), both of which are more difficult to maintain than they seem. Both the therapist and the client are imperfect human beings, with obvious limitations. Therefore, a therapist, even a person-centered therapist, cannot be expected to always be real, accepting, and understanding (with congruence, unconditional positive regard, and accurate empathic understanding) with and for every client. However, the person-centered therapist will attempt to develop these therapeutic conditions and attitudes toward a client.

Rogers realized that his theory of psychotherapy is radical and controversial because he strongly asserted that his six conditions of therapeutic personality change are the only sufficient and necessary ones for clients, as well as for other people, to grow and become more fully functioning. He therefore disagreed with therapists who insisted on other necessary conditions, such as specific therapeutic techniques, to bring about therapeutic change. However, even when therapists view Rogers's core conditions of congruence, unconditional positive regard, and empathic understanding as neither necessary nor sufficient, or as necessary but not sufficient, to produce therapeutic change, most of them still appreciate these conditions as helpful. They are often taught as the clinical foundations for any effective approach to counseling and psychotherapy, and therefore they have been incorporated into almost every contemporary school of counseling and psychotherapy. Congruence or genuineness, unconditional positive regard or acceptance, and empathic understanding or accurate empathy will now be covered in more detail as crucial components of the therapeutic relationship, especially in person-centered therapy.

Congruence

Congruence in the therapist is also referred to as genuineness, or authenticity and transparency. In other words, a person-centered therapist who is congruent or integrated in the therapeutic relationship with the client is real, honest, and open, engaging in appropriate self-disclosure to the client, involving both positive as well as negative feelings. When the congruent therapist is genuine with the client, the client is enabled to be more real as well, and hence to be more truly in touch with his or her real self. Congruence or genuineness is therefore essential for effective counseling and psychotherapy from a person-centered perspective (see C. R. Rogers 1961).

Unconditional Positive Regard

Unconditional positive regard is also referred to as acceptance, warmth, prizing, or respect. It is a nonpossessive deep and real caring for the client that is nonjudgmental and positive, allowing and accepting the client to have the feelings he or she is experiencing at the moment in the therapeutic relationship. There is also a total prizing or valuing of the client in an unconditional way, respecting the client regardless of his or her behavior. Such unconditional positive regard of the therapist for the client will more likely lead to forward movement or therapeutic change according to Rogers (1986, 198). Fall, Holden, and Marquis (2004, 202) have noted, however, that unconditional positive regard actually goes beyond acceptance because it is a total respect for the client and his or her humanity, regardless of the behavior the client may be showing at the moment. This unconditional positive regard of the therapist for the client will enhance the client's own unconditional self-regard and therefore help the client to grow and become a more fully functioning person, because conditions of worth have been reduced or removed. Rogers was aware that therapists are not perfect people, and therefore cannot experience and communicate unconditional positive regard to all their clients all the time. However, it is essential from a person-centered therapy perspective for therapists to have deep respect and genuine caring or warmth for their clients in effective therapy (C. R. Rogers 1977; see Corey 2009, 175).

Empathic Understanding or Accurate Empathy

Empathic understanding, or accurate empathy, refers to the therapist's ability to enter deeply into the client's subjective world or internal frame of reference and feel *with* the client as sensitively and accurately as possible. Although it involves deep listening, it is more than just reflection of the client's feelings. It is an entering into the client's subjective experiences, feeling the client's feelings without losing the therapist's own identity or being overwhelmed by the client's feelings. Such empathic understanding experienced and expressed by the therapist to the client will help the client be in deeper touch and understanding of his or her own subjective experiences or feelings, including those that may not be as clear or obvious initially.

There are therefore at least two levels of accurate empathy, or empathic listening (see C. R. Rogers 1975, 1980): empathic understanding of what the client is feeling or experiencing, and deeper empathic listening and understanding of meanings of the client's experiences of which the client is hardly aware or conscious. This latter deeper empathy is sometimes called advanced empathy, whereby the therapist deeply hears the message behind the message (Egan 2002).

Empathy is actually a multidimensional rather than a simple construct, with several components (see Buie 1981; J. Sommers-Flanagan and Sommers-Flanagan 2003). The three main ones are *intellectual empathy*, which is viewing the world from the client's perspective but in an objective, intellectual, or distant way; *emotional empathy*, which is the therapist's emotional response to a client's feelings or words; and *imaginative empathy*, which refers to a therapist's asking the empathy question posed by Carkhuff (1987): "How would I feel if I were in my client's situation?" (see J. Sommers-Flanagan and Sommers-Flanagan 2004, 185). Empathy has been the most researched and discussed of the three core therapeutic conditions of congruence, unconditional positive regard, and empathic understanding described by Rogers in person-centered therapy (see Bohart and Greenberg 1997; J. C. Watson 2002). It has

Sidebar 8.2

Techniques in Person-Centered Therapy
(see J. Sommers-Flanagan & Sommers-Flanagan 2004, 190–98)

1. Experiencing and expressing congruence
2. Experiencing and expressing unconditional positive regard
3. Experiencing and expressing empathic understanding

been acknowledged by almost every major approach to counseling and psychotherapy as a crucial factor in effective therapy.

However, in reviewing the writings of Rogers on these three core therapeutic or therapist conditions, Jerald Bozarth concluded that genuineness and empathic understanding can be viewed as the two contextual attitudes for the primary condition of therapeutic change: unconditional positive regard (1996, 44). Bozarth therefore believes that unconditional positive regard, together with genuineness and empathic understanding, should all be considered a single crucial condition for therapeutic change to occur in the client, and this condition is essentially an *attitude* that the therapist must have toward the client for effective counseling and therapy to take place (see also Tyler 1999). Person-centered therapy ultimately requires this kind of therapeutic *attitude* on the part of the therapist, and not techniques; only when the therapist thus successfully communicates positive regard can the client be therapeutically changed.

Major Therapeutic Techniques and Interventions

Person-centered therapy as developed by Rogers does not espouse specific therapeutic techniques or interventions. It also does not formally engage in psychological diagnosis but rather treats each client as a unique individual (although some contemporary practitioners of person-centered therapy may provide diagnoses for their clients for the sake of medical insurance reimbursement). Rogers himself felt that formal psychological diagnosis is not necessary for therapy and may even have deleterious effects on the process of therapy (C. R. Rogers 1957, 220).

More traditional person-centered therapy following Rogers emphasizes that only six conditions are necessary for therapeutic change to occur in the client. The first two conditions focus on a client who is experiencing incongruence, with feelings of vulnerability or anxiety, but who is in psychological contact or therapeutic relationship with a therapist. The other three conditions focus on the therapist being congruent, experiencing unconditional positive regard for the client, and experiencing empathic understanding of the client's internal frame of reference and communicating this to the client. The final condition requires the congruent therapist communicating empathic understanding and unconditional positive regard to the client to the degree that the client perceives and experiences this understanding and regard. The key therapeutic "technique" or intervention in person-centered therapy thus concerns the therapist having the right therapeutic *attitude* toward the client and effectively communicating or expressing it to the client.

Although there are no specific techniques in the practice of traditional person-centered therapy, the therapeutic attitude of the person-centered therapist toward the client can be described as consisting of three major "techniques" or interventions: experiencing and expressing congruence, experiencing and expressing unconditional positive regard, and experiencing and expressing empathic understanding (J. Sommers-Flanagan and Sommers-Flanagan 2004, 190–98).

Experiencing and Expressing Congruence

For the therapist to be congruent means that the therapist is real, open, genuine, and honest in relating to the client. However, this does not mean that the therapist engages in total self-disclosure or shares every thought or feeling that he or she may have during the therapy session with the client. Some discernment and self-control are still needed so that the therapist shares only what is appropriate and helpful to the client. It can include sharing negative feelings such as feeling bored, but some feelings, such as sexual attraction for the client, may be better shared with a clinical supervisor or consultant than with the client, who may feel threatened by the therapist's disclosure of such feelings.

Rogers seems to have believed that therapists can use techniques in therapy but only if they occur spontaneously, and not in a preplanned way (J. Sommers-Flanagan and Sommers-Flanagan 2004, 193). In other words, if techniques are ever appropriate in therapy, they should come up in a genuine and spontaneous way, consistent with the behavior of a congruent therapist. More-contemporary practitioners of person-centered therapy, therefore, may use techniques at times but in a genuine way appropriate to particular clients (see Bozarth, Zimring, and Tausch 2002; Cain 2002a).

Experiencing and Expressing Unconditional Positive Regard

Experiencing and expressing unconditional positive regard for the client is another core therapeutic condition according to Rogers. Bozarth (1996) concluded that unconditional positive regard is *the primary condition* for therapeutic change to occur in the client. It is an attitude of warmth, respect, deep caring for, and acceptance of the client, in which the client is valued simply for who he or she is as a person, without any conditions of worth (C. R. Rogers 1959). Rogers clarified that such unconditional positive regard is a kind of love that is equivalent to *agape*, a term used by theologians, but not related to the romantic and possessive meanings usually associated with the word "love" (see C. R. Rogers 1962, 422).

Since there are no perfect human beings or perfect therapists, it is impossible in practice for even person-centered therapists to experience and express unconditional positive regard for every client all the time. However, the person-centered therapist will strive as much as possible for an attitude of unconditional positive regard for a client.

Unconditional positive regard can be communicated or expressed to a client in various ways. The more direct way of simply saying, for example, "I value and prize you as a whole person" or "I accept you and care about you for who you are as a person" or "I won't judge you" oftentimes may not be the most appropriate means of expressing unconditional positive regard. Clients may be overwhelmed by such direct statements and react with unrealistic expectations of perfect caring and even romantic love from the therapist or respond with fear or distancing because of their discomfort with such caring intimacy offered by the therapist (see J. Sommers-Flanagan and Sommers-Flanagan 2004, 195). However, sometimes a direct expression of unconditional positive regard or warmth and deep caring can be helpful, for example, when Rogers himself responded to a client who didn't care what happened with: "You just don't care what happens. And I guess I'd just like to say—*I* care about you. And *I* care what happens" (C. R. Rogers, Gendlin, Kiesler, and Truax 1967, 409).

Other appropriate ways of indirectly expressing unconditional positive regard include establishing a relationship of respect and warmth with the client by keeping appointments, addressing him in the way he would like to be addressed, and listening intently and caringly to him; letting the client freely talk about herself in whatever manner is comfortable for her; hearing and remembering particular details of the client's story, for example, by using paraphrases, summaries, and occasionally interpretations; responding with empathy and compassion when the client expresses emotional pain and conflicts; and making an intentional effort to accept and respect the client in a warm and caring way (see J. Sommers-Flanagan and Sommers-Flanagan 2003, 108).

Experiencing and Expressing Empathic Understanding

Although it is impossible to fully and directly experience another person's feelings (C. R. Rogers 1959), person-centered therapists do their best to experience and express empathic understanding of their client's internal frame of reference or subjective feelings with as accurate empathy as possible. Based on Rogers's description of what being empathic really means (see C. R. Rogers 1975, 4), J. Sommers-Flanagan and Sommers-Flanagan briefly describe the following four major components of experiencing and expressing empathic understanding to the client: "*Entering and Becoming at Home in the Client's Private Perceptual World; Being Sensitive from Moment to Moment with the Client's Changing Meanings and Emotions; Temporarily Living and Moving*

About Delicately in the Client's Life; and *Sensing Deep Meanings, but Not Uncovering Feelings That Are Too Far Out of Awareness"* (2004, 197, italics as set in original).

With regard to *temporarily* living and moving about delicately in the client's personal world, there is a real danger of the therapist becoming too involved, so much so that the empathic therapist loses his or her own sense of self in a way that is unhealthy and potentially harmful to the therapist as well as to the client. Rogers himself became too involved in the subjective world of one of his female clients and ultimately lost his sense of self in the relationship (see C. R. Rogers 1967, 367; see also C. R. Rogers 1972).

Nevertheless, empathic understanding of, or accurate empathy for, the client is a core therapeutic condition in person-centered therapy, and virtually every school of counseling has acknowledged it as an integral part of effective therapy. It is crucial to remember that empathic understanding is more than merely reflecting feelings or paraphrasing the feelings expressed by a client, what has been described as the basic counseling technique of active listening. Rogers himself stopped writing about reflection of the client's feelings early in his professional career because many clinicians erroneously concluded that empathy simply involves paraphrasing and summarizing the feelings expressed by the client. Rogers chose instead to emphasize the need for a person-centered therapist to have an *empathic attitude* rather than focus on reflecting a client's feelings or listening empathically (C. R. Rogers 1975).

Carkhuff (1971, 170–71) has extended Rogers's three core therapeutic conditions to six core conditions: the *facilitative* conditions of *empathy* (or understanding), *respect* (or unconditional positive regard), and *concreteness* (or being specific); and the *action* conditions of *genuineness* (or being real or congruent), *confrontation* (or telling it like it is), and *immediacy* (or what is really going on between the therapist and the client). The extra core therapeutic condition that is most often added to congruence (or genuineness), unconditional positive regard (or respect), and empathic understanding (or empathy) is *concreteness or specificity* (see, e.g., Egan 2006). Traditional person-centered therapy still focuses on the three core therapeutic conditions and the six necessary and sufficient conditions of therapeutic personality change first described by Rogers (1957). It has been applied not only in individual therapy but also in play therapy (Axline 1947) and client-centered work with children (K. Moon 2002), client-centered group process, classroom teaching, the intensive group or basic encounter group, and peace and conflict resolution between larger groups and even nations (see Raskin, Rogers, and Witty 2008, 172–74).

As noted, more-contemporary versions of person-centered therapy have built on and gone beyond Rogers's approach, with a wider array of therapeutic techniques and practices. Such innovations include person-centered expressive arts therapy (N. Rogers 1993, 1995; J. Sommers-Flanagan 2007); "focusing" as an experiential technique to deeper client experiencing (Gendlin 1996); evocative techniques to help clients reexperience crucial troubling feelings that still bother them (Rice and Greenberg 1984); perceptual psychology (Combs 1988, 1989, 1999); new frontiers in the theory and practice of person-centered therapy (Mearns and Thorne 1999, 2000); collaborative gender and power issues in the person-centered approach (Natiello 2001); facilitation of emotional change in therapy and more-advanced methods of person-centered therapy (L. S. Greenberg, Korman, and Paivio 2002; L. S. Greenberg, Rice, and Elliott 1993); focus on the inner workings of the process of therapy (Rennie 1998); deeper understanding of empathy in the practice of therapy (Bohart 2003; Bohart and Greenberg 1997; Bohart and Tallman 1999); empathy when functioning in all its multifaceted dimensions (cognitive, affective, and interpersonal) as one of the most potent tools of the therapist (J. C. Watson 2002); client-centered therapy as a universal system of therapy (C. H. Patterson 1995); and the client-centered relationship understood as essential in all approaches to therapy (Hubble, Duncan, and Miller 1999), to name but a few (see Corey 2009, 190).

Motivational interviewing (MI) is a well-known and more specific contemporary version of a person-centered approach to therapy that includes specific techniques. It was developed by William R. Miller, based on his clinical work and research on problem drinking and addiction. Described by Miller as Carl Rogers in new clothes (Prochaska and Norcross 2010, 147), MI has been defined as "a directive, client-centered counseling style for eliciting behavior change by helping clients to explore and resolve ambivalence" (Rollnick and Miller 1995, 326). It focuses on enhancing the intrinsic motivation to change in a client by using a person-centered style with warmth, empathy, and an egalitarian therapeutic relationship, in conjunction with person-centered "techniques" such as reflective listening and asking key questions. However, MI also adds other therapeutic techniques that go beyond traditional person-centered therapy, such as using specific therapeutic interventions to help clients move toward behavior change and including the therapist's goals for therapeutic changes in the client (Moyers and Rollnick 2002).

William Miller and Stephen Rollnick (1991, 2002) have identified and described four major principles for the practice of MI (see Prochaska and Norcross 2010, 148) based on their view of Rogers's approach to person-centered therapy (which they felt was not nondirective because Rogers did guide his clients, though gently, to explore their pain, agitation, or confusion, and stay with such experiences in order to work through them):

1. *Express empathy* by using reflective listening skills to understand the client and convey such empathic understanding as well as genuine caring to the client.
2. *Develop discrepancy* between the client's deep values and present behavior. The therapist helps the client to perceive or notice such a dis-

crepancy, which can powerfully motivate the client to initiate change that the client desires. It is the client who argues for change and talks about changing, not the therapist.

3. *Roll with resistance* by responding to client resistance with reflection instead of confrontation. Client resistance is viewed as an expression of ambivalence about change, and the therapist should not confront it directly or try to persuade the client to change. The therapist should instead roll with the resistance by using empathic reflection and understanding.

4. *Support self-efficacy* by actively communicating to the client that he or she is capable of change, building optimism, using brief and small interventions that allow change to successfully occur, and reinforcing optimism for further change. However, the therapist still lets the client lead in coming up with possible solutions for change.

More recently, a new series of books focusing on applications of MI is being published, including MI for treating psychological problems such as anxiety, posttraumatic stress disorder, obsessive-compulsive disorder, depression, suicidal tendencies, eating disorders, problem and pathological gambling, medication adherence in schizophrenia, patients with dual diagnoses, and patients in the criminal justice or correctional system (Arkowitz, Westra, Miller, and Rollnick 2008); and MI in health-care contexts, helping patients change behavior to improve their health in areas such as weight loss, exercise, smoking cessation, medication adherence, and safer sex practices (Rollnick, Miller, and Butler 2008). A practitioner workbook is also available for building MI skills (Rosengren 2009). William Miller and Gary Rose recently proposed a theory of MI with two major components: "a relational component focused on empathy and the interpersonal spirit of MI, and a technical component involving the differential evocation and reinforcement of client change talk" (2009, 527).

Person-Centered Therapy in Practice

A Hypothetical Transcript

Client: I lost my job again . . . the second time in just a month! I feel like a loser, and that people must be laughing at me and thinking that I'm a failure, that I'm good for nothing.

Person-Centered Therapist: You just lost your job, twice in one month . . . and you're feeling lousy about it, like being a loser, and you feel that others are looking down on you, thinking of you as no good and a failure.

Client: Yeah, . . . and it hurts real bad inside because I've tried very hard to keep my jobs . . . but I guess I'm not good enough and never will be good enough . . . (with tears welling up)

Person-Centered Therapist: Um-hmm . . . It's really painful, especially when you tried so hard to keep your jobs, and feeling you're not good enough . . . and will never be good enough? . . . (silence for a few moments, with more tears from the client)

Client: It's . . . It's really hard . . . to feel like no matter how much I try, it's no use . . . it's not going to make a difference at all . . . because I'm no good at all at keeping a job . . . or even at anything else . . . I'm such a failure, such a loser . . . (weeps a little).

Person-Centered Therapist: Um-hmm . . . Here are some Kleenex if you'd like some. . . . You really feel crushed inside . . . like you're a total failure, and no matter what you do or how hard you try, it's not going to work out . . . it's not going to be good enough . . . about your job . . . as well as about anything else in your life. . . . Is that what you said? Am I getting it right?

Client: Yeah, yeah . . . that's right. I don't know where to go from here and what to do . . . but I feel I'm just a total nothing, a big zero . . . who can't do anything right . . . (weeps a little more) (silence for a few more moments)

Person-Centered Therapist: Sounds like you're experiencing an overwhelming feeling of being a complete failure . . . being a total nobody . . . and you feel stuck, not knowing what to do or where to go from here . . . and it just hurts . . . and hurts . . . and hurts . . . more and more deeply . . . (client begins to weep more)

Client: Yeah . . . it's just so hard . . . and it hurts so much deep inside . . . (sobs for a few seconds) (silence for a few moments)

Person-Centered Therapist: Um-hmm . . . so much pain inside . . . it hurts so badly and deeply that the tears just flow . . .

Client: Um-hmm . . . (weeps for a few more seconds)

Person-Centered Therapist: (remains quiet for a few seconds while handing more Kleenex to the client)

This hypothetical transcript of a small part of a traditional person-centered therapy session demonstrates the experience and expression of unconditional positive regard (warmth and deep caring) as well as empathic understanding by a genuine or congruent person-centered therapist for a client who is struggling with much deep emotional pain and feels overwhelmed by it. The person-centered therapist engages in intense reflective listening and conveys unconditional positive regard and empathic understanding by using para-phrases and brief summaries of the client's feelings and experiences, as well as by being present in deeply caring moments of silence and offering the client Kleenex at appropriate times when the client is crying. The person-centered therapist does not use other specific therapeutic techniques such as problem solving of the job situation, or cognitive restructuring of the client's thinking, or behavioral methods for emotional control.

Critique of Person-Centered Therapy: Strengths and Weaknesses

Person-centered therapy has several strengths, many of them similar to the strengths of existential therapy covered in the previous chapter of this book. First, person-centered therapy involves a genuine and deep respect for the cli-ent as a person. It is thus client centered, with a deep trust in the individual's actualizing tendency to learn and grow to become a more fully functioning person. It has a basically positive view of the goodness of human nature. As a humanistic approach similar to existential therapy, it strongly opposes any therapeutic attempt to dehumanize or objectify the client and therefore does not focus on therapeutic techniques per se or on formal diagnosis and psy-chological testing and assessment of the client.

Second, it emphasizes the therapeutic relationship as the key factor in effec-tive counseling and therapy for all clients. In fact, according to Rogers, there are only six necessary and sufficient conditions for therapeutic personality change to occur in the client, chief among them: congruence, unconditional positive regard, and empathic understanding, which the therapist needs to experience and communicate to the client. Traditional person-centered therapy therefore exalts such a therapeutic relationship to the highest level of necessity for therapeutic change in the client to occur, without the need for any other therapeutic techniques or interventions. No other approach to counseling and therapy places such a premium on the therapeutic relationship as the es-sential and only healing factor in effective counseling and therapy. Empathy in particular has received tremendous attention and research support for its crucial and essential role in effective therapy (J. C. Watson 2002).

Third, a related strength of person-centered therapy is its focus on the person of the therapist and the need for congruence or genuineness and ma-turity on the part of therapists so that they effectively experience and express unconditional positive regard and empathic understanding to their clients. The person of the therapist is more important than techniques.

Fourth, Rogers has been credited with opening the counseling and therapy field to empirical scrutiny and research. He tried to put his person-centered ideas into hypotheses that could be empirically tested in research (see Cain 2002a, 2002b; Combs 1988). He also insisted on allowing therapy sessions to be recorded and then objectively rated by impartial judges or researchers to investigate the relationship of the core therapeutic conditions of genuineness, unconditional positive regard, and empathic understanding or empathy to therapeutic outcomes. Person-centered therapy has therefore contributed significantly to research on therapy process and outcome, despite its eschewing of technique and diagnosis.

Fifth, person-centered therapy has greatly influenced virtually every major approach to counseling and therapy, but this impact has not always been explicitly acknowledged or sufficiently appreciated (Farber 1996). Nevertheless, innovations in more-contemporary person-centered approaches to therapy have been made, with appropriate acknowledgments of the pioneering work and influence of Rogers, a partial list of which was briefly reviewed earlier in this chapter.

Sixth, and finally, person-centered therapy may be particularly helpful to clients who need space and deep acceptance and genuine caring from a therapist, in order to explore issues and their own inner experiences and feelings, without being judged or having external conditions of worth imposed on them. Such clients have typically included middle-class college students and others struggling with developmental and identity issues, many of whom were seen in early client-centered therapy, the forerunner of person-centered therapy.

Person-centered therapy also has several weaknesses. First, the radical focus on the individual and deep respect and trust in his or her innate goodness and actualizing tendency can result in an overly optimistic reliance on the client to provide self-appraisals that are accurate and to engage in healthy growth or actualization as a person. Such an individualistic focus on the self and its ultimate importance and autonomy may well lead to grosser forms of individualism and inflated views of the self that are unhealthy and may even become pathological. Human beings are capable not only of healthy and constructive growth but also of more negative and destructive actions such as crime and war, and not only because of conditions of worth imposed on them (see Parrott 2003, 190–91).

Second, the individualistic focus on person-centered therapy tends to neglect the importance of other factors such as social, cultural, political, economic, and biological forces that can lead to psychopathology in individuals. A more holistic and contextual view of an individual's functioning and dysfunctioning is needed for person-centered therapy to be more balanced and comprehensive.

Third, the emphasis on self-actualization and the importance and autonomy of the self in person-centered therapy is also problematic in a cross-cultural context and from a multicultural perspective. It may reflect a Western cultural bias in valuing individualism. Other cultures, such as those of Asia, value social and family relationships more than Western cultures do, and hence personality theories from Asian cultural perspectives emphasize more the importance of relationships in the development of the individual (Pedersen 1983). For some Asian theories of personality, a focus on self-actualization is viewed as detrimental to a person's optimal development (see Todd and Bohart 2006, 215).

Fourth, traditional person-centered therapy's radical emphasis on the therapeutic relationship based on the core conditions of congruence, unconditional positive regard, and empathic understanding, as the essential healing factor in effective counseling and therapy, is too exclusive and extreme. Although the therapeutic relationship is an important factor in effective therapy, it is not the only factor. In fact, based on earlier research (see, e.g., Lambert, DeJulio, and Stein 1978; Parloff, Waskow, and Wolfe 1978), even person-centered therapists have acknowledged that the core conditions described by Rogers are not necessary or sufficient, but can be helpful for therapeutic change to occur in clients (see Raskin 1992).

Fifth, traditional person-centered therapy's shunning of specific therapeutic techniques has been questioned. Although techniques are not always the most important factor in effective therapy, they are still important, and in some psychological disorders they are crucial for effective treatment. Examples of specialized therapy techniques that empirical research has found to be superior in their effectiveness in the treatment of particular psychological disorders include exposure treatments for specific phobias, response prevention for obsessive-compulsive disorders, cognitive restructuring and exposure for agoraphobia, gradual practice with some sexual disorders, and use of a more supportive approach in interpretation in short-term psychodynamic therapy, taking client symptom severity into consideration (Lambert and Barley 2002; Lambert and Ogles 2004). A related weakness of person-centered therapy is its eschewing of formal diagnosis and psychological assessment and its assumption that it can be effective for all clients and all psychological disorders. It is clear that one size does not fit all in this context; hence, diagnosis and assessment are important, and so are some therapeutic techniques crucial to the effective treatment of particular psychological disorders.

Sixth, the emphasis on the person of the therapist and the need for the therapist to exhibit the core therapeutic conditions in person-centered therapy is a tall order for any therapist. No therapist is perfect; hence, no therapist can experience and express unconditional positive regard and empathic understanding all the time to all clients, with therapist congruence required as well. The other danger is the possibility that a person-centered therapist will try so hard to empathically enter into the client's internal frame of reference or subjective world of experience that the therapist ends up losing his or her own sense of self and clinical objectivity. Rogers himself had such an experience with a woman client, as mentioned earlier in this chapter.

Seventh, another closely related weakness of person-centered therapy is its claim to be nondirective and unconditional in the positive regard or valuing of the client. In reality it is impossible for a therapist to be completely nondirective or value free and unconditional in his or her positive regard for the client. Every therapist, as a person, has values, even if they are not stated explicitly or verbally. Values, of course, should not be imposed on the client, but they must be clarified and shared openly when appropriate. Even Rogers has been observed in his therapy sessions with his clients to be directive at times, however gently, responding to them with more interest or empathy whenever they expressed their feelings more openly or seemed to be moving in a more actualizing direction.

Eighth, clients with physical disabilities (See 1985), more severe psychological disorders, or more specific symptoms such as simple phobias, sexual dysfunction, and obsessive-compulsive disorders may need more than what traditional person-centered therapists can offer in terms of the core therapeutic conditions. In the broader arena of dealing with racial conflicts and political tensions between nations, Rogers still focused on providing the core therapeutic conditions to facilitate group discussion and understanding. Although this practice may be helpful to some extent, it is a rather naive or simplistic approach to peacemaking that does not take into sufficient consideration other powerful historical, political, economic, cultural, tribal, and social forces that may make conflict resolution and constructive change very difficult, if not impossible.

Finally, although Rogers was instrumental in advancing empirical research in the process and outcome of therapy, and specifically of person-centered therapy, there are methodological weaknesses and flaws in many of the research studies that have been conducted on person-centered therapy. Examples of such methodological weaknesses include the absence of no-treatment and attention-placebo control groups, and assessment that depends on ratings of the client's subjective experiences rather than the actual functioning or behavior of clients (see Prochaska and Norcross 2010, 153).

A Biblical Perspective on Person-Centered Therapy

Person-centered therapy has several philosophical perspectives, similar to existential therapy, that can be appreciated from a biblical, Christian perspective, including its deep respect and genuine caring for the person and its emphasis on the individual's freedom to choose and to grow. However, several significant and serious problems with person-centered therapy emerge when it is critiqued from a biblical perspective.

First, Rogers had too optimistic a view of human beings as innately good with an actualizing or growth tendency. A biblical perspective on human nature will also emphasize the darker side of human nature that is sinful and fallen

(Jer. 17:9; Rom. 3:23). Human beings are therefore also capable of evil and sin. They do not automatically engage in constructive growth because of an innately good actualizing tendency.

Second, person-centered therapy's supreme regard for the primacy and autonomy of the self or the individual is problematic because it can lead to self-worship and even self-obsession, which is at odds with true worship and love of God and loving community with others (Mark 12:29–31). The eventual result may be allowing and even encouraging the client to "slide into a self-gratifying, narcissistic world" as Vitz (1994, 110) has pointed out. Hurding drew the following conclusion about Rogers and his person-centered therapy from a Christian perspective: "Francis Schaeffer has described humanity not only as a ruin, but as a glorious ruin. Rogers' optimistic views, although compatible with the 'glory,' do not accord with the 'ruin' of mankind. Schaeffer's 'glorious ruin' has become a 'do-it-yourself' structure where men and women do not bear the divine image but are made in the image of themselves. Sadly, such an edifice is built on the shaky ground of human autonomy and is doomed to ultimate collapse" (1985, 123).

Third, Rogers also viewed God or biblical authority as secondary, if not unnecessary in an individual's self-actualization, placing the highest authority instead in the subjective experience of the person. Rogers wrote these strong words: "Experience is, for me, the highest authority. The touchstone of validity is my own experience. No other person's ideas and none of my own ideas are as authoritative as my experience. It is to experience that I must return again and again; to discover a closer approximation to truth as it is in the process of becoming in me. Neither the bible nor the prophets—neither Freud nor research—neither the revelations of God nor man—can take precedence over my own direct experience" (1961, 23). Such a view of the ultimacy and highest authority of personal experience is seriously flawed from a biblical perspective, which emphasizes the ultimacy of God, and the highest authority in the Bible, God's inspired Word. Person-centered therapy emphasizes the sovereignty of the human person (Raskin, Rogers, and Witty 2008, 181) whereas the Bible emphasizes the sovereignty of God.

Fourth, unconditional positive regard is often equated with agape love as described in Scripture (1 Cor. 13). Rogers himself described unconditional positive regard as a kind of love that is equivalent to agape (C. R. Rogers 1962, 422). Although his therapeutic conditions of congruence, unconditional positive regard, and empathic understanding as a triad come close to agape love, they are not equivalent to agape love (S. L. Jones and Butman 1991, 270). Agape love in Scripture is deeper, purer, divine love (1 Cor. 13) that is truly other centered and focused on the ultimate welfare and well-being of others. It also firmly holds people accountable to ultimate biblical truth, which does not ignore sin and evil. Agape love will therefore caringly and compassionately confront the client when necessary.

Fifth, person-centered therapy's radical emphasis on the therapeutic relationship and the person of the therapist in effective counseling and therapy is overall a good one that is consistent with the Bible's focus on the importance of the relational dimension in life. However, the need for the Holy Spirit's power and presence in producing the spiritual fruit or virtue of agape love in the therapist is crucial from a biblical perspective (see Tan 1999b), so that the genuinely caring therapist can maintain a deeply empathic relationship with the client in a healthy and holy way, without losing his or her sense of self or falling into a more sexualized version of love. The burden is too heavy for the imperfect human therapist to try on his or her own strength to be congruent with unconditional positive regard and empathic understanding all the time with every client.

Sixth, the ultimate human need is not for so-called unconditional positive regard from another human being, but for eternal agape love from God himself, which has been demonstrated through Jesus Christ, who loved us and gave himself for us in his death and resurrection (Gal. 2:20; Rom. 5:8). Furthermore, self-actualization of the deepest kind can only be realized and experienced in a personal relationship with Jesus Christ as our Lord and Savior. We then will discover our true self in Christ, as we surrender to him and his agape love, aligning ourselves with his will and his heart, which always desire the best for us and our ultimate and eternal welfare (see Benner 2003, 2004, 2005a). This is the Christian, biblical answer to unconditional positive regard and self-actualization. It holds in balance sin and grace as Mark McMinn (2008) has emphasized, whereas Rogers seems to focus solely on grace without adequately dealing with the reality of sin and fallen human nature. In fact, as McMinn has noted, God's grace is so amazing only because our sin is so great.

Finally, agape love includes mutual love for others that involves loving others for their own sake and not for the sole purpose of self-actualization. Mutual love therefore requires a degree of self-transcendence that is not present in person-centered therapy and other humanistic therapies. Person-centered therapy is based on "nonhedonistic ethical egoism," in which self-actualization is the major goal and regard for others is only a secondary consequence, as Browning and Cooper (2004, 81–82) have pointed out. They thus conclude that if we were to take the humanistic therapies, including person-centered therapy, seriously, the eventual result would be more social turmoil and confusion rather than more health (85).

Research: Empirical Status of Person-Centered Therapy

Research on person-centered therapy can be categorized into two main types: empirical studies of the importance of the core conditions of congruence (genuineness), unconditional positive regard (warmth or acceptance), and empathic understanding (empathy) for therapeutic personality change; and empirical studies on the effectiveness of person-centered therapy compared to other therapies and/or control conditions such as a no-treatment, wait-list control group, or an attention-placebo control group.

Research on the core conditions has included the development of scales to measure them, with subsequent criticisms of the scales and their shortcomings (see Barkham and Shapiro 1986). A more recent measure that may be particularly helpful for assessing clients' perceptions of the core conditions in therapy is the Client Evaluation of Counselor Scale (Hamilton 2000). Empirical evidence has shown a moderate relationship between empathy and positive therapeutic outcome in a meta-analysis of forty-seven studies (Bohart, Elliott, Greenberg, and Watson 2002), a moderately positive relationship between unconditional positive regard (warmth) and therapeutic outcome (Farber and Lane 2002; see also W. R. Miller 2000), and a more mixed but still positive relationship between congruence (genuineness) and therapeutic outcome (M. H. Klein, Kolden, Michels, and Chrisholm-Stockard 2002). However, such moderate to mixed relationships between these three core conditions and therapeutic outcome are not strong enough to conclude that they are necessary and sufficient conditions for therapeutic personality change (see also Beutler, Crago, and Arezmendi 1986; Lambert, DeJulio, and Stein 1978; Parloff, Waskow, and Wolfe 1978). They are certainly facilitative or helpful and thus important (Raskin 1992; see also Kirschenbaum and Jourdan 2005), but Rogers's assertion that these core conditions are necessary and sufficient has not been supported by research to date.

Rogers seems to have overstated his case about the core therapeutic conditions. However, his view that the therapeutic relationship is the essential factor in effective therapy has received more consistent research support from empirical studies that have shown the therapeutic alliance to be more important overall than techniques across different therapies such as psychodynamic, cognitive, and humanistic (Lambert 1992; see also Todd and Bohart 2006, 213). Therapist empathy in particular has been found to be an essential factor in effective therapy regardless of the therapeutic modality; it also appears to be the strongest predictor of client therapeutic progress when client ratings of therapist empathy are used (J. C. Watson 2002).

Research on the effectiveness of person-centered therapy has yielded the following conclusions to date, based mainly on meta-analyses (M. L. Smith and Glass 1977; M. L. Smith, Glass, and Miller 1980; see also Grawe, Donati, and Bernauer 1998; Kirschenbaum and Jourdan 2005; Shapiro and Shapiro 1982; Weisz, Weiss, Alicke, and Klotz 1987; Weisz et al. 1995): (1) person-centered therapy is more effective than no treatment; (2) it is somewhat more effective than placebo treatment; and (3) it is somewhat less effective than cognitive and behavioral treatments (see J. Sommers-Flanagan and Sommers-Flanagan 2004, 205). Person-centered therapy has been found overall to be effective in the treatment of a wide variety of psychological disorders including anxiety disorders and personality disorders (Bohart 2003). Earlier outcome research on person-centered therapy was limited primarily to college students and clients who were mildly disturbed (Prochaska and Norcross 2010, 152).

The research on *motivational interviewing* (MI) should also be briefly mentioned (see Prochaska and Norcross 2010, 149–50). In a large therapy outcome study called Project MATCH, two major randomized clinical trials conducted in parallel but independently, compared an early, brief version of MI (four sessions) to Cognitive-Behavioral Coping Skill Training (twelve sessions) and to Twelve-Step Facilitation Therapy (twelve sessions), with 952 alcohol-dependent clients seen in outpatient therapy in one study, and 774 clients seen in aftercare therapy after their alcohol inpatient treatment in the other study (Project MATCH Research Group 1993, 1997). Of the four sessions, MI was a significant component of the first two sessions, with the last two sessions serving mainly as booster sessions (W. R. Miller, Zweben, DiClemente, and Rychtarik 1992). The brief form of MI was found to be as effective as the two longer treatments at each follow-up period.

The outcome literature on MI is now larger than that on person-centered therapy, with over one hundred randomized clinical trials on MI (Prochaska and Norcross 2010, 150). MI has been found to have large effects even with the use of small or brief interventions (Burke, Arkowitz, and Dunn 2002). In fact, MI was as effective as longer and active treatments for a variety of target behaviors, but especially for substance or alcohol abuse, according to the results of a meta-analysis of seventy-two controlled clinical trials (Hettema, Steele, and Miller 2005; see also Burke, Arkowitz, and Menchola 2003). However, MI was not found to be effective for smoking cessation. Ethnic-minority clients and resistant clients did particularly well with MI and its supportive and nonconfrontational style (Hettema, Steele, and Miller 2005). MI can also be successfully taught to licensed substance-abuse professionals or counselors through systematic training, especially if it involves a clinical workshop plus feedback and coaching (W. R. Miller et al. 2004).

Future Directions

On the one hand, person-centered therapy and its emphasis on the core therapeutic conditions and the therapeutic relationship as well as on the person of the therapist, rather than on technique, have been incorporated into many other approaches to counseling and therapy. On the other hand, person-centered therapy has also been challenged to adapt and integrate other approaches to therapy into its own practice, especially focusing-oriented, experiential, and existential therapies that share much in common with person-centered therapy (P. Sanders 2004b). Although person-centered therapy in its traditional practice generally shuns techniques, there have been attempts to integrate behavioral interventions such as relaxation techniques (Tausch 1990) and cognitive-behavioral therapy (Keijsers, Schaap, and Hoogduin 2000) with person-centered therapy.

Motivational interviewing (MI) has been a particularly powerful and effective integration of person-centered therapy with techniques to help clients change behavior to enhance their physical and mental health or to overcome addictions. MI is a relatively brief or short-term approach that has recently shown afresh how therapist empathy and the autonomy of the client are crucial factors in effective counseling and therapy.

Rogers has thus often been ranked as the psychologist who has most greatly impacted the field of counseling and psychotherapy (D. Smith 1982) because of the pervasive way in which person-centered therapy has been incorporated into virtually every major approach to therapy. However, only a small percentage of clinical psychologists (1 percent), counseling psychologists (3 percent), social workers (1 percent), and counselors (10 percent) in the United States identified themselves as person-centered therapists in recent surveys (Prochaska and Norcross 2010, 3). Nevertheless, the development of person-centered therapy has progressed, despite Rogers's own reluctance to form a formal association or school of person-centered therapy. The Association for the Development of the Person-Centered Approach (ADPCA) was inaugurated in September 1986 with a meeting at International House, University of Chicago, which Rogers attended only months before his death. The first workshop on the person-centered approach was held February 11–15, 1987, in Warm Springs, Georgia, a week after the death of Rogers, and it has been held annually in Warm Springs since 1987. The ADPCA also holds annual meetings; further information can be found at the organization's Web site (www.adpca.org) (Raskin, Rogers, and Witty 2008, 150–51).

David Cain founded the *Person-Centered Review* in 1986; in 1992, it was renamed the *Person-Centered Journal*, with Jerold Bozarth and Fred Zimring serving as coeditors. The World Association for Person-Centered and Experiential Psychotherapy and Counseling (WAPCEPC) was formed in Portugal at the International Forum for the Person-Centered Approach (for more information, visit www.pce-world.org). A recently launched reviewed journal, *Person-Centered and Experiential Psychotherapies*, publishes theoretical, qualitative, and empirical articles that are of interest to humanistic researchers and practitioners (Raskin, Rogers, and Witty 2008, 151; see also Kirschenbaum and Jourdan 2005).

Person-centered therapy is nevertheless on the decline in the United States at the present time, although it is still going strong in Europe (Prochaska and Norcross 2010, 157). Formal training in person-centered therapy is difficult to obtain in the United States, since the Chicago Counseling Center is the only institution currently offering a formal training program. More training programs in person-centered therapy are available in Europe and Great Britain.

For example, the University of Strathclyde in Scotland has a well-developed model for training in person-centered therapy that uses a person-centered approach (Mearns 1997a, 1997b). There are approximately thirty-five training programs available in Great Britain; formal training programs are also offered in other countries, including France, Germany, Greece, Switzerland, and the Slovak Republic (Sharf 2008, 208).

A final trend concerns the continued work on using person-centered therapy principles with large groups to deal with political tensions, international conflict, and racial problems. Some successful work has been done in South Africa with governmental groups (Cilliers 2004), and with racially mixed South Africans in exile (Saley and Holdstock 1993). The Carl Rogers Institute for Peace in La Jolla, California, has continued to sponsor such work in conflict resolution and peacemaking (Sharf 2008, 207).

Person-centered therapy will continue to be a significant part of contemporary counseling and psychotherapy (see Cain 2010), but its distinctiveness may ironically be reduced as its influence on other approaches to counseling and therapy becomes even more pervasive and widespread.

Recommended Readings

Cain, D. J. (2010). *Person-centered psychotherapies*. Washington, DC: American Psychological Association.

Levitt, B. E. (Ed.). (2005). *Embracing non-directivity: Reassessing person-centered theory and practice in the 21st century*. Ross-on-Wye, England: PCCS Books.

Rogers, C. R. (1951). *Client-centered therapy*. Boston: Houghton Mifflin.

Rogers, C. R. (1961). *On becoming a person*. Boston: Houghton Mifflin.

Rogers, C. R. (1980). *A way of being*. Boston: Houghton Mifflin.

Sanders, P. (Ed.). (2004). *The tribes of the person-centered nation*. Ross-on-Wye, England: PCCS Books.

Thorne, B. (2003). *Carl Rogers* (2nd ed.). London: Sage.

9

Gestalt Therapy

rederick Solomon "Fritz" Perls is often credited as the founder of Gestalt therapy. However, in a more recent account of the historical development of Gestalt therapy, Charles Bowman notes that two other names are crucial in the founding and establishing of Gestalt therapy: Laura Perls (Fritz's wife, whose maiden name was Lore Posner) and Isadore From. Bowman emphasizes that "if Frederick Perls was the father of Gestalt therapy, Laura Perls was certainly the first lady and Isadore From the dean of the school" (2005, 11). From played an important role in the historical development of Gestalt therapy not only because of his deep commitment to Gestalt therapy and his articulate teaching of it, but also because Paul Goodman, another key figure in early Gestalt therapy, abandoned Gestalt therapy and had an untimely death at age sixty-one in 1972 (Bowman 2005, 11–12).

Gestalt therapy has roots in psychoanalysis but developed into a unique and independent approach to therapy that is grounded in the experiential and existential or humanistic perspectives. It focuses particularly on enhancing the client's awareness, with the Gestalt therapist taking a very active and even directive role, fully engaging in authentic dialogue and relationship with the client. Gestalt therapy is a holistic, integrative approach to therapy that uses a variety of therapeutic techniques or interventions to help the client develop greater awareness in order to more freely choose his or her own direction in life (Yontef and Jacobs 2008).

Gestalt therapy focuses more on experiential methods rather than merely verbal ones. Examples of well-known Gestalt therapy techniques include the empty chair, converting questions into statements, and experiential dream work (Parrott 2003).

Biographical Sketch of Fritz Perls

Fritz Perls, the main developer of Gestalt therapy, was born in 1893 in Berlin, the only son and middle child of lower middle-class German Jewish parents. His parents had frequent and intense arguments. Perls was close to his mother but did not respect his father, who was a heavy drinker and a traveling wine salesperson. He was also closer to Grete, his younger sister, but disliked Elsie, his older sister, who later died in a concentration camp (Shepard 1975).

Perls was difficult to manage as a child, creating trouble at school and at home. He failed seventh grade twice and even had to leave school for a while, during which time he briefly worked for a merchant. He returned to school when he was fourteen years old. Perls eventually managed to attend medical school and obtained his medical degree. He served as a medic in the German army during World War I.

After the war, Perls spent time working as an assistant with Kurt Goldstein in Frankfurt at the Institute for Brain Injured Soldiers. Perls learned a Gestalt psychology, or holistic perspective, from Goldstein, viewing the soldiers' perceptions of themselves and their environment as crucial, with the whole consisting of more then merely the sum of its parts. Perls also met other people who later greatly influenced him, including Laura, whom he married in 1930.

Perls received psychoanalytic training at the Vienna and Berlin Institutes of Psychoanalysis. He was particularly affected by Wilhelm Reich, his training analyst. Other psychoanalysts who influenced Perls at this time include Otto Fernichel, Karen Horney, and Helene Deutsch. Perls also came into personal contact with Jung, Adler, and Freud.

Due to the rise of Nazism and Hitler's anti-Semitic policies in Germany in the 1930s, Perls, with his wife and their two-year-old daughter, immigrated to Amsterdam, where they lived for a year under miserable conditions. In 1934, they left Amsterdam for South Africa, where Perls accepted a psychoanalytic position in Johannesburg that Ernst Jones had announced. Perls established his psychoanalytic practice, and in 1935 founded the South African Institute for Psychoanalysis. He and Laura had a thriving psychoanalytic practice in Johannesburg for over a decade and enjoyed an affluent lifestyle. Perls was exposed to the holistic ideas of South African prime minister Jan Christian Smuts, who wrote an influential book, *Holism and Evolution* (Smuts 1926/1996), that strongly impressed Perls (Bowman 2005, 9).

Perls met Freud in 1936 at an international psychoanalytic conference, but only for a brief few minutes. Perls described it as a negative experience in which he felt shock and disappointment at being so badly treated by Freud, who seemed to have brushed him off (Perls 1969c, 56). This was a significant experience for Perls, who then felt free to let go of traditional Freudian or psychoanalytic thinking and begin developing his own unique approach to psychotherapy and counseling (with significant help from his wife, Laura): Gestalt therapy.

Perls left South Africa in 1946 after living there for twelve years because of the rise of apartheid and moved to New York City. He eventually established the New York Institute for Gestalt Therapy, together with Laura Perls and Paul Goodman, in 1952. Perls lived in New York for nine years, after which he moved and traveled extensively, setting up Gestalt therapy training centers in US cities such as Los Angeles, San Francisco, and Miami, as well as in Canada, Japan, Israel, and other countries. He also separated from his wife at this time.

Perls then became involved with the Esalen Institute in Big Sur, California, and worked as an associate psychiatrist there from 1964 to 1969. In 1969, he moved to Cowichan Lake on Vancouver Island, in British Columbia, where he set up a therapeutic community, or a special "Gestalt community," as a training center where therapists could study with him for longer periods of time (e.g., for a few months). Perls died shortly thereafter, in 1970.

Some of the important books that Perls authored or coauthored in developing Gestalt therapy include *Ego, Hunger, and Aggression*, first published in 1947 (F. Perls 1947/1969a), with Laura Perls contributing a couple of chapters, but her significant work was not sufficiently acknowledged, due partly to Fritz Perls's own flamboyant and somewhat egotistical style (see Rosenfeld 1978); *Gestalt Therapy: Excitement and Growth in the Human Personality*, coauthored with Ralph F. Hefferline and Paul Goodman in 1951 (Perls, Hefferline, and Goodman 1951/1994); *Gestalt Therapy Verbatim* (F. Perls 1969b); and *In and Out of the Garbage Pail* (F. Perls 1969c), which includes much autobiographical material summarized in this biographical sketch of Fritz Perls (see also Sharf 2008, 220–21; and Parrott 2003, 202–3). Two other books were published posthumously: *The Gestalt Approach* (F. Perls 1973) and *Legacy from Fritz* (Baumgardner 1975).

Laura Posner Perls (1905–90), wife of Fritz Perls, deserves recognition as a cofounder and developer of Gestalt therapy. She was born in Pforzheim, Germany. Music and modern dance were crucial parts of her life, both as a child and as an adult. She was a gifted pianist, with a varied and rich educational background, having studied law, Gestalt psychology, philosophy, and psychoanalysis. She cofounded the New York Institute for Gestalt Therapy in 1952, with Fritz Perls and Paul Goodman, and made significant contributions in the development of Gestalt therapy and in training Gestalt therapists. In fact, at the twenty-fifth anniversary of the New York Institute for Gestalt Therapy, she insisted that without the support and help of her and other friends, Fritz Perls would not have written or founded anything (see L. Perls 1990, 18).

Laura focused on relationships and the importance of support and contact, in contrast to Fritz's emphasis on awareness and the individual. She also underscored the need for each Gestalt therapist to develop his or her own unique style in therapy (Humphrey 1986; see also Corey 2009, 199).

Major Theoretical Ideas of Gestalt Therapy

Perspective on Human Nature

Gestalt therapy is an experiential therapy that seeks to increase the client's awareness, especially of the here and now as well as the holistic and balanced integration of mind and body. Fritz Perls focused on helping clients to be self-sufficient so that they can deal with their problems in living by themselves (Perls 1969b). In order to achieve this autonomy, Perls worked with clients in a directive, active, and even confrontational style to move them from depending on others or their environment (environmental support) to depending on themselves (self-support) and to facilitate the reintegration of disowned or blocked off parts of their personalities.

Gestalt therapy assumes that clients have an inherent capacity to become more aware and in contact with their internal and external worlds, so that they are able to solve their problems in their own way and time and engage in self-regulation. It therefore has a somewhat positive perspective on human nature and its potential for change and growth and hence is rooted in existential and humanistic worldviews. Gestalt therapy's emphasis on self-sufficiency and self-support in the self-actualization of the individual person, however, reflects a harshly realistic and somewhat pessimistic view of human relationships (S. L. Jones and Butman 1991, 307). This is more true of Fritz Perls's original views, whereas contemporary Gestalt therapists emphasize more the importance of the interpersonal dimensions and a more mutual and dialogical relationship between the Gestalt therapist and the client.

Basic Theoretical Principles of Gestalt Therapy

Corey has summarized the basic theoretical principles of Gestalt therapy as "Holism, Field Theory, the Figure-Formation Process, Organismic Self-Regulation, The Now, Unfinished Business, Contact and Resistances to Contact, Energy and Blocks to Energy" (2009, 201–6).

Holism. Gestalt therapists focus on the whole person, emphasizing that the whole is more than the sum of its parts. Thus they do not regard any one part of a client's experiences as more important than other parts. A client's feelings, behaviors, thoughts, bodily sensations, dreams, and other experiences are all considered by the Gestalt therapist with equal weight. *Gestalt* is a German word that means a complete whole that cannot be broken down into its particular parts without losing its essential nature, and Gestalt therapy is rooted in such holism.

Field Theory. Field theory is closely related to holism. It emphasizes that one's experience is influenced by one's environment or context, that is, one's field, with interconnected parts or elements. According to Gary Yontef and Lynne Jacobs, "Holism asserts that humans are inherently self-regulating, that they are growth-oriented, and that persons and their symptoms cannot be understood apart from their environment. Holism and field theory are interrelated in gestalt theory. Field theory is a way of understanding how one's context influences one's experiences" (2008, 329).

> **Sidebar 9.1**
>
> **Principles of Gestalt Therapy**
> **(Corey 2009, 201–6)**
>
> 1. Holism
> 2. Field theory
> 3. The figure-formation process
> 4. Organismic self-regulation
> 5. The now
> 6. Unfinished business
> 7. Contact and resistances to contact
> 8. Energy and blocks to energy

The Figure-Formation Process. The notion of figure-formation process is based on the work of Gestalt psychologists in the area of visual perception; it refers to how a person organizes his or her experience, moment by moment, depending on what comes to the foreground, that is, the figure, and what stays or recedes in the background, that is, the ground. This process is strongly influenced by the particular needs of a person at a specific moment of experience.

Organismic Self-Regulation. Organismic self-regulation is an individual's capacity to move in the direction of growth and wholeness, by being consciously aware of or in touch with his or her present experience and needs or wants and working toward equilibrium. Organisms or individuals regulate themselves so that they experience equilibrium, growth, and change as urgent needs in the foreground are met. Yontef and Jacobs emphasize that organismic self-regulation "requires knowing and owning—that is, identifying with—what one senses, feels emotionally, observes, needs or wants, and believes," and moving toward wholeness further includes "being honest with self and others about what one is actually able and willing to do—or not willing to do" (2008, 329).

The Now. Gestalt therapists emphasize the power of the now, or the present, to help clients not become mired in the past or preoccupied with the future. This emphasis on the now is also evident in Gestalt therapy's focus on the what and how, and not on the why. Gestalt therapists engage in *phenomenological inquiry*, in which they ask clients "what" and "how" questions to help clients be in touch with the present moment and their immediate experience; and they do not ask "why" questions which often result in intellectualizing or cognitive reasoning that may impede the awareness of current experience. Gestalt therapists use a variety of therapeutic interventions to help clients focus on the here and now, and the what and how. These therapeutic interventions will be described later in the chapter.

Unfinished Business. Clients experience unfinished business when unexpressed feelings or unresolved issues from the past affect their present experience, for example, having unexpressed feelings, such as anger, hatred, fear, guilt, grief, and abandonment, of which they are not fully aware. Unfinished business can also be manifested in obsessions with sex or money or in problematic physical sensations and blockages within one's body.

Gestalt therapists help their clients to deal with unfinished business by encouraging them to stay with the *impasse*, or point where they are stuck; to fully experience their impasse and be in touch with their frustrations; and to accept themselves and their experiences more fully. As clients do this, without being rescued or too frustrated by the Gestalt therapist, they are better able to complete the Gestalt, that is, resolve the unfinished business from the past by feeling, thinking, and acting in new ways that are more self-actualizing. Gestalt therapy assumes that individuals have inherent self-actualization or growth-oriented tendencies and capacities.

Contact and Resistances to Contact. Contact refers to the connection or relationship between a person and others and between a person and his or her environment. Contact involves using the senses such as hearing, touching, seeing, smelling, and moving. In Gestalt therapy, contact is viewed as crucial for growth and change. The Gestalt therapist therefore helps the client to have constructive and authentic contact with people and with the environment, without the client losing a sense of self, so that the client does not become fused with others or the environment (Polster and Polster 1973). Appropriate healthy boundaries must be maintained for two main reasons: boundaries help people to be in contact; and they help people to separate so that fusion with others or the environment does not take place.

Perls (1969b, 1969c, 1970) described various levels of contact as five layers of neuroses that people must remove so that they can grow into psychological maturity by being in greater contact with others and their environment. These five layers are: (1) the *phony* layer, which involves interacting with others in patterned or inauthentic ways, for example, being nice to others to get something from them; (2) the *phobic* layer, which avoids or denies emotional pain, for example, not admitting that a close relationship with someone has ended; (3) the *impasse* layer, that is, the point where a person feels stuck and afraid to make a move or change, for example, no longer being in love with one's spouse and feeling stuck in the marriage; (4) the *implosive* layer, where one begins to be aware of one's real self and experiences feelings more, but may still not do much about them; and (5) the *explosive* layer, where the person is more authentic and real, without pretense, and experiences feelings fully. A person will be in more authentic contact with self, others, and the environment if all five layers of neuroses are experienced and eventually stripped away, so that he or she can experience the present more fully (see Sharf 2008, 225–26).

Contact boundaries are processes by which a person connects with or separates from others or the environment. Erving Polster and Miriam Polster (1973) have described the following types of contact boundaries: (1) *body boundaries*, which make certain bodily sensations off-limits or at least restricts them; (2) *value boundaries*, or values that people hold strongly or rigidly that are difficult to change; (3) *familiarity boundaries*, which involve behaviors or events that occur frequently and routinely without much thought or challenge, such as driving the same route to work every day for many years; (4) *expressive boundaries*, which involve behaviors learned early in life, such as not yelling or whining, and—particularly for men in American culture—not crying (see Sharf 2008, 226).

Contact boundaries can be broken, resulting in resistances to contact, so that one's experiences of the present are curtailed. Polster and Polster (1973) have described five types of *contact boundary disturbances* (see Sharf 2008, 227): (1) *introjection*, the wholesale or uncritical acceptance of the views and values of others by an individual without further reflection or integration, for example, a child introjecting or taking in all of the parents' values and standards without further critical reflection; (2) *projection*, the disowning of particular aspects of oneself by assigning them to others or the environment, for example, blaming others for one's own faults or mistakes; (3) *retroflection*, in which an individual does to herself what she actually wants to do to someone else, or an individual does for himself something that he actually wants someone else to do for him, for example, a man who engages in self-injurious behavior because he directs aggression at himself instead of directing it outward toward others; such self-directed retroflection can lead to depression and other psychosomatic symptoms (Corey 2009, 205); (4) *deflection*, which involves different degrees of avoiding contact with others or the environment, for example, talking incessantly about details and beating around the bush, talking constantly, and being extremely polite, all of which enable a person to avoid authentic contact with others or the environment; (5) *confluence*, in which the boundary between oneself and others or the environment is lessened and blurred, so that the demarcation between inner experiences or feelings of oneself and the experiences and feelings of others in external reality is no longer clear, for example, when the people involved in interpersonal relationships perceive that they all share exactly the same feelings and thoughts, and there is no conflict or anger whatsoever. Individuals who engage in confluence usually have an extreme need to be liked and accepted, and they therefore allow enmeshment and blurred boundaries to occur between them and others. Genuine contact with such persons is very difficult. Gestalt therapists try to help their clients become aware of such contact boundary disturbances or resistances to authentic contact because they regard contact as crucial for genuine growth and self-actualization to take place.

Energy and Blocks to Energy. The Gestalt therapist pays special attention to the location of energy in the client, where and how it may be blocked, and how it may be better used by the client. Blocked energy is viewed as another manifestation of defensive behavior on the part of the client. Examples of blocked energy include tension in certain parts of the body, shallow breathing, not looking at people when interacting with them, cutting off certain sensations or feelings, and closing off or tightening one's body.

The Gestalt therapist will help clients become more aware of where and how they are blocking their energy, so that they can release their energy and use it in more constructive ways to facilitate growth and self-actualization. One way of doing this involves the Gestalt therapist encouraging clients to more fully experience tension in their bodies by exaggerating tension states such as tightened jaws and shaking legs rather than ignoring them (Corey 2009, 206).

Therapeutic Process and Relationship

Gestalt therapists do not have preset goals for clients. However, they do have a fundamental aim or goal of helping clients achieve deeper awareness and hence more freedom to choose (Corey 2009, 206) so that clients can grow toward self-actualization and personal integration. A good therapeutic relationship is seen as essential in this process of helping clients (see Sharf 2008, 229).

Perls (1969b, 16) believed that awareness in and of itself can be curative for clients. Gestalt therapists therefore focus on enhancing clients' awareness of both themselves and their environments. J. Zinker (1978, 96–97) has provided the following specific examples of increased awareness in clients: experiencing deeper awareness of their emotions, physical sensations, and environment; owning their experiences rather than making others responsible for them; learning to be conscious of their needs and having the skills to fulfill such needs without violating the rights of others; having more contact with all their senses (sight, hearing, smell, touch, and taste) so that they more fully experience themselves in every aspect; being able to support themselves rather than blaming others, complaining, or making others feel guilty; becoming more sensitive to their environments but with appropriate protection from what may be dangerous to them; and developing responsibility for their behaviors and consequences.

Sharf (2008) has noted that Gestalt therapy may be especially helpful for clients who are inhibited or overly socialized and constricted, such as phobic, depressed, or perfectionistic individuals.

The *process of therapeutic change and growth* in clients undergoing Gestalt therapy has been described by Miriam Polster (1987) as a three-stage integration sequence. The first stage of *discovery* involves clients achieving a new view of themselves or a new perspective on an old situation. The second stage of *accommodation* involves clients realizing that they have choices, and therefore they can experiment with new or different behaviors, especially with therapeutic support that is crucial at this stage. Finally, the third stage of *assimilation* involves clients learning how to impact their environment, including being more assertive in expressing and obtaining what they want from others or from their environment.

The *therapeutic relationship* is crucial in effective Gestalt therapy, which emphasizes an existential approach to the client. Gestalt therapy has been influenced by Carl Rogers and his emphasis on empathy and the need for the therapist to be sensitively attuned to the client's subjective experience. It has also been influenced by Martin Buber's emphasis on an authentic I-Thou relationship between the therapist and the client. More recently, Gestalt therapy has also been affected by intersubjectivity theory, which has emphasized a more mutually respectful and interactional relationship between client and therapist in psychoanalytic therapy. A meaningful relationship with the therapist is therefore essential for facilitating growth in the client through deepened awareness (Yontef and Jacobs 2008). This therapeutic relationship has been described as a *dialogic* relationship focusing on an authentic meeting and understanding of the other person, and not on any particular outcomes (see Hycner and Jacobs 1995).

Gestalt therapy has developed several unique therapeutic techniques to help clients develop deeper awareness. However, it is important to emphasize that the *therapeutic relationship* is seen as the crucial factor in effective Gestalt therapy, rather than simply the techniques. As Corey has observed, "Contemporary Gestalt therapists place increasing emphasis on factors such as presence, authentic dialogue, gentleness, more direct self-expression by the therapist, decreased use of stereotypic exercises, and great trust in the client's experiencing" (2009, 211). Thus Gestalt therapy today has gone beyond the therapeutic practices of its earlier history, when Fritz Perls emphasized confrontation and more specific techniques.

Major Therapeutic Techniques and Interventions

Gestalt therapy emphasizes the experiential rather than the verbal and doing more than talking. It focuses especially on the here and now, or present moment. It has developed some of the most creative and innovative therapeutic techniques and interventions available (Parrott 2003). Before we examine the major Gestalt therapy techniques, it may be helpful to clarify the difference between *experiments* and *exercises* (or techniques). *Exercises* refer to set techniques that can be used to produce specific outcomes during a therapy session or to attain a therapeutic goal. *Experiments* are more spontaneous and emerge from the dialogic interaction between the Gestalt therapist and the client. They help to facilitate experiential learning for clients and are one-of-a-kind

Sidebar 9.2

Techniques of Gestalt Therapy

(see Parrott 2003, 213–17, and J. Sommers-Flanagan and Sommers-Flanagan 2004, 159–60)

1. Experiential dream work
2. Converting questions to statements
3. Using personal pronouns
4. Assuming responsibility
5. Playing the projection
6. The empty-chair technique
7. Making the rounds
8. Exaggeration
9. Confrontation
10. "May I feed you a sentence?"
11. Staying with the feeling
12. The Reversal Technique

interventions creatively tailored for particular clients. Experiments have often been confused with exercises (Melnick and Nevis 2005).

The experiment is a crucial and foundational part of Gestalt therapy as it is practiced today. In full collaboration with the client, the Gestalt therapist creatively develops experiments to help the client experience deeper levels of awareness and emotions in order to gain fresh insight (Strümpfel and Goldman 2002). Miriam Polster (1987) has specifically focused on how an experiment can help a client work through his or her sticking points, by encouraging spontaneous and innovative ways of dramatizing an internal conflict or sticking point, in the safety and immediacy of the therapy session. Examples of such Gestalt therapy experiments include visualizing a future event that may be threatening, role-playing an interaction between the client and another important person, playing out the experience of a painful memory, role-playing one's father or mother, and creating a dialogue between two parts of an individual that are in conflict. Experiments must be implemented in a supportive, timely, and customized way for a specific client. They should challenge a client without overwhelming him or her (see Corey 2009, 212–13).

Important therapeutic techniques or interventions often used in Gestalt therapy include experiential dream work; converting questions to statements; using personal pronouns; assuming responsibility; playing the projection; the empty-chair technique; making the rounds; exaggeration; confrontation; asking, "May I feed you a sentence?" (see Parrott 2003, 213–17); and staying with the feeling and the reversal technique (see J. Sommers-Flanagan and Sommers-Flanagan 2004, 159–60).

Experiential Dream Work

Dream work is a crucial part of Gestalt therapy. Fritz Perls believed that the dream is "the royal road to integration" (F. Perls 1947/1969a, 66) and the mainstay of Gestalt therapy. However, Gestalt therapists do not engage in the interpretation of dreams. Instead, they believe that dreams are to be experienced; hence Gestalt dream work is experiential and not analytical. The client is fully responsible for his or her dreams and shares them with the Gestalt therapist, who then encourages the client to identify himself or herself with every aspect of each dream. Every character and detail of each dream is viewed as representing some part of the client that the client needs to own in fully experiencing the dream.

Gestalt experiential dream work involves four steps. First, the client describes his or her dream to the therapist. Second, the client is asked by the therapist to talk about the dream in the present tense instead of the past tense. Third, the client is encouraged to play the role of a director, organizing the dream like a play and describing its details and sequence, including its characters and objects. Finally, in the fourth step, the client acts out as fully as possible the dream, identifying with each character or object by using "I" language to personalize the identification and more deeply experience the dream. Perls also often asked his clients to add the following repetitive statement after each brief phrase describing a dream (or fantasy or image): "and this is my existence," even though this may initially feel fake or silly to the client. He did this to help facilitate deeper client insight and experience of the dream (see J. Sommers-Flanagan and Sommers-Flanagan 2004, 163–64).

Gestalt experiential dream work is meant to help clients be more in touch with themselves, especially parts of themselves they may have blocked from awareness, by identifying personally with different characters or objects and details in their dreams. Clients can then become more integrated persons as they grow in their self-awareness and take more responsibility for themselves and their experiences.

Converting Questions to Statements

The Gestalt therapist, following Perls, often asks clients to change their questions into statements, so that clients cannot hide behind questions that may reflect manipulation, denial of personal responsibility, passivity, and so forth. For example, when a client asks a question like "Do you really feel that?" the Gestalt therapist will ask the client to convert this question into a statement, so that the client says: "I don't think you really feel that." This technique of asking clients to convert questions to statements is meant to help clients acknowledge their own beliefs and feelings and take responsibility for them.

Using Personal Pronouns

Clients tend to talk about themselves by using words such as "you," "we," or "it," thereby distancing themselves from fully experiencing what they are describing about themselves. For example, a client might say: "It's so boring to attend this meeting." The Gestalt therapist will then ask the client to use the personal pronoun "I" instead of the word "it," and say instead: "I find it is so boring to attend this meeting," thus owning his or her own experience or behavior and taking responsibility for it.

Assuming Responsibility

Employing a method similar to using personal pronouns, the Gestalt therapist also often instructs clients to add the following statement at the end of every expression of feelings or thoughts: "And I take responsibility for it." To use the previous example again, the client will now say: "I find it so boring to attend this meeting, and I take responsibility for it." Another method for helping clients to assume responsibility is to ask them to change the word "can't" to "won't," and the word "but" to "and." For example, a client might say: "I *can't* do that!" The Gestalt therapist will ask the client to say instead: "I *won't* do that!" As another example, a client might say: "I want to attend the concert, *but* I haven't purchased a ticket for it yet." The Gestalt therapist will instruct the client to say instead: "I want to attend the concert, *and* I have not purchased a ticket for it yet." These techniques for helping clients assume responsibility are important because clients eventually realize that they do not have to depend so much on others or the environment.

Playing the Projection

Clients often project onto others what they themselves are experiencing or struggling with, but at an unconscious level. Gestalt therapists will ask clients to role-play or act out a particular quality they don't like in someone else, that is, "play the projection." For example, if a client says, "My friend is a really loud and aggressive person," the Gestalt therapist will ask the client to take on the role of the friend and act in a loud and aggressive way. Perls believed that projection frequently occurs in interpersonal relationships. Playing the projection is an important Gestalt intervention to help clients acknowledge their projections and gain deeper awareness of their own experience and behavior, including their tendency to project onto others.

The Empty-Chair Technique

The empty-chair technique is the best-known and best-researched Gestalt therapy intervention (L. S. Greenberg and Foerster 1996; L. S. Greenberg and Malcolm 2002; Paivio and Greenberg 1995). It has been used not only in Gestalt therapy but also in other approaches to therapy. Gestalt therapy uses the empty-chair technique in two ways to help clients become more aware of and reclaim parts of themselves that they may have blocked from consciousness. The first way involves instructing the client to role-play two polarized parts of his or her personality that are in conflict with each other: the "top dog," representing the legalistic side or the righteous conscience or superego of one's personality, and the "underdog," representing the side that is weak and often frustrating to the person (F. Perls 1973, 125). The top dog is therefore the moralistic, demanding, and critical side of the client, and the underdog is the passive, weak, and needy side (Strümpfel and Goldman 2002). In the empty-chair technique, the Gestalt therapist asks the client to sit in one chair and assume the role of the top dog talking to the empty chair in front of the client. The client is then asked to move to the previously empty chair and assume the role of the underdog talking to the chair that is now empty. The client moves from chair to chair, repeating this process several times while guided by the Gestalt therapist. Eventually, the client experiences both sides or polarities of his or her personality that are often in conflict and begins to better integrate the top dog and underdog parts of himself or herself, finding more-effective compromise solutions to unfinished business (L. S. Greenberg and Malcolm 2002; see also Elliott, Watson, Goldman, and Greenberg 2004).

The second way of using the empty-chair technique in Gestalt therapy involves asking a client who is experiencing a real-life conflict with a significant other to role-play the two people involved in the conflict (i.e., the client and someone else) by using two chairs facing each other. For example, if a woman client is having a conflict with a rude brother, with feelings of hurt and anger toward this brother, she is asked to first assume the role of herself and express those feelings to the brother, whom she imagines to be sitting in the empty chair across from her. She is then instructed to move into the previously empty chair and take on the role of the brother and speak to the client now imagined to be sitting in the chair across. This process is repeated several times with the guidance of the Gestalt therapist, so that the client is helped to more fully experience the conflict, with deeper awareness of her own feelings as well as more empathy for the feelings of her brother. This can help the client to reintegrate parts of herself that may have been blocked before.

The empty-chair technique seems to be more effective in helping clients resolve unfinished business when it involves highly emotional experiencing and processing by the client (L. S. Greenberg and Malcolm 2002).

Making the Rounds

This Gestalt therapy technique is often used in the context of group therapy. For example, if a client says, "Everyone is so cold in this group," the Gestalt therapist will ask the client to go around and say this to each member of the group: "You are so cold." The client thus engages in "making the rounds" with each member of the group and thereby more fully experiences his own inner feelings and becomes more aware of what is happening within himself. Making the rounds can also be used with positive feelings, not just with negative feelings.

Exaggeration

This Gestalt therapy technique involves the therapist asking the client to exaggerate, or act out more intensively and expansively, a particular behavior, usually nonverbal, to help the client become more in touch with underlying feelings and thus increase self-awareness. For example, a client may start biting her fingernails every time she talks about the harsh boss at work. The Gestalt therapist, in using exaggeration as an intervention, will ask the client to bite her fingernails even more while continuing to talk about the boss, and to focus more attention on what this exaggerated behavior of fingernail biting feels like and may mean to the client. Previously blocked feelings of fear and anger toward the boss may surface into the client's awareness.

Confrontation

When clients show discrepancies in their feelings and behaviors, the Gestalt therapist will often use the technique of *confrontation*, by pointing out these contradictions to the client. The therapist will use *how* and *what* questions rather than *why* to avoid intellectualization or rationalization. For example, a client may say very softly, "I don't like it when my mother criticizes me for little, petty things." The Gestalt therapist will then point out the discrepancy between the very soft voice and the strong feeling of dislike and possibly even anger at the mother by asking the client, "What are you experiencing deep inside when you state your dislike of your mother's criticism of you in such a soft voice? How are you really feeling?" This gentle confrontation can help the client become more aware of inner feelings and better integrate them.

May I Feed You a Sentence?

A Gestalt therapist may suggest a sentence for the client to repeat, to help the client verbalize an underlying, implicit message or attitude that is unclear. The therapist will then say to the client, "May I feed you a sentence?" and ask the client to repeat that sentence. For example, if the therapist senses that the client is having some trouble verbalizing feelings of being hurt by a friend, the therapist may say to the client: "May I feed you a sentence?" and "Here's the sentence I want you to repeat after me: 'I feel deeply hurt and disappointed by my friend Joan, who is very precious to me.'" The client will repeat this sentence aloud and in doing so, may become more aware of her own inner feelings and grow in insight as well.

Staying with the Feeling

Gestalt therapists use this general strategy with all clients to help them stay with and experience their immediate feelings in the present, instead of blocking them or avoiding them.

Several specific techniques can be used in Gestalt therapy to help clients stay with the feeling. First, particular questions can be used repeatedly, such as, "What are you experiencing now?" or "What are you aware of at this very moment?" Second, the therapist can instruct clients to let their feelings speak for themselves or to give "voice" to their feelings (e.g., "Let your depression have a voice and speak now"). Third, the therapist can encourage clients to act out or role-play their feelings right in the session at the moment of experiencing them (see J. Sommers-Flanagan and Sommers-Flanagan 2004, 159).

Staying with the feeling helps clients to be more in touch with their previously blocked feelings and to own them and reintegrate them into their current awareness and functioning.

The Reversal Technique

Therapists use this Gestalt therapy technique to help clients become more in touch with aspects of themselves that have been blocked or denied. For example, the Gestalt therapist will ask a client who is very loud and aggressive to reverse his behavior and talk and act in a more gentle, quiet way. The reversal technique can be used in group therapy as well as in individual therapy. For instance, the Gestalt therapist will ask a very passive and introverted client who hardly talks in group therapy to reverse such behavior by talking the most in the group therapy session.

Gestalt Therapy in Practice

A Hypothetical Transcript

Client: I have an article to write for a scientific journal with a deadline in a few days. I've tried to write it, but I get stuck. . . . I just can't do it!

Gestalt Therapist: Please change the word "but" to "and," and the word "can't" to "won't" and make your statement again!

Client: OK . . . I've tried to write it, *and* I get stuck. . . . I just *won't* do it!

Gestalt Therapist: I would like you to repeat your statement but this time add, "And I take responsibility for it" at the end of the statement.

Client: Well, I'll try again. . . . I have tried to write it, and I get stuck. . . . I just won't do it! And I take responsibility for it!

Gestalt Therapist: How do you feel now? What's going on within you at this moment?

Client: I'm feeling my stuckness more and also that I'm responsible for it . . . that I've somehow chosen *not* to write the article instead of that I cannot write it . . .

that maybe I can do something about it . . . and yet
I still struggle inside me with a part of me that says,
"Come on, you have to do it!" and another part of me
that says, "Yes, I'll try, but I don't think I can make it!"
It's a real conflict!

Gestalt Therapist: It's tough to have these two sides or parts of you
fighting each other, like a top dog demanding that
you get the article done and an underdog helplessly
pleading weakness and inability to do so. Let me
suggest an experiment for you to try that may help you
deal with these two sides of you. You're now sitting in
one chair, and I would like you to speak and express
the part of you that is harshly demanding that you
finish writing the article by the deadline, the top dog in
you, in this chair. Then move to the empty chair across
from you, and in this second chair I would like you
to speak and express the part of you that is weak and
helpless, feeling that you can't make it by the deadline,
the underdog in you. I would like you to continue this
dialogue or interaction between the two parts of you
by switching back and forth between the two chairs,
and let's see what happens, OK?

Client: OK, I'll try.

Gestalt Therapist: OK, go ahead and speak to the other part of you in
the empty chair as you look at the empty chair.

Client: (sitting in the first chair) You really need to pull
yourself together and get this article written on time.
You're wasting a lot of time worrying about it, and
then watching a lot of TV as an escape. You're being
lazy and flaky again. You will really blow it if you
don't get this article done! Your chances of getting
promoted to associate professor will be badly affected!
So, come on and get going and just do it!

Gestalt Therapist: Good! Now move into the empty chair and express the
other part of you while looking at the first chair you
sat in.

Client: (moves to the empty chair and sits in it) OK, OK . . . I
know I have to finish writing the article by the deadline
. . . but it's too much work and too much pressure
for me! I don't think that I can finish it on time. . . . I
only have a few days left before the deadline, and this
is driving me crazy! I need a break and that's why I
watch TV. I'm not flaky or lazy, and I do want to get
promoted in my department!

Gestalt Therapist: OK, now move back to the first chair and switch back to the harsh, demanding part of you again, and see what happens. . . .

This hypothetical transcript of a small part of a Gestalt therapy session demonstrates the Gestalt therapist's use of assuming responsibility as well as the empty-chair technique to help the client take more responsibility and also to be more aware of the top dog and underdog parts of himself or herself that are in conflict and need to be more integrated (e.g., by coming up with compromise solutions such as planning a more specific schedule of writing interspersed with some breaks to watch TV and asking for a short extension of the deadline from the journal's editor).

Critique of Gestalt Therapy: Strengths and Weaknesses

Gestalt therapy has several strengths. First, it emphasizes focusing on the here and now and experiencing the present moment. Many clients are stuck in the past and its pain and regrets or are preoccupied with worry about the future and its concerns. The Gestalt therapist's focus on helping clients experience the now, in the present moment, is a good corrective and balance. It is also consistent with the growing contemporary emphasis on mindfulness, or attending to present experience, with gentle acceptance in various approaches to therapy (see, e.g., Baer 2006; Germer, Siegel, and Fulton 2005). Second, Gestalt therapy highly values awareness and being in touch with one's feelings and present experience. This is a good corrective to therapeutic approaches that tend to overemphasize the cognitive processes of thinking, which can lead to the client intellectualizing and rationalizing as defenses against painful experiences that he or she may want to deny, distort, or disown.

Third, Gestalt therapy attempts to facilitate self-actualization or self-regulation in the client, who is assumed to have an inherent capacity toward integration and self-actualization. The client therefore ultimately depends much less on others or the environment to fulfill his or her own needs and becomes more self-reliant and self-sufficient. However, while growing to be more mature and less dependent on external sources of support can be a healthy development for a person, there is a danger of falling into gross individualism and self-centeredness.

Fourth, Gestalt therapy focuses on helping clients finish or resolve unfinished business in their lives. The Gestalt therapist will thus confront clients (even if more gently in contemporary Gestalt therapy than Fritz Perls did) with their self-deceptions, layers of neuroses, and other discrepancies, in order to frustrate their neuroses so that they can face reality and grow toward self-actualization. Authenticity is crucial in Gestalt therapy, which is also a form of existential therapy that is humanistic and experiential. Clients are therefore helped to overcome playing games with themselves and others.

Fifth, Gestalt therapy has more recently emphasized the importance of the therapeutic relationship and a more reciprocal, gentle, and dialogical interaction between the therapist and the client. This is a good balance and a corrective to the often flamboyant, authoritarian, and even abrasive style of Fritz Perls and his earlier followers in their practice of Gestalt therapy, which was more confrontational and less relational.

Sixth, Gestalt therapy has developed several helpful and creative therapy interventions or methods, including the widely known and researched empty-chair technique. As an existential and experiential therapy, it has more concrete and specific therapy interventions than other existential therapies. However, this is both a strength and a potential weakness since Gestalt therapy techniques can be misused when they are insensitively applied to clients, without appropriate understanding or training.

Seventh, Gestalt therapy is a flexible, open, and creative approach to therapy, and it can be adapted for use with different ethnic groups and cultures, nationally and internationally, especially in group work and group therapy contexts (see Corey 2009, 219–21).

Finally, Gestalt therapy has recently been subjected to more empirical research evaluating its effectiveness or efficacy in terms of therapeutic outcomes (see, e.g., Strümpfel and Goldman 2002; see also Elliott, Greenberg, and Lietaer 2004). Fritz Perls was not interested in conducting such research in the earlier years of Gestalt therapy, instead emphasizing individual cases with subjective reports of therapeutic growth. However, the empirical evidence related to Gestalt therapy has grown in recent years, including more research on specific therapeutic interventions such as the empty-chair technique.

Gestalt therapy also has several weaknesses. First, as a humanistic and existential therapy, it tends to regard too positively human nature and an individual's inherent capacity to grow toward self-actualization or self-regulation. Its focus on helping a client become more self-sufficient can easily lead to narcissistic self-centeredness and gross individualism. Gestalt therapy does not sufficiently consider the darker side of human nature that is capable of evil and destructive behavior such as crime and war (Parrott 2003). However, it does confront clients with their self-deception, layers of neuroses, and discrepancies that reflect efforts at denying, disowning, or distorting reality in their lives.

Second, Gestalt therapy's emphasis on focusing on the here and now and one's experience in the present moment may result in a client not adequately dealing with the past or the future. Clients are motivated or affected by future goals and concerns as well as by past issues. Although Gestalt therapists do work with clients on resolving or finishing unfinished business from the past, their emphasis is still on the present experience of the client. Such a focus can overemphasize present experience, resulting in therapy that is imbalanced or insufficiently holistic.

Third, Gestalt therapy's focus on enhancing the client's awareness and helping him or her more fully experience feelings can also be imbalanced, since this focus usually ignores or even negates rational thinking. One's thoughts can affect one's feelings and behaviors, as the cognitive-behavioral therapists have emphasized. Gestalt therapy's eschewing of rational thinking or cognition is a weakness. Reasonable or rational thinking is not always equivalent to rationalization or intellectualization as a defense as Fritz Perls assumed and asserted in his anti-intellectual stance (Perls 1947/1969a). Another related weakness is the "philosophical sloppiness" of Gestalt therapy's theoretical views, which are not rigorously systematic or comprehensive and are philosophically weak. Gestalt therapy is primarily a pragmatic approach to therapy that combines ideas and methods from various sources but not always in a coherent way (see Day 2004, 230). Some of the terms Gestalt therapy uses, borrowed from Gestalt psychology and other existential schools, are also sometimes loosely used with meanings that may be somewhat different from their original sources.

Fourth, Gestalt therapy, although more gentle and relational now than in its earlier years, is still a somewhat confrontational and directive therapy. Clients are confronted with their unfinished business, defenses, and layers of neuroses and self-deception. There is a danger of such confrontation being too overwhelming for some clients and therefore potentially harmful. This is a potential danger for all confrontational, intensely emotional types of therapy (Lilienfeld 2007; see also Tan 2008c).

Fifth, Gestalt therapy may be helpful to clients who are inhibited and out of touch with their deeper feelings and impulses, but it may not be appropriate for those who are impulsive, reckless, and insensitive to others' feelings and needs, such as sociopaths, delinquents, and individuals who lack empathy for others (see Day 2004, 221–22; Shepherd 1970).

Sixth, Gestalt therapy, unlike some other approaches to existential therapy such as logotherapy (see, e.g., Wong, Wong, McDonald, and Klaassen 2007), does not adequately address the larger questions of life concerning meaning and purpose in life. Gestalt therapists do not ask "Why," but "How" and "What" questions. However, many clients do struggle with the existential questions of life that are related to fear of death and meaning in life. Asking the bigger "Why" questions may therefore be crucial at times for some clients, and Gestalt therapy is weak in dealing with such questions (see S. L. Jones and Butman 1991, 313).

Seventh, although Gestalt therapy has developed some useful specific techniques such as the empty-chair technique, a weakness lies in therapists misusing or abusing them. Inexperienced or inadequately trained therapists can apply such Gestalt techniques in a simplistic and mechanical manner, without being sufficiently sensitive to clients and their actual needs and struggles. The appropriate and ethical use of Gestalt therapy interventions must be safeguarded (see Lee 2004) because of the potential harm clients can suffer when these techniques are misused or abused.

Eighth, although Gestalt therapy can be flexibly adapted for use with other ethnic groups or cultures, it nonetheless tends to be saturated with middle-class North American culture and values, focusing on self-actualization, self-sufficiency, and even self-centeredness. Clients from countries with more collectivistic and collaborative cultures may value family and social relationships more highly. In fact, some Asian cultures view an emphasis on self-actualization negatively, because it is seen as being detrimental to a person's healthy development (Todd and Bohart 2006, 215). A related weakness in Gestalt therapy's focus on the individual is the tendency to neglect other important factors that can also contribute to the development of psychopathology in people, such as social, cultural, political, economic, spiritual, and biological forces.

Finally, empirical research on the effectiveness or efficacy of Gestalt therapy is still limited. Although more research has been done on specific Gestalt interventions such as the empty-chair technique, more controlled outcome research is needed to evaluate the effectiveness of Gestalt therapy as a whole for different clients with different disorders.

A Biblical Perspective on Gestalt Therapy

Gestalt therapy has a number of strengths that have already been mentioned, some of which are consistent with a biblical perspective or worldview. For example, the emphasis on being real and authentic, confronting and overcoming self-deception and layers of neuroses, and taking responsibility for oneself and one's growth can be appreciated from a biblical, Christian perspective, which also affirms the need to face and experience truth in order to be set free (John 8:32) and to take responsibility for one's choices and behaviors. The focus on the here and now and present experience, in the moment, is also a good corrective to being stuck in the past or preoccupied with the worries of the future. It is somewhat consistent with a biblical, Christian view of attending to the "sacrament of the present moment" (Caussade 1989) and focusing on one day at a time and not worrying about tomorrow, as Jesus taught in the Sermon on the Mount (Matt. 6:34). However, Gestalt therapy also presents several significant problems when it is critiqued from a biblical perspective.

First, the focus of Gestalt therapy on the here and now, recently popularized even more by Eckhart Tolle (2005) with the support of Oprah Winfrey, can be overemphasized to the point of negating a biblical hope for the future, including eternity in heaven because of what Jesus Christ has done for those of us who believe in him. True and eternal hope encourages an appropriate and biblical focus on the future to help us live more faithful and obedient lives now on earth for God and his kingdom (see Matt. 6:33; Rom. 8:18; 2 Cor.

4:16–18). It should be noted that there are other serious problems with Tolle's views from a biblical perspective (see Abanes 2008).

Second, Gestalt therapy's emphasis on present experience to deepen awareness, valuing intense emotional processing, and negating the importance of thinking, including rational and intellectual processing, is another serious problem from a biblical perspective. The Bible emphasizes instead the whole person and values the importance of thinking (as well as feelings and behaviors) in the transformation of the person. We are transformed by the renewing of our minds (Rom. 12:2), and we are set free knowing and experiencing the truth (John 8:32). Biblical thinking and sound doctrine are crucial to true Christian spirituality and personal transformation into deeper Christlikeness, which is God's ultimate will for us (Rom. 8:29).

Third, Gestalt therapy holds too positive a view of human nature, with its assumption that individuals have an inherent capacity to grow toward self-regulation or self-actualization. A biblical perspective on human nature will also consider the darker side of human nature, which is sinful, fallen, and capable of evil (Jer. 17:9; Rom. 3:23). As human beings we are not simply inclined toward growth and self-actualization. We also have a tendency toward sin and evil from which only Jesus Christ can adequately redeem and heal us.

Fourth, Gestalt therapy, as advocated by Fritz Perls, emphasizes individual self-actualization or self-regulation so much that it can easily deteriorate into gross individualism and even sinful self-worship (Vitz 1994). The well-known Gestalt prayer written and popularized by Perls in the 1960s captures this attitude well:

> I do my thing and you do your thing.
> I am not in this world to live up to your expectations
> And you are not in this world to live up to mine.
> You are you and I am I. If by chance we find each other, it's beautiful.
> If not, it can't be helped.
>
> (see Day 2004, 229)

A biblical perspective emphasizes instead agape love (1 Cor. 13) and loving God and loving others (Mark 12:29–31). The interdependent and community aspects of human interpersonal interaction and functioning are therefore viewed as essential to human fulfillment and harmony (see 1 Cor. 12), and in overcoming the sinful tendency toward selfishness and gross individualism (see also Phil. 2:3–4), which ultimately leads to isolation and moral decay. Similar to person-centered therapy, Gestalt therapy is based on "nonhedonistic ethical egoism" (Browning and Cooper 2004, 81), with its ultimate value of self-actualization or self-regulation, which reduces caring or concern for others to only a secondary consequence. True agape love, however, is characterized by self-transcendence and mutual love for others that involves loving others for their own welfare, and not for self-actualization itself. Such a degree of self-transcendence is not present in Gestalt therapy and the other humanistic therapies, which can eventually lead to more confusion and social turmoil rather than health (see Browning and Cooper 2004, 81–85).

Fifth, Gestalt therapy does not adequately deal with the larger existential and spiritual or religious questions about death and the ultimate meaning to life: the "why" questions (see S. L. Jones and Butman 1991, 313). A biblical perspective will seriously and authentically deal with these larger-meaning questions (see Wong, Wong, McDonald, and Klaassen 2004), but it will center the answers ultimately in Jesus Christ as the way, the truth, and the life (John 14:6). Recent developments in Gestalt therapy, however, have included attempts to integrate generic or personal spirituality with Gestalt therapy (see, e.g., Ingersoll 2005).

Sixth, Gestalt therapy's focus on subjective experience as the foundation of one's life and growth toward self-actualization negates moral absolutes of right and wrong, thus resulting in a radical "situational ethics." There is no ultimate truth or meaning in life and no moral absolutes to follow (see Hurding 1985, 206–7). A biblical perspective will uphold absolute truth and moral absolutes as revealed in the Bible as the inspired Word of God (Matt. 24:35; 2 Tim. 3:16), but with careful interpretation of Scripture.

Gestalt therapy therefore presents several serious problems from a biblical perspective. However, as Jones and Butman (1991) have commented, "perhaps Gestalt therapy has something to teach us about what it means to love one another in truth and honesty" (1991, 321), in what Clinton McLemore (1984) has called "honest Christianity," because of its emphasis on being real and authentic and confronting and overcoming self-deception or layers of deceit. Yet the Bible's balanced teaching is that truth should always be spoken in love, so that we will grow up into Christ and deeper spiritual maturity (Eph. 4:15).

Research: Empirical Status of Gestalt Therapy

Mary Lee Smith, Gene Glass, and Thomas Miller (1980), in an earlier quantitative review of research on the outcomes of various approaches to therapy, found that Gestalt therapy had an average effect size of .64, which is in the moderate effect range. Such an effect size means that Gestalt therapy is better than no treatment but not much better than placebo interventions. More-recent reviews of the limited number of outcome studies on Gestalt therapy have concluded that it is significantly better than no-treatment and waitlist control groups, with no direct comparisons to an "active" placebo group (Elliott, Greenberg, and Lietaer 2004). Gestalt therapy has been evaluated with other forms of therapy in five direct comparisons, with Gestalt therapy showing slightly inferior outcomes in four of them (Greenberg, Elliott, and Lietaer 1994). Gestalt therapy is therefore more effective than no treatment, but it is not more effective than other forms of therapy with adult clients. Its effectiveness with children and adolescents has not been adequately researched to date (see Prochaska and Norcross 2010, 185–87; Todd and Bohart 2004, 239–40).

In the comparisons of Gestalt therapy and other experiential therapies with cognitive-behavioral therapies, the slight statistical superiority of cognitive behavioral therapies may have been partly due to methodological problems, especially what has been called the researcher allegiance effect (Luborsky et al. 1999). Robert Elliott, Leslie Greenberg, and Germain Lietaer (2004) have noted that a researcher allegiance effect occurs when advocates of experiential therapies, including Gestalt therapy, find significantly better outcomes of these therapies compared to cognitive-behavioral therapies. Similarly, this effect occurs when proponents of nonexperiential therapies, including cognitive-behavioral therapies, report significantly better outcomes for such therapies compared to experiential therapies, including Gestalt therapy.

It should be noted that research on experiential therapies includes more than just Gestalt therapy; hence, conclusions based on such research cannot be over-generalized to Gestalt therapy. For example, L. Beutler, A. Consoli, and G. Lane (2005) reported the results of several studies that compared a Gestalt-based group treatment called focused expressive psychotherapy (Daldrup, Beutler, Engle, and Greenberg 1988) with cognitive therapy and supportive self-directed therapy in group therapy with depressed outpatients, meeting weekly for twenty weeks. There were no significant differences in overall effectiveness of the three group treatments. However, overly socialized, low-resistant, internalizing clients did better with Gestalt-based therapy. The Gestalt-based therapy was an experiential-focused expressive therapy that went beyond standard Gestalt therapy. It intensi-fied emotional arousal by enhancing awareness and the processing of unwanted feelings. The important work of Leslie Greenberg and his colleagues on process-experiential therapy, recently developed into a more integrative approach called emotion-focused therapy (see Elliott, Watson, Goldman, and Greenberg 2004), is another example of an experiential therapy that is *not* synonymous with Gestalt therapy. It includes elements of Gestalt therapy *and* person-centered therapy, as well as other experiential therapies, and therefore goes beyond Gestalt therapy (see Sharf 2008, 219; see also Pos, Greenberg, and Elliott 2008, 87).

In another review of outcome research on Gestalt therapy, Uwe Strümpfel and Rhonda Goldman (2002) optimistically reported the following signifi-cant results: Gestalt therapy is equal to or better than other therapies for a number of disorders; Gestalt therapy is effective with personality disorders, substance addictions, psychosomatic problems, and various other psycholog-ical disorders; and Gestalt therapy has lasting therapeutic effects, according to follow-up evaluations conducted from one to three years after the end of treatment (see also Strümpfel and Courtney 2004). Some of these conclusions may be too positive in light of more-nuanced conclusions from other recent reviews already mentioned.

More research has also been done to evaluate the effectiveness of specific Gestalt therapy techniques, especially the empty-chair technique (L. S. Greenberg and Foerster 1996; L. S. Greenberg and Malcolm 2002; Paivio and Greenberg 1995). For example, the empty-chair technique has been found to be effective in helping clients resolve conflictual feelings. It has also helped clients to be experientially involved in the therapeutic process more quickly than the technique of reflection of feelings as developed in person-centered therapy. Although more empirical research on the effectiveness of Gestalt therapy has been conducted in recent years, the number of controlled outcome studies available is still relatively small. More and better controlled outcome research is needed in order to expand and strengthen the empirical base for the efficacy of Gestalt therapy. However, Gestalt therapists may not embrace such quantitative approaches to outcome research, especially randomized controlled trials (RCTs). Yontef and Jacobs (2008) therefore recently asserted: "When qualitative research—research not governed by the RCT protocol—is included, there is considerable evidence of the efficacy of gestalt therapy" (2008, 354).

Future Directions

Only 1 percent of clinical psychologists and social workers and 2 percent of counseling psychologists and counselors surveyed in the United States indicate Gestalt/experiential therapy as their primary theoretical orientation (see Prochaska and Norcross 2010, 3). The number of "purist" Gestalt therapists is therefore small in the United States. However, the influence of Gestalt therapy as an experiential and humanistic therapeutic approach in the field of counseling and psychotherapy in general has recently increased again. Emotion has become a major focus in psychotherapy in the last decade or so, whereas cognition was predominant in the 1980s and 1990s and behavior in the 1970s (Prochaska and Norcross 2010). Gestalt therapy is therefore being incorporated in various ways, large and small, into other therapeutic approaches that are essentially experiential (e.g., emotion-focused therapy) as well as those that are not (e.g., cognitive-behavioral therapies that utilize some Gestalt methods such as the empty-chair technique to help clients access emotionally laden or "hot" cognitions).

However, one must be cautious with the use of Gestalt therapy and other experiential therapies that focus on evoking intense emotional experiences, which may not be appropriate for certain types of vulnerable clients who can be negatively affected by such therapies (see Lilienfeld 2007). Overcontrolled and inhibited clients with relatively low resistance may nevertheless respond well to Gestalt therapy.

Yontef and Jacobs (2008) have observed that Gestalt therapy has recently undergone some significant shifts in its view of personality and therapy. For example, a greater appreciation of interdependence and a deeper understanding of shame processes have led Gestalt therapists to become less confrontational and more supportive in their therapeutic style with their clients.

Yontef and Jacobs (2008) also describe the significant growth or proliferation of Gestalt therapy training institutes or centers and literature available all over the world. In 2007 there were approximately 120 Gestalt therapy training institutes in the United States, with at least one in every major US city. Around 180 Gestalt therapy training institutes operate in Europe, South America, Canada, and Australia (see Yontef and Jacobs 2008, 336; Corey 2009, 227). The International Gestalt Therapy Association (IGTA) (www.gestalt.org/igta .htm) was founded in 2000 (Sharf 2008, 221) and held its first conference in Montreal, Quebec, Canada, in 2002 (Fall, Holden, and Marquis 2004, 243). Other well-known professional organizations include the Association for the Advancement of Gestalt Therapy (AAGT) (www.aagt.org) in the United States, the European Association for Gestalt Therapy (EAGT) (www.eagt.org), and Gestalt Australia and New Zealand (GANZ) (www.ganz.org.au).

The *Gestalt Journal* and its successor, the *International Gestalt Journal*, are no longer published, but two major English language Gestalt therapy journals are available today: the *Gestalt Review* (www.gestaltreview.com) and the *British Gestalt Journal* (www.britishgestaltjournal.com). The *Gestalt Directory*, containing information about Gestalt therapists and training programs worldwide, can be obtained at no cost from the Center for Gestalt Development, Inc. (www.gestalt.org). The center also offers audiotapes, videotapes, and books on Gestalt therapy (Corey 2009, 228–29).

As previously noted, Gestalt therapy has recently experienced renewed interest and growth that will likely continue into the near future. Although the actual number of Gestalt therapists may be small, the influence of Gestalt therapy has increased and become more pervasive in the field of counseling and psychotherapy, which is becoming more focused on emotion.

Recommended Readings

Passons, W. R. (1975). *Gestalt approaches in counseling*. New York: Holt, Rinehart & Winston.

Perls, F. (1969). *Gestalt therapy verbatim*. Moab, UT: Real People Press.

Perls, F. (1969). *In and out of the garbage pail*. Moab, UT: Real People Press.

Polster, E., & Polster, M. (1973). *Gestalt therapy integrated: Contours of theory and practice*. New York: Brunner/Mazel.

Wheeler, G. (1991). *Gestalt reconsidered: A new approach to contact and resistance*. New York: Gardner.

Woldt, A. S., & Toman, S. M. (Eds.). (2005). *Gestalt therapy: History, theory, and practice*. Thousand Oaks, CA: Sage.

10

Reality Therapy

William Glasser is the founder of reality therapy (W. Glasser 1965), an approach to therapy that focuses on the present and emphasizes a client's strengths and ability to make choices and control his or her behavior. Reality therapy is based on choice theory as developed by Glasser and his revisions and modifications of control theory. Glasser asserts that people are responsible for choosing their own thinking and actions that then directly affect their emotional and physiological functioning. According to choice theory, all human beings have five basic needs: survival, love and belonging, power or achievement, freedom or independence, and fun, with the need to love and to belong being the primary need (W. Glasser 2001, 2005).

Reality therapy helps clients to become more responsible and realistic and therefore more successful in achieving their goals and meeting their needs. Glasser was disappointed with the weaknesses and limitations of psychoanalysis. He developed reality therapy in the 1960s as a more rational and direct approach to therapy that also has existential and humanistic roots in its emphasis on one's freedom and capacity to choose and also one's responsibility to authentically make choices in one's life. Reality therapy has a basically positive view of human nature and potential for change.

Several therapeutic techniques often used in reality therapy include structuring, confrontation, contracts, instruction, role-playing, support, skillful questioning (e.g., asking, "Does your present behavior enable you to get what you want now, and will it take you in the direction you want to go?"), and emphasizing choice (e.g., by changing nouns and adjectives into verbs) (see Parrott 2003).

Biographical Sketch of William Glasser

William Glasser was born on May 11, 1925, in Cleveland, Ohio, the youngest of three children of Ben and Betty Glasser. His father, who owned a small business, had emigrated to the United States as a child with his Russian Jewish family to escape persecution. Glasser has described his mother as very controlling, whereas his father was the opposite, the personification of choice theory (W. Glasser 1998a, 90). He noted that despite such a basic incompatibility between his parents, they were consistently loving in their relationship with him.

Glasser went to college, like his older brother and sister, and majored in chemical engineering. He was still a student when he married Naomi Judith Silver, his first wife, who during forty-six years of marriage was also his professional collaborator until her death in 1992. Glasser enrolled in a PhD program in clinical psychology, but his dissertation was rejected. He graduated with a master's degree in clinical psychology in 1948, after which he attended medical school at Case Western Reserve University and obtained his MD degree in 1953, at the age of twenty-eight.

Glasser moved to southern California for his psychiatric residency at UCLA and at the West Los Angeles Veterans Administration Hospital, which he completed in 1957. He was board certified in psychiatry in 1961. His supervisor and mentor at UCLA was a psychiatrist named G. L. Harrington, who supported Glasser's serious struggles with traditional psychiatry and psychoanalytic theory and the subsequent development of reality therapy in the early 1960s (W. Glasser 1961, 1965).

Glasser also worked at the Ventura School for Girls, a residential institution for delinquent adolescent girls, in 1956. He conducted individual and group therapy and was also involved in training staff. He focused on fostering a kind and respectful relationship with the girls at the school while expecting them to be responsible for their own choices and behavior. He also verbally praised them for appropriate behaviors. His new approach to helping them proved to be very effective, which prompted him to begin consulting in the California school system. Glasser has significantly impacted teachers and school systems here and abroad with the application of his reality therapy principles and methods or choice theory to the positive development and learning of students (see W. Glasser 1969, 1986, 1998b, 2000a). He founded an education training center as a further extension of the William Glasser Institute established in California. He also kept a full schedule of teaching, lecturing, and conducting a private practice, in addition to consulting with school systems as he continued to further develop reality therapy. He published his classic book, *Reality Therapy*, in 1965.

Glasser was exposed in 1977 to the work of William Powers through his book *Behavior: The Control of Perception* (1973) and began using some of Powers's ideas for further theoretical development of reality therapy using control theory. Glasser wrote *Stations of the Mind* (1981) as a somewhat technical version of control theory and its applications to people's lives. A more popular book on control theory was published as *Control Theory: A New Explanation of How We Control Our Lives* (W. Glasser 1985). Glasser thus based reality therapy on control theory as he described it. The main theoretical idea he borrowed from Powers was the notion that "people's choices are attempts to control their perception that their needs are being met in the world" (Fall, Holden, and Marquis 2004, 249).

However, Glasser eventually revised his theory and renamed it choice theory instead of control theory in the late 1990s (W. Glasser 1998a). He did not want people to misunderstand *control* theory by erroneously thinking that it involves controlling others when it really concerns self-control and making one's own decisions in a responsible way. He therefore replaced the word "control" with "choice," which better reflects reality therapy's emphasis on making responsible choices for oneself; hence, choice theory is now the theoretical foundation for reality therapy. Glasser has written several other books on choice theory and its applications, including *Counseling with Choice Theory* (2001); *The Language of Choice Theory*, with his second wife, Carleen, who is involved in the use of reality therapy in schools (W. Glasser and Glasser 1999); and *Getting Together and Staying Together*, also with Carleen (W. Glasser and Glasser 2000). A more recent book, *Warning: Psychiatry Can Be Hazardous to Your Mental Health* (W. Glasser 2003), advances his critical view of the use of psychiatric medications in dealing with personal problems, based on his belief that such medications can adversely affect the process by which people make choices in a responsible way. It should be noted that Glasser's first wife, Naomi, was involved in editing several of his books, as well as editing two significant texts herself on the practical applications of reality therapy (N. Glasser 1980), including case studies (N. Glasser 1989).

Glasser is still actively involved in teaching choice theory and reality therapy around the world. He founded the Institute of Reality Therapy in 1967 but changed its name to the William Glasser Institute in 1996 since his development of choice theory and its applications have gone beyond reality therapy. Glasser has even applied his choice theory ideas to a community of twenty thousand people in Corning, New York, beginning in 1997. He remains an energetic and visionary advocate for choice theory and reality therapy (see W. Glasser 2002, 189–90). (For further biographical information on William Glasser, see Fall, Holden, and Marquis 2004, 247–49; Parrott 2003, 341–42; Sharf 2008, 374–76; and J. Sommers-Flanagan and Sommers-Flanagan 2004, 297–98, 329–30.)

Major Theoretical Ideas of Reality Therapy

Perspective on Human Nature

Reality therapy has existential roots. Glasser was influenced by the ideas of Hellmuth Kaiser, one of the earliest existential therapists in the United States (Prochaska and Norcross 2010, 119). However, since reality therapy also combines existential ideas such as the individual's freedom to choose and ability to control his or her own behavior with practical behavioral techniques for implementing behavioral change and action, it is sometimes viewed as a behavioral therapy or an eclectic therapy. It is nevertheless unique in its emphasis on human freedom and choice and hence cannot be easily categorized as a behavioral or eclectic therapy. Reality therapy is probably best described as a unique therapy with existential roots (Wubbolding 2000).

Glasser himself strongly opposes behaviorism or the philosophical foundation of behavioral approaches to therapy because of their focus on external control of behavior, which he critiques as *external control psychology* (W. Glasser 1998a). He believes that such external control psychology is actually the cause of much of the human suffering and social problems today. In reality therapy or choice theory, Glasser advocates an internal control psychology that emphasizes human choice. He also asserts that we can control only our own behavior, and not the behaviors of others. Reality therapy therefore has a basically positive view of human nature and an individual's capacity for change. It also focuses more on the present and emphasizes a client's strengths.

Basic Theoretical Principles of Reality Therapy

Reality therapy is grounded in choice theory (W. Glasser 1998a, 2001), which is a revision of control theory (W. Glasser 1985). The following are the basic theoretical principles of reality therapy or choice theory: basic human needs, one's quality world or inner picture album, total behavior, choosing behavior, and the Ten Axioms of Choice Theory (see Fall, Holden, and Marquis 2004, 250–54; Sharf 2008, 376–79; and J. Sommers-Flanagan and Sommers-Flanagan 2004, 300–311).

Basic Human Needs

Glasser (1998a) believes that all human behavior is basically motivated or governed by five basic human needs that are genetically encoded in every individual:

1. Survival
2. Love and belonging
3. Power (achievement)

4. Freedom (independence)

5. Fun (enjoyment)

Survival is a basic human need that is mainly biological: a need for current survival as well as future survival. It can be met by engaging in behaviors that enhance an individual's probability of survival, for example, eating, exercising, and having adequate shelter, as well as those that increase the probability of the survival of the human race, for example, sexual behavior.

Glasser (1998a) considered *love and belonging* to be the most important or primary of all the five basic human needs, because we usually must first have relationships with others in order to meet the other four basic needs. This need for love and belonging is expressed in behaviors such as socializing with people, establishing deep and caring friendships, and being involved in sexually intimate relationships. However, choice theory notes that this primary human need for love and belonging can be adversely affected by another basic human need: the need for power.

The basic human need for *power* is often regarded as negative, but Robert Wubbolding (2000) has provided more positive alternatives for describing it as a need for *achievement, accomplishment*, or *internal control*. The need for power can conflict with the need for love and belonging, especially in a close relationship such as marriage, in which a power struggle between the marital partners leads to a lack of compromise and an ultimate breakdown of a loving and caring relationship with each other (W. Glasser 1985, 1998a; W. Glasser and Glasser 2000). However, the need for power can be fulfilled in constructive ways such as getting good grades in college, doing well in athletic events, or effectively helping others. Nevertheless, Glasser warns against the excessive need for power that is still prevalent in Western culture; its destructive effects can be seen in the power struggles in almost every area of life as pecking orders are established (see W. Glasser 1998a, 38).

The basic human need for *freedom* (or *independence*) is a longing in every individual for autonomy and the ability to choose from a variety of possibilities, relatively unhampered by others. Adolescents in particular often manifest this basic need for freedom by wanting to do things their own way, sometimes even rebelling against their parents' external control. According to choice theory, human creativity is clearly connected to the fulfillment of the need for freedom. Without a sense of freedom, it is difficult to be creative

---

Sidebar 10.1

Principles of Reality Therapy

1. Basic human needs
2. One's quality world or inner picture album
3. Total behavior
4. Choosing behavior
5. The Ten Axioms of Choice Theory

in a constructive way. When the need for freedom is not met, other destructive behaviors can result, including symptoms of psychopathology such as hysteria.

Finally, the basic human need for *fun* involves the quest or longing for enjoyment and playfulness. Glasser (1998a) directly connects this need for fun to play, and play to learning. People learn through play that is enjoyable or fun. He also views the need for fun as the easiest one to fulfill and notes that laughter is the best definition of fun. Fun is also usually closely connected with the primary human need for love and belonging.

All five basic human needs can be met in responsible and constructive ways or in irresponsible and destructive behaviors. Reality therapists help clients to fulfill these five basic needs in healthy, responsible, and constructive ways that do not harm others in the process of meeting one's own needs. Clients are also reminded that they can control only their own choices and behaviors; they cannot control others, although they can influence them. When one (or more) of these five basic human needs is not fulfilled, people feel bad and are motivated to try to meet the unsatisfied needs.

One's Quality World or Inner Picture Album

According to choice theory, shortly after birth and throughout our lives our basic needs are not directly satisfied. Instead, because we are only somewhat aware of our five basic needs in general, we keep track more specifically of whatever we do that makes us feel very good. Over time, we build our own mental list of specific wants and needs, a kind of *inner picture album* of specific memories and images of people, things, or experiences, and beliefs that have made us feel good because they satisfied our basic needs (see W. Glasser 1998a; Wubbolding 2000).

This inner picture album is also called one's *quality world*, or personal Shangri-la, an ideal world in which one would like to live if possible (see Corey 2009, 318). The quality world, or inner picture album, differs from person to person and also within a person over time. In other words, it can be revised as an individual has new experiences.

It is therefore crucial for reality therapists to empathically understand each client's subjective quality world. They also need to enter into the client's quality world by establishing genuine, caring, and respectful therapeutic relationships with him or her so that the client experiences love and belonging in therapy and allows the therapist to enter into that quality world.

Total Behavior

Choice theory emphasizes that the key characteristic of all human beings from birth to death is the fact that they *behave*. Such behavior is described by choice theory as *total behavior* consisting of four specific but connected parts that are always functioning simultaneously: acting, thinking, feeling, and physiology. *Acting* refers to particular behaviors such as walking, moving, talking, and eating, and may be voluntary or involuntary. *Thinking* refers to all types of thoughts, voluntary or involuntary, including dreams. *Feeling* refers to emotional experience, both pleasant or painful, such as joy, sadness, anger, and satisfaction. *Physiology* refers to bodily functions, voluntary or involuntary, such as heart rate and sweating.

The total behavior of an individual in acting, thinking, feeling, and physiology has often been described using Glasser's car analogy (1990). The engine of the car contains the individual's basic needs (survival, love and belonging, power, freedom, and fun), which provide the power for the whole system of the car. The wants of the person are like the steering wheel moving the car in the direction of his or her quality world. Acting and thinking are like the two front wheels of the car, which an individual can directly control in order to satisfy particular wants and needs. Thoughts and behaviors are both chosen by a person according to Glasser. Feelings and physiology are like the two rear wheels of the car, which can be indirectly controlled by an individual. Glasser (2000b) emphasizes that one can directly choose only one's actions and thoughts, but one can also indirectly control one's feelings and physiology by choosing to change one's actions and thoughts.

Choosing Behavior

Glasser holds the radical view that so-called mental illness does not exist (see W. Glasser 1965, 85; 2002, 2) except for extreme conditions where there is obvious brain pathology, for example, brain trauma and Alzheimer's disease. His critical view on mental illness echoes similar views voiced by other well-known psychiatrists such as Thomas Szasz (1970, 1971) and Peter Breggin (1991). Glasser believes instead that psychological disorder is due to an individual's personal choice. He is also very critical of the use of psychiatric medications to treat psychopathology (W. Glasser 2003). He holds an extreme position that people choose their own behavior and are therefore fully responsible for their problems, whether behavioral, emotional, or physical.

Glasser advocates using active verbs to describe human suffering and problems. Instead of the usual way of saying that "I am depressed" or "I have a headache" or "I am angry" or "I am anxious," all of which reflect passivity and tend to be incorrect and to reinforce a denial of personal responsibility, Glasser prefers to use more accurate verb forms in saying "I am depressing," or "I am headaching," or "I am angering," or "I am anxietying"! This way of speaking challenges clients to remember that they are choosing their own behavior, and hence they are actually depressing themselves, or angering themselves, or making themselves anxious. They are thus held responsible for choosing their own suffering within a range of *"paining" behaviors*, the best behaviors they can manage to try to meet their wants and needs (Corey 2009, 318–19).

Glasser's radical view of *choosing behavior*, including psychopathology and human suffering, as an all-pervasive freedom and responsibility for every human being can sound harsh and may not be fully accepted by all therapists, including some reality therapists. However, this radical view of choice theory and psychopathology can still be communicated in an empathic way in the therapeutic process of reality therapy, which is based on the therapist having a caring, genuine, and respectful relationship with the client. Ultimately, reality therapy uses choice theory to empower the client to make his or her own choices in a responsible and constructively fulfilling way (see J. Sommers-Flanagan and Sommers-Flanagan 2004, 307–10).

Glasser (1985) provides four main reasons for why individuals may choose pathological behavior or human suffering and misery. First, many people choose to make themselves anxious or depress themselves in order to *control or restrain anger*. For example, people usually achieve more control or power over others by depressing themselves than by angering. Second, individuals may choose to make themselves anxious or depressed in an attempt to *get help from others*. Depressing oneself especially can be an effective means of getting help and sympathy from others, including mental health professionals, as well as of controlling significant people in one's life, in order to meet one's basic needs for love and belonging and also for power. Third, people may choose to depress themselves or make themselves anxious in order *to avoid things* that they do not want to deal with or face in their lives. It may be easier for someone who has been laid off from work to remain frozen in fear or to be anxious than to take difficult steps toward finding a job. Glasser would challenge people trying to avoid dealing with a difficult situation like this to either change what they want or to change their behavior (W. Glasser 1998a, 83). Fourth and finally, people may choose to make themselves anxious or depress themselves in order to achieve significant control over other people and get others to do things for them.

Glasser (1985, 2001) also views so-called crazy behavior, such as hallucinations and delusions, as creative behavior with the purpose of gaining control over one's life, in a desperate way.

Ten Axioms of Choice Theory

Glasser summarizes the basic theoretical principles of reality therapy as the *Ten Axioms of Choice Theory* (1998a):

1. The only person's behavior we can control is our own.
2. All we can give another person is information.
3. All long-lasting psychological problems are relationship problems.
4. The problem relationship is always part of our present life.
5. What happened in the past has everything to do with who we are today, but we can only satisfy our basic needs right now and plan to continue satisfying them in the future.

6. We can satisfy our needs only by satisfying the pictures in our quality world.
7. All we do is behave.
8. All behavior is total behavior and is made up of four components: acting, thinking, feeling, and physiology.
9. All total behavior is chosen, but we have direct control only over the acting and thinking components. We can control our feeling and physiology only indirectly through how we choose to act and think.
10. All total behavior is designated by verbs and named by the part that is the most recognizable (see J. Sommers-Flanagan and Sommers-Flanagan 2004, 311).

Therapeutic Process and Relationship

Glasser (1965) emphasizes three major foundational principles of reality therapy: reality, responsibility, and right and wrong. He believes that when individuals choose to engage in responsible behavior within the limits of reality in order to meet their basic needs in ways that do not hurt others, their behavior is right or moral. They will then be able to give and receive love and have a deep sense of self-worth. Reality therapists help their clients have satisfying relationships with others so that their own basic needs for survival, love and belonging, power, freedom, and fun can be fulfilled in responsible and constructive ways.

The reality therapist functions like a mentor, teacher, or coach to the client and therefore often assumes a directive and educational role in therapy. However, it is still crucial for the reality therapist to establish a genuine, caring, and connected therapeutic relationship with the client. Reality therapy emphasizes the therapeutic alliance based on an empathic and supportive relationship with the client but does not view it as sufficient for effective therapy to occur. Reality therapists, following Glasser, believe that a friendly therapeutic relationship that also includes firmness helps to provide an appropriate counseling environment for the client, who basically has unsatisfying relationships or no relationships with others. The reality therapist connects with the client by engaging in a genuine, caring, and supportive relationship and attempts to enter the client's quality world. Specific techniques are then also needed to further help clients choose and change their behavior, in addition to establishing a friendly therapeutic relationship in what is called the *cycle of counseling* (see Sharf 2008, 381).

Glasser (1998a) has provided more guidelines for establishing a good therapeutic relationship with the client by describing "seven caring habits" that reality therapists would do well to cultivate: supporting, encouraging, listening, accepting, trusting, respecting, and negotiating differences. Glasser (2002, 13) also lists "seven deadly habits" of harsh confrontation that should be avoided by reality therapists: criticizing, blaming, complaining, nagging, threatening, punishing, and rewarding to control (see J. Sommers-Flanagan and Sommers-

Flanagan 2004, 324–25). Reality therapists, however, also do not accept excuses from clients, do not criticize or argue, and are persistent in caring for their clients and therefore do not give up easily. Instead, they try to always be courteous, determined, enthusiastic, firm, and genuine with their clients, to focus on the present, to use humor, and to appropriately use empathic confrontation (see Wubbolding 1988; Wubbolding and Brickell 1998).

The process of reality therapy has been further elaborated and described by Wubbolding (2000, 2007, 2008) using the *WDEP system* of reality therapy. W stands for wants and needs, D for direction and doing, E for self-evaluation, and P for planning (see Corey 2009, 325–29).

In the W stage or component of reality therapy, the therapist helps the client to explore her wants, needs, and perceptions. The key question that the reality therapist asks the client is: "What do you want?" The client's answers about her wants will be related to the five basic human needs: survival, love and belonging, power, freedom, and fun. The reality therapist uses skillful questioning to encourage the client to explore her internal picture album and further clarify her deeper wants and needs, which may not be currently fulfilled.

In the D stage or component of reality therapy, the therapist helps the client to focus on the present and on what he is doing, asking the key question: "What are you doing?" The reality therapist will also help the client to explore and clarify the future direction of his life, by asking another crucial question: "What do you see for yourself at this time and in the future?" The client therefore focuses on direction and doing, or on present actual behavior and direction for the future, rather than dwelling on feelings or on the past.

In the E stage or component of reality therapy, the core part of therapy is covered, with the therapist helping the client to engage in the following crucial self-evaluation: "Does your present behavior enable you to get what you want now, and will it take you in the direction you want to go?" Usually the client is struggling with serious relationship problems that are causing her much emotional pain. Another key question the reality therapist often asks the client is: "Is your present behavior bringing you closer to people who are important to you, or is it driving you farther apart from them?" The reality therapist uses skillful questioning to help the client evaluate her total behavior in terms of her acting (doing), thinking, feeling, and physiology, and empower her to choose more-constructive ways of behaving and thinking that will help her satisfy her wants and needs.

In the P stage or component of reality therapy, the therapist helps the client to focus on planning and action in a specific and concrete way, with the goal of meeting the client's wants and needs that were earlier expressed. The client is again empowered to make responsible plans to fulfill his wants and needs without hurting others. The reality therapist will help the client to devise an effective plan of action that follows the acronym SAMIC[3] described by Wubbolding (1988, 2000, 2007, 2008): simple, attainable, measurable, immediate,

Sidebar 10.2

**Eight Steps of the Process
of Reality Therapy
(see Parrott and Tan 2003, 347)**

1. Being involved with the client in a caring and encouraging relationship
2. Focusing on behavior
3. Focusing on the present
4. Making a specific plan
5. Getting a commitment
6. Accepting no excuses
7. Eliminating punishment
8. Never giving up

controlled (by the planner), committed to, and continuously done.

The WDEP system of reality therapy can be used in both individual and group therapy contexts. More specific techniques used in reality therapy will now be discussed. It should be noted that the reality therapist has much freedom to be flexible and creative in conducting therapy with clients.

Major Therapeutic Techniques and Interventions

Glasser (1965, 1981) originally described the process of reality therapy as consisting of eight steps but with much flexibility on the part of the reality therapist in applying them to clients. The eight steps of reality therapy are (1) being involved with the client in a caring and encouraging relationship; (2) focusing on behavior (and not just feelings); (3) focusing on the present (and not the past); (4) making a specific plan; (5) getting a commitment; (6) accepting no excuses; (7) eliminating punishment; (8) and never giving up (see Parrott and Tan 2003, 347).

The major therapeutic techniques and interventions often used by reality therapists are structuring, confrontation, contracts, instruction, skillful questioning (e.g., "Does your present behavior enable you to get what you want now, and will it take you in the direction you want to go?"), emphasizing choice (e.g., by using verbs in place of adjectives and nouns), role-playing, support, constructive debate, humor, self-disclosure, positive addictions, and assessment (see Parrott 2003, 348–52), as well as the use of metaphors and paradoxical techniques (see Sharf 2008, 387–90).

Structuring

Structuring is the technique of helping clients set up their expectations for therapy, including specific aspects of therapy such as fees, anticipated number of sessions, goals of therapy, and what reality therapy involves. Through such structuring, the reality therapist helps the client to have more realistic expectations as well as hope for possible change.

Confrontation

Confrontation is an intervention that will eventually be used because client excuses are not accepted by reality therapists, who persevere and do not quickly give up in their therapeutic work with clients. Confrontation, however, does not have to be conducted in a harsh way. Reality therapists often use confrontation in the form of empathic yet firm questions or comments that challenge clients to acknowledge their own responsibility in choosing to act or think in particular ways and to honestly face the consequences of their actions. Clients are also confronted with how seriously committed they are to their choices. The following is an example of the use of confrontation by a reality therapist with a client:

> Client: I didn't call my brother as I planned to, for the purpose of trying to resolve a conflict we had recently. But it's OK, because this is not that important to me anyway!
>
> Reality Therapist: You said last week that this was really important to you, but if it isn't that important, then what is really important to you?

The reality therapist can also respond to this client by saying, "You talked a lot about making this call to your brother in our last session, and you said it was really important to you to make the call. I believe that it still is important to you!"

Confrontation is thus a technique that can be used in different forms and ways depending on the style and personality of the reality therapist, as well as the particular client.

Contracts

Contracts involve the use of written agreements signed by the client and the reality therapist, with clear descriptions of what the client has freely committed himself or herself to doing, as a plan of action, for meeting the client's wants and needs in a responsible way that does not hurt others. A signed contract can help clients to make their commitment to follow through with their plans of action more concrete and firm. It can also be a record of their successful execution of their plans and achievement of their goals.

Instruction

Reality therapists will often function in a teaching or coaching role, instructing clients in specific skills so that they can execute their plans and meet their needs and goals in a responsible way. If a particular client needs instruction in an area of knowledge that the reality therapist lacks, the therapist will refer the client to another person or agency.

Skillful Questioning

A key question used by reality therapists in conducting skillful questioning is: "Does your present behavior enable you to get what you want now, and will it take you in the direction you want to go?" (see Parrott 2003, 350). This question will help a client to reflect on his or her behavior, wants and needs, as well as goals and plans, and therefore to engage in productive self-evaluation. Other direct questions that reality therapists can use in skillful questioning include the following suggested by Wubbolding (1988, 2000): "Is what you are doing now what you want to be doing? Is your behavior working for you? Is what you want against the rules? Is what you want realistic or attainable? After carefully examining what you want, does it appear to be in your best interest and in the best interest of others? How committed are you to the therapeutic process and to changing your life?" (see Corey 2009, 327). Such skillful questioning enables the reality therapist to understand the client's world more empathically and empowers the client to assume more responsibility and control for his or her life and choices. However, questions should not be overused but rather be integrated with other types of responses such as active and reflective listening (Wubbolding 1996).

Emphasizing Choice

Reality therapy emphasizes the freedom of the client to choose his or her own values. The client is confronted with personal *responsibility* for his or her own total behavior (directly for actions and thoughts and indirectly for feelings and physiology). Emphasizing choice is a technique in which the therapist uses verbs in place of adjectives or nouns in order to strongly emphasize the client's responsibility in choosing his or her own behaviors. For example, when a client says, "I'm angry," the reality therapist will ask the client to replace "angry" with "angering" and say instead, "I'm angering." Similarly, "I'm depressed" will be replaced with "I'm depressing" and "I have a headache" with "I'm headaching." The reality therapist uses such verb forms of expression in emphasizing choice to the client and helping the client to realize that he or she is actually choosing to "depress" (for depression) or to "anxietize" (for anxiety) himself or herself.

Clients therefore learn to choose more-constructive and healthier ways of acting, thinking, feeling, and physically functioning when they realize they have choices and are not totally under the control of external forces. This radical emphasis on choice in reality therapy can be too extreme at times when biological, spiritual, or other factors may actually be controlling the client's behavior and experiences. Emphasizing choice is a therapeutic intervention that must be used in an empathic and sensitive way rather than in a harsh manner, so that the client feels empowered to make choices responsibly, rather than crushed and blamed.

Role-Playing

Role-playing is the technique of practicing and rehearsing specific behaviors that the client wants to try out in real life, in the safety of therapy first, with the reality therapist providing coaching and encouragement. Role-playing in reality therapy also includes rehearsing the possible consequences of specific behaviors in which the client wants to engage, such as his or her feelings after executing the behaviors. J. R. Cockrum (1993) has described how role-playing concrete situations with a reality therapist often helps clients with problems in interpersonal relationships.

Support

As clients learn to accept personal responsibility for their choices and behaviors, they need support from the reality therapist in order to follow through with their action plans. Clients with a history of past failures and a "failure identity" that expects failure as a way of life are especially in need of support from the reality therapist. Support therefore is the technique of providing encouragement and positive feedback to clients so that they feel more empowered and motivated to make changes in their lives in constructive ways.

Constructive Debate

Constructive debate is the technique in which the reality therapist challenges the client's ideas and values, and vice versa. This challenging is done with respect for the client and without forcing the therapist's own values on the client. In constructive debate, the reality therapist encourages the client to speak up and have her own strong voice as she expresses personal ideas and values, which the reality therapist takes seriously, even as they engage in healthy and mutual debate. The client is also empowered to make significant contributions to therapy by speaking up.

Humor

Humor is a therapeutic intervention in reality therapy that involves the therapist and the client laughing together at a joke or at themselves or others in a sensitive and appropriate way. Since fun is a basic human need according to Glasser, it is often experienced in a playful context, with laughter. Humor in therapy can help meet the client's need for fun in a small way. The reality therapist also engages in a friendly, caring therapeutic relationship with the client in which humor can more naturally occur. However, humor must be used carefully and cannot be forced, and the therapist must be willing to laugh at himself or herself first. If used appropriately, humor can help clients to be more objective and to be able to laugh at themselves and take themselves less seriously so that they can enjoy life more (W. Glasser and Zunin 1979). If humor involves sarcasm or demeans the client, it is being used inappropriately in a way that can harm the client. Such destructive humor should be avoided in therapy.

Self-Disclosure

Reality therapy emphasizes a collaborative, friendly, caring, and mutually open therapeutic relationship between the therapist and the client. Reality therapists therefore engage in self-disclosure, or sharing their own feelings, struggles, and weaknesses. Such therapist vulnerability in honest self-disclosure helps the client to feel less vulnerable and more empowered to live more realistically and responsibly.

Positive Addictions

Glasser (1976) has described positive addictions as activities or behaviors that lead to a natural or healthy high, on a regular basis, that do not require excessive time or concentration. Examples of positive addictions include jogging, meditation, or visiting with friends. Reality therapists encourage their clients to choose positive addictions in their lives so that they can live in a more fulfilling and healthy way.

Assessment

Reality therapists do not typically use formal testing to diagnose clients, but they do engage in assessment or monitoring of their clients' progress in therapy and in achieving their goals. Reality therapists will especially note any step that clients have successfully taken to live in a more responsible way. Clients are considered ready for termination of therapy when they accept responsibility and act more responsibly in meeting personal needs without hurting others or themselves (W. Glasser and Zunin 1979).

Metaphors

Metaphors involve the reality therapist using the client's specific language, especially metaphorical or symbolic language, in order to communicate deeper empathy to the client (Wubbolding and Brickell 1998). An example of the use of metaphors in reality therapy is when a client says, "When I got the promotion at work and a pay raise, life just seemed brighter!" and the reality therapist responds with, "Tell me more about what it feels like to be in such bright sunshine" (see Sharf 2008, 388).

Paradoxical Techniques

Usually reality therapists help their clients make plans and execute them in direct ways. However, sometimes clients may resist change. At such times, reality therapists may use paradoxical techniques, referring to the provision of contradictory instructions to clients in order to help them overcome resistance and move in the direction of further therapeutic change (Wubbolding and Brickell 1998). One example is instructing a client obsessed with not making mistakes at work to go ahead and make mistakes at work. If the client attempts to make mistakes at work as instructed, he has shown some control over the target behavior. If the client does not follow the therapist's instructions, then his undesirable behavior ends up being controlled or terminated (Sharf 2008, 389). Paradoxical techniques are complex and not easy to conduct. They also present ethical and clinical dangers. Two specific types of paradoxical techniques are reframing and prescriptions (see Sharf 2008, 390). Reframing involves helping clients change their way of thinking about something. For example, if a husband complains of his wife's nagging, he can be instructed to reframe her nagging as caring. Paradoxical prescriptions refer to instructing the client to actually perform a particular symptom (i.e., prescribing the symptom). For example, if a client is afraid of having a panic attack, she is instructed to go ahead and try to have a panic attack. Or if a client is afraid of blushing, she is told to go ahead and blush as much as possible and tell people around her how much and how often she blushes. Paradoxical techniques can thus help clients to regain a sense of control and choice over their symptoms.

Paradoxical techniques can be confusing and potentially dangerous if they are used inappropriately and insensitively. Gerald Weeks and Luciano L'Abate (1982) have emphasized that involvement and safety are essential in the effective use of paradoxical techniques. They should therefore not be used with suicidal, sociopathic, or paranoid clients, or with those who are in crises such as suffering the loss of a loved one or a job. Nevertheless, paradoxical techniques can be helpful therapeutic interventions that reality therapists can use with their clients to help them achieve more control over their symptoms and to overcome their resistance.

Reality Therapy in Practice

A Hypothetical Transcript

Client: I often feel anxious, especially when I have to give a talk or do a presentation before an audience . . . I have this anxiety creeping up . . . and then I have headaches too!

Reality Therapist: We often express our feelings and experiences such as anxiety and having headaches as if they just happen to us, as if they are way beyond our control, as if we have absolutely no choice. But we do have a choice, and to help you remember that you always have a choice I would like you to try saying, "I'm anxietizing myself when I have to give a talk" instead of "I often feel anxious when I have to give a talk." Change the word "anxious" into a verb "anxietize"! Go ahead and try saying this.

Client: OK . . . I'm anxietizing myself when I have to give a talk or do a presentation in public . . .

Reality Therapist: Good! Now go on and try saying, "I'm headaching myself" instead of "I have headaches" too.

Client: OK . . . I'm headaching myself . . .

Reality Therapist: You're getting the hang of it pretty well! Now combine both sentences about anxietizing and headaching yourself and see how you feel.

Client: Well . . . I'm anxietizing myself especially when I have to give a talk or do a presentation before an audience. . . . I anxietize myself more and more . . . and then I am headaching myself too!

Reality Therapist: Good . . . now that you are able to say that you are anxietizing yourself and headaching yourself, how do you feel?

Client: It feels kind of weird . . . but I do feel that I have some choice in my anxiety and headaches . . . that I have some responsibility and control, instead of being a passive victim to my feelings and physical sensations.

Reality therapist: You're doing really well. . . . You realize now that you do have some choice in your anxietizing and headaching. Now do you think that what you're doing—anxietizing and headaching yourself—is helping or hurting you?

Client: It's definitely hurting me because I want to be able to give an effective presentation that will really help the people listening. I guess I do have a basic need for some power or achievement. I also want to connect with my audience, to feel appreciated and liked or loved by my listeners, to meet my basic need for love and belonging, I guess.

Reality Therapist: You've expressed it well and have a good understanding of basic needs that are motivating you to give an effective and helpful presentation that will actually help your listeners as well as connect you and bond you with them. Yet anxietizing and headaching yourself is hurting you instead of helping you. What else can you choose to do to help you meet your needs in a responsible way that does not hurt you or others?

Client: Well, I guess I can choose to relax myself rather than anxietize myself, to perhaps tell myself I'll be able to do a good job in my presentation. Also, I can choose to put in a bit more time and effort in preparing my presentation instead of procrastinating and doing it at the last minute or the eleventh hour.

Reality Therapist: Excellent ideas and suggestions! Now how committed are you to making these changes and following through with your plans, which we can discuss further to make them even more concrete and specific?

This hypothetical transcript of a small part of a reality therapy session demonstrates the reality therapist's use of the techniques of emphasizing choice and skillful questioning. The therapist also provides support and encouragement by verbally praising the client for responding well to the therapist's interventions. The therapist continues to use skillful questioning to challenge the client to commit to making changes and to lead the client on to further discussion of how to develop even more concrete and specific plans for action and therapeutic change.

Critique of Reality Therapy: Strengths and Weaknesses

Reality therapy has several strengths (see Corey 2009, 330–36; Fall, Holden, and Marquis 2004, 264–69; Parrott 2003, 354–56). First, its versatility and adaptability have resulted in its application to diverse populations including children, adolescents, adults, and older adults as well as to a variety of settings such as schools, prisons, hospitals, and crisis centers (N. Glasser 1989). It is a relatively short-term therapy approach that is direct and therefore has been used for helping clients with addictions and those in recovery programs for over three decades (Wubbolding and Brickell 2005). It is also consistent with managed care's emphasis today on short-term treatments and brief therapy.

Second, reality therapy is concrete and specific, focusing on particular behavioral goals, with contracts often spelled out and signed, so that progress toward achieving client goals can be monitored and measured. Again, it is a relatively short-term approach to therapy that deals directly with client needs and goals.

Third, reality therapy focuses on present behavior and needs and helps clients make concrete plans for the future. It is therefore a good corrective to therapeutic approaches that may focus too much on the past with the danger of clients getting stuck there. It also emphasizes exploration of behaviors and thoughts more than feelings or symptoms so that clients do not become mired in whining or complaining about their symptoms.

Fourth, reality therapy is still an existential approach to therapy that emphasizes choice on the part of the client. It challenges clients to choose their own values and behaviors in order to meet their basic human needs or wants in ways that are consistent with responsibility, reality, and right and wrong so that others will not be hurt.

Fifth, reality therapy as developed by Glasser, emphasizing choice theory, radically opposes the medical model of psychological disorder or mental illness and its treatment with psychiatric medications. Glasser is extremely critical of psychiatric treatment of psychological disorders centered on the use of psychotropic medications. He believes that such psychiatric treatment can be harmful to the mental health of clients (W. Glasser 2003). Although Glasser's approach to reality therapy and choice theory is radical and extreme in this regard, it is nevertheless empowering to clients, who can choose to change their maladaptive behaviors and thoughts and eventually their total behavior including feelings and physiology. There is a real danger in the medical model of psychopathology that reduces all psychological disorders to mental illnesses and the premature and sometimes mistaken use of psychiatric medications to treat such disorders in clients. The myth of mental illness has been misapplied to many clients who may be better helped with approaches to therapy such as reality therapy, which emphasizes their own choice and responsibility in bringing about therapeutic change (see also Breggin 1991; Szasz 1970, 1971).

Sixth, reality therapy has developed and described several therapeutic techniques and interventions that can be of much practical help to many clients. Reality therapists can therefore use these techniques in concrete ways to facilitate client therapeutic change, based on choices made by the client in setting goals for such change.

Seventh, reality therapy's emphasis on client choice has been found to be helpful in cross-cultural counseling. Clients are encouraged to choose their own values and ways of meeting their needs that are culturally sensitive and consistent. Furthermore, reality therapy's focus on thoughts and actions rather than feelings is helpful to clients from cultures that do not value or express individual feelings as openly as Western culture does. Nevertheless, reality therapy has required adaptation in work with clients from other countries and cultures, as Wubbolding has pointed out in his experience conducting reality therapy workshops internationally (Wubbolding 2000; Wubbolding et al. 1998, 2004), in places such as Japan, Taiwan, Singapore, India, Korea, Kuwait, Australia, Slovenia, Croatia, and other European countries.

Eighth, reality therapy has been found to be useful in helping clients with disabilities and their rehabilitation (see, e.g., Ososkie and Turpin 1985; G. Walker 1987), with a focus on clients making realistic and responsible choices in their personal, social, and vocational goals and plans (see Parrott 2003, 356).

Reality therapy also has several weaknesses and limitations. First, reality therapy, as an existential and humanistic therapy, shares the same weakness as other similar therapies such as existential therapy, person-centered therapy, and Gestalt therapy, in having too positive a view of human nature and an individual's capacity to change in responsible and realistic ways. The darker side of human nature, which is capable of sin and evil and thus of hurting and harming others, is not adequately dealt with in reality therapy. It is not as easy for clients to simply choose in responsible ways or to change as reality therapy purports.

Second, reality therapy does not sufficiently deal with the past. Some clients have experienced trauma in their past that requires more therapeutic attention and help from the therapist. Although reality therapy's emphasis on dealing with the present and making plans for the future is a good corrective to getting stuck in the past, it nevertheless commits the mistake of not paying enough attention to unresolved pain and issues in the client's past that can still interfere with his or her present functioning and problem solving for the future.

Third, reality therapy's ignoring of unconscious processes, such as transference and dreams, can limit its comprehensiveness and effectiveness. Paying adequate attention to these unconscious processes can help clients gain deeper insight into their thoughts, behaviors, and feelings, and make more constructive therapeutic change in their lives (see Corey 2009, 334–35).

Fourth, reality therapy as expounded by Glasser, takes an extreme and radical view of psychological disorders as steeped in behavioral choices made by the client, negating biological or genetic factors in such psychological disorders and rejecting the reality of mental illnesses and the need for psychiatric medications to treat them. Some reality therapists do not take as extreme a view as Glasser does, especially regarding severe psychological disorders such as schizophrenia, bipolar disorder, or major depressive disorder, where psychotropic medications have helped and even saved the lives of patients suffering from these disorders. The myth of mental illness is therefore sometimes a myth too (i.e., the myth of the myth of mental illness). There is such a thing as mental illness for some clients who have severe psychological disorders, and it can be harsh, if not cruel, to assume that they are freely choosing their severe symptoms.

Fifth, the reality therapist risks imposing his or her values on the client since the therapist functions as a coach, mentor, and teacher (see Wubbolding 2008). The reality therapist must be careful to let the client engage in self-evaluation and self-choice rather than directing, lecturing, or moralizing the client.

Sixth, the specific, concrete therapeutic techniques in reality therapy can be misused by inadequately trained or inexperienced therapists. Although these techniques can be of practical help to clients and useful for therapists, they must be used in the context of an empathic relationship with the client and a comprehensive understanding of the client's clinical problems. Appropriate and adequate training, experience, and supervision are therefore essential in the effective, efficient, and ethical use of reality therapy techniques (Wubbolding 2007).

Seventh, Glasser's radical emphasis on clients being able to freely choose their thoughts and actions, values, and plans to fulfill their basic needs in a responsible way may not be sensitive enough to clients who are experiencing actual social, political, or environmental oppression or discrimination, especially clients from certain ethnic minority cultures. Such clients are not truly free to choose in many instances and contexts. Reality therapists in such situations focus on the areas in which clients still have some limited choice (Wubbolding 2008). However, such clients may still need to openly share their experiences of oppression or discrimination and be encouraged to take small steps to help change external factors that are objectively oppressive (see Corey 2009, 333). Furthermore, the therapist must consider other factors such as biological or spiritual forces that may be strongly affecting, if not controlling, the client.

Eighth, some clients from other cultures and countries who have more collectivistic values may not be as comfortable or assertive in expressing individual needs and goals and plans to fulfill them. They may be more comfortable with expressing more communal and familial needs and values. Reality therapy thus may not be sensitive enough to such multicultural diversity and contexts. Wubbolding (2000), however, has tried to adapt reality therapy for use in other cultures and countries. For example, he has advocated less-direct questioning and gentler and more-careful confrontation, use of words other than "plan" and "accountability," and acceptance of "I'll try" as a genuine expression of commitment (rather than as an excuse) with Japanese clients because of the unique characteristics of Japanese culture, including the inappropriateness of assertive language, especially between parent and child and employer and employee (see Corey 2009, 331).

Finally, reality therapy has not focused sufficiently on research and empirical outcome studies to evaluate its effectiveness or efficacy in treating clients with various disorders. Although some empirical research has been done to date, it is still quite limited.

A Biblical Perspective on Reality Therapy

Reality therapy has several strengths, some of which are consistent with a biblical perspective. In fact, reality therapy had a significant influence on the early development of various Christian counseling approaches because of its emphasis on responsibility, reality, and right and wrong (see Hurding 1985, 276–77; Morris 1980, 232; see also S. L. Jones and Butman 1991, 247–50). Paul Morris, for example, who developed love therapy as a Christian counseling approach, years ago wrote: "When I read this book [*Reality Therapy*], it dawned on me that what he was saying was verbatim what Scriptures taught: Loving involvement with a focus on responsibility" (1980, 232). Reality therapy's emphasis on a caring therapeutic relationship with a client, with a focus on choice and responsibility, therefore resonated with many Christian therapists and pastors (see Young 1982) because a biblical perspective also emphasizes agape love (1 Cor. 13) and choice and responsibility (see Josh. 24:15; Luke

13:3). However, reality therapy's basically positive view of human nature and an individual's capacity to choose and change, relying on his or her own strength, is ultimately too optimistic and not fully consistent with a biblical perspective on human nature, which also emphasizes the darker side of human beings that is capable of sin (Rom. 3:23). Furthermore, the Bible teaches the need for God's grace (cf. 2 Cor. 12:9–10), salvation through Jesus Christ (Rom. 6:23), and the power of the Holy Spirit (cf. Zech. 4:6; Eph. 5:18) in genuine transformation of one's life, exposing the futility and vanity of self-effort. Agape love (1 Cor. 13) is also deeper and purer than an involved and caring therapeutic relationship.

Second, reality therapy's focus on present behavior and future plans is somewhat consistent with the biblical view of taking life one day at a time (Matt. 6:34), with genuine hope for the future because of eternal life in Christ both now and forever in heaven (see Matt. 6:33; Rom. 8:18; 2 Cor. 4:16–18). However, its ignoring of the past must be balanced with an appropriate dealing with the past in order to leave the past behind or to "forget" what is behind (see Phil. 3:13–14). Sometimes this may require the judicious use of inner-healing prayer or the healing of memories (see Tan 2003b, 2007b). It may also require patiently working through unresolved issues and painful unfinished business from the past, some of which may be unconscious.

Third, reality therapy's emphasis on meeting individual needs and wants as long as others are not hurt in the process is a relativistic and somewhat self-centered form of ethics. The potential conflict between meeting one's needs and interfering with meeting the needs of others is more substantial and problematic than Glasser has acknowledged. A biblical perspective calls us to a higher standard of ethical living governed and guided by a self-transcendent agape love (1 Cor. 13) that genuinely cares more about the welfare and well-being of others than those of oneself. Such agape love is the fruit of the Holy Spirit (Gal. 5:22–23), who empowers Christians to love; it is not the result of self-effort.

Fourth, the needs and values of individuals seem to be of paramount importance in choice theory and reality therapy. There is no transcendent, spiritually objective truth such as inspired revelation in the Bible (2 Tim. 3:16). Our needs and values ultimately find their deepest fulfillment and greatest clarification in God and his eternal truth as revealed in Scripture. Attempts in reality therapy to integrate spirituality still subject spiritual truth or experience to reality therapy's judgment of what is responsible and what is not (see Linnenberg 1997; Mickel and Liddle-Hamilton 1996). Although reality therapists may positively approach the spirituality of clients as a crucial part of many clients' particular quality worlds, they will still assess whether such spirituality helps or hinders clients' fulfillment of their needs in a responsible way (see Fall, Holden, and Marquis 2004, 268). In other words, a transcendent and real spirituality are not embraced. Biblical spirituality in Christ transcends meeting one's needs.

There is a spiritual reality that is greater than needs and greater than oneself. Paradoxically, our deepest God-shaped inner vacuum and need can only be met in a real, transcendent relationship with God through Jesus Christ.

Fifth, reality therapy can be dangerous in the hands of an authoritarian, moralistic, or legalistic therapist who simplistically misuses or abuses its techniques and ultimately imposes his or her own values on the client. Because reality therapy emphasizes what is responsible, realistic, and "right," it can also be reduced to a moralistic system. This danger is similarly present in some authoritarian approaches to biblical counseling (see S. L. Jones and Butman 1991, 249–50). The Bible emphasizes the need to speak the truth with love (Eph. 4:15) and the need for patience, encouragement, and support, in addition to admonishment, in helping others (1 Thess. 5:14). It also teaches the need to comfort others with God's loving comfort (2 Cor. 1:3–4). Reality therapy has more recently embraced a gentler approach in place of its earlier, somewhat confrontational stance in challenging clients to take responsibility for themselves and to choose. This is a positive development and more consistent with a biblical perspective on helping others.

Finally, reality therapy's radical view of freedom to choose for each individual, including choosing symptoms of psychological disorder, negates the possibility of other factors that may cause such symptoms, including environmental, social, political, biological, and even spiritual or demonic forces. The reality of spiritual warfare (see Eph. 6) and the possibility of demonization in some cases from a biblical perspective cannot be accommodated or accepted by reality therapy.

Research: Empirical Status of Reality Therapy

Glasser has not focused on research as a priority, and the training of certified reality therapists does not include research training in the curriculum. The research base for the empirical status of reality therapy is therefore limited, although some research studies have been conducted (see Sharf 2008, 400–401). Most of the available data on the effectiveness of reality therapy have been in the form of case studies covering a wide variety of psychological disorders (W. Glasser 2000b; see also N. Glasser 1980, 1989).

Wubbolding (2000) has reviewed the research on the effectiveness of reality therapy with clients suffering from addiction and depression and with juvenile and adult offenders. Research studies have also been conducted in different types of educational institutions in several countries internationally. R. J. Kim and J. G. Hwang (1996) in a small study in Korea with 11 middle-school girls who received group reality therapy and 12 students in a control group found that those who received group reality therapy showed improvements in discipline, motivation for achievement, and locus of control. In another study of reality therapy, involving 25 seventh-grade students, R. Edens and T. Smyrl (1994) found a significant decrease in disruptive behavior. A. V. Peterson, C. Chang, and P. L. Collins (1997, 1998), in a larger study of 217 undergraduate students in Taiwan, divided their sample into three groups: those who received group reality therapy for eight weeks, those who received teaching or classes on choice theory for eight weeks, and those in a no-treatment control group. Significant positive effects on self-concept and locus of control were obtained for the students in both the therapy and the teaching groups when compared to the no-treatment control group. J. R. Petra (2000) found positive effects on children with discipline difficulties at school after their parents (45 of them) received reality therapy and parenting education for thirteen hours.

A specific topic that has received some attention in research on reality therapy is domestic violence. A. Gilliam (2004) divided men who had committed domestic violence into two groups of fifteen each: one group received twelve weeks of group reality therapy, while the other group received twelve weeks of structured cognitive-behavioral therapy. The group that received reality therapy showed a significant change on a self-control over violence scale, whereas the other group did not. However, no significant differences between the two groups were found on several other measures of psychological and social functioning. Robert Rachor (1995) evaluated the effectiveness of a twenty-one session program for domestic violence with twenty-two men and twenty-three women, using reality therapy concepts and reality therapy for families. The results showed very little or no reported domestic violence for the women, but some violence was reported for the men. A no-treatment control group was unfortunately not used in this study.

D. H. Lawrence (2004) conducted a study on self-determination in adults with developmental disabilities, dividing them into two groups of fifteen each: one group received six sessions of reality therapy, whereas the other group received six sessions of mutual support. The reality therapy group showed significant changes in self-determination, but the other group did not.

There are therefore some positive findings on the effectiveness of reality therapy with students with discipline and other achievement problems, with adult domestic-violence offenders, with adults with developmental disabilities, and others (see Wubbolding 2000). However, not all these research studies had adequate control groups. In a meta-analysis of over twenty outcome studies on reality therapy, L. Radtke, M. Sapp, and W. Farrell (1997) found a medium effect for reality therapy. Controlled outcome research on reality therapy, using randomized clinical trials (RCTs), is still very limited. Thus no definitive conclusions can be presently made on the effectiveness of reality therapy, but preliminary findings so far are encouraging. More controlled outcome research on purer forms of reality therapy conducted by properly trained and certified reality therapists is needed for the empirical status of reality therapy to be further strengthened (see L. Murphy 1997; Wubbolding 2000).

Future Directions

Although the percentage of psychotherapists surveyed in the United States who indicate the existential approach to therapy as their primary orientation is small, ranging from 1 percent of clinical psychologists to 5 percent of counseling psychologists and counselors (see Prochaska and Norcross 2010, 3), the actual number of reality therapists today is probably much higher. In fact, since William Glasser originally used the term "reality therapy" in 1962 (O'Donnell 1987), reality therapy's popularity has significantly increased. Glasser established the Institute for Reality Therapy in 1967 in Los Angeles, and in 1975 it began certifying reality therapists who completed an eighteen-month training program. An international organization for certified reality therapists was founded in 1981; the group has grown significantly and now holds annual conventions. At present, over six thousand people have completed the training program and are reality therapy certified (RTC). The Institute of Reality Therapy was renamed the William Glasser Institute in 1996 (see Sharf 2008, 399) and is now located in Chatsworth, California (www.wglasser.com). There is also a Center for Reality Therapy directed by Robert E. Wubbolding in Cincinnati, Ohio (www.realitytherapywub.com).

Reality therapy has had a large following since 1965, particularly among teachers, rehabilitation counselors, youth guidance counselors, and substance-abuse treatment counselors (Parrott 2003, 356). It has also established itself as a major approach to counseling and psychotherapy that has been used in many practice settings with different clients and clinical problems.

The leading journal for reality therapy today is the *International Journal of Reality Therapy* (which was called the *Journal of Reality Therapy* when it began publication in 1981); further information about this journal can be obtained at its Web site (www.journalofrealitytherapy.com). The official journal of the William Glasser Institute is the *International Journal of Choice Theory*; further details about this journal can be found at the institute's Web site (www.wglasser.com/internat.htm) (see Corey 2009, 336–37).

Reality therapy and choice theory will continue to be a major school of counseling and therapy as well as an important approach to school consultation and the positive development and learning of students. Glasser has established an education training center as a further extension of the William Glasser Institute, and he continues to be a visionary and energetic advocate for choice theory and reality therapy in the United States and abroad (see W. Glasser 2002, 189–90).

Recommended Readings

Glasser, W. (1965). *Reality therapy: A new approach to psychiatry*. New York: Harper & Row.

Glasser, W. (1998). *Choice theory: A new psychology of freedom*. New York: HarperCollins.

Glasser, W. (2001). *Counseling with choice theory: The new reality therapy*. New York: HarperCollins.

Wubbolding, R. E. (1988). *Using reality therapy*. New York: Harper & Row.

Wubbolding, R. E. (2000). *Reality therapy for the 21st century*. Philadelphia: Brunner-Routledge.

11

Behavior Therapy

Behavior therapy first appeared as a systematic approach to counseling
and psychotherapy in the treatment of psychological disorders in the
late 1950s and 1960s. It was initially defined as "the application of modern learning theory to the treatment of clinical problems" (Wilson 2008, 223),
with an emphasis on classical and operant conditioning. However, behavior
therapy has developed in significant ways over the past several decades, with
greater sophistication and complexity. Contemporary behavior therapy applies
not only principles of learning but also experimental findings from scientific
psychology to the treatment of specific behavioral disorders. It is an empirically
based approach to therapy that is broadly social-learning-oriented in theory.
By the 1970s, behavior therapy had become a major approach to counseling
and therapy (Spiegler and Guevremont 2003, 25).

Behavior therapy does not have a single founder. Instead, it has several key
figures, including Joseph Wolpe, Hans Eysenck, B. F. Skinner, Arnold Lazarus,
Albert Bandura, and Donald Meichenbaum (see Corey 2009, 233–34; Day 2004,
244–45; Fishman and Franks 1992, 161–69; Glass and Arnkoff 1992, 587–99;
Parrott 2003, 267–69; Prochaska and Norcross 2010, 246–48, 470–71; Sharf 2008,
256–59; Wilson 2008, 230–32). Behavior therapy can be characterized as consisting of three major thrusts, or three Cs according to Prochaska and Norcross
(2010): (1) counterconditioning (Wolpe); (2) contingency management (Skinner);
and (3) cognitive behavior modification (Meichenbaum). Behavior therapists view
human beings as products of their environments and unique learning histories.
Human nature is therefore seen as neither positive nor negative.

The behavior therapist plays an active and directive role in therapy, often acting as coach or teacher. Some examples of well-known behavior therapy techniques or interventions include positive reinforcement (reward for desirable behavior), assertiveness training (role-playing with clients to help them learn how to express their thoughts and feelings more freely and appropriately), systematic desensitization (pairing of a neutral or pleasant stimulus with one that has been conditioned to elicit fear or anxiety), and flooding (exposing the client to stimuli that elicit maximal anxiety for the purpose of eventually extinguishing the anxiety) (see Parrott 2003).

Biographical Sketches of Key Figures in Behavior Therapy

Joseph Wolpe was born in Johannesburg, South Africa, on April 20, 1915. Although he had a religious Jewish upbringing, Wolpe also read other philosophers such as Immanuel Kant, David Hume, and the atheist Bertrand Russell, and eventually ended up embracing physical monism instead of his earlier Jewish faith. He grew up in South Africa and earned his medical degree from the University of Witwatersrand in Johannesburg.

Wolpe had some psychoanalytic influence earlier in his training in psychiatry but eventually gravitated to the conditioning theories of Ivan Pavlov and his work on classical conditioning (or respondent conditioning) in Russia, and especially to the theoretical work of Clark Hull on conditioning as explicated in his book, *Principles of Behavior* (Hull 1943).

Wolpe did his MD thesis research on animal neuroses and discovered counterconditioning processes and procedures when he found that the eating response in cats could be used to inhibit, or countercondition, a classical conditioned anxiety response to a buzzer that was initially paired with electric shock. In 1958, he wrote a groundbreaking book, *Psychotherapy by Reciprocal Inhibition*, in which he described a learning-based approach to therapy based on counterconditioning. More specifically, he used deep relaxation to countercondition anxiety and hence developed systematic desensitization as a unique behavioral intervention for treating phobias and anxiety problems. He also used assertive responses to inhibit social anxiety, leading to the development of assertiveness training. Wolpe reviewed more than two hundred cases of patients with different behavioral problems that had been treated with his counterconditioning procedures with about 90 percent success rates (see Prochaska and Norcross 2010, 246–48). He influenced a group of students and colleagues who met often with him at the University of Witwatersrand. Arnold Lazarus and Stanley Rachman participated in this group, and they eventually helped bring Wolpe's systematic desensitization to the United States and Great Britain. Wolpe himself moved to the United States in 1963 (Glass and Arnkoff 1992).

Wolpe taught at the University of Virginia and Temple University Medical School in Philadelphia, where he was a professor of psychiatry from 1965 until his retirement in 1988. He then went to Pepperdine University in California, where he spent nine more years as a distinguished professor of psychiatry until his death on December 4, 1997, due to lung cancer. Wolpe also directed the behavior therapy unit at the Eastern Pennsylvania Psychiatric Institute when he was teaching at Temple University.

Wolpe was a leading figure in behavior therapy and wrote a well-known text, *The Practice of Behavior Therapy* (1990), that went through four editions. He also helped found the Association for Advancement of Behavior Therapy (AABT), now called the Association for Behavioral and Cognitive Therapies (ABCT), as well as the *Journal of Behavior Therapy and Experimental Psychiatry*. He coauthored one of the first books on techniques of behavior therapy with Arnold Lazarus, *Behavior Therapy Techniques* (1966). Wolpe was always an advocate for a purer and less diluted version of behavior therapy that preserved its foundations in learning theory (Wolpe 1989). He therefore did not support expanding the boundaries of behavior therapy to make it more cognitive-behavioral, eclectic, or multimodal as Arnold Lazarus and others have done (see Glass and Arnkoff 1992, 608).

Hans Jürgen Eysenck was born in Berlin, Germany, on March 4, 1916, but moved to England in the 1930s because of the Nazi movement in Germany. He obtained his PhD in psychology from the Department of Psychology at University College London, with Sir Cyril Burt as his mentor and dissertation supervisor. Eysenck taught at the Institute of Psychiatry, Maudsley Hospital, University of London, as professor of psychology from 1955 to 1983. He was one of England's best-known psychologists, having made significant contributions to several areas of psychology, including personality and individual differences, intelligence and the role of genetics in IQ differences, and behavior therapy.

Eysenck was a strong advocate for a scientific psychology. In 1952, he published a scathing critique of psychotherapy as practiced in the 1950s with mainly psychoanalytic and client-centered approaches. He asserted, based on the studies he had reviewed, that there was no empirical support for the effectiveness of psychotherapy for patients with neurotic disorders. He drew the shocking conclusion that psychotherapy was not more effective than spontaneous remission rates found in no-treatment control patients (i.e., around two-thirds of neurotic patients will recover or significantly improve over a two-year period without therapy). More-recent research has contradicted Eysenck's earlier sweeping conclusions (Eysenck 1952); this research indicates that spontaneous remission rates are actually closer to 43 percent and finds psychotherapy to be effective (Bergin and Lambert 1978). However, his 1952 critique of traditional psychotherapy as being ineffective prepared the field of counseling and psychotherapy to be more open to behavior therapy as a systematic approach for treating psychological disorders.

Eysenck played a very significant role in helping to establish behavior therapy worldwide. He met weekly with colleagues and students at his home to further discuss and develop this new approach to therapy, based on the learning theories and conditioning views of Hull and Pavlov, that he eventually labeled *behaviour therapy* (or *behavior therapy*). He defined it as the application of modern learning theory to the understanding and treatment of behavioral or behaviorally related disorders (Eysenck 1959). Lazarus (1958) in South Africa also used this term, behavior therapy, to describe Wolpe's approach to treating neurotic patients with reciprocal inhibition techniques. Interestingly enough, B. F. Skinner, H. C. Solomon, and O. R. Lindsley (1953) in the United States initially used the term "behavior therapy" in an unpublished status report, to refer to their use of operant conditioning techniques to increase social interactions among psychotic inpatients (see Fishman and Franks 1992, 172).

In the 1960s, Eysenck also published two significant books that helped advance behavior therapy and its practice: *Behavior Therapy and the Neuroses* (1960) and *The Causes and Cures of Neurosis*, with Stanley Rachman (Eysenck and Rachman 1965). Eysenck himself did not treat patients, but he was instrumental in supporting the development of behavior therapy techniques at the Maudsley Hospital in the late 1950s and 1960s, when other well-known behavior therapists such as Cyril Franks and Stanley Rachman were there. Eysenck was given much support and encouragement by M. B. Shapiro, the head of the clinical section at the Maudsley Hospital, who therefore also played a significant role in the birthing of the behavior therapy movement in England (see Glass and Arnkoff 1992, 594).

Eysenck died on September 4, 1997, in London, England, having achieved the special status around the time of his death of being the most frequently cited living psychologist in scientific journals (Haggbloom et al. 2002). He also launched the first journal devoted solely to behavior therapy, *Behaviour Research and Therapy*, in 1963, and it is still being published today. Further details on Eysenck's life and the development of behavior therapy can be found in his autobiography, *Rebel with a Cause* (Eysenck 1990).

B. F. Skinner, whose full name was Burrhus Frederick Skinner, has been listed as the most influential psychologist of the twentieth century (Haggbloom et al. 2002). He was born in Susquehanna, Pennsylvania, in 1904. He had a younger brother, Edward, who died when Skinner was visiting home from college in 1923. After Edward's death, Skinner, who was then known as Fred, drew closer to his parents and became more actively involved with the family. He graduated from Hamilton College in Clinton, New York, in 1926 with a BA in English literature.

Skinner had aspired to be a writer, but after pursuing a writing career for a year, he abandoned the notion (see Day 2004, 244–45). He had always been a bright student, with a special interest in building things, such as gadgets and machines. He eventually made several significant inventions in experimental psychology that helped researchers to monitor and record behaviors in an unobtrusive way. Skinner earned a PhD in psychology from Harvard University in 1931, after which he continued his work in laboratory research until 1936, when he left Harvard for a time to teach and do research at other universities. In 1936, he wed Yvonne Blue, and they remained married until her death in 1997. They had two daughters, one of whom became an artist and the other an educational psychologist (Corey 2009, 233).

Skinner was a radical behaviorist who did not believe in human free will. He is often viewed as the father of behavioral psychology. He believed that behavior is determined by environmental events, and especially that behavior is governed by its consequences. Rewards, or positive consequences, reinforce or maintain specific behaviors, whereas punishment, or aversive consequences, decrease or eliminate particular behaviors. Skinner therefore developed *operant conditioning* techniques, or the use of reinforcement contingencies to modify behavior; hence the term "behavior modification" is often used for his approach. The label "behavior therapy" was initially used by Skinner and his colleagues in an unpublished status report at the Metropolitan State Hospital, in Waltham, Massachusetts (Skinner, Solomon, and Lindsley 1953). Skinner, like Wolpe, did not favor introducing more cognitive concepts and techniques into the field of behavior therapy because he felt that they are unnecessary and would weaken the behavioral approach (Skinner 1990).

Skinner did most of his work in experimental studies in the laboratory, focusing on the behaviors of pigeons and rats, but he ultimately applied his principles and procedures to human beings as well, especially in areas such as education, behavior modification as a therapeutic approach for the treatment of psychological disorders, and social planning. He has written several important books, including *Walden Two* (Skinner 1948), about a utopian community, *Science and Human Behavior* (Skinner 1953), about the application of behavioral principles to all areas of human behavior, and *Beyond Freedom and Dignity* (Skinner 1971), about the need for drastic changes using science and technology for the survival of our society (Corey 2009, 233). Skinner kept up his active schedule as a lecturer and writer until his death in 1990 from leukemia, at the age of eighty-six.

Arnold Allan Lazarus was born in 1932 in South Africa, where he grew up and received his education (see Prochaska and Norcross 2010, 470–71). He obtained his PhD in 1960 from the University of Witwatersrand in Johannesburg. His mentor was Joseph Wolpe, one of the pioneers of behavior therapy. Lazarus wrote his dissertation on the effectiveness of group systematic desensitization in the treatment of phobic conditions.

Lazarus received his early training in behavior therapy and initially conducted his clinical practice using mainly behavioral interventions. He is credited with being one of the first authors to use the term "behavior therapy" in a published article (Lazarus 1958), and he coauthored an early text on behavior therapy techniques with Joseph Wolpe (Wolpe and Lazarus 1966). However, Lazarus found that the behavioral interventions he used with his clients often produced significant therapeutic outcomes that did not last at follow-up. Although he is often considered a pioneer in behavior therapy, he was also one of the first to advocate broad-spectrum behavior therapy that incorporated cognitive interventions rather than narrow-band purist behavior therapy (Lazarus 1966, 1971).

Lazarus eventually became dissatisfied even with broad-spectrum behavior therapy and went on to develop a more distinctive approach to therapy that he called *multimodal behavior therapy*, in which he added to behavior and cognition several other domains such as imagery, affect, sensation, interpersonal, and biological, or the BASIC I.D. (Lazarus 1973, 1976). He refined his approach even more, advocating technical eclecticism but not theoretical eclecticism, and finally called his new approach to therapy *multimodal therapy* (Lazarus 1981, 1985, 1989, 1997, 2008). He continues to add new therapeutic techniques to the repertoire of multimodal therapy interventions, while emphasizing the need to match the therapist's approach and techniques to the specific needs of the individual client.

Lazarus has taught at Stanford, Temple, and Yale universities, but he eventually settled at the Graduate School of Applied and Professional Psychology at Rutgers University in Piscataway, New Jersey. He is now a distinguished professor emeritus but continues to present workshops and training seminars on multimodal therapy. He also directs the Lazarus Institute in Princeton, New Jersey. He is highly regarded and often cited as one of the most influential psychotherapists today, and remains a particularly significant voice for technical eclecticism (Prochaska and Norcross 2010, 471).

Albert Bandura was born in 1925 in Mundare, Alberta, Canada, the youngest of six children from an Eastern European family background. He obtained his BA from the University of British Columbia in Vancouver, and then went to the University of Iowa for graduate school, where he earned a PhD in clinical psychology in 1952. After a year of clinical internship, he accepted a faculty position at Stanford University, where he has remained.

Bandura has made significant contributions to several areas of psychology, including authoring an early key text on behavior therapy and behavior modification, *Principles of Behavior Modification* (1969). He is well known for his research on observational learning (modeling) and his development of social learning theory (Bandura 1977b), or social cognitive theory, which has had a tremendous influence on counseling and psychotherapy. He also published a groundbreaking article in 1977 on self-efficacy as a unifying theory of behavioral change (Bandura 1977a). Since then he has further developed his theory of self-efficacy (Bandura 1986, 1997), which has been the subject of numerous doctoral dissertations in diverse areas.

Perceived self-efficacy, or a self-efficacy expectation, is the belief that one can successfully perform the behavior required to produce a particular outcome, and such perceived self-efficacy will determine one's persistence and ultimate success in coping with threats (Bandura 1977a). Perceived self-efficacy can therefore be simply defined as one's belief that one can succeed at a task (Spiegler and Guevremont 2003, 291). Bandura (1997) has more recently described the wide-range applications of his self-efficacy theory to many areas, including psychology, psychiatry, education, health, medicine, human development, business, athletics, as well as international affairs and political and social change (see Corey 2009, 233). His self-efficacy theory of behavioral change greatly influenced the further development of behavior therapy into broader-spectrum cognitive-behavioral therapy. Bandura has advocated a more open reciprocal determinism that allows for some degree of self-reflection and self-regulation or choice (Bandura 1986, 1997).

Bandura served as president of the American Psychological Association in 1974 and has received many honors, including the Outstanding Lifetime Contribution to Psychology Award from the American Psychological Association in 2004. In a survey conducted in 2002, he was found to be the fourth most frequently cited psychologist of all time (Haggbloom et al. 2002).

Donald Meichenbaum was born in 1940 and raised in New York City. He completed his undergraduate studies at the City College of New York and obtained a PhD in clinical psychology from the University of Illinois, Urbana-Champaign. Shortly thereafter, in 1966, he joined the faculty at the University of Waterloo in Waterloo, Ontario, and continued his teaching and research there for thirty-three years until he retired in 1998. He is now a distinguished professor emeritus at the University of Waterloo, and a distinguished visiting professor at the School of Education at the University of Miami in Florida. He is also the research director of the Melissa Institute for Violence Prevention and Treatment of Victims in Miami, Florida.

Meichenbaum has helped to further develop behavior therapy into a broader-based cognitive-behavioral approach by emphasizing the crucial role of self-instruction, or self-talk, in the regulation of one's emotions and behaviors. He conducted important research on *self-instructional training* as a cognitive-behavioral intervention to help people instruct themselves to cope better with different types of problems such as impulsive behavior in children and bizarre speech and thoughts in schizophrenic patients (see Spiegler and Guevremont 2003, 344). He also expanded self-instructional training into a more comprehensive intervention called *stress inoculation training* to help clients cope more effectively with stressful situations and problems such as anxiety, anger, and pain (see Meichenbaum 1977, 1985, 2003, 2007). His book *Cognitive-Behavior Modification*, first published in 1977, has become a classic in the field of cognitive behavior therapy.

Meichenbaum has also done significant work in the areas of posttraumatic stress disorder (Meichenbaum 1994); anger-control problems and aggressive behaviors (Meichenbaum 2002); treatment adherence (Meichenbaum and Turk 1987); stress prevention and management (Meichenbaum and Jaremko

1982); and suicide (Meichenbaum 2005). He was one of the founders of the journal *Cognitive Therapy and Research*.

Meichenbaum has received many honors and awards, including the prestigious Izaak Killiam Fellowship Award from the Canada Council. He is also a fellow of the Royal Society of Canada. He was voted by clinicians as one of the ten most influential therapists of the twentieth century and was also found to be the most frequently cited psychology researcher at Canadian universities during his academic career. He has lectured and conducted workshops as well as consulted widely, both nationally and internationally. He continues to make contributions in the areas of education, violence prevention, trauma, and suicide.

In addition to Wolpe, Eysenck, Skinner, Lazarus, Bandura, and Meichenbaum, other important figures associated with the development of behavior therapy include Cyril Franks and Stanley Rachman, mentioned earlier, and Hobart and Willie Mowrer. Early experimental work that provided the initial learning and conditioning foundations for behavior therapy was done by well-known researchers such as Ivan Pavlov, John B. Watson, Mary Cover Jones, and Edward Thorndike in the 1920s and 1930s (see Spiegler and Guevremont 2003, 16–25). A key figure who significantly contributed to the development of behavior therapy in Canada in the 1960s and later is Ernest G. Poser, who was a professor of psychology at McGill University and director of the behavior therapy unit at the Douglas Hospital Centre in Montreal, one of the first clinical treatment and teaching facilities of its kind (see Poser 1977). He is now retired in Vancouver, British Columbia.

Major Theoretical Ideas of Behavior Therapy

Perspective on Human Nature

The history of the development of behavior therapy consists of three major generations or waves (Hayes et al. 2006). The first wave was traditional behavior therapy, which emerged in the late 1950s and developed further in the 1960s and early 1970s; it emphasized what Prochaska and Norcross (2010) have described as counterconditioning (Wolpe) and contingency management (Skinner) thrusts. So-called modern learning theories, particularly classical conditioning following the work of Ivan Pavlov and operant conditioning based on B. F. Skinner's work, dominated the field of behavior therapy in the first wave. Conditioning theories of learning viewed human beings as being controlled by classical or operant conditioning; therefore, early behavior therapy tended to have a deterministic view of human nature, with little or no freedom to choose. Human nature was also seen as primarily neutral, neither positive nor negative.

The second wave of behavior therapy began in the late 1970s and involved the development of a broader-based cognitive behavior therapy that incorporated the thinking dimension of individuals, rather than only focusing narrowly on environmental factors. Cognitive behavior therapy, however, is now more than thirty years old (Hayes et al. 2006). It is the predominant approach today in behavior therapy but has expanded to include newer treatment approaches that incorporate mindfulness and acceptance (see Hayes, Follette, and Linehan 2004).

The third wave of behavior therapy that has recently developed in the 1990s and the early twenty-first century involves relatively contextualistic approaches that are based to some extent on concepts such as mindfulness and acceptance (Hayes et al. 2006). The major approaches in this third wave of behavior therapy include dialectical behavior therapy (DBT) (Linehan 1993); mindfulness-based cognitive therapy (MBCT) (Segal, Williams, and Teasdale 2002); and acceptance and commitment therapy (ACT) (Hayes and Strosahl 2004).

The more recent approaches to behavior therapy in its second and third waves have moved beyond the earlier mechanistic and radically behavioristic views of human nature espoused by traditional behaviorists such as Skinner. Contemporary behavior therapy and cognitive behavior therapy tend to view human beings as having some capacity for choice and self-reflection and self-control (Kazdin 2001; D. L. Watson and Tharp 2007). Bandura's social learning or social cognitive theory and in particular his concepts of self-efficacy and reciprocal determinism (Bandura 1977a, 1977b, 1986, 1997) have resulted in a more complex view of human nature as having a greater capacity for self-regulation and choice and therefore some free will. Human beings are still seen as neutral, however, neither inherently good nor inherently evil.

Basic Theoretical Principles of Behavior Therapy

Contemporary behavior therapy can no longer be easily defined. Marvin Goldfried and Gerald Davison have broadly described behavior therapy as "reflecting a general orientation to clinical work that aligns itself philosophically with an experimental approach to the study of human behavior" (1994, 3). The four major features of development in behavior therapy are classical conditioning, operant conditioning, social learning theory, and cognitive behavior therapy (see Corey 2009, 235–37).

Classical conditioning, or respondent conditioning, refers to the way behavior is controlled by its *antecedents*, or what has happened before the behavior. For example, in his early experimental work, Ivan Pavlov found that putting food into a dog's mouth will lead the dog to salivate. This salivation is called the respondent behavior, or the unconditioned response (UCR) to the food, which is the unconditioned stimulus (UCS). However, if the UCS of food is then repeatedly paired with the sound of a bell as a conditioned stimulus (CS), presented just before the food, eventually the sound of the bell itself (CS), presented without the food (UCS), will elicit salivation as the conditioned response (CR) of the dog to the CS. However, if this process is done repeatedly, presenting the CS without the UCS, the CR of salivation will eventually decrease and be eliminated. In this way, through the process of classical (or respondent) conditioning, neutral stimuli, such as a sound, can elicit conditioned responses. Fear responses can be conditioned through classical conditioning processes. Wolpe's systematic desensitization technique, or reciprocal inhibition approach to treating phobias and anxiety disorders, is based on classical conditioning and counterconditioning processes.

Operant conditioning involves learning processes in which one's behavior is controlled by the *consequences* that follow the behavior. B. F. Skinner's work helped to explicate the principles and schedules of operant conditioning. If a behavior is followed by pleasant or rewarding consequences (positive reinforcement) or the elimination of negative, aversive stimuli (negative reinforcement), then it is more likely to increase or be maintained. On the other hand, if a behavior is followed by aversive or negative consequences (punishment) or no reinforcement at all, then it is likely to decrease or be eliminated. Reinforcement contingencies, that is, the techniques of positive and negative reinforcement, punishment, and extinction, are powerful interventions used in behavior therapy for the modification of behavior, based on operant conditioning principles and processes.

Earlier views of classical and operant conditioning did not refer to more-cognitive processes that could mediate such conditioning. Bandura's *social learning theory*, or social-cognitive approach, paid much more attention to symbolic processes such as observational learning or modeling, and his subsequent development of self-efficacy theory greatly influenced behavior therapy to move beyond simplistic notions of classical and operant conditioning. Behavior therapy today has incorporated mediational concepts such as an individual's cognitions and perceptions including self-efficacy expectations, which can significantly affect one's emotions and behavior. The interpretation of environmental events, as opposed to only the tangible influence of environmental events, is therefore viewed as a crucial determinant of human behavior.

Contemporary behavior therapy has therefore developed predominantly into *cognitive behavior therapy*, influenced by social learning theory and self-efficacy. Cognitive behavior therapy has been simply defined as "a more purposeful attempt to preserve the demonstrated efficiencies of behavior modification within a less doctrinaire context, and to incorporate the cognitive activities of the client in the efforts to produce therapeutic change" (Kendall and Hollon 1979, 1).

Contemporary behavior therapy has accepted the importance of an individual's self-talk, attitudes, expectations, beliefs, and values or one's cognitions or thoughts in influencing one's feelings and behavior, and has incorporated techniques to modify maladaptive cognitions or thinking in bringing about behavioral change.

Development of Psychopathology

Behavior therapists often view maladaptive behavior, or psychopathology, as attributable to an individual's particular learning history. Such behavior is either detrimental or dangerous to oneself and/or to others (see Parrott 2003, 273). More specifically, early behavior therapists such as Wolpe (1990) defined psychopathology, or neurosis, as consisting of maladaptive habits that have been acquired through conditioning. For example, fear and anxiety have been considered conditioned responses to certain stimuli and can thus be deconditioned or counterconditioned. Maladaptive habits that an individual has learned through past experiences can therefore be unlearned, and more adaptive habits or behaviors can then be relearned or learned anew.

Similarly, Skinner and the behavior modification practitioners who followed him viewed maladaptive behavior as attributable to operant conditioning processes. For example, a young boy's temper tantrums may be due to the profuse attention his parents give him when he acts out, even if they are scolding him. They are reinforcing his negative behavior of whining, crying, and yelling by attending to him, thus strengthening such maladaptive behavior. Behavior therapists, following Skinner, will use operant conditioning procedures, that is, rearrange the reinforcement contingencies in deliberate, purposeful ways to decrease the temper tantrums by teaching the parents to ignore them and to provide social reinforcement, or positive praise and attention, to the boy when he is behaving himself.

Contemporary behavior therapists, however, do not view psychopathology simply as learned maladaptive habits. They tend to be more cognitive-behavioral in orientation and consider maladaptive behavior and feelings as resulting from internal dialogues, or the self-talk, of the individual, focusing more on the person's thoughts and images. Negative, irrational, extreme, unreasonable, and illogical thinking is often seen as underlying problematic feelings and behaviors. Such thinking must be identified, challenged, and modified with more rational, reasonable, and logical thinking that can then lead to better adaptive behavior and emotional experiencing. Self-criticism or self-contempt in one's thinking in particular can cause much emotional pain and problem behavior (see Bandura 1977b, 1986). Behavior therapists today pay more attention to how observational learning or modeling can contribute to maladaptive behavior, and to how such modeling can be used to promote more prosocial and appropriate behavior.

Therapeutic Process and Relationship

The behavior therapist is active and directive in conducting therapy with clients. He or she functions as a problem solver as well as a coping model for and with the client (Wilson 2008, 238). Although the therapeutic relationship is important in behavior therapy, and the behavior therapist does show genuine concern and respect for the client, the therapeutic alliance itself is not sufficient for effective therapy to occur (see DeRubeis, Brotman, and Gibbons 2005). In accounting for the efficacy of behavior therapy, therapeutic interventions have been found to be more significant than the therapeutic alliance (Loeb et al. 2005). Nevertheless, a strong, positive therapeutic alliance that is warm, empathic, genuine, and collaborative is still essential for the effectiveness of behavior therapy (see, e.g., J. S. Beck 2005; A. T. Beck, Rush, Shaw, and Emery 1979; P. Gilbert and Leahy 2007), even in manual-based versions of behavior therapy (Wilson 2008, 238).

The process of behavior therapy is relatively more structured and systematic than many other approaches to therapy (see Miltenberger 2008; Spiegler and Guevremont 2003; Wilson 2008). It consists of several steps or stages. First, the behavior therapist conducts a *functional assessment* or *behavioral analysis* (Wolpe 1990) of the major complaints, or *target behaviors*, that the client wants to deal with and change. This involves a concrete definition of the client's expressed problem behaviors and clarification of the antecedents as well as the consequences of the target behaviors. The therapist usually asks specific questions such as *how, when, where,* and *what* rather than *why* regarding the problem behavior being discussed. The behavior therapist may also use other methods of assessment (see Wilson 2008, 239–40) such as *guided imagery* (in which the client imagines a particular situation and shares the thoughts and feelings it may trigger); *role-playing; physiological recording* (e.g., heart rate); *self-monitoring* (which involves the client keeping careful daily records of specific behaviors such as frequency of hand washing); *behavioral observation* (in which the client observes his or her own behavior or others observe the client's behavior and record it with rating scales); and sometimes *psychological tests and questionnaires* (e.g., the Beck Depression Inventory [see A. T. Beck, Rush, Shaw, and Emery 1979] as a self-report measure of depression).

Second, the behavior therapist obtains a developmental history of the client and the problem behaviors being presented, to further assess the client's past learning or conditioning experiences as well as possible organic or biological bases for the problems (see Parrott 2003, 274).

Third, the behavior therapist helps the client set specific goals for therapy in a collaborative way. It is important ethically for the behavior therapist to empower the client to ultimately choose his or her own goals, with the therapist functioning as the expert or coach in helping the client achieve them. As G. T. Wilson has emphasized: "The client controls what; the therapist controls how" (2008, 238).

Fourth, and finally, the behavior therapist helps the client choose the most effective therapeutic interventions to best enable the client to change the identified problem behaviors and to achieve the goals the client has set. The behavior therapist then administers these therapeutic techniques to help the client in direct and systematic ways, while monitoring the client's progress. The therapist is sensitive and flexible enough to use other techniques if the current interventions are not working effectively for the client.

Major Therapeutic Techniques and Interventions

Behavior therapy is a unique approach to therapy that focuses on solving problems and overcoming symptoms presented by the client. It therefore emphasizes the use of specific techniques that have received empirical support. Behavior therapy (see Emmelkamp 2004) and cognitive behavior therapy (see Butler, Chapman, Forman, and Beck 2006; Hollon and Beck 2004) are among the most empirically supported treatments for a wide range of psychological disorders (Chambless and Ollendick 2001; Nathan and Gorman 2007; Roth and Fonagy 2005).

The number of behavior therapy techniques has dramatically increased since the late 1950s and 1960s, when behavior therapy first emerged as a systematic therapeutic approach. Published in 1987, the *Dictionary of Behavior Therapy Techniques* (Bellack and Hersen 1987) already listed and described over 150 behavior therapy techniques. Today, with broader-spectrum behavior therapy and cognitive behavior therapy as well as even more comprehensive multimodal therapy as developed by Lazarus (1971, 1976, 1981, 1997), behavior therapy interventions have increased exponentially. It is thus impossible to describe most of them in this chapter. However, the major behavior therapy techniques will now be briefly described. They include behavioral assessment; operant conditioning techniques (e.g., positive reinforcement, negative reinforcement, extinction, and punishment); token economies; social skills training and assertiveness training; modeling; relaxation training; systematic desensitization; flooding and in vivo exposure; self-modification programs and self-directed behavior; multimodal therapy; and mindfulness and acceptance-based cognitive behavior therapy (see Corey 2009, 241–57; Parrott 2003, 277–86; see also Miltenberger 2008; Spiegler and Guevremont 2003).

Behavioral Assessment

The first stage of behavior therapy involves conducting a comprehensive behavioral assessment of the client and his or her target problems and symptoms (e.g., anxiety, anger, or depression). This process has also been described as performing a functional assessment or behavioral analysis (Wolpe 1990); some details of functional or behavioral assessment have already been provided in the previous section of this chapter on the therapeutic process of behavior therapy.

Operant Conditioning Techniques

Operant conditioning techniques include positive reinforcement, negative reinforcement, extinction, positive punishment, and negative punishment (see Kazdin 2001; Miltenberger 2008).

Positive reinforcement involves the *addition* of something that rewards an individual following a target behavior that is to be strengthened or increased. For example, in order to increase the target behavior of writing, a person is reinforced with verbal praise from a close friend whenever she completes several pages of writing. The positive reinforcement can be anything that the person finds rewarding, such as verbal praise, food, money, or attention.

Negative reinforcement involves the *removal* of unpleasant or aversive stimuli following the occurrence of a target behavior that is to be increased or strengthened. For example, a person's writing can be negatively reinforced when after she has written a few pages, a close friend stops nagging her about writing. The removal of the nagging, which is an aversive or unpleasant stimulus, negatively reinforces the person's writing so that this behavior is strengthened. Both positive and negative reinforcement are meant to increase or strengthen the target behavior that is seen as desirable.

Extinction refers to removing reinforcement from a particular target behavior or response that has been previously reinforced. For example, a child's temper tantrums that have been previously reinforced by the attention his parents provided can be extinguished by the parents withholding their attention from their child whenever he acts out with temper tantrums. Extinction is usually combined with positive reinforcement of other, more desirable behaviors (Kazdin 2001). In the example just described, the parents will now positively reward their child with attention and praise whenever he behaves well and ignore him when he throws temper tantrums.

Punishment is another operant conditioning technique, also called aversive control, aimed at decreasing an undesirable

---

Sidebar 11.2

Behavior Therapy Techniques
(see Corey 2009, 241–57; Parrott 2003, 277–86)

1. Behavioral assessment
2. Operant conditioning techniques
3. Token economies
4. Social skills training and assertiveness training
5. Modeling
6. Relaxation training
7. Systematic desensitization
8. Flooding and in vivo exposure
9. Self-modification programs and self-directed behavior
10. Multimodal therapy
11. Mindfulness and acceptance-based cognitive behavior therapy

target behavior. There are two main kinds of punishment: *positive punishment* and *negative punishment* (Miltenberger 2008). *Positive punishment* involves the *addition* of an aversive stimulus after a particular target behavior has occurred, in order to decrease or weaken that behavior, that is, make it less likely to occur in the future. For example, when a boy engages in aggressive behavior in class by hitting someone else, he then must do twenty push-ups as a form of unpleasant positive punishment, which should lead to less frequent aggressive behavior.

Negative punishment involves the removal of a pleasant or positively re-inforcing stimulus following the occurrence of a target behavior in order to decrease or weaken it, that is, make it less likely to occur in the future. For example, when a child misbehaves, her parents take away her television-watching time, thus negatively punishing her misbehavior, making it less likely that she will misbehave again in the future.

Extinction and punishment can lead to certain side effects, such as aggression and anger. In applied behavior analysis or operant conditioning, positive reinforcement is the major intervention, with the use of punishment or aversive control only when necessary (Kazdin 2001; Miltenberger 2008). Skinner (1948) himself advocated the use of positive reinforcement for modifying behavior and believed that punishment should rarely be used because it was undesirable and had limited utility in changing behavior (see Corey 2009, 243).

More recently, behavioral activation has been found to be particularly effective as a treatment for more severely depressed clients and for prevention of relapse (Dimidjian et al. 2006; K. S. Dobson et al. 2008; see also Coffman et al. 2007). R. E. Zinbarg and J. W. Griffith (2008) have described behavioral activation as a specific behavior therapy technique based primarily on positive reinforcement of healthy behaviors and activity in depressed clients (see also Lewinsohn 1974; Martell, Addis, and Jacobson 2001; Martell, Dimidjian, and Herman-Dunn 2010). Another recent randomized controlled trial of behavioral activation for moderately depressed university students using only a structured single-session intervention, with a no-treatment control group, yielded strong effect sizes, reflecting significant decreases in depression and increased environmental reward (Gawrysiak, Nicholas, and Hopko 2009).

Token Economies

Token economies refer to a specific application of operant conditioning in which tokens are given to clients when they engage in appropriate behaviors, so that these behaviors are reinforced by the tokens earned. Tokens can also be lost because of inappropriate or undesirable client behaviors. Clients can then choose specific reinforcers for which they can exchange their tokens, such as food, candy, toys, or the privilege to watch a movie. Token economies have been effectively used to shape and reinforce appropriate social behaviors in institutionalized patients and clients in residential homes, but also in the classroom and for individuals (Spiegler and Guevremont 2003, 176–94).

Social Skills Training and Assertiveness Training

Social skills training is a behavioral intervention that comprehensively covers helping clients with interpersonal difficulties or deficits in social skills when interacting with other people. The behavior therapist coaches and teaches the client how to interact more effectively and appropriately with others, especially in social situations. Several specific techniques are used in social skills training, including providing information about appropriate ways of interacting with others, modeling of such social skills for the client, reinforcing the client with verbal praise for trying more effective ways of social interaction through behavioral rehearsal, role-playing, and providing feedback and further instruction and coaching to the client. Social skills training can also be used as a significant intervention in *anger management training* for clients who have difficulty controlling their tempers or those with aggressive behavior. Social skills training has been used with children and adolescents as well as with adults, including adults with schizophrenia (Spiegler and Guevremont 2003, 273–78).

Assertiveness training, or assertion training, is a type of social skills training (Spiegler and Guevremont 2003, 278–86) used to help clients who have trouble expressing themselves freely, whether in making requests of others, saying "no" to others, stating positive or negative sentiments (e.g., affection or anger), or interacting with other people in social situations. Clients are taught to differentiate between passive, aggressive, and appropriately assertive behaviors or responses. The behavior therapist then uses instruction, modeling of assertive responses, practice of such responses by the client, role-playing with the client, and further feedback and coaching to help the client improve his or her assertiveness responses; the therapist provides appropriate positive reinforcement by verbally praising the client when he or she effectively performs assertive responses. Clients therefore learn that it is their right to stand up, speak out, and talk back where and when appropriate (see Alberti and Emmons 2008).

Modeling

The behavioral techniques of modeling are based mainly on Bandura's significant work on observational learning (1969, 1971, 1977b, 1986, 1997). Modeling involves a client observing another person's behavior and its consequences and then imitating that behavior.

Modeling has five major functions when it is used in behavior therapy to help clients: teaching, prompting, motivating, reducing anxiety, and discouraging (Spiegler and Guevremont 2003, 263–64). *Teaching* through modeling occurs when the client learns a new behavior by observing a model. For example, a child learns language by watching and hearing an adult model speak. *Prompting* through modeling occurs when the client is reminded or cued to do a particular behavior after watching a model perform that behavior. For example, a client watches a model take a slow, deep breath to relax and then does likewise, being reminded to relax in a stressful situation. *Motivating* through modeling occurs when the client sees a model receiving positive reinforcement or some reward for performing a particular behavior and then is motivated to engage in that behavior too due to the vicarious reinforcement that the client has experienced. For example, a student volunteers to answer a question in class because she has observed other students doing so and being praised by the teacher. *Reducing anxiety* through modeling occurs when the client watches a model performing an anxiety-provoking behavior safely and with little or no anxiety, with anxiety reduction vicariously experienced by the client. For example, a client with aquaphobia, or a fear of water and swimming, overcomes this fear by watching a model enjoy going into the pool and swimming. Finally, *discouraging* the client through modeling occurs when the client watches a model's behavior that is followed by negative or unpleasant consequences, which discourages the client from engaging in such behavior. For example, a child observes a classmate being punished by the teacher for hitting others, and the child is then discouraged from engaging in hitting behavior too. These five functions of modeling are not always independent, and several of them can occur at once.

Modeling can be used in various ways: *live modeling*, in which the client observes an actual person or the therapist; *symbolic modeling*, in which the client is exposed to models indirectly through videos or movies and books, or *modeling in imagination*, called *covert modeling*, in which the client imagines someone else or even himself successfully performing a particular desirable behavior such as making an effective sales presentation or speech; *role-playing*, in which the therapist models specific behaviors that the client wants to perform more effectively and appropriately by playing the role of the client and then reversing roles so that the client can practice the behaviors as herself, that is, by engaging in *behavior rehearsal*; and *participant modeling*, in which the therapist first models a particular behavior for the client by executing it well. For example, the therapist will pet a well-trained dog and then guide the client, who has a fear of dogs, to gradually pet the dog too, so that the client becomes a participant in the modeling by the therapist (see Sharf 2008, 272–73).

Relaxation Training

Relaxation training is an important or core behavior therapy technique. It is used to help clients suffering from a number of different clinical disorders such as anxiety disorders, stress, insomnia, headaches and other chronic pain conditions, asthma, hypertension, eczema (skin inflammation), irritable bowel syndrome, side effects of chemotherapy, postsurgical distress, and panic disorder (see Cormier, Nurius, and Osborn 2009; Spiegler and Guevremont 2003). It should be noted, however, that relaxation training for some panic-prone clients can be harmful rather than helpful (Lilienfeld 2007). Relaxation training should therefore be conducted in a clinically sensitive way, adapted and tailor-made for each client. Relaxation training targets tension and its alleviation as critical for the management and reduction of emotionally intense states such as anxiety and anger. There are various techniques for relaxation training, but an important one is *progressive muscle relaxation*, based on the earlier work of Edmund Jacobson (1938). It involves the alternate tensing and relaxing or letting go of major muscle groups. Jacobson's original version of progressive muscle relaxation was very elaborate and time consuming to follow, with almost two hundred hours of training required. Behavior therapists have shortened progressive muscle relaxation to around sixteen muscle groups (see Goldfried and Davison 1994; Wolpe 1990), and sometimes even to four major muscle groups (Tan 1996a). Frank Dattilio (2006) has made available an excellent audiotape demonstration of progressive muscle relaxation.

Here is an example of progressive muscle relaxation training, using four major muscle groups, that can be done by a client at home:

> This relaxation technique involves the alternate tensing and then relaxing or letting go of various muscle parts of your body. . . . First, sit in a comfortable chair or recliner, in a room and at a time when you will not be disturbed. Give yourself at least 15–20 minutes of uninterrupted "relaxation time" to practice the relaxation exercises, beginning with the leg muscles and ending with the arm muscles.
>
> *Leg muscles*. You can tense your thigh and calf muscles by pointing your toes toward your face and tensing these muscles hard. Hold the tension for 7–10 seconds by counting slowly up to 5. Then let go and allow the muscles to go limp. Now use self-talk: tell yourself to "just relax, let go of all the tension . . . allow the muscles to smooth out . . . take it easy . . . just unwind and relax more and more . . ." Continue with this relaxation patter for 20 seconds or so before proceeding to repeat this exercise. Do this exercise a total of 4 times. Then proceed to the next one.
>
> *Upper-body muscles*. After completing the exercise for the leg muscles, focus your attention on the muscles of your upper body—your chest, stomach, shoulders, and back. Tense them by taking in a slow, deep breath, holding it for a count up to 5 (about 7–10 seconds), pulling your stomach in, and arching your back (unless you have a back injury or back pain, in which case you should not arch your back). When you reach a count of 5, slowly exhale and let got of all the muscle tension, again telling yourself mentally to relax and take it easy, using the relaxation patter or self-talk for about 20 seconds or so before repeating the exercise. Do it a total of 4 times. . . .

Face and neck muscles. Focus your attention on the muscles of your face and neck regions. Tense these muscles by closing your eyes tightly, biting your teeth, smiling back, pushing your chin down as if to touch your chest but not allowing it to touch your chest. Hold the tension for a count up to 5 (7–10 seconds), and then relax and let go of these muscles, again using the relaxation patter or self-talk for up to 20 seconds or so. Repeat this exercise for a total of 4 times before proceeding to the final exercise.

Arm muscles. Now focus your attention on the muscles of your arms. Tense them by clenching your fists and flexing your biceps. . . . Hold the tension for a count up to 5 (7–10 seconds), and then relax and let your arms flop down limp by your sides. Again, engage in the relaxation patter or self-talk for 20 seconds or so before repeating the exercise, doing it a total of 4 times. . . .

At the end you should give yourself a couple more minutes to just sit quietly and enjoy the feelings of deeper and more complete muscle relaxation that you are experiencing by this time. Then, count from 1 to 5 as you slowly move your muscles, and eventually open your eyes at the count of 5, feeling very relaxed and refreshed. (Tan 1996a, 59–61)

This version of progressive muscle relaxation training can also be conducted in the reverse order, starting with the arm muscles, then the face and neck muscles, then the upper body muscles, and ending with the leg muscles.

Another form of relaxation training often used by behavior therapists today is an even more abbreviated version based on the work of Meichenbaum (1977, 1985) on stress inoculation training. In this stress management, or *stress inoculation approach to relaxation training*, the following three major relaxation techniques are used: (1) *slow, deep breathing*: the client is instructed to take in a slow, deep breath, hold it for a few seconds, and then exhale the tension out slowly; this is repeated a few times; (2) *calming self-talk*: the therapist instructs the client to say several calming and relaxing statements to himself or herself, that is, to use self-talk such as: "Just relax, take it easy, let go of all the tension, allow the muscles to smooth out. . . ."; (3) *pleasant imagery*: the therapist instructs the client to imagine or visualize as clearly and as vividly as possible a very pleasant, relaxing, enjoyable, and peaceful scene, such as lying on the beach in Hawaii, watching a beautiful sunset or sunrise, or taking a walk in the woods.

Finally, another well-known relaxation technique that can be used to help clients relax away tension and anxiety is a passive, quiet meditative exercise developed by Herbert Benson for activating what he has called "the relaxation response" (Benson 1975). It involves a few simple steps: sit quietly in a comfortable position with your eyes closed; deeply relax all your muscles from your feet up to your face; breathe through your nose and then say a word such as "one" or "peace" when exhaling or breathing out; maintain a quiet and passive attitude throughout for a total time of about twenty minutes, even if you have distracting thoughts at times.

Systematic Desensitization

Systematic desensitization is another core behavior therapy technique that has received much empirical support for its effectiveness as a behavioral treatment for anxiety disorders and specific phobias (Cormier, Nurius, and Osborn 2009; Spiegler and Guevremont 2003). It has also been used to treat other problems such as anger, insomnia, asthma, motion sickness, nightmares, and sleepwalking (Spiegler 2008). It was originally developed by Joseph Wolpe over fifty years ago when he used classical conditioning principles and processes to conduct psychotherapy by reciprocal inhibition (Wolpe 1958) in the treatment of neurotic disorders, such as anxiety problems and phobias. Systematic desensitization was therefore the first major behavior therapy intervention (Spiegler and Guevremont 2003). It involves pairing an anxiety-provoking stimulus that usually elicits an anxiety response (as the conditioned response, or CR) with a competing response, usually relaxation. This process is done repeatedly until eventually the particular anxiety-provoking stimulus no longer elicits anxiety because it is now associated more with relaxation as a competing response that has replaced fear. This is the usual process and explanation for *traditional systematic desensitization*, which consists of three steps: (1) The behavior therapist teaches the client a response that competes with anxiety, usually relaxation. (2) The specific stimuli or events that provoke anxiety in the client are listed from the least anxiety provoking to the most anxiety provoking, thus constructing an *anxiety hierarchy*. A simple *Subjective Units of Discomfort scale (SUDs)* is used to rate the anxiety level that the client experiences on a 0 (no anxiety) to 100 (maximum, extreme anxiety) for each of the anxiety-provoking items on the anxiety hierarchy. (3) The behavior therapist then guides the client to repeatedly visualize the anxiety-provoking items, in order of increasing anxiety, while engaging in the competing response, usually relaxation (see Spiegler and Guevremont 2003, 204–11).

Goldfried and Davison (1994, 124–26) describe Wolpe's traditional systematic desensitization as consisting of conducting deep relaxation, constructing an anxiety hierarchy (usually with one to two dozen items), and presenting an item from it (in order of increasing anxiety) for five, ten, or fifteen seconds to the client in imagination while the client is in a deeply relaxed state. If the client signals anxiety while visualizing the item or scene, he or she is asked to remove the scene from imagination and return to a deeply relaxed state, at which point the item will be presented again. This process is repeated until the client's SUDs rating of anxiety for that particular item goes down to about 0. Then, the next item from the client's anxiety hierarchy is presented in this manner repeatedly until the client rates it also with a SUDs rating of 0. Then another item is presented. Usually, two to five items from a hierarchy are presented in each session of traditional systematic desensitization. It is therefore a tedious and time-consuming behavior therapy technique that may

---

Sidebar 11.3

Systematic Desensitization Procedure Using an Anxiety Hierarchy

An example of an anxiety hierarchy for a client with a phobia or fear of spiders might include the following items in order of increasing anxiety with SUDs ratings in parentheses:

1. Reading the word "spider" in a book (10).
2. Seeing a picture/drawing of a small spider in a book (20).
3. Seeing a picture/drawing of a large spider in a book (30).
4. Seeing a small dead spider (40).
5. Seeing a large dead spider (50).
6. Seeing a small live spider (60).
7. Seeing a large live spider (70).
8. Touching a small dead spider with a pen (80).
9. Touching a large dead spider with a pen (85).
10. Touching a small live spider with a pen (90).
11. Touching a large live spider with a pen (95).
12. Touching a small or large live spider with a finger (100).

---

take between ten and thirty sessions to successfully help a client overcome a specific phobia or anxiety problem. It is, however, an effective intervention. Clients usually find traditional systematic desensitization acceptable because they are exposed to anxiety-provoking scenes only in a gradual way and at their own pace and have control of when they want to end the exposure to such scenes (Spiegler and Guevremont 2003).

Wolpe originally explained the effectiveness of traditional systematic desensitization by the process of counterconditioning, or reciprocal inhibition of the anxiety response with the competing response of relaxation. He emphasized the need for a thorough anxiety hierarchy consisting of one to two dozen items in order of gradually increasing anxiety, and for the client's complete relaxation with virtually no anxiety, a SUDs rating of about 0, before proceeding to the next item in the anxiety hierarchy. Research, however, has shown that Wolpe's approach and explanations are not necessarily valid for the effective treatment of anxiety disorders. The *essential* element in systematic desensitization and its effectiveness has been found instead to be "*repeated exposure to anxiety-evoking situations without the client experiencing any negative consequences*" (Spiegler and Guevremont 2003, 213, italics as set in original). Items on the anxiety hierarchy can therefore be presented out of order, and relaxation training can be omitted in effective systematic desensitization. In fact, *emotive imagery* involving the use of pleasant images and thoughts as well as humor and laughter have been found to be alternative effective competing responses to anxiety (see Spiegler and Guevremont 2003, 214).

There are also variations in systematic desensitization that go beyond Wolpe's traditional version, such as *coping desensitization* developed by Marvin Goldfried (1971), which focuses more on the bodily sensations of anxiety and using coping responses (such as muscle relaxation but also calming self-talk and other techniques); *anxiety management training*, developed by Richard Suinn and Frank Richardson (1971), which is similar to coping desensitization but does not use an anxiety hierarchy; and *interoceptive exposure* and cognitive behavior therapy, developed by David Barlow and his colleagues (Barlow 1988, 2002; Craske and Barlow 2008), for treating panic attacks, which includes artificially inducing the somatic symptoms (e.g., increased heart rate and dizziness) of panic attacks while the client imagines panic-provoking events, cognitive restructuring or use of coping self-talk, and breathing retraining, especially slow, deep, and steady diaphragmatic breathing (see Spiegler and Guevremont 2003, 214–17).

Flooding and In Vivo Exposure

Flooding, like systematic desensitization, is another form of exposure therapy in which the client with a phobia or anxiety disorder is exposed to the anxiety-provoking stimulus or event without the feared consequences occurring. However, unlike systematic desensitization, flooding is a behavior therapy technique that exposes the client to maximal anxiety from the start (rather than to minimal anxiety initially). While being exposed to the anxiety-provoking event, the client is encouraged to tolerate the high anxiety levels until the anxiety subsides. Flooding can be conducted in real life, in which case it is called *flooding in vivo*, or in imagination, in which case it is called *imaginal flooding*. Likewise, systematic desensitization can be conducted in imagination, which is usually the case, but it can also be conducted in vivo. An example of flooding in vivo is when a client with a balloon phobia is exposed to dozens of balloons at one time in the treatment room, with no recourse to leaving the room as an escape response, until the high anxiety level experienced by the client is significantly reduced before the session is terminated. Such flooding in vivo is also called *in vivo exposure with response prevention*, because the client is prevented from engaging in any maladaptive responses for anxiety reduction (e.g., avoiding the anxiety-provoking situation, or performing ritualistic or obsessive-compulsive behaviors such as checking or hand washing) during the exposure therapy. An example of imaginal flooding would be asking a client with a balloon phobia to visualize dozens of balloons before him, without his being able to leave or avoid the situation. This imaginal flooding session is continued until the client's high anxiety level has substantially subsided. Thomas Stampfl and Donald Levis

Sidebar 11.4

Eye Movement Desensitization and Reprocessing (EMDR)

Eye movement desensitization and reprocessing (EMDR) is a relatively new exposure-based therapy that is still somewhat controversial. It was originally developed by Francine Shapiro to treat emotionally disturbing thoughts and memories of traumatic events such as combat-related trauma, sexual assault, and robbery at gunpoint (see Shapiro 2001, 2002). EMDR involves imaginal flooding during which the client is instructed to watch and visually track the index finger of the therapist as it moves back and forth (from left to right about twice per second, for a dozen to two dozen times) in a rapid and rhythmic fashion within the client's visual field. Such eye movements, according to Shapiro, result in a neurological effect, similar to rapid eye movements seen in intense dreaming, that helps the client to better process intense and stressful experiences and memories. EMDR also involves cognitive restructuring of the client's thinking, focusing on adaptive beliefs associated with the traumatic images presented to the client in imaginal flooding.

EMDR has been touted as an effective breakthrough exposure treatment that produces rapid and significant therapeutic results with clients who have trauma-based anxiety disorders. However, the controlled outcome studies conducted so far have not supported the effectiveness of EMDR beyond that of its imaginal flooding component, and the eye movements have not been found to be necessary for its effectiveness (see Spiegler and Guevremont 2003, 247–49). It is therefore still a controversial exposure-based treatment in need of further well-controlled outcome studies before more definitive conclusions about its efficacy as a treatment can be made.

developed an earlier variant of imaginal flooding called *implosive therapy*, in which the prolonged or intense exposure included therapist-hypothesized cues and exaggerated imaginary scenes, often with psychodynamic themes, that went far beyond the client-reported scenes (Stampfl and Levis 1967, 1973). Implosive therapy is practiced less frequently today.

Systematic desensitization in vivo involves gradually exposing the client in real life to an increasing number of anxiety-provoking items from the client's anxiety hierarchy.

Effective exposure treatments can be conducted in gradual or intense ways, in vivo or in imagination, and with individual clients or in groups. Effective exposure treatments are usually prolonged in duration, frequent, and comprehensive (see Persons 1989, 94–95). They are typically conducted by therapists, in which case they are called *therapist-directed exposure*. Clients can also perform their own exposure treatments in what is called *self-managed exposure*. Some types of phobias, such as fears of natural disasters (e.g., fires, floods, earthquakes), cannot be practically treated with in vivo exposure;

hence imaginal exposure is more appropriate and feasible in treating these kinds of phobias. More recently, since the 1980s and 1990s, exposure therapy has also been conducted using computer-based virtual reality technology in exposing clients to specific anxiety-provoking scenes. Such *virtual reality exposure therapy* was pioneered by Barbara Rothbaum and Larry Hodges (see Rothbaum and Hodges 1999). It has been used to treat panic disorder, agoraphobia, obsessive-compulsive disorder, social phobia, posttraumatic stress disorder, and specific phobias such as fears of flying, public speaking, driving, spiders, heights, enclosed spaces, and several medical procedures (Wiederhold and Wiederhold 2005). Although it is still costly, it is a promising approach to exposure treatment that warrants further research and evaluation of its effectiveness (Spiegler and Guevremont 2003). Recent meta-analyses have, in fact, shown substantial decreases in symptoms of anxiety after virtual reality exposure therapy (Parsons and Rizzo 2008) and large average effect sizes (M. B. Powers and Emmelkamp 2008).

Self-Modification Programs and Self-Directed Behavior

Self-modification or *self-management programs* in behavior therapy focus on developing clients' *self-directed behavior*, empowering them to choose their own goals with specific target behaviors they want to modify, with some guidance from the behavior therapist, who coaches the clients with specific behavioral change techniques.

Self-modification interventions usually include self-monitoring, self-contracting, self-reward, stimulus control, and self-as-model (Corey 2009, 250). Clients are taught coping skills they can use in dealing with difficult problems or stressful situations. David Watson and Roland Tharp (2007) have described the following steps that a client needs to take in order to successfully implement a self-modification program: (1) *select goals* that are realistic, attainable, measurable, and meaningful to him or her; (2) *translate goals into target behaviors* that are clear and concrete; (3) *engage in self-monitoring* in which he or she keeps a daily behavioral diary of systematic observations of his or her own target behaviors and their antecedents and consequences; (4) *develop a specific plan for behavioral change* and use self-reinforcement when desirable target behaviors occur; (5) *evaluate each action plan*, and make adjustments or revisions to it where necessary, to keep it realistic and attainable.

Self-modification programs have been used to help clients struggling with depression, panic attacks, fear of the dark, social anxiety, and public speaking anxiety as well as for enhancing creativity and productivity, controlling smoking, and increasing exercise (D. L. Watson and Tharp 2007). Self-modification has also been evaluated with clients suffering from health problems such as asthma, arthritis, cardiac disease, cancer, diabetes, headaches, substance abuse, and vision loss (Cormier, Nurius, and Osborn 2009).

Multimodal Therapy

Arnold Lazarus is a key figure in the development of behavior therapy and especially in expanding it to *broad-spectrum behavior therapy* (Lazarus 1966, 1971), then *multimodal behavior therapy* (Lazarus 1973, 1976), and eventually to *multimodal therapy* (Lazarus 1981, 1985, 1989, 1997, 2008). Multimodal therapy as developed by Lazarus is a comprehensive and systematic approach to therapy that has gone beyond clinical broad-spectrum behavior therapy, although it is still largely based in social learning theory and social cognitive theory and uses many cognitive and behavioral techniques in treating a broad range of clinical problems.

Lazarus strongly advocates *technical eclecticism*, or using whatever therapeutic techniques have been found to be effective. However, he does not advocate theoretical eclecticism, which can be confusing, inconsistent, and incoherent. Multimodal therapists, like behavior therapists and cognitive behavior therapists, are very active and directive in conducting therapy, comfortably functioning as coaches, consultants, educators, trainers, and role models for their clients. They also engage in appropriate levels of self-disclosure and will openly provide instructions, suggestions, and constructive feedback as well as offer positive reinforcement or verbal praise to their clients (Corey 2009, 252).

The multimodal approach to therapy is based on a view of human personality as consisting of seven major dimensions of functioning that can be summarized as one's *BASIC I.D.* (or basic identity). BASIC I.D. stands for the following: B=Behavior; A=Affect; S=Sensations; I=Images; C=Cognitions; I=Interpersonal Relationships; and D=Drugs/Biology (Lazarus 1981, 1989, 1997, 2008). All seven modalities or areas of human functioning can interact among themselves, but they can also be seen as separate dimensions. The seventh modality, drugs and biology, also includes nutrition and exercise.

Multimodal therapy emphasizes the need for a comprehensive assessment of the client across the BASIC I.D., covering each modality or dimension, which yields a BASIC I.D. profile unique to the client. A multimodal life history inventory (Lazarus and Lazarus 1991) is often used by multimodal therapists in exploring a client's history. Lazarus (2008) believes that effective therapy should be comprehensive, covering all the modalities of a client's BASIC I.D., using as many therapeutic interventions as needed to help the client learn as broad a repertoire of coping skills as possible to deal with his or her problems and to prevent relapse.

Mindfulness and Acceptance-Based Cognitive Behavior Therapy

The third wave of behavior therapy has expanded the behavioral and cognitive-behavioral approach to therapy to include mindfulness and acceptance-based therapies (Hayes, Follette, and Linehan 2004; Roemer and Orsillo 2009). Such therapies emphasize *mindfulness*, or focusing attention on one's immediate experience in the present moment, with acceptance or an open, curious, and receptive orientation, and not with a judgmental or evaluative attitude.

There are four major approaches to third-wave behavior therapy (see Corey 2009, 255–57).

Dialectical behavior therapy (DBT). DBT was developed by Marsha Linehan (1993) for the treatment of borderline personality disorder. It emphasizes acceptance and mindfulness in helping clients to regulate their intense emotions. DBT's major components are regulating affect, tolerating distress, improving interpersonal relationships, and training in mindfulness that is based on Zen practice (Corey 2009, 255). Clients need enough time to learn such skills in DBT, and therapy therefore usually lasts for at least a year, involving individual therapy as well as group skills training. DBT has more recently been applied across different disorders and settings (Dimeff and Koerner 2007), including in private practice (Marra 2005).

Mindfulness-based stress reduction (MBSR). MBSR was developed by Jon Kabat-Zinn (1990). It is a group intervention that usually lasts for eight to ten weeks, during which clients are taught sitting meditation and mindful yoga as well as a body-scan meditation to help them observe and experience all their bodily sensations. Clients practice mindfulness meditation on a daily basis for about forty-five minutes and learn to attend to their present or immediate experience in coping more effectively with stress and thus improve their health.

Mindfulness-based cognitive therapy (MBCT). MBCT was developed by Zindel Segal, Mark Williams, and John Teasdale (2002), based on Kabat-Zinn's MBSR. It combines mindfulness training with cognitive-behavioral therapy in an eight-week program for the treatment of depression and its recurrence. It seems to be effective especially for clients who have had three or more previous episodes of depression. However, further controlled outcome research is needed before more definitive conclusions can be made about the effectiveness of MBCT for depression and its recurrence (see Coelho, Canter, and Ernst 2007; Williams, Russell, and Russell 2008).

Acceptance and commitment therapy (ACT). ACT was developed by Steven C. Hayes and his colleagues (Hayes and Strosahl 2004; Hayes, Strosahl, and Wilson 1999; see also Hayes and Smith 2005; Luoma, Hayes, and Walser 2007). This approach to therapy helps clients to accept painful experiences rather than fight to modify or control unpleasant feelings. It emphasizes acceptance as well as commitment to one's own values and taking action to live according to one's values. ACT has six major components: acceptance, cognitive defusion (emphasizing flexibility in place of rigidity), being present, self as context focusing on a transcendent sense of self, values, and committed action. It is a promising approach to third-wave behavior therapy that is receiving increasing empirical support for its effectiveness in treating a wide range of clinical problems (Hayes et al. 2006; Hayes et al. in press; Ost 2008).

Cognitive Behavior Modification

Prochaska and Norcross have described three major thrusts or categories of behavior therapy techniques: (1) *counterconditioning* (Wolpe), including systematic desensitization, assertiveness training, sexual arousal, behavioral activation, and stimulus control (Prochaska and Norcross 2010, 246–57); (2) *contingency management* (Skinner), including institutional control, self-control, mutual control, therapist control, and aversive control (Prochaska and Norcross 2010, 257–65); and (3) *cognitive behavior modification* (Meichenbaum) including Meichenbaum's *self-instructional training* (Meichenbaum 1977) and *stress inoculation training* (Meichenbaum 1985) as well as biofeedback and problem-solving therapy (Prochaska and Norcross, 265–71).

Cognitive behavior modification (CBM) as developed by Meichenbaum is a broad-spectrum behavior therapy that includes both behavioral coping skills such as relaxation techniques as well as cognitive strategies such as calming and coping self-talk or self-instructional training. It can also be considered a major approach to cognitive behavior therapy. Prochaska and Norcross (2010) have chosen to categorize cognitive behavior modification (CBM) as part of the contemporary behavior therapies. CBM will be discussed only briefly here, in the form of stress inoculation training, because it will receive more detailed coverage in the next chapter of this book, which covers cognitive behavior therapy and rational emotive behavior therapy.

Meichenbaum went beyond self-talk or self-instructional training when he developed a more comprehensive approach to therapy that he called *stress inoculation training (SIT)*, which is a substantial part of CBM (see Meichenbaum 1985, 1993, 2003, 2007). It consists of three phases: a conceptual educational phase; a skills acquisition, consolidation, and rehearsal phase; and an application phase with follow through. In the conceptual educational phase, clients are provided with a meaningful rationale for stress inoculation training aimed at helping them cope more effectively with stressful situations in their lives by anticipating stress and practicing coping skills for stress management. In the second phase of skills acquisition, consolidation, and rehearsal, various coping skills are reviewed with clients, and they choose and practice the ones most relevant and helpful to them (e.g., problem-solving, assertiveness training, cognitive reframing, relaxation techniques, calming self-talk, pleasant imagery). In the final phase of application and follow through, the client uses the coping skills to manage experimental or actual stressors, or through role-playing and imagery rehearsal (Meichenbaum 1985, 2003).

SIT has been successfully used in helping clients cope with a wide range of stressful situations, including acute stressors such as medical procedures and surgery, traumatic events; chronic intermittent stressors such as athletic competitions and evaluations; and chronic stressors such as chronic pain, anxiety and anger problems, and persistent exposure to occupational challenges such as those in police work, nursing, teaching, and combat (Meichenbaum 2003).

Behavior Therapy in Practice

A Hypothetical Transcript

Client: I was at the grocery store the other day, waiting in line to pay the cashier for a couple of things. Another customer then cut right in front of me. I felt really angry but couldn't bring myself to say anything to him. He paid for his stuff and then walked away as if nothing had happened. I was fuming mad inside but kept it all to myself. . . . I wish I could be bolder and had told him off for cutting in front of me!

Behavior Therapist: Sounds like you really felt upset at this guy for cutting in front of you, but you have trouble speaking up though you want to. What do you think holds you back? What's getting in the way of you saying what you want to say to this guy?

Client: Well . . . I have trouble asserting myself or speaking up when I want to. . . . I get nervous, and I'm not sure what to say. . . . I also am afraid of losing my temper and getting really mad and shouting at the guy.

Behavior Therapist: So you have some feelings of nervousness as well as fear of blowing up in anger at the guy.

Client: Yeah . . . I'm not sure how to control my feelings, except to stuff them. . . . I'm also not sure what to say to express myself appropriately to the guy, to let him know that what he did wasn't right.

Behavior Therapist: OK, let's see if we can help you first to manage your feelings of nervousness and fear of blowing up. Some simple relaxation and coping techniques for calming ourselves down may be helpful. For example, you can take a slow, deep breath, hold it for a few moments, and then breathe out slowly and relax. You can then tell yourself quietly, "Just relax, take it easy, I can handle this without blowing up." You can also briefly visualize or imagine yourself lying on the beach in Hawaii to relax yourself more. What do you think?

Client: Yeah, that sounds good!

Behavior Therapist: Let's try practicing these three simple but powerful stress control techniques of slow, deep breathing, calming self-talk, and pleasant imagery. I want you to take in a slow, deep breath now, hold it for a few moments as you notice the tension rising . . . and now just relax and breathe out slowly . . . quietly tell yourself, "Just relax, take it easy . . . I can handle this . . ." and then briefly picture or imagine yourself lying on the beach in Hawaii. . . . Just relax more and more deeply. . . . How are you feeling?

Client: I'm feeling much more relaxed. . . . These techniques are really helpful!

Behavior Therapist: Good! Now do you think it would also be helpful to you if we practice in a role-play several times what you could actually say to this guy in an appropriate and bold or assertive way without losing your cool?

Client: Yeah . . . I need some suggestions and coaching from you!

Behavior Therapist: OK . . . let's do a brief role-play with you being yourself and with me playing the role of the guy cutting in front of you. So here goes . . . I've just cut in front of you . . . and you go ahead and try saying what you want to say, to me . . .

Client: Well . . . excuse me, do you mind waiting in line like the rest of us instead of cutting in like this?

Behavior Therapist: That's not bad at all for a first try. How do you feel about what you said and how might we improve on it?

Client: I'm not sure . . . but maybe I don't have to say the last part about cutting in like this, especially since I'm raising my voice too.

Behavior Therapist: That's a good observation! Let me play the role of you now, and you take the role of the guy so that I can provide you an example of what to say. . . . "Excuse me but I would appreciate it if you wait in line like the rest of us. . . . Thanks!"

Client: Yeah, that sounds much better and like what I really want to say!

Behavior Therapist: OK . . . Let's practice it again but now you play the role of yourself and I'll play the role of the guy again . . . go ahead . . .

Client: "Excuse me . . . I would appreciate it if you wait in line like the rest of us . . . there's a line here . . . Thanks!"

Behavior Therapist: That's great! Well done! How do you feel now?

This hypothetical transcript of a small part of a behavior therapy session demonstrates the therapist's use of several behavioral techniques. They include brief relaxation and coping skills training and assertiveness training with coaching, modeling, role-playing, providing constructive feedback, and giving positive reinforcement in the form of verbal praise and encouragement. The behavior therapist used these techniques to help the client overcome nervousness and anxiety about possibly getting angry and learn how to respond in an appropriately assertive way. The behavior therapist also interacted with the client in a warm and empathic manner.

Critique of Behavior Therapy: Strengths and Weaknesses

Behavior therapy has several strengths (see Corey 2009, 259–66; Fall, Holden, and Marquis 2004, 291–95; Parrott 2003, 289–91; Prochaska and Norcross 2010, 287–90), many of which are similar to the strengths of reality therapy, covered in the previous chapter of this book. First, behavior therapy is a versatile and comprehensive approach to therapy that has been applied to diverse populations including children, adolescents, adults, and older adults; in various settings such as schools, hospitals, rehabilitation centers, residential homes, clinics, private practice offices, prisons, and private homes; and for a wide range of clinical problems (see Kazdin 2001; Miltenberger 2008; Spiegler and Guevremont 2003; Wilson 2008). Behavior therapy is usually relatively short-term and is therefore also consistent with managed care's emphasis on effective short-term treatments and brief therapy.

Second, behavior therapy is a concrete and specific approach to therapy that focuses on particular behavioral goals set by the client and how to achieve them, using the most empirically supported or effective behavioral and cognitive-behavioral interventions. Behavior therapists engage in regular monitoring and measurement of client progress toward desirable therapeutic or behavioral change. It is an approach to therapy that is accountable and focused on achieving the goals of the client in a clear and measurable way.

Third, behavior therapy primarily addresses the current environmental situation and the problems or symptoms of the client, with emphasis on making specific behavioral changes according to the goals and needs of the client. It is therefore a good corrective to other approaches to therapy that may focus too much on the past or on exploration of feelings and achievement of insight, without sufficient attention to present environmental conditions affecting the client and actual behavioral change.

Fourth, behavior therapy emphasizes client choice in setting the goals for therapy, although it is not an existential approach to therapy, like reality therapy or existential therapy, that makes one's freedom to choose, in an authentic and responsible way, an all-pervasive capacity and necessity for every human being. Although behavior therapy does not overemphasize choice as reality therapy tends to do, it does empower clients to choose their own goals for therapy.

Fifth, behavior therapy is open to the use of psychiatric medications for certain severe psychological disorders such as major depressive disorder, bipolar disorder, and schizophrenia, unlike Glasser's extreme and radical stance against the use of psychiatric medications in treating such disorders due to his overemphasis on client choice, even asserting that people choose their symptoms and misery and suffering (W. Glasser 2003). Behavior therapists have explored the use of combined treatments for certain clinical problems, such as antidepressants with behavior therapy including exposure therapy for helping clients with obsessive-compulsive disorder (OCD) (see Prochaska and Norcross 2010, 282–83).

Sixth, behavior therapy is a unique approach that offers a wide array, or armamentarium, of therapeutic interventions and techniques to help clients with many different types of psychological and behavioral disorders, with empirical support for the effectiveness of the majority of the techniques. Clients who want specific and effective help to overcome particular problems or symptoms including somatic symptoms (e.g., hypertension, migraine headaches, irritable bowel syndrome) and psychological symptoms (e.g., anxiety disorders, depression, eating disorders) can get it from behavior therapists who have developed effective therapeutic interventions and techniques for treating such problems (Prochaska and Norcross 2010, 287).

Seventh, behavior therapy takes empirical research very seriously and subjects its techniques and therapeutic interventions to controlled outcome studies as much as possible. It is therefore, together with cognitive behavior therapy, the most empirically supported approach to therapy today.

Finally, behavior therapy can be easily used with clients from different cultures and countries in a multicultural counseling context because it focuses on treating symptoms and problems that cut across cultures. It also gives clients the freedom to choose their own goals in a culturally sensitive way. It is a problem-solving approach to therapy that is direct, systematic, and relatively short-term without the need for much introspection and exploration of the past. Behavior therapy and cognitive behavior therapy, with some modification and adaptation, can be especially helpful with ethnic minority clients (see Hays and Iwamasa 2006), including Chinese American clients (Chen and Davenport 2005). There is now some accumulating research evidence supporting the effectiveness of cognitive-behavioral therapy with adult ethnic minority clients (Voss Horrell 2008; see also Miranda et al. 2005).

Behavior therapy also has several limitations and weaknesses. First, it tends to treat symptoms and problems rather than focus holistically on the whole person of the client. It can therefore be conducted in a mechanistic way, without adequate attention to the person and the life context of the client. However, contemporary behavior therapy tends to be more comprehensive in its behavioral assessment of the client and his or her life context (see, e.g., Lazarus 1976, 1989, 1997; Wilson 2008).

Second, behavior therapists emphasize their techniques and empirically supported interventions more than the therapeutic relationship with clients, although they do acknowledge the importance of having a warm, empathic, and supportive relationship with the client (see Wilson 2008). Again, the danger exists for behavior therapy to be conducted in a mechanistic way that is not sufficiently sensitive to the intricacies and complexities of the therapeutic relationship between the behavior therapist and the client. However, behavior therapists and cognitive behavior therapists have recently begun paying more attention to the importance of the therapeutic relationship in the cognitive-behavioral therapies (see P. Gilbert and Leahy 2007; see also Safran and Segal 1990).

Third, behavior therapy does not adequately focus on the past and its unresolved issues or painful memories, since it is a problem-solving approach that mainly treats the presenting problems and current symptoms of the client. Some clients will need more time to process and deal with past issues and pain than behavior therapists typically provide.

Fourth, behavior therapy is still based mainly on social learning or social cognitive theory. It tends to ignore unconscious processes such as transference and dreams, which can be rich sources of helpful insights for clients and for facilitating further therapeutic change. Behavior therapists and cognitive behavior therapists, however, have tried to deal with such unconscious processes and dreams but within a cognitive-behavioral framework of understanding rather than from a psychodynamic or psychoanalytic perspective (see, e.g., K. S. Bowers and Meichenbaum 1984; Rosner, Lyddon, and Freeman 2003).

Fifth, behavior therapy does not adequately deal with existential issues, which some clients may be struggling with, such as seeking meaning in life, choosing authentic values, and overcoming the fear of death. Furthermore, traditional secular behavior therapy also does not seriously incorporate spirituality and religion, which may be of crucial importance to religious clients. However, significant attempts and advances have been made in recent years to develop a more spiritually oriented behavior therapy (see, e.g., W. R. Miller and Martin 1988) or cognitive-behavioral therapy (see, e.g., Tan 1987a; Tan and Johnson 2005; see also Propst 1988) that seriously integrates religion and spirituality into therapy. The third wave of behavior therapy also includes approaches such as DBT, MBCT, and ACT that are mindfulness based and acceptance based (Hayes, Follette, and Linehan 2004), centered in some form of contemplative or meditative spirituality, usually within a Zen Buddhist framework (but it can also be some other religious framework such as Roman Catholic or Eastern Orthodox).

Sixth, behavior therapy is a directive and systematic approach to therapy in which the behavior therapist functions as a coach, trainer, teacher, consultant, and role model in helping the client to achieve his or her therapeutic goals. There is a real danger of the behavior therapist acting like an expert and ultimately influencing the client with the therapist's own values, or even worse, imposing the therapist's values on the client, a potential ethical problem that also plagues other directive therapies such as reality therapy (see Wubbolding 2008). Behavior therapists try to avoid this potential danger by encouraging the client to actively participate in therapy and to choose his or her own treatment goals (Wilson 2008).

Seventh, behavior therapy techniques can be simplistically and easily misused and abused by inadequately trained or inexperienced therapists. Some behavioral interventions such as flooding and in vivo exposure require adequate training and careful clinical supervision before therapists make independent attempts to conduct them. Proper training and supervision in behavior therapy are therefore needed for the competent and ethical use of behavior therapy techniques.

Eighth, although behavior therapy can be adapted for effective use with clients from other cultures and countries, it may still not be sensitive enough to the larger sociopolitical and environmental contexts within which clients live. In other words, behavior therapists may still pay too much and too narrow attention to the client and his or her symptoms and target complaints, without adequately considering factors such as discrimination, oppression, and marginalization in the larger sociopolitical context of the client's life, which can have a substantial negative impact on the client's functioning. The client may need to be empowered to deal more directly with factors such as discrimination and oppression.

Finally, behavior therapists may not be sensitive enough to the possibility that successful behavioral change in the client may negatively impact those around him or her, even though the client's own treatment goals may be achieved (e.g., becoming more assertive). Conflicts between the client's goals and the cultural and social values of significant others in his or her life will require more attention and sensitivity on the part of the behavior therapist working with such clients in a multicultural counseling context or from a diversity perspective (see Corey 2009, 260).

A Biblical Perspective on Behavior Therapy

Behavior therapy has both strengths and weaknesses from a biblical perspective (Tan 1987a; see also Browning and Cooper 2004, 86–105; S. L. Jones and Butman 1991, 154–70).

First, behavior therapy or behavior modification, in its earlier version, was more deterministic and naturalistic in its basic philosophy, following Skinner and his radical behaviorism, which had no place for human free will. This version also had no place for transcendence and the supernatural since behavioral approaches to therapy tend to be reductionistic in their naturalistic and materialistic assumptions (S. L. Jones and Butman 1991). These earlier philosophical assumptions of behavior therapy are problematic from a biblical perspective, which assumes at least some free will and freedom to choose for human beings (see Josh. 24:15; Luke 13:3). The Bible also affirms self-transcendence and the reality of God and the supernatural, including eternity. However, more recent versions of behavior therapy are based more on Bandura's social cognitive theory, which includes reciprocal determinism that allows for some limited degree of free will and choice on the part of the individual person. There have also been serious attempts to integrate religion and spirituality, including transcendence and the supernatural, into behavior therapy (e.g., W. R. Miller and Martin 1988) and cognitive behavior therapy (e.g., Tan 1987a; Tan and Johnson 2005; see also Propst 1988).

Second, behavior therapy's emphasis on environmental control on human behavior and the importance of conditioning, including operant conditioning and reinforcement contingencies, is a good reminder of how human beings are not totally free, even as creatures made in the image of God the creator (Gen. 1:26–27). Being human means that our nature also has an animal side that is subject to conditioning to a certain extent (see Bufford 1981; Browning and Cooper 2004; S. L. Jones and Butman 1991). The Bible also talks about rewards and incentives, but it has a higher ultimate view of eternal rewards to come in heaven that transcends immediate gratification or positive reinforcement of specific behaviors now. Paul can therefore talk about enduring and even embracing present suffering and trials in anticipation of future glory and eternal joy in heaven (see Rom. 8:18; 2 Cor. 4:16–18). Although we are creatures with conditioned habits, we are not totally conditioned. We are also created in the image of God (Gen. 1:26–27), with some freedom to choose, although our capacity to choose is not absolute, as existential therapists and reality therapists may want us to believe. Behavior therapists have correctly reminded us of our limited freedom to choose.

Third, behavior therapists' empowerment of clients to choose their own goals, based on their own values, is a good corrective to the potential danger of imposing the therapist's values and goals on the client because behavior therapy is such a directive approach to therapy. However, ultimate values from a biblical perspective can only come from God and his inspired Word or the Scriptures (2 Tim. 3:16).

Fourth, behavior therapy's focus on powerful and effective techniques of behavior change can result in not only self-efficacy but also sinful self-sufficiency and overdependency on one's skills to cope effectively with the problems in one's life. A biblical perspective will emphasize instead sufficiency and strength in Christ (Phil. 4:13) and dependence on the filling and power of the Holy Spirit (Zech. 4:6; Eph. 5:18) in bringing about lasting behavioral change.

Fifth, behavior therapy's emphasis on techniques of behavior change may not focus enough attention on the therapeutic relationship, although recently there have been more deliberate attempts to make the therapeutic relationship more central in behavior therapy and cognitive behavior therapy (see, e.g., P. Gilbert and Leahy 2007; see also Safran and Segal 1990). A biblical perspective will emphasize the primacy of agape love (1 Cor. 13) in the therapeutic relationship and the importance of establishing a warm, empathic, and genuine relationship with the client.

Sixth, behavior therapy tends to focus on current symptoms and the presenting problems of the client, with less attention paid to the past. Although this emphasis is a good corrective to the endless exploring of past issues and experiences, a biblical perspective will nevertheless deal more adequately with the past, especially with unresolved developmental issues and painful memories, and include the judicious use of the healing of memories or inner-healing prayer when appropriate (see Tan 2003b, 2007b).

Seventh, behavior therapy does not pay much attention to unconscious processes, including the darker, fallen side of human nature, which is capable of sin and evil, as well as more complex internal conflicts, in what the Bible calls the inner "heart" of a person (see Jer. 17:9; Rom. 3:23). A biblical perspective will deal with such complex struggles, including unconscious conflicts, more adequately.

Eighth, one of behavior therapy's major techniques is exposure therapy for treating various anxiety disorders. The Bible also emphasizes the need to confront the truth in order to be set free (cf. John 8:32), and exposure therapy is consistent with this teaching, which also underscores the need for cognitive restructuring and renewal of the mind (Rom. 12:1–2) using biblical truth in cognitive behavior therapy (Tan 1987a).

Ninth, behavior therapy needs to focus more on larger contextual factors such as familial, social, religious, cultural, and even political influences affecting a particular client's life and functioning. A biblical perspective will emphasize the need to make use of community resources in therapeutic interventions with a client, including the church as a body of believers available for mutual support, help, and ministry to one another (1 Cor. 12; 1 Pet. 2:5, 9).

Finally, behavior therapy's hallmark of subjecting its techniques to controlled outcome research and using empirically supported therapeutic interventions is a strength that can be appreciated. However, from a biblical perspective, empirical support cannot be accepted as the ultimate criterion for using specific behavioral or other therapeutic techniques. A Christian therapist will not simply use whatever works. The therapeutic interventions chosen for use must ultimately be consistent with biblical truth, morality, and ethics. Furthermore, the amelioration or reduction of symptoms and emotional suffering is not the ultimate goal of therapy from a biblical perspective. The ultimate goal of Christian therapy or counseling is more transcendent and eternal, centered in becoming more Christlike (Rom. 8:29) and therefore in holiness rather than simply in happiness. This perspective means that some temporal suffering has ultimate meaning (cf. Rom. 8:18; 2 Cor. 4:16–18).

Research: Empirical Status of Behavior Therapy

One of the hallmarks of behavior therapy is its emphasis on empirical research, especially controlled outcome studies or randomized clinical trials (RCTs). Behavior therapy and cognitive behavior therapy have therefore been subjected to more controlled outcome studies than other approaches to therapy. Close to two-thirds of controlled outcome studies on therapy with children and adolescents have involved behavior therapy interventions (Kazdin 1991; Weisz, Hawley, and Doss 2004), and a majority of such studies with adults have involved behavioral and cognitive-behavioral interventions (Grawe, Donati, and Bernauer 1998; Wampold 2001).

Prochaska and Norcross (2010, 277–87) have provided a helpful overview of the many meta-analyses that have evaluated the effectiveness of behavior therapy in general as well as several specific behavior therapy interventions, and a few clinical disorders in particular, which will now be briefly summarized. Meta-analyses of controlled outcome studies on the effectiveness of *behavior therapy with children and youth* (covering the behavioral methods of operant conditioning [e.g., reinforcement], desensitization/relaxation, modeling, social skills training, cognitive-behavioral, and multiple behavioral) showed effect sizes indicating the greater effectiveness of behavior therapy compared to placebo treatment and no treatment. Behavior therapy has also been found to be more effective than other treatments such as insight-oriented therapy and play therapy (see Weiss, Hawley, and Doss 2004). Meta-analyses of controlled outcome studies on the effectiveness of *behavior therapy with adults* (covering behavioral methods of rehearsal and self-control, covert behavioral, relaxation, desensitization, reinforcement, modeling, and social skills training) have yielded large effect sizes demonstrating the superiority of behavior therapy over no treatment and placebo treatment (see Shapiro and Shapiro 1982). An extensive meta-analysis of controlled outcome studies (Grawe, Donati, and Bernauer 1998) found positive and substantial effect sizes for behavior therapy and cognitive-behavioral therapy (e.g., social skills training, stress inoculation, and problem-solving therapy), which indicated their superiority over control treatments as well as their superiority over psychodynamic treatments when direct comparisons were conducted. More specifically, Thomas Bowers and George Clum (1988) found that the specific effects of behavior therapies were double the nonspecific effects of placebo treatments.

Meta-analyses of controlled outcome studies on the effectiveness of *behavior therapy with couples*, called behavioral marital therapy (BMT) (e.g., communication skills training, problem-solving training, and modification of dysfunctional relationship attributions and expectations), have shown BMT to be significantly more effective than no treatment (see Hahlweg and Markman 1988; Dunn and Schewebel 1995; Shadish and Baldwin 2005). The effectiveness of *behavior therapy with families*, or behavioral family therapy, has also been supported by a meta-analysis of controlled outcome studies (Shadish and Baldwin 2003) that yielded moderate to large effect sizes for behavioral family therapy, thus indicating its superiority over no treatment and control treatment and at times even over other nonbehavioral approaches to family therapy (see Prochaska and Norcross 2010, 279).

Prochaska and Norcross also reviewed meta-analyses of controlled outcome studies on the effectiveness of specific behavioral methods such as relaxation training, social skills training, stress inoculation, biofeedback, behavioral activation, self-statement modification, contingency management, behavioral parent training, and problem solving, mainly with positive results showing their superiority over no treatment or control conditions (2010, 280–82). They further reviewed meta-analyses of controlled outcome studies on the effectiveness of behavior therapy for specific disorders such as obsessive-compulsive disorder (OCD), panic disorder, mental retardation, eating disorders, attention-deficit hyperactivity disorder (ADHD), schizophrenia, anger disorders, cigarette smoking, nocturnal enuresis (bed-wetting at night), hypertension, migraine headache, insomnia, and irritable bowel syndrome, mainly with positive results (282–87). The results of several RCTs also showed that DBT in particular is an effective treatment for borderline personality disorder and better than no treatment or treatment as usual (283).

The controlled outcome research therefore shows that behavior therapy and cognitive-behavioral therapy are often effective in treating both psychological symptoms (e.g., anxiety, depression, eating disorders) and somatic symptoms (e.g., hypertension, migraine headaches, irritable bowel syndrome). Behavior therapy is an effective treatment not only for psychological or mental disorders but also for some general health conditions.

Prochaska and Norcross also reviewed the controlled outcome research on the effectiveness of three exposure therapies: implosive therapy, exposure therapy, and eye movement desensitization and reprocessing (EMDR). Implosive therapy has been found to be significantly better than no treatment and placebo treatment, and equally effective, if not better, than certain other therapies (see 2010, 228). Exposure therapy has been shown to be an effective treatment and one of the treatments of choice for posttraumatic stress disorder (PTSD), obsessive-compulsive disorder (OCD), social phobia, and other anxiety disorders, with greater effectiveness than no treatment and several other treatments, and greater or similar effectiveness when compared to pharmacotherapy or medications (see 228–31). Finally, EMDR has been found to be an effective treatment, especially for PTSD, comparable to exposure therapy and better than no treatment and nonexposure therapies (see

236–37). However, the eye movements in EMDR may not be necessary for its effectiveness, which may be mainly due to the exposure component of this treatment, with further research needed to clarify the essential components of EMDR responsible for its effectiveness (see Perkins and Rouanzoin 2002). A recent meta-analysis of thirty-three randomized therapy studies involving psychological approaches in the treatment of specific phobias showed exposure based treatments to be superior over other treatments (Wolitzky-Taylor, Horowitz, Powers, and Telch 2008).

Wilson (2008, 246–51) has also recently reviewed the research evidence supporting the effectiveness of behavior therapy for a wide range of psychological disorders in various populations and settings, including education, medicine, and community living. He included behavior therapy for anxiety disorders (e.g., panic disorder, OCD, PTSD), depression (especially the use of behavioral activation), eating and weight disorders (e.g., binge eating and bulimia nervosa, obesity), schizophrenia, childhood disorders, behavioral medicine, prevention and treatment of cardiovascular disease, and other applications to diverse health-related problems (e.g., headaches, pain conditions, asthma, epilepsy, sleep disorders, nausea reactions in cancer patients receiving radiation treatment, children's fears regarding hospitalization and surgery, and treatment compliance).

Wilson (2008) noted that the most thorough and rigorous evaluations of both psychological and pharmacological treatments and their effectiveness or efficacy for various clinical disorders are those done by the National Institute for Clinical Excellence (NICE) in the United Kingdom (see, e.g., National Institute for Clinical Excellence 2004). Treatment guidelines issued by NICE, based on research data, are graded from A (with rigorous empirical support from well-controlled RCTs) to C (with expert opinion and strong empirical data). Behavior therapy has done very well, usually receiving A ratings from the NICE evaluations. Behavioral interventions are recommended by NICE as the psychological treatments of choice for specific anxiety and mood disorders and evaluated as being equivalent to pharmacological treatment in effectiveness. Behavior therapy has also been rated as more effective than medication for eating disorders (Wilson and Shafran 2005).

Behavior therapy has also fared very well in the list of empirically supported treatments first established in 1995 by Division 12 (Society of Clinical Psychology) of the American Psychological Association, still dominating a recent update of such a list together with cognitive behavior therapy (see Woody, Weisz, and McLean 2005). More-recent third-wave versions of behavior therapy are receiving more empirical support for their therapeutic effectiveness, such as DBT for borderline personality disorder (Linehan et al. 2006), and ACT as a promising treatment but still needing further research and empirical support from additional controlled outcome studies (Hayes et al. 2006). A more recent meta-analytic review of mindfulness-based therapy (e.g., MBSR, MBCT) that included thirty-nine studies involving a total of 1,140 participants found robust effect sizes for improving anxiety and mood symptoms in patients with anxiety and mood disorders (Hofmann, Sawyer, Witt, and Oh 2010). Wilson (2008) notes that recent research has shown that behavior therapy is also effective in real-life community-based clinical settings (e.g., Foa et al. 2005; see also Van Ingen, Freiheit, and Vye 2009; Stewart and Chambless 2009) and with ethnic minority clients (e.g., Miranda et al. 2005; see also Voss Horrell 2008).

Behavior therapy is therefore the most empirically researched approach to therapy and also the most empirically supported treatment (together with cognitive behavior therapy) available today. Its empirical status is substantial and solid, and it will continue to be the most empirically studied of all the major approaches to therapy.

Future Directions

Behavior therapy is still a significant primary theoretical orientation of psychotherapists surveyed in the United States as evidenced in the following percentages of therapists indicating it as such (see Prochaska and Norcross 2010, 3): clinical psychologists (10 percent), counseling psychologists (5 percent), social workers (11 percent), and counselors (8 percent). Behavioral interventions are also often used by therapists who indicate cognitive therapy or eclectic/integrative therapy as their primary theoretical orientation.

The Association for Advancement of Behavior Therapy (AABT), founded in 1966 in the United States as a multidisciplinary group interested in behavior therapy (Glass and Arnkoff 1992, 597), changed its name in 2005 to the Association for Behavioral and Cognitive Therapies (ABCT), reflecting the trend of behavior therapy toward a more cognitive-behavioral orientation. It has a membership of over 4,500, consisting of psychologists and other mental health professionals and students with an interest in behavior therapy, cognitive behavior therapy, behavioral assessment, and applied behavioral analysis. It publishes two journals, *Behavior Therapy* and *Cognitive and Behavioral Practice*, and a newsletter, the *Behavior Therapist*. Further information about training in behavior therapy and membership in ABCT can be obtained through its Web site (www.abct.org) (see Corey 2009, 266).

There are now numerous behavior therapy societies and organizations worldwide, including the European Association of Behaviour Therapy, which has organized annual conferences in different European countries since 1970. Their tenth annual meeting, held in Jerusalem, became the first World Congress in Behavior Therapy. Since the publication of *Behaviour Research and Therapy* as the first journal solely devoted to behavior therapy in 1963, the number of journals focusing primarily or solely on behavior therapy and its various offshoots now exceed fifty (Fishman and Franks 1992, 169). It should be noted that another major behavioral organization in the United States, the Association for Behavior Analysis International (www.abainternational.org), focuses on the application of Skinner's operant conditioning approach and resists the development of behavior therapy toward a more cognitive-behavioral orientation (Fishman and Franks 1992, 169).

Wilson (2008) has described two major challenges to behavior therapy in the twenty-first century. The first challenge is to spread the use of empirically supported behavioral interventions and techniques for various common clinical disorders more widely and effectively, with the concomitant need to further develop simpler behavioral methods so that more mental health professionals can easily learn to use them. The second challenge is to develop even more effective behavioral treatments for a wider range of clinical problems, with a focus on determining why they work. Wilson also emphasizes the need for behavior therapy to be more rooted in the latest developments in experimental psychology as well as biology, especially in the areas of genetics and neuroscience. Behavior therapists must better understand brain mechanisms and their impact on clinical disorders (e.g., Baxter et al. 1992) so that they can develop more-sophisticated theories and more-effective behavioral treatments to enable behavior change.

Prochaska and Norcross (2010) have predicted that behavior therapy will continue to expand and grow in many directions in the coming years as one of the premier contemporary approaches to therapy. They anticipate two future directions for behavior therapy that will be more enduring. The first involves the greater integration of behavior therapy and its many effective techniques for behavioral change into health-care practice and the health-care system, focusing on not only mental health problems but also medical problems, including those encountered in the fields of pediatrics and cardiology. The second involves the more widespread use of acceptance-based versions of third-wave behavior therapy (see, e.g., Hayes, Follette, and Linehan 2004; Roemer and Orsillo 2009). Both behavior therapists and their clients will come to more realistic terms about what can be changed and what cannot, and therefore what should be accepted with gentleness and openness. Furthermore, a growing emphasis on mindfulness and acceptance in general in behavior therapy may paradoxically lead to increased therapeutic results. The third wave of behavior therapy will continue to develop in significant and exciting ways in the years ahead.

Recommended Readings

Barlow, D. H. (Ed.). (2008). *Clinical handbook of psychological disorders: A step-by-step treatment manual* (4th ed.). New York: Guilford Press.

Goldfried, M. R., & Davison, G. C. (1994). *Clinical behavior therapy* (Expanded ed.). New York: Wiley.

Kazdin, A. E. (2001). *Behavior modification in applied settings* (6th ed.). Pacific Grove, CA: Brooks/Cole.

Miltenberger, R. G. (2008). *Behavior modification: Principles and procedures* (4th ed.). Belmont, CA: Wadsworth.

Roemer, L., & Orsillo, S. M. (2009). *Mindfulness- and acceptance-based behavioral therapies in practice*. New York: Guilford Press.

Spiegler, M. D., & Guevremont, D. C. (2003). *Contemporary behavior therapy* (4th ed.). Belmont, CA: Wadsworth.

12

Cognitive Behavior Therapy and Rational Emotive Behavior Therapy

ognitive behavior therapy (CBT) has been defined as "a more purposeful attempt to preserve the demonstrated efficiencies of behavior modification within a less doctrinaire context, and to incorporate the cognitive activities of the client in the efforts to produce therapeutic change" (Kendall and Hollon 1979, 1). Much of contemporary behavior therapy, as noted in the previous chapter, has become cognitive-behavioral in orientation and approach. The three major approaches to CBT are *cognitive therapy* (CT), founded by Aaron Beck; *rational emotive behavior therapy* (REBT), founded by Albert Ellis; and to a lesser extent, *cognitive behavior modification* (CBM) including *stress inoculation training* (SIT), developed by Donald Meichenbaum.

Beck's cognitive therapy approach emphasizes how maladaptive and dysfunctional thinking affects feelings and behavior. It helps clients overcome emotional problems such as depression, anxiety, and anger by teaching them to identify, challenge, and modify errors in thinking or cognitive distortions (A. T. Beck 1976). Similarly, Ellis developed REBT as an active and directive approach to therapy that focuses on helping clients change their irrational beliefs, which are viewed as the root of emotional problems (Ellis 1962). Meichenbaum's CBM and SIT approach, with its emphasis on self-talk and other coping skills in teaching clients to more effectively manage stress and other emotional problems (Meichenbaum 1977), has already been briefly described in the previous chapter on behavior therapy.

Besides Beck, Ellis, and Meichenbaum, other important figures in the earlier development of cognitive behavior therapy based on integrating cognitive mediational constructs with behavioral theory include Albert Bandura (1977a, 1977b), Marvin Goldfried (see Goldfried and Merbaum 1973), George Kelly (1955), Arnold Lazarus (1976, 1981), Michael Mahoney (1974), Walter Mischel (1973), Lynn Rehm (1977), and Martin Seligman (1975); Kelly's (1955) personal construct theory of emotional disorders was a crucial forerunner of CT and CBT (see Reinecke and Freeman 2003, 227).

CBT, including CT, REBT, and CBM, tends to have a neutral view of human nature, but it does assume that clients have the capacity to change their maladaptive thinking and hence to change problem feelings and behaviors. CBT has been earlier described as consisting of *cognitive learning therapies* (Mahoney and Arnkoff 1978) that include three major categories: (1) *cognitive restructuring* (helping clients to change or modify maladaptive, dysfunctional thoughts); (2) *coping skills therapies* (helping clients use cognitive and behavioral skills to cope more effectively with stressful situations); and (3) *problem-solving therapies* (helping clients explore options and implement particular solutions to specific problems and challenges). More specifically, REBT employs cognitive-behavioral techniques such as the *use of the A-B-C theory of REBT* (**A** refers to **A**ctivating Events, **B** to **I**rrational **B**eliefs, and **C** to **C**onsequences, emotional and/or behavioral, of such beliefs), with the client keeping an A-B-C diary of daily experiences; disputation of irrational beliefs; and action homework.

Biographical Sketches of Key Figures in Cognitive Behavior Therapy

As with behavior therapy, cognitive behavior therapy has no single founder. However, there are at least three major figures in CBT: Aaron Beck, the founder of CT; Albert Ellis, the founder of REBT; and Donald Meichenbaum, who developed CBM and SIT. Donald Meichenbaum's biographical sketch appears in the previous chapter on behavior therapy. Biographical sketches of Aaron Beck and Albert Ellis will now be provided (see Corey 2009, 273–74; Fall, Holden, and Marquis 2004, 300–301, 337–38; Prochaska and Norcross 2010, 296–97, 312–13; Sharf 2008, 300–302; 334–35; see also Ellis 2004, 2008; Padesky 2004; Weiner 1988; Weishaar 1993; Yankura and Dryden 1994).

Aaron Temkin Beck, the founder of cognitive therapy, was born on July 18, 1921, in Providence, Rhode Island, the youngest child of Jewish immigrant parents from Russia. He had a difficult childhood that included breaking his arm when he was seven years old, which resulted in a bone and blood infection requiring major surgery that brought him close to death. As a result, he developed several fears and phobias, such as blood/injury phobia and public speaking anxiety. He also had to cope with an emotionally unstable mother who struggled with depression as well as an abusive teacher in first grade. Such childhood experiences helped him to have a special sensitivity toward others and their unpredictable changes in mood (Weishaar 1993).

Beck was able to overcome problems in school resulting from his health issues and ultimately did excellent academic work. One of his high school friends nicknamed him "Tim," from his middle name, Temkin, and his wife and close friends have continued to use this nickname (Weishaar 1993, 11).

Beck graduated from high school first in his class. While attending Brown University, he met Phyllis Whitman, who eventually became a Pennsylvania Superior Court judge. Whitman and Beck married in 1950. Beck graduated from Brown in 1942 and then entered Yale University School of Medicine, where he obtained his MD degree in 1946. He then trained in pathology and neurology but eventually completed his residency training in psychiatry. Beck was certified in psychiatry by the American Board of Psychiatry and Neurology in 1953. He received further training in psychoanalysis and graduated from the Philadelphia Psychoanalytic Institute in 1956.

Beck became a faculty member in the Department of Psychiatry at the University of Pennsylvania Medical School in 1954, where he is now University Professor Emeritus of Psychiatry. He is also president of the Beck Institute for Cognitive Therapy and Research in Bala Cynwyd, Pennsylvania, and honorary president of the Academy of Cognitive Therapy, which is responsible for certifying cognitive therapists with appropriate qualifications. Although Beck initially tried to validate some of Freud's psychoanalytic views on depression, he eventually parted ways with his Freudian psychoanalytic training and background. He developed his own unique approach to treating depression and other emotional disorders that focused on modifying dysfunctional thinking, involving cognitive errors or distortions, as a root cause of such disorders. Beck is thus the founder of cognitive therapy (A. T. Beck 1961, 1963, 1964, 1967, 1976), which has become a major approach to therapy and a crucial part of contemporary cognitive behavior therapy. He has authored or coauthored over five hundred articles and more than twenty-five books on cognitive therapy and the treatment of a wide range of emotional disorders (Sharf 2008, 334), including depression, bipolar disorder, anxiety disorders and phobias, suicidality, alcoholism and substance abuse, eating disorders, marital problems and relationship difficulties, schizophrenia and psychotic disorders, personality disorders, pain and anger, hostility and violence problems (see, e.g., A. T. Beck 1988, 1999; A. T. Beck and Emery, with Greenberg 1985; A. T. Beck, Freeman, Davis, and associates 2003; A. T. Beck, Rector, Stolar, and Grant 2009; A. T. Beck, Rush, Shaw, and Emery 1979; A. T. Beck, Wright, Newman, and Liese 1993; Clark and Beck 2009; Newman et al. 2001; Wenzel, Brown, and Beck 2009; Winterowd, Beck, and Gruener 2003; Wright, Thase, Beck, and Ludgate 1993; see also Fairburn 2008; Leahy 2004; Scott, Williams, and Beck 1989). He has also developed several widely used assessment scales such as those for depression, suicidal risk, and anxiety (Corey 2009, 274). Cognitive therapy, as a substantial part of cognitive behavior therapy, is one of the most empirically supported therapies today (see Butler, Chapman, Forman, and Beck 2006).

Beck and his wife, Phyllis, have four children. Their daughter, Judith Beck, is also a well-known figure in contemporary cognitive therapy (see J. S. Beck 1995, 2005). She is currently the director of the Beck Institute for Cognitive Therapy and Research and clinical associate professor of psychology in psychiatry at the University of Pennsylvania.

Beck has made substantial and revolutionary conceptual and empirical contributions to cognitive therapy and the treatment of various emotional disorders that have greatly impacted the field of psychiatry and psychotherapy. He has been awarded more than twenty-five prestigious awards of special recognition, four of them lifetime achievement awards (Padesky 2004, 3). In 2006, he won the Lasker Prize, an outstanding award that some consider America's Nobel Prize, for his development of cognitive therapy (Kellogg and Young 2008, 73). He has also been recognized as one of the ten most influential psychotherapists (see Fall, Holden, and Marquis 2004, 301), and is the only psychiatrist today to have been awarded the highest research awards from the American Psychiatric Association as well as the American Psychological Association (Weishaar 1993, 43). His achievements are all the more amazing given his earlier struggles with childhood difficulties, health problems, and fears and phobias, as well as the initial negative reactions of many psychiatrists and therapists to his novel cognitive therapy ideas.

Beck continues to help further develop cognitive therapy and its applications to an ever-widening range of emotional and psychological disorders. His vision for the cognitive therapy community is that it become global, inclusive, collaborative, empowering, and benevolent. Beck has always had an international or global vision for cognitive therapy; he hosted the first World Congress of Cognitive Therapy in Philadelphia, inspiring the formation of the International Association of Cognitive Psychotherapy, and helped to establish the global Academy of Cognitive Therapy, which certifies appropriately qualified cognitive therapists. He was never interested in setting up a solely American cognitive therapy association (Padesky 2004, 17).

Albert Ellis, the founder of rational emotive therapy (RET), now called rational emotive behavior therapy (REBT), was born to a Jewish family on September 27, 1913, in Pittsburgh, Pennsylvania, but the family moved to New York City when he was four years old. His father was a businessman who was often away from home, and his mother was emotionally absent and neglected the family. The oldest of three children, Ellis learned to be independent at a young age and took care of his siblings as well as himself. He was frequently sick as a child, mainly with kidney problems, and was hospitalized nine times.

He developed renal glycosuria when he was nineteen years old and diabetes when he was forty. Ellis developed and applied REBT principles and methods to himself in effectively coping with his medical problems, family difficulties, and personal fears (e.g., of rejection by women and of public speaking), and was able to live a full and energetic life until the last two years, which were overshadowed by serious illness.

Ellis completed his undergraduate studies at City College of New York and received a BA degree in business in 1934. He had a short career in business and also tried writing fiction for a while but without success. He then began graduate studies in clinical psychology at Teachers College, Columbia University, in 1942. He earned his PhD in 1947, after training primarily in Freudian psychoanalytic therapy. He acquired further psychoanalytic training by undergoing his own personal analysis with Richard Hulbeck, a psychiatrist who had undergone analysis with Hermann Rorschach, the developer of the well-known Rorschach inkblot test. Hulbeck also supervised Ellis in his early psychoanalytic work. From 1947 to 1953, Ellis practiced psychoanalysis and psychoanalytic therapy but became dissatisfied with Freud's approach to therapy and its inefficiency and ineffectiveness with many clients. This experience led him to found and develop a more direct and rational approach to therapy that focused on changing clients' irrational beliefs, which he regarded as the root cause of emotional problems.

Ellis presented his first paper on what he then called *rational therapy* in 1956 at the annual convention of the American Psychological Association. He quickly changed the name of his new rational, directive approach to therapy to RET so that he would not be misunderstood as a therapist who ignored emotions or feelings (see Ellis 1962). In 1993, Ellis decided to rename his approach REBT at a two-day conference titled "A Meeting of the Minds: Is Integration Possible?" (Kernberg et al. 1993). He prefers REBT as a more accurate term than RET for his therapy approach (Ellis 1999, 2008) because of its cognitive, emotive, and behavioral components (Ellis 1993a).

Ellis had liberal views and values, advocating long-term hedonism or the maximizing of pleasure (Ellis 2008). He was antidogmatic and antireligious in his earlier years, espousing probabilistic atheism and humanism (see Ellis 1960, 1971, 1973, 1980). He was also abrasive, direct, and humorous in his flamboyant style in public presentations and workshops. He even wrote and sang humorous rational songs (Corey 2009, 273). However, in his later years, Ellis became a bit more open to the notion that some devout religious or spiritual beliefs can be healthy and consistent with REBT, but he remained skeptical of dogmatic and rigid beliefs (Ellis 2000; see also Nielsen, Johnson, and Ellis 2001).

Ellis established the Albert Ellis Institute in 1959 in New York City to disseminate the REBT approach through courses and workshops on rational living, training programs at the postgraduate level, reasonably priced clinics providing individual and group REBT, and special publications, including the *Journal of Rational-Emotive and Cognitive-Behavior Therapy*, as well as audiovisual materials. However, Ellis's relationship with the institute he had founded became strained when its board of trustees removed him from the board and relieved him of all his responsibilities at the institute in September 2005. He was reinstated after the State Supreme Court in Manhattan in January 2006 ruled that the board was wrong in dismissing Ellis at a meeting at which he was not present. In the same year the Albert Ellis Foundation was established to promote and protect REBT and Ellis's works. It is not related in any way to the Albert Ellis Institute, and Ellis stated in 2006 that the Institute was no longer following a program consistent with REBT (see Ellis 2008, 193–94).

Ellis married Debbie Joffe, an Australian psychologist, in 2004. He called her the greatest love of his life (Ellis 2008, 194). She assisted him in his work and collaborated with him as he continued to maintain his hectic schedule, often working sixteen hours a day. He saw numerous clients for therapy, engaged in prolific writing, and traveled extensively, presenting workshops and talks nationally and internationally. He authored or coauthored over eighty books and twelve hundred articles in his lifetime. However, illness forced him to slow down in the last two years of his life. Ellis died on July 24, 2007.

Ellis received numerous awards from many professional organizations, including the Award for Distinguished Professional Contributions from the American Psychological Association. He was ranked the second most influential psychotherapist in history after Carl Rogers and ahead of Sigmund Freud in a 1982 professional survey (D. Smith 1982). REBT continues to be a major and influential approach to therapy and a crucial part of contemporary cognitive behavior therapy.

Major Theoretical Ideas of Cognitive Behavior Therapy (CBT) and Rational Emotive Behavior Therapy (REBT)

Perspective on Human Nature

CBT, which includes CT, REBT, and CBM/SIT, differs from behavior therapy and behavior modification, especially those therapies following B. F. Skinner, in that it does not assume radical behaviorism and the absence of free will in human beings. CBT has a more complex view of human nature and pays more attention to how one's thoughts influence and affect one's behavior and feelings. Its perspective on human nature thus includes some capacity for choice as well as for self-reflection and self-control (Kazdin 2001; D. L. Watson and Tharp 2007). Bandura's social learning or social cognitive theory has significantly influenced CBT, with its emphasis on *self-efficacy* and *reciprocal determinism*, which assume that human beings have some degree of free will and choice and therefore a greater capacity for self-regulation (Bandura 1977a,

1977b, 1986, 1997). The CBT approach, however, still views human beings as basically neutral, neither inherently good nor inherently evil.

More specifically, Ellis's REBT approach emphasizes that one's maladaptive thinking in the form of irrational beliefs leads to emotional problems. By vigorously disputing such irrational beliefs, an individual can engage in more-constructive, rational thinking so that he or she can become less emotionally disturbed (Ellis 2008). Individuals therefore have the capacity to change their irrational thinking to more rational thinking, realizing that their ideas, attitudes, or beliefs greatly affect their feelings and experiences. Ellis (2008) acknowledges the influence of Alfred Adler (see, e.g., Adler 1964) on the development of such views in REBT.

Basic Theoretical Principles of CBT

CBT, or cognitive-behavioral interventions, has, at minimum, six basic tenets or characteristics: (1) the human organism responds primarily to cognitive representations of its environments rather than to these environments per se; (2) most human learning is cognitively mediated; (3) thoughts, feelings, and behaviors are causally interrelated; (4) attitudes, expectancies, attributions, and other cognitive activities are central to producing, predicting, and understanding

---

Sidebar 12.1

Basic Tenets of Cognitive Behavior Therapy
(Kendall and Bemis 1983, 565–66)

1. The human organism responds primarily to cognitive representations of its environments rather than to these environments per se.
2. Most human learning is cognitively mediated.
3. Thoughts, feelings, and behaviors are causally interrelated.
4. Attitudes, expectancies, attributions, and other cognitive activities are central to producing, predicting, and understanding psychopathological behavior and the effects of therapeutic interventions.
5. Cognitive processes can be cast into testable formulations that are easily integrated with behavioral paradigms, and it is possible and desirable to combine cognitive treatment strategies with enactive techniques and behavioral contingency management.
6. The task of the cognitive-behavioral therapist is to act as diagnostician, educator, and technical consultant who assesses maladaptive cognitive processes and works with the client to design learning experiences that may remediate these dysfunctional cognitions and the behavioral and affective patterns with which they correlate.

---

psychopathological behavior and the effects of therapeutic interventions; (5) cognitive processes can be cast into testable formulations that are easily integrated with behavioral paradigms, and it is possible *and* desirable to combine cognitive treatment strategies with enactive techniques and behavioral contingency management; and (6) the task of the cognitive-behavioral therapist is to act as diagnostician, educator, and technical consultant who assesses maladaptive cognitive processes and works with the client to design learning experiences that may remediate these dysfunctional cognitions and the behavioral and affective patterns with which they correlate (Kendall and Bemis 1983, 565–66).

In another earlier review of CBT approaches, Michael Mahoney and D. B. Arnkoff (1978) have described them as contemporary cognitive learning therapies in three major categories: (a) *cognitive restructuring*, including rational-emotive therapy (RET) (Ellis 1962), self-instruction (Meichenbaum 1977), and cognitive therapy (CT) (A. T. Beck 1976); (b) *coping skills therapies*, including covert modeling (Cautela 1971; Kazdin 1973), coping skills training (Goldfried 1971), anxiety management training (Suinn and Richardson 1971), and stress inoculation (Meichenbaum 1977); and (c) *problem-solving therapies*, including behavioral problem solving (D'Zurilla and Goldfried 1971), problem-solving therapy (Spivack, Platt, and Shure 1976), and personal science (Mahoney 1977). CBT therefore includes many cognitive and behavioral techniques and interventions that are subsumed under these three major categories of contemporary cognitive learning therapies.

CBT has been defined as an approach to therapy that attempts to preserve the empirically supported effectiveness and efficiency of behavior modification but in a less behavioristic context that includes the crucial role of the client's thoughts in the therapeutic process (see Kendall and Hollon 1979, 1). The basic theoretical principles of behavior therapy already covered in the previous chapter thus apply to CBT, but with more emphasis on the cognitive processes of the client and not on behavioral aspects alone, as with Wolpe's counterconditioning and Skinner's contingency management (Prochaska and Norcross 2010). CBT is therefore supposedly grounded in a more comprehensive social cognitive, or social learning, theory of human functioning and change, while incorporating operant and classical conditioning, modeling, and other, earlier learning-based principles.

More recently, the CBT tradition has been expanded in the third wave of behavior therapy to include mindfulness-based and acceptance-based therapies such as DBT, MBCT, and ACT (Hayes, Follette, and Linehan 2004; see also Hayes et al. 2006), which have been briefly covered in the previous chapter.

Development of Psychopathology

Going beyond traditional behavior therapy's view of psychopathology as consisting of conditioned or learned maladaptive habits (Wolpe 1990), contemporary CBT emphasizes the crucial role of maladaptive, irrational thinking, or cognitive distortions, in the development of psychopathology. The internal dialogues, or self-talk, of a person can lead to maladaptive behavior and feelings, especially if negative, irrational, extreme, unreasonable, and illogical thinking is present. CBT helps clients to identify, challenge, and modify such maladaptive thinking into more rational, realistic, reasonable, and logical thinking.

More specifically, *Beck's cognitive therapy (CT) approach* focuses on how an individual's *automatic thoughts* reflect his or her underlying *basic assumptions* about life and even early maladaptive *schemas* set in his or her mind because of early childhood experiences. One's automatic thoughts often contain logical errors, or *cognitive distortions*, that lead to emotional difficulties and behavioral problems. Some examples of such cognitive distortions include (see A. T. Beck and Weishaar 2008, 272) *arbitrary inference* (making a conclusion without sufficient evidence or even with contradictory evidence, e.g., a working mother, after a very busy and demanding day, says to herself, "I'm an awful mother"); *selective abstraction* (coming to a conclusion based only on a detail taken out of context while ignoring other relevant information, e.g., a man who becomes upset and jealous of his girlfriend at a party because he sees her talking to another man, who is actually her cousin); *overgeneralization* (applying a general rule from isolated incidents to other inappropriate or unrelated situations, e.g., after being turned down for a date, a man concludes, "All women are alike; I'll never get a date with any of them"); *magnification and minimization* (viewing something as much greater or significantly less than it really is, e.g., when a student catastrophizes in magnification by saying, "If I fail this test, it'll be the end of the world or a disaster for me," or a woman engages in minimization by saying, "My mother will recover soon from the infection" when her mother has terminal cancer); *personalization* (relating external events to oneself without any evidence for such a causal relationship, e.g., a man waves to a friend in a crowded mall with no response, and concludes, "I must have done something that upset him and made him dislike me"); and *dichotomous thinking* (viewing things in one of two extreme categories, such as total success or complete failure, e.g., a student concludes, "If I don't ace this exam, then I am a total failure as a student").

Beck's CT approach also describes the systematic bias in cognitively processing information that is found in specific emotional disorders (see A. T. Beck and Weishaar 2008, 273). For example, in depression, it is a negative view of self, experience, and the future, whereas in panic disorder, it is a catastrophic interpretation of bodily and/or mental experiences.

Ellis's REBT approach also emphasizes how maladaptive thinking is at the root of emotional problems. However, Ellis is more specific about the *content* of such dysfunctional thinking as consisting of the following *irrational beliefs* (Ellis 1962):

(1) It is essential that a person be loved or approved by virtually everyone in the community; (2) A person must be perfectly competent, adequate, and achieving to be considered worthwhile; (3) Some people are bad, wicked, or villainous and therefore should be blamed and punished; (4) It is a terrible catastrophe when things are not as a person wants them to be; (5) Unhappiness is caused by outside circumstances, and a person has no control over it; (6) Dangerous or fearsome things are cause for great concern, and their possibility must be continually dwelt upon; (7) It is easier to avoid certain difficulties and self-responsibilities than to face them; (8) A person should be dependent on others and should have someone stronger on whom to rely; (9) Past experiences and events are the determinants of present behavior; the influence of the past cannot be eradicated; (10) A person should be quite upset over other people's problems and disturbances; and (11) There is always a right or perfect solution to every problem, and it must be found or the results will be catastrophic. (See Day 2004, 304–5)

Ellis (2008) viewed these irrational beliefs and childish demandingness as responsible for human unhappiness and neurosis or emotional problems. REBT therefore strongly challenges clients to give up such "masturbatory" thinking consisting of terms such as "must," "should," "ought to," "have to," or "got to," and catastrophizing conclusions (see Prochaska and Norcross 2010, 300–301).

Although CT and REBT are similar in their focus on the crucial role of maladaptive, dysfunctional thinking in the development of psychopathology or emotional disorders, there are also some important differences between Beck's CT approach and Ellis's REBT. Ellis (2008, 119–200) has briefly described the following eight differences between REBT and CT: (1) REBT usually challenges clients' irrational beliefs more strongly and directly than CT; (2) REBT focuses more on absolutist or dogmatic *musts* and *shoulds* than CT; (3) REBT uses psychoeducational interventions such as books, audiovisual tapes, talks, and workshops more than CT; (4) REBT clearly differentiates between healthy negative emotions such as sadness and frustration and unhealthy negative emotions such as depression and hostility; (5) REBT uses other emotive-evocative therapeutic interventions (e.g., shame-attacking exercises, imagery, and vigorous self-talk) more than CT; (6) REBT uses in vivo desensitization and implosive techniques more than CT; (7) REBT uses penalties and rewards to motivate clients to complete their homework assignments; (8) REBT emphasizes deep philosophical acceptance of oneself, others, and the world more than CT.

Meichenbaum's cognitive behavior modification (CBM) approach, which includes stress inoculation training (SIT), also emphasizes the importance of constructive and calming self-talk as well as coping skills in effective management of emotional problems. CBM similarly views negative self-talk and a lack of coping skills as contributing to the development of psychological disorders (Meichenbaum 1977, 1985).

Therapeutic Process and Relationship

The cognitive behavior therapist, like the traditional behavior therapist, is active and directive in conducting therapy with clients. The therapist in CBT, whether CT, REBT, or CBM, functions as a diagnostician, educator, and technical consultant in helping the client to identify and change maladaptive cognitions and their correlated behavioral and affective patterns (Kendall and Bemis 1983).

The process of CBT is also similar to that of behavior therapy described in the previous chapter. It is a structured and systematic approach to therapy that begins by helping the client identify target complaints on a problem list and then set his or her own goals for therapy in collaboration with the therapist (see Persons 1989, 2008). The connections between thoughts, behaviors, and feelings are clarified, with emphasis on how thoughts affect behaviors and feelings. The cognitive behavior therapist can also choose to do a more comprehensive assessment of the client and his or her problems by using the BASIC I.D. framework from *multimodal therapy* (Lazarus 1981), covering the seven major dimensions of a person's functioning: behavior, affect, sensations, images, cognitions, interpersonal relationships, and drugs/biology.

Cognitive therapists in particular usually begin a session of CT by setting an agenda with the client as well as reviewing any homework assignments from a previous session (A. T. Beck, Rush, Shaw, and Emery 1979). Therapists conducting CBT will then help clients to deal with specific problems on their problem list by using empirically supported cognitive-behavioral interventions. Client progress is continuously assessed throughout the process of CBT, and therapeutic methods are adjusted as the therapist conducts CBT in a flexible and sensitive way. Therapy is gradually phased out as the client increasingly achieves goals, with therapy sessions reduced from weekly to once every two weeks or monthly before termination of regular therapy. Follow-up sessions at three months or six months or even longer periods after termination of regular therapy can also be conducted. Clients can always contact the therapist for an appointment if there is an emergency or a special need arises (see Reinecke and Freeman 2003, 251).

The therapeutic relationship is considered important in CBT but not as the most crucial element in effective CBT. Beck views a positive therapeutic relationship between the therapist and the client as a necessary but not sufficient condition for successful CBT or CT (A. T. Beck, Rush, Shaw, and Emery 1979). Ellis (2008), however, does not believe in the therapist having too much empathy for the client because it can be counterproductive in REBT, which requires strong, vigorous disputation of irrational beliefs and demandingness in the client in order for it to be effective. CBT therefore emphasizes the importance of specific cognitive and behavioral interventions that go beyond the therapeutic effects of a positive therapeutic relationship. A warm and collaborative therapeutic relationship is nevertheless still helpful in CBT or CT (Persons 1989), and more attention is being paid to the therapeutic relationship as a crucial factor even in these therapies (see, e.g., Safran and Segal 1990; P. Gilbert and Leahy 2007), especially in schema therapy, a specific form of CT that focuses on early maladaptive schemas and the treatment of personality disorders, including borderline personality disorder (see Kellogg and Young 2006, 2008; Young 2002; Young, Klosko, and Weishaar 2003). The major therapeutic techniques used in CBT will now be reviewed.

Major Therapeutic Techniques and Interventions

Just as there are numerous techniques and therapeutic interventions in behavior therapy, all of which can be used if and when appropriate in CBT, there are also many CBT methods available today. The traditional behavior therapy techniques have already been described in the previous chapter. The major CBT interventions include those used in cognitive restructuring, coping skills therapies, and problem solving therapies (Mahoney and Arnkoff 1978). They will now be reviewed under the following three major approaches to CBT: CT (Beck), REBT (Ellis), and CBM/SIT (Meichenbaum).

Cognitive Therapy (CT) (Beck)

Aaron Beck, the founder of CT, works in a collaborative and respectful way with clients (J. Sommers-Flanagan and Sommers-Flanagan 2004, 262) that is called *collaborative empiricism*, or mutual working together to help clients identify and change their cognitive distortions (A. T. Beck, Rush, Shaw, and Emery 1979; see also Kuyken, Padesky, and Dudley 2009). Beck's approach is gentler than Albert Ellis's REBT approach, in which Ellis is often much more forceful and disputational in vigorous dialogue and even debate with clients to help them challenge their irrational beliefs. Beck does not have a predetermined set of irrational beliefs. Instead, he helps clients discover and modify cognitive distortions by engaging in Socratic dialogue with them that often includes the use of open-ended questions.

CT has various *cognitive* and *behavioral* techniques that can be used to help clients with a wide range of emotional disorders (see Reinecke and Freeman 2003, 244–50; A. T. Beck and Weishaar 2008, 284–87; see also J. S. Beck 1995; K. S. Dobson 2009; D. Dobson and Dobson 2009; Leahy 2004; McMullin 1999; Persons 1989, 2008; Persons, Davidson, and Tompkins 2001).

Cognitive techniques help clients to identify and directly modify their dysfunctional thoughts or cognitions that are associated with their emotional distress. They include the following (Reinecke and Freeman 2003, 245–48; see also A. T. Beck and Weishaar 2008, 284–85):

Idiosyncratic Meaning. Cognitive therapists ask clients to explore and clarify the personal or idiosyncratic meaning of specific words they use to describe their thoughts and feelings. Active listening skills and wise Socratic questioning and dialogue are used by the therapist to sensitively understand the idiosyncratic meaning of the client's words and thoughts.

Questioning the Evidence. Clients are taught to question the evidence that they are using to support their particular conclusions or beliefs. The cognitive therapist asks key questions such as: "On what basis do you say this?" and "Where is the evidence for your view or conclusion?" Evidence for as well as evidence against a specific belief the client has assumed is examined. Clients are encouraged to question and modify their belief in the face of contradictory evidence.

Reattribution. In this technique, clients are encouraged to test their automatic thoughts and assumptions by exploring other possible ways of looking at things or alternative causes of events. The cognitive therapist may ask: "Is there another way of looking at this?" For example, a male client might erroneously conclude that his boss does not like him and may fire him because his boss did not smile back at him when he greeted him at work. When asked by the therapist if there is another way of looking at this event, the client may realize that his boss was anxious about a board meeting later that day and actually did not smile at any of the staff that morning. The client may then reattribute responsibility for his boss not smiling to his boss's anxiety, and not personalize it and blame himself.

Rational Responding. This is one of the most powerful techniques in CT for helping clients to challenge their maladaptive thinking. Rational responding consists of four steps: (1) systematically exploring the evidence for and against a particular client belief; (2) developing an alternative view or explanation that is more adaptive or reasonable; (3) modifying the belief to be less extreme or less catastrophic, that is, decatastrophizing it; and (4) coming up with concrete behavioral steps that can be used by the client to more effectively cope with the problem.

Examining Options and Alternatives. This technique refers to the cognitive therapist helping the client to brainstorm other options or alternative solutions to the client's problem, so that the client can see beyond his or her initial limited range of possible solutions.

Decatastrophizing. The cognitive therapist uses Socratic questioning to help the client see if he or she is blowing things out of proportion and hence *catastrophizing*, or making extreme conclusions about a situation or outcome. If so, the therapist encourages the client to put things in proper and realistic perspective and thus engage in decatastrophizing.

Fantasized Consequences. In this technique, the cognitive therapist guides the client to describe a fantasy of a feared situation and its possible consequences, often exposing the irrationality of the fantasized consequences. However, if such imagined consequences are deemed realistic, then the therapist will help the client learn coping strategies to better manage the problem.

Advantages and Disadvantages. This is a problem-solving technique that the cognitive therapist can use to help clients look at the pros and cons of an option, so that they can acquire a broader and clearer perspective as well as take more reasonable steps of action.

Turning Adversity to Advantage. Clients are helped in this technique to see how a negative experience can be turned into a positive outcome. For example, a client who has been laid off due to cutbacks at work can be encouraged to see how this initially negative experience is opening up opportunities to pursue another job or career.

Guided Association/Discovery. This intervention is also referred to as the *vertical/downward arrow* technique in which the cognitive therapist guides the client to discover more connections between his or her automatic thoughts and possible underlying basic assumptions or deeper schemas. The therapist using guided association and discovery will ask questions such as "And then what?" in response to the client's expressions of his or her automatic thoughts, so that the client can discover a series of connected automatic thoughts as well as their possible underlying schemas.

Use of Exaggeration or Paradox. In this technique the cognitive therapist will take an idea or thought that the client has verbalized to its extreme either by using exaggeration or a paradoxical intervention (e.g., prescribing the symptom) to help the client move back to a more reasonable view. The therapist must be careful and sensitive in the use of exaggeration or paradox and should not use this technique if it is inappropriate for certain clients.

Scaling. For clients who tend to view things in extreme all-or-nothing categories, the technique of scaling may be helpful. The cognitive therapist asks the client to rate himself or herself on a scale of 0 (nothing) to 100 (all) on a particular dimension the client is having trouble with. For example, a depressed client may think of herself as incompetent. The client is asked to identify the most incompetent person in the world to be rated as 0, and the most competent and highly skilled person in the world to be rated as 100 on the scale of 0 to 100. The client then rates herself on this 0-to-100 competency scale and will often achieve a less extreme view of herself in terms of competence, with some strengths and weaknesses (and not all weaknesses and no competence).

Externalization of Voices. In this technique, the cognitive therapist helps the client to externalize his or her internal self-talk, consisting of dysfunctional thoughts, by first verbalizing such thoughts and then having the therapist model rational responses for the client. The therapist can proceed to model a progressively more dysfunctional and harsher voice for the client so that the client can more clearly see and hear the rational as well as the maladaptive voices now externalized and choose to respond in more adaptive ways.

Self-Instruction. Based on the work of Meichenbaum (1977), this self-instruction technique involves the cognitive therapist modeling for the client specific self-statements that the client can use to more effectively cope with stressful situations or emotional problems. Clients learn to practice and use coping or calming self-statements such as "Relax. Take one step at a time. I can handle this."

Thought Stopping. This technique is used by the cognitive therapist to help the client stop a series of maladaptive automatic thoughts or ruminations that lead to more emotional distress. When the upsetting emotional state is initially noticed with its accompanying negative automatic thoughts, the therapist suggests to the client to strongly say to himself or herself, "Stop!" or else imagine a huge red stop sign, to momentarily stop the ruminations. The client can then engage in other coping strategies such as rational responding to prevent further negative self-talk and emotional disturbance.

Distraction. This technique involves instructing clients to refocus their attention on other things such as doing complex math, or counting people in a store, or engaging in pleasant mental imagery (e.g., lying on the beach in Hawaii), instead of focusing on anxiety-provoking thoughts. Distraction is a short-term technique that works only for a while, but like thought stopping, it provides the client with some time to relax and the opportunity to use other cognitive coping techniques.

Direct Disputation. Cognitive therapists use this technique at appropriate times to directly challenge a client and his or her dysfunctional thinking by engaging in vigorous debate. This technique is more often used in REBT than in CT because CT emphasizes a more collaborative, gentle style, with the use of Socratic questioning, rather than direct disputation, which Ellis advocates in REBT. Nevertheless, direct disputation may be necessary and appropriate with certain clients, such as suicidal clients, who are obviously at risk of harming themselves.

Labeling of Distortions. This technique involves teaching clients the main cognitive distortions such as arbitrary inference, selective attention, overgeneralization, magnification and minimization, personalization, and dichotomous thinking covered earlier in this chapter, and how to identify and label them when they occur in the clients' thinking. A specific way of helping clients label their cognitive distortions is to have them keep a daily thought record or diary of their automatic thoughts, especially when they are experiencing emotional distress such as anger, anxiety, or depression. Their recorded automatic thoughts can then be reviewed and cognitive distortions identified when they occur. Clients can eventually cognitively restructure such dysfunctional thoughts and replace them with more realistic, reasonable, and rational thoughts.

Developing Replacement Imagery. Clients who have anxiety problems often also experience frightening images during stressful times that exacerbate their anxiety. The technique of developing replacement imagery involves helping clients to visualize or imagine calming and coping imagery in place of the frightening imagery. With some practice, clients can learn to use calming and coping imagery whenever they begin to experience anxiety-provoking imagery.

Bibliotherapy. This technique involves the cognitive therapist assigning self-help homework reading for the client to help the client continue to make therapeutic progress between sessions. Several excellent, popular books, such as *Feeling Good* (Burns 1988), *Love Is Never Enough* (A. T. Beck 1988), and *Mind Over Mood* (Greenberger and Padesky 1995), can be used as bibliotherapy for clients in CT.

Behavioral techniques are also frequently used as major therapeutic interventions in CT or CBT. They include *activity scheduling* (scheduling weekly activities that bring a sense of mastery or accomplishment, pleasure or enjoyment, and social connection) with *mastery, pleasure and social ratings, social skills or assertiveness training, graded task assignments* (taking small, gradual steps to achieve a particular goal), *behavior rehearsal or role-playing, in vivo exposure*, and *relaxation training* (Reinecke and Freeman 2003, 248–49; see also A. T. Beck and Weishaar 2008, 286–87). Many of these behavioral techniques have already been discussed in the previous chapter. Another crucial CT technique is the use of *homework*, whether in the form of a reading assignment or bibliotherapy, doing relaxation exercises daily, completing a daily thought record, calling someone for a social event together, or some other task. There are many possible homework assignments involving both cognitive and behavioral tasks. They should be clear, relevant, helpful, feasible, and manageable, with a high probability of successful completion between therapy sessions, for the benefit of the client. Homework assignments should be monitored at each therapy session, and the therapist should give the client appropriate verbal positive reinforcement and other rewards for completing the homework assigned. Difficulties in accomplishing homework assignments also warrant discussion and guidance from the cognitive therapist, to help modify the specific homework given in collaboration with the client to increase the probability of the client's successful completion of the homework.

Rational Emotive Behavior Therapy (REBT) (Ellis)

Albert Ellis, the founder of REBT, was a charismatic, often flamboyant, and strong personality who gave REBT a more forceful, active, directive, vigorous, and disputational therapeutic style than Beck's collaborative, gentle Socratic style in CT. REBT employs cognitive, emotive, and behavioral or behavioristic techniques to help clients modify their irrational beliefs and minimize their core philosophies of life that are absolutistic, rigid, and dogmatic (Ellis 2008, 201).

The following are some of the major therapeutic techniques used in REBT in three major categories: cognitive techniques, emotive techniques, and behavioral or behavioristic techniques (see Corey 2009, 282–85; Sharf 2008, 311–13; see also Ellis 1996, 2004; Ellis and Dryden 1997; Ellis and MacLaren 1998).

Cognitive techniques are major therapeutic interventions in REBT, which focuses on irrational beliefs as the root of emotional disorders. They include the following (see Corey 2009, 282–83):

Disputing Irrational Beliefs. This is a core cognitive technique in REBT. Clients are first taught the A-B-C model or theory of personality functioning, in which A stands for Activating Events, or situations encountered by them; B for the Beliefs that are triggered by the activating events, and such beliefs are usually irrational, dogmatic, absolutistic, and negative; and C for the Consequences (emotional and behavioral) of the beliefs, for example, feelings of depression or anxiety, and avoidance of feared situations. Clients thus learn that A does not lead to C, but rather A triggers B, which then leads to C. They realize that their *irrational beliefs*, triggered by activating events in their lives, lead to their emotional disturbance and upset as well as to their behavioral problems. The therapist in REBT then helps the client to go on to D, for Disputing their irrational beliefs in a vigorous, active, and directive way, first by the therapist, and then by the client. Finally, clients learn to identify E, or the Effect, of their strong and vigorous disputing of their irrational beliefs, usually ultimately experiencing less emotional disturbance or feelings such as depression and anxiety, and more satisfying and stable feelings such as sadness, concern, and even happiness and contentment. Clients therefore learn the A-B-C-D-E approach in REBT to dispute their irrational beliefs (see Sharf 2008, 311–14).

A specific example of an irrational belief (B) is: "It's the end of the world and awful if I don't get the promotion at work that I have been working so hard for." Disputing this irrational belief (D) may involve the therapist teaching the client to say instead: "It'll be disappointing and sad if I don't get the promotion at work that I have been working so hard for, but it won't be awful and it certainly won't be the end of the world." The activating event (A) in this case may be the client's anticipation of a job performance review in a couple of days to determine if he or she will get a much desired and substantial job promotion. The consequences (C) of the irrational belief (B) of the client may include anxiety and depression. The eventual effect (E) of disputing the irrational belief (D) may include feelings of disappointment and sadness but no longer anxiety or depression.

Doing Cognitive Homework. Clients are often asked to do cognitive homework by completing a daily A-B-C diary of events that trigger certain irrational beliefs leading to particular negative feelings and then to vigorously dispute their irrational beliefs (D) and to note the effect (E) of such disputation. Ultimately they compile an A-B-C-D-E diary that helps them to practice identifying and disputing their irrational beliefs on a daily basis. This diary has also been called an REBT Self-Help Form (see Sharf 2008, 309–10). Clients are encouraged by the therapist to put themselves in somewhat risky or stressful situations so that they can face their emotional disturbance connected with particular irrational beliefs and modify them in order to reduce their emotional upset.

Cognitive homework in REBT also often includes bibliotherapy or self-help reading to reinforce rational thinking and further challenge clients' irrational thinking. Some REBT self-help books that are used for homework reading include *A New Guide to Rational Living* (Ellis and Harper 1997, 3rd ed.), *Feeling Better, Getting Better, and Staying Better* (Ellis 2001), and *Rational Emotive Behavior Therapy: It Works for Me—It Can Work for You* (Ellis 2004). Clients are also often asked to listen to tapes of their own REBT sessions and reflect on them, so that they can continue to learn and change between therapy sessions.

Changing One's Language and Self-Statements. Use of language or self-statements that contain preferences rather than absolutistic demands is another cognitive technique often used by therapists and clients in REBT. Clients are taught to change their use of specific language from words such as "must," "ought," and "should" that reflect dogmatic and rigid *demandingness* to softer words that reflect *preferences*. For example, instead of saying, "I *must* pass this exam or else I'm a failure, and it's horrible and awful to fail," a client is taught instead to say, "I would like to pass the exam, but even if I fail it, it's not the end of the world."

Psychoeducational Methods. Ellis (2008) has emphasized that REBT uses psychoeducational interventions such as books, audiovisual tapes, talks, and workshops more than CT. Clients are encouraged to avail themselves of such psychoeducational materials and methods to further reinforce and strengthen their efforts at identifying and vigorously challenging their irrational beliefs and to maintain their therapeutic improvements and changes.

Teaching Others. Clients are also encouraged to teach and apply REBT principles and methods to other people, when appropriate (Sharf 2008, 315). One of the best ways of learning and reinforcing what one has learned is to teach others, and REBT uses this as a technique to help clients further strengthen their learning of REBT principles and procedures. It is also sometimes easier for clients to identify irrational beliefs in others (Ellis and Dryden 1997).

Emotive techniques are also significant therapeutic interventions used in REBT. They tend to be emotionally evocative and strong, but they still seek to dispute the irrational beliefs of clients. Ellis (2008) emphasizes, however, the goal of clients learning to have *unconditional self-acceptance* (USA), and the therapist offers such acceptance to clients while helping them to challenge their irrational beliefs and modify their self-destructive behaviors. Emotive techniques used in REBT include the following (see Corey 2009, 283–85):

Rational Emotive Imagery. This emotive technique in REBT involves teaching clients to use vivid and intense mental imagery to visualize themselves behaving, thinking, and feeling the way that they would like to in their actual lives. They can also use such imagery to visualize negative emotional experiences that upset them and then to change their irrational beliefs so that they eventually experience less-disturbing feelings. Ellis (2001, 2008) believes that regular use of rational emotive imagery a few times a week for several weeks can help individuals to overcome feeling upset about negative situations.

Use of Humor. The use of humor in an appropriate way is another unique emotive technique often used in REBT to help clients take themselves less seriously and to put things in proper perspective. Making fun of or poking fun at irrational beliefs and exposing their absurdities by jokes, strong language, and even the singing of humorous rational songs to well-known tunes are examples of how Ellis and other therapists have used humor in REBT in therapeutic ways with clients (see, e.g., Ellis 2001).

Role-Playing. This technique has cognitive, behavioral, and emotive aspects, but it can be helpful to clients to role-play or rehearse with the therapist in REBT an emotionally upsetting or stressful situation, so that they become more aware of their negative feelings as well as associated irrational beliefs. Clients can then learn to dispute their irrational beliefs and practice more-effective coping skills and behaviors to overcome their emotional distress.

Shame-Attacking Exercises. These are unique emotive techniques developed by Ellis and used in REBT to help clients intentionally engage in behaviors about which they usually feel shame or embarrassment (see Ellis 2001). The purpose of shame-attacking exercises is to enable clients to be less concerned about other people's reactions when they perform such behaviors and therefore to attack the shame or embarrassment that they usually feel. Examples of shame-attacking exercises include speaking loudly in a store, talking to strangers, asking silly questions in class, or wearing very colorful clothes that others will notice. They involve breaking social conventions in small ways. They do not include illegal acts or behaviors that will be dangerous to others or oneself. Clients learn that they self-create their own feelings of humiliation, and that they can be less sensitive to others' negative opinions or disapproval of them. They therefore learn to be less inhibited and more spontaneous in their behaviors.

Use of Force and Vigor in Self-Dialogue. This REBT emotive technique involves teaching clients to challenge and dispute their irrational beliefs in very strong, forceful ways, even raising their voices to talk back to their irrational beliefs. The therapist in REBT can also role-play with the client, including using reverse role-playing in which the therapist role-plays the client and expresses the client's irrational beliefs, with the client playing the role of the therapist and trying energetically and vigorously to strongly dispute the client's own irrational beliefs that the therapist is role-playing. Ellis (2008) emphasizes that REBT uses such vigorous self-talk and other emotive-evocative techniques with force and energy more than CT does.

Behavioral techniques are also part of the therapeutic interventions often used in REBT. They include standard behavior therapy techniques such as *operant conditioning, self-modification strategies, social skills training, relaxation training, in vivo exposure*, and *systematic desensitization* (see Corey 2009, 285), many of which have been described in the previous chapter. *Homework assignments* are often given to clients in REBT, so that they can practice between sessions the coping skills they have learned in therapy. *Action homework* or *activity homework* (see Parrott 2003, 317; Sharf 2008, 317) usually involves the client engaging in some risky behavior such as asking for a date, or exposing himself or herself to anxiety-provoking situations in vivo or in real life, in order to become desensitized to them.

The therapist in REBT therefore has a wide variety of cognitive, emotive, and behavioral techniques that can be used to help clients deal with different emotional disorders, but with one main focus: to strongly dispute irrational beliefs and eventually replace them with more-rational thinking that reflects preferences rather than dogmatic and absolutistic demands (Ellis 2008).

Cognitive Behavior Modification (CBM) and Stress Inoculation Training (SIT) (Meichenbaum)

Donald Meichenbaum developed an approach to CBT called cognitive behavior modification (CBM) that includes stress inoculation training (SIT). CBM is a coping skills therapy approach that includes relaxation and other coping skills training as well as constructive and calming self-talk and cognitive restructuring. CBM and SIT have been briefly reviewed in the previous chapter on behavior therapy. A more detailed description of SIT will now be provided.

SIT was developed by Meichenbaum as a more comprehensive approach to CBM than simply self-instructional or self-talk therapy (see Meichenbaum 1977, 1985, 1993, 2003, 2007). It has been effectively used to treat a wide range of problems (Meichenbaum 2003). SIT consists of three main phases, each with specific therapeutic techniques that can be flexibly tailored to fit particular clients and their needs as well as preferences. Meichenbaum (2003) has noted that flexibility is one of the unique strengths of SIT, which has been used with individuals, couples, and groups. The length of treatment in SIT varies, from only twenty minutes in preparing patients for surgical procedures to forty sessions in therapy with psychiatric patients and patients with chronic medical conditions. Typically, SIT lasts from eight to fifteen sessions, with booster or follow-up sessions spread over a period of three to twelve months (Meichenbaum 2003, 409).

Phase 1, or the *Conceptual-Educational Phase*, of SIT consists of several therapeutic interventions, including: (1) interviewing the client and his or her significant others, using imagery to help the client to describe a typical stressful situation, and using psychosocial and behavioral assessments to help the client, in a collaborative way, to describe his or her presenting problems or stressors in more specific behavioral terms; (2) helping the client to provide a narrative account of his or her experiences with stress and coping, noting unique coping resources and strengths, and identifying more specific goals for therapy; (3) asking the client to do self-monitoring to clarify the connections between his or her thoughts, behaviors, and feelings; (4) exploring with the client how problems in coping may be due to specific deficits in coping skills or to other factors such as negative thinking, maladaptive beliefs, low self-efficacy, and secondary gains; (5) helping the client, in a collaborative way, to conceptualize stress reactions as typically going through several phases: preparing for the stressor, confronting the stressor, coping with the feeling of being overwhelmed, and reflecting on how the client coped with the stressor, using reinforcing self-statements where appropriate; and (6) clearing away any misconceptions about stress and coping (Meichenbaum 2003, 409).

Phase 2, or the *Skills Acquisition, Consolidation, and Rehearsal Phase*, of SIT includes the following therapeutic interventions: (1) providing skills training tailor-made to a specific client population and length of training: (2) discovering the client's preferred coping style and techniques as well as blocks to effective coping; (3) training the client in the use of problem-focused instrumental coping skills such as problem-solving, assertiveness training, and use of appropriate social support; (4) teaching the client emotionally focused coping skills such as cognitive restructuring or reframing, perspective taking, and emotional regulation; (5) using imagery and behavioral practice to help the client rehearse coping skills; and (6) using generalization methods, including anticipating possible blocks to employing coping skills, and learning ways to overcome such barriers (Meichenbaum 2003, 409–10).

Phase 3, or the *Application and Follow-Through Phase*, of SIT involves the use of several therapeutic interventions, including: (1) encouraging the client to use coping skills in more difficult stressful situations; (2) using relapse prevention strategies; (3) enhancing the self-efficacy of the client by attributing successful coping to the client's own efforts; (4) phasing out treatment sessions in a gradual way, with booster and follow-through sessions; (5) involving the client's significant others in the treatment plan; (6) asking the client to coach someone else with a similar problem, thus empowering the client to assume a consultative role; and (7) helping the client to view stressors differently and more adaptively either by himself or herself or with others' help (Meichenbaum 2003, 410).

More recently, Meichenbaum has moved beyond traditional CBT or CBM to a more philosophical-constructivist or narrative approach to CBM and SIT that focuses on how clients actively construct their own reality or their own stories (see, e.g., Meichenbaum 1997; Meichenbaum and Fitzpatrick 1993). Based on this *constructive narrative perspective (CNP)*, Meichenbaum has emphasized that SIT therapists or trainers not only teach coping skills to clients but they also help clients to construct new life stories that show them as "survivors," or even "thrivers," rather than "victims" (2007, 500). Mahoney (1991, 2003) has similarly gone beyond traditional CBT (Mahoney 1974) in developing a broader and more philosophical-constructivist approach to therapy called *constructive psychotherapy* (Mahoney 2003).

Cognitive Behavior Therapy in Practice

A Hypothetical Transcript of CT (Beck)

Client: I felt pretty down and depressed again this past week. It was a bad week for me.

Cognitive Therapist: Tell me more about it. . . . What happened, and what went through your mind? What were you thinking about when you felt depressed?

Client: Well, I tried to ask this woman out on a date. Her name is Joan, and she's an attractive and nice person that I met at a friend's birthday party a couple of weeks ago. We had a good time chatting, and I even got her phone number. But when I called to ask her out for a movie, she turned me down pretty quickly!

Cognitive Therapist: How did you feel about her turning you down?

Client: I felt bad . . . and rejected. It really got to me, and I started feeling depressed and lousy.

Cognitive Therapist: What thoughts were you thinking as you were feeling lousy and depressed?

Client: I thought to myself: "I must be pretty unattractive. This is the second time in a month that I've been turned down for a date by two different women. It feels really lousy to be rejected again. I'll probably never get a date and won't be able to find someone to marry." It's a horrible and scary feeling—seeing the future as so bleak and hopeless for me, almost like it's the end of the world!

Cognitive Therapist: Um-hmm . . . it feels really lousy and scary, and you say it's like the end of the world and there's no future for you, no hope for finding a wife. On what basis do you say that, or where's the evidence for your conclusion?

Client: As I said, I've been turned down twice already by two different women—Joan last week, and Mary a couple of weeks ago. I think that this proves no woman would find me attractive enough to date me. That's why I've lost hope and the future looks bleak!

Cognitive Therapist: So, you feel it looks hopeless because two women have turned you down for a date. You've concluded that they've rejected you, that you're unattractive, and that you won't be able to find a wife in the future. Is there another way of looking at all this, another perspective or different conclusion that one can come to?

Client: I can't quite see it any other way. Twice is enough rejection!

Cognitive Therapist: Let's pause for a moment and really look at the situation as best and as objectively as we can. You remember our discussion from the last session about some of the most common errors we tend to make in our thinking—cognitive distortions, so to speak? What do you think may be happening here in your thinking? Based on two rejections, you conclude you'll never get another date in the future.

Client: I guess I may be jumping to conclusions too quickly, based on only two samples—I may be overgeneralizing, which is a cognitive distortion or common error in thinking that we had discussed last week. I guess I'm doing it again. But it does feel like there's no hope!

Cognitive Therapist: Um-hmm . . . it does feel like it's hopeless, if you think it's hopeless, based on two cases. Again, is there another way of looking at this more objectively and accurately?

Client: I guess I can tell myself that it's only two cases. I can't tell for sure that the third woman I ask out for a date will definitely turn me down. I can stop jumping to conclusions or overgeneralizing and wait for more cases or data before I make a more definite conclusion like I'll never find someone to marry. I can see now that I'm going too far ahead, too fast. Maybe, just maybe, there's a little bit of hope.

Cognitive Therapist: Good! You're really telling yourself the truth more objectively and putting the whole situation in better or more proper perspective, seeing it from another angle. How are you feeling now?

Client: A bit better . . . with a bit of hope.

Cognitive Therapist: Good! You can see how your thinking can really affect your feelings. We can also discuss further your reasons for concluding that Joan was rejecting you, when she simply turned you down for a date. . . . What do you think?

Client: Well . . . yeah . . . I felt rejected . . . I concluded she was rejecting me, but are you suggesting she may

Cognitive Therapist: have refused my request for a date but this does not necessarily mean that she doesn't like me at all or that she is rejecting me as a person? After all, we did enjoy talking together for quite a while at the birthday party, and she did give me her telephone number . . .

Cognitive Therapist: That's a good logical analysis of what happened. Again, is there another way of looking at Joan's turning you down for a date, besides rejection?

Client: Maybe she didn't feel like it, or was too busy or tired last week. She did say that, but I felt it was only an excuse or cover-up.

Cognitive Therapist: You may want to check that out next week by asking her out again, but only if you want to.

Client: Yeah, yeah . . . I see the point.

Cognitive Therapist: Let's take this discussion one step further, to really help you deal with your underlying thinking or basic assumptions about life. Just suppose that you ask Joan again and she is really rejecting you, then what would this mean to you? What does rejection mean to you?

This hypothetical transcript of a small part of a typical cognitive therapy (or cognitive behavior therapy) session demonstrates the use of cognitive restructuring by the cognitive therapist to help the client identify dysfunctional thinking and a specific cognitive distortion of overgeneralization, and to challenge it and modify it to more reasonable, rational, and realistic thinking. The cognitive therapist uses the traditional cognitive therapy questions: "On what basis do you say that, or where's the evidence for your conclusion?" "Is there another way of looking at all this?" and "Suppose this is true (rejection), what would it mean to you?" The cognitive therapist is using the downward arrow technique to help the client not only to identify cognitive distortions and change them but also to uncover the client's underlying basic assumptions or schema, in this case about rejection and why it's so horrible. The cognitive therapist also shows empathy for the client and engages in a warm and collaborative therapeutic relationship with the client, using Socratic dialogue and gentle questioning (rather than directive vigorous disputing of the client's dysfunctional thinking, which is more characteristic of Ellis's REBT approach).

Critique of CBT: Strengths and Weaknesses

The strengths and weaknesses of CBT are similar to those of behavior therapy that have been covered in the previous chapter. However, there are some other strengths and weaknesses more unique to CBT (see Corey 2009, 300–309; Parrott 2003, 328–29; Prochaska and Norcross 2010, 328–30).

First, CBT, like behavior therapy, is a comprehensive and versatile approach to therapy that has been used with diverse populations (e.g., children, adolescents, adults, and older adults), to address a wide range of psychological disorders and clinical problems, in a variety of practice settings (see Leahy 2004; Spiegler and Guevremont 2003; Wilson 2008; see also Kazdin 2001; Miltenberger 2008). CBT is typically a relatively short-term therapy and therefore easily fits with managed care's emphasis on effective brief therapy and short-term treatments.

Second, CBT, like behavior therapy, focuses on specific therapy goals set by the client in collaboration with the therapist, with regular monitoring of client progress in therapy. It is therefore a therapy approach that is accountable, as client improvement or lack thereof is assessed and measured in a consistent and clear way.

Third, CBT, somewhat like behavior therapy, focuses more on the present complaints of the client, with an emphasis on both the client's internal cognitive activities as well as environmental conditions that may be contributing to the client's present symptoms and problems. CBT does not emphasize the past or exploration of feelings at length and is thus a good corrective to therapy approaches that may invest too much time and energy in past issues and feelings.

Fourth, CBT, like behavior therapy, empowers the client to set his or her own goals for therapy, in collaboration with the therapist, and therefore gives the client choice regarding treatment goals as well as preferred treatment options.

Fifth, CBT, like behavior therapy, is open to the use of pharmacotherapy or psychiatric medication in the treatment of severe psychological disorders such as major depressive disorder, bipolar disorder, OCD, and schizophrenia, and hence to the use of combined treatments of CBT and psychiatric medications for clients with such disorders.

Sixth, CBT has a wide repertoire of therapy techniques that include many cognitive and behavioral interventions as well as some emotive ones (as in REBT) that can be used to effectively treat specific psychological disorders and somatic conditions. Clients with such focused symptoms and a desire for structured, directive, and empirically supported interventions in a relatively short-term therapy context can receive effective and systematic help through CBT.

Seventh, CBT, like behavior therapy, greatly values empirical, controlled outcome research and, together with behavior therapy, is the most empirically supported therapy approach today for a wide range of clinical problems.

Eighth, CBT is flexible enough to be sensitively used with clients from diverse cultures and different countries in a multicultural counseling context, because it focuses on treating symptoms and problems that are prevalent across cultures and nations and empowers clients to freely choose their own treatment goals, consistent with their cultural and societal values. CBT is a directive, structured, and problem-solving approach to therapy that does not require too much introspection or lengthy exploration of feelings and past issues; therefore, it fits the preferences of many clients from non-Western cultures. CBT with culturally diverse clients (see, e.g., Hays and Iwamasa 2006; Chen and Davenport 2005) is receiving more empirical support for its effectiveness (Voss Horrell 2008; see also Miranda et al. 2005). However, CBT, perhaps more than traditional behavior therapy, may also be at greater risk for insensitively challenging so-called irrational beliefs of clients from non-Western cultures because of its focus on changing such thinking in clients. CBT may therefore inadvertently challenge cherished cultural values that seem irrational to the Western mind. Hays (2009) has specifically suggested questioning the *helpfulness* rather than the validity or rationality of particular thoughts and beliefs of culturally diverse clients in order to show them respect in culturally responsive CBT.

Finally, CBT can be helpful to clients with physical disabilities or challenges. CBT's focus on modifying negative expectations and challenging irrational beliefs that clients may have about their physical disabilities and limitations, and its problem-solving and skills training approach can be of particular benefit to such clients as they learn to cope more effectively with life (see Parrott 2003, 329; Halligan 1983; Radnitz 2000).

CBT also has several weaknesses, similar to those of behavior therapy. First, CBT tends to focus on the treatment of the client's presenting problems or symptoms, such as anxiety, depression, anger, stress, and marital difficulties, and may not pay sufficient attention to the whole person and the client's total life context. CBT can therefore be conducted in a rather mechanistic way. However, CBT does include a somewhat comprehensive assessment of the client in terms of cognitions, emotions, and behaviors and can also include a broader consideration of the client's functioning in the BASIC I.D. framework of multimodal therapy (Lazarus 1981, 1997, 2008).

Second, CBT, like behavior therapy, may place too much emphasis on techniques and not pay adequate attention to the therapeutic relationship. To be fair, CBT does emphasize the importance of establishing a warm, empathic, and collaborative relationship with the client, but this is not considered a sufficient condition for therapeutic change (A. T. Beck, Rush, Shaw, and Emery 1979; Wilson 2008). However, CBT has recently focused more on the importance of the therapeutic relationship in effective CBT (see P. Gilbert and Leahy 2007; see also Safran and Segal 1990).

Third, CBT tends not to pay much attention to the past and the unresolved issues or painful experiences in the client's life and history. Some clients will require more time to adequately process unresolved issues from their past.

Fourth, CBT, like behavior therapy, is supposedly still mainly based on social learning or social cognitive theory; hence it tends to ignore unconscious processes, including transference and dreams, that can provide helpful insights to clients and facilitate further therapeutic improvements. However, CBT has attempted to deal with such unconscious processes and dreams but not within a psychoanalytic framework (see, e.g., K. S. Bowers and Meichenbaum 1984; Rosner, Lyddon, and Freeman 2003). It should be noted that CBT's supposed grounding in social cognitive theory or any other specific theory (see Kazantzis, Reinecke, and Freeman 2009) has been strongly criticized as inaccurate (see, e.g., McMinn and Campbell 2007, 92–94).

Fifth, CBT, similar to behavior therapy, does not typically deal with existential issues, such as seeking meaning in life, choosing authentic values, and facing the fear of death, in a focused way because its problem-solving approach deals more directly with the client's presenting problems and symptoms. Clients struggling with such existential concerns, and even spiritual issues, may not find traditional CBT sufficiently helpful. However, serious attempts have recently been made to pay more attention to existential concerns (see, e.g., Dattilio 2002), and especially to integrate religion and spirituality, including Christian and Muslim spirituality, into CBT (see, e.g., Tan 1987a, 2007b; Tan and Johnson 2005; see also Propst 1988; McMinn and Campbell 2007; Walker, Reese, Hughes, and Troskie 2010). Even Ellis became more open to integrating religion and REBT (see Ellis 2000; Nielsen, Johnson, and Ellis 2001). The CBT tradition has also recently been expanded to include mindfulness-based and acceptance-based therapies such as DBT, MBCT, and ACT, which have some roots in contemplative or meditative spirituality, such as Zen Buddhism (Hayes, Follette, and Linehan 2004; see also Roemer and Orsillo 2009).

Sixth, CBT, similar to behavior therapy, is a directive, structured, and systematic therapy approach in which the therapist functions as a teacher, coach, consultant, and role model. There is, therefore, a real danger that the therapist in the role of expert and trainer may impose his or her values on the client. For example, an overenthusiastic therapist in REBT can end up debating with a client in challenging the client's irrational beliefs defined according to the therapist's criteria of rationality and irrationality, based on Western cultural values. This can be a serious problem in conducting CBT within a multicultural context. However, CBT does empower the client to choose his or her own treatment goals and to collaborate in the therapeutic process with the therapist (A. T. Beck, Rush, Shaw, and Emery 1979; see also Kuyken, Padesky, and Dudley 2009; Wilson 2008).

Seventh, the emphasis in CBT on teaching specific skills (e.g., relaxation and coping self-talk, and problem-solving) to the client assumes that the best way for clients to learn and change in therapeutic ways is to be directly instructed. For example, Meichenbaum's SIT has been criticized by C. H. Patterson and C. Edward Watkins (1996) for making this assumption, which may not hold true for all clients, because some of them do better by learning through gradual self-discovery and more reflection and processing of their feelings (see Corey 2009, 308–9).

Eighth, CBT employs many cognitive and behavioral techniques that can be simplistically misused or abused by inexperienced or inadequately trained therapists. Proper training and supervision in CBT techniques is needed in order for therapists to conduct effective, efficient, and ethical CBT.

Ninth, CBT, similar to behavior therapy, may not pay enough attention to other, larger sociopolitical and environmental factors that may contribute to a client's psychological problems in certain cultural and national contexts. Such factors can include oppression, discrimination, and marginalization experienced by the client, who therefore must be empowered to deal more directly with such external stressors, and not focus only on his or her own irrational beliefs.

Finally, CBT needs to be particularly sensitive to how therapeutic changes in behavior and thinking, including values, in the client can negatively affect others in the client's familial and social network of relationships. This negative result is a likely outcome if the client's new way of thinking clashes with the cultural and social values of the significant others in the client's life.

A Biblical Perspective on CBT

A biblical perspective on CBT will include much of what has already been covered in the previous chapter regarding a biblical perspective on behavior therapy. See sidebar 12.2 for a succinct summary of a biblical approach to CBT that incorporates a biblical critique of CBT.

Key questions often asked in a Christian approach to CBT that uses biblical truth as the basis for cognitive restructuring of dysfunctional or unbiblical thinking include: "What does God have to say about this?" "What do you think the Bible has to say about this?" and "What does your faith tradition or church or denomination have to say about this?" (see Tan 2007b, 108).

Jones and Butman have also written thoughtful, biblically based critiques of RET or REBT and CBT. They conclude that RET or REBT is problematic from a Christian perspective primarily because of its very humanistic definition of rationality, its vision of human health that is individualistic, hedonistic, and rationalistic, and its troubling views on rationality and emotion (1991, 193). With regard to CBT, Jones and Butman raise important questions that secular CBT needs to deal with more adequately, for example, questions concerning transcendence and spirituality, self-deception and evil, complex human relationships, internal conflicts within the person, the nature of emotion, and the meaning of being fully and truly human. They conclude, however, that CBT still has many strengths, and therefore it "is likely to be one of the more fruitful models for Christians to explore for its integrative potentials" (S. L. Jones and Butman 1991, 223).

Sidebar 12.2

A Biblical Approach to CBT

A biblical approach to cognitive behavior therapy will:

- Emphasize the primacy of agape love (1 Cor. 13) and the need to develop a warm, empathic, and genuine relationship with the client.
- Deal adequately with the past, especially with unresolved developmental issues or childhood traumas, and will use inner healing or healing of memories judiciously and appropriately.
- Pay special attention to the meaning of spiritual, experiential, and even mystical aspects of life and faith, according to God's wisdom as revealed in Scriptures and by the Holy Spirit's teaching ministry (John 14:26), and will not overemphasize the rational, thinking dimension, although biblical, propositional truth will be given its rightful place of importance. The possibility of demonic involvement in some cases will also be seriously considered and appropriately addressed.
- Focus on how problems in thoughts and behavior may often (*not* always, because of other factors, e.g., organic or biological) underlie problem feelings (Rom. 12:1–2; Eph. 4:22–24; Phil. 4:8) and use biblical truth (John 8:32), not relativistic, empirically oriented values, in conducting cognitive restructuring and behavioral change interventions.
- Emphasize the Holy Spirit's ministry in bringing about inner healing as well as cognitive, behavioral, and emotional change. It will use prayer and affirmation of God's Word in facilitating dependence on the Lord to produce deep and lasting personality change and will be cautious not to inadvertently encourage sinful self-sufficiency (cf. Phil. 4:13).
- Pay more attention to larger contextual factors, such as familial, societal, religious, and cultural influences, and hence utilize appropriate community resources in therapeutic intervention, including the church as a body of believers and fellow "priests" to one another (1 Cor. 12; 1 Pet. 2:5, 9).
- Use only those techniques that are consistent with biblical truth and not simplistically use whatever techniques work. It will reaffirm scriptural perspectives on suffering, including the possibility of the "blessings of mental anguish" (Evans 1986), with the ultimate goal of counseling being holiness or Christlikeness (Rom. 8:29), not necessarily temporal happiness (Grounds 1976). However, such a goal will include being more open to receiving God's love and grace and thereby becoming more Christlike and overcoming mental anguish due to unbiblical, erroneous beliefs (i.e., misbeliefs).
- Utilize rigorous outcome research methodology before making definitive statements about the superiority of cognitive behavior therapy (Tan 1987a, 108–9).

More recently, Mark McMinn and Clark Campbell (2007), in their attempt to develop a comprehensive Christian approach to therapy called *integrative therapy*, included a helpful and insightful critique of secular CBT, affirming the need to integrate behavioral, cognitive, and interpersonal models of therapy within a Christian theological framework for a more balanced, holistic, and biblically consistent approach to Christian therapy.

The recent expansion of CBT to incorporate mindfulness and acceptance-based therapies such as DBT, MBCT, and ACT, which are rooted in contemplative and meditative spirituality such as Zen Buddhism, can be of serious concern from a Christian or biblical perspective. Eastern or Buddhist spiritual traditions can be at odds with Christian understandings of ultimate truth and the Bible. However, mindfulness and acceptance are not necessarily Buddhist concepts. They can also be found in Christian contemplative spirituality and Christian meditation (see, e.g., Caussade 1989; Finley 2004).

Research: Empirical Status of CBT

As noted in the previous chapter, a crucial characteristic of CBT and behavior therapy is the emphasis on empirical research, especially controlled outcome studies or randomized clinical trials (RCTs) on the effectiveness of the therapeutic interventions used to treat particular clinical problems. More controlled outcome research has been conducted on CBT and behavior therapy than on any other therapy approach.

Prochaska and Norcross (2010, 281, 321–28) have provided a helpful review of the major meta-analyses and controlled outcome studies that have been done on REBT (Ellis) and CT (Beck) as well as a meta-analysis of thirty-seven studies done on SIT (Meichenbaum), which will now be briefly summarized. They note that hundreds of controlled outcome studies have been completed to date on cognitive therapies, including REBT and CT.

Empirical Status of REBT

Smith, Glass, and Miller (1980), in their earlier meta-analysis of 475 studies with 25,000 patients, reported an average effect size of .68 for REBT, and 1.13 for CBT. L. C. Lyons and P. J. Woods (1991) in a later meta-analysis found an overall effect size of .95 for REBT, indicating that REBT was significantly better than control groups and no treatment. However, the outcome of REBT was no different from that of behavior therapy and cognitive behavior modification. Similar findings were obtained in another meta-analysis of 28 well-controlled studies that showed REBT to be better than no treatment and placebo, but no different from other behavioral and cognitive therapies (Engels, Garnefski, and Drekstra 1993). REBT with a behavioral emphasis did not achieve better results than REBT with a more cognitive emphasis.

More specifically, REBT and other cognitive and cognitive-behavioral treatments have been found to be effective with older children and adolescents. A meta-analysis of 150 outcome studies with children and adolescents (Weisz et al. 1995) found that cognitive and cognitive-behavioral therapy (in 38 treatment groups) had an average effect size of .67, which is moderately large and better than the nonbehavioral treatments. Another meta-analysis of 19 outcome studies on rational emotive therapy (RET) or REBT with 1,021 children and adolescents found an effect size of .50 for RET or REBT, a moderate and respectable effect, especially for disruptive and conduct disorders (Gonzalez et al. 2004).

REBT has thus been found to be an effective therapy for adults as well as for children and adolescents, with significantly better outcomes than no treatment and placebo, but usually equivalent to other cognitive and behavioral treatments.

Empirical Status of CT and CBT

Beck's CT and more generic CBT have been the most researched treatments with numerous controlled outcome studies as well as meta-analyses conducted in the last decade or so. The meta-analyses done for specific clinical disorders or problems will now be briefly discussed.

For *depression*, several meta-analyses have been conducted on outcome studies on the effectiveness of CT and other related CBT treatments for adults, adolescents, and older adults. Cognitive therapy (CT or CBT) is clearly superior to no treatment and placebo treatments for depression, for adults, children, adolescents, and older adults, and probably equivalent in effectiveness to other psychotherapies for depression (see Prochaska and Norcross 2010, 322–24). Continuation of cognitive therapy reduces the likelihood of later relapse-recurrence (see Vittengl, Clark, Dunn, and Jarrett 2007). More recently, however, *behavioral activation*, a specific behavior therapy approach that includes positive reinforcement of healthy behaviors and activity, has been found to be more effective than CT in the treatment of more severely depressed clients and also almost as effective as CT for the prevention of relapse (Dimidjian et al. 2006; K. S. Dobson et al. 2008; see also Coffman et al. 2007). The effectiveness of behavioral activation in the treatment of depression, especially moderate to severe depression, raises the question of whether it is the behavioral component (e.g., activity scheduling) rather than the cognitive restructuring component in CT and CBT that is the crucial factor in effective CBT for depression.

A more recent meta-analysis of comparative outcome studies on the efficacy or effectiveness of seven major psychotherapies (cognitive behavior therapy, nondirective supportive treatment, behavioral activation treatment, psychodynamic treatment, problem-solving therapy, interpersonal therapy, and social skills training) for *mild to moderate depression* in adults revealed few significant differences among them, except for interpersonal therapy being somewhat more efficacious and nondirective, and supportive treatment being somewhat less efficacious (Cuijpers, Van Straten, Andersson, and Van Oppen 2008). Cognitive behavior therapy had a significantly higher dropout rate, whereas problem-solving therapy had a significantly lower dropout rate. CBT is therefore not superior to other major therapies for mild to moderate depression in adults.

For *anxiety disorders*, the meta-analyses of controlled outcome studies show that CT and CBT are more effective than wait-list and placebo control groups, with large average effect sizes found for CT used for generalized anxiety disorder and social phobia, but not better than behavioral treatments. CT and CBT also outperform medication in the treatment of anxiety disorders in the long run with better maintenance of treatment gains. For obsessive-compulsive disorder (OCD), CT and CBT have actually done as well as exposure therapy in therapeutic effectiveness. For social phobia, the largest effect sizes have been found when CT was combined with exposure therapy (see Prochaska and Norcross 2010, 324).

For *panic disorder*, meta-analyses and controlled outcome studies have shown that the most effective treatment involves a combination of cognitive restructuring (CT) and exposure, and especially panic control therapy (PCT), a CBT approach developed by David Barlow and his colleagues that includes aspects of CT, behavior therapy, and exposure (Barlow and Lehman 1996; see also Craske and Barlow 2008). CBT has been found to be a treatment of choice for panic disorder, and the most cost-effective treatment for panic disorder as well as generalized anxiety disorder (see Prochaska and Norcross 2010, 324–25).

For *posttraumatic stress disorder (PTSD)*, meta-analyses have shown CBT to be as effective as exposure therapy and EMDR for both adults and children.

For *eating disorders*, results from a meta-analysis and other controlled outcome studies indicate that CBT is a treatment of choice for bulimia; it is more effective than medication alone, no treatment, and control treatments, and evidences more enduring therapeutic effects at follow-up. For *chronic pain*, meta-analyses show multicomponent CBT treatments to be effective for chronic pain reduction in both adults and children. For *body dysmorphic disorder*, a meta-analysis found antidepressant medications to be effective, but cognitive therapy was more effective (see Prochaska and Norcross 2010, 325–26).

For *personality disorders*, a meta-analysis and controlled outcome studies have yielded results that support the effectiveness of dialectical behavior therapy (DBT) (Linehan 1993) for borderline personality disorder, as well as CBT for personality disorders, but it is not superior to psychodynamic therapy. For *psychotic disorders*, meta-analyses have shown CBT to be effective for speeding recovery from acute schizophrenia and delaying reoccurrences, although more research is needed.

For *marital therapy*, a meta-analysis has shown that couples treated with CBT marital therapy did significantly better than couples who received no treatment, but not better than couples who were treated with insight-oriented marital therapy or who had received behavioral marital therapy. A meta-analysis of *group CBT* found it to be effective, similar to CBT marital therapy (see Prochaska and Norcross 2010, 326–27).

For *domestic violence*, a meta-analysis has revealed sobering results showing the lack of effectiveness of CBT for reducing domestic violence in men, as well as no differences in the effect sizes found for CBT and other treatments. Finally, a meta-analysis of studies conducted on the effectiveness of homework assignments in CBT found that homework assignments did produce better therapeutic results than treatments limited to only in-session intervention (see Prochaska and Norcross 2010, 327).

Empirical Status of SIT

A meta-analysis involving thirty-seven studies with 1,837 clients has been done on the effectiveness of SIT (Saunders, Drishell, Johnson, and Salas 1996). The overall effect size of .37 on state anxiety and .51 on performance anxiety indicate that SIT is moderately effective, and significantly better than no treatment or control treatments (see Prochaska and Norcross 2010, 281).

Meichenbaum noted that in some two hundred studies SIT has been used with different populations (2003, 407–8; see also Meichenbaum 2007). SIT has been successfully used as a *preventative intervention* with clients such as surgical patients, patients having to undergo stressful medical procedures, hemodialysis patients, several stressful occupational groups (e.g., flight attendants, firefighters, police officers, teachers, nurses, soldiers, oil rig workers), stepparents, parents of children with cancer, and international students facing the stress of adjustment. SIT has also been used as a *treatment intervention* with *medical* patients such as those suffering from pain conditions, cancer, ulcers, hypertension, burns, genital herpes, AIDS, childhood asthma, and traumatic brain injury. It has been successfully employed to treat *psychiatric* patients (children, adolescents, and adults) who have anxiety disorders (e.g., phobias, PTSD, dental anxiety, and performance anxiety), anger control problems, addictive disorders, and other chronic psychiatric disorders. More controlled outcome research is obviously needed to further strengthen the empirical base supporting the effectiveness of SIT for a wide range of clinical problems and applications, both as a preventive intervention and a treatment approach.

A recent review of sixteen methodologically rigorous meta-analyses (involving 332 studies with 9,995 subjects) conducted on the outcomes of CBT, including CT, for a wide range of psychiatric disorders yielded the following findings: (1) large effect sizes were obtained for CBT for unipolar depression, generalized anxiety disorder, panic disorder with or without agoraphobia, social phobia, posttraumatic stress disorder (PTSD), and childhood depressive and anxiety disorders; (2) effect sizes in the moderate range were found for CBT of marital distress, anger, childhood somatic disorders, and chronic pain; (3) CBT was somewhat better than antidepressants in the treatment of depression in adults; (4) CBT was as effective as behavior therapy in the treatment of depression and obsessive-compulsive disorder (OCD) in adults; and (5) large uncontrolled effect sizes were obtained for CBT for bulimia nervosa and schizophrenia (Butler, Chapman, Forman, and Beck 2006, 17). Butler and his colleagues (2006) concluded that these sixteen meta-analyses provide empirical support for the efficacy or effectiveness of CBT for many psychiatric disorders, although some limitations are inherent in the use of a statistical method such as meta-analysis. A more recent meta-analysis of 11 effectiveness studies with a total of 973 clients found that cognitive-behavioral interventions for anxiety disorders generalize in their effectiveness to real-world clinical practice (Van Ingen, Freiheit, and Vye 2009). Another recent meta-analysis of 56 effectiveness studies of CBT for adult anxiety disorders in actual clinical practice similarly concluded that CBT is robustly effective in clinically representative conditions, with large effect sizes found (Stewart and Chambless 2009).

A recent Dutch study (Giesen-Bloo et al. 2006) has provided empirical support for the effectiveness of *schema therapy*, a specific form of CT that deals with early maladaptive schemas (Young, Klosko, and Weishaar 2003), for treating borderline personality disorder. This three-year study evaluated the effectiveness of schema therapy versus that of transference-focused therapy based on Otto Kernberg's work (Levy et al. 2006). Both treatments showed reductions in borderline personality disorder symptomatology, with schema therapy being more effective (45.5 percent of schema therapy patients had full recovery compared to 23.8 percent of transference-focused therapy patients). Schema therapy patients also had significantly greater reductions of other personality dysfunction measures, with a lower likelihood of dropping out of treatment (see Kellogg and Young 2008, 69).

Future Directions

CBT should be more accurately called cognitive behavior therapies, because various versions of CBT are available today, including the three major approaches covered in this chapter: CT, REBT, and CBM/SIT. CBT, especially CT, is a major and significant school of therapy today, with 28 percent of clinical psychologists and 29 percent of counselors in the United States indicating CT as their primary theoretical orientation (see Prochaska and Norcross 2010, 3). CBT is also the most popular and fastest growing as well as the most empirically researched of all the contemporary systems of counseling and psychotherapy available. There are two main reasons for CBT or CT's present dominant position: its openness to incorporating other empirically supported therapeutic techniques (see Alford and Beck 1997) and its solid grounding in empirical research, especially controlled outcome evaluation (Prochaska and Norcross 2010, 333). Cognitive and cognitive-behavioral approaches are among the leading therapy orientations predicted by a Delphi poll to thrive in the next decade, when therapy is expected to be more directive, psychoeducational, problem focused, technological, and short term (see Prochaska and Norcross 2010, 517–19).

CBT has already been successfully and effectively applied to a wide range of psychological and medical disorders and will continue to be a prominent approach to treatment as well as prevention of such disorders, including the more severe conditions such as personality disorders, schizophrenia and other psychoses, and bipolar disorder. CBT's ever widening empirical base supporting its effectiveness will continue to make it a crucial and substantial part of contemporary evidence-based treatment that is becoming increasingly important to managed care and insurance companies.

CBT has begun to incorporate the third wave of behavior therapy, consisting of mindfulness and acceptance-based therapies such as DBT, MBCT, and ACT, which have some roots in contemplative or meditative spirituality, such as Zen Buddhism (Hayes, Follette, and Linehan 2004; Hayes et al. 2006; Hayes et al. in press; see also Roemer and Orsillo 2009). Serious attempts have also been made to develop a more spiritually or religiously oriented CBT, including Christian and Muslim versions (see, e.g., Tan and Johnson 2005). The integration of religion and spirituality with CBT is an area that will see further refinement and development as well as require more and better empirical research (see T. B. Smith, Bartz, and Richards 2007).

Another area deserving further development in the future is the integration of positive psychology and CT, focusing on issues of positive affect or happiness, life satisfaction, and contentment, including the use of cognitive therapy or CBT techniques to treat clinical problems, in what has recently been called *quality of life therapy*, developed by Michael Frisch (2006).

Schema therapy, as a specific form of CT that has been found to be effective for borderline personality disorder (see Kellogg and Young 2008; see also Kellogg and Young 2006; Young 2002; Young, Klosko, and Weishaar 2003), will also receive more attention and further refinement and development in the years ahead.

The Association for Advancement of Behavior Therapy (AABT) changed its name to the Association for Behavioral and Cognitive Therapies (ABCT) in 2005, reflecting the significant impact CBT (including CT) has had on behavior therapy. More specifically, there is also the International Association for Cognitive Therapy (www.cognitivetherapyassociation.org or www.the-iacp.com) representing Beck's CT approach, with the *Journal of Cognitive Psychotherapy: An International Quarterly* as its major publication. Other primary journals in CT include *Cognitive Therapy and Research* and *Cognitive and Behavioral Practice*. The *International Cognitive Therapy Newsletter* was launched in 1985, and it serves as a newsletter network through which therapists from five continents can exchange information related to CT. A non-profit organization, the Academy of Cognitive Therapy, was founded in 1999 to certify therapists skilled or appropriately trained in CT. The Beck Institute for Cognitive Therapy and Research (www.beckinstitute.org) in Bala Cynwyd, Pennsylvania, provides training programs in CT and outpatient services. Ten other therapy training centers in the United States also provide training in CT. The Center for Cognitive Therapy, affiliated with the University of Pennsylvania Medical School, is a research institute that also provides outpatient services (see A. T. Beck and Weishaar 2008, 269–70). Leahy (2004, x) has noted that cognitive therapy centers exist today in most major cities in the United States and CBT organizations in every major country worldwide. The World Congress of Cognitive Psychotherapy in 2004 was held in Kobe, Japan.

With regard to REBT, its major journal is the *Journal of Rational-Emotive and Cognitive-Behavior Therapy*. The Albert Ellis Institute, founded by Ellis in 1959, is no longer associated with Ellis, who established the Albert Ellis Foundation in 2006 to better protect and promote his works and REBT (Ellis 2008). Further information about REBT and available training programs may be obtained online (www.rebtnetwork.org; see Corey 2009, 309).

CBT, and especially CT, will continue to grow and expand in significant and substantial ways in the years ahead. Its future looks extremely bright as a primary, if not the premier, contemporary approach to therapy.

Recommended Readings

Beck, A. T., Rush, A. J., Shaw, B. F., & Emery, G. (1979). *Cognitive therapy of depression*. New York: Guilford Press.

Beck, J. S. (1995). *Cognitive therapy: Basics and beyond*. New York: Guilford Press.

Beck, J. S. (2005). *Cognitive therapy for challenging problems*. New York: Guilford Press.

Dobson, K. S. (Ed.). (2008). *Handbook of cognitive-behavioral therapies* (3rd ed.). New York: Guilford Press.

Ellis, A., & MacLaren, C. (1998). *Rational emotive behavior therapy: A therapist's guide*. Atascadero, CA: Impact.

Leahy, R. L. (Ed.). (2004). *Contemporary cognitive therapy: Theory, research, and practice*. New York: Guilford Press.

Meichenbaum, D. (1977). *Cognitive-behavior modification: An integrative approach*. New York: Plenum.

Persons, J. B. (2008). *The case formulation approach to cognitive-behavior therapy*. New York: Guilford Press.

13

Marital and Family Therapy

Marital and family therapy (MFT) actually refers to over twenty diverse therapeutic approaches to marital and family problems (Levant 1984). Today it is more often referred to as *couple and family therapy* (Lebow 2008), *systemic therapies* (Prochaska and Norcross 2010), *family systems therapy* (Corey 2009), and *family therapy* (Goldenberg and Goldenberg 2008a, 2008b). More specifically, *marital therapy* is now often called *couple therapy* (Gurman 2008a). MFT has also been more accurately referred to as *marital therapies* (Gurman 2003) and *family therapies* (N. J. Kaslow, Dausch, and Celano 2003) to reflect the many therapy approaches that are included in MFT.

MFT is therefore an umbrella term for over twenty systemic therapies that assume that the crucial factor in helping individuals to change is to understand and work with the interpersonal systems within which they live and function. The couple and family must be addressed and seen in effective therapy for individual problems as well as for marital or couple and family issues. MFT has no single founder, but the key figures and approaches in this area include Salvador Minuchin, the founder of the *structural* approach; Jay Haley and the Milan Group, who developed the *strategic* approach; Murray Bowen, who developed family systems theory and transgenerational (multigenerational) family therapy; Virginia Satir, who developed conjoint family therapy; and Susan Johnson and Leslie Greenberg, who developed emotionally focused therapy (EFT) for couples; as well as others such as Carl Whittaker, Ivan Boszormenyi-Nagy, Steve de Shazer, Michael White, Neil Jacobson, Andrew

Christensen, John Gottman, and Alan Gurman, and earlier innovators like Alfred Adler and Nathan Ackerman.

MFT had its beginnings in the 1940s; systemic family therapy took root in the 1950s (Becvar and Becvar 2006). However, its significant growth and development occurred only in the late 1970s and 1980s (Parrott 2003), following psychodynamic (first force), behavioral (second force), and humanistic (third force) approaches. MFT can therefore be considered the "fourth force" in the field of therapy (Corey 2009, 411), although family therapy or counseling as ministry has informally been around for three hundred years, since the early 1700s (Yarhouse and Sells 2008, 46–47; see also Gladding 2007, 56).

Numerous therapeutic techniques are used in MFT, including *reframing* (seeing problems in a more constructive or positive way); *boundary setting* (either to establish firmer limits or lines of separation, or to build more flexible boundaries to facilitate deeper connection); *family sculpting* (asking a couple or family members to physically put themselves in particular positions to reflect their family relationships); and constructing a *genogram* (a three-generational family tree or history) (see Parrott 2003, 378–80).

Biographical Sketches of Key Figures in MFT

The following are biographical sketches of several key figures in MFT: Alfred Adler, Nathan Ackerman, Murray Bowen, Jay Haley, Salvador Minuchin, Carl Whitaker, Virginia Satir, Cloé Madanes, Ivan Boszormenyi-Nagy, Steve de Shazer, Michael White, Susan Johnson, and Leslie Greenberg, as well as Neil Jacobson, Andrew Christensen, John Gottman, and Alan Gurman (see Corey 2009, 374, 410–11, 418–19; Day 2004, 342–44; Fall, Holden, and Marquis 2004, 367–76; Goldenberg and Goldenberg 2008a, 2008b; Gurman 2003; N. J. Kaslow, Dausch, and Celano 2003; Lebow 2008; Prochaska and Norcross 2010, 335–74; Yarhouse and Sells 2008, 38–286).

Alfred Adler (1870–1937), the founder of *individual psychology*, or Adlerian therapy (see chapter 5 of this book), was one of the first therapists to use a systemic approach in family therapy. After World War I, he established over thirty child guidance clinics in Vienna. Rudolph Dreikurs later applied Adlerian concepts and methods in the United States when he set up family education centers. Adler conducted family therapy sessions in front of other families so they could learn how to deal with problems that Adler believed were common among families (O. C. Christensen 2004).

Nathan Ackerman has been called "the unofficial founder of family therapy" (Gurman 2003, 464) and "the parent figure of psychodynamic family therapy" (Yarhouse and Sells 2008, 151), who earlier asserted that marital therapy was "the core approach to family change" (Ackerman 1970a, 124), but family therapy has not embraced his view. Ackerman was trained in doing psychoanalytic therapy with children, but he eventually advocated seeing the whole family as a unit in therapy in order to assess and help troubled families (Ackerman 1966, 1970b). His book *The Psychodynamics of Family Life* (Ackerman 1958) is often considered the landmark text that helped to define the new field of family therapy (Goldenberg and Goldenberg 2008a, 410).

Ackerman was born in Bessarabia, Russia, on November 22, 1908, but his family moved to the United States in 1912. He obtained his BA in 1929 and his MD in 1933 from Columbia University. He became chief psychiatrist at the Menninger Child Guidance Clinic in 1937. After World War II, Ackerman became a clinical professor of psychiatry at Columbia University.

Ackerman established the Institute for Family Studies and Treatment in 1960 and served as its director until his death in 1971, at which time it was renamed the Nathan W. Ackerman Institute, or simply the Ackerman Institute, which is now world renowned as a center for family psychology. It publishes *Family Process*, the first major family therapy journal. Ackerman died on June 12, 1971.

Murray Bowen was born on January 13, 1913, in Waverly, Tennessee, the oldest of five children in a family that was relatively large and close-knit. He graduated with a BS from the University of Tennessee in Knoxville in 1934 and obtained his MD from the University of Tennessee Medical School in Memphis in 1937. Bowen served in the U.S. Army for five years, during which his interests shifted from surgery to psychiatry. He trained in psychiatry and psychoanalysis at the Menninger Foundation in Topeka, Kansas, from 1946 to 1954. Bowen focused on schizophrenic patients and their mothers, and this work eventually resulted in his concept of *differentiation of self*, or the development of autonomy of the individual.

In 1954, Bowen accepted a position at the National Institute of Mental Health, where he became the first director of the new Family Division. He began treating the whole family as a unit seen together in therapy sessions and therefore became a major figure in the development of systemic family therapy. He moved to Georgetown University in Washington, DC, in 1959, where he remained until he died in 1990 of lung cancer, at the age of seventy-seven. He was a clinical professor of psychiatry in the Department of Psychiatry as well as director of family programs at Georgetown University. He also established a family center. Bowen further developed his family systems theory, including key concepts such as *differentiation of self*, *triangulation*, and *multigenerational or transgenerational transmission*, which are now widely accepted in the MFT field. His well-known approach to therapy has been variously labeled *extended family systems therapy, transgenerational or multigenerational family therapy*, or simply *Bowenian family therapy* (Yarhouse and Sells 2008).

Bowen also helped found the American Family Therapy Association and served as its first president from 1978 to 1982. His most significant publication is *Family Therapy in Clinical Practice* (1978).

Jay Douglas Haley (1923–2007) helped develop *strategic family therapy*, another major approach to MFT (see Haley 1963, 1976; Haley and Richeport-Haley 2003, 2007). Strategic family therapy is a pragmatic, problem-solving approach that deals with the present problems of couples and families without delving into the past to achieve insight. Haley developed ideas relating to power, hierarchy, and strategic interventions including directive as well as paradoxical techniques. He was influenced by Milton Erickson and his therapeutic techniques (Haley 1973). The Milan Group, led by Mara Selvini-Palazzoli (see Selvini 1988) at the Center for Family Studies in Milan, Italy, also contributed to the further development of strategic family therapy into what is called *systemic family therapy* (Boscolo, Cecchin, Hoffman, and Penn 1987; Selvini-Palazzoli, Boscolo, Cecchin, and Prata 1978), which is especially successful with psychotic and anorectic patients (Goldenberg and Goldenberg 2008a, 412).

Haley was born in Midwest, Wyoming, but moved with his family to Berkeley, California, when he was four years old. He obtained a BA in theater arts from UCLA, a bachelor of library science degree from UC Berkeley, and a master's degree in communication from Stanford University. He married his first wife, Elizabeth, in 1950, and they had three children.

Haley met Gregory Bateson, an anthropologist, while he was at Stanford and was invited to be involved in the Double Bind Communications Project—later called the Bateson Project—together with Bateson, who launched the project in 1952; John Weakland; and Donald Jackson. Jackson founded the Mental Research Institute (MRI) in Palo Alto in 1958 (with the involvement of Virginia Satir and Paul Watzlawick), and when the Bateson Project ended in 1962, Haley joined MRI, together with Weakland. This very creative and productive group produced many publications (see Prochaska and Norcross 2010, 339–40), including a landmark article that helped develop the field of family therapy, titled, "Toward a Theory of Schizophrenia" (Bateson, Jackson, Haley, and Weakland 1956), that focused on how double binds or conflicting communications in a family system could lead to schizophrenic symptoms.

In the mid-1960s, Haley took a position at the Philadelphia Child Guidance Clinic, where he worked closely with Salvador Minuchin, who developed *structural family therapy*. He then founded the Family Therapy Institute in Washington, DC, in 1976, with Cloé Madanes, his second wife, and they continued to further develop strategic family therapy (see Madanes 1981). During this time, he published *Problem-Solving Therapy* (Haley 1976), which became one of the most significant books in the MFT field.

Haley eventually left the Family Therapy Institute and moved to San Diego, where in the last few years of his life he collaborated with his third wife, Madeleine Richeport-Haley, in producing several films on anthropology and psychotherapy. They also coauthored two important books: *The Art of Strategic Therapy* (Haley and Richeport-Haley 2003) and *Directive Family Therapy* (Haley and Richeport-Haley 2007). Haley was a scholar in residence at the California School of Professional Psychology, Alliant International University, when he died on February 13, 2007, at the age of eighty-three (see Ray 2007).

Salvador Minuchin developed *structural family therapy* in the 1960s, initially based on his work in therapy and research with delinquent youths from poor families at the Wiltwyck School in New York (S. Minuchin et al. 1967). Structural family therapy can be briefly described as "a systemic approach to family interventions that focuses on identifying the underlying patterns or rules that regulate or dictate the space between people in the relationship" (Yarhouse and Sells 2008, 122). Minuchin believed that structural changes in the organization of families in terms of their usual patterns of interaction and types of relationships are necessary before the symptoms of individual members of the family can be reduced (Corey 2009, 411). It had a preeminent place in family therapy and theory in the 1970s and 1980s and is still a major approach to MFT today (see Yarhouse and Sells 2008, 122–23, for more details on Minuchin and the history of structural family therapy).

Minuchin was born in 1921 in Argentina, where his parents had immigrated from Europe. He obtained his medical training in Buenos Aires and served as a military physician in the Israeli army in the late 1940s, as Israel attempted to achieve statehood. He then trained to be a psychiatrist in New York before returning to Israel in 1952 to help families and orphans in the aftermath of the Holocaust.

Minuchin returned to the United States in 1954 and received psychoanalytic training at the William Alanson White Institute in Manhattan. He also served as the psychiatrist at the Wiltwyck School for delinquent boys, where he collaborated with a clinical social worker, Braulio Montalvo, in developing structural family therapy and theory. Minuchin has referred to Montalvo as his most influential teacher (Goldenberg and Goldenberg 2008b).

Minuchin moved to the Philadelphia Child Guidance Clinic in 1965 to become its director. He invited Montalvo and Jay Haley to join him there, and their collaboration further advanced the integration of structural and strategic family therapy ideas and techniques. The clinic grew under Minuchin's leadership and had become very well known by the time he left in 1981. Minuchin has authored and coauthored several significant books in the MFT field, including the classic *Families and Family Therapy* (1974) on structural family therapy and theory (see also P. Minuchin, Colapinto, and Minuchin 2007; S. Minuchin, Rosman, and Baker 1978; S. Minuchin and Fishman 1981; S. Minuchin, Lee, and Simon 2006; S. Minuchin, Nichols, and Lee 2007). His structural approach has also been more specifically applied to helping troubled couples in what is called *structural couple therapy* (Simon 2008). He has continued to write and train family therapists at the Minuchin Center for the Family in New York City (see Prochaska and Norcross 2010, 349).

Carl Whitaker, another well-known figure in the MFT field (see Yarhouse and Sells 2008, 195–97), is credited with Virginia Satir for independently developing *experiential family therapy* or *symbolic-experiential family therapy*. His approach is more intuitive and spontaneous, with the family therapist functioning actively and creatively as a coach and participant with the troubled family, helping its members to be more open and autonomous as individuals while maintaining a sense of connection or belonging in the family (Corey 2009, 410).

Whitaker was born in 1912 and grew up in upstate New York on a dairy farm. He was not very outgoing but had a few close friends as an adolescent who were helpful to him as he made decisions and went through his teen years, college, medical training, and medical practice. Friendship was crucial for him, and his relationships with Muriel, his wife, and with his six children, were of particular significance to him (Whitaker 1989; Whitaker and Keith 1981). Whitaker valued cotherapy and advocated having two or more therapists, or cotherapists, when treating a troubled family, because a therapist working alone is more prone to mistakes and can be less objective. Cotherapy was also a good balance and corrective for Whitaker's often unconventional and radical interventions, for he was well known "for being spontaneous, unpredictable, funny, bold, confrontational and direct" (Yarhouse and Sells 2008, 195).

Whitaker obtained his medical training at Syracuse University and specialized in psychiatry after initially trying obstetrics and gynecology. He then became a faculty member at the University of Louisville. During World War II, he was involved as a physician in the Oak Ridge Research facility in eastern Tennessee, where the US government was secretly developing the atomic bomb. He and his cotherapist, John Warkentin, experienced very strong transference relationships with their patients who might have had posttraumatic stress disorder symptoms. Whitaker therefore learned to function as a symbolic mother and father to deal with the transference needs of family members seen in family therapy by him and his cotherapist. He used a combination of warmth, humor, self-disclosure, confrontation, and even radical and absurd interventions in order to do this. He believed that a mature therapist will function like a foster parent and be appropriately parental to the patients and families they see in therapy. He founded and developed what came to be known as *symbolic-experiential family therapy* (Whitaker and Bumberry 1988; Whitaker and Keith 1981).

Whitaker became chair of the Department of Psychiatry at Emory University in Atlanta in 1946 and remained there until 1955. He coauthored an important book with Thomas Malone in 1953, titled *The Roots of Psychotherapy*, in which they emphasized that psychotherapy is essentially a sacred relationship and involves a learning experience that is culturally based and should not be quantified or objectified. Psychotherapy should therefore not be considered a branch of medical science (Whitaker and Malone 1953).

Emory University preferred a more psychoanalytic approach to therapy, so Whitaker left and set up a private practice clinic in Atlanta with his colleagues, including Thomas Malone and John Warkentin. In 1965, he then moved to the University of Wisconsin Medical School in Madison, Wisconsin, to become a professor of psychiatry, a position he occupied until his retirement in 1989. This was a very productive period of his professional life during which he and his students further developed many of his ideas on symbolic-experiential family therapy. He died in 1995.

Virginia Satir was also responsible for developing *experiential family therapy*, with which Carl Whitaker is usually associated (see Yarhouse and Sells 2008, 193–95). They made their significant contributions to this major approach to MFT independently of each other.

Satir was born Virginia Pagenkopf on June 26, 1916, in Neillsville, Wisconsin, a rural farming town, the eldest of five children. She and her family moved to Milwaukee in 1929 so that she could attend high school. Satir graduated from high school when she was sixteen years old and then attended Milwaukee Teachers College, where she obtained a BA in education in 1936. She began her graduate studies at Northwestern University, but completed her master's degree in social work administration at the University of Chicago in 1943. Satir married and divorced twice, the second time to Norman Satir, whom she married in 1951 and divorced in 1957.

Satir began her clinical work with families in 1951 and set up a clinical psychiatric training program at the Illinois Psychiatric Institute with Dr. Calmest Gyros. Ivan Boszormenyi-Nagy, who developed contextual family therapy, was one of Satir's supervisees then. Her significant clinical work in experiential family therapy put her in touch with Murray Bowen, who connected her with Don Jackson. Satir became the clinical director of the Mental Research Institute (MRI) at Jackson's invitation in 1959. Several years later, in 1966, she moved to the Esalen Institute in Big Sur, California, where she served as its clinical director. This was a significant move for Satir, who also shifted from being a purist in systemic theory and therapy to being more a humanistic therapist who focused on self-esteem as the crucial factor in human growth. She had a professional rift with Salvador Minuchin in the 1970s, which resulted in her emphasizing human potential and growth even more, with less emphasis on family systems. Satir was well known for her charisma as well as her warm and gentle style (see Yarhouse and Sells 2008, 194–95).

Satir specifically developed *conjoint family therapy* as a process of human validation, based on communication and emotional experiencing and centered in the therapeutic relationship between the therapist and the family rather than in techniques, which are viewed as being secondary (see Satir and Bitter 2000). Although she made use of Bowen's multigenerational or transgenerational model, she focused more on making current patterns of family interaction come to life in the therapy session by using interventions such as *sculpting* and *family reconstructions* (see Corey 2009, 410). She has authored or coauthored several significant books that have greatly influenced the MFT field (e.g., Satir 1964, 1972, 1983, 1988; Satir and Baldwin 1983; Satir, Bauman, Gerber, and Gamori 1991). Satir is considered one of the most influential therapists as well as the "most celebrated humanist" (Nichols 2006, 199). She received numerous awards and honors, including an honorary doctorate in social sciences from the University of Wisconsin-Madison in 1978. She died on September 10, 1988.

Cloé Madanes founded the Family Therapy Institute in Washington, DC, in 1976 with her then-husband, Jay Haley. She collaborated with Haley in further developing strategic family therapy and authored an important text on this approach, *Strategic Family Therapy* (Madanes 1981; see also Madanes 1984). In the 1980s, strategic family therapy as a short-term, problem-solving treatment became the most popular approach in the MFT field (Corey 2009, 411).

Madanes and Haley eventually divorced, but she went on to establish her own unique work and voice in other related areas such as sex, love, and violence (Madanes 1990). More recently, she has published a collection of her papers focusing on her work as a therapist who is a humanist, a social activist, and a systemic thinker (Madanes 2006).

Madanes is currently president of the Robbins-Madanes Center for Strategic Intervention and the Madanes Institute in La Jolla, California. She is also the director of the Program for the Prevention of School and Family Violence and the Council for Human Rights of Children, at the Center for Child and Family Development, University of San Francisco.

Ivan Boszormenyi-Nagy (pronounced Boz-er-men-yee-Naj) founded and developed *contextual family therapy* (see Yarhouse and Sells 2008, 171–73), which is a major approach to MFT. His contextual family therapy approach (Boszormenyi-Nagy and Krasner 1986; see also Boszormenyi-Nagy and Spark 1984; Hargrave and Pfitzer 2003) consists of four major dimensions (Van Heusden and Van den Eerenbeemt 1987, xiv): *facts* (e.g., genetic roots and features, physical health, and events such as adoption, divorce, unemployment, and disability); *individual psychologies* (e.g., basic needs and internal motivations of the individual); *transactions* (systemic interaction or behavioral and communication patterns observed between people, e.g., structures, subsystems, rules, roles, power alignments); and *relational ethics* (referring to fairness or justice in a relationship or the balance between obligations and earned merit, with a focus on trust, loyalty, trustworthiness and entitlement, and the influence of previous generations and implications for future generations).

Boszormenyi-Nagy (professionals often refer to him as Nagy) was born in Budapest, Hungary, on May 19, 1920. After graduating from medical school in Hungary, he completed his residency training in psychiatry at the University of Budapest. In 1950, he moved to the United States and worked under Kalman Gyarfas, a relationship-oriented dynamic therapist, at the Illinois Psychiatric Institute in Chicago; he was also supervised in his clinical work by Virginia Satir. While Boszormenyi-Nagy was influenced by psychoanalytic and psychodynamic theories, including Freudian psychoanalysis and the object relations views of Ronald Fairbairn, he had never been a trained psychoanalyst (Van Heusden and Van den Eerenbeemt 1987, 5). He was also influenced by the work of well-known therapists in the 1950s who were treating patients with schizophrenia, and especially by Martin Buber and his humanistic emphasis on the I-Thou relationship, which Boszormenyi-Nagy believed is achieved in a family context by building trust (Yarhouse and Sells 2008, 172).

In 1957, Boszormenyi-Nagy moved to the Eastern Pennsylvania Psychiatric Institute (EPPI) and worked in a research inpatient service for psychotic patients, where he and his staff did intensive individual therapy. However, in 1958, he introduced the use of family therapy for all patients. At EPPI, he was able to recruit a group of talented researchers and therapists who made significant contributions to the field of family therapy, including James Framo, Gerald Zuk, Geraldine Spark, and John Rosen. He also had contact with other early family therapists such as Nathan Ackerman, Murray Bowen, Lyman Wynne, and later, Carl Whitaker (Van Heusden and Van den Eerenbeemt 1987, 5–6). He died on January 28, 2007.

Steve de Shazer was one of the originators of *solution-focused family therapy* (see Corey 2009, 374; Yarhouse and Sells 2008, 223–25). He and his wife, Insoo Kim Berg, another well-known figure in the MFT field, codeveloped the solution-focused approach to MFT and were involved for many years with the Brief Family Therapy Center in Milwaukee, Wisconsin, where de Shazer was director of research and Berg served as director of the center. He wrote several significant books (see de Shazer 1985, 1988, 1991, 1994; de Shazer and Dolan 2007) as did Berg (see Berg 1994; Berg and Miller 1992; De Jong and Berg 2008). Solution-focused family therapy focuses specifically "on *solutions*, on *what works for clients*" (Hoyt 2008, 259), with the therapist helping clients to think differently about their problems and finding solutions by asking key questions such as: "Suppose that one night, while you were asleep, there was a miracle and this problem was solved. How would you know? What would be different?" (de Shazer 1988, 10). There is no attempt to dig deeper for insight into unconscious processes. The solution-focused approach developed by de Shazer and Berg can also be applied to individual therapy and couple therapy (see Hoyt 2008, 262–63).

Steve de Shazer was born on June 25, 1940, in Milwaukee, Wisconsin. He was a musician before he became a therapist. He graduated with a bachelor's degree in fine arts from the University of Wisconsin, Milwaukee; he loved jazz music and played the saxophone. He later obtained a master's degree in social work from the same university. De Shazer's spontaneity in jazz music influenced his development of solution-focused family therapy, with its emphasis on creativity and spontaneity in both the therapist and the client in exploring solutions for the client in relatively brief therapy. His work, together with his wife, at the Brief Family Therapy Center in Milwaukee, Wisconsin, was very productive and had a significant impact on MFT and its practice. He died on September 11, 2005, in Vienna while he was on a teaching tour in Europe. His wife died in 2007.

Michael Kingsley White was the cofounder of the narrative therapy movement, together with David Epston, who is codirector of the Family Therapy Centre in Auckland, New Zealand (see Corey 2009, 357; Yarhouse and Sells 2008, 266). White was codirector of the Dulwich Centre in Adelaide, Australia, and began developing narrative therapy in the late 1980s through his work and writings at the center. He is widely considered the major figure of the narrative therapy movement (Lebow 2008, 325). He founded the Adelaide Narrative Therapy Centre in January 2008 to provide clinical services and further training in narrative therapy, not only with families and couples but also with individuals, groups, and communities. He authored or coauthored several significant books that have greatly influenced the practice of MFT (see, e.g., M. White 2007; M. White and Epston 1989, 1990).

David Epston's writings have also made substantial contributions to the development of narrative therapy (see, e.g., M. White and Epston 1989, 1990; see also Freeman, Epston, and Lobovits 1997; Monk, Winslade, Crocket, and Epston 1997), including the technique of letter writing, in which letters written by the family therapist can be repeatedly read by clients to help them maintain therapeutic gains (Yarhouse and Sells 2008, 266). Narrative family therapy, as developed by White and Epston (see also C. Brown and Augusta-Scott 2007), was influenced by the French postmodern philosophers Michel Foucault and Jacques Derrida as well as by the therapeutic ideas of Gregory Bateson (Yarhouse and Sells 2008, 266). As a major approach to MFT, it emphasizes empowering family members to re-author their own life stories in more constructive and less oppressive ways so that they see more options as they learn to view their problems as being outside themselves, a process called *externalization* (Goldenberg and Goldenberg 2008a, 413).

Michael White was born on December 29, 1948, in Adelaide, South Australia. He obtained a bachelor's degree in social work from the University of South Australia in 1979 and then joined the staff of Adelaide Children's Hospital as a psychiatric social worker. In 1983, he helped found the Dulwich Centre in Adelaide and also began a private practice in family therapy.

White received several honors and awards in recognition of his significant and influential work in the MFT field, particularly in cofounding and developing narrative family therapy, which also includes narrative couple therapy (see Freedman and Combs 2002, 2008). He was awarded an honorary doctorate of humane letters by John F. Kennedy University in Orinda, California, as well as the Distinguished Contribution to Family Therapy, Theory, and Practice Award from the American Family Therapy Academy in 1999. White died on April 4, 2008.

Susan M. Johnson, better known as Sue Johnson, is one of the originators and the main proponent of emotionally focused therapy, or emotion-focused therapy (EFT), and experiential couple and family therapy (see Goldenberg and Goldenberg 2008a, 411). Together with Leslie Greenberg, Johnson has developed EFT, which has experienced phenomenal growth since the 1990s (Yarhouse and Sells 2008, 198). Greenberg and Johnson in their earlier collaborative work in developing EFT, and Johnson in her later work that integrated more attachment theory into *emotionally focused couple therapy*, made use of therapeutic interventions derived from Gestalt therapy. Clients are thus helped to express intense emotions such as anger, deal with defenses, and work toward a softening of feelings so that connection between a couple or members of a family can be restored and deepened (see Lebow 2008, 325). Johnson has authored or coauthored several significant books (see S. M. Johnson 2008a) on emotionally focused couple and family therapy that have greatly impacted the MFT field (see, e.g., S. M. Johnson 2002, 2004, 2008b; S. M. Johnson et al. 2005; see also L. S. Greenberg and Johnson 1988). Greenberg has also written more generally on EFT as emotion-focused therapy, which helps clients to work through their feelings (L. S. Greenberg 2002).

Johnson received her doctorate (EdD) degree in counseling psychology from the University of British Columbia in 1984. She is a professor of clinical psychology at the University of Ottawa and director of the Ottawa Couple and Family Institute and of the International Center for Excellence in Emotionally Focused Therapy in Ottawa, Ontario. She annually conducts EFT externships in Ottawa to train others in EFT. She is also a registered psychologist in Ontario and a research professor at Alliant University in San Diego, California, where she conducts training in EFT every January. Johnson is considered the main proponent of emotionally focused couple therapy and emotionally focused family therapy. She has received several honors and awards for her well-known work in the MFT field, including the American Association of Marriage and Family Therapy Outstanding Contribution to the Field award in 2000 and the award for research in family therapy from the American Family Therapy Academy in 2005. She has a private practice in Ottawa, where she lives with her husband and two children (see S. M. Johnson et al. 2005, 395).

Leslie Samuel Greenberg, who helped develop EFT with Sue Johnson, is a professor of psychology at York University in Toronto, Ontario. He is the cofounder of EFT for couples and families (see L. S. Greenberg and Johnson 1988; see also L. S. Greenberg and Goldman 2008) as well as EFT to help clients work through their feelings (L. S. Greenberg 2002), including dealing with depression (L. S. Greenberg and Watson 2006). Greenberg is also a well-known and prominent leader in *experiential psychotherapy* (see, e.g., L. S. Greenberg, Watson, and Lietaer 1998; Pos, Greenberg, and Elliott 2008).

Greenberg was born on September 30, 1945, in Johannesburg, South Africa, but eventually emigrated to Canada. He is married with two children and currently lives in Toronto. He has made substantial contributions to the MFT field as well as to experiential psychotherapy, in his development of EFT with couples and families and also with individuals.

Neil S. Jacobson (1949–99) initially made significant contributions to the development of *behavioral marital therapy* (BMT) or *traditional behavioral couple therapy* (TBCT) based on social learning and behavior exchange principles (N. S. Jacobson and Margolin 1979). TBCT is still the only couple therapy that currently meets the strictest criteria (efficacy and specificity) for an empirically supported treatment (see Dimidjian, Martell, and Christensen 2008, 73). Jacobson later helped develop *integrative behavioral couple therapy* (IBCT) with Andrew Christensen (N. S. Jacobson and Christensen 1998; see also A. Christensen and Jacobson 2000). Jacobson was a professor of psychology at the University of Washington in Seattle until his death in 1999. He was a prolific author of nine books and two hundred articles and is one of the most widely cited family therapists. He made substantial and cutting-edge contributions not only to the MFT field but also to the treatment of depression and domestic violence. He received many honors, including prestigious research awards from the American Association for Marriage and Family Therapy, the American Family Therapy Academy, and the National Institutes of Health.

Andrew Christensen is well known for codeveloping *integrative behavioral couple therapy* (IBCT) with Neil Jacobson (see A. Christensen and Jacobson 2000; N. S. Jacobson and Christensen 1998; see also Dimidjian, Martell, and Christensen 2008). He has also done substantial research, funded by the National Institute of Mental Health, on evaluating the relative effectiveness of IBCT versus TBCT (traditional behavioral couple therapy) (see A. Christensen et al. 2004; A. Christensen, Atkins, Yi, Baucom, and George 2006; A. Christensen, Atkins, Baucom, and Yi 2010). Christensen is a professor of psychology at the University of California, Los Angeles (UCLA). He has published widely on couple therapy and couple conflict.

John Mordecai Gottman (1942–) developed his research-based approach, now called the *Gottman method couple therapy*, in collaboration with his wife, Julie Schwartz Gottman (see Gottman and Gottman 2008). Gottman's method of couple therapy endeavors to integrate different approaches to MFT, such as analytic, behavioral, existential, emotionally focused, narrative, and systems, into a theory (the sound relationship house theory) that is empirically derived, based on years of research on what makes relationships succeed or fail. The Gottman method couple therapy uses various therapeutic interventions to achieve the following goals: "down-regulate negative affect during conflict, up-regulate positive affect during conflict, build positive affect during non-conflict, bridge meta-emotion mismatches, and create and nurture a shared meaning system" (Gottman and Gottman 2008, 143–61).

John Gottman is an emeritus professor of psychology in the Department of Psychology at the University of Washington and director of the Relationship Research Institute in Seattle, Washington. He has authored or coauthored several significant books that have greatly impacted the MFT field (see, e.g., Gottman 1994a, 1994b, 1999; Gottman and Gottman 2007; Gottman and Silver 1999).

Alan S. Gurman is a pioneer in the development of integrative approaches to couple therapy (see Gurman 2008a, vii). He has described his *integrative couple therapy* (ICT) as a depth-behavioral approach that seriously considers both interpersonal and intrapersonal factors in helping couples with relationship difficulties. ICT is based on general family systems theory and adult developmental theory (especially attachment theory) and more specifically grounded in applied social learning theory (or behavior therapy) and object relations theory (see Gurman 2008b, 383). Gurman has independently refined and developed his integrative approach to couple therapy for the past three decades, although ICT shares some similarities with other integrative models of couple therapy. ICT was previously called *brief integrative marital therapy* (BIMT) (Gurman 2002).

Gurman has coauthored or coedited several influential books on family therapy, marital or couple therapy, brief therapy, and essential psychotherapies that have greatly influenced the MFT field as well as the broader field of counseling and psychotherapy (see, e.g., Budman and Gurman 1988; Gurman 2008a; Gurman and Jacobson 2002; Gurman and Kniskern 1981, 1991; Gurman and Messer 2003).

Gurman is an emeritus professor of psychiatry and director of Family Therapy Training at the University of Wisconsin School of Medicine and Public Health in Madison. He has served for two terms as editor of the *Journal of Marital and Family Therapy* and was president of the Society for Psychotherapy Research. He has made substantial contributions to the MFT field and received many awards and honors, including awards for Distinguished Contributions to Family Psychology from the American Psychological Association, Distinguished Achievement in Family Therapy Research from the American Family Therapy Academy, and Distinguished Contribution to Research in Family Therapy from the American Association for Marriage and Family Therapy. He was also recently the recipient of a national teaching award for Excellence in Internship Training/Distinguished Achievement in Teaching and Training from the Association of Psychology Postdoctoral and Internship Centers. He has an active clinical practice in Madison, Wisconsin.

Major Theoretical Ideas of Marital and Family Therapy

Perspective on Human Nature

MFT actually has over twenty diverse systemic therapies that have been developed to help distressed couples and troubled families. It is therefore difficult to identify a particular perspective on human nature that can adequately represent such different MFT approaches. For example, psychodynamic family therapy (see Yarhouse and Sells 2008), or more specifically object relations couple and family therapy, will have a perspective on human nature that is more in line with a psychoanalytic or psychodynamic view. Cognitive-behavioral family therapy will have a perspective on human nature that is consistent with a cognitive behavior therapy (CBT) view. Such views on human nature of the major approaches to counseling and psychotherapy have already been covered in previous chapters and will not be repeated here.

There are, however, some basic perspectives on human nature that are consistent across most MFT approaches that take a *systemic* view of human functioning. Systemic approaches in MFT focus on the family as a unit and apply *general systems theory* as developed by Ludwig von Bertalanffy (1968) beginning in the 1940s to family functioning and dysfunctioning, emphasizing the significance of interrelations between parts of a system that can result in *circular causality* (e.g., A may cause B, but B also affects A, which then affects B, and so on). A specific example of such family systems thinking is the view that symptoms in one member of the family actually reflect family dysfunction instead of the individual's own psychopathology (see Goldenberg and Goldenberg 2008a, 409). Systemic MFT approaches such as strategic family therapy, structural family therapy, Bowenian or transgenerational (multigenerational) family therapy, contextual family therapy, and psychodynamic or object relations family therapy (see Yarhouse and Sells 2008) tend to have a more pessimistic view of human nature and of families as having tendencies toward dysfunction. The therapist therefore must intervene as an expert, giving directives or providing interpretations that may help families and family members to change. The potential to change is there but in limited degree.

Other, more recent approaches to MFT that have a systems approach but are modified to include a more respectful view of human nature and families as being capable of choice, change, creative problem-solving, and meaning making, include experiential family therapy, solution-focused family therapy, narrative therapy, and to a certain extent, cognitive-behavioral family therapy and emotionally focused couple and family therapy (see Yarhouse and Sells

2008). The family therapist in these approaches does not assume an expert stance but rather collaborates with the family members, in mutually respectful and egalitarian therapeutic relationships, empowering them to develop their own creative solutions to their family problems, while providing some gentle guidance. Cognitive-behavioral family therapy and emotionally focused couple and family therapy, however, usually involve relatively more directive family therapist action and intervention.

Thus the major MFT approaches differ in their views of human nature and the nature of families. Some have more positive perspectives on human nature and the potential for change in families, whereas others have somewhat more pessimistic perspectives on human nature and the limited capacity of families to choose and make therapeutic changes.

Major Approaches to MFT

Irene Goldenberg and Herbert Goldenberg (2008b) have identified eight major approaches to MFT: (1) object relations family therapy; (2) experiential family therapy; (3) transgenerational family therapy; (4) structural family therapy; (5) strategic family therapy; (6) cognitive behavior family therapy; (7) social constructionist family therapy; and (8) narrative therapy (see also Goldenberg and Goldenberg 2008a, 411–14).

Object Relations Family Therapy. This psychodynamic family therapy developed by David Scharff and Jill Scharff (1987, 1991; see also J. S. Scharff and D. E. Scharff 2008) assumes an object relations approach to couple and family therapy emphasizing that the basic need in life is to have a satisfying relationship with some "object" or another person. Family members bring *introjects* (or memories of loss or lack of fulfillment in childhood) into their present interactions with others, attempting to find fulfillment but also affecting current family relations in negative ways at times. Family members unconsciously relate to one another based on childhood expectations and motivations. The object relations family therapist attempts to help family members understand how they internalized objects from their past and gain insight into how these internalized objects are still affecting their present relationships, so that they can change in constructive ways.

Experiential Family Therapy. Experiential family therapy includes the *human validation process model* (Satir and Bit-

Sidebar 13.2
Approaches to Marital and Family Therapy *(see Goldenberg and Goldenberg 2008a, 411–14)*
1. Object relations family therapy
2. Experiential family therapy
3. Transgenerational family therapy
4. Structural family therapy
5. Strategic family therapy
6. Cognitive behavior family therapy
7. Social constructionist family therapy
8. Narrative therapy

ter 2000), better known as *conjoint family therapy* developed by Satir (1964, 1983), and the *symbolic-experiential family therapy* developed by Whitaker (Whitaker and Bumberry 1988; Whitaker and Keith 1981; see also Whitaker 1989). Both Satir and Whitaker emphasized that disturbed families need a growth experience in deeply connecting with an authentic, involved, and appropriately self-disclosing family therapist (or two in cotherapy), thus helping such families to open up and be more honest about their real feelings and needs, and empowering them to choose to change in more constructive ways. Satir focused more on building self-esteem and teaching open and adequate communication with families, whereas Whitaker used his own fantasies and instincts to help family members accept their own subjective experiences and explore their inner world of symbolic meanings in order to grow. Goldenberg and Goldenberg (2008a, 411) included *emotion-focused couple therapy* (EFT) (L. S. Greenberg 2002; S. M. Johnson 2004, 2008a) as a current representation of experiential family therapy, grounded in attachment theory and integrated with humanistic and systemic perspectives, that helps couples to soften their negative interactions and strengthen their emotional connection with each other.

Transgenerational Family Therapy. This approach has also been called *multigenerational family therapy* or simply *Bowenian family therapy* (Yarhouse and Sells 2008) because it was developed by Bowen (1978). He believed that family members are connected to their family system, and those with the strongest emotional connections, or *fusion*, with the family are more susceptible to experiencing their own emotional reactions to family struggles. *Differentiation of self*, or one's ability to have a separate sense of self independent from the family and also one's ability to differentiate between one's intellect and one's feelings, is crucial for the healthy functioning of the individual in his or her family.

Triangulation is another key concept described by Bowen, referring to a process in which three people are involved in a *two-against-one* experience (see Corey 2009, 415), for example, when a married couple with marital conflict and tension pull in their teenage daughter as a third person to help stabilize their conflict rather than dealing with it more directly by themselves. Their attention is now diverted to their daughter, who may end up acting out in rebellious ways (see Yarhouse and Sells 2008, 76, 78).

Bowen also described how a family's emotional processes and problems, especially low levels of differentiation of self, are passed down from one generation to another in what he called a *multigenerational transmission process*. An example is when a family member with low differentiation of self marries a spouse who also has a low differentiation of self, and their offspring who is least differentiated also ends up marrying someone with low differentiation of self. The low differentiation of self thus continues through succeeding generations.

Goldenberg and Goldenberg (2008a, 412) included *contextual family therapy* (see Boszormenyi-Nagy 1987; Boszormenyi-Nagy and Krasner 1986; Boszormenyi-Nagy and Spark 1984) as developed by Ivan Boszormenyi-Nagy as another example of *transgenerational family therapy*. However, Boszormenyi-Nagy focused more on the ethical dimension in family relationships, in an intergenerational context, with aspects such as trust, loyalty, entitlements, and indebtedness. Contextual family therapists help families to maintain fairness and to fulfill each family member's personal sense of claims, rights, and obligations in his or her relationships with the other members of the family.

Structural Family Therapy. This approach to MFT was developed by Minuchin (1974), who described a structural view that focused on the organization of families and the rules that govern the interactions between family members. Attention is especially given to family rules, roles, alignments, and coalitions, and also to how the overall family system is composed in terms of its subsystems and boundaries. Structural family therapists try to help families free themselves from their usual rigid and repetitive patterns of interaction so that they can engage in more constructive and healthy reorganization of the family.

Strategic Family Therapy. This approach to MFT was developed mainly by Haley (1963, 1976). It is a pragmatic, problem-solving therapy that involves the use of creative strategies by the strategic family therapist to reduce or eliminate unwanted behavior in the family. The specific therapeutic techniques used can be direct or indirect, such as paradoxical techniques (e.g., prescribing the symptom). Haley's approach does not focus on helping family members gain insight into the past or unconscious processes. Instead, it focuses on the presenting problems of the family and on directively attempting to solve them in creative and constructive ways.

Mara Selvini-Palazzoli and her colleagues (Selvini-Palazzoli, Boscolo, Cecchin, and Prata 1978) in Milan, Italy, developed a variation of strategic family therapy called *systemic family therapy*, which has been successfully used especially with psychotic and anorectic patients. Selvini-Palazzoli (1986) views behavioral symptoms in children as part of "dirty games" in which parents and their symptomatic children engage in power struggles. Children thus use their symptoms in attempts to defeat one parent in order to help the other parent. Boscolo and Cecchin (Boscolo, Cecchin, Hoffman, and Penn 1987) have further developed interviewing techniques (e.g., *circular questioning*) to empower family members to explore their family belief system and make constructive changes and new choices. Luigi Boscolo and Gianfranco Cecchin also viewed the family therapist no longer as the expert who knows objectively what is best for the family being seen in therapy but simply as a participant with the rest of the family. They therefore helped to facilitate the development of more postmodern, social constructionist approaches to MFT (see Goldenberg and Goldenberg 2008a, 412).

Cognitive Behavior Family Therapy. This approach to MFT includes the behavioral perspective, which focuses on using reinforcement contingencies to increase desirable behaviors and decrease dysfunctional behaviors in couples and families and on teaching communication and problem-solving skills (see, e.g., N. S. Jacobson and Margolin 1979). It also incorporates cognitive therapy, which focuses on identifying and restructuring distorted thinking or irrational beliefs that influence feelings and behaviors (see, e.g., Baucom and Epstein 1990; Baucom, Epstein, LaTaillade, and Kirby 2008; Dattilio 2009; Epstein and Baucom 2002; Epstein, Schlesinger, and Dryden 1988). More-recent versions of behavioral and cognitive behavior family therapy place greater emphasis on acceptance, for example, in integrative behavioral couple therapy (IBCT) (see N. S. Jacobson and Christensen 1998; A. Christensen and Jacobson 2000; see also Dimidjian, Martell, and Christensen 2008) versus traditional behavioral couple therapy (TBCT).

Social Constructionist Family Therapy. This approach to MFT is a more recent development, influenced mainly by postmodern views, which emphasize subjective perceptions of reality that differ from person to person or family to family, depending on important diversity factors such as ethnicity, culture, gender, and sexual orientation (see Goldenberg and Goldenberg 2008, 413). Social constructionist family therapy therefore values diversity and challenges traditional systems perspectives that emphasize a simple cybernetic model of family functioning with the family therapist as expert in assessing and treating troubled families. The social constructionist approach to MFT advocates mutually respectful and truly collaborative therapeutic relationships between family therapists and family members. Families are empowered to develop their own creative solutions to their problems, with only some gentle guidance from the therapist, who does not function as the expert. Well-known examples of social constructionist family therapy include *solution-focused therapy*, developed by Steve de Shazer (see, e.g., de Shazer 1985, 1988, 1991; de Shazer and Dolan 2007), and the *collaborative language systems approach*, developed by Harlene Anderson (1997).

Narrative Therapy. This approach to MFT emphasizes that the stories individuals and families tell or believe about themselves greatly influence their subjective sense of reality and how it is organized and experienced. Michael White was the major proponent of narrative therapy (see, e.g., M. White 2007; M. White and Epston 1989, 1990; see also Monk, Winslade, Crocket, and Epston 1997). The narrative approach to MFT helps family members reduce the power of stories that are negative, oppressive, and problem-centered by empowering them to re-author their lives with other stories that are more constructive, so that they can explore and try new options and possibilities in their lives. Narrative family therapists focus more on how a particular problem has impacted the family rather than on how particular family patterns may have caused the problem. A specific intervention often used is *externalization*, which is the process of helping family members see the problem as being outside themselves instead of being an internal part of their basic identity. Such externalization can help empower the family to explore other more constructive stories or options that they can choose in order to overcome their problems and feelings of helplessness (see Goldenberg and Goldenberg 2008a, 413).

Mark Yarhouse and James Sells (2008) have similarly summarized and described nine major approaches to MFT that are similar to the eight approaches mentioned by Goldenberg and Goldenberg (2008a). The nine MFT approaches are (1) Bowenian family therapy; (2) strategic family therapy; (3) structural family therapy; (4) psychodynamic family therapy; (5) contextual family therapy; (6) experiential family therapy; (7) solution-focused family therapy; (8) cognitive-behavioral family therapy; (9) and narrative family therapy.

Therapeutic Process and Relationship

The therapeutic process and relationship in MFT will depend greatly on the specific approach to MFT that is being considered. As already mentioned, some approaches to MFT such as strategic family therapy, structural family therapy, transgenerational or Bowenian family therapy, contextual family therapy, psychodynamic or object relations family therapy, cognitive-behavioral family therapy, and emotionally focused family therapy tend to emphasize the role of the family therapist as somewhat of an expert in assessing and treating couple and family dysfunction. A warm, caring therapeutic relationship is still valued by such MFT approaches, but specific therapeutic techniques of family therapy, direct or indirect, are also valued and emphasized.

Other approaches to MFT, especially those influenced mainly by postmodern perspectives that value subjective perceptions of reality and diversity, such as social constructionist family therapy including solution-focused family therapy, narrative family therapy, and some forms of experiential family therapy (e.g., Satir's conjoint family therapy), emphasize the centrality of the therapeutic relationship between the family therapist and the family members. The family therapist in these MFT approaches does not assume the role of expert. Instead, he or she participates with the family in a warm, caring, and mutually respectful therapeutic relationship that seeks to empower family members to devise their own creative ways of dealing with their family problems. The family is therefore viewed as the expert, and the therapist assumes a "not-knowing," nonexpert approach to therapy (see H. Anderson and Goolishian 1992).

The process of MFT also varies in terms of length of therapy, depending on the specific approach to MFT that is being considered. Many MFT approaches are relatively short term, while others such as psychodynamic or object relations family therapy can be long-term. Usually the couple or the family are seen together. The process of therapy in MFT typically involves four major movements: "forming a relationship, conducting an assessment (using multiple

Sidebar 13.3

**Characteristics of Strong
or Healthy Families**

Jones and Butman (1991, 353) provided the following characteristics of strong or healthy families from a general family therapy perspective:

1. Respond positively to challenges and crises
2. Have a clearly articulated worldview
3. Communicate well
4. Choose to spend time together in a variety of tasks
5. Make promises and honor commitments to one another
6. Know how to express their love and appreciation for one another

lenses or perspectives), hypothesizing and sharing meaning, and facilitating change" (Corey 2009, 428–33).

The goals of MFT will also vary, depending on the needs of particular couples and families as well as the specific approach to MFT that is being used. MFT approaches attempt to help couples and families reduce their problems and grow to become healthier and more functional in a systemic way (see Parrott 2003, 376–77). The needs and problems of families will vary, depending on which stage of their *family life cycle* they have reached. There are at least six major stages of the family life cycle (B. Carter and McGoldrick 2005): "1. A single, young adult leaves home to live a more or less independent life. 2. Individuals marry or become a couple to build a life together. 3. The couple has children and starts a family. 4. The children become adolescents. 5. The parents launch their children into the world and prepare to live a life without children. 6. The family reaches its later years where children may have to care for parents as well as their own children, and the parents prepare for the end of their lives" (Corey 2009, 424).

Major Therapeutic Techniques and Interventions in MFT

There are many approaches to MFT and even more techniques available to modify family functioning and facilitate therapeutic change (see, e.g., J. Carlson, Sperry, and Lewis 2005; S. Minuchin and Fishman 1981; see also Bitter 2009; J. Patterson et al. 2009). Some of the best-known therapeutic techniques often used by family therapists are reframing, therapeutic double binds, enactment, family sculpting, circular questioning, cognitive restructuring, miracle question, and externalization (Goldenberg and Goldenberg 2008a, 422–23) as well as boundary setting and genogram (see Parrott 2003, 378).

In order to provide a more coherent framework within which to practice family therapy that integrates the major approaches to MFT and their techniques, Douglas Breunlin, Richard Schwartz, and Betty MacKune-Karrer (1997) have described their perspective of *metaframeworks* for transcending the differ-

ent models of family therapy. They have
proposed the following six original main
metaframeworks, which serve as therapeutic lenses that family therapists can use to
assess and help a family system in trouble:
internal family systems (i.e., individual),
sequences (i.e., interaction patterns), *organization* (of the family system), *developmental*, *multicultural*, and *gender*. More
recently, two more metaframeworks or
lenses have been added: *teleological* (i.e.,
goal-orientation), and *process* (see Corey
2009, 417–32). All or any of these eight
lenses can be used to guide the family therapist to select specific techniques to meet
the particular needs of the family (see, e.g.,
J. Carlson, Sperry, and Lewis 2005).

> **Sidebar 13.4**
>
> **Some Family Therapy Techniques**
> *(see Goldenberg and Goldenberg
> 2008a, 422–23; Parrott 2003, 378)*
>
> 1. Reframing
> 2. Therapeutic double binds
> 3. Enactment
> 4. Family sculpting
> 5. Circular questioning
> 6. Cognitive restructuring
> 7. Miracle question
> 8. Externalization
> 9. Boundary setting
> 10. Genogram

We will now examine some of the
major family therapy techniques often
used by family therapists (see Goldenberg and Goldenberg 2008a, 422–23;
Parrott 2003, 378).

Reframing. This family therapy technique involves relabeling behavior
that is problematic with a new, alternative description that is more positive,
emphasizing especially the good intention of the particular behavior being
discussed. For example, a teenage son who is upset by his mother's nagging
behavior may respond more constructively (rather than with anger and rebellion) if his mother's behavior is relabeled or reframed to be an expression of
her caring and concern for his welfare, rather than calculated simply to bug
him with repeated "nagging." Reframing is used to restructure the meaning
given to a particular behavior without modifying or denying the reality of the
actual behavior itself. It is often used by strategic family therapists to help
family members view problematic behavior from a more positive perspective,
thus enabling them to change their family system or interactions in more
constructive ways.

Therapeutic Double Binds. This technique is often used by strategic and
systemic family therapists who may directively instruct families to persist in
their problem behaviors, thus putting them into a *therapeutic double bind*.
This is usually done by using paradoxical interventions that prescribe the
symptom, for example, a couple who often argue are encouraged to argue even
more. If they do so, they are admitting that they are in control to increase or
decrease their problem behavior of arguing. If they do not do so, then their
problem behavior will eventually be eliminated. This technique is therefore
a double bind in which the clients will benefit therapeutically whether or not
they follow the paradoxical intervention.

Enactment. This family therapy technique is often used by structural family therapists following Minuchin; it refers to conducting a role-play of an actual family dysfunctional pattern of interaction. In such *enactments*, or *attempts at role-playing actual family situations*, in the family therapy session itself, the family therapist can observe the dysfunctional pattern and provide feedback to help the family members "unfreeze" or break out of their unhealthy, destructive family interactions and replace them with more constructive ways of family interaction. Goldenberg and Goldenberg (2008a, 423) provide an example of Minuchin doing an enactment (see S. Minuchin, Rosman, and Baker 1978) with a family consisting of two parents and an anorectic adolescent daughter; Minuchin arranged the first session with them to include bringing lunch so that they were faced with an enactment of their usual family interaction around eating. He could then observe the parents' struggles and dysfunctional ways of trying to deal with their daughter's refusal to eat and point out the ineffectiveness of the parental subsystem in handling their daughter's eating problem. He could then guide the parents to cooperate with each other more (rather than fighting with or contradicting each other) in encouraging their daughter to eat, thus forming a more united front that is stronger and more effective. The daughter would then also be relieved of the position of power and destructive manipulation that she had been maintaining. This enactment in the therapy session, with directive suggestions and feedback from a family therapist with a structural approach such as Minuchin, can force the family to more clearly see their dysfunctional family system that they have created so far and to explore more-constructive ways of interaction.

Family Sculpting. This family therapy technique involves asking family members to take turns acting as a "director" in getting the different family members to place themselves in particular positions physically in space in the therapist's office to represent their family relationships. Thus they express themselves and their attitudes toward each other in active, nonverbal behavior rather than in words. The family members' views of family, roles, alliances, boundaries, and subsystems can be further clarified for the whole family to see by using family sculpting, a technique that is often used by experiential family therapists following Satir's approach.

Circular Questioning. This technique is frequently used by systemic family therapists (see Boscolo, Cecchin, Hoffman, and Penn 1987) to draw attention to family interactions instead of individual pathology. The family therapist will ask each family member the same question about his or her perceptions of the same issue, whether it is an event or a relationship. By going around to each family member using this technique of circular questioning, the family therapist is able to explore more deeply each family member's perceptions and feelings without being confrontational. The family can then be more comfortable in examining the underlying root of their family conflict. Such nonconfrontational questioning is used by systemic family therapists as a therapeutic process to help the family deal with their family problems by sharing their views of their difficulties and modifying them into more constructive perspectives (see Goldenberg and Goldenberg 2008a, 423).

Cognitive Restructuring. This cognitive therapy technique is often used by cognitive-behavioral family therapists to help family members identify and challenge their individual maladaptive, distorted thoughts about themselves and their family problems, and to replace such dysfunctional thoughts with more accurate, realistic, and rational beliefs. For example, a couple may initially think that because they are arguing so often, they are personally failures and their marriage is doomed to end in divorce. Cognitive restructuring of such negative and catastrophic thinking is designed to help the couple to think more rationally by telling themselves that although they do have serious conflicts that they need to work out and resolve more effectively, they are not personal failures and their marriage is not doomed to end in divorce. In fact, they may realize that many couples struggle with conflicts, and such conflicts may actually be opportunities for them to learn better communication and conflict resolution skills and therefore even strengthen their marriage. One's thinking strongly influences one's feelings and behavior.

Miracle Question. This is a solution-focused family therapy technique described by de Shazer in which clients are asked the following *miracle question*: "Suppose that one night, while you were asleep, there was a miracle and this problem was solved. How would you know? What would be different?" (1988, 10). Each family member is asked to answer this miracle question and therefore speculate how different things would be as well as how each family member's behavior would change. The use of the miracle question can help families break out of old, problem-saturated ways of looking at their family problems and choose new goals and find potential solutions to their old problems that are more creative, novel, and constructive.

Externalization. This technique of *externalization* is often used by narrative family therapists following the work of Michael White and David Epston to help families free themselves from their old, problem-saturated stories that have dead ends and failures as outcomes and that often result in self-blame for family members. The therapist uses externalization to help family members see that the problem resides outside the family instead of attributing the problem to an internal family deficit or a particular family member's personal psychopathology. The whole family is encouraged to view the problem as external to them and to pull together to see how they can deal with the problem with more-constructive solutions. For example, instead of viewing the problem of the mother's depression as "Mother is depressed," the family is helped by the family therapist to externalize the problem by saying, "Depression is trying to control Mother's life." The family members can then explore other creative ways of dealing more effectively with the depression that is affecting the whole family (see Goldenberg and Goldenberg 2008a, 423–24).

In addition to these eight major therapeutic techniques or interventions of family therapy mentioned by Goldenberg and Goldenberg (2008a), Parrott added at least two more: *boundary setting* and *genogram* (2003, 378).

Boundary Setting. This family therapy technique involves either establishing firmer limits or lines of separation (i.e., "walls") in families where the family members are too enmeshed with one another, or building more flexible or permeable boundaries (i.e., "bridges") to facilitate deeper connection among family members who may be too disengaged from one another. The family therapist can use boundary setting in various ways, for example, by directing communication so that only one family member speaks at a time to help each family member to have his or her own voice, or by helping the family negotiate and set up family rules that respect an adolescent's need for personal space and privacy and the family's need for time together and connection.

Genogram. A *genogram* is a three-generational family tree that is often used by family therapists to help family members see more clearly family patterns that may have been transmitted or passed down from generation to generation. Genograms are graphic tools that can help family members discover how their family history has impacted them and their present struggles and problems.

There are many more family therapy techniques, but the ones just described are examples of some of the better-known and more frequently used therapeutic interventions in couple and family therapy. Recently, common factors in couple and family therapy have been emphasized as the overlooked foundation for effective practice (Sprenkle, Davis, and Lebow 2009).

MFT in Practice

A Hypothetical Transcript

Client (Father): My son, John, never tells me anything about what's going on in his life! I have to ask him many times but he still says almost nothing!

Client (Son, named John): But Dad, that's because you bug me so much with all your nagging, and you just get in my face all the time and come into my room any time you want to without even knocking!

Client (Mother): Yeah, they get on each other's nerves so often, I'm tired and fed up with all this!

Family Therapist: Wow, you are all really upset about this situation. Dad, you want John to share more of what's going on in his life with you. John, you feel dad is nagging you too much and not respecting your privacy and not giving you enough space. And Mom, you're frustrated and

	tired with all of this—am I on the right track with each of you?
Client (Father):	Uh-huh . . .
Client (Son):	Yup, you got it!
Client (Mother):	Yes.
Family Therapist:	I can't help but wonder if all this nagging from Dad is really his way of showing you, John, that he cares about you and what's going on in your life; that's why he's asking, even if it's too many times. What do you think, John?
Client (Father):	That's right! I do care about him but he doesn't appreciate it . . .
Client (Son):	There he goes again, and I think that you asked me the question, and not him, right?
Family Therapist:	That's right actually, so if you can wait just a moment, Dad, let me hear what John has to say, OK?
Client (Father):	OK. . . .
Family Therapist:	Good! So go ahead, John . . .
Client (Son):	Well, I guess my dad's nagging is a way of his showing me that he's interested in me and my life and what's going on with me, and if I look at it this way, it doesn't feel as bad or negative as when I look at it usually as nagging and then it really bugs me! I still wish he would not ask me questions so often or so repeatedly!
Family Therapist:	Can you say this directly to your dad?
Client (Son):	OK . . . well, Dad, I guess your nagging is your way of showing me you're interested in my life and that you care about how I'm doing. I do appreciate it! But it would be nice if you didn't ask me questions so often, OK? . . .
Client (Father):	Well, I'm glad you realize that I really do care about you, and that you finally appreciate it! I'll try to ask you less often, but it would help too if you just tell me things more spontaneously and just be more open with me and talk to me more without me having to ask you.
Client (Son):	I'll try . . .
Family Therapist:	Good! You're beginning to connect with each other in more-constructive and helpful ways, and you're really listening to each other and getting it! Mom, what do you think about what's happening here?
Client (Mother):	I'm glad! They're finally talking to each other or with each other rather than talking at each other! I think there's another issue about giving John a bit more space and privacy since he is already sixteen years old!

Family Therapist: OK, what do you have to say about this, Dad?

Client (Father): Well . . . I'm OK with giving John a bit more space or privacy, but it'll be easier if he tells me what's happening more often . . .

Client (Son): I'll try, Dad, but I would appreciate it if you don't just walk into my room any time you feel like it, especially if my door is closed, and you don't knock. I may be taking a nap or just need some down time to be quiet. Please knock if you need to talk to me before you come into my room, OK?

Client (Father): OK . . .

Family Therapist: That's great! You're both setting appropriate boundaries or guidelines that allow you to communicate and still be connected while respecting John's need for a bit more space and privacy because he's growing up fast! So, Dad, you're OK with knocking before entering John's room, if you want to talk to him?

Client (Father): Yeah, I'll try to remember.

Family Therapist: Good! And John, you're OK with telling Dad what's up with you and your life a bit more often, without him having to ask all the time?

Client (Son): Yeah, I guess I'll try too, like Dad! (smiles a bit here and looks at Dad)

Family Therapist: And Mom, you're OK with all this?

Client (Mother): Sure! I've been trying to tell my husband that he should do something like what we agreed on today, because John is already sixteen years old, and not to treat him like a ten-year-old!

Client (Father): But you don't tell me nicely and sometimes you nag me too! (with a smile)—But I agree, and we can work together to connect better with you, John.

Client (Mother): That's good.

Family Therapist: It is good! Dad and Mom working together more, and Dad and John agreeing to communicate and connect more openly and spontaneously, with Dad respecting John's space more, and John realizing that his Dad really does care for him even through his nagging! Are you all OK with doing this for homework until our next session?

Client (Father): Yeah, I'll try.

Client (Son): Sure.

Client (Mother): I'll do my best to support them!

Family Therapist: Great! Let's see what else is on your agenda that you want to cover or deal with for the rest of today's session . . .

This hypothetical transcript of a small part of a family therapy session with a sixteen-year-old adolescent son and his parents demonstrates the family therapist's use of reframing (of the father's nagging and frequent questions as caring for and interest in the son and what's happening in his life) and boundary setting (by encouraging the father to respect his son's request for more space and privacy by knocking before entering his son's room, and encouraging the son to more spontaneously share what's happening in his life with his father). The family therapist directed and monitored so that each family member had a chance to talk during the session. The family therapist also engaged in a warm, respectful, and empathic therapeutic relationship with each of the family members by summarizing what they said, asking them if it was OK with them when the therapist made specific suggestions after exploring possible solutions with them, and empowering the family members to come up with their own creative problem-solving ideas.

Critique of MFT: Strengths and Weaknesses

Again, it is difficult to critique MFT because of the many different approaches to couple and family therapy that are included in this field. However, in general, MFT has several strengths as well as weaknesses (see Corey 2009, 433–34, 439–40; Parrott 2003, 387–88; Prochaska and Norcross 2010, 366–70).

In terms of strengths, MFT, based on a broad systems perspective on couples and families, focuses on the family as a unit and therefore transcends the individualistic emphasis often found in other approaches to therapy. MFT does not place blame on individual psychopathology and therefore avoids scapegoating or holding a particular person responsible for the problems of the whole family system. It also avoids blaming the family itself for its struggles because it tends to look instead at the bigger picture of the family system and subsystems.

Second, MFT has numerous family therapy techniques that can be used to effectively help couples and families with their problems in practical ways. Whether it is reframing, therapeutic double binds, enactment, family sculpting, circular questioning, cognitive restructuring, asking the miracle question, externalization, boundary setting, constructing a genogram, communication skills training, problem solving, or other therapeutic interventions, MFT is a practical, usually relatively short-term therapy of twenty sessions or less (Lebow 2008, 328) that deals with the problems of couples and families in a direct and concrete way. An exception would be the psychodynamic or object relations family therapy approach, which can be relatively long term because it focuses on the unconscious processes and childhood experiences of the individual members of the family system. Many couples and families who want effective and efficient help for their difficulties can find it from practitioners of MFT.

Third, MFT takes into serious consideration the systems and subsystems of families, including the significant role of factors such as ethnicity, culture, gender, values, beliefs, spirituality, and religion (see, e.g., McGoldrick, Giordano, and Garcia-Preto 2005; McGoldrick and Hardy 2008; F. Walsh 2009). It therefore attempts to be multiculturally sensitive and attentive to larger systems such as racial, social, cultural, gender, and spiritual or religious contexts and influences.

Fourth, MFT is a field that is still open to experimentation and the further development of more creative and novel ways of helping couples and families. It will continue to evolve and contribute new ideas and therapeutic techniques to the theory and practice of counseling and psychotherapy.

Fifth, although earlier MFT approaches (e.g., structural family therapy, strategic family therapy, contextual family therapy, Bowenian or transgenerational family therapy, and psychodynamic family therapy) emphasized the role of the family therapist as an expert with specialized knowledge and skills for assessing and treating family problems systemically, more recent versions of MFT, especially those based on postmodern, social constructionist perspectives (e.g., solution-focused family therapy, narrative family therapy, and experiential or conjoint family therapy), focus on the client or the family as the expert, not the family therapist. They emphasize the centrality of a mutually respectful, fully collaborative, and deeply caring therapeutic relationship in effective family therapy. This gentler approach that empowers the family to develop its own creative and constructive narratives and solutions to its problems is a strength of MFT today.

Sixth, the social constructionist approaches to MFT focus more on narratives and the big-picture stories of family members and their lives, empowering them to engage in more-constructive meaning making of their lives and experiences. This more existential emphasis, including a respectful use of spiritual and religious resources (see F. Walsh 2009), reflects a greater openness in MFT today to dealing with deeper issues relating to meaning in life, and this is another one of its strengths.

Seventh, MFT tends to assume a systemic perspective on families and family functioning and dysfunctioning. It has a clear model of what healthy family functioning is and what dysfunctional families look like, especially enmeshed or disengaged families from a structural viewpoint. This perspective is a strength in terms of systematic assessment and treatment of family dysfunction within a systemic and structural framework, but it can also be a potential weakness if such a structural model is imposed on all families.

Eighth, MFT deals with the whole family, including extended family when appropriate, in family therapy sessions. Many cultures place significant value on the family, especially the extended family. MFT can therefore be seen as more relevant and sensitive to cultures that do not emphasize individualistic values or self-focused fulfillment but instead value community and extended family relationships. Practitioners of MFT can help families and extended families in such cultures better than more Westernized therapists who practice individual approaches to therapy focusing more on the self and self-actualization and less on the interpersonal contexts of family and community.

Finally, many MFT approaches have been subjected to controlled outcome evaluations and have overall been found to be effective treatments (see, e.g., Prochaska and Norcross 2010, 361–66; Sharf 2008, 510–12; Todd and Bohart 2006, 358–59). The empirical outcome research that has been done and that continues to be conducted on MFT is therefore another strength.

MFT also has several significant weaknesses. First, its focus on the family as a unit from a systems perspective can lead to a loss of appreciation for the personhood of the individual family member. In other words, the pendulum can swing too far from individualistic self-focused therapy to systems-focused MFT, which can result in losing the person of the client or family member. Systemic MFT approaches can become mechanistic in treating the family as a whole like a "machine" that needs only to be tweaked with the right technique, using the right systems terminology, and forgetting that ultimately the family still consists of individual family members who are important persons in their own right.

Second, MFT has numerous therapeutic techniques that can be used to help troubled couples and families, but such techniques can be superficially used or misused and abused, especially by inadequately trained or inexperienced family therapists who do not pay sufficient attention to the deeper unconscious struggles of each individual family member. Furthermore, individual psychopathology is often ignored by MFT practitioners, who focus more on family pathology or dysfunction. Some individual family members may have severe forms of psychopathology such as borderline personality disorder, bipolar disorder, major depressive disorder, or psychotic disorders and therefore may be especially vulnerable to family therapy interventions that are too confrontational or even confusing and paradoxical. Such interventions may be potentially dangerous and harmful to these clients. It should be noted, however, that more attempts have recently been made in MFT to pay more attention to individual psychopathology in couple and family therapy, for example, in treating difficult couples who have coexisting mental and relationship disorders (see Snyder and Whisman 2003).

Third, although MFT takes seriously the importance of factors such as ethnicity, culture, gender, values, beliefs, spirituality, and religion in dealing with the systems and subsystems of families, certain MFT approaches still tend to be more patriarchal, male-oriented, and "white" in their practice. Feminist therapists have particularly criticized most of the pioneers of family therapy as being insensitive to gender, ethnicity, and culture, because the majority of them were males (e.g., Murray Bowen and Salvador Minuchin), with the exception of Virginia Satir. The influence of such "fathers" of MFT, with their masculine bias, is still present in family therapy (see Prochaska and Norcross 2010, 369; see also Silverstein and Goodrich 2003). This weakness needs to be rectified by paying more sensitive attention to race, culture, and gender in the clinical practice of MFT today, in what has been called the challenge of "revisioning family therapy" (McGoldrick and Hardy 2008).

Fourth, MFT's openness to experimentation and further development of creative and novel therapeutic techniques has a corresponding weakness: the lack of more-substantial and coherent theories with adequate empirical support. Advances in theory development are significantly lagging behind developments in family therapy techniques that are not based in solid or adequate theoretical conceptualizations.

Fifth, although more-recent social constructionist MFT approaches emphasize the central importance of the therapeutic relationship in effective family therapy, including a deep respect for the family as expert, the tendency of MFT practitioners to function as experts and to impose their systemic views and techniques on all families is still present. This weakness is potentially dangerous and harmful to some families that may not find such systemic (e.g., structural and strategic) views and techniques helpful at all.

Sixth, the flip side of the fifth weakness just mentioned is that some families do need a more direct, structured, and directive form of MFT to help them with their problems in practical and concrete ways. They may be limited in their awareness of how to help themselves and may not be able to devise creative solutions to deal with their difficulties. Social constructionist approaches to MFT such as solution-focused family therapy and narrative family therapy may thus be too optimistic and positive in assuming that such families are their own experts and can develop their own solutions to their problems. The expertise of the family therapist is still needed for such families, which can benefit most from a more directive and structured MFT approach that affirms the role of the family therapist as an expert, yet in a collaborative and warm fashion (e.g., cognitive-behavioral family therapy).

Seventh, some MFT approaches such as structural and strategic family therapy tend to have clear-cut models of healthy families versus dysfunctional families and specific family therapy techniques for effecting change in the family system and subsystems in ways that are consistent with their models. There is a potential danger here of imposing such models and techniques on all families, without paying adequate attention to the diversity of families in terms of race, culture, and gender considerations. One size does not fit all in helping families. Lewis, Beavers, Gossett, and Philips (1976), in fact, found in their intensive study of psychological health in family systems that there was no single way or particular structure characterizing how these healthy families functioned. MFT must be more inclusive in its theorizing and practice for pluralistic societies, including the United States, where there are now significant numbers of single-parent families, families with no children, cohabiting couples, gay-couple families, blended families, extended families, and immigrant families (see Prochaska and Norcross 2010, 369).

Eighth, another weakness of MFT is that the systemic perspective can be taken too far and therefore be misleading. For example, the systemic view present in most MFT approaches treats the family as a system or unit. It is often assumed that if the identified patient or scapegoat in a dysfunctional family system gets better and no longer has symptoms, another family member will now become the new scapegoat and develop symptoms. This scenario is MFT's version of "symptom substitution" in individual therapy, where one symptom, if eliminated, may lead to a new symptom (usually a psychodynamic or psychoanalytic assumption that has not received empirical support), except in MFT it is now "patient substitution": if the scapegoat or identified patient in a family system gets better and is no longer symptomatic, then there will be "patient substitution," with another family member now being the new scapegoat and therefore being symptomatic. Although this sometimes happens in a family where one family member's improvement leads to another family member's worsening, it does not always happen. In fact, the whole family may get better when the identified patient or scapegoat improves (e.g., recovers from substance abuse). In other words, not every problem in a family is always a systems problem. Systems theory can be misapplied, and it can also at times be wrong (see Prochaska and Norcross 2010, 370).

Finally, while MFT has a strong empirical base generally supporting its overall effectiveness, some approaches to MFT still lack sufficient controlled outcome evaluations. More and better empirical research evaluating the therapeutic effectiveness of some of these MFT approaches for specific disorders is therefore needed to address this weakness.

A Biblical Perspective on MFT

The strengths and weaknesses of MFT in general have already been covered. A biblical perspective and critique of MFT will now be provided (see, e.g., S. L. Jones and Butman 1991, 360–72; W. H. Watson 1997; Yarhouse and Sells 2008, 287–310, 493–502).

First, MFT's focus on the couple or family as the unit for therapy is a good corrective to the emphasis on the individual in most major therapy approaches and the accompanying danger of individualism and self-obsession. MFT's unique systems perspective is somewhat consistent with the Bible's emphasis on community and body life of the church (see, e.g., 1 Cor. 12), including a healthy family life (see, e.g., Eph. 5:21–6:4; Col. 3:18–21). However, the Bible contains many more passages on the body life of the church as a community of believers in Christ, and on how to love and encourage one another, than on marriage or family life in particular (see, e.g., Collins 2007, 588–90). Nevertheless, such biblical passages also generally apply to marriage and family life (see, e.g., Getz 1976).

Second, the systemic focus of MFT on the family can nevertheless be over-emphasized to the point where the personhood of the individual or family member can be lost. Paradoxically, the Bible also emphasizes the worth and personhood of the individual human being, who is deeply loved by God and whom Jesus came to save through his death and resurrection (see, e.g., Luke 15:3–7 on the parable of the one lost sheep, and Luke 15:11–32 on the parable of the lost son; John 3:16). A biblical perspective will therefore still retain a balanced focus on the individual as a special person created in the image of God (Gen. 1:26–27) as well as on community and body life in the church (see, e.g., Bolsinger 2004; Wilhoit 2008), including marriage and family life.

Third, MFT's focus on the couple or family may also not extend far enough to larger systems or interpersonal contexts such as the church as the body of Christ (see, e.g., 1 Cor. 12) or the kingdom of God wherever and whenever and in whomever God rules and reigns. In other words, a biblical perspective will emphasize the larger body life of the church as community perspective and not narrowly overemphasize the couple or the nuclear family or even the individual in a self-centered way. Attention should also be adequately given to additional contextual factors such as sociopolitical, cultural, economic, religious, spiritual, and other environmental factors that may impact family life.

Fourth, MFT approaches tend to have their own theoretical views of what constitutes healthy family functioning and what does not, but such models may be limited, deficient, and even erroneous at times, depending on the families being seen in family therapy. The Bible has various examples of troubled as well as functional families and how God still worked in and through them, in the diversity of families that he has created (see Yarhouse and Sells 2008, 15–36). The few biblical guidelines available on marriage and family life must be considered and applied, but overall, the Bible gives ample room for families to grow and function in various and diverse ways, culturally and spiritually. MFT practitioners must be careful not to impose a particular model of how healthy families should look and what they be like, especially if the model is culturally biased with a white, male perspective.

Fifth, although MFT approaches have developed numerous effective therapeutic techniques to practically help troubled couples and families, a Christian family therapist will be discerning and not use any and all techniques simply because they work according to empirical research. Some family therapy techniques such as paradoxical interventions and other strategic family therapy approaches may involve an element of manipulating, tricking, and even lying, in the therapist's attempts to bring about therapeutic change in the family quickly and effectively. Biblical values, ethics, and morality must be upheld and respected, and some of these techniques may be questionable and should be questioned by the Christian family therapist, even if they have been found empirically to be effective and efficient. The key question from a biblical perspective is whether they are also ethical.

Sixth, a biblical perspective will emphasize loving God and loving others as oneself or one's family (Mark 12:29–31) and the primacy of agape love (1 Cor. 13) as the fruit of the Holy Spirit (Gal. 5:22–23), which is genuinely self-transcendent and sacrificial, divinely inspired, and other-centered, although it does include an appropriate kind of self-care or love for oneself and one's family (see, e.g., Browning 2006, 143–45; see also Roberts 1993, 12). A Christian perspective on MFT will therefore go beyond models or goals that focus on balance, healthy functioning, happiness or fulfillment, and symptom alleviation. It will emphasize sacrificial love and appropriate servanthood (see Tan 2006b) based on mutual submission in Christ, in sacred marriage (Thomas 2000a) and sacred parenting (Thomas 2004) that strive more for holiness and growing in Christlikeness than simply for happiness. Helpful biblical or Christian models are available for marriage based on covenant, grace, empowerment, and intimacy (e.g., Balswick and Balswick 2006) and for the family (e.g., Balswick and Balswick 2007; see also R. S. Anderson and Guernsey 1985; Ouellet 2006).

Seventh, a biblical perspective on MFT will include not only a Christian understanding of marriage and the family but also an integrative approach to Christian family therapy. Yarhouse and Sells (2008, 15–37, 287–310, 493–502) have provided a helpful description of such an integrative Christian family therapy that is biblically based in terms of three major aspects of marital and family life: *family functioning* (e.g., individual and systematic; family rules; and family pattern or sequences of interaction); *family relationships* (e.g., intrapersonal, interpersonal, and generational relationships); and *family identity* (e.g., culture, gender, religion, socioeconomic status; definition, locating self in the world, and worldview; and meaning, significance), based on the themes of function, structure, and relationship as aspects of the image of God, or *imago Dei*, in which human beings are created (see McMinn and Campbell 2007). The Christian family therapist can be eclectic in using various MFT approaches and techniques but is clearly committed to a biblical perspective on marriage and the family. Based on biblical texts such as Ruth 1:16–18, Ephesians 5:21–33, and 2 Timothy 1:5, Yarhouse and Sells (2008) emphasize the following crucial characteristics of Christian family relationships: *dependence on God, mutuality, self-denial, perseverance* or *resilience*, and *integrity* (2008, 28–32).

Eighth, more-recent social constructionist MFT approaches such as solution-focused and narrative family therapy have a collaborative therapeutic relationship with the family, affirming each family member's capacity to choose and to engage in growth and therapeutic change by developing their own creative solutions and constructive narratives. Although this emphasis on the family member's free will and creative capacities is somewhat consistent with a biblical perspective, which also affirms one's freedom to choose (Josh. 24:15) as well as the image of God in each human person created by God (Gen. 1:26–27), it does not adequately acknowledge and deal with the fallen, sinful nature of a human being, which is capable of evil and even cruelty (Jer. 17:9; Rom. 3:23). Systemic approaches to MFT also do not focus sufficient attention on the inner part or "heart" of each family member (see, e.g., Pss. 51:6; 139:23–24; Jer. 17:9; Matt. 15:18–19), where internal conflicts and unconscious motives and evil motivations may be present and therefore must be addressed. The need for salvation through faith in Jesus Christ as Lord and Savior (John 3:16; Rom. 6:23) and the empowering presence and filling of the Holy Spirit (Zech. 4:6; Eph. 5:18) in order to be truly transformed as persons, including couples and families, is emphasized in Scripture instead of self-sufficiency. Creative solutions and meaningful narratives also must be biblically based and grounded in the objective, eternal truth of the Bible, which contains God's metanarrative, or big story (cf. 2 Tim. 3:16).

Ninth, a biblical perspective will emphasize the crucial importance of forgiveness and realistic attempts at reconciliation where appropriate (see, e.g., Matt. 5:23–24; 18:15–17; Rom. 12:18; Eph. 4:32). A Christian approach to MFT will therefore go beyond justice or fairness and focus on practicing agape love, including forgiveness (see, e.g., Hargrave 1994; Worthington 2003, 2005a, 2005b).

Finally, MFT tends to have pragmatic and utilitarian emphases in helping couples and families, focusing mainly on doing what works, and "fixing things," which can result in family members being treated as objects rather than valued and respected as persons created in the image of God (see S. L. Jones and Butman 1991, 370). A biblical approach to MFT will focus more on scriptural values and standards and spiritual, even mystical, aspects of the Christian life, which are not always consistent with pragmatic and utilitarian emphases (cf. Tan 1987a).

Research: Empirical Status of MFT

Outcome research on the empirical status of MFT, referring usually to the format of seeing couples or families together for therapy as well as to more specific MFT approaches to therapy, will now be briefly summarized (see Prochaska and Norcross 2010, 361–66; Sharf 2008, 510–12; Todd and Bohart 2006, 358–59).

At least twenty meta-analyses have now been published on the overall effectiveness of MFT. W. R. Shadish and S. A. Baldwin (2003), in a quantitative review of twenty meta-analyses, reached the following conclusions about the empirical status of MFT (see Prochaska and Norcross 2010, 362–63):

1. The average effect size of MFT was found to be .65 compared to no treatment controls, showing MFT to be generally effective with a 65 percent

treatment success rate compared to only 34 percent in no-treatment control groups.

2. Treatment effects of MFT decrease somewhat over time with an effect size of .52 at follow-up.

3. The average effects for marital or couple therapy (d = .84) are somewhat higher than the effects of family therapy, with a treatment success rate of about 80 percent for marital or couple therapy compared to 30 percent for no-treatment control groups.

4. Most MFT approaches when directly compared to one another showed no significant differences among them in terms of their relative effectiveness. However, Satir's approach and person-centered treatments were found to be relatively inferior and behavioral marital therapy to be relatively superior in treatment effectiveness.

5. MFT approaches have been found to be as effective as, and sometimes more effective than, other types of treatment, such as individual psychotherapy and group therapy. Shadish and his colleagues (Shadish, Ragsdale, Glaser, and Montgomery 1995) earlier concluded that the empirical evidence from meta-analyses available then indicated a tie between individual therapy and family therapy in terms of treatment effectiveness, with moderate and frequently clinically significant effects.

The field of MFT continues to develop diverse methodologies in actively conducting research on family therapy (see Sprenkle and Piercy 2005).

Alan Gurman (2003) and Gurman and Peter Fraenkel (2002), in their reviews of the outcome research more specifically focused on marital or couple therapy, found the average effect size to be .80 or greater, similar to that reported by Shadish and Baldwin (2003). Todd and Bohart (2006, 358) noted that the two marital or couple therapy approaches with the most outcome research support for their treatment effectiveness are behavioral marital therapy (see also Shadish and Baldwin 2005) and emotion-focused therapy (or emotionally focused therapy), with *some* empirical support for the effectiveness of structural or strategic approaches. For behavioral marital or couple therapy, the results of a recent five-year follow-up study showed that integrative behavioral couple therapy had significantly but not dramatically better outcomes than traditional behavioral couple therapy for the first two years after treatment termination, but subsequent findings yielded more similarity and nonsignificant differences in outcome over longer periods of follow-up between integrative behavioral couple therapy and traditional behavioral couple therapy (A. Christensen, Atkins, Baucom, and Yi 2010).

With regard to the more specific area of family therapy, positive and equivalent treatment effects have been found for behavioral, systemic, psychodynamic, and eclectic approaches to family therapy (Shadish, Ragsdale, Glaser, and Montgomery 1995). However, for specific disorders, Thomas Sexton, James

Alexander, and Alyson Mease (2004) reported that *functional family therapy* (Sexton and Alexander 1999) and *multisystemic therapy* or (MST) (Henggeler et al. 1998, 2009) both of which are behaviorally oriented family therapies, are more effective than other family therapy approaches for treating conduct disorder and substance abuse, especially in adolescent family members (see Todd and Bohart 2006, 359; see also Sexton, Weeks, and Robbins 2003). MST has also been found to be an effective treatment for juvenile sexual offenders (see Borduin, Schaeffer, and Heiblum 2009).

Sharf (2008, 510) concluded that reviews of outcome research on the effectiveness of family therapy have generally shown family therapy to be helpful for various types of clinical problems and to be at least equivalent in effectiveness to other approaches to therapy (see, e.g., Friedlander and Tuason 2000; Pinsof, Wynne, and Hambright 1996). He also noted that *some* research (not all controlled outcome studies) supports the effectiveness of Bowenian, behavioral, MRI (Mental Research Institute), structural, the Milan Group, and psychoeducational approaches to family therapy. Lebow (2008, 329), however, observed that there is very little research support for several widely practiced MFT approaches including Bowen, narrative, strategic, and solution focused.

The controlled outcome research on the effectiveness of MFT approaches has also been reviewed for five specific disorders: alcohol dependence, drug abuse, childhood obesity, conduct disorder, and schizophrenia. Overall, the empirical evidence available tends to support the effectiveness of some MFT approaches for treating these disorders (Prochaska and Norcross 2010, 363–65).

More specifically, Satir's conjoint family therapy or communication approach has been evaluated in only a few direct outcome studies, which have found nonsignificant effect sizes (Shadish et al. 1993). Strategic family therapy has been found in meta-analyses to be robust in its therapeutic effectiveness for treating substance abusers (Shadish et al. 1993; Stanton and Shadish 1997) but uncertain for treating schizophrenia, anxiety disorders, and psychosomatic conditions (Gurman, Kniskern, and Pinsof 1986; Sandberg et al. 1997). Based on a few controlled outcome studies, structural family therapy is probably effective in treating substance abuse, conduct disorders, and psychosomatic conditions (Sandberg et al. 1997; Stanton and Shadish 1997), but it has not been sufficiently evaluated for its effectiveness with schizophrenia, anxiety disorders, mood disorders, and other childhood disorders (Shadish and Baldwin 2003). Bowenian family therapy has apparently not been evaluated in randomized, controlled outcome studies (Sandberg et al. 1997; Shadish and Baldwin 2003) and therefore remains largely untested (see Prochaska and Norcross 2010, 365–66).

The empirical status of MFT is therefore generally solid, with controlled outcome research supporting the overall therapeutic effectiveness of most MFT approaches. However, further controlled outcome research is still needed to evaluate the effectiveness of some MFT approaches that have only anecdotal data or uncontrolled case studies relating to their potential usefulness.

Future Directions

MFT has contributed a unique systemic perspective on treating the couple or the family as a unit and doing so mainly in a relatively short-term, problem-solving, or solution-oriented way, using numerous therapeutic techniques to effectively help couples and families. MFT will therefore continue to receive greater attention in the years ahead as increasing numbers of couples and families seek concrete, practical help for their problems. It also fits managed care's preference for funding empirically supported, short-term therapy approaches (see Goldenberg and Goldenberg 2008a, 433).

MFT can develop in several promising directions in the near future (see Prochaska and Norcross 2010, 372–73). First, it will continue to extend the application of a systemic perspective and therapy to areas other than the nuclear family, including larger systems and contexts such as organizations, including religious institutions (see, e.g., Friedman 1985), schools, and communities. Paradoxically, MFT will also be applied more frequently to the treatment of the individual client who has coexisting mental and relationship disorders (see, e.g., Snyder and Whisman 2003), so that individual psychopathology will also be more adequately addressed in MFT. It will continue to be applied to medical areas such as family systems medicine, which involves the integration of family medicine and family therapy. More specifically, family therapy has been effectively used to treat clients with alcohol dependence and drug abuse problems, and couple therapy for those with dementia, sexual difficulties, and cardiovascular disease (Pinsof, Wynne, and Hambright 1996; Snyder, Castellani, and Whisman 2006).

Second, further work will likely be done to establish a more consensual and consistent diagnostic system for the assessment of dysfunctional families. The DSM-IV (American Psychiatric Association 1994), the commonly used traditional diagnostic system for psychiatric or mental disorders, does not adequately focus on the relational context of individual psychopathology. Assessment of relational functioning and dysfunctioning may be included in the next DSM edition. A substantial effort has already been made by various organizations in publishing the *Handbook of Relational Diagnosis and Dysfunctional Family Patterns* (F. Kaslow 1996), which will be of significant help in further developing a more consensual and formal diagnostic system for dysfunctional families.

Third, MFT approaches have gradually become less distinct and more integrative over the years, and this movement toward greater integration and eclecticism will probably continue to grow in the coming decades. In fact, between one-third and one-half of family therapists who responded to large surveys indicated that their theoretical orientation is eclectic (see, e.g., Lebow 1997).

Fourth, MFT approaches will become more sensitive to race, culture, and gender issues in clinical practice as more family therapists respond to the challenge of revisioning family therapy (McGoldrick and Hardy 2008; see also McGoldrick, Giordano, and Garcia-Preto 2005).

Fifth, just as the broader field of counseling and psychotherapy has become more sensitive to spiritual and religious issues and the appropriate use of spiritual and religious resources in therapy in recent years, the MFT field will also continue to be involved in developing and using spiritual and religious resources in family therapy (see F. Walsh 2009).

Finally, training and certification as a marital and family therapist in the United States will increasingly require the completion of a graduate degree in MFT from an accredited program and being licensed in the state in which the MFT practitioner is residing and engaging in independent clinical practice. However, many graduate programs in professional psychology (such as clinical and counseling psychology doctoral programs), social work, and counseling or counselor education include some training in MFT. The influence of systemic theories and therapy approaches will continue to be significant in the broader field of counseling and psychotherapy, although the more formal certification and recognition of MFT practitioners who are licensed in specific states in the United States will become stricter and more institutionalized.

There are many MFT organizations worldwide, but two important ones are the American Association for Marriage and Family Therapy (AAMFT), founded in 1942, which publishes the *Journal of Marital and Family Therapy* and the *Family Therapy Magazine*, which its more than twenty-four thousand members receive as part of their membership benefits (www.aamft.org); and the International Association of Marriage and Family Counselors (IAMFC), a division of the American Counseling Association (ACA), which publishes the *Family Journal*, which its members receive as part of their membership benefits (www.iamfc.com) (see Corey 2009, 440–41). There is also the Division of Family Psychology (Division 43) of the American Psychological Association (www.apa.org/divisions/div.43/). MFT will therefore continue to grow as a diverse field in the years to come.

Recommended Readings

Bitter, J. R. (2009). *Theory and practice of family therapy and counseling.* Belmont, CA: Brooks/Cole.

Goldenberg, I. & Goldenberg, H. (2008). *Family therapy: An overview* (7th ed.). Belmont, CA: Brooks/Cole.

Gurman, A. S. (Ed.). (2008). *Clinical handbook of couple therapy* (4th ed.). New York: Guilford Press.

Sexton, T. L., Weeks, G. R., & Robbins, M. S. (Eds.). (2003). *Handbook of family therapy: The science and practice of working with families and couples.* New York: Brunner-Routledge.

Walsh, F. (Ed.). (2009). *Spiritual resources in family therapy* (2nd ed.). New York: Guilford Press.

Yarhouse, M. A., & Sells, J. N. (2008). *Family therapies: A comprehensive Christian appraisal.* Downers Grove, IL: IVP Academic.

Part 3

A Christian Approach to Counseling and Psychotherapy

14

Christian Theology in Christian Counseling

A Biblical Perspective on Human Nature and Effective Counseling and Psychotherapy

A significant contemporary development in clinical practice is the integration of religion or spirituality and psychotherapy (see, e.g., Aten and Leach 2009; Cashwell and Young 2005; Dowd and Nielsen 2006; Frame 2003; Griffith and Griffith 2001; G. Miller 2003; W. R. Miller 1999; Nelson 2009; Paloutzian and Park 2005; Pargament 1997, 2007; Plante 2009; Richards and Bergin 2000, 2004, 2005; Shafranske 1996; Sorenson 2004; Sperry and Shafranske 2005; F. Walsh 2009).

More specifically, the integration of Christian faith and psychotherapy, or Christian therapy, has also witnessed tremendous growth in recent years (see N. T. Anderson, Zuehlke, and Zuehlke 2000; Benner 1998; Clinton and Ohlschlager 2002; Clinton, Hart, and Ohlschlager 2005; Collins 2007; I. F. Jones 2006; Malony and Augsburger 2007; McMinn 1996; McMinn and Campbell 2007; Pugh 2008; see also R. S. Anderson 1990; S. L. Jones and Butman 1991; Stevenson, Eck, and Hill 2007; Yarhouse, Butman, and McRay 2005; Yarhouse and Sells 2008).

The next four chapters of this book will focus specifically on a Christian approach to therapy that is Christ centered, biblically based, and Spirit filled (see Tan 2001b; see also Tan 1996c). In this chapter, a biblical perspective on human nature and effective therapy will be discussed. It emphasizes the crucial and central role of Christian theology or Scripture in Christian counseling (Tan 1991, 2001b; see also Collins 1993; Crabb 1977, 1987; Farnsworth 1996; Hurley and Berry 1997a, 1997b; Porter 2010a, 2010b; Welch and Powlison 1997a, 1997b).

Christian Theology in Christian Counseling: Approaches to Integration of Christian Faith and Psychology

Although there are various approaches to Christian counseling, the role of Christian theology based on Scripture or the Bible in Christian counseling is crucial and central (Tan 2001b). Such integration of Christian faith or Christian theology and counseling can be conceptualized using many different models. B. E. Eck (1996) has provided a helpful summary of twenty-seven models of *integration of Christian theology and psychology* (including counseling and psychotherapy) that can be organized into three major paradigms: the nonintegrative paradigm, the manipulative paradigm, and the nonmanipulative paradigm. The following is his succinct description of these three major paradigms of integration:

> The *Non-Integrative Paradigm* does not seek integration of the data but rather builds its understanding of God's truth on one discipline alone. The *Manipulative Paradigm* seeks to integrate the data of both disciplines, but the data of one discipline must be altered before becoming acceptable to the other discipline. The final paradigm, the *Non-Manipulative Paradigm*, accepts the data from both disciplines directly into the integrative process. Each paradigm contains certain processes that define the method for how the data of each discipline will be integrated. The Non-Integrative Paradigm contains only the *Rejects Process*; the Manipulative Paradigm contains both the *Reconstructs Process* and the *Transforms Process*; and the Non-Manipulative Paradigm utilizes the *Correlates Process* and the *Unifies Process*. (Eck 1996, 103)

Another way of summarizing the various models or paradigms of integration is to describe them in terms of four basic approaches (see J. D. Carter 1996; J. D. Carter and Narramore 1979): *Christianity against psychology* (usually held by biblically militant and conservative Christians); *Christianity of psychology* (usually held by those with more liberal theological views); the *parallels model* or *approach* (Christianity and psychology are seen as equally important but essentially separate fields); and *Christianity integrates psychology*. Lawrence J. Crabb (1977) has more simply described these four basic approaches to integration thus: (1) separate but equal; (2) tossed salad (equal and mixable); (3) nothing buttery (psychology is unnecessary and irrelevant because only the Bible is needed to deal with human problems and needs); and (4) spoiling the Egyptians (using whatever concepts or techniques from secular psychology that are consistent with Scripture or the Bible, with the Bible having final authority).

Another description of four major views on the relationship of psychology and Christianity is the following (see E. L. Johnson and Jones 2000; see also E. L. Johnson 2010): (1) a levels-of-explanation (scientific) view (Myers 2000); (2) an integration view (Collins 2000); (3) a Christian psychology view (Roberts 2000); and (4) a biblical counseling view (Powlison 2000).

The approach to Christian counseling that I propose and describe in this book is consistent with the Christianity integrates psychology approach (J. D. Carter and Narramore 1979) or the spoiling the Egyptians (Crabb 1977) approach to integration of Christian faith and psychology (including counseling and psychotherapy). However, it is also consistent with a recent emphasis on going beyond integration to develop a distinctly *Christian psychology* that is more substantially grounded in biblical and historical theology and ultimately in Scripture itself, as Eric Johnson (2007) has advocated and described (see also Roberts 2000). The role of Scripture or Christian theology is therefore central to my description of a Christian counseling approach that is Christ centered, biblically based, and Spirit filled (Tan 2001b; see also Tan 1991). Thus Scripture has ultimate authority because it is the inspired Word of God that does deal with the major issues and problems of human beings, especially when properly interpreted in thematic and extended application contexts (Crabb 1977, 1987; see also Farnsworth 1996; Porter 2010a, 2010b). The Bible is comprehensive, even if it is not exhaustive (cf. S. L. Jones 1996), regarding human beings and their functioning and dysfunctioning, and therefore it is foundational for a truly Christian psychology and Christian counseling and soul care (E. L. Johnson 2007). Basic Christian theology must be carefully understood, with the best of biblical interpretation, and then applied to the context of Christian therapy, thus providing the biblical basis of Christian counseling for people helpers (Collins 1993; see also Collins 2007). My approach to Christian counseling resonates most with the integration (Collins 2000), Christian psychology (Roberts 2000; see also E. L. Johnson 2007), and biblical counseling (Powlison 2000) views on the relationship of psychology and Christianity (see also Dueck and Lee 2005; Entwistle 2010; McMinn and Phillips 2001; Moriarty 2010; Worthington 2010). It builds bridges with biblical counselors and appreciates all that is truly biblical (see Monroe 1997). It also emphasizes *personal or intrapersonal integration* (i.e., a person's own appropriation of psychological and spiritual experience, including one's spirituality in Christ) as the most foundational area of integration (Tan 2001b), with the three major areas of integration (Malony 1995) being *principled* (theoretical-conceptual and research), *professional* (clinical or practice), and *personal* (intrapersonal, including spirituality).

Basic Christian theology usually covers the following major topics as Collins (1993) has briefly described and applied to Christian counseling: Bibliology (the doctrine of Scripture), theology proper (the doctrine of God the Father), Christology (the doctrine of God the Son), pneumatology (the doctrine of God the Holy Spirit), anthropology (the doctrine of human beings), hamartiology (the doctrine of sin), soteriology (the doctrine of salvation), ecclesiology (the doctrine of the church), angelology (the doctrine of angels), and eschatology (the doctrine of the future). These are major Christian doctrines usually explained in some detail in systematic theology books (see, e.g., Grudem 1994). Much more work must be done in understanding and applying such Christian theology to Christian therapy contexts, especially with more theological depth and sophistication (see J. R. Beck 2006).

A crucial topic covered in previous chapters on the major approaches to therapy concerns their perspective on human nature. In Christian therapy, a biblical perspective on human nature is also a critical and foundational topic. Much integrative work in this area of biblical anthropology has been recently published, with some substantial and helpful attempts at theological and psychological integration (e.g., Balswick, King, and Reimer 2005; J. R. Beck and Demarest 2005; W. S. Brown, Murphy, and Malony 1998; Brugger and the Faculty of Institute for the Psychological Sciences 2008; Corcoran 2006; Green 2008; L. W. Hoffman and Strawn 2009; Lints, Horton, and Talbot 2006; Puffer 2007).

A Biblical Perspective on Human Nature

A biblical perspective on human nature (biblical anthropology) focuses on the essential or unique characteristics of human beings, based on Scripture (see Puffer 2007, 45). Biblically based views of human nature vary even among Christian theologians and therapists. For example, an important topic in biblical anthropology that has received much attention and debate in recent years is the nature of the soul, and even whether a human being has a soul (see, e.g., N. Murphy 2006). The more traditional views assume some form of *dualism* in a human being with body-soul or body-mind composition, or even *trichotomism* with body, soul, and spirit composition (see N. Murphy 2006, 95–98). An alternative view that has been recently gaining support is *nonreductive physicalism* (N. Murphy 2006) which assumes that a human being's essential nature is basically synonymous with his or her physical body (including the brain), and thus there is no separate soul of the person, with "soul" referring instead to the capacity to relate to God (see also W. S. Brown, Murphy, and Malony 1998; Corcoran 2006; Green 2008; Jeeves and Brown 2009). However, this debate continues, with strong criticisms of the nonreductive physicalism view (which attempts to take neuroscience seriously in a theological context) by other well-known Christian scholars who espouse a more traditional dualistic view of the human being, who does have a body and a soul or is a body-soul in composition (see J. R. Beck and Demarest 2005, 203–9; J. W. Cooper 1989; Green and Palmer 2005).

Whether one accepts a more traditional dualistic view of the human being or espouses a nonreductive physicalism view of human nature, it is still crucial to have a basic biblical perspective on human nature to guide the process and practice of Christian counseling. Keith Puffer has recently described a modest proposal of *seven essential biblical assumptions about human nature* and summarized them in the following statement: "Humans are created beings fashioned into God's image. Fallen with a sinful nature and striving to find meaning, people are also redeemable, dwellable by God's Spirit, and transformable for God's purposes" (2007, 46).

He provides further implications of the following seven essential biblical assumptions about human beings or human nature: they are (1) created beings; (2) fashioned in the image of God; (3) fallen with a sin nature; (4) striving to find meaning; (5) redeemable; (6) dwellable by the Spirit of God; (7) transformable for God's purposes (Puffer 2007, 47–53).

In proposing and describing a biblical model for effective lay counseling some years ago, I included the following summary of a *basic view of humanity or human nature from a biblical perspective*:

1. Basic psychological and spiritual needs include needs for security (love), significance (meaning/impact), and hope (forgiveness).
2. Basic problem is sin—but not all emotional suffering is due to personal sin.
3. Ultimate goal of humanity is to know God and have spiritual health.
4. Problem feelings are usually due to problem behavior and, more fundamentally, problem thinking—however, biological and demonic factors should also be considered.
5. Holistic view of persons—all have physical, mental/emotional, social, and spiritual dimensions. (Tan 1991, 50–51)

This basic view of human nature from a biblical perspective is not an exhaustive or even comprehensive treatment of the vast and complex topic of biblical anthropology. It is an attempt to describe five basic biblically based assumptions of human nature that have particular relevance to effective Christian counseling (see Tan 1991, 34–39, 50–51), which will now be covered in more detail.

First, the *basic psychological and spiritual needs* of human beings include the needs for *security (love)* and *significance (purpose)* (Crabb 1977) and for *hope (forgiveness)* (Adams 1973). The basic human needs for security and significance have been rephrased by Crabb as "deep longings in the human heart for relationship and impact" (1987, 15), which can only be fully met in the context of a personal relationship with Jesus Christ as one's Lord and Savior. Such longings or needs will not be completely satisfied while one lives in a sinful, fallen world that is imperfect; hence, complete fulfillment of them in the Lord can only be experienced in heaven to come. However, they can be substantially satisfied by surrendering our self-protective defenses and depending more fully on Jesus Christ to empower us to live our lives according to his will, including being involved in a caring community of believers in a local church context. Although the basic psychological and spiritual needs of human beings can be described in various ways, depending on one's theoretical and theological viewpoint, such basic human longings include the needs for security (love/relationship), significance (purpose/impact), and hope (forgiveness).

Second, from a biblical perspective humanity's *basic problem is sin*. All human beings have sinned and therefore are fallen people (Rom. 3:23), yet they have been created in the image of God (Gen. 1:26–27), with a freedom or capacity to choose (Deut. 30:19; Josh. 24:15). Disobeying God's moral laws as revealed in Scripture and believing the satanic deception or lie that we can handle our own lives and fulfill our basic needs and longings without God underlie most psychological or emotional problems that do not have obvious organic bases (Crabb 1977; see also Adams 1970). However, this does not mean that all emotional suffering is due to personal sin or even the sins of others. Sometimes, emotional pain is simply part of living in a fallen, sinful, imperfect world. Paradoxically, emotional anguish can also at times have nothing to do with sin at all; it may instead result from the process of being perfected by God into deeper Christlikeness (i.e., sanctification) and thus from *obedience* to God's will, and *not* sinful disobedience. Jesus himself experienced deep anguish and emotional and spiritual suffering in the Garden of Gethsemane (see Grounds 1976) as he struggled with the Father's will for him to go to the cross and die for sinful humanity in order to save us (Matt. 26:36–39; Mark 14:32–36; Luke 22:40–44). Yet he never sinned (Heb. 4:15). We must therefore discern and differentiate between sin-induced emotional suffering and anguish that is sometimes part of the process of growing as a Christian into deeper Christlikeness and obedience to God's will.

There are "mystical" aspects of the spiritual life in Christ that include processes and experiences that are not easily comprehended, such as the "dark night of the soul" according to St. John of the Cross (cf. Isa. 50:10). Richard Foster has described such an experience thus:

> The "dark night" . . . is not something bad or destructive. . . . The purpose of the darkness is not to punish or afflict us. It is to set us free. . . .
>
> What is involved in entering the dark night of the soul? It may be a sense of dryness, depression, even lostness. It strips us of overdependence on the emotional life. The notion, often heard today, that such experiences can be avoided and that we should live in peace and comfort, joy and celebration, only betrays the fact that much contemporary experience is surface slush. The dark night is one of the ways God brings us to a hush, a stillness, so that He can work on inner transformation of the soul. . . . Recognize the dark night for what it is. Be grateful that God is lovingly drawing you away from every distraction so that you can see Him. (Foster 1978, 89–91)

I have thus previously written about the need for Christian counselors and therapists to better understand and thus more appropriately help clients who are experiencing mystical aspects of the spiritual life in Christ, such as the dark night of the soul:

> From a psychological perspective, Christian psychologists need to have a better acquaintance with such processes of the spiritual life as the dark night of the soul . . . so that they do not naively or prematurely attempt to reduce all painful symptoms, but rather to appropriate their meaning first. This will require not only psychological assessment skills but spiritual wisdom and discernment as well. Sometimes there is no easy solution or therapy or healing, but to trust God and His grace to help people grow through such deepening and painful spiritual experiences. The best therapy then is to provide understanding, support, and much prayer. (Tan 1987b, 37)

More attention has recently been given to the phenomenon of *spiritual struggle*, which includes experiences such as the dark night of the soul, in the literature on psychology and religion (Pargament, Murray-Swank, Magyar, and Ano 2005) and in spiritually integrated psychotherapy (Pargament 2007).

Third, the *ultimate goal of humanity is to know God and enjoy him forever*; hence *spiritual health is primary*. The end goal in life for a Christian is to obey God's will and grow in maturity in Christ or to become more like Christ (Rom. 8:29). This may involve suffering at times, but God has promised to provide sufficient grace and to empower us in our weakness (2 Cor. 12:7–9). Although mental and physical health are worthwhile and acceptable goals to achieve, for the Christian they are always secondary and subordinate to the end goal of spiritual health and maturity in Christ. The absence of emotional pain, or happiness at all costs, is therefore not the ultimate goal of life on earth for the Christian. Biblical perspectives on suffering, including what C. S. Evans (1986) has called "the blessings of mental anguish," need to be affirmed. Evans has also noted that "the primary goal of a Christian counselor is not to help people become merely 'normal,' but to help them love God with all their hearts, minds and souls" (1986, 29). The ultimate goal of life on earth and also of Christian counseling should therefore be holiness, not temporal happiness, and spiritual health or wholeness, not just mental or physical health (see Grounds 1976, 105–11).

Fourth, a biblical perspective on human nature assumes that *problem feelings are usually due to problem behavior* (cf. Gen. 4:3–7) and, more fundamentally, to problem thinking (John 8:32; Rom. 12:1–2; Eph. 4:22–24; Phil. 4:8). Crabb (1977) has emphasized that at the root of nonorganically caused mental and emotional problems are unbiblical, erroneous basic assumptions or beliefs, or what Backus (1985) has called "misbeliefs" (see also Backus and Chapian 1980), reflecting a Christian approach to cognitive therapy or rational emotive behavior therapy. However, this does not mean that problem feelings are always due to problem behavior and problem thinking. Problem feelings can at times be due to biological or physical factors, even if no known organic cause can be found, since current knowledge of such biological factors is limited but ever expanding. Medical or psychiatric help, where appropriate, should be sought. Problem feelings (as well as thoughts and behaviors) can also sometimes be due to demonic activity (demonization), whether demonic oppression or possession, in which case when properly discerned, prayer for deliverance may be necessary (e.g., Bufford 1988; MacNutt 1995). Some helpful criteria (though not foolproof) for discerning the presence of the demonic versus mental illness include the following: the afflicted person's strong, negative reaction to the name of Jesus (or the reading of Scripture or the singing of hymns); a foreboding or almost overwhelming sense of evil on the part of the therapist; the afflicted person's history of involvement with the occult and/or cults; and possibly an olfactory criterion involving a smell of sulfur or rotten eggs associated with the afflicted person. These are not definitive differential diagnostic criteria for demonization versus mental illness. They should be used in consultation with other pastors or Christian counselors experienced in deliverance ministries and pastoral care and counseling, as well as with much prayer and dependence on the Holy Spirit and his gift of discerning of spirits (1 Cor. 12:10).

In a broader sense, from a biblical perspective counseling and psychotherapy can be viewed as involving *spiritual warfare* because they inevitably deal with good and evil, including the demonic. In this context, Marguerite Shuster (1987) has emphasized the need for agape love, humility, weakness, and dependence on the Lord's grace and power on the part of the counselor or therapist so that he or she can conquer evil with good.

The need to keep a good balance in focusing not only on problem thinking but on all three major areas of human experience, that is, feelings, behavior, and thoughts, has been emphasized by Gary Collins (1976). Similarly, Crabb (1987) has noted the need to attend to all four major circles or dimensions of a person's functioning: the personal, rational, volitional, and emotional areas. Nevertheless, the crucial role of problem thinking and problem behavior in the development of problem feelings must not be lost or negated.

Fifth and finally, a biblical perspective on human nature assumes *a holistic view of people with physical, mental-emotional, social, and spiritual dimensions* (cf. Luke 2:52). As Jay Adams has observed, a client's problem (e.g., depression or anxiety) must be viewed in the context of all areas of his or her life, and biblical restructuring should also involve all these areas in what he calls "total structuring": (1) church, Bible, prayer, witness; (2) work, school; (3) physical health, exercise, diet, sleep; (4) marriage, sex; (5) finances, budget; (6) family, children, discipline; (7) social activities, friends; (8) other (e.g., reading) (see 1973, 409–12).

A similar comprehensive but secular approach to viewing human functioning and dysfunctioning is the multimodal therapy perspective advocated by

Arnold Lazarus, which was discussed in chapter 11 of this book. Lazarus (1989, 2008) has described seven major dimensions of human personality functioning, summarized as an individual's BASIC I.D. (or basic identity): *B*ehavior, *A*ffect, *S*ensations, *I*mages, *C*ognitions, *I*nterpersonal relationships, *D*rugs/Biology. The BASIC I.D. does not specifically include or focus on the crucial spiritual dimension of life. Christian counselors can add *S* for the spiritual dimension so that it now reads the BASIC I.D.S. (see Tan 1991, 39), or as Jeffrey Bjorck has suggested, use the seven dimensions of the BASIC I.D. to assess the spiritual realm and one's experience of God (2007, 145).

Basic Principles of Effective Counseling and Psychotherapy: A Biblical Perspective

I have further proposed and described thirteen basic principles of effective counseling and psychotherapy from a biblical perspective. They are also based on empirical research and counseling theories that are consistent with biblical views. Here is my summary of the thirteen principles:

1. The Holy Spirit's ministry as counselor is crucial; depend on him.
2. The Bible is a basic and comprehensive (not exhaustive) guide for counseling.
3. Prayer is an integral part of biblical counseling.
4. The ultimate goal of counseling is maturity in Christ and fulfilling the Great Commission.
5. The personal qualities of the counselor are important, especially spiritual ones.
6. The client's attitudes, motivations, and desire for help are important.
7. The relationship between counselor and client is significant.
8. Effective counseling is a process involving exploration, understanding, and action phases, with a focus on changing problem thinking.
9. The style or approach in counseling should be flexible.
10. Specific techniques or methods of counseling should be consistent with Scripture; cognitive-behavioral ones may be especially helpful, with qualifications.
11. Cultural sensitivity and cross-cultural counseling skills are required.
12. Outreach and prevention skills in the context of a caring community are important.
13. Awareness of limitations and referral skills are also important. (Tan 1991, 50–52)

These thirteen basic principles of effective counseling and psychotherapy from a biblical perspective will now be covered in more detail (see Tan 1991, 41–52).

First, *the Holy Spirit's ministry as counselor or comforter is crucial in effective Christian counseling* (Tan 1999b). As Adams (1973) has emphasized, there are always at least three persons involved in every situation of counseling: the client, the counselor, and the Holy Spirit. Prayerful dependence on the Holy Spirit and his work as counselor is essential in effective Christian counseling (cf. John 14:16–17). The Christian counselor must be filled with the Holy Spirit (Eph. 5:18) and depend on the Spirit's power, gifts, truth, and fruit in order to help clients in a Christ-centered, biblically based, and Spirit-led way (Tan 1999b; see also Pugh 2008).

Second, *the Bible is the basic guide for dealing with problems in living* (cf. 2 Tim. 3:16–17). It is a comprehensive (though not exhaustive) guide for counseling because it speaks meaningfully to human problems and needs when it is carefully interpreted in terms of its contents, categories, implications, and images as well as its extended applications to the complex problems with which people struggle (Crabb 1987; see also Adams 1973). The Bible therefore requires not only as accurate and appropriate interpretation as possible (exegesis and hermeneutics), but also practical application to life and its difficulties for it to function as a basic guide for counseling. The Christian counselor must have at least some basic knowledge of Scripture and theology, because Christian theology is foundational for effective Christian counseling (Collins 1993; Hurding 1992; I. F. Jones 2006; see also Collins 2007; Kruis 2000; P. A. Miller 2002; P. A. Miller and Miller 2006). However, the Bible is *not* an exhaustive guide for counseling. Hence, theories and techniques from secular therapy can be used in Christian counseling as long as they do *not* contradict Scripture or biblical values. This view affirms that "all truth is God's truth" or the unity of truth, and that God's general revelation and common grace allow his truth to be discovered even by those who are not Christians, for example, through good research. However, ultimate authority is still given to Scripture.

Third, *prayer is an integral part of effective Christian counseling that is biblically based* (cf. James 5:16). The Christian counselor can also use prayer in various ways, such as praying for the client before and in between counseling sessions and silently during counseling sessions. Prayer can also be used explicitly during counseling sessions when the Christian counselor prays aloud with the client. Informed consent from the client must be obtained before using spiritual resources such as prayer and Scripture in counseling sessions (see Tan 1996b).

Fourth, *the ultimate goal of Christian counseling is to make disciples or disciplers of clients* (see Collins 1976). With informed consent from clients, Christian counselors can sensitively point clients to Christ and thus help to fulfill the Great Commission (Matt. 28:18–20). Collins (1976) has therefore described Christian counseling as "discipleship counseling" (see also N. T. Anderson 2003). Crabb (1977) has similarly emphasized that the basic goal of Christian counseling is to help free people to better worship and serve God by guiding them toward maturity in Christ.

Fifth, *the personal qualities of the Christian counselor are important for effective Christian counseling*. For example, Christian counselors need to have qualities such as goodness (goodwill or love), knowledge of God's Word, and wisdom in applying it in practical ways (Rom. 15:14; Col. 3:16) (Adams 1973). They may be particularly gifted for counseling ministries with spiritual gifts such as encouragement (Rom. 12:8) (see Tan 1999b). Christian counselors must also be spiritually mature to be effective in helping clients with their problems in living (cf. Gal. 6:1–2). The fruit of the Spirit manifested especially in agape love (Gal. 5:22–23; see 1 Cor. 13) is also essential in the Christian counselor, who must be, at minimum, warm, empathic, and genuine in relating to clients.

Sixth, *the client's attitudes, motivations, and desire for help are also crucial factors for determining the outcome of counseling and psychotherapy* (see Collins 1976). For example, according to research findings from the Vanderbilt Psychotherapy Study, the process variable that most consistently predicted the outcome of counseling or therapy was the extent of client involvement in therapy (Gomes-Schwartz 1978). More specifically, clients who were not hostile or mistrustful and who actively participated in their therapy showed more therapeutic changes compared to clients who were defensive, withdrawn, or unwilling to be actively involved in their therapy (see Gomez-Schwartz 1978, 1032).

Seventh, *the relationship between the counselor and the client is another significant variable for determining the outcome of counseling and psychotherapy*. Carkhuff (1971) has emphasized the importance of good rapport and communication in the relationship between the counselor and the client for effective counseling. He describes six "core conditions" for therapeutic change: the facilitative conditions of (1) empathy (or understanding); (2) respect (or caring or warmth); and (3) concreteness (or being specific); and the action conditions of (4) genuineness (or being real); (5) confrontation (or telling it like it is); and (6) immediacy (or what's really going on between the two of you). Ephesians 4:15, in a similar vein, emphasizes speaking the truth (similar to concreteness, immediacy, confrontation, and genuineness) in love (similar to respect or warmth, empathy, and genuineness). More-recent research on empirically supported therapy relationships (ESRs) has shown that empathy, therapeutic alliance, cohesion in group therapy, and goal consensus and collaboration are demonstrably effective, and positive regard (or respect or warmth), congruence/genuineness, feedback, repair of alliance ruptures, self-disclosure, management of countertransference, and quality of relational interpretations are promising and probably effective as general elements of the therapy relationship (see Norcross 2002, 441).

Eighth, *effective counseling is a process involving exploration, understanding, and action phases that unfold cyclically*. It therefore requires the counselor to explore and understand the client and his or her problems before undertaking specific courses of action to help the client (see Carkhuff 1971; Egan 1986). Crabb (1977) has expanded the three major phases of exploration, understanding, and action in the counseling process into a seven-stage model of effective biblical counseling: (stage 1) identify problem feelings; (stage 2) identify problem behavior; (stage 3) identify problem thinking; (stage 4) teach and clarify biblical thinking; (stage 5) secure commitment; (stage 6) plan/carry out biblical behavior; and (stage 7) identify Spirit-controlled feelings.

Ninth, *directive, or nouthetic, counseling is an important part of Christian counseling, but the style or approach taken in Christian counseling and therapy should be flexible.* Nouthetic counseling that is directive and involves caring confrontation to bring about client change in a biblical way, as developed by Adams (1970, 1973), is an important part but not the whole of Christian counseling. Biblically based Christian counseling is more appropriately based on *parakaleo* and *paraklesis* rather than only on *noutheteo* and *nouthesia*, Greek words found in the New Testament that are most relevant to counseling. Biblical counseling therefore includes not only the nouthetic, or directive, confrontational, approach but also the *parakaleo* components such as encouraging, supporting, and comforting (J. D. Carter 1975). The specific style or approach that a Christian counselor takes in helping clients should be flexible and appropriate to the specific client with a particular problem. First Thessalonians 5:14 provides wise biblical guidance that supports such sensitive flexibility in counseling: "And we urge you, brothers, warn those who are idle, encourage the timid, help the weak, be patient with everyone." D. E. Carlson (1976) has also observed from Scripture that Jesus's style of relating was flexible, ranging from his prophetic, confrontational style to his priestly, accepting style, with his pastoral style in between, depending on the person to whom he was relating.

Tenth, *there is flexibility with regard to specific techniques or therapeutic methods to be used in counseling and therapy, but they should be consistent with Scripture.* A certain technical eclecticism in the use of specific therapy techniques is acceptable provided that the Scriptures are used as the ultimate screening device for deciding whether to accept or reject particular therapeutic interventions (cf. 1 Thess. 5:21). Whatever is deemed unbiblical or antibiblical should be rejected, but whatever is seen as consistent with Scripture, even if it is not in the Bible, can be used. Cognitive-behavioral and behavioral techniques can be particularly helpful to many clients across a range of clinical problems, as already covered in chapters 12 and 13 of this book. However, a biblical approach to, and critique of, cognitive-behavioral interventions should still be used (see Tan 1987a). McMinn and Campbell (2007) have recently described a more comprehensive Christian approach to therapy called *integrative psychotherapy*, which integrates behavioral, cognitive, and interpersonal models of therapy within a Christian theological framework.

Eleventh, *effective Christian counseling requires cultural sensitivity and cross-cultural or multicultural counseling skills.* American society has become even more pluralistic, diverse, and multicultural in recent years. Christian counseling, as well as counseling and therapy in general, must be culturally sensitive and use cross-cultural or multicultural counseling skills to be effective in helping clients from diverse backgrounds (see, e.g., Ridley 2005; D. W. Sue and D. Sue 2008; D. Sue and D. M. Sue 2008; for Christian perspectives, see also Augsburger 1986; Dueck and Reimer 2009; Hesselgrave 1984; Ridley 1986; Uomoto 1986; Tan 1999a; Yang 1996).

Twelfth, *outreach and prevention skills in the context of a caring community or the local church are important in effective Christian counseling.* J. S. Prater (1987) made the following six proposals, originally for lay Christian counselors to be trained in interventions that go beyond individual counseling; they are also relevant to professional Christian counselors and therapists: (1) Christian counselors should be trained to assess the role of environmental stressors (e.g., poverty, unemployment, racism, sexism, and lack of social support) in the development and maintenance of emotional problems; (2) Christian counselors should be trained in the techniques of community outreach and empowerment; (3) Christian counselors should be trained in cultural awareness and sensitivity; (4) Christian counselors should be trained to be aware of and to make use of existing support systems and services within churches; (5) Christian counselors should be trained in skills to develop new support systems within the church where needed (e.g., prevention-oriented seminars on topics such as stress management, parenting skills, and conflict resolution); and (6) Christian counselors should be trained to communicate more actively and regularly with other leaders involved in outreach ministries of the church so that a coordinated package of ministries can be established.

Thirteenth and finally, *awareness of limitations and referral skills are also important in effective Christian counseling.* Every counselor or therapist has limitations and needs to be aware of them so that he or she can skillfully and sensitively make appropriate referrals of clients to other professionals (e.g., other therapists or counselors, lawyers, psychiatrists, physicians, financial consultants) who can better help such clients because of their expertise. Some examples of counseling situations that may require referring clients to other professionals include those involving clients who are severely disturbed or suicidal, need medical or psychiatric help, have serious financial needs or legal problems, show extremely aggressive behavior, use drugs or alcohol in excessive and harmful ways, or want to see another therapist (see Collins 1976, 113).

The crucial and essential role of Christian theology in Christian counseling and therapy has been emphasized in this chapter. A biblical perspective on human nature, with five basic assumptions, and a biblical approach to effective counseling, with thirteen basic principles that I have previously described in the context of lay Christian counseling (Tan 1991), have also been summarized and updated in this chapter for application to Christian counseling and therapy as a whole, whether professional or lay.

Recommended Readings

Beck, J. R., & Demarest, B. (2005). *The human person in theology and psychology: A biblical anthropology for the twenty-first century*. Grand Rapids: Kregel.

Collins, G. R. (1993). *The biblical basis of Christian counseling for people helpers*. Colorado Springs: NavPress.

Crabb, L. J. (1987). *Understanding people: Deep longings for relationship*. Grand Rapids: Zondervan.

Johnson, E. L. (2007). *Foundations for soul care: A Christian psychology proposal*. Downers Grove, IL: IVP Academic.

Johnson, E. L., & Jones, S. L. (Eds.). (2000). *Psychology and Christianity: Four views*. Downers Grove, IL: InterVarsity.

Stevenson, D. H., Eck, B. E., & Hill, P. C. (Eds.). (2007). *Psychology and Christianity: Seminal works that shaped the movement*. Batavia, IL: Christian Association for Psychological Studies.

Tan, S. Y. (1991). *Lay counseling: Equipping Christians for a helping ministry*. Grand Rapids: Zondervan.

15

Christian Faith in Clinical Practice

Implicit and Explicit Integration

Christian faith in clinical practice, as a specific example of religion or spirituality in clinical practice (Tan 1996c), refers to integration in the therapy room (M. E. L. Hall and Hall 1997; see also Eck 2002). Such integration has also been called professional integration (Tan 2001b) or the practical integration of theology and psychology (N. T. Anderson, Zuehlke, and Zuehlke 2000). It involves the actual conducting of Christian counseling and psychotherapy that is Christ centered, biblically based, and Spirit led (Tan 2001b). As noted in the previous chapter, this area of Christian counseling and therapy has witnessed significant growth and development in recent years, as has the more general area of religiously oriented and spiritually oriented therapy, especially in the last decade or so. Relatively contextualistic approaches in the so-called third wave of behavior therapy and cognitive behavior therapy, including acceptance and commitment therapy (ACT), mindfulness-based cognitive therapy (MBCT), and dialectical behavior therapy (DBT), have also recently emphasized mindfulness and acceptance, which have spiritual roots in Zen Buddhism (Hayes et al. 2006) as well as other contemplative religious or spiritual traditions (see Tan 2007b).

Implicit and Explicit Integration in Christian Therapy

Christian therapy has been described as consecrated counseling with the following distinctives: "Counseling is most truly Christian when the counselor has a deep faith; counsels with excellence; holds a Christian world view; is guided by Christian values in choosing the means, goals and motivations of counseling: actively seeks the presence and work of God; and actively utilizes spiritual interventions and resources within ethical guidelines" (Bufford 1997, 120). Two major models of professional integration in the actual clinical practice of Christian therapy are implicit and explicit integration, which can be described as two ends of a continuum: "*Implicit integration* . . . refers to a more covert approach that does not initiate the discussion of religious or spiritual issues and does not openly, directly or systematically use spiritual resources. . . . *Explicit integration* . . . refers to a more overt approach that directly and systematically deals with spiritual or religious issues in therapy, and uses spiritual resources like prayer, Scripture or sacred texts, referrals to church or other religious groups or lay counselors, and other religious practices" (Tan 1996c, 368). A Christian therapist will practice implicit or explicit integration or move along the continuum between implicit and explicit integration, depending on the needs and problems of the client as well as the training, inclination, and personality of the Christian therapist. It is crucial to note that *both* implicit and explicit integration are equally substantial and important. Intentional and prayerful integration is the critical factor, whether it involves implicit or explicit integration or both. It should be conducted in dependence on the Holy Spirit, in a professionally competent, ethically responsible, and clinically sensitive way, with clear informed consent from the client (Tan 2001b).

Implicit Integration in Christian Therapy

The Christian therapist who practices implicit integration in Christian therapy does not initiate discussion of religious or spiritual issues with the client and does not openly, directly, or systematically employ spiritual resources or interventions such as prayer and Scripture in therapy with the client. Implicit integration is a more covert approach to integrating Christian faith in clinical practice. However, it is still a crucial and substantial approach that is intentional and prayerfully dependent on the Holy Spirit for his guidance and healing grace as clients are helped in therapy. The Christian therapist using an implicit integration approach will still be silently praying for the client and be authentic in showing agape love to the client. The Christian therapist thus will reflect biblical values and convictions without imposing them on the client or explicitly discussing such religious issues in a verbal way with the client.

Implicit integration is particularly helpful and appropriate when the Christian therapist is helping clients who are not believers or Christians and who are not interested in discussing spiritual or religious issues or using spiritual resources such as prayer and Scripture. It is also appropriate in counseling with Christian clients who are not interested in a more explicit approach to

Christian therapy, whether they are presently in active rebellion against God, or experiencing a significant spiritual struggle, or simply feeling indifferent or cold toward God and the spiritual life. However, as therapy progresses, such clients may become more interested in discussing spiritual or religious issues in a more direct and open way, including the possible use of spiritual resources such as prayer and Scripture, in which case the Christian therapist may move in the continuum to a more explicit integration approach in therapy.

Implicit integration in Christian therapy may also be more easily adopted by Christian therapists who practice from psychodynamic and psychoanalytic perspectives, since these approaches to therapy require the therapist to be more of a "blank slate" and nondirective. Explicit integration, on the other hand, may be more easily adopted by Christian therapists who practice from cognitive-behavioral and humanistic-existential perspectives, since these approaches to therapy are consistent with the therapist assuming a more directive stance (see I. R. Payne, Bergin, and Loftus 1992).

Recently, C. Jeffrey Terrell (2007) has challenged the definition of implicit integration presented so far, following the original formulation of implicit and explicit integration that I provided in an earlier work (Tan 1996c). Terrell describes instead an intentional incarnational integration approach in relational psychodynamic psychotherapy (see also S. A. Rogers 2007), which is usually viewed as implicit integration according to my original formulation (Tan 1996c). However, it can be conceptualized as "explicit" integration in another sense because the therapist's use of the therapeutic relationship as a catalyst for bringing about deeper change in the client's relational patterns is very intentional. Terrell states:

> In making this argument, I realize that I *am* blurring the boundaries of explicit and implicit integration. . . . It is "explicit" in its avowal that our patient is worthy of love. It is "explicit" in its awareness of imperfection and failure in him or her. It is "explicit" in its unflinching description of his or her attempts to manipulate the world. It is "explicit" in its acceptance of our patient, despite his or her worst, most humiliating experiences. In this way, intentional and incarnational integration is being practiced, whether implicit or explicit in its verbal expression. (2007, 162)

Terrell therefore emphasizes that such an intentional incarnational integration approach in relational psychodynamic Christian therapy can be conceptualized as "explicit" as well as implicit integration. He concludes: "When we engage relationally, our patients believe we *get* them. We hear the worst and still accept them. Modeling the gospel story, our work is incarnational (Benner 1983). It is redemptive, integrative, and intentional (Tan 2001b), 'explicit' even when it doesn't involve the direct use of scriptural texts or in session prayer" (2007, 164). In a similar vein, Steven Rogers (2007) has emphasized that a focus on the process and the here-and-now within therapy can itself be described as a powerful spiritual intervention in object relations psychotherapy, a psycho-dynamic approach to therapy. This process orientation includes therapist skills such as the therapist acknowledging his or her own errors while conducting therapy with the client, and the therapist using his or her own feelings in ap-propriate self-disclosure during a therapy session. Rogers views this process orientation and focus on the here-and-now within a therapy session as a highly spiritual intervention because it reflects God's way of relating to human be-ings and creates a sacred space for clients to develop deeper understanding of themselves, others, and God.

Explicit Integration in Christian Therapy

Explicit integration is a more overt approach to integrating Christian faith into clinical practice. It views the spirituality of both the therapist and the client to be foundational for effective therapy as well as for growth and wholeness. It integrates psychological therapy with spiritual guidance or direction to some extent, in the context of therapy (Tan 1996c; see also Tan 2003c). The Chris-tian therapist who practices explicit integration in Christian therapy will more verbally, directly, and systematically deal with spiritual issues in therapy and use spiritual resources such as prayer, Scripture, referrals to church or other support groups or lay counselors, and other religious practices.

Explicit integration in Christian therapy should be conducted in a clini-cally sensitive, ethically responsible, and professionally competent way, since it can potentially be misused by overenthusiastic therapists who may unethi-cally impose their religious values and spiritual interventions on clients (Tan 1996c). Several ethical guidelines are available for the appropriate practice of explicit integration in Christian therapy (see, e.g., Tan 2003c). They include the following three basic practices proposed by A. A. Nelson and W. P. Wilson (1984), who state that it is ethical for therapists to use their religious faith in therapy if (1) they are dealing with clinical problems that can be helped by religious or spiritual interventions; (2) they are not imposing their own religious beliefs and values on the client and are thus working within the client's belief system; and (3) they have obtained informed consent from the client to use religious or spiritual resources and interventions as part of a clearly defined therapy contract with the client.

A Christian therapist therefore needs to openly and sensitively discuss with the client in the initial intake interview how the client would like to deal with religious or spiritual issues, if at all, so that the therapist can then decide whether to use an explicit or implicit integration approach in therapy. The therapist can ask helpful questions in the intake interview, such as: "What is your religion or religious affiliation, if any?" and "Are religious or spiritual issues and resources such as prayer important for you and me to address in our therapy sessions?" If the client is not interested in dealing with religious or spiritual issues in therapy, then the therapist needs to respect the client's wishes. If the client expresses an interest in having a more explicit integration approach in therapy, then the therapist can proceed to obtain informed consent from the client, preferably in written form. The therapy contract clearly agreed upon, with full and free informed consent from the client, will therefore include open and direct discussion of religious or spiritual issues and the use of spiritual resources and interventions such as prayer and Scripture. It will also include the goals set by the client for his or her therapy. However, if the therapist does not feel adequately trained or experienced in using an explicit integration approach in therapy, then the therapist should refer the client to another Christian therapist who may be more experienced in conducting explicit Christian therapy (Tan 1996c).

> **Sidebar 15.1**
>
> **Three Aspects of Explicit Integration**
> *(see Tan 1996c)*
>
> 1. Using religious and spiritual resources in therapy
> 2. Dealing with spiritual issues in therapy
> 3. Fostering intrapersonal integration and the development of spirituality in the therapist and the client

It is important to note that implicit and explicit integration are not two mutually exclusive models for integrating Christian faith in therapy. They are actually two ends of a continuum of integration. A Christian therapist's approach can range from being implicit to explicit in addressing religious or spiritual issues and using spiritual resources in therapy. The therapist can also move along the continuum with the client at different stages of the therapy or even during a particular session, depending on the needs and openness of the client. The therapist must respond to the client in an appropriate, sensitive, and empathic way. As Terrell (2007) has emphasized, a more relational psychodynamic approach to therapy, while relatively more implicit, can also be considered to have "explicit" features in that it is very intentional in its Christian integration approach, which is essentially incarnational in nature, even if it is not always verbal in dealing with religious issues.

Explicit integration in Christian therapy has various components. Three major aspects of explicit integration are: (1) using religious and spiritual resources in therapy; (2) dealing with spiritual issues in therapy; and (3) fostering intrapersonal integration and the development of spirituality in the therapist and the client (see Tan 1996c).

Explicit Integration: Use of Religious and Spiritual Resources in Therapy

A major component of explicit integration is the direct, open, and systematic use of religious and spiritual resources in therapy. There are many examples of such resources (see, e.g., Pargament 2007; Plante 2009; Richards and Bergin

2005; Sperry and Shafranske 2005), but three main ones are prayer, Scripture, and referral to religious groups (Tan 1996c).

Prayer

Prayer is a major spiritual resource or intervention often used in explicit integration. It can be described simply as communing with God but it also refers to other ways of experiencing or focusing on God (C. B. Johnson 1987). It includes *meditative* (waiting and worshiping in God's presence), *ritualistic* (involving the use of rituals), *petitionary* (making specific requests), and *colloquial* (conversational and relational, with gratitude) prayer (Poloma and Pendleton 1989, 1991), as well as *intercessory* (asking on behalf of others, e.g., for their healing and blessing) prayer (McCullough and Larson 1999). A specific form of prayer has been termed "holy name repetition," and Christian examples include "Lord Jesus Christ, Son of God, have mercy on me," "Lord Jesus have mercy," or simply "Jesus," all variants of the Jesus prayer (see Oman and Driskill, 2003). Richard J. Foster (1992) in fact describes twenty-one types of prayer. They help us in *moving inward* (seeking the transformation we need), *moving upward* (seeking the intimacy we need), and *moving outward* (seeking the ministry we need). Many Christians have memorized the different types of prayer as consisting of **A**doration, **C**onfession, **T**hanksgiving, and **S**upplication (including both petition for oneself and intercession for others), or ACTS. There are therefore different types of prayer that can be used in Christian therapy with a client (e.g., quiet, meditative, or contemplative prayer; general prayer aloud with the client; specific prayer aloud with and for the client; inner-healing prayer; or prayer for healing of memories). A Christian therapist can also use prayer at different times, such as before, during, or after the therapy session, at the beginning or at the end of the therapy session, or any other time connected with the therapy session.

The use of Christian contemplative prayer in psychotherapy refers to a type of prayer that focuses one's full attention on relating to God in an open, passive, nondefensive, and nondemanding way (see Finney and Malony 1985a, 1985b, 1985c). Such contemplative prayer, or any other form of prayer, should not be used simply as a therapeutic technique or coping strategy for managing anxiety more effectively (Finney and Malony 1985b), but should be used only if spiritual development is also a goal of therapy. Prayer should be viewed as an end in itself and not just as a tool, technique, or strategy (see Hunsinger 2006). Prayer is to be a way of life for the Christian in relationship with God (C. B. Johnson 1987). Prayer is ultimately "the transforming friendship" with God (Houston 1989) in which we find our heart's true home in loving, intimate relationship with God (Foster 1992). Relational prayer therefore comes before petitionary prayer (Crabb 2006). Prayer can also be described as a "tree of life" that unifies Christian spirituality, with five major models of prayer: conversation, relationship, journey, transformation, and presence (Chase 2005).

Inner-healing prayer or *healing of memories* is a specific type of prayer that can be defined as "a form of prayer designed to facilitate the client's ability to process affectively painful memories through vividly recalling those memories and asking for the presence of Christ (or God) to minister in the midst of this pain" (Garzon and Burkett 2002, 42). Fernando Garzon and Lori Burkett have reviewed four major models of healing of memories developed by David Seamands (1985), myself (Tan 1996c), Leanne Payne (1991), and Edward M. Smith (2002/2005), the founder of Theophostic Ministry, and described their commonalities as well as differences. They noted that the history of healing of memories can be traced back to Agnes Sanford and her work in the 1950s, followed by others such as Francis MacNutt, Ruth Carter Stapleton, and John and Paula Sandford (see also Flynn and Gregg 1993; Kraft 1993; Richardson 2005; Wardle 2001). Inner-healing prayer is a distinctively Christian type of prayer that can also be used as a spiritual intervention in explicit integration in Christian therapy. It can be especially helpful to clients who have unresolved painful memories from their past that may involve deprivation or neglect, abandonment, rejection, harsh treatment or criticism, physical or sexual abuse, and trauma. It is usually not conducted as a stand-alone spiritual intervention but rather used in the process of ongoing therapy or pastoral care and counseling (Tan 2003b).

Inner-healing prayer should be used in a clinically sensitive way, always with informed consent obtained from the client. It should not be used, or used only with caution, with certain types of clients, for example, those with substance abuse problems, thought disorders, severe depression, or burnout (Garzon and Burkett 2002). In such cases, it is crucial for the therapist to engage in adequate client assessment, proper timing, and comprehensive treatment.

I have developed a seven-step model for inner-healing prayer that I first described in 1992 (see Tan 1992; see also Tan 2003b; Tan and Ortberg 2004, 64–71). This model does not have a set script for the client and does not directively instruct the client to visualize specific images of Jesus, unlike some other approaches to inner-healing prayer or healing of memories (e.g., Seamands 1985). Instead, it places the focus on prayer and the Holy Spirit's presence and ministry during the inner-healing prayer process, emphasizing waiting upon the Lord to minister to the client in whatever way the Spirit leads. The following are the seven steps for inner-healing prayer:

1. Begin with prayer for protection from evil, and ask for the power and healing ministry of the Holy Spirit to take control of the session.
2. Guide the client into a relaxed state, usually by brief relaxation strategies (e.g., slow, deep breathing, calming self-talk, pleasant imagery, prayer, and Bible imagery).

3. Guide the client to focus attention on a painful past event or traumatic experience, and to feel deeply the pain, hurt, anger, and so forth.
4. Prayerfully ask the Lord, by the power of the Holy Spirit, to come to the client and minister his comfort, love, and healing grace (even gentle rebuke where necessary). It may be Jesus imagery or other healing imagery, music (song/hymn), Scriptures, a sense of his presence or warmth, or other manifestation of the Spirit's working. No specific guided imagery or visualization is provided or directively given at this point.
5. Wait quietly upon the Lord to minister to the client with his healing grace and truth. Guide and speak only if necessary and led by the Holy Spirit. In order to follow or track with the client, the counselor will periodically and gently ask, "What's happening? What are you feeling or experiencing now?"
6. Close in prayer.
7. Debrief and discuss the inner-healing prayer experience with the client. (Tan 2003b, 20–21)

Homework inner-healing prayer can also be assigned to the client to be used during his or her own times of prayer at home. This seven-step model for inner-healing prayer can be modified or adapted where necessary (Tan 2007b).

Inner-Healing Prayer

A Hypothetical Transcript

The following is a hypothetical transcript of an inner-healing prayer intervention during a later therapy session with a client named Jane, who was experiencing fatigue, mild depression, and a superficial, distant relationship with God:

Therapist: As we discussed in our last session, and you have read about the seven steps of inner-healing prayer, do you feel ready today to begin this prayer intervention, focusing on the painful memory you still have of your emotionally distant father?

Client: Yes, I would like to begin inner-healing prayer for this painful memory.

Therapist: Good. Before we begin, let's remember that this is prayer and not a technique per se. We will come before the Lord with your need and painful memory and let him minister to you in whatever way he wants to and knows you need. Let's be open and receptive to what he may want to do today, with no specific expectations or demands on our part, OK?

Client: OK.

Therapist: Good. I'll begin with the first step. Please close your eyes and be in a receptive, prayerful mode, as I begin in prayer: "Dear Lord, we pray that you will protect us from evil, and come in the presence and power of the Holy Spirit, and minister to Jane your healing grace and truth for the painful memory she has. Thank you for your love and presence with us. In Jesus's name we pray. Amen." Now keep your eyes closed and continue in a prayerful mode, as I move on to the second step.

Client: OK.

Therapist: Now, Jane, I'd like you to use the relaxation techniques that you learned a couple of sessions ago, to help you relax as deeply and as comfortably as possible. . . . I'd like you now to take in a slow, deep breath . . . hold it for a few seconds . . . and now breathe out slowly and relax . . . letting go of all tension . . . just relax deeply. . . . Now, Jane, again take in a slow, deep breath . . . hold it . . . and relax, breathing out slowly and letting go of all tension. . . . Now go back to normal breathing, as you use the second relaxation technique of calming, relaxing self-talk . . . saying quietly to yourself . . . Just relax . . . take it easy . . . letting go of all tension . . . so that from the top of your head all the way down to your toes . . . you are allowing yourself to relax as deeply and as comfortably as possible . . . good. . . . Now, Jane, use the third relaxation technique of pleasant imagery. . . . In your mind's eye I want you to visualize or imagine as vividly and as clearly as possible a very relaxing, calming, peaceful, enjoyable, and pleasant scene . . . like lying on the beach on a beautiful sunny day . . . allow this pleasant and enjoyable scene to relax you even more deeply . . . even more comfortably. . . . How are you feeling now, Jane?

Client: I'm feeling very relaxed and calm, feeling pretty good.

Therapist: OK, good. Now I'd like you to switch the focus of your attention to something that is not as pleasant. I would like you to go back in your imagination and see yourself as a young girl in elementary or primary school and picture your father at home sitting in his chair and reading the newspapers and not paying much attention to you. . . . Can you relive that scene in your imagination. . . . Is it clear?

Client: Yes. I can see it happening again . . . it's actually quite painful (with eyes beginning to tear up a bit) . . .

Therapist: OK . . . I would like you to continue to see that scene clearly and to experience your feelings as fully as possible, and not avoid them or block them out. Do not just look at yourself in that scene but try to actually be yourself in that scene, so that you're actually experiencing those feelings yourself afresh at this moment.

Client: I can feel the painful emotions . . . (with some more tears)

Therapist: I know this is hard for you, but it's important for you to continue to experience these painful feelings and stay with the scene with your father still reading the newspapers . . .

Client: OK . . .

Therapist: Also, please tell me aloud while keeping your eyes closed, Jane, . . . what are you experiencing now, how are you feeling, and what's happening? . . . so I can follow you and track with you.

Client: I'm feeling lonely . . . and deeply hurt . . . that my father is still hiding behind his newspapers and not noticing me although I try to get his attention. . . . I wonder if he really loves me although he does provide material things for me and my family. . . . I feel alone and isolated and ignored and I feel like crying (with tears) . . .

Therapist: (after some time has passed) Jane, continue with that painful scene in imagery and continue to feel the painful emotions. . . . At this point, I'd like to pause here and pray for the Lord to come and minister to you, by the power and presence of the Holy Spirit, and to touch you with his healing grace and truth, OK?

Client: OK . . .

Therapist: "Dear Lord, I pray that you will now come by the power of the Holy Spirit, to walk with Jane into this painful memory, and lovingly minister your healing grace and truth to her in whatever way is needed or appropriate, according to your will. Thank you, in Jesus's name. Amen." Now, Jane, just wait for a few moments and be in a receptive, open, prayerful mode allowing the Lord to minister to you, to speak to you . . .

Client: OK . . .

Therapist: (after a few moments have passed) Jane, please tell me now what's going on. . . . What are you experiencing? . . . What are you feeling?

Client: (with some tears but a smile on her face) It's deeply touching and healing what I'm experiencing. . . . I actually sense the presence of Jesus with me, although I can't see his face clearly. . . . He is having lunch with me, spreading out a blanket with a picnic basket . . . and he eats a leisurely lunch with me, giving me his full and loving attention . . . and he speaks to me and tells me that I am his beloved child and very precious to him (with some tears) . . . I feel really close to him, and my heart is experiencing some warmth and joy and . . . deep peace. . . . I feel that I can experience God more now as a loving and present heavenly Father or Parent . . .

Therapist: Good . . . just continue to let the Lord minister . . . to you . . . continue to receive from him . . .

Client: OK . . .

Therapist: (after some more moments have passed) Can you tell me now what's happening, what you're feeling or experiencing now?

Client: Yes . . . I continue to experience the presence of Jesus. . . . I also sense that he is gently telling me to let go of any resentment I may have toward my father, and to forgive him . . . at least he works hard to provide for my material needs. . . . I can also see more clearly now with God's help that this is the way my father expresses his love for me . . . and I actually feel more gratitude and some warmth toward him now, as I let go of any resentment toward him and forgive him. . . . I also ask God to forgive me of any resentment or wrong attitudes I may have had toward my father all these years. . . . I feel more released and at peace.

Therapist: That's beautiful, Jane . . . anything else before we close in prayer?

Client: No . . . I'm ready to pray.

Therapist: OK, let's close in prayer. Would you like to start?

Client: OK . . . "Dear Lord, thank you so much for this deeply touching and healing time with you . . . for giving me such a healing image of you having lunch just with me. . . . Please continue to heal me and make me more whole so that I can know you more deeply and serve you better. Thank you in Jesus's name. Amen."

Therapist: "Dear Lord, we thank you for your healing grace and loving truth that you allowed Jane to experience today. . . . Continue your healing work in her life, and be with us and lead us as we go on with the therapy sessions here. In Jesus's name. Amen." Jane, just before you go, do you have any comments or questions about this experience in inner-healing prayer that you've just had? Let's debrief and discuss it now.

Client: It was a deeply touching and healing experience for me, thank you. Could I use these steps of inner-healing prayer on my own, in my daily quiet time with the Lord?

Therapist: Yes, that's a good idea. I was about to ask you to do exactly this as a "homework assignment." Are you OK with doing this?

Client: Yes, and thank you again!

Therapist: You're welcome, Jane. Take care and God bless! See you again next week. (adapted from Tan 2007b, 105–7)

It is important to note that inner-healing prayer does not always go so well. Some clients may have difficulty recalling their painful memories in a vivid way in imagery and may need a more narrative approach in which they simply tell their painful stories verbally and pray over them. Another option is to role-play the painful situation with such clients, ending with prayer. Clients should not be forced to keep trying to recall or relive their painful memories when they are having trouble doing so. Clients who do not experience any significant healing after an inner-healing prayer time need to be reassured that the Lord has promised grace sufficient for their need, even if they do not experience significant healing (cf. 2 Cor. 12:9–10). The importance of forgiveness also needs to be addressed. Inner-healing prayer is therefore not a panacea for all painful memories and their associated problems, but it can be a potentially helpful spiritual intervention in Christian therapy, including Christian cognitive behavior therapy (CBT). It can help facilitate deeper levels of emotional processing and cognitive restructuring and change. It emphasizes a more receptive and contemplative prayerful mode on the part of both the client and the therapist, consistent with more recent versions of CBT, which are based on mindfulness and acceptance (Tan 2007b).

Although there is some research support for the effectiveness of Christian CBT that includes the use of religious or Jesus imagery with Christian clients suffering from depression (e.g., Propst 1980; Propst et al. 1992), controlled outcome studies that specifically evaluate the effectiveness of inner-healing prayer are still lacking. Furthermore, the religious or Jesus imagery used in the Propst studies involved dealing with present and future-oriented situations, and not with painful memories from the past (Garzon and Burkett 2002). Inner-healing prayer also does not necessarily include Jesus imagery (Tan 2007b). Further research is needed to better evaluate the effectiveness specifically of inner-healing prayer.

A recent development that combines inner-healing prayer with the repeated use of a timeline of a client's life consisting of actual memories has been described as "the healing timeline" by Catherine Thorpe in her so-titled book (2008). The three basic steps of this new approach are:

1. Clients present a current problem or situation to a counselor. The client and counselor ask God through prayer to lead them to a former memory which needs healing in order to bring relief to the current problem.
2. The client invites Jesus *into* the memory scene. The client listens and watches as Jesus intervenes and speaks into the situation.
3. After the internal interaction with Jesus, the counselor leads the client through a timeline of his or her life consisting of real memories. The client nods when these memories are recalled and the timeline continues without discussion until the client's current age. Seeing Jesus in the memory scene and repetitions of the timeline are alternated until no distress remains in the memory scene. (Thorpe 2008, 8–9)

This new approach of the healing timeline also needs further research.

Prayer for deliverance is another form of prayer that needs to be briefly mentioned (Tan 1996c). Sometimes also called exorcism, prayer for deliverance may be necessary if a client seen in Christian therapy shows signs of being demonized or oppressed by demons or evil spirits (see Bufford 1988; MacNutt 1995; see also Appleby 2006). This is a controversial area, and many Christian therapists may prefer to refer such clients to pastors, pastoral counselors, or prayer ministry teams, who may have more training in dealing with such cases. Nevertheless, a Christian therapist may at times have to deal with an obviously demonized client by praying a prayer of deliverance such as: "In the name of Jesus, I command you to leave this person now, and go where Jesus sends you, never to return again to afflict or oppress this person." Informed consent from such a client should of course first be obtained, if possible, before prayer for deliverance or any other form of prayer is used as a spiritual intervention in explicit integration in Christian therapy.

Prayer can be potentially misused or abused in therapy, and there are dangers inherent in superficial inner-healing prayer approaches (see Alsdurf and Malony 1980; Malony 1987), including using prayer as an escape from dealing more deeply with painful issues in therapy. Christian therapists therefore differ in how explicitly they integrate spiritual interventions, such as prayer and the use of Scripture and other spiritual disciplines, into therapy sessions with clients, with some advocating caution but not censure (e.g., McMinn 1996; McMinn and McRay 1997). However, prayer, including inner-healing prayer, can be used in a spiritually meaningful and therapeutically helpful way in therapy, especially with highly spiritual or religious clients such as orthodox Christians, who may prefer the explicit use of prayer and Scripture (Gass 1984) and open discussion of religious and spiritual issues (Rose, Westefeld, and Ansley 2001). When appropriate, explicit integration in Christian therapy should be conducted in a clinically sensitive, ethically responsible, and professionally competent way, with full informed consent from the client and appropriate caution and careful timing following the client's lead and preferences (see Tan 1996b, 1996c). This is important because some highly religious clients may not find in-session prayer helpful (see, e.g., Martinez, Smith, and Barlow 2007 regarding a study of 152 Church of Jesus Christ of Latter-Day Saints [LDS] clients seen at a university counseling center); therefore, such prayer should not be imposed on them (see also Magaletta and Brawer 1998). However, a recent survey specifically of first-visit Christian clients and their therapists found that 82 percent of such clients wanted audible prayer in counseling, but more-liberal, Catholic, and younger clients may be less interested in having prayer included in counseling sessions (Weld and Erikson 2007). Christian therapists therefore must be cautious in how they use prayer in therapy sessions.

More broadly, Nathaniel Wade, Everett Worthington, and David Vogel (2007) found that clients with high religious commitment had greater improvement in their presenting problem after receiving religiously tailored interventions in Christian therapy compared to clients with low religious commitment. A client's level of religious commitment is therefore important to assess before using religious interventions, such as prayer, in Christian therapy.

It should also be noted that a recent study on prayer and subjective well-being found that of six prayer types (adoration, confession, thanksgiving, supplication, reception, and obligatory prayer), three forms of prayer (adoration, thanksgiving, and reception involving a contemplative attitude of openness, receptivity, and surrender) were positively related to measures of well-being (Whittington and Scher 2010). These three forms of prayer seem to be more God-focused and less ego-focused. In another study on the functions of prayer in the coping process, the prayer functions of seeking guidance and expressing gratitude were reported by participants to be the most effective (Bade and Cook 2008).

Scripture

A second major example of the use of religious and spiritual resources in explicit integration in Christian therapy is the use of Scripture or the Bible (and other sacred texts in other religious approaches to therapy), especially in Christian CBT (Tan 2007b; Tan and Johnson 2005; see also Garzon 2005). The Bible is God's inspired Word (2 Tim. 3:16) and can be used in therapy with Christian clients who want to discuss biblical truths relevant to their struggles in life, for various purposes, such as: "to comfort, clarify (guide), correct (cognitively restructure), change character, cleanse, convict (convert), and cure (or heal) (e.g., see 2 Tim. 3:16; John 15:3; Ps. 119:9, 11; Heb. 4:12; 1 Pet. 2:2; Ps. 119:105; Ps. 119:97–100; 1 Pet. 1:2, 3; Rom. 10:17; John 8:32)" (Tan 2007b, 108).

Scripture can be used in different ways in Christian therapy, including the following: indirectly by alluding to biblical truth; directly but generally by referring to examples or teachings in the Bible without citing chapter and verse; directly but specifically by referring to particular texts of Scripture, citing chapter and verse; by reading, meditating, memorizing, hearing, or studying Scripture (see Tan and Gregg 1997, 79–91); or by assigning Scripture for homework reading, study, meditation, or memorization (see Tan 2007b, 108).

The use of Scripture in Christian therapy is especially relevant in Christian CBT, which focuses on cognitive restructuring of dysfunctional thinking that often includes unbiblical or sinful assumptions. In addition to standard CBT questions used in cognitive restructuring (e.g., "On what basis do you say this? Where is the evidence for your conclusion?" "Is there another way of looking at this?" and "If your conclusion is true, what does it mean to you?"), Christian CBT that uses Scripture to challenge unbiblical thinking will include other questions such as: "What do you think the Bible has to say about this?" or "What do you think God has to say about this?" (see Tan 2007b, 108). There are several helpful resources that a Christian therapist can consult about using Scripture with clients in therapy, with careful biblical interpretation (see, e.g., Kruis 2000; P. A. Miller 2002; P. A. Miller and Miller 2006; see also Clinton and Hawkins 2007; Hurding 1992; Hutchison 2005; McKnight 2008; Osborne 2006; Monroe 2008; Takle 2008).

Scripture can also potentially be abused or misused in Christian therapy (C. B. Johnson 1987). The thoughtless and superficial use of Scripture in therapy can lead to harmful consequences. P. G. Monroe (2008) has emphasized the need to pay careful attention to issues relating to contextualization in the use of the Bible in therapy. He suggests several key questions that Christian therapists need to ask themselves in order to clarify why they may want to use Scripture in therapy with clients, such as: "Why do I want to have them read this text? What do I hope to accomplish through it (e.g., to be provoked, taught, comforted, connected to something greater than self, to change one's focal point, etc.)? What barriers might hinder this goal? How might they misinterpret my intervention?" (2008, 56).

Use of Scripture in Therapy

A Hypothetical Transcript

The following is another hypothetical transcript showing how Scripture was used to help Jane challenge and change her distorted and unbiblical way of thinking about anger.

Client: I feel badly whenever I experience even mild anger at my father for not being more expressive of affection toward me when I was a child growing up. I tend to block the anger out or deny it because I believe that it's wrong or sinful for me as a Christian to get angry at all. . . . But the anger doesn't really go away and I feel more fatigued and depressed eventually.

Therapist: Let's take a closer look at your specific thought or belief that anger is always wrong or sinful. . . . On what basis do you believe it is true? What do you think the Bible has to say about this?

Client: I remember there are verses in different parts of the Bible commanding us to put away anger and wrath and malice, but I can't recall the specific references now. I feel guilty whenever I feel anger . . .

Therapist: OK, would you like to look at the Bible more closely and see what it actually says or teaches about anger?

Client: Oh yes! I've been struggling with this issue for quite a while . . .

Therapist: Can you think of any other Bible verses or passages that are relevant to our discussion?

Client: Not really . . . hmmm . . . wait a minute. I do recall Jesus throwing out the money changers in the temple . . . so maybe there is a type of anger like when God gets angry . . . or Jesus gets angry, and it's not sinful, it's OK . . . but I still feel that when I get angry, it's not OK, because I'm not God.

Therapist: So, you already see that at the very least, when Jesus or God gets angry, it is not sinful or wrong, so there is a type of anger that may not be sinful. Some call this righteous indignation. Can you think of other Bible verses or passages that may teach this more directly?

Client: Come to think of it, didn't Paul say something in the Bible like, "Be angry but do not sin"?

Therapist: That's a good text you recalled. It's actually found in Ephesians 4:26. . . . Would you like to read this passage?

Client: Sure. (reads from the Bible the therapist hands over to her)

Therapist: What do you think Ephesians 4:26 means?

Client: Well, at least it says we can be angry but must not sin in our anger.

Therapist: It sounds like you are seeing now that anger is not always wrong or sinful . . . (adapted from Tan 2007b, 108–9)

This conversation demonstrates how a Christian therapist can use the Bible in a therapy session with a Christian client who wants to openly and directly discuss scriptural teaching (see also Tan and Johnson 2005). Scripture can be used in a sensitive and effective way to help in the cognitive restructuring of clients' unbiblical or dysfunctional thinking. It is interesting to note that the late Albert Ellis, founder of rational emotive behavior therapy (REBT), actually acknowledged that the Bible as a self-help book has probably helped more people than all therapists combined, in terms of facilitating significant changes in personal functioning (Ellis 1993b).

Referral to Religious Groups

A third major example of the use of religious and spiritual resources in explicit integration in Christian therapy is referral of the client to religious groups such as churches or parachurch groups within the client's religious belief system. These religious groups often provide fellowship, support, and prayer that can facilitate deeper healing and growth for clients. They can also help clients to make a more effective transition through the termination phase of therapy. Examples of such groups include "small groups, Bible study groups, recovery groups, prayer groups, fellowship groups, religiously oriented or Christ-centered 12-step programs, youth groups, and so forth" (Tan 1996c, 376).

Many churches and parachurch organizations also provide lay counseling services without charge, to which clients can be referred for further help and support. The lay or paraprofessional counselors are usually selected, trained, and supervised in a systematic and careful way (see Tan 1991, 2002b). Referral to lay counselors in churches and parachurch groups can be particularly helpful to clients who may not be able to afford to continue professional therapy because of financial difficulties.

Referral to religious groups should be done in a sensitive and supportive way, in full collaboration with the client, and for the benefit and welfare of the client.

Explicit Integration: Dealing with Spiritual Issues in Therapy

A second major component of explicit integration is dealing with spiritual issues in therapy. Clients often see counselors and psychotherapists for help with problems that have spiritual or moral aspects and even causes (see, e.g., Crabb 1987; F. J. White 1987). Explicit integration in psychotherapy will involve dealing with such spiritual and religious issues presented by the client in an open and direct way, with the client's full informed consent. This will first require an initial and adequate spiritual assessment of the client and his or her problems. Kenneth Pargament has suggested the following key questions for use in an initial spiritual assessment of the client in an intake session:

"Do you see yourself as a religious or spiritual person? If so, in what way?" (assessing the salience of spirituality to the client); "Are you affiliated with a religious or spiritual denomination or community? If so, which one?" (assessing the salience of a religious affiliation to the client); "Has your problem affected you religiously or spiritually? If so, in what way?" (assessing the salience of spirituality to the problem); and "Has your religion or spirituality been involved in the way you have coped with your problem? If so, in what way?" (assessing the salience of spirituality to the solution). (2007, 211)

Other suggestions for conducting an initial spiritual or religious assessment of the client can be found in H. N. Malony's (1988) religious status interview approach and M. Scott Peck's (1993) questions for taking a spiritual history. Peck actually advocated that all psychiatry residents should be taught how to obtain a spiritual history of their clients in their first month of training, alongside learning how to take a more general history and conducting a mental status exam.

Spiritual and religious issues can also emerge during the course of therapy with clients. They include broad existential struggles such as searching for meaning in life, dealing with the fear of death and mortality, and choosing authentic values in life (see, e.g., Wong, Wong, McDonald, and Klaassen 2007). They can also be more specific spiritual and religious issues such as doubts, sins, struggles with guilt, bitterness, and unforgiveness, "dark nights of the soul" and other spiritual struggles (see, e.g., Pargament 2007), and even possible demonization. Negative aspects of spiritual and religious experiences such as so-called toxic faith (Arterburn and Felton 1991) or religious addiction (Booth 1991) are other spiritual issues that may need to be explicitly explored and dealt with in therapy.

Neil Anderson has emphasized the essential need for Christian clients to understand and appropriate their *identity in Christ* from a biblical perspective in order to live a victorious Christian life, in the following three main areas: *"I am accepted in Christ"* (John 1:12; 15:15; Rom. 5:1; 1 Cor. 6:17, 19–20; 12:27; Eph. 1:1, 5; 2:18; Col. 1:14; 2:10); *"I am secure in Christ"* (Rom. 8:1–2, 28, 33–34, 35; 2 Cor. 1:21; Phil. 1:6; 3:20; Col. 3:3; 2 Tim. 1:7; Heb. 4:16; 1 John 5:18); *"I am significant in Christ"* (Matt. 5:13–14; John 15:16; Acts 1:8; 1 Cor. 3:16; 2 Cor. 5:17–20; 6:1; Eph. 2:6, 10; 3:12; Phil. 4:13) (2003, 75–76). He has also described seven steps to freedom in Christ in which a negative element in the fallen world is replaced with a biblical answer:

1. counterfeit versus real
2. deception versus truth
3. bitterness versus forgiveness
4. rebellion versus submission
5. pride versus humility
6. bondage versus freedom
7. acquiescence versus renunciation (see N. T. Anderson, Zuehlke, and Zuehlke 2000, 152–63, 384–411)

Collins has listed and described several important spiritual issues often encountered in Christian therapy, including "sinful thoughts and actions; legalism; self-sufficiency; pride; bitterness; non-Christian values; lack of: understanding of spiritual issues, spiritual nourishment, giving, balance, commitment, simplicity, Holy Spirit power, spiritual disciplines, and involvement with the church; suffering; and spiritual warfare" (2007, 825).

It is crucial for the Christian therapist to handle spiritual and religious issues in an empathic way, with gentleness and respect for the client. The therapist should not impose his or her own religious convictions on the client.

Timing is also important in helping clients deal with their spiritual and religious issues, especially if they involve conflict and spiritual struggles. If such issues are confronted too soon or insensitively, the client's faith may be impacted in a negative way (F. J. White 1987). The Christian therapist will therefore be sensitive to the client's readiness for discussing these issues in an open and direct way and follow the client's pace. The client's freedom to choose and ultimate responsibility in making decisions must always be respected. For more-severely disturbed clients, the therapist will wisely refrain from confronting and challenging their religious convictions, even if they are clearly dysfunctional, until such clients have emotionally stabilized and are better able and ready to deal with their dysfunctional religious beliefs (see Tan 1996c).

Christian therapists also must learn how to help clients from diverse religious and cultural backgrounds deal with more general religious and spiritual issues by having some understanding of other religions (see, e.g., Richards and Bergin 2000; see also Dowd and Nielsen 2006; Lovinger 1984, 1990). Robert Lovinger (1984) has provided some helpful examples of countertransference on the part of the therapist when dealing with religious issues in therapy with clients who are religiously committed. Therapists must be careful not to fall into these therapeutic mistakes that come from their own countertransference or unconscious negative reactions toward clients; examples of such mistakes include arguing with clients about doctrinal issues; having long discussions about philosophical and theological topics with no therapeutic purpose; and not adequately exploring the reasons for a client having made a significant change in religious orientation, especially in the direction of the therapist's own religion or denomination (Lovinger 1984).

Explicit Integration: Fostering Intrapersonal Integration and the Development of Spirituality in the Therapist and the Client

Intrapersonal integration or personal integration (i.e., one's own appropriation of faith and integration of psychological and spiritual experience) and the spiritual development of the therapist and the client are also crucial aspects of explicit integration in Christian therapy (Tan 1996c). Explicit integration will often include discussion and application of spiritual disciplines as a means of God's grace for helping both the therapist and the client to grow in deeper Christlikeness (Rom. 8:29) and spiritual maturity (see Tan 1996b, 1998). Several helpful books are available that clearly describe spiritual disciplines for spiritual growth and transformation (see, e.g., Foster 1988; Ortberg 2002; Tan and Gregg 1997; Whitney 1991; Willard 1988; see also A. A. Calhoun 2005). *Disciplines of the Holy Spirit* (Tan and Gregg 1997) identifies the following spiritual disciplines as disciplines of the Holy Spirit: disciplines of solitude in drawing near to God (e.g., solitude and silence, listening and guidance, prayer and intercession, study and meditation); disciplines of surrender in yielding to God (e.g., repentance and confession, yielding and submission, fasting, and worship); and disciplines of service in reaching out to others (e.g., fellowship, simplicity, service, and witness).

Spiritual disciplines can, however, be potentially dangerous (cf. Plummer 2009). If they are practiced in a way that is legalistic, dogmatic, and self-absorbed, they can lead to pride, self-sufficiency, and self-righteousness, and thus ultimately harm one's spiritual life and development. A Christian therapist will therefore also emphasize what Gary Thomas (2002) has called the *authentic disciplines* or *circumstantial spiritual disciplines* (Tang 2008) that are not within our voluntary control, as vital additions to the traditional spiritual disciplines. These so-called authentic disciplines include selflessness, waiting, suffering, persecution, social mercy, forgiveness, mourning, contentment, sacrifice, and hope and fear (Thomas 2002). They focus more on God seeking the face of men and women and emphasize a God-ordained spirituality, under his sovereignty and not our own control. Their ultimate goal is to learn "to love with God's love and . . . serve with God's power" (Thomas 2002, 12). Such authentic disciplines, including suffering and painful experiences that lead to ultimate spiritual formation and growth into deeper Christlikeness, have recently been cited in the more general psychological literature as highly stressful life events and trauma that lead to perceived growth, labeled "post-traumatic growth," "stress-related growth," and "benefit-finding" (see, e.g., see Helgeson, Reynolds, and Tomich 2006; Park and Helgeson 2006; see also L. G. Calhoun and Tedeschi 2006; Park 2010). Biblical meaning making and benefit finding can be part of dealing with experiences of authentic disciplines that clients may have in their lives.

The traditional spiritual disciplines should be used in a grace-filled, non-legalistic way in the Christian therapist's life to facilitate the therapist's own spiritual growth so that he or she can more effectively help the client to also grow spiritually. The ultimate goal of Christian therapy is not only to alleviate symptoms but also to deepen spiritual maturity in the client. Appropriate spiritual self-disclosure by the Christian therapist (see Denney, Aten, and Gingrich 2008) is an important part of sharing traditional spiritual disciplines and how they can be used in sessions as well as in between sessions as home-

---

Sidebar 15.2

Spiritual Disciplines and Practices
(see Eck 2002, 273)

Eck has comprehensively listed thirty-nine spiritual disciplines and practices that include both traditional spiritual disciplines and authentic disciplines and has explored their therapeutic use in clinical practice. He divides them into three major categories:

Cognitive: meditation, listening, Scripture, study, prayer, discernment
Behavioral: simplicity, frugality, fasting, chastity, body care, saying no/yes, slowing, Sabbath, solitude, silence, secrecy, service, servanthood, sacrifice, suffering, dying well
Interpersonal: confession, repentance, forgiveness, submission, humility, worship, Eucharist, singing, celebration, fellowship, community, hospitality, healing, witnessing, testimony, intercession, guidance.

He emphasizes that the use of spiritual disciplines and practices in therapy should be done with "a grace filled, God empowered focus as a means of grace and mercy, and not as a legalistic or coercive process" (Eck 2002, 272). They should therefore be used in ethical and appropriate ways for the spiritual formation and therapeutic benefit of the client and with his or her full informed consent (see Chapelle 2000; Tan 2003c).

---

work assignments. It is also a significant part of engaging in biblical meaning making and benefit finding as the therapist and the client explore and discuss experiences of authentic disciplines, including suffering and painful events in their lives that can lead to deeper spiritual formation and growth in Christ. Some degree of spiritual direction, or the process of discerning and surrendering to God's will and deepening one's personal relationship with God in the context of one's life experiences by meeting with someone for prayer and spiritual conversation (see Benner 2002, 94), is therefore an appropriate part of explicit integration in Christian therapy (see Tan 2003c; see also Kellemen 2005a, 2005b).

Some leaders in the Christian therapy field do not advocate integrating spiritual direction into Christian therapy (e.g., McMinn and Campbell 2007). However, many others support integrating spiritual direction, including the use of spiritual disciplines, into Christian therapy (see Tan 2003c; see also Benner 2005b; Crabb 2003; G. W. Moon and Benner 2004). Although Benner (1988) earlier felt that Christian therapy and spiritual direction cannot be integrated because they are so different in their focus and role demands, he has subsequently changed his view and is supportive of a Christian psychospiritual therapy that includes spiritual direction (Benner 1998). In fact, he has developed an approach called the *intensive soul care retreat* (see Benner 2005b). He also cites Bernard Tyrell's *Christotherapy* as another example of combining spiritual direction and psychotherapy (see Tyrell 1982).

Gary Moon and his colleagues (G. W. Moon, Willis, Bailey, and Kwasny 1993) found that out of a list of twenty spiritual guidance techniques, those most frequently used by Christian psychotherapists, pastoral counselors, and spiritual directors were spiritual history, discernment, forgiveness, solitude or silence, intercessory prayer, and teaching from Scripture. These findings are consistent with previous research conducted in this area. Moon and his colleagues also reported that doctoral-level religious mental health clinicians were less likely than master's-level practitioners to use such explicit spiritual guidance techniques. In a more recent general study of ninety-six psychologists and their reported use of twenty-nine recommended religious/spiritual psychotherapy behaviors, Royce Frazier and Nancy Hansen (2009) found that in general, and for 90 percent of the twenty-nine behaviors, the psychologists practiced them less frequently than their importance ratings indicated they should. Also, the greater the psychologists' religious/spiritual self-identification, the higher the likelihood of them reporting engaging in these behaviors in psychotherapy.

A study with 100 therapists sampled mainly from alumni of an APA-accredited Christian doctoral program in clinical psychology (Walker, Gorsuch, and Tan 2005) found that course work in integration and theology was not significantly related to the explicit use of religious and spiritual interventions in therapy. Instead, it reported that clinical training with religious clients (i.e., number of contact hours with religious clients) and intervention-specific training with religious and spiritual interventions (i.e., number of clinical supervision hours devoted to religious and spiritual interventions in therapy) were significantly correlated with more-frequent use of religious and spiritual interventions in therapy and also self-reported competency. A later study of 162 student therapists from three APA-accredited Christian doctoral programs in clinical psychology (Walker, Gorsuch, Tan, and Otis 2008) similarly found intervention-specific training to be potentially the most efficient way for training therapists to explicitly use religious and spiritual interventions in clinical practice. The role of Christian clinical supervision is therefore crucial in developing therapist integration skills, including the explicit use of Christian spiritual interventions and spiritual disciplines in therapy (Tan 2009a; see also Tan 2007c).

Some cautions, mentioned earlier in this chapter, are needed in the practice of explicit integration in Christian therapy, which includes the use of spiritual interventions such as prayer, Scripture, and the spiritual disciplines (see, e.g., Martinez, Smith, and Barlow 2007; Magaletta and Brawer 1998; Weld and Eriksen 2007). Further research on the effectiveness of such explicitly Christian spiritual interventions in therapy is also needed, although outcome research to date has yielded empirical support for both the efficacy (Worthington and Sandage 2001) and the effectiveness in actual clinical settings (Wade, Worthington, and Vogel 2007) of Christian therapy (see also Pargament 2007; T. B. Smith, Bartz, and Richards 2007). A recent meta-analytic review of thirty-one outcome studies (eighteen with true experimental designs and six with quasi-experimental designs) of religiously or spiritually oriented therapies with a total of 1,845 clients yielded an average effect size of 0.56 (T. B. Smith, Bartz, and Richards 2007). Some empirical support was therefore found for the effectiveness of such therapies, especially in treating clients suffering from depression, anxiety, stress, and eating disorders. The majority of the clients were Christian (73 percent) and Muslim (24 percent) in their religious affiliation, with most of the outcome studies involving Christian or Muslim therapy (see Abu Raiya and Pargament 2010; Tan and Johnson 2005). A more recent and larger meta-analytic review of fifty-one samples (including twenty-four CBT samples) from forty-six separate outcome studies of religious and spiritual therapies with a total of 3,290 clients came to similar conclusions, further supporting the efficacy or effectiveness of such therapies (Worthington, Hook, Davis, and McDaniel in press).

A recent review of empirically-supported treatments (ESTs) for Christian counseling concluded that Christian ESTs include Christian cognitive therapy for depression and three marriage enrichment interventions (PREP, Interpersonal Communication Program, and Hope-Focused Couple Approach). A few other Christian therapies have received some support for their efficacy but are not ESTs yet, including Christian CBT for eating disorders, Christian lay counseling in general, Christian group treatment for unforgiveness, and Christian devotional meditation for anxiety (Worthington, Hook, Davis, and Ripley 2008). A more recent review of empirically supported religious and spiritual therapies in general concluded that Christian accommodative cognitive therapy for depression and twelve-step facilitation for alcoholism were efficacious and Muslim psychotherapy for depression as well as for anxiety was efficacious when used with medication. The following were deemed possibly efficacious treatments: Christian devotional meditation for anxiety, Taoist cognitive therapy for anxiety, Christian accommodative group treatment for unforgiveness, spiritual group treatment for unforgiveness, Christian accommodative group cognitive-behavioral therapy for marital discord, and Christian lay counseling for general psychological problems. Spiritual group therapy for eating disorders when combined with existing inpatient treatment and Buddhist accommodative cognitive therapy for anger in a prison setting were also deemed possibly efficacious (Hook et al. 2010).

Explicit integration in Christian therapy that includes the appropriate and ethical use of spiritual interventions and resources in therapy and incorporates the process of spiritual direction to a certain degree can have great potential "for deep blessing and greater wholeness and shalom for the client who freely chooses such a psychospiritual therapy that aims toward both psychological and spiritual growth as well as the reduction of psychological distress" (Tan 2003c, 20). It should be conducted in an ethically responsible, clinically sensitive, and professionally competent way, for the benefit and well-being of the client (Tan 1996c).

This chapter on Christian faith in clinical practice has focused mainly on individual therapy, but it can also be applied to couple and family therapy (see, e.g., Worthington 2005b; Yarhouse and Sells 2008), and group therapy and care groups (see, e.g., Greggo 2008).

Recommended Readings

Anderson, N. T., Zuehlke, T. E., and Zuehlke, J. S. (2000). *Christ-centered therapy: The practical integration of theology and psychology*. Grand Rapids: Zondervan.

Benner, D. G. (1998). *Care of souls: Revisioning Christian nurture and counsel*. Grand Rapids: Baker.

Bufford, R. K. (1988). *Counseling and the demonic*. Dallas: Word.

Collins, G. R. (2007). *Christian counseling: A comprehensive guide* (3rd ed.). Nashville: Thomas Nelson.

Crabb, L. J. (1977). *Effective biblical counseling*. Grand Rapids: Zondervan.

McMinn, M. R., & Campbell, C. D. (2007). *Integrative psychotherapy: Toward a comprehensive Christian approach*. Downers Grove, IL: IVP Academic.

Moon, G. W., & Benner, D. G. (Eds.). (2004). *Spiritual direction and the care of souls*. Downers Grove, IL: InterVarsity.

Pargament, K. I. (2007). *Spiritually integrated psychotherapy: Understanding and addressing the sacred*. New York: Guilford Press.

16

The Holy Spirit and Christian Spirituality
in Counseling and Psychotherapy

Christian counseling or psychotherapy can be simply described as counseling conducted by a Christian who is Christ centered, biblically based, and Spirit filled (see Tan 1999b). The role of the Holy Spirit, the third person of the Triune God (Father, Son, and Holy Spirit), is crucial and central in Christian counseling. Numerous works are available on the Holy Spirit from a theological perspective (see Fee 1994; Karkkainen 2002; Moltmann 1997; Pinnock 1996). There is also a small but growing literature on the ministry of the Holy Spirit in the context of Christian therapy and personality functioning, both articles in journals (see Coe 1999; Dodds 1999; Ingram 1996; Parker 2008; see also Decker 2002) and books (see Coe and Hall 2010; M. G. Gilbert and Brock 1985, 1988; Pugh 2008; Vining 1995a, 1995b; Vining and Decker 1996).

The crucial role of the Holy Spirit in Christian therapy is supported by Scripture that describes the Holy Spirit as the Counselor, Comforter, Helper, or Advocate (John 14:16–17). In every counseling or therapy situation, at least three persons are involved: the counselor, the client or counselee, and the Holy Spirit, who is the Counselor par excellence (see Adams 1973). The Holy Spirit is also described as the giver of life by the Nicene Creed, supported by Scriptures in both the Old Testament and the New Testament (see Parker 2008, 286). His key role in Christian therapy as the Counselor, as well as the giver of life, means that Christian therapists must acknowledge and depend on the Spirit's presence and healing power in every counseling situation, with a basic biblical understanding of the work and ministry of the Holy Spirit (Tan 1999b).

The Work and Ministry of the Holy Spirit

The work and ministry of the Holy Spirit can be described and biblically understood in at least three major ways: the Spirit's power (and gifts), the Spirit's truth, and the Spirit's fruit (see Tan 1999b, 568).

The Spirit's Power and Gifts

The power of the Holy Spirit is essential in Christian life and ministry, including witnessing and evangelism (Acts 1:8). Christians are commanded in Scripture to be continually filled with the Holy Spirit (Eph. 5:18), moment by moment on a daily basis. This means that we confess our sins and yield to Jesus Christ as Lord of our lives and ask for the Holy Spirit to fill us and take control of us, so that we can be empowered by him to become more like Jesus and to do the works of Jesus (see Hayford 2005), including counseling and helping others.

As we prayerfully yield to the Spirit's control, he empowers us and guides us in our Christian lives and ministries. He also sovereignly and supernaturally gives us spiritual gifts according to God's will, to enable us to be fruitful and faithful in the areas of ministry to which he has called us, including counseling (see Rom. 12; 1 Cor. 12; Eph. 4; 1 Pet. 4). These spiritual gifts are God's droplets of grace, which he freely gives us to empower us to have an effective ministry with love, gratitude, and humility, that glorifies him and blesses others for eternity. They include the following spiritual gifts that are especially relevant for an effective counseling ministry led by the Holy Spirit: exhortation or encouragement (Rom. 12:8); healing (1 Cor. 12:9, 28); wisdom (1 Cor. 12:8); knowledge (1 Cor. 12:8); discerning of spirits (1 Cor. 12:10); and mercy (Rom. 12:8) (see Tan 1999b, 568). Other spiritual gifts that are often viewed as important for counseling ministries, especially from a more charismatic or Pentecostal perspective include prophecy, teaching, faith, miracles, tongues, and intercession. Helpful definitions of twenty-seven spiritual gifts and a spiritual gifts questionnaire to help Christians discern and discover their spiritual gifts can be found in *Your Spiritual Gifts Can Help Your Church Grow* (Wagner 1994).

The Spirit's Truth

The Holy Spirit is the Spirit of truth who will teach us and guide us into all truth (John 14:26; 16:13), including psychotheological truth. Ultimately, such eternal truth is what will set us free (John 8:32), centered in Jesus Christ, who is the Truth (John 14:6) as well as the Way and the Life. The Holy Spirit inspired the writing of Scripture as God's Word. His work and ministry, including in the counseling context, will never contradict the truth of Scripture when it is properly interpreted. The Holy Spirit will therefore always uphold the eternal validity of Scripture. His ministry in counseling will be consistent with the moral and ethical aspects of biblical teaching and truth.

The Spirit's Fruit

The Holy Spirit produces the fruit of the Spirit that is characteristic of mature Christlikeness (Rom. 8:29) and that is mentioned in Galatians 5:22–23: love, joy, peace, patience, kindness, goodness, faithfulness, gentleness, and self-control. This fruit refers basically to the fruit of *agape*, or Christlike love, produced by the Spirit in Christian lives that are yielded to his control and empowering. The Spirit's fruit of *agape* is powerfully therapeutic in counseling situations.

All three aspects of the Holy Spirit's ministry are essential and crucial in the Christian life as well as in Christian therapy. They need to be present in biblical balance. Power without love often results in abuse. Power without truth can become heresy. However, power based on biblical truth and used with Christlike love can produce renewal and revival as well as the deep and substantial healing of broken lives.

The Work of the Holy Spirit in Counseling

The Holy Spirit can work in many different ways during a counseling session itself. In more-implicit integration approaches to Christian therapy, such as in psychodynamic or psychoanalytic therapy, the Holy Spirit's work as giver of life may be more emphasized. Stephen Parker (2008), for example, has described the Holy Spirit's creative work in therapy using Winnicott's object relations theory and the concepts of transitional phenomena and object usage (see Winnicott 1966, 1971). Parker focuses especially on how the Spirit can help clients by "conferring a sense of identity and providing an environment for emergence of a strong spiritual self. The work of the Holy Spirit was also seen as tapping into the creative potential of what Winnicott (1971) calls 'transitional phenomena,' and in engendering new life by making God real in ways that transcend our imaginings" (Parker 2008, 292). Parker also emphasizes that the life-giving work of the Holy Spirit enables a client to still have a basic sense of hope even when all the client's "wishes, dreams, disappointments, fears, and frustrations have been spent" (Parker 2008, 292), making God real to the client despite his or her experiencing the absence of God.

Similarly, the Holy Spirit can work in implicit integration that is intentional and incarnational, such as in relational psychodynamic therapy. The Spirit's work is quietly but intentionally embraced and expressed by the Christian therapist in the avowal that the client is worthy of love and the acceptance of the client's worst experiences (see Terrell 2007, 162). Stephen Rogers (2007) has also described how a focus on the process and the here-and-now during a therapy session in object relations therapy can be understood as a powerful spiritual intervention, quietly guided and empowered by the Holy Spirit. Transcendent moments and creative experiences in Christian therapy may therefore reflect the deep but quiet work of the Holy Spirit in counseling. Psychotherapy itself can be theologically viewed as "work in the Spirit" (Kunst and Tan 1996) in bringing wholeness to broken lives. John Pugh has emphasized that the Holy Spirit works in and through the day-to-day "awful experiences of human existence" (2008, 280).

The Holy Spirit can also work in explicit integration in Christian therapy, which deals with religious and spiritual issues more directly and uses spiritual resources and religious interventions more overtly and systematically with clients. There are at least five ways that the Holy Spirit can work during a Christian therapy session in which the therapist uses a more explicit integration approach (Tan 1999b).

First, the Holy Spirit can directly help the Christian therapist quickly and accurately discern the root problems of the client by providing the Christian therapist with specific and relevant words of knowledge or wisdom (1 Cor. 12:8). From a more conservative evangelical perspective, Swindoll (1994) has referred to such experiences of receiving words of knowledge or wisdom from the Spirit (see Deere 1993, 1996) as "inner promptings" or nudges of the Spirit within the Christian counselor who is prayerfully attentive to the Spirit's leading. Such promptings can also help the Christian therapist to engage in deeper spiritual conversation with the client, or "soultalk" (Crabb 2003). The Christian therapist can be more mindfully and attentively dependent on the Holy Spirit during a counseling session by periodically praying "flash prayers" in his or her heart such as "Spirit of God, please guide me"; "Holy Spirit, touch the client with your healing grace"; "Holy Spirit, help us at this point of impasse"; "Spirit of God, protect us and empower us"; "Holy Spirit, please comfort and strengthen the client."

Second, the Holy Spirit can provide spiritual direction regarding God's will to both the Christian therapist and the client as they participate in more-explicit integration practices during a therapy session, such as praying together, discussing Scripture, and openly exploring spiritual issues. As noted earlier, the Holy Spirit can also guide in more-implicit integration approaches to Christian therapy during a therapy session.

Third, the Holy Spirit can directly touch a client in a powerful way with his healing grace and power. This experience can occur anytime spontaneously and supernaturally in God's sovereignty and by his grace and goodness, often leading to significant or "quantum change," as when sudden insights and epiphanies bring transformation of ordinary lives (see W. R. Miller and C'de Baca 2001). However, explicit use of prayer, and especially inner-healing prayer or healing of memories (see Tan 2003b; Tan and Ortberg 2004; see also Garzon and Burkett 2002), can be especially helpful in facilitating the occurrence of such transcendent moments.

Fourth, the Holy Spirit can enable the Christian therapist to discern the presence of the demonic if there is demonization or demonic oppression in the client's life. The spiritual gift of discerning of spirits or distinguishing between spirits (1 Cor. 12:10) can be particularly helpful to the Christian therapist, especially in making an accurate differential diagnosis between demonization and mental disorder. At times, both demonization and mental illness may afflict a particular client. The Holy Spirit can also empower the Christian therapist to engage in effective prayers for deliverance and protection from the demonic, if this is called for, with proper informed consent and full collaboration from the client. It may be more appropriate at times to refer the client with possible demonization to a pastor or prayer ministry team experienced in deliverance work preferably in the client's own church or denomination.

Fifth, and finally, the Holy Spirit can work deeply in spiritual transformation of both the client and the therapist into greater Christlikeness as they practice the spiritual disciplines (e.g., solitude and silence, listening and guidance, prayer and intercession, study and meditation, repentance and confession, yielding and submission, fasting, worship, fellowship, simplicity, service, and witness) in the power of the Spirit (Tan and Gregg 1997). Some of these spiritual disciplines can be practiced in the therapy session and others as homework assignments for the client between sessions. They can help both the therapist and the client to access more of the presence and power of the Spirit for the client's growth and healing. It is therefore not totally true that a therapist can lead a client only as far as the therapist has gone spiritually or psychologically. The Spirit can bring both of them beyond their present level. This is the sovereign work of God and his grace alone.

The work of the Holy Spirit in Christian therapy is therefore central and crucial. Although training and competence in therapy skills are needed, Christian therapists will use such skills in dependence on the Holy Spirit.

The Holy Spirit and Christian Spirituality in Counseling

A distinctive goal of Christian therapy is to help the client to grow spiritually into deeper Christlikeness (Rom. 8:29), that is, to develop the client's Christian spirituality (in addition to reducing his or her psychological distress). The Holy Spirit's work is also essential in developing Christian spirituality, which needs further definition and description.

Christian Spirituality: Definition and Description

In recent years, much has been written about spirituality in general, and Christian spirituality in particular (see Augsburger 2006; Benner 2002; Bloesch

2007; Boa 2001; Chan 1998, 2006; Foster 1998; Foster and Beebe 2009; Howard 2008; McKnight 2004; E. H. Peterson 2005, 2006, 2007, 2008, 2010; Webber 2006; Willard 1998, 2002). There are also two relatively new journals devoted to Christian spirituality: *Conversations: A Forum for Authentic Transformation* and *Journal of Spiritual Formation & Soul Care*.

Spirituality in a more generic and psychological sense has different meanings (Zinnbauer and Pargament 2005). However, it has been defined as a search for the sacred, that is, that which transcends the self (P. C. Hill et al. 2000). Steven Sandage and F. LeRon Shults (2007) have emphasized *relational spirituality* and defined it as "ways of relating to the sacred" (Shults and Sandage 2006, 161). Also, a recent movement in the mental health and general health-care arenas has focused on the significant relationship, often positive (but not always), between religion/spirituality and health or mental health (e.g., Koenig 1998; Koenig, McCullough, and Larson 2001; Plante and Sherman 2001; see also P. C. Hill and Pargament 2003; W. R. Miller and Thoresen 2003; Powell, Shahabi, and Thoresen 2003; Seeman, Dubin, and Seeman 2003), but there are critics of this movement (e.g., Sloan and Bagiella 2002).

Christian spirituality can also be defined and described in various ways. Alister McGrath has defined the essential meaning of Christian spirituality as consisting of "the shaping, empowering, and maturing of the 'spiritual person' (1 Cor. 2:14–15)—that is, the person who is alive to and responsive to God in the world, . . . and evangelical spirituality will thus be Bible-centered, and it will be concerned more with the facilitation and enhancement of the personal redemptive encounter of the believer with Christ" (1995, 125). He particularly emphasizes the lordship of the Holy Spirit and the importance of Christian community for the spiritual growth of Christians (see Tan 2008a, 28). He also suggests that evangelical Christian spirituality will have the following four major characteristics: "be Scripture-centered; place considerable emphasis on the transforming character of the knowledge of God; rest on a solid and reliable foundation in the self-revelation of God; and rediscover the importance of spiritual discipline" (McGrath 1995, 134–37).

Christian spirituality can also be defined as "the disposition or internal condition of people when in such a state as prepares them to recognize and fully appreciate spiritual realities, and such true spirituality is ultimately the result of the inworking of the Holy Spirit (1 Cor. 2:14, 15; 3:1, 16—see Unger 1981, p. 1043)" (Tan 1987b, 36).

E. B. Howard has recently provided a comprehensive description of Christian spirituality consisting of three levels: "the level of *practice*, which refers to our actual cultivation and experience of relationship with God; the level of *dynamics*, which refers to our formulation of the patterns of lived divine-human relationship; and the level of *academic discipline*, which refers to the formal field of study that explores the first two levels in a systematic manner" (2008, 24).

Christian spirituality, from a biblical, evangelical perspective, has many aspects and facets (see Tan 1987b, 36–38). First, it means having a *deep hunger or thirst for God* (Ps. 42:1–2; Matt. 5:6). The Holy Spirit inspires such a sincere longing to know God in a personal and intimate way (see Packer 1973). In every person, there is a God-shaped vacuum that only God can fill and fulfill.

Second, it means having a *love for God* based on personal knowledge of God, which eventually results in *worship* of God and *obedience* to his good and perfect will (Matt. 22:37, 38; John 14:21, 23; cf. Rev. 2:1–7).

Third, it means *being filled with the Holy Spirit and surrendering to God's deepening work of grace in our hearts and not yielding to the sinful nature* or *the flesh in us* (Eph. 5:18; Gal. 5:16; Rom. 6:12–13). The regular, grace-filled, nonlegalistic practice of the spiritual disciplines involving both individual and community life will help us connect more to the presence and power of the Holy Spirit (see Tan and Gregg 1997) and experience God's deepening work of grace in transforming us to become more like Jesus.

Fourth, it means *discovering and using the spiritual gifts given by the Holy Spirit for God's purposes and glory* (see Rom. 12; 1 Cor. 12; Eph. 4; 1 Pet. 4), *bearing forth the fruit of the Spirit that is ultimately agape or Christlike love* (Gal. 5:22–23), and *becoming more Christlike in every way in our lives and character* (Rom. 8:29).

Fifth, it means *developing biblical thinking and having a worldview that is consistent with God's eternal perspective as revealed in the Bible, his inspired Word* (cf. Rom. 12:2; Phil. 4:8; Col. 3:16a; 2 Tim. 3:16–17). Such biblical thinking will lead to a balanced ministry to the whole person, involving evangelism, missions, discipleship training including servanthood and leadership (see Tan 2006b, 2009), pastoral care and counseling, social action, and an eschatological hope and longing for the Lord's return and the final consummation of the kingdom of God.

Sixth, it means *being involved in spiritual warfare that requires the use of supernatural power and resources from God* (cf. 1 Cor. 4:20; Eph. 6:10–18), especially the use of prayer and Scripture in the power of the Holy Spirit to overcome the world, the flesh, and the devil (Eph. 2:2–3). This will include the crucifixion of our own ministry and the surrendering of our ambitions to the service of Christ (Purves 2007), actualizing the truth that we have been crucified with Christ and it is he who lives in us (Gal. 2:20).

Finally, it means that there are *mystical aspects and experiences* in the depths of Christian spirituality, which transform us to be more Christlike, including sharing in the fellowship of Christ's sufferings (Phil. 3:10). At times, it may include experiencing the "dark night of the soul" as described by St. John of the Cross (cf. Isa. 50:10) and discussed in chapter 15 of this book. It is important for Christian therapists, guided by the Holy Spirit through Scripture and writings on Christian spirituality, to understand such mystical and painful experiences of the spiritual life in Christ, so that clients can be better helped and empathically supported when they are going through dark nights. God uses these experiences to lovingly draw us away from the many distractions of our lives and closer to him so that he can work a deeper inner transformation of the soul (see Foster 1978, 89–91). When helping clients who are experiencing such spiritual struggles, the Christian therapist, guided by the Holy Spirit, will learn that the best therapy is to provide empathic understanding, caring support, and much prayer (see Tan 1987b, 37).

There are other aspects and dimensions of Christian spirituality that center on loving God and loving others (Mark 12:29–31; see McKnight 2004; see also Augsburger 2006), but the major ones just described can help Christian therapists provide Christian counseling that also aims at spiritual growth and Christlike maturity in the client.

In a similar vein, Parker has recently emphasized the crucial life-giving work of the Holy Spirit in the development of true Christian spirituality. He notes:

> In the Old Testament, the dominant metaphor for the Spirit is *ruach* (wind, breath) and hence an early connection to the idea of the Spirit's life-giving quality. . . . In the New Testament this metaphor of the Spirit (Greek: *pneuma*; cf. English "wind") creating new life is addressed in the context of the regeneration of the believer (Rom. 8:11; 1 Cor. 6:11; Titus 3:5). St. Paul further connects the life-giving work of the Spirit to the transformation of the believer into the very image or likeness of Christ (2 Cor. 3:17–18). Thus, for Paul, the new life of the Christian can be characterized as one in which the old life of the "flesh" is exchanged for a new life dominated by the Spirit (Rom. 8). (2008, 286)

Christian Spirituality: Types and Approaches

While Christian spirituality can be defined and described to some degree (see Howard 2008), there are different types of, and approaches to, Christian spirituality.

One way of further elaborating on the types of Christian spirituality available to us is to focus on the six major traditions of Christian faith as streams of living water, as Foster (1998) has done. He has described the following six traditions as essential to a balanced approach to Christian spirituality: *the contemplative tradition*, emphasizing *the prayer-filled life*; *the holiness tradition*, emphasizing *the virtuous life*; *the charismatic tradition*, emphasizing *the Spirit-empowered life*; *the social justice tradition*, emphasizing *the compassionate life*; *the evangelical tradition*, emphasizing *the Word-centered life*; and *the incarnational tradition*, emphasizing *the sacramental life* (see Foster 1998).

Similarly, Kenneth Boa (2001) has provided descriptions of twelve major biblical and practical approaches to spiritual formation, each focusing on a distinctive facet of Christian spirituality. They are (1) *relational spirituality*, focusing on loving God completely, ourselves correctly, and others compassionately; (2) *paradigm spirituality*, focusing on cultivating an eternal versus a temporal perspective; (3) *disciplined spirituality*, focusing on engaging in the historical disciplines; (4) *exchanged life spirituality*, focusing on grasping our true identity in Christ; (5) *motivated spirituality*, focusing on a set of biblical incentives; (6) *devotional spirituality*, focusing on falling in love with God; (7) *holistic spirituality*, focusing on every component of life under the lordship of Christ; (8) *process spirituality*, focusing on process versus product, being versus doing; (9) *Spirit-filled spirituality*, focusing on walking in the power of the Spirit; (10) *warfare spirituality*, focusing on overcoming the world, the flesh, and the devil; (11) *nurturing spirituality*, focusing on a lifestyle of evangelism and discipleship; (12) *corporate spirituality*, focusing on encouragement, accountability, and worship (see Boa 2001, 11–13).

> **Sidebar 16.1**
>
> **Twelve Major Approaches to Spiritual Formation**
> *(see Boa 2001, 11–13)*
>
> 1. Relational spirituality
> 2. Paradigm spirituality
> 3. Disciplined spirituality
> 4. Exchanged life spirituality
> 5. Motivated spirituality
> 6. Devotional spirituality
> 7. Holistic spirituality
> 8. Process spirituality
> 9. Spirit-filled spirituality
> 10. Warfare spirituality
> 11. Nurturing spirituality
> 12. Corporate spirituality

While certain varieties of Christian spirituality focus on becoming more mature in Christ, there are also personal preferences regarding how we approach God and develop our spiritual maturity. Spiritual temperaments also vary among us, with different preferences in spiritual pathways to God. Thomas (2000b) has therefore emphasized that Christian spirituality is not "one-size-fits-all." Instead, he describes nine sacred or spiritual pathways from which people may choose according to their preferences, in order to grow in Christ: tradition, vision, relationships, intellectual thought, service, contemplation, activism, nature, and worship. Acceptance of one another's approach to Christian spirituality and spiritual formation in Christ is crucial. In such spiritual formation into deeper Christlikeness, the work of the Holy Spirit is essential, including spiritual formation that occurs in the context of Christian therapy (see, e.g., Coe and Hall 2010).

Concluding Comments

In order for the Holy Spirit to do his crucial work in Christian therapy that also focuses on Christian spirituality and the spiritual formation of clients into deeper Christlikeness (Rom. 8:29), Christian therapists must have faith in Christ as Lord of all professional and academic disciplines, including psychology and counseling (E. L. Johnson 1997). As Spirit-filled servants of Jesus Christ, Christian therapists will exercise faith or trust and full confidence in Christ as the most brilliant person in the universe who is also both master and maestro of our field and profession of counseling and psychotherapy (Tan 2008b; see also Willard 2006).

Christian therapists who practice by faith a Christ-centered, biblically based, and Spirit-filled approach to counseling will experience and help their clients experience the eternal life that Jesus came to give us (John 3:16; 10:10). As Dallas Willard has written:

> Many counselors today are learning that for their own work, deep immersion in the disciplines is necessary, both for developing their own character, and beyond that, accessing special powers of grace for their work in counseling people. Many psychologists are learning how to use techniques of prayer and various kinds of ministry to have a much greater effect than they could have if all they had to go on were just the things they learned in their clinical training programs. . . . I think the most important and the most solid way is to begin to integrate prayer and spiritual teaching into the therapy process as it seems appropriate. . . . I think the issue here lies deeper than even matters of integration as we commonly discuss it. It is a matter of our understanding of the gospel of Jesus Christ as one which breaks through the natural world and brings it into the spiritual world and invites us as individuals to learn to live an eternal kind of life now. (Willard 1996, 19–20)

It is interesting to note that three decades ago, J. D. Frank (1982) and Isaac Marks (1978), two prominent leaders in the field of secular psychotherapy, had already challenged therapy researchers to pay more attention to the role of "healing power" or faith healing, involving faith and religious processes, in psychotherapy and its effects or outcomes. Further research is obviously needed, focusing more specifically on religious and spiritual healing interventions, including inner-healing prayer, and their effectiveness, especially in Christian therapy conducted by Christian therapists, who are empowered by the Holy Spirit. We need to prayerfully depend on the Holy Spirit and his power and gifts and truth and fruit in order to be Spirit-filled servants of Jesus Christ in counseling and psychotherapy. The Holy Spirit will enable us to continue to develop and practice a truly Christian psychology that is biblically based. This endeavor will require involvement with a community of Christian scholars and Christian counselors and psychologists. Only by the grace of God will we thus keep the faith or be kept in the faith in him in our work in counseling and psychotherapy (see Tan 2008b, 67).

Recommended Readings

Decker, E. (2002). The Holy Spirit in counseling: A review of Christian counseling journal articles (1985–1999). *Journal of Psychology and Christianity* 21, 21–28.

Fee, G. D. (1994). *God's empowering presence: The Holy Spirit in the letters of Paul*. Peabody, MA: Hendrickson.

Gilbert, M. G., & Brock, R. T. (Eds.). (1985). *The Holy Spirit and counseling, Vol. 1: Theology and theory*. Peabody, MA: Hendrickson.

Gilbert, M. G., & Brock, R. T. (Eds.). (1988). *The Holy Spirit and counseling, Vol. 2: Principles and practice*. Peabody, MA: Hendrickson.

Howard, E. B. (2008). *The Brazos introduction to Christian spirituality*. Grand Rapids: Brazos.

Tan, S. Y., & Gregg, D. H. (1997). *Disciplines of the Holy Spirit*. Grand Rapids: Zondervan.

Vining, J. K. (1995). *Spirit-centered counseling: A pneumascriptive approach*. East Rockaway, NY: Cummings & Hathaway.

17

Legal and Ethical Issues in Christian Counseling and Psychotherapy

L egal and ethical issues in the general field of counseling and psychotherapy have already been discussed in chapter 3. In this final chapter,
the legal and ethical issues that pertain more specifically to Christian
counseling and psychotherapy will be discussed.

Legal issues involving the particular laws of a country, state, or province
that are relevant to the professional practice of counseling and psychotherapy
also apply to the professional practice of Christian therapy. Examples provided in chapter 3 in the context of American society include the prohibition
of sex with clients; the requirement to protect client confidentiality (with a
few exceptions relating to mandatory reporting laws, such as in cases of child
abuse and elder abuse); the need to assure the competency of therapists in
the professional services they provide; and the mandate to refrain from insurance fraud (see Knapp, Gottlieb, Berman, and Handelsman 2007, 54). Christian therapists must be aware of laws that govern the professional practice
of counseling and psychotherapy (see, e.g., Levicoff 1991; Ohlschlager and
Mosgofian 1992). Since laws can be changed or revised, and new ones can be
enacted, it is imperative for Christian therapists, like all therapists, to keep
up-to-date regarding legal and ethical issues in counseling and psychotherapy.
In many states in the United States, professional therapists are required to
take a continuing education course in legal and ethical issues pertaining to

Sidebar 17.1

AACC Code of Ethics

The AACC Code of Ethics is built on seven biblical-ethical foundations:

1st Foundation: Jesus Christ and his revelation in the Old and New Testaments of the Bible is the preeminent model for Christian counseling practice, ethics, and caregiving activities.

2nd Foundation: Christian counseling maintains a committed, intimate, and dedicated relationship with the worldwide church, and individual counselors with a local body of believers.

3rd Foundation: Christian counseling, at its best, is a Spirit-led process of change and growth, geared to help others mature in Christ by the skillful synthesis of counselor-assisted spiritual, psychosocial, familial, biomedical, and environmental interventions.

4th Foundation: Christian counselors are dedicated to Jesus Christ as their "first love," to excellence in client service, to ethical integrity in practice, and to respect for everyone encountered.

5th Foundation: Christian counselors accord the highest respect to the biblical revelation regarding the defense of human life, the dignity of human personhood, and the sanctity of marriage and family life.

6th Foundation: The biblical and constitutional rights to religious freedom, free speech, and free association protect the Christian counselor's public identity, and the explicit incorporation of spiritual practices into all forms of counseling and intervention.

7th Foundation: Christian counselors are mindful of their representation of Christ and his church and are dedicated to honor their commitments and obligations in all social and professional relations. (see AACC 2004, 5)

their area of professional practice before they can be licensed or relicensed for independent practice.

The rest of this chapter will focus more on *ethical issues and guidelines* that apply to the practice of Christian therapy. These guidelines are discussed in the final version of the American Association of Christian Counselors (AACC) Code of Ethics drafted by the AACC Law and Ethics Committee chaired by George Ohlschlager and made available in 2004 (see American Association of Christian Counselors [AACC] 2004). It was publicly presented to its fifty thousand members in all fifty states of the United States and fifty other nations as of winter 2003–4 (AACC 2004, 2). Ethical issues and challenges relevant to the incorporation of spirituality and religion into psychotherapy in general have also received increased attention in recent years (see e.g., Gonsiorek, Richards, Pargament, and McMinn 2009; Hathaway and Ripley 2009; Plante 2007).

AACC Code of Ethics: A Brief Review of the Y2004 Final Code

A code of ethics can be defined as "a systematic statement of ethical standards that represent the moral convictions and guide the practice behavior of a group—in this case, the various counseling disciplines" (Ohlschlager and Clinton 2002, 245), referring to Christian and counseling ethics.

George W. Ohlschlager and Timothy E. Clinton have also provided the following Christian counselor's golden rule based on Romans 13:8–10 to reflect the core values and rules of Christian counseling ethics:

> Christian counselor, hear this:
> - Do not be indebted to any client . . . except the debt to love them.
> - For if you love your clients, you honor all your professional . . . duties.
>
> You know the rules of counseling . . . :
> - Do not engage in any form of sexual misconduct with your clients, whether current or past.
> - Do not, as far as it is possible with you, let them kill or harm themselves or anyone else.
> - Do not steal your client's money or disregard your time with them.
> - Do not harm or envy or look down on or manipulate or fight with or in any way exploit those Christ has sent to you for help.
>
> In fact, to sum it up and state it conclusively:
> - Practice the Golden Rule with all wisdom and grace.
> - Love your clients as yourself.
> - Don't do anything to your clients or those they love that you wouldn't want done to yourself.
> - For love does no wrong to any client. Therefore, to *love your clients as Christ loves you* is to fulfill all your obligations—all your moral-ethical-legal duties—as a Christian counselor. (2002, 247)

The crucial emphasis in Christian counseling ethics (see also Browning 2006; R. K. Sanders 1997; Tjeltveit 1992, 1999) is therefore to follow the biblical command to love one another with *agape* or Christlike love (John 13:34–35) and to love our neighbor as ourselves (Mark 12:31).

The AACC Code of Ethics (AACC 2004) contains eight major sections, five of them relating to ethical standards, and three of them relating to procedural rules. The five sections on ethical standards are: I. Ethical standards for Christian counselors; II. Ethical standards for supervisors, educators, researchers, and writers; III. Standards and exemptions for ordained ministers and pastoral

---

Sidebar 17.2

Sections in the AACC Code of Ethics

Ethical Standards

  I. Ethical standards for Christian counselors
  II. Ethical standards for supervisors, educators, researchers, and writers
  III. Standards and exemptions for ordained ministers and pastoral counselors
  IV. Standards and exemptions for lay helpers and other ministers
  V. Standards for resolving legal-ethical conflicts

Procedural Rules

  VI. Authority, jurisdiction, and operation of the Law and Ethics Committee
  VII. Procedures for the adjudication of complaints against AACC members
  VIII. Procedures following action by churches, courts, and other bodies (AACC 2004)

---

counselors; IV. Standards and exemptions for lay helpers and other ministers; and V. Standards for resolving legal-ethical conflicts. The three sections on procedural rules are: VI. Authority, jurisdiction, and operation of the Law and Ethics Committee (LEC); VII. Procedures for the adjudication of complaints against AACC members; and VIII. Procedures following action by churches, courts, and other bodies.

Ethical Standards for Christian Counselors

The first section of the AACC Code of Ethics covers ethical standards for Christian counselors (see AACC 2004, 6–18). The first major standard is ES1–100, First, Do No Harm. It covers affirming the God-given dignity of all persons; avoiding client harm, intended or not; refusal to participate in the harmful actions of clients; prohibition of sexual misconduct; and dual and multiple relationships.

The second major standard is ES1–200, Competence in Christian Counseling. It covers honoring the call to competent Christian counseling; duties to consult and/or refer; duties to study and maintain expertise; maintaining integrity in work, reports, and relationships; and protective action when personal problems interfere.

The third major standard is ES1–300, Informed Consent in Christian Counseling. It covers securing informed consent; consent for the structure and process of counseling; and consent for biblical-spiritual practices in counseling.

The fourth major standard is ES1–400, Confidentiality, Privacy, and Privileged Communication. It covers maintaining client confidentiality; asserting confidentiality or privilege following demands for disclosure; protecting persons from deadly harm: the rule of mandatory disclosure; disclosures in cases of third-party payment and managed care; disclosures for supervision, consultation, teaching, preaching, and publication; maintaining privacy and preserving written records; and advocacy for privacy rights against intrusive powers.

The fifth major standard is ES1–500, Ethical Practice in Christian Counseling and Evaluation. It covers fees and financial relationships in Christian counseling; case notes and proper record keeping; ethics in testing, assessment, and clinical evaluation; working with couples, families, and groups; working with persons of different faiths, religions, and values; continuity of care and service interruption; and avoiding abandonment and improper counseling termination.

The sixth major standard is ES1–600, Ethical Relations in the Professional Workplace. It covers honorable relations between professional and ministerial colleagues; maintaining honorable professional and employment relations; Christian counselors as employers; and Christian counselors as employees.

The seventh major standard is ES1–700, Ethics in Advertising and Public Relations. It covers unethical statements in public communications; communication of association with the AACC and other groups; communication of work products and training materials; and ethical guidelines in public statements by others.

The eighth and final standard is ES1–800, Ethical Relations with the State and Other Social Systems. It covers ethical relations to other professions and institutions; working for a caring church, a just government, and a better society; and being salt and light in a post-Christian culture.

Ethical Standards for Supervisors, Educators, Researches, and Writers

The second section of the AACC Code of Ethics focuses on ethical standards for supervisors, educators, researchers, and writers (AACC 2004, 19–23) that are relevant to Christian counseling. The first major standard is ES2–100, Base Standards for Supervisors and Educators. It covers ethics and excellence in supervision and teaching; and the duty of supervisors and educators not to exploit students and trainees.

The second major standard is ES2–200, Ethical Standards for Christian Counseling Supervisors. It covers counselor supervision programs; the duty of supervisors to provide a varied experience; and supervision evaluation and feedback.

The third major standard is ES2–300, Ethical Standards for Christian Counseling Educators. It covers counselor education and training programs; student and trainee evaluation; integration study and training; and field placement, practicum, and intern training.

The fourth major standard is ES2–400, Ethical Standards for Christian Counseling Researchers. It covers respecting standards of science and research; protecting human research participants and human rights; informed consent and confidentiality in research; and reporting research results.

The fifth and final major standard is ES2–500, Writing and Publication Ethics in Christian Counseling. It covers integrity in writing and publication; submission of manuscripts; and avoiding ghost writers.

Standards for Resolving Ethical-Legal Conflicts

Section five of the AACC Code of Ethics focuses on standards for resolving ethical-legal conflicts (AACC 2004, 25-27) that are relevant to Christian counseling. The first major standard is ES5–100, Base Standards for Ethical Conflict Resolution. It covers the base rule for resolving ethical-legal conflicts. The second major standard is ES5–200, Resolving Conflicts with Employers and Colleagues. It covers ethical and value differences with employers and colleagues; and law and ethics violations by colleagues and employers. The third major standard is ES5-300, Resolving Professional and Organizational Conflicts, which covers the higher ethics of Jesus Christ. The fourth and final standard is ES5–400, Resolving Conflicts with the State and Its Laws, which covers the higher law of Jesus Christ.

These three major sections of the AACC Code of Ethics (I, II, and V) are the most relevant ones for Christian counselors and therapists to use in guiding them in their professional work.

Ethical Issues and Guidelines for Integrating Christian Faith and Spiritual Direction into Psychotherapy

There are more specific ethical issues and guidelines that pertain to integrating Christian faith, including spiritual direction and spiritual disciplines, into psychotherapy (Tan 1994, 2003c, 2004; see also Richards and Bergin 1997, 143–69; Richards and Bergin 2005; R. K. Sanders 1997).

The following potential pitfalls or dangers exist in religious psychotherapy, which includes integrating Christian faith and spiritual direction into psychotherapy.

1. Imposing the therapist's religious beliefs or values on the client, thus reducing client freedom to choose.
2. Failing to provide sufficient information regarding therapy to the client.
3. Violating the therapeutic contract by focusing mainly or only on religious goals rather than therapeutic goals, and thus obtaining third-party reimbursement inappropriately. (It is, however, difficult sometimes to

clearly differentiate between spiritual and therapeutic goals because they tend to overlap for religious clients.)

4. Lacking competence as a therapist in the area of converting client values ethically or conducting religious psychotherapy appropriately.
5. Arguing over doctrinal issues rather than clarifying them.
6. Misusing or abusing spiritual resources such as prayer and Scriptures, thus avoiding dealing with painful issues in therapy.
7. Blurring important boundaries or parameters necessary for the therapeutic relationship to be maintained.
8. Assuming ecclesiastical authority and performing ecclesiastical functions inappropriately, when referral to ecclesiastical leaders may be warranted.
9. Applying only religious interventions to problems that may require medication or other medical or psychological treatments. (see Tan 1994, 390)

The ethical issue of whether it is appropriate to charge fees and receive third-party reimbursement for the use of spiritual disciplines and religious interventions in psychotherapy has been raised by Mark McMinn and Barrett McRay (1997). They especially emphasize the need to obtain empirical support for the efficacy of spiritual interventions in therapy. It is also important to keep intact the goal of helping to reduce the psychological distress of clients and not completely replace therapy with only spiritual direction (Tan 2003c). It is therefore ethical to integrate Christian faith and spiritual direction and the use of spiritual resources into therapy if: the client and the therapist share similar religious or spiritual beliefs, the client has expressed a desire for spiritual interventions to be used in therapy and thus has given informed consent, and there is a valid reason for using a specific spiritual intervention in therapy because it is relevant to the client's clinical problem and it will help to reduce the client's psychological symptoms and distress (see A. A. Nelson and Wilson 1984).

In a case where a client still wants to continue to see his or her therapist for only spiritual direction after the client's psychological symptoms have been significantly reduced and therapy goals have been substantially achieved, then the Christian therapist has several ethical options from which to choose. First, the therapist can agree to continue to see the client for spiritual direction and growth, with the client paying for these sessions, with no third-party reimbursements. Second, the therapist can provide a few more sessions of spiritual direction to the client pro bono, or free of charge. Finally, the therapist can switch to a suggested donation voluntarily made by the client, without any third-party reimbursements (see Tan 2003c). It may therefore be ethically simpler to integrate spiritual direction into lay Christian counseling because fees are not charged by lay counselors in such a context (Tan 1991; see also Tan 1997a).

P. Scott Richards and Allen E. Bergin (1997, 143–69) have covered ethical guidelines and issues related to a theistic, spiritual approach to therapy (see also Richards and Bergin 2005). They deal with five important difficult and challenging ethical issues: dual relationships (religious and professional); the danger of displacing or usurping religious authority; the danger of imposing religious values on clients; the danger of violating work-setting (church-state) boundaries; and the danger of practicing outside the boundaries of competence. They also mention two other significant concerns: becoming enmeshed in superstition, and trivializing the sacred or numinous (see Tan 2003c, 16). Their many cautious but helpful ethical guidelines for dealing with these five major ethical issues will now be briefly summarized (see Tan 2003c, 17–18).

First, regarding the ethical issue of *dual relationships*, Richards and Bergin (1997, 147–48) recommend several ethical guidelines. They include the following recommendations: Therapist-religious leader dual relationships should be avoided as a general guideline. Consultation with a supervisor or professional colleagues should be sought and agreement obtained before a therapist becomes involved in a dual relationship with a client that the therapist has deemed is in the best interest of the client. The limits and risks of the dual relationship need to be clearly explained to the client. The therapist should continue to seek frequent consultation from professional colleagues or a supervisor and be ready to terminate the dual relationship and make a proper referral if the client appears to be harmed by the dual relationship. Proper and careful documentation is crucial in this situation.

Second, regarding *the danger of displacing or usurping religious authority*, Richards and Bergin (1997, 151–53) recommend several ethical guidelines for *collaborating with religious authorities*. They include the following considerations: A client's religious or denominational tradition, if any, should be assessed by a therapist and the question of whether a client views his or her religious leaders as potential sources of help must be clarified. If a client agrees and gives written informed consent, the therapist can contact the client's religious leaders to consult with them and enlist their support in helping the client. This should be done with proper respect for and clear communication with the client's religious leaders, as well as with appreciation for their help and cooperation. Before spiritual interventions (including spiritual direction and spiritual guidance techniques) are used in therapy, the therapist should also clearly communicate to the client that he or she does not have any ecclesiastical authority over the client. Ecclesiastical functions to be performed only by the religious leaders of the client (e.g., hearing confessions and absolving sins) should not be usurped by the therapist. A client should feel that a particular spiritual intervention (e.g., use of prayer or religious imagery) is appropriate in therapy *before* it is used by the therapist. The therapist should not criticize a client's religious leaders but instead inform the client that the therapist generally views religious leaders and communities as potential sources of help and support.

Third, regarding *the danger of therapists imposing their religious values on clients*, Richards and Bergin (1997, 158–59) recommend several ethical guidelines for *respecting client values*. They include the following suggestions: A therapist should respect a client's right to have religious beliefs and convictions that are different from those held by the therapist. A therapist should therefore not attempt to proselytize or convert a client to the therapist's own religious faith or denomination. A therapist can engage in open and honest discussion of the moral and spiritual dimensions and consequences of a client's value choices and behaviors if the client is interested in pursuing such a discussion. However, the therapist should avoid arrogantly condemning a client's choices or behaviors with which the therapist does not agree. When such value conflicts occur in therapy, the therapist can express his or her own views but should preserve the client's right to have different values. The therapist also needs to assess with the client whether their value conflicts may have a negative effect on therapy and hence whether referral of the client to another therapist with more similar values may be the best option. Religious and spiritual goals should only be set and spiritual interventions used in therapy if the client is interested in such goals and interventions and informed consent is obtained from the client.

Fourth, regarding *the danger of violating work-setting (church-state) boundaries*, Richards and Bergin (1997, 162–63) recommend several ethical guidelines for *respecting church-state boundaries*: A therapist working in civic settings must comply with the policies and laws concerning the separation of church and state in such work-settings. A therapist in a civic setting should not use spiritual interventions in such a way as to impose a particular religious tradition on a client. Instead, a therapist should work within a client's value system, as far as possible. Written consent from both supervisor and client should be obtained by the therapist before he or she uses religious or spiritual interventions in therapy. A therapist also must obtain written parental consent before using any spiritual or religious intervention in therapy with children or adolescents. A therapist working in public schools or other civic settings involving children or adolescents is advised not to use religious or spiritual interventions such as prayer with clients, discussing Scripture with them, or distributing religious literature for bibliotherapy.

Fifth and finally, regarding *the danger of practicing outside the boundaries of competence*, Richards and Bergin (1997, 166) recommend several ethical guidelines for *education and training standards* for professional therapists who want to use a theistic, spiritual approach in their therapeutic work. They include the following recommendations: A therapist should be trained in the foundations of multicultural counseling attitudes and skills (see, e.g., D. W. Sue and D. Sue 2008; see also Sue et al. 2007; Whaley and Davis 2007). Relevant and helpful scholarly literature including journals and books on religious and spiritual issues in therapy and on the psychology and sociology of religion should be read by therapists who wish to use a theistic, spiritual approach to therapy. Such therapists should also attend at minimum a workshop or a course on religion and mental health and spiritual issues in therapy, and take a class or read books on world religions. They should gain more knowledge of particular religions and spiritual traditions and practices that may often be encountered in therapy (see, e.g., Richards and Bergin 2000; see also Dowd and Nielsen 2006). A therapist must obtain supervision or consultation when he or she first sees a client from a religious or spiritual tradition that the therapist is not familiar with and involving issues that the therapist has not dealt with previously. Such supervision or consultation is also important when a therapist first begins to use religious or spiritual interventions, especially if they are new, untried ones, in therapy with clients.

The ethical guidelines recommended by Richards and Bergin (1997) are cautious and conservative, and not everyone will agree with all that they have suggested. For example, sometimes it is ethical for a Christian therapist to share his or her faith in Christ and the gospel if the client asks for such specific information and gives his or her full informed consent for the gospel to be shared. This may happen in the context of a client seeking meaning in life and an answer to his or her fear of death—key existential questions and spiritual struggles that sometimes emerge in therapy. Although aggressive proselytization or directive efforts to convert the client to the therapist's Christian faith is not appropriate in therapy, as Richards and Bergin have noted, there is an ethically appropriate place for gentle, noncoercive sharing of the gospel when requested by a client who gives full informed consent to openly discuss the Christian faith.

Another example is the ethical concern raised by Richards and Bergin (1997) about dual relationships with the client on the part of the therapist. Great care and clinical caution should be exercised in engaging in dual relationships with clients, because clients may be potentially harmed by such relationships. However, there are ethical ways in which a therapist can enter into a dual relationship with a client, for the benefit of the client (see, e.g., Barnett 2007b; Lazarus 1994, 2007; Lazarus and Zur 2002). Furthermore, in the special case of lay or paraprofessional helping, dual relationships are usually acceptable in the context of peer or friendship counseling in which peers help one another with their problems (see Tan 1991, 1997). For example, peer helping can occur in schools or youth groups where teens counsel other teens who are acquaintances or friends (see Sturkie and Tan 1992, 1993).

Virtue Ethics: Focusing on the Character of the Christian Therapist

W. B. Johnson (2007a) has emphasized *virtue ethics*, which focus more on the character and moral virtues of the therapist, rather than only *principle ethics*

Sidebar 17.3

Virtues That Should Characterize the Christian Therapist
(From Jones, Butman, Dueck, and Tan 1988 and summarized in Jones and Butman 1991, 410–12)

Compassion as opposed to elitism
Servanthood as opposed to superiority
Community as opposed to isolation
Accountability as opposed to independence and autonomy
Transparency as opposed to impression management
Love as opposed to Rogerian positive regard
Stewardship as opposed to profit maximization
Holiness as opposed to anonymity or wholeness
Wisdom as opposed to mere secular brilliance
Integrity as opposed to mere ethical compliance (to ethical codes)

Above all, the key characteristic or virtue of the Christian therapist should be *a true depth of spirituality* centered in Christ and empowered by the Holy Spirit (see Tan 1987b).

(Corey, Corey, and Callanan 2007), which focus on the ethical guidelines and rules governing right and appropriate behavior in particular clinical situations (see also Dueck 1995).

Collins (2007, 83–99) has provided several suggestions to help Christian counselors deal with legal, ethical, and moral issues in their practice in biblical and God-honoring ways, respecting the client as a person of worth and always seeking the client's welfare. More specifically, Collins warns about the danger of falling into unethical and sinful sexual intimacies with clients. He recommends the following helpful means of counselor self-control: "spiritual protection; knowing one's vulnerabilities; being aware of danger signals; setting limits; telling oneself the truth; finding support and accountability with others" (2007, 99).

Future Directions in Christian Counseling and Psychotherapy and Implications for Ethical Practice

In bringing this chapter and this book to a close, it is appropriate to look ahead into possible future directions in Christian counseling and psychotherapy and identify some of the implications for ethical practice in this field.

First, in a more general context, James R. Beck (2006) has made several predictions about how the integration of psychology, including counseling and psychotherapy, and Christian faith may develop in the next fifty years. After providing brief snapshots of the state of psychology, theology, and integration in 1956 and in 2006, he has courageously made snapshot predictions about their possible state in 2056.

More specifically in the area of *integration*, Beck has made the following predictions for 2056:

1. Christian therapists will be challenged to widen their understanding of psychotherapy to include other modalities such as coaching, spiritual formation, and discipleship;
2. Theoreticians who work in the area of the integrative enterprise will make great progress in synthesizing what now seem to be distinct models of integration;
3. Christian psychology will display an increased need for sophisticated empirical research to undergird its efforts to deliver quality services . . . ;
4. Christian integrators must upgrade the level of understanding and utilization of psychological science . . . in their work of integration;
5. Integrators must likewise upgrade the sophistication of the biblical and theological material they utilize in their work. (J. R. Beck 2006, 327–28)

The need to stay abreast of the latest developments in psychology and theology in the integration enterprise as well as the need to obtain empirical support for the effectiveness of Christian therapeutic approaches and interventions with more sophisticated outcome research (see Worthington 2006) are clear ethical challenges for integrators in the next few decades.

Second, Clinton and Ohlschlager (2006) have also made several predictions more specifically about the future of Christian counseling, as the field matures. They include the following twenty-five trends:

1. A 21st century code of ethics;
2. Sure advocacy for client and the marginalized;
3. National credentialing;
4. Academic and clinic accreditation;
5. Lay helping ministry;
6. Spiritual and relationship formation;
7. Biblical and theological depth;
8. e-Counseling and use of Internet technologies;
9. Expanding cutting-edge modes of care;
10. Interprofessional relations;
11. Working with faith-based initiatives;
12. Intensive care for counselors and pastors;
13. Distance and on-line education;

14. Continuing education and focused certificate programs;
15. Doctoral programs for Christian counseling leaders;
16. Heightened multicultural sensitivity;
17. New and more refined research;
18. Salt and light ministry;
19. Glocalization ("thinking global, acting local");
20. Flowering into a mature interdisciplinary profession;
21. Theoretical integration reaching maturity;
22. Integration with medicine and law;
23. Brain imaging and neuroscience;
24. Positive psychology movement;
25. Spiritual hunger and the emerging church. (see Clinton and Ohlschlager 2006, 33–35)

These are possible trends in the future of Christian counseling as it matures as a field. However, the need for high ethical and biblical standards is obvious as new strategies, practices, and other innovations are used, especially in technological areas. One example is e-counseling or telephone and Internet therapy, which raises ethical and legal questions about issues such as confidentiality, helping suicidal or dangerous clients, and counseling clients from different states in the United States (Centore 2006; see also McMinn, Orton, and Woods 2008). The positive psychology movement in particular holds promise for further development in the Christian therapy context (see, e.g., Hart and Hart-Weber 2006; see also Hackney 2007). However, it also must be carefully and biblically critiqued, because it can overemphasize strengths, virtues, and happiness, and downplay the human capacity for sin and evil and the importance of godly sorrow and repentance (Tan 2006a). Clinton and Ohlschlager have encouraged Christian counselors to see that "the door to the future is wide open to us as Christian counselors, but there are many challenges and adversaries. We must join hands now and go forward together" (2006, 35).

Finally, Collins has similarly described ten counseling waves of the future that apply to the field of Christian counseling. They include the waves of technology, globalism, biotechnology, whole-brain thinking, postmodernism, change in spirituality, changing churches, changing professionalism, nontraditional education, and positive psychology (see 2007, 849–61). Again, there is a need for clear and high standards of ethics and biblical values to guide Christian counselors and therapists in the years ahead as they navigate such significant waves of change in the counseling field.

It is interesting to note that twelve emerging directions for the general field of psychotherapy have also been described by James Prochaska and John Norcross in the following areas: economics of mental health care or the industrialization of mental health care; evidence-based practice; therapy relationship;

technological applications; self-help resources; neuroscience; behavioral health; proactive treatment of populations; faith-based practices; positive psychology; integration of psychotherapy and pharmacotherapy; and the effectiveness of psychotherapy (see 2010, 520–32).

The future of Christian counseling and psychotherapy therefore looks bright and promising, as spiritually or religiously oriented therapy in general continues to grow and develop in the coming decades. The challenge for Christian counselors and therapists is to remain faithful and fruitful in Christ, by the power of the Holy Spirit and the grace of God. Christian therapy must always be Christ centered, biblically based, and Spirit filled (Tan 1999b, 2001b), whatever the waves of change may be in the counseling and psychotherapy field in the years to come. We should regard these possible future directions with humility and some tentativeness, because only God knows the future with certainty. Christian therapy must also be ethically characterized by *agape* or Christlike love (Mark 12:31; John 13:34–35), upholding the highest of biblical virtue ethics, manifested as the fruit of the Holy Spirit (Gal. 5:22–23).

Recommended Readings

American Association of Christian Counselors. (2004). *AACC code of ethics: The Y2004 final code*. Forest, VA: AACC.

Browning, D. S. (2006). *Christian ethics and the moral psychologies*. Grand Rapids: Eerdmans.

Levicoff, S. (1991). *Christian counseling and the law*. Chicago: Moody Press.

Ohlschlager, G. W., & Clinton, T. E. (2002). The ethical helping relationship: Ethical conformation and spiritual transformation. In T. E. Clinton & G. W. Ohlschlager (Eds.), *Competent Christian counseling* (Vol. 1, pp. 244–293, 750–751). Colorado Springs, CO: WaterBrook Press.

Ohlschlager, G. W., & Mosgofian, P. (1992). *Law for the Christian counselor*. Dallas: Word.

Sanders, R. K. (Ed.). (1997). *Christian counseling ethics: A handbook for therapists, pastors, and counselors*. Downers Grove, IL: InterVarsity.

Tjeltveit, A. C. (1999). *Ethics and values in psychotherapy*. New York: Routledge.

Appendix

Is Psychotherapy Effective?

Methods of Research

Research methods are usually categorized as *quantitative* or *qualitative*. The *quantitative* approach has been more widely and traditionally used thus far. It focuses on measuring the *outcomes* of counseling and psychotherapy as well as the *processes* that occur in therapy interactions that may be related to such outcomes. Outcome research is used to evaluate the *efficacy* or *effectiveness* of therapy. The terms "efficacy" and "effectiveness" are usually used interchangeably. However, in recent years some authors have used the term "efficacy" to refer to the results of scientifically controlled outcome studies that show whether a particular therapeutic technique or intervention works better than no treatment or an "attention-placebo" condition. Such studies typically involve *random assignment of patients or clients* who meet the diagnostic criteria for specific psychological disorders and the use of *detailed treatment manuals or manualized treatments* in systematically and consistently carrying out the particular therapeutic intervention whose efficacy is being evaluated. These studies are also called *randomized controlled trials* (RCTs) by experimental or scientific design and are basically quantitative in nature.

The term "effectiveness" has recently been used to refer more specifically to how successful a particular therapy or technique is in *real-life, clinical situations in actual practice*, and not in carefully controlled scientific experimental studies such as the RCTs often used in *efficacy* outcome research (see M. E. P. Seligman 1995). However, most authors and texts still use the terms "efficacy" and "effectiveness" synonymously and interchangeably, as I do in the book you are now reading. It is nevertheless important to evaluate how effective a particular therapy or technique is in both carefully controlled scientific outcome studies and in real-life clinical practice. J. Hunsley and C. M. Lee (2007) have recently reviewed thirty-five *effectiveness* studies for adult disorders (N = 21) and child and adolescent disorders (N = 14) and found that the improvement rates in these *effectiveness* studies were comparable to those reported in *efficacy* studies involving randomized controlled trials. These initial data therefore provide encouraging support for the application or transportability of treatments with established efficacy to real-life clinical settings.

Qualitative research is more difficult to define and evaluate, but it is an important complement to quantitative research. Qualitative research usually involves intense study of individual cases using data collection methods such as repeated interviews, questionnaires or surveys, and tapes. It is more often used to investigate the *processes* of therapy that may be related to the *outcomes* or efficacy and effectiveness of therapy. Qualitative research is still not as valued as well-controlled quantitative research, but there are also some significant problems and issues with quantitative research involving RCTs that will be covered later in this appendix (see Westen, Novotny, and Thompson-Brenner 2004). Qualitative research tends to be valued more by researchers evaluating approaches such as psychodynamic, humanistic, and constructivistic therapies that are more relational and open-ended (Todd and Bohart 2006).

Results of Research: The Effectiveness of Counseling and Psychotherapy

Is counseling or psychotherapy effective, that is, efficacious? This question is difficult to answer. However, many outcome studies have now been done, with some important results every counselor or therapist needs to know and use in his or her clinical practice.

It is well known that Hans Eysenck's original 1952 scathing critique of the (in)effectiveness of psychotherapy as practiced at that time (mainly Freudian and Rogerian therapies) is no longer valid. He asserted about six decades ago (Eysenck 1952) that psychotherapy was not more effective than spontaneous remission rates (i.e., around two-thirds of neurotic patients will recover or significantly improve over a two-year period without therapy) found among no-treatment control patients. Since then, more outcome research has been done, and the results of such research are quite different from Eysenck's early claims. For example, Bergin and Lambert (1978) have shown that spontaneous remission rates actually range from 43 to 65 percent of "untreated" patients, and noted that rates closer to 43 percent would be more accurate.

In a well-known review of therapy outcome studies that introduced the use of a statistical method called *meta-analysis*, M. L. Smith, Glass, and Miller (1980) identified 475 studies at that time that compared some therapy approach or intervention to a control group of some kind. Meta-analysis is a statistical method used to calculate an *effect size* based on the results of all available studies (regardless of the methodological quality of a particular study) on a subject of interest, in this case, the effectiveness of counseling and psychotherapy. The effect size gives us the average effect of a specific treatment that is above or better than the average effect for those who did not receive the treatment. M. L. Smith, Glass, and Miller reported that psychotherapy had an overall effect size of 0.85: the average person who had therapy did better than 80 percent of those who did not have therapy, a far cry from the no significant difference between treated and untreated patients that Eysenck had boldly claimed in 1952.

More recently, Michael J. Lambert and Benjamin M. Ogles (2004) have reviewed the results of research on the effectiveness and efficacy of psychotherapy, including meta-analyses conducted since the one done by M. L. Smith, Glass, and Miller (1980). Effect sizes reported range from 0.47 to 1.05. Despite some inconsistent results, as well as methodological problems with meta-analysis (e.g., this statistical procedure does not take into consideration the quality of each outcome study but lumps all available studies together in calculating an effect size), the current conclusion is that psychotherapy is moderately effective, to say the least.

Lambert and Ogles (2004) also found that various therapies did not significantly differ from one another in terms of their effectiveness. This conclusion again echoes what Lester Luborsky, Barton Singer, and Lise Luborsky (1975) found over three decades ago: among the different therapies no particular approach is superior since they are all roughly equivalent in their effectiveness. Therefore, they all have won, and all must have prizes, to paraphrase the Dodo bird in Alice's Wonderland. This has come to be known as the "Dodo Bird Effect" of no significant difference in the effectiveness of the various approaches to counseling and psychotherapy (see also Wampold et al. 1997). The Dodo Bird Effect, however, has not been universally accepted by researchers in this field. In fact, it has recently been strongly challenged by those who advocate empirically supported treatments (ESTs) and the use of specific techniques for particular psychological disorders. ESTs will be discussed in more detail later in this appendix.

Despite the general conclusion that counseling or psychotherapy is effective overall, it is important to note two other facts from the research results: a significant minority of clients (5–10 percent) actually get worse or deteriorate while undergoing psychotherapy (Lambert and Ogles 2004); and about 20 percent of clients do not improve or respond to therapy (M. L. Smith, Glass, and Miller 1980). Using this rough estimate Ty Tashiro and Laura Mortensen (2006) have recently concluded that about 6,273,000 adults and 3,024,000 children in the United States annually continue to have debilitating symptoms even after undergoing and completing psychotherapy. Therapy therefore does not help a significant number of people (about 20 percent) and may even harm a certain percentage (5–10 percent) of them. There is still much work to be done to improve the effectiveness of psychotherapy and to reduce its potential harmful effects on some people.

Scott Lilienfeld (2007) has recently provided a provisional list of psychological treatments that can cause harm, *potentially harmful therapies* (PHTs) (see also Tan 2008c). They include the following Level I PHTs that are *probably* harmful for some clients: critical incident stress debriefing (with heightened risk for posttraumatic stress symptoms); Scared Straight interventions (with risk of exacerbation of conduct problems); facilitated communication (with risk of false accusations of child abuse against family members); attachment therapies, for example, rebirthing (with risk of death and serious injury to children); recovered memory techniques (with risk of false memories of trauma); dissociative identity disorder–oriented therapy (with risk of induction of "alter" personalities); grief counseling for clients with normal bereavement reactions (with risk of increases in depressive symptoms); expressive-experiential therapies (with risk of worsening of painful emotions); boot-camp interventions for conduct disorder (with risk of worsening of conduct problems); and DARE programs (with risk of increased intake of alcohol and other substances such as cigarettes). Level II PHTs that are *possibly* harmful for some clients include: peer-group interventions for conduct disorder (with possible worsening of conduct problems); and relaxation treatments for panic-prone clients (with possible induction of panic attacks) (see Lilienfeld 2007, 58). More attention is therefore being focused on the potential harmful or negative effects of psychological treatment (see Barlow 2010; Castonguay, Boswell, Constantino, Goldfried, and Hill 2010; Dimidjian and Hollon 2010).

Tashiro and Mortensen (2006) note that results of clinical outcome research show that about 80 percent of clients in psychotherapy do better than those who do not receive treatment (M. L. Smith, Glass, and Miller 1980), and about 55–66 percent of clients in treatment will improve compared with those in active control groups (Baskin, Tierney, Minami, and Wampold 2003). Yet the causal mechanisms or processes responsible for why psychotherapy works are still unclear (Westen, Novotny, and Thompson-Brenner 2004). Tashiro and Mortensen also point out that the dose-response research literature estimates that for at least 50 percent of clients to improve, around thirteen sessions of therapy are needed; for 83 percent of clients to improve, around twenty-six sessions are required (Hansen, Lambert, and Forman 2002).

Why Psychotherapy Works: The Common Factors Approach

The Dodo Bird Effect, when accepted, has led several researchers to conclude that counseling or psychotherapy works because of some common factors that are operative across the different approaches to therapy. The following are common therapeutic factors and the associated percentage of improvement in clients as a function of such factors (Lambert and Barley 2002): *extratherapeutic change* (outside therapy, including receiving help from friends, family, clergy members, self-help literature, and self-help groups, and client characteristics such as severity and chronicity of the client's condition; the presence of an underlying personality disorder; the nature, strength, and quality of social supports; and the client's diagnosis), 40 percent; *common factors or relationship factors* (e.g., therapist attributes and facilitative conditions such as warmth, empathy, and congruence or genuineness, and the therapeutic alliance), 30 percent; *techniques* (specific therapeutic methods or interventions), 15 percent; and *expectancy* (placebo effect), 15 percent (see also Hubble, Duncan, and Miller 1999; Duncan, Miller, Wampold, and Hubble 2010).

Michael J. Lambert and Dean E. Barley (2002) therefore conclude, as others have, that specific therapeutic techniques contribute much less (15 percent) to the outcome of psychotherapy than relationship or interpersonal factors (30 percent) common to all therapies (see also Lambert and Ogles 2004). However, they do acknowledge that a few specialized therapy techniques have been found to be superior in their effectiveness with clients with specific diagnostic types or categories. The following are some examples: exposure treatments for specific phobias, gradual practice with particular sexual disorders, response prevention for obsessive-compulsive disorders, cognitive restructuring and exposure for agoraphobia, and using a more supportive approach in interpretation in short-term psychodynamic therapy, taking client symptom severity into consideration. Other researchers have put more emphasis on such techniques in producing therapeutic change. In fact, a whole movement began in 1995, when the first list of *empirically validated treatments* was published by a task force of Division 12 (Society of Clinical Psychology) of the APA. Since then, the list has been relabeled *empirically supported treatments* (ESTs), and it has grown to over 145 (see Chambless and Ollendick 2001; Tan 2001a).

Why Psychotherapy Works: Empirically Supported Treatments (ESTs)

The list of ESTs has grown to beyond the 145 well-established efficacious and probably efficacious treatments (108 for adults and 37 for children) listed several years ago by Diane L. Chambless and Thomas H. Ollendick (2001). Since then, there have been more recent updates of these treatments that work (e.g., Nathan and Gorman 2007; Roth and Fonagy 2005). The following are the original criteria that the Task Force on Promotion and Dissemination of Psychological Procedures of Division 12 of APA provided for defining *well-established efficacious treatments* (Task Force 1995; see also Chambless et al. 1998):

I. At least two good between-group design experiments demonstrating efficacy in one or more of the following ways:
   A. Superior (statistically significantly so) to pill or psychological placebo or to another treatment.
   B. Equivalent to an already established treatment in experiments with adequate sample sizes.

OR

II. A large series of single case design experiments (nine or more) demonstrating efficacy. These experiments must have:
  A. Used good experimental designs and
  B. Compared the intervention to another treatment as in IA.

III. Experiments must be conducted with treatment manuals.
IV. Characteristics of the client samples must be clearly specified.
 V. Effects must have been demonstrated by at least two different investigators or teams.

Probably efficacious treatments are defined as:

I. Two experiments showing the treatment is superior (statistically significantly so) to a waiting-list control group.

OR

II. One or more experiments meeting the well-established treatment criteria IA or IB, III, and IV but not V.

OR

III. A small series of single case design experiments (three or more) otherwise meeting well-established treatment criteria II, III, and IV.

Some of these criteria have been somewhat modified in attempts by others to compile similar lists of ESTs (see Chambless and Ollendick 2001).

It should be noted that of the 145 well-established efficacious and probably efficacious ESTs summarized by Chambless and Ollendick (2001), the majority are behavioral, cognitive-behavioral, and cognitive interventions. However, the list of ESTs also includes brief dynamic therapy, interpersonal therapy, hypnosis, family systems therapy, emotion-focused couples therapy, insight-oriented marital therapy, systemic therapy, long-term family therapy, and functional family therapy for different disorders (Tan 2001a).

Although the EST movement has gained momentum, there have also been some criticisms of ESTs. For example, questions have been raised about whether they are effective in real-life clinical settings with patients who have not been screened or preselected for research outcome studies (Nathan, Stuart, and Dolan 2000), and whether they focus too much on technique and not enough on other crucial variables such as therapist, client, and relationship factors (Norcross 2002). Another criticism of ESTs is that empirical support for their efficacy with ethnic minority clients is still lacking (G. C. N. Hall 2001). However, there is more-recent empirical support for the efficacy of cognitive-behavioral therapy with adult ethnic minority clients (Voss Horrell 2008).

Hyun-Nie Ahn and Bruce E. Wampold (2001) did a meta-analysis of twenty-seven component studies and have concluded that theoretically based significant components were found not to be responsible for therapeutic effects, thus raising further doubts about the specificity of psychological treatments. They emphasize instead that the efficacy of therapies is due more to common pathways found in all valid treatments such as the context for healing, the belief in the efficacy of treatment, the therapeutic alliance, therapeutic interventions consistent with the client's perception of his or her problems, the development of self-efficacy, and remoralization (Ahn and Wampold 2001, 255).

More recently, Drew Westen, Catherine Novotny, and Heather Thompson-Brenner (2004) have provided a critical review of the assumptions and findings of RCTs used to provide research support for ESTs. They advocate meta-analytic studies as more appropriate and nuanced for evaluating treatment efficacy rather than a dichotomous judgment of supported versus unsupported treatments in establishing ESTs. They also recommend changes in reporting practices to maximize the clinical utility of RCTs, describe alternative methodologies that may be useful when the assumptions underlying EST methodology are violated, and suggest moving from validating treatment packages to evaluating intervention strategies and theories of change that practitioners can integrate into *empirically informed therapies* (631).

A specific reaction to the EST movement was the formation of another task force, this time of APA Division 29 (Psychotherapy), commissioned by John Norcross in 1999 to identify, operationalize, and disseminate information about empirically supported therapy relationships (ESRs). This task force focused more on psychotherapy relationships rather than on techniques in effective therapy.

Why Psychotherapy Works: Empirically Supported Therapy Relationships (ESRs)

Norcross (2002) has edited a book on psychotherapy relationships that work summarizing what was done by the APA Division 29 task force. It focuses on therapist contributions and responsiveness to clients or patients, that is, on ESRs, to counterbalance the emphasis on ESTs since 1995 (see Tan 2003a). In the final chapter of the edited volume, the steering committee of this task force makes the following conclusions and recommendations regarding ESRs (see Steering Committee 2002, 441–43): With regard to *general elements of the therapy relationship* mainly provided by the therapist, the empirical evidence indicated that the following factors are *demonstrably effective*: therapeutic alliance, cohesion in group therapy, empathy, and goal consensus and collaboration. The evidence reviewed also indicated that the following factors are *promising and probably effective*: positive regard, congruence/genuineness, feedback, repair of alliance ruptures, self-disclosure, management of countertransference, and quality of relational interpretations.

With regard to *customizing the therapy relationship to individual clients* based on their qualities or behaviors, the empirical evidence indicated that the following factors are *demonstrably effective*: resistance and functional impairment. The evidence reviewed also indicated that the following factors are *promising and probably effective* as a *means of customizing therapy*: coping style, stages of change, anaclitic/sociotropic and introjective/autonomous styles, expectations, and assimilation of problematic behaviors. *Insufficient* empirical evidence was found for a definitive conclusion to be presently made for the following client or patient characteristics: attachment style, gender, ethnicity, religion and spirituality, preferences, and personality disorder.

The steering committee strongly recommends that therapists make the creation and cultivation of the therapy relationship based on the factors found to be demonstrably and probably effective a major goal in their therapeutic work with clients. It also suggests that the concurrent use of both ESRs and ESTs tailored to the client's disorder and characteristics will lead to the best therapeutic outcomes (Steering Committee 2002, 442).

Another approach to answering the question of why psychotherapy works is to more broadly extract empirically informed principles of treatment selection that go beyond techniques or single-theory views as Larry E. Beutler (2000) has done (see also Beutler, Clarkin, and Bongar 2000; Beutler and Harwood 2000). Beutler suggests eighteen guiding principles for treating clients with depression, with ten basic guidelines (e.g., the likelihood of improvement is a positive function of social support level and a negative function of functional impairment) and eight optimal and enhancing guidelines (e.g., therapeutic change is most likely if change efforts initially focus on building new skills and disrupting symptoms) (see Tan 2002a). More recently, this approach has been expanded in work done by yet another task force jointly sponsored by APA Division 12 (Society for Clinical Psychology) and the North American Society for Psychotherapy Research, between 2002 and 2004. Louis G. Castonguay and Larry E. Beutler (2006b) have summarized what this task force has done in an edited volume on principles of therapeutic change that work or empirically based principles of therapeutic change (see also Tan 2007a).

Why Psychotherapy Works: Empirically Based Principles of Therapeutic Change

The two major questions that the task force focusing on empirically based principles of therapeutic change attempted to answer are: "(1) What is known about the nature of the participants, relationship, *and* procedures within treatment that induce positive effects across theoretical models and methods? (2) How do the factors or variables that are related to participants, relationships, and treatments, work together to enhance change?" (Castonguay and Beutler 2006b, v–vi).

Castonguay and Beutler (2006b) cover both common and unique principles of therapeutic change that are empirically based or grounded, but they include only psychosocial treatments with *adult* clients (with four major disorders: dysphoric disorders, anxiety disorders, personality disorders, and substance use disorders). They note that these principles are not empirically supported by experimental studies per se. These empirically based principles of therapeutic change that work should therefore be considered more as hypotheses and not yet as established factual processes of change. Gerald M. Rosen and Gerald C. Davison (2003) have recently advocated that psychology list empirically supported principles of change (ESPs) instead of credentialing trademarked therapies or other treatment packages.

Castonguay and Beutler (2006a) have summarized sixty-one empirically based principles of therapeutic change covering the work of the task force. The following are some examples of these sixty-one principles under their three major headings (see Tan 2007a): *participant (client and therapist) characteristics* (e.g., dropout rates are reduced and improvement is better if clients and therapists are from the same or similar social/ethnic backgrounds; if clients have a preference for religiously oriented therapy, therapeutic effects are enhanced if this preference is accommodated by therapists; therapists are likely to enhance their effectiveness if they have attitudes of flexibility, open-mindedness, and creativity, and if they are patient); *therapeutic relationship* (e.g., therapy tends to be helpful if a strong working alliance is formed and maintained during therapy; therapists should relate to their clients with empathy; an attitude of congruence or authenticity on the part of the therapist is likely to promote change); and *technique factors* (e.g., therapeutic change is likely to occur if therapists provide a structured treatment and stay focused in the application of the interventions; positive therapeutic outcome tends to occur when therapists help clients change their cognitions or thinking and help them engage in self-exploration; therapeutic change is likely if therapists help clients accept, tolerate, and even fully experience their feelings).

The research literature has therefore included ESTs, ESRs, and even ESPs (and PHTs). The work of the latest task force on empirically based principles of therapeutic change has helped to broaden the focus to include participant (client and therapist) characteristics, therapeutic relationship, and technique factors that cut across theoretical models and methods. In fact, the latest development in empirically based counseling and psychotherapy is the even broader concept of *evidence-based practice* (EBP). More specifically, EBP that relates to the clinical practice of psychology is now called evidence-based practice in psychology (EBPP).

Evidence-Based Practice in Psychology (EBPP)

The empirically based principles of therapeutic change that Castonguay and Beutler (2006a, 2006b) have recently summarized are consistent with the latest development of EBPP. An APA presidential task force (yes, another one!) has defined EBPP as the integration of the best available research with clinical expertise in the context of patient or client characteristics, culture, and preferences (APA Presidential Task Force on Evidence-Based Practice 2006; see also Norcross, Beutler, and Levant 2006). EBPP is therefore broader than ESTs, ESRs, or even ESPs. It takes into consideration not only the best available research (from various sources that include RCTs as well as correlational and qualitative studies) but also the clinical expertise of the therapist, and especially client characteristics, culture, and preferences, including religious and spiritual values and preferences. EBPP emphasizes the application of empirically supported principles of psychological assessment, case formulation, therapeutic relationship, and intervention in order to promote effective psychological practice and enhance public health (see also Kazdin 2008; Levant and Hasan 2008). Alan E. Kazdin (2008) has noted that *evidence-based practice* (EBP) is the broader term that includes *evidence based treatment* (EBT), which is synonymous with EST (see McHugh and Barlow 2010). At times some authors (e.g., Gotham 2006) have erroneously used the term *evidence-based practices* (EBPs) to refer to ESTs (or EBTs), thus confusing EBPP (or EBP) with ESTs, as Ronald F. Levant and Nadia T. Hasan (2008) have noted.

The National Institute of Mental Health (NIMH) has recently attempted to generate innovative treatments for mental or psychological disorders. It has specifically targeted *translational research* for alleviating mental illness as a major priority for research funding. Tashiro and Mortensen (2006) have therefore provided some helpful suggestions for translating basic science from social psychology in particular into innovative treatments for mental disorders. NIMH has defined translational research in the behavioral and social sciences as research that deals with how basic behavioral processes inform the diagnosis, prevention, treatment, and delivery of services for mental illness, and also how knowledge of mental illness increases our understanding of basic behavioral processes (see Tashiro and Mortensen 2006, 959).

A Biblical Perspective on ESTs, ESRs, ESPs, and EBPP

ESTs and therapeutic relationships (ESRs) as well as principles of therapeutic change or ESPs are all based on good scientific research. As such, they can be appropriately respected and used in clinical practice by Christian counselors and therapists. However, biblical guidelines for effective, efficient, and ethical therapy must have first priority. For example, we should use ESTs, ESRs, or ESPs that work only if they are consistent with biblical truth, ethics, and values. Whatever contradicts the Bible and its teachings, even if empirically supported, should not be accepted or applied in clinical practice by Christian therapists (Tan 2001a). The primacy of agape love (1 Cor. 13) as the foundation and center of Christian counseling and psychotherapy means that ESTs cannot be used without ESRs, including the importance of a good therapeutic alliance between therapist and client based on empathy, which is a crucial component of agape love (see Tan 2002a, 2003a).

Appropriate respect and appreciation for good scientific research, including the use of RCTs, should challenge Christian therapists and researchers to conduct additional empirical outcome studies on the effectiveness of Christian therapeutic interventions (Tan 2001a). However, a Christian biblical perspective on outcome or efficacy studies will take a broader approach to the research methods used in such studies. We can value experimental methods such as RCTs without viewing them as the only valid research methods to use. More-qualitative research methods such as phenomenological, hermeneutical, and narrative approaches can also be validly used, especially in investigating religious or spiritual phenomena and experiences (e.g., see Vande Kemp 1996; Wulff 1998), even in therapy outcome studies. It is important not to fall into a psychological reductionism that is based too much on logical positivism, which views reality only in physicalistic, naturalistic ways. However, we can still have a healthy respect for good science without embracing scientism (the worship of science and naturalism) and thereby excluding the supernatural or spiritual realm.

EBPP is a more comprehensive approach to using ESTs, ESRs, and ESPs. EBPP not only stresses the need to use the best available research or empirically supported variables in effective therapy. It also emphasizes the need to use the clinical expertise of the therapist and to incorporate the client's characteristics, culture, and preferences, including religious and spiritual values and preferences. This is a more balanced and broad-based approach to conducting effective, efficient, and ethical therapy. As such, EBPP is relatively more consistent with a biblical perspective on effective therapy or a Christian counseling approach that affirms biblical values and ethics (Tan 1987a, 1987b, 2007a).

Results of Research: The Effectiveness of Lay or Paraprofessional Counseling

In concluding this discussion on research in counseling and psychotherapy, it is important to note the results of dozens of outcome studies that have evaluated the effectiveness of lay or paraprofessional counseling (see Tan 1991, 1997b, 2002b for reviews of the research; see also Egan 2010). Such counseling is done by untrained or minimally trained lay counselors who do not have graduate degrees in counseling and related mental health fields and who therefore are not licensed mental health professionals. Briefly, the results of the majority of outcome studies that have compared the effectiveness of professional counselors to lay counselors have shown that lay counselors are generally as effective as professional counselors for most common problems (see Atkins and Christensen 2001; Bickman 1999; Christensen and Jacobson 1994; Lambert and Bergin 1994; see also Ali, Rahbar, Naeem, and Gul 2003; Neuner, Onyut, Ertl, Odenwald, Schauer, and Elbert 2008).

However, some results from research indicate that professionally trained and experienced therapists or counselors do better than paraprofessionals in outpatient settings in terms of having fewer client dropouts (Stein and Lambert 1995). Other results favoring professional experience have been found in research on the use of manualized treatments with children with conduct disorders (Kendall et al. 1990), in a study of group cognitive-behavioral therapy for depression at six month follow-up (Bright, Baker, and Neimeyer 1999), and in a study on relaxation training administered by professionals, paraprofessionals, or audiotape for cancer chemotherapy patients (Carey and Burish 1987).

More recently, Barlow (2004) has asserted that contrary to some assumptions, results from recent research indicate that significant clinical expertise and a strong therapeutic relationship are essential to maximize the efficacy of psychological treatments, especially for clients who have more severe psychopathology (D. N. Klein et al. 2003; Norcross 2002). Furthermore, therapist variables, such as experience, do contribute to beneficial outcome in these psychological interventions (Huppert et al. 2001). Barlow therefore strongly advocates the use of highly trained and experienced therapists or counselors, preferably a psychologist, in the treatment of clients with more severe psychopathology (see also Beutler and Kendall 1995).

These more recent data, however, do not totally negate previous findings that lay counselors are generally as effective as professional therapists. In fact, after briefly reviewing relevant research, Leonard Bickman has concluded: "Until additional research demonstrates consistent results, we should consider the belief that degree programs produce better clinicians a myth" (1999, 971). Further research is therefore needed before more-definitive conclusions can be made regarding the greater effectiveness of professionally trained and experienced counselors or therapists. It is still fair and valid to conclude that lay counselors can generally be effective helpers (Tan 1991, 2002b). However, the empirical evidence more specifically for the effectiveness of lay Christian counseling is very limited (e.g., Toh and Tan 1997) with a need for better-controlled outcome studies (Garzon and Tilley 2009).

References

Abanes, R. (2008). *A new earth, an old deception*. Minneapolis: Bethany House.

Abu Raiya, H., & Pargament, K. I. (2010). Religiously integrated psychotherapy with Muslim clients: From research to practice. *Professional Psychology: Research and Practice, 41,* 181–188.

Abzug, R. H. (1996). Rollo May as friend to man. *Journal of Humanistic Psychology, 36,* 17–22.

Ackerman, N. W. (1958). *The psychodynamics of family life*. New York: Basic Books.

Ackerman, N. W. (1966). *Treating the troubled family*. New York: Basic Books.

Ackerman, N. W. (1970a). Family psychotherapy today. *Family Process, 9,* 123–126.

Ackerman, N. W. (1970b). *Family therapy in transition*. Oxford: Little, Brown.

Adams, J. E. (1970). *Competent to counsel*. Grand Rapids: Baker Academic.

Adams, J. E. (1973). *The Christian counselor's manual*. Grand Rapids: Baker Academic.

Adler, A. (1917). *Study of organ inferiority and its psychical compensation*. New York: Nervous and Mental Diseases Publishing.

Adler, A. (1958). *What life should mean to you*. New York: Capricorn.

Adler, A. (1959). *Understanding human nature*. New York: Premier Books.

Adler, A. (1964). *Social interest: A challenge to mankind*. New York: Capricorn.

Ahn, H. N., & Wampold, B. E. (2001). Where oh where are the specific ingredients? A meta-analysis of component studies in counseling and psychotherapy. *Journal of Counseling Psychology, 48,* 251–257.

Alberti, R. E., & Emmons, M. L. (2008). *Your perfect right: A guide to assertive behavior* (9th ed.). Atascadero, CA: Impact.

Alcorn, R. (2004). *Heaven*. Wheaton: Tyndale.

Alford, B. A., & Beck, A. T. (1997). *The integrative power of cognitive therapy*. New York: Guilford Press.

Ali, B. S., Rahbar, M. H., Naeem, S., & Gul, A. (2003). The effectiveness of counseling on anxiety and depression by minimally trained counselors: A randomized controlled trial. *American Journal of Psychotherapy, 57*, 324–336.

Alsdurf, J. M., & Malony, H. N. (1980). A critique of Ruth Carter Stapleton's ministry of "inner healing." *Journal of Psychology and Theology, 8*, 173–184.

American Association of Christian Counselors. (2004). *AACC code of ethics: The Y2004 final code*. Forest, VA: AACC.

American Psychiatric Association. (1994). *Diagnostic and statistical manual of mental disorders* (4th ed.). Washington, DC: American Psychiatric Association.

American Psychological Association. (2002). Ethical principles of psychologists and code of conduct. *American Psychologist, 57*, 1060–1073.

Anderson, H., & Goolishian, H. (1992). The client is the expert: A not-knowing approach to therapy. In S. McNamee & K. J. Gergen (Eds.), *Therapy as social construction* (pp. 25–39). Newbury Park, CA: Sage.

Anderson, H. D. (1997). *Conversation, language, and possibilities: A postmodern approach to therapy*. New York: HarperCollins.

Anderson, N. T. (2003). *Discipleship counseling*. Ventura, CA: Regal.

Anderson, N. T., Zuehlke, T. E., & Zuehlke, J. S. (2000). *Christ-centered therapy: The practical integration of theology and psychology*. Grand Rapids: Zondervan.

Anderson, R. S. (1990). *Christians who counsel: The vocation of wholistic therapy*. Grand Rapids: Zondervan.

Anderson, R. S., & Guernsey, D. B. (1985). *On being family: A social theology of the family*. Grand Rapids: Eerdmans.

Ansbacher, H. L. (1992). Alfred Adler's concepts of community feeling and social interest and the relevance of community feeling for old age. *Individual Psychology, 48*, 402–412.

Ansbacher, H. L., & Ansbacher, R. (Eds.). (1956). *The individual psychology of Alfred Adler*. New York: Basic Books.

APA Presidential Task Force on Evidence-Based Practice. (2006). Evidence-based practice in psychology. *American Psychologist, 61*, 271–285.

Appleby, D. W. (2006). Deliverance in the 21st century. *Christian Counseling Today, 14* (4), 56–59.

Arkowitz, H., Westra, H. A., Miller, W. R., & Rollnick, S. (Eds.). (2008). *Motivational interviewing in the treatment of psychological problems*. New York: Guilford Press.

Arterburn, S., & Felton, J. (1991). *Toxic faith: Understanding and overcoming religious addiction*. Nashville: Thomas Nelson.

Aten, J. D., & Leach, M. M. (Eds.). (2009). *Spirituality and the therapeutic process: A comprehensive resource from intake to termination*. Washington, DC: American Psychological Association.

Atkins, D. C., & Christensen, A. (2001). Is professional training worth the bother? A review of the impact of psychotherapy training on client outcome. *Australian Psychologist, 36*, 122–131.

Augsburger, D. (1986). *Pastoral counseling across cultures*. Philadelphia: Westminster.

Augsburger, D. (2006). *Dissident discipleship: A spirituality of self-surrender, love of God, and love of neighbor*. Grand Rapids: Brazos.

Axline, V. M. (1947). *Play therapy*. Boston: Houghton Mifflin.

Backus, W. (1985). *Telling the truth to troubled people*. Minneapolis: Bethany House.

Backus, W., & Chapian, M. (1980). *Telling yourself the truth*. Minneapolis: Bethany House.

Bade, M. K., & Cook, S. W. (2008). Functions of Christian prayer in the coping process. *Journal for the Scientific Study of Religion, 47*, 123–133.

Baer, R. A. (Ed.). (2006). *Mindfulness-based treatment approaches: Clinician's guide to evidence base and applications*. San Diego: Elsevier.

Bair, D. (2003). *Jung: A biography*. Boston: Little, Brown.

Balswick, J. O., & Balswick, J. K. (2006). *A model for marriage: Covenant, grace, empowerment and intimacy*. Downers Grove, IL: IVP Academic.

Balswick, J. O., & Balswick, J. K. (2007). *The family: A Christian perspective on the contemporary home* (3rd ed.). Grand Rapids: Baker Academic.

Balswick, J. O., King, P. E., & Reimer, K. S. (2005). *The reciprocating self: Human development in theological perspective*. Downers Grove, IL: InterVarsity.

Bandura, A. (1969). *Principles of behavior modification*. New York: Holt, Rinehart & Winston.

Bandura, A. (Ed.). (1971). *Psychological modeling: Conflicting theories*. Chicago: Aldine Atherton.

Bandura, A. (1977a). Self-efficacy: Toward a unifying theory of behavioral change. *Psychological Review, 84*, 191–215.

Bandura, A. (1977b). *Social learning theory*. Englewood Cliffs, NJ: Prentice Hall.

Bandura, A. (1986). *Social foundations of thought and action: A social cognitive theory.* Englewood Cliffs, NJ: Prentice Hall.

Bandura, A. (1997). *Self-efficacy: The exercise of control.* San Francisco: W. H. Freeman.

Bankart, C. P. (1997). *Talking cures: A history of Western and Eastern psychotherapies.* Pacific Grove, CA: Brooks/Cole.

Barkham, M., & Shapiro, D. A. (1986). Exploratory therapy in two-plus-one sessions: A research model for studying the process of change. In G. Lietner, J. Rombauts, & R. an Balen (Eds.), *Client-centered and experiential psychotherapy in the nineties* (pp. 429–445). Leuven, Belgium: Leuven University Press.

Barlow, D. H. (1988). *Anxiety and its disorders: The nature and treatment of anxiety and panic.* New York: Guilford Press.

Barlow, D. H. (2002). *Anxiety and its disorders: The nature and treatment of anxiety and panic* (2nd ed.). New York: Guilford Press.

Barlow, D. H. (2004). Psychological treatments. *American Psychologist, 59,* 869–878.

Barlow, D. H. (2005). Clarification on psychological treatments and psychotherapy. *American Psychologist, 60,* 734–735.

Barlow, D. H. (2006). Psychotherapy and psychological treatments: The future. *Clinical Psychology: Science and Practice, 13,* 216–220.

Barlow, D. H. (2010). Negative effects from psychological treatments: A perspective. *American Psychologist, 65,* 13–26.

Barlow, D. H., & Lehman, C. L. (1996). Advances in the psychosocial treatment of anxiety disorders. *Archives of General Psychiatry, 53,* 727–735.

Barnett, J. E. (2007a). Seeking an understanding of informed consent. *Professional Psychology: Research and Practice, 38,* 179–182.

Barnett, J. E. (2007b). Whose boundaries are they anyway? *Professional Psychology: Research and Practice, 38,* 401–405.

Barnett, J. E., Baker, E. K., Elman, N. S., & Schoener, G. R. (2007). In pursuit of wellness: The self-care imperative. *Professional Psychology: Research and Practice, 38,* 603–612.

Barnett, J. E., Doll, B., Youngren, J. N., & Rubin, N. J. (2007). Clinical competence for practicing psychologists: Clearly a work in progress. *Professional Psychology: Research and Practice, 38,* 510–517.

Barnett, J. E., & Johnson, W. B. (2008). *Ethics desk reference for psychologists.* Washington, DC: American Psychological Association.

Barnett, J. E., Lazarus, A. A., Vasquez, M. J. T., Moorehead-Slaughter, O., & Johnson, W. B. (2007). Boundary issues and multiple relationships: Fantasy and reality. *Professional Psychology: Research and Practice, 38,* 401–410.

Barnett, J. E., Wise, E. H., Johnson-Greene, D., & Bucky, S. F. (2007). Informed consent: Too much of a good thing or not enough? *Professional Psychology: Research and Practice, 38*, 179–186.

Baskin, T. W., Tierney, S. C., Minami, T., & Wampold, B. E. (2003). Establishing specificity in psychotherapy: A meta-analysis of structural equivalence of placebo controls. *Journal of Consulting and Clinical Psychology, 71*, 973–979.

Bateson, G., Jackson, D. D., Haley, J., & Weakland, J. (1956). Toward a theory of schizophrenia. *Behavioral Science, 1*, 251–264.

Baucom, D. H., & Epstein, N. (1990). *Cognitive-behavioral marital therapy*. New York: Brunner/Mazel.

Baucom, D. H., Epstein, N. B., LaTaillade, J. J., & Kirby, J. S. (2008). Cognitive-behavioral couple therapy. In A. S. Gurman (Ed.), *Clinical handbook of couple therapy* (4th ed., pp. 31–72). New York: Guilford Press.

Baumgardner, P. (1975). *Legacy from Fritz*. Palo Alto, CA: Science and Behavior Books.

Baxter, L. R., Schwartz, J. M., Bergman, K. S., Szuba, M. P., Guze, B. H., Mazziotata, J. C., et al. (1992). Caudate glucose metabolic rate changes with both drug and behavior therapy for obsessive-compulsive disorder. *Archives of General Psychiatry, 49*, 681–689.

Beck, A. T. (1961). A systematic investigation of depression. *Comprehensive Psychiatry, 2*, 162–170.

Beck, A. T. (1963). Thinking and depression: Idiosyncratic context and cognitive distortions. *Archives of General Psychiatry, 9*, 324–333.

Beck, A. T. (1964). Thinking and depression. 2. Theory and therapy. *Archives of General Psychiatry, 10*, 561–571.

Beck, A. T. (1967). *Depression: Clinical, experimental, and theoretical aspects*. New York: Hoeber.

Beck, A. T. (1976). *Cognitive therapy and the emotional disorders*. New York: International Universities Press.

Beck, A. T. (1988). *Love is never enough: How couples can overcome misunderstandings, resolve conflicts, and solve problems through cognitive therapy*. New York: Harper & Row.

Beck, A. T. (1999). *Prisoners of hate: The cognitive basis of anger, hostility, and violence*. New York: HarperCollins.

Beck, A. T., & Bhar, S. S. (2009). Analyzing effectiveness of long-term psychodynamic psychotherapy. *Journal of the American Medical Association, 301*, 931.

Beck, A. T., & Emery, G., with Greenberg, R. L. (1985). *Anxiety disorders and phobias: A cognitive perspective*. New York: Basic Books.

Beck, A. T., Freeman, A., Davis, D. D., & associates. (2003). *Cognitive therapy of personality disorders* (2nd ed.). New York: Guilford Press.

Beck, A. T., Rector, N. A., Stolar, N., & Grant, P. (2009). *Schizophrenia: Cognitive theory, research, and practice.* New York: Guilford Press.

Beck, A. T., Rush, A. J., Shaw, B. F., & Emery, G. (1979). *Cognitive therapy of depression.* New York: Guilford Press.

Beck, A. T., & Weishaar, M. E. (2008). Cognitive therapy. In R. J. Corsini & D. Wedding (Eds.), *Current psychotherapies* (8th ed., pp. 263–294). Belmont, CA: Brooks/Cole.

Beck, A. T., Wright, F. D., Newman, C. F., & Liese, B. S. (1993). *Cognitive therapy of substance abuse.* New York: Guilford Press.

Beck, J. R. (2006). Integration: The next 50 years. *Journal of Psychology and Christianity, 25,* 321–330.

Beck, J. R., & Demarest, B. (2005). *The human person in theology and psychology: A biblical anthropology for the twenty-first century.* Grand Rapids: Kregel.

Beck, J. S. (1995). *Cognitive therapy: Basics and beyond.* New York: Guilford Press.

Beck, J. S. (2005). *Cognitive therapy for challenging problems.* New York: Guilford Press.

Becker, E. (1973). *The denial of death.* New York: Free Press.

Becker, W. W. (1987). The paraprofessional counselor in the church: Legal and ethical considerations. *Journal of Psychology and Christianity, 6* (2), 78–82.

Becvar, D. S., & Becvar, R. J. (2006). *Family therapy: A systemic integration* (6th ed.). Needham Heights, MA: Allyn & Bacon.

Bellack, A. S., & Hersen, M. S. (Eds.). (1987). *Dictionary of behavior therapy techniques.* New York: Pergamon.

Benner, D. G. (1983). The incarnation as a metaphor for psychotherapy. *Journal of Psychology and Theology, 11,* 287–294.

Benner, D. G. (1988). *Psychotherapy and the spiritual quest.* Grand Rapids: Baker Academic.

Benner, D. G. (1998). *Care of souls: Revisioning Christian nurture and counsel.* Grand Rapids: Baker Academic.

Benner, D. G. (2002). *Sacred companions: The gift of spiritual friendship and direction.* Downers Grove, IL: InterVarsity.

Benner, D. G. (2003). *Surrender to love: Discovering the heart of Christian spirituality.* Downers Grove, IL: InterVarsity.

Benner, D. G. (2004). *The gift of being yourself: The sacred call to self-discovery.* Downers Grove, IL: InterVarsity.

Benner, D. G. (2005a). *Desiring God's will: Aligning our hearts with the heart of God*. Downers Grove, IL: InterVarsity.

Benner, D. G. (2005b). Intensive soul care: Integrating psychotherapy and spiritual direction. In L. Sperry & E. P. Shafranske (Eds.), *Spiritually oriented psychotherapy* (pp. 287–306). Washington, DC: American Psychological Association.

Benson, H. (1975). *The relaxation response*. New York: William Morrow.

Berg, I. K. (1994). *Family-based services: A solution-focused approach*. New York: Norton.

Berg, I. K., & Miller, S. D. (1992). *Working with the problem drinker: A solution-focused approach*. New York: Norton.

Bergin, A. E. (1980). Psychotherapy and religious values. *Journal of Consulting and Clinical Psychology, 48*, 95–105.

Bergin, A. E., & Lambert, M. J. (1978). The evaluation of therapeutic outcomes. In S. L. Garfield & A. E. Bergin (Eds.), *Handbook of psychotherapy and behavior change* (2nd ed., pp. 139–189). New York: Wiley.

Bertalanffy, L. von. (1968). *General systems theory: Foundations, development, applications* (Rev. ed.). New York: George Braziller.

Beutler, L. E. (2000). David and Goliath: When empirical and clinical standards of practice meet. *American Psychologist, 55*, 997–1007.

Beutler, L. E., Clarkin, J. F., & Bongar, G. (2000). *Guidelines for the systematic treatment of the depressed patient*. New York: Oxford University Press.

Beutler, L. E., Consoli, A. J., & Lane, G. (2005). Systematic treatment selection and prescriptive psychotherapy. In J. C. Norcross & M. R. Goldfried (Eds.), *Handbook of psychotherapy integration* (2nd ed, pp. 121–143). New York: Oxford University Press.

Beutler, L. E., Crago, M., & Arezmendi, T. G. (1986). Research on therapist variables in psychotherapy. In S. L. Garfield & A. E. Bergin (Eds.), *Handbook of psychotherapy and behavior change* (3rd ed., pp. 257–310). New York: Wiley.

Beutler, L. E., & Harwood, T. M. (2000). *Prescriptive psychotherapy: A practical guide to systematic treatment selection*. New York: Oxford University Press.

Beutler, L. E., & Kendall, P. C. (1995). Introduction to the special section: The case for training in the provision of psychological therapy. *Journal of Consulting and Clinical Psychology, 63*, 179–181.

Bickman, L. (1999). Practice makes perfect and other myths about mental health services. *American Psychologist, 54*, 965–978.

Binswanger, L. (1963). *Being-in-the-world: Selected papers of Ludwig Binswanger*. New York: Basic Books.

Bitter, J. R. (2009). *Theory and practice of family therapy and counseling.* Belmont, CA: Brooks/Cole.

Bitter, J. R., Christensen, O. C., Hawes, C., & Nicoll, W. G. (1998). Adlerian brief therapy with individuals, couples, and families. *Directions in Clinical and Counseling Psychology, 8,* 95–111.

Bitter, J. R., & Nicoll, W. G. (2000). Adlerian brief therapy with individuals: Process and practice. *Journal of Individual Psychology, 56,* 31–44.

Bjorck, J. P. (2007). A Christian application of multimodal therapy. *Journal of Psychology and Christianity, 26,* 140–150.

Bloesch, D. (2007). *Spirituality old & new: Recovering authentic spiritual life.* Downers Grove, IL: InterVarsity.

Blomberg, J., Lazar, A., & Sandell, R. (2001). Long-term outcome of long-term psychoanalytically oriented therapies: First findings of the Stockholm Outcome of Psychotherapy and Psychoanalysis Study. *Psychotherapy Research, 11,* 361–382.

Boa, K. (2001). *Conformed to His image: Biblical and practical approaches to spiritual formation.* Grand Rapids: Zondervan.

Bohart, A. C. (1995). The person-centered psychotherapies. In A. S. Gurman & S. B. Messer (Eds.), *Essential psychotherapies* (pp. 85–127). New York: Guilford Press.

Bohart, A. C. (2003). Person-centered psychotherapy and related experiential approaches. In A. S. Gurman & S. B. Messer (Eds.), *Essential psychotherapies* (2nd ed., pp. 107–148). New York: Guilford Press.

Bohart, A. C., Elliot, R., Greenberg, L. S., & Watson, J. C. (2002). Empathy. In J. C. Norcross (Ed.), *Psychotherapy relationships that work* (pp. 89–108). New York: Oxford University Press.

Bohart, A. C., & Greenberg, L. S. (Eds.). (1997). *Empathy reconsidered: New directions in psychotherapy.* Washington, DC: American Psychological Association.

Bohart, A. C., & Tallman, K. (1999). *How clients make therapy work: The process of active self-healing.* Washington, DC: American Psychological Association.

Bolsinger, T. E. (2004). *It takes a church to raise a Christian: How the community of God transforms lives.* Grand Rapids: Brazos.

Book, H. E. (1998). *How to practice brief psychodynamic psychotherapy: The Core Conflictual Relationship Theme method.* Washington, DC: American Psychological Association.

Booth, L. (1991). *When God becomes a drug: Breaking the chains of religious addiction and abuse.* New York: Jeremy P. Tarcher/Pedigree Books.

Borduin, C. M., Schaeffer, C. M., & Heiblum, N. (2009). A randomized clinical trial of multisystemic therapy with juvenile sexual offenders: Effects on youth ecology and criminal activity. *Journal of Consulting and Clinical Psychology, 77*, 26–37.

Boscolo, L., Cecchin, G., Hoffman, L., & Penn, P. (1987). *Milan systemic family therapy: Conversations in theory and practice.* New York: Basic Books.

Boss, M. (1963). *Daseinanalysis and psychoanalysis.* New York: Basic Books.

Boszormenyi-Nagy, I., & Krasner, B. R. (1986). *Between give and take: A clinical guide to contextual therapy.* New York: Brunner/Mazel.

Boszormenyi-Nagy, I., & Spark, G. (1984). *Invisible loyalties: Reciprocity in intergenerational family therapy* (2nd ed.). New York: Brunner/Mazel.

Bottome, P. (1957). *Alfred Adler.* New York: Vanguard.

Bowen, M. (1978). *Family therapy in clinical practice.* New York: Jason Aronson.

Bowers, K. S., & Meichenbaum, D. (1984). *The unconscious reconsidered.* New York: Wiley.

Bowers, T. G., & Clum, G. A. (1988). Relative contribution of specific and nonspecific treatment effects: Meta-analysis of placebo-controlled behavior therapy research. *Psychological Bulletin, 103*, 315–323.

Bowman, C. E. (2005). The history and development of Gestalt therapy. In A. L. Woldt & S. M. Toman (Eds.), *Gestalt therapy: History, theory, and practice* (pp. 3–20). Thousand Oaks, CA: Sage.

Bozarth, J. D. (1996). A theoretical reconceptualization of the necessary and sufficient conditions for therapeutic change. *Person-Centered Journal, 3*, 44–51.

Bozarth, J. D., Zimring, F. M., & Tausch, R. (2002). Client-centered therapy: The evolution of a revolution. In D. J. Cain & J. Seeman (Eds.), *Humanistic psychotherapies: Handbook of research and practice* (pp. 147–188). Washington, DC: American Psychological Association.

Breggin, P. R. (1991). *Toxic psychiatry: Why therapy, empathy and love must replace the drugs, electroshock and biochemical theories of the "new psychiatry."* New York: St. Martins.

Breunlin, D. C., Schwartz, R. C., & MacKune-Karrer, B. (1997). *Metaframeworks: Transcending the models of family therapy* (Rev. ed.). San Francisco: Jossey-Bass.

Bright, J. I., Baker, K. D., & Neimeyer, R. A. (1999). Professional and paraprofessional group treatments for depression: A comparison of cognitive-behavioral and mutual support interventions. *Journal of Consulting and Clinical Psychology, 67*, 491–501.

Brown, C., & Augusta-Scott, T. (Eds.). (2007). *Narrative therapy: Making meaning, making lives.* Thousand Oaks, CA: Sage.

Brown, W. S., Murphy, N., & Malony, H. N. (Eds.). (1998). *Whatever happened to the soul? Scientific and theological portraits of human nature.* Minneapolis: Fortress.

Browning, D. S. (2006). *Christian ethics and the moral psychologies.* Grand Rapids: Eerdmans.

Browning, D. S., & Cooper, T. D. (2004). *Religious thought and the modern psychologies* (2nd ed.). Minneapolis: Fortress Press.

Brugger, E. C., & the Faculty of the Institute for the Psychological Sciences. (2008). Anthropological foundations for clinical psychology: A proposal. *Journal of Psychology and Theology, 36,* 3–15.

Budman, S. H., & Gurman, A. S. (1988). *Theory and practice of brief therapy.* New York: Guilford Press.

Bufford, R. K. (1981). *The human reflex: Behavioral psychology in biblical perspective.* San Francisco: Harper & Row.

Bufford, R. K. (1988). *Counseling and the demonic.* Dallas: Word.

Bufford, R. K. (1997). Consecrated counseling: Reflections on the distinctives of Christian counseling. *Journal of Psychology and Theology, 25,* 111–122.

Bugental, J. F. T. (1981). *The search for authenticity: An existential-analytic approach to psychotherapy* (Rev. ed.). New York: Holt, Rinehart & Winston.

Bugental, J. F. T. (1987). *The art of the psychotherapist.* New York: Norton.

Bugental, J. F. T. (1999). *Psychotherapy isn't what you think: Bringing the psychotherapeutic engagement into the living moment.* Phoenix: Zeig, Tucker.

Bugental, J. F. T., & Bracke, P. E. (1992). The future of existential-humanistic psychotherapy. *Psychotherapy, 29,* 28–33.

Buie, D. H. (1981). Empathy: Its nature and limitations. *Journal of the American Psychoanalytic Association, 29,* 281–307.

Burke, B. L, Arkowitz, H., & Dunn, C. (2002). The efficacy of motivational interviewing and its adaptations: What we know so far. In W. R. Miller & S. Rollnick (Eds.), *Motivational interviewing: Preparing people for change* (2nd ed., pp. 217–250). New York: Guilford Press.

Burke, B. L., Arkowitz, H., & Menchola, M. (2003). The efficacy of motivational interviewing: A meta-analysis of controlled clinical trials. *Journal of Consulting and Clinical Psychology, 71,* 843–861.

Burns, D. (1988). *Feeling good: The new mood therapy.* New York: Signet.

Butler, A. C., Chapman, J. E., Forman, E. M., & Beck, A. T. (2006). The empirical status of cognitive-behavioral therapy: A review of meta-analyses. *Clinical Psychology Review, 26,* 17–31.

Cain, D. J. (1987a). Carl Rogers' life in review. *Person-Centered Review*, 2, 476–506.

Cain, D. J. (1987b). Carl R. Rogers: The man, his vision, his impact. *Person-Centered Review*, 2, 283–288.

Cain, D. J. (2002a). Defining characteristics, history, and evolution of humanistic psychotherapies. In D. J. Cain & J. Seeman (Eds.), *Humanistic psychotherapies: Handbook of research and practice* (pp. 3–54). Washington, DC: American Psychological Association.

Cain, D. J. (2002b). Preface. In D. J. Cain & J. Seeman (Eds.), *Humanistic psychotherapies: Handbook of research and practice* (pp. xix–xxvi). Washington, DC: American Psychological Association.

Cain, D. J. (2010). *Person-centered psychotherapies*. Washington, DC: American Psychological Association.

Calhoun, A. A. (2005). *Spiritual disciplines handbook: Practices that transform us*. Downers Grove, IL: InterVarsity.

Calhoun, L. G., & Tedeschi, R. G. (Eds.). (2006). *Handbook of posttraumatic growth: Research and practice*. Mahwah, NJ: Erlbaum.

Carey, M. P., & Burish, T. G. (1987). Providing relaxation training to cancer chemotherapy patients: A comparison of three delivery techniques. *Journal of Consulting and Clinical Psychology*, 55, 732–737.

Carkhuff, R. R. (1971). *The development of human resources*. New York: Holt, Rinehart & Winston.

Carkhuff, R. R. (1987). *The art of helping* (6th ed.). Amherst, MA: Human Resource Development Press.

Carlson, D. E. (1976). Jesus' style of relating: The search for a biblical view of counseling. *Journal of Psychology and Theology*, 4, 181–192.

Carlson, J., & Englar-Carlson, M. (2008). Adlerian therapy. In J. Frew & M. D. Spiegler (Eds.), *Contemporary psychotherapies for a diverse world* (pp. 93–140). Boston: Lahaska Press.

Carlson, J., Sperry L., & Lewis, J. A. (2005). *Family therapy techniques: Integrating and tailoring treatment*. Belmont, CA: Brooks/Cole.

Carlson, J., Watts, R. E., & Maniacci, M. (2006). *Adlerian therapy: Theory and practice*. Washington, DC: American Psychological Association.

Carter, B., & McGoldrick, M. (Eds.). (2005). *The expanded family life cycle: Individual, family, and social perspectives* (3rd ed.). Boston: Allyn & Bacon.

Carter, J. D. (1975). Adams' theory of nouthetic counseling. *Journal of Psychology and Theology*, 3, 143–155.

Carter, J. D. (1996). Success without finality: The continuing dialogue of faith and psychology. *Journal of Psychology and Christianity*, 15, 116–122.

Carter, J. D., & Narramore, S. B. (1979). *The integration of psychology and theology*. Grand Rapids: Zondervan.

Cashwell, C. S., & Young, J. S. (Eds.). (2005). *Integrating spirituality and religion into counseling: A guide to competent practice*. Alexandria, VA: American Counseling Association.

Castonguay, L. G., & Beutler, L. E. (2006a). Common and unique principles of therapeutic change: What do we know and what do we need to know? In L. G. Castonguay & L. E. Beutler (Eds.), *Principles of therapeutic change that work* (pp. 353–369). New York: Oxford University Press.

Castonguay, L. G., & Beutler, L. E. (2006b). *Principles of therapeutic change that work*. New York: Oxford University Press.

Castonguay, L. G., Boswell, J. F., Constantino, M. J., Goldfried, M. R., & Hill, C. E. (2010). Training implications of harmful effects of psychological treatments. *American Psychologist, 65*, 34–49.

Caussade, J. P. de (1989). *The sacrament of the present moment*. New York: Harper & Row.

Cautela, J. R. (1971). Covert conditioning. In A. Jacobs & L. B. Sachs (Eds.), *The psychology of private events: Perspectives on covert response systems* (pp. 109–130). New York: Academic Press.

Centore, A. J. (2006). The ecounseling controversy: Advantages and disadvantages of telephone and Internet therapy. *Christian Counseling Today, 14* (4), 26–30.

Chambless, D. L., Baker, M. J., Baucom, D. H., Beutler, L. E., Calhoun, K. S., Crits-Christoph, P., et al. (1998). Update on empirically validated therapies, II. *Clinical Psychologist, 51*, 3–16.

Chambless, D. L., & Ollendick, T. H. (2001). Empirically supported psychological interventions: Controversies and evidence. *Annual Review of Psychology, 52*, 685–716.

Chan, S. (1998). *Spiritual theology: A systematic study of the Christian life*. Downers Grove, IL: InterVarsity.

Chan, S. (2006). *Liturgical theology: The church as worshiping community*. Downers Grove, IL: IVP Academic.

Chapelle, W. (2000). A series of progressive legal and ethical decision-making steps for using Christian spiritual interventions in psychotherapy. *Journal of Psychology and Theology, 28*, 43–53.

Chase, S. (2005). *The tree of life: Models of Christian prayer*. Grand Rapids: Baker Academic.

Chen, S. W.-H., & Davenport, D. S. (2005). Cognitive-behavioral therapy with Chinese American clients: Cautions and modifications. *Psychotherapy: Theory Research, Practice, Training, 42*, 101–110.

Christensen, A., Atkins, D. C., Baucom, B., & Yi, J. (2010). Marital status and satisfaction five years following a randomized clinical trial comparing traditional versus integrative behavioral couple therapy. *Journal of Consulting and Clinical Psychology, 78,* 225–235.

Christensen, A., Atkins, D. C., Berns, S., Wheeler, J., Baucom, D. H., & Simpson, L. E. (2004). Traditional versus integrative behavioral couple therapy for significantly and chronically distressed married couples. *Journal of Consulting and Clinical Psychology, 72,* 176–191.

Christensen, A., Atkins, D. C., Yi, J., Baucom, D. H., & George, W. H. (2006). Couple and individual adjustment for two years following a randomized clinical trial comparing traditional versus integrative behavioral couple therapy. *Journal of Consulting and Clinical Psychology, 74,* 1180–1191.

Christensen, A., & Jacobson, N. S. (1994). Who (or what) can do psychotherapy: The status and challenge of nonprofessional therapies. *Psychological Science, 6,* 8–14.

Christensen, A., & Jacobson, N. S. (2000). *Reconcilable differences.* New York: Guilford Press.

Christensen, O. C. (Ed.). (2004). *Adlerian family counseling* (3rd ed.). Minneapolis: Educational Media.

Cilliers, F. (2004). A person-centered view of diversity in South Africa. *Person-Centered Journal, 11* (1–2), 33–47.

Clark, D. A., & Beck, A. T. (2009). *Cognitive therapy of anxiety disorders: Science and practice.* New York: Guilford Press.

Clinton, T., Hart, A., & Ohlschlager, G. (Eds.). (2005). *Caring for people God's way.* Nashville: Thomas Nelson.

Clinton, T., & Hawkins, R. (2007). *Biblical counseling quick reference guide: Personal and emotional issues.* Nashville: Thomas Nelson.

Clinton, T., & Ohlschlager, G. (Eds.). (2002). *Competent Christian counseling* (Vol. 1). Colorado Springs: WaterBrook Press.

Clinton, T., & Ohlschlager, G. (2006). The maturation of Christian counseling: Reprise on a preferred future. *Christian Counseling Today, 14* (4), 32–35.

Cockrum, J. R. (1993). Teaching role playing and critiquing. *Journal of Reality Therapy, 12,* 70–75.

Coe, J. (1999). Beyond relationality to union: Musing toward a pneumadynamic approach to personality and psychotherapy. *Journal of Psychology and Christianity, 18,* 109–128.

Coe, J. H., & Hall, T. W. (2010). *Psychology in the Spirit: Contours of a transformational psychology.* Downers Grove, IL: IVP Academic.

Coelho, H. F., Canter, P. H., & Ernst, E. (2007). Mindfulness-based cognitive therapy: Evaluating current evidence and informing future research. *Journal of Consulting and Clinical Psychology, 75*, 1000–1005.

Coffman, S. J., Martell, C. R., Dimidjian, S., Gallop, R., & Hollon, S. D. (2007). Extreme nonresponse in cognitive therapy: Can behavioral activation succeed where cognitive therapy fails? *Journal of Consulting and Clinical Psychology, 75*, 531–541.

Cohn, H. W. (1997). *Existential thought and therapeutic practice: An introduction to existential psychotherapy*. London: Sage.

Collins, G. R. (1972). *Effective counseling*. Carol Stream, IL: Creation House.

Collins, G. R. (1976). *How to be a people helper*. Santa Ana, CA: Vision House.

Collins, G. R. (1993). *The biblical basis of Christian counseling for people helpers*. Colorado Springs: NavPress.

Collins, G. R. (2000). An integration view. In E. L. Johnson & S. L. Jones (Eds.), *Psychology and Christianity: Four views* (pp. 102–129). Downers Grove, IL: InterVarsity.

Collins, G. R. (2007). *Christian counseling: A comprehensive guide* (3rd ed.). Nashville: Thomas Nelson.

Combs, A. W. (1988). Some current issues for person-centered therapy. *Person-Centered Review, 3*, 263–276.

Combs, A. W. (1989). *A theory of therapy: Guidelines for counseling practice*. Newbury Park, CA: Sage.

Combs, A. W. (1999). *Being and becoming*. New York: Springer.

Cooper, J. W. (1989). *Body, soul and life everlasting: Biblical anthropology and the monism-dualism debate*. Grand Rapids: Eerdmans.

Cooper, M. (2003). *Existential therapies*. Thousand Oaks, CA: Sage.

Corcoran, K. J. (2006). *Rethinking human nature: A Christian materialist alternative to the soul*. Grand Rapids: Baker Academic.

Corey, G. (2009). *Theory and practice of counseling and psychotherapy* (8th ed.). Belmont, CA: Brooks/Cole.

Corey, G., Corey, M., & Callanan, P. (2007). *Issues and ethics in the helping professions* (7th ed.). Belmont, CA: Brooks/Cole.

Cormier, S., Nurius, P. S., & Osborn, C. (2009). *Interviewing and change strategies for helpers: Fundamental skills and cognitive behavioral interventions* (6th ed.). Belmont, CA: Brooks/Cole.

Corsini, R. J., & Wedding, D. (Eds.). (2008). *Current psychotherapies* (8th ed.). Belmont, CA: Brooks/Cole.

Crabb, L. J. (1977). *Effective biblical counseling*. Grand Rapids: Zondervan.

Crabb, L. J. (1987). *Understanding people: Deep longings for relationship*. Grand Rapids: Zondervan.

Crabb, L. (2003). *Soultalk: The language God longs for us to speak*. Brentwood, TN: Integrity.

Crabb, L. (2006). *The PAPA prayer: The prayer you've never prayed*. Brentwood, TN: Integrity.

Craske, M. G., & Barlow, D. H. (2008). Panic disorder and agoraphobia. In D. H. Barlow (Ed.), *Clinical handbook of psychological disorders: A step-by-step treatment manual* (4th ed., pp. 1–64). New York: Guilford Press.

Crumbaugh, J. C. (1968). Cross validation of Purpose-in-Life Test based on Frankl's concept. *Journal of Individual Psychology, 24,* 74–81.

Crumbaugh, J. C., & Henrion, R. (1988). PIL Test: Administration, interpretation, uses, theory and critique. *International Forum for Logotherapy Journal of Search for Meaning, 11,* 76–88.

Cuijpers, P., Van Straten, A., Andersson, G., & Van Oppen, P. (2008). Psychotherapy for depression in adults: A meta-analysis of comparative outcome studies. *Journal of Consulting and Clinical Psychology, 76,* 909–922.

Daldrup, R. J., Beutler, L. E., Engle, D., & Greenberg, L. S. (1988). *Focused expressive psychotherapy: Freeing the overcontrolled patient*. New York: Guilford Press.

Dattilio, F. M. (2002). Cognitive-behaviorism comes of age: Grounding symptomatic treatment in an existential approach. *Psychotherapy Networker, 26* (1), 75–78.

Dattilio, F. M. (2006). *Progressive muscle relaxation* (CD program). Available from http://www.dattilio.com.

Dattilio, F. M. (2009). *Cognitive-behavioral therapy with couples and families: A comprehensive guide for clinicians*. New York: Guilford Press.

Day, S. X. (2004). *Theory and design in counseling and psychotherapy*. Boston: Houghton Mifflin.

DeCarvalho, R. J. (1996). Rollo R. May (1909–1994). *Journal of Humanistic Psychology, 36,* 8–16.

DeCaussade, J. P. (1989). *The sacrament of the present moment*. New York: Harper & Row.

Decker, E. (2002). The Holy Spirit in counseling: A review of Christian counseling journal articles (1985–1999). *Journal of Psychology and Christianity, 21,* 21–28.

Deere, J. (1993). *Surprised by the power of the Spirit*. Grand Rapids: Zondervan.

Deere, J. (1996). *Surprised by the voice of God*. Grand Rapids: Zondervan.

De Jong, P., & Berg, I. K. (2008). *Interviewing for solutions* (3rd ed.). Belmont, CA: Brooks/Cole.

Demorest, A. (2005). *Psychology's grand theorists: How personal experience shaped professional ideas.* Mahwah, NJ: Erlbaum.

Denney, R. M., Aten, J. D., & Gingrich, F. C. (2008). Using spiritual self-disclosure in psychotherapy. *Journal of Psychology and Theology, 36,* 294–302.

Derlega, V. J., Winstead, B. A., & Jones, W. H. (2005). *Personality: Contemporary theory and research* (3rd ed.). Belmont, CA: Wadsworth.

DeRubeis, R. J., Brotman, M. A., & Gibbons, C. J. (2005). A conceptual and methodological analysis of the nonspecifics argument. *Clinical Psychology: Science and Practice, 12,* 174–183.

de Shazer, S. (1985). *Keys to solution in brief therapy.* New York: Norton.

de Shazer, S. (1988). *Clues: Investigating solutions in brief therapy.* New York: Norton.

de Shazer, S. (1991). *Putting differences to work.* New York: Norton.

de Shazer, S. (1994). *Words were originally magic.* New York: Norton.

de Shazer, S., & Dolan, Y. M. (with Korman, H., Trepper, T., McCullom, E., & Berg, I. K.). (2007). *More than miracles: The state of the art of solution-focused brief therapy.* New York: Haworth Press.

Dimeff, L. A., & Koerner, L. (Eds.). (2007). *Dialectical behavior therapy in clinical practice: Applications across disorders and settings.* New York: Guilford Press.

Dimidjian, S., & Hollon, S. D. (2010). How would we know if psychotherapy were harmful? *American Psychologist, 65,* 21–33.

Dimidjian, S., Hollon, S. D., Dobson, K. S., Schmaling, K. B., Kohlenberg, R. J., Addis, M. E., et al. (2006). Randomized trial of behavioral activation, cognitive therapy, and antidepressant medication in the acute treatment of adults with major depression. *Journal of Consulting and Clinical Psychology, 74,* 658–670.

Dimidjian, S., Martell, C. R., & Christensen, A. (2008). Integrative behavioral couple therapy. In A. S. Gurman (Ed.), *Clinical handbook of couple therapy* (4th ed., pp. 73–103). New York: Guilford Press.

Dinkmeyer, D. C., & Sperry, L. (2000). *Counseling and psychotherapy: An integrated Individual Psychology approach* (3rd ed.). Upper Saddle River, NJ: Merrill/Prentice-Hall.

Dinkmeyer, D. C., Dinkmeyer, D. C., Jr., & Sperry, L. (1987). *Adlerian counseling and psychotherapy* (2nd ed.). Columbus, OH: Merrill.

Dobson, D., & Dobson, K. S. (2009). *Evidence-based practice of cognitive-behavioral therapy.* New York: Guilford Press.

Dobson, K. S. (Ed.). (2009). *Handbook of cognitive-behavioral therapies* (3rd ed.). New York: Guilford Press.

Dobson, K. S., Hollon, S. D., Dimidjian, S., Schmaling, K. B., Kohlenberg, R. J., Gallop, R. J., et al. (2008). Randomized trial of behavioral activation, cognitive therapy, and antidepressant medication in the prevention of relapse and recurrence in major depression. *Journal of Consulting and Clinical Psychology, 76,* 468–477.

Dodds, L. (1999). The role of the Holy Spirit in personality growth and change. *Journal of Psychology and Christianity, 18,* 129–139.

Douglas, C. (2008). Analytical psychotherapy. In R. J. Corsini & D. Wedding (Eds.), *Current psychotherapies* (8th ed., pp. 107–140). Belmont, CA: Brooks/Cole.

Dowd, E. T., & Nielsen, S. L. (Eds.). (2006). *The psychologies in religion: Working with the religious client.* New York: Springer.

Dreikurs, R. (1967). *Psychodynamics, psychotherapy, and counseling: Collected papers.* Chicago: Alfred Adler Institute of Chicago.

Dreikurs, R. (1997). Holistic medicine. *Individual Psychology, 53,* 127–205.

Dreikurs, R., & Mosak, H. H. (1966). The tasks of life: I. Adler's three tasks. *Individual Psychologist, 4,* 18–22.

Dreikurs, R., & Mosak, H. H. (1967). The tasks of life: II. The fourth task. *Individual Psychologist, 4,* 51–55.

Dueck, A. C. (1995). *Between Jerusalem and Athens: Ethical perspectives on culture, religion, and psychotherapy.* Grand Rapids: Baker Academic.

Dueck, A., & Lee, C. (Eds.). (2005). *Why psychology needs theology: A radical-reformation perspective.* Grand Rapids: Eerdmans.

Dueck, A., & Reimer, K. (2009). *A peaceable psychology: Christian therapy in a world of many cultures.* Grand Rapids: Brazos.

Duncan, B. L., Miller, S. D., Wampold, B. E., & Hubble, M. A. (Eds.). (2010). *The heart and soul of change: Delivering what works in therapy* (2nd ed.). Washington, DC: American Psychological Association.

Dunn, R. L., & Schewebel, A. I. (1995). Meta-analytic review of marital therapy outcome research. *Journal of Family Psychology, 9,* 58–68.

D'Zurilla, T. J., & Goldfried, M. R. (1971). Problem solving and behavior modification. *Journal of Abnormal Psychology, 78,* 107–126.

Eck, B. E. (1996). Integrating the integrators: An organizing framework for a multifaceted process of integration. *Journal of Psychology and Christianity, 15,* 101–115.

Eck, B. E. (2002). An exploration of the therapeutic use of spiritual disciplines in clinical practice. *Journal of Psychology and Christianity, 21,* 266–280.

Edens, R. & Smyrl, T. (1994). Reducing disruptive classroom behaviors in physical education: A pilot study. *Journal of Reality Therapy, 13*, 40–44.

Egan, G. (1986). *The skilled helper: A systematic approach to effective helping* (3rd ed.). Monterey, CA: Brooks/Cole.

Egan, G. (2002). *The skilled helper* (7th ed.). Pacific Grove, CA: Brooks/Cole.

Egan, G. (2006). *Essentials of skilled helping: Managing problems, developing opportunities*. Belmont, CA: Brooks/Cole.

Egan, G. (2010). *The skilled helper: A problem-management and opportunity-development approach to helping* (9th ed.). Belmont, CA: Brooks/Cole.

Ellenberger, H. F. (1970). *The discovery of the unconscious*. New York: Basic Books.

Elliott, R., Greenberg, L. S., & Lietaer, G. (2004). Research on experiential psychotherapies. In M. J. Lambert (Ed.), *Bergin and Garfield's handbook of psychotherapy and behavior change* (5th ed., pp. 493–539). New York: Wiley.

Elliott, R., Watson, J. C., Goldman, R. N., & Greenberg, L. S. (2004). *Learning emotion-focused therapy: The process-experiential approach to change*. Washington, DC: American Psychological Association.

Ellis, A. (1960). There is no place for the concept of sin in psychotherapy. *Journal of Counseling Psychology, 7*, 188–192.

Ellis, A. (1962). *Reason and emotion in psychotherapy*. Secaucus, NJ: Lyle Stuart.

Ellis, A. (1970). Tribute to Alfred Adler. *Journal of Individual Psychology, 26*, 11–12.

Ellis, A. (1971). *The case against religion: A psychotherapist's view*. New York: Institute for Rational Living.

Ellis, A. (1973). *Humanistic psychotherapy: A rational-emotive approach*. New York: Institute for Rational Living.

Ellis, A. (1980). Psychotherapy and atheistic values: A response to A. E. Bergin's "Psychotherapy and religious values." *Journal of Consulting and Clinical Psychology, 48*, 635–639.

Ellis, A. (1993a). RET becomes REBT. *IRETletter, 1*, 4.

Ellis, A. (1993b). The advantages and disadvantages of self-help therapy materials. *Professional Psychology: Research and Practice, 24*, 335–339.

Ellis, A. (1996). *Better, deeper, and more enduring brief therapy: The rational emotive behavior therapy approach*. New York: Brunner/Mazel.

Ellis, A. (1999). Why rational-emotive therapy to rational-emotive behavior therapy? *Psychotherapy, 36*, 154–159.

Ellis, A. (2000). Can rational emotive behavior therapy (REBT) be effectively used with people who have devout beliefs in God and religion? *Professional Psychology: Research and Practice, 31*, 29–33.

Ellis, A. (2001). *Feeling better, getting better, staying better.* Atascadero, CA: Impact.

Ellis, A. (2004). *Rational emotive behavior therapy: It works for me—It can work for you.* Amherst, NY: Prometheus.

Ellis, A. (2008). Rational emotive behavior therapy. In R. Corsini & D. Wedding (Eds.), *Current psychotherapies* (8th ed., pp. 187–222). Belmont, CA: Brooks/Cole.

Ellis, A., & Dryden, W. (1997). *The practice of rational-emotive therapy* (Rev. ed.). New York: Springer.

Ellis, A., & Harper, R. A. (1997). *A guide to rational living* (3rd ed.). North Hollywood, CA: Melvin Powers (Wilshire Books).

Ellis, A., & MacLaren, C. (1998). *Rational emotive behavior therapy: A therapist's guide.* Atascadero, CA: Impact.

Emmelkamp, P. M. G. (2004). Behavior therapy with adults. In M. J. Lambert (Ed.), *Bergin and Garfield's handbook of psychotherapy and behavior change* (5th ed., pp. 393–446). New York: Wiley.

Engels, G. L., Garnefski, N., & Drekstra, R. F. W. (1993). Efficacy of rational-emotive therapy: A quantitative analysis. *Journal of Consulting and Clinical Psychology, 61*, 1083–1090.

Entwistle, D. N. (2010). *Integrative approaches to psychology and Christianity: An introduction to world-view issues, philosophical foundations, and models of integration* (2nd ed.). Eugene, OR: Cascade.

Epstein, N., & Baucom, D. H. (2002). *Enhanced cognitive-behavioral therapy for couples: A contextual approach.* Washington, DC: American Psychological Association.

Epstein, N., Schlesinger, S. E., & Dryden, W. (Eds.). (1988). *Cognitive-behavioral therapy with families.* New York: Brunner/Mazel.

Erikson, E. H. (1950). *Childhood and society.* New York: Norton.

Erikson, E. H. Extended by Erikson, J. M. (1997). *The life cycle completed.* New York: Norton.

Evans, C. S. (1986). The blessings of mental anguish. *Christianity Today, 30* (1), 26–29.

Evans, C. S. (1989). *Wisdom and humanness in psychology.* Grand Rapids: Baker Academic.

Evans, C. S. (1990). *Søren Kierkegaard's Christian psychology.* Grand Rapids: Zondervan.

Eysenck, H. (1952). The effects of psychotherapy: An evaluation. *Journal of Consulting Psychology, 16*, 319–324.

Eysenck, H. J. (1959). Learning theory and behaviour therapy. *Journal of Mental Science, 105*, 61–75.

Eysenck, H. J. (Ed.). (1960). *Behaviour therapy and the neuroses*. London: Pergamon Press.

Eysenck, H. J. (1990). *Rebel with a cause*. London: W. H. Allen.

Eysenck, H. J., & Rachman, S. (1965). *The causes and cures of neurosis*. London: Routledge & Kegan Paul.

Fairbairn, W. R. D. (1954). *An object relations theory of the personality*. New York: Basic Books.

Fairburn, C. G. (2008). *Cognitive behavior therapy and eating disorders*. New York: Guilford Press.

Fall, K. A., Holden, J. M., & Marquis, A. (2004). *Theoretical models of counseling and psychotherapy*. New York: Brunner-Routledge.

Farber, B. A. (1996). Introduction. In B. A. Farber, D. C. Brink, & P. M. Raskin (Eds.), *The psychotherapy of Carl Rogers: Cases and commentary* (pp. 1–14). New York: Guilford Press.

Farber, B. A., & Lane, J. (2002). Positive regard. In J. C. Norcross (Ed.), *Psychotherapy relationships that work* (pp. 175–194). New York: Oxford University Press.

Farnsworth, K. E. (1996). The devil sends errors in pairs. *Journal of Psychology and Christianity, 15*, 123–132.

Farson, R. (1975). Carl Rogers, quiet revolutionary. In R. I. Evans (Ed.), *Carl Rogers: The man and his ideas* (pp. xxviii–xliii). New York: Dutton.

Fee, G. D. (1994). *God's empowering presence: The Holy Spirit in the letters of Paul*. Peabody, MA: Hendrickson.

Finch, J. G. (1982). *Nishkamakarma*. Pasadena, CA: Integration Press.

Finch, J. G., & Van Dragt, B. (1999). Existential psychology and psychotherapy. In D. G. Benner & P. C. Hill (Eds.), *Baker encyclopedia of psychology and counseling* (2nd ed., pp. 412–416). Grand Rapids: Baker Academic.

Finley, J. (2004). *Christian meditation: Experiencing the presence of God*. San Francisco: HarperSanFrancisco.

Finney, J. R., & Malony, H. N. (1985a). An empirical study of contemplative prayer as an adjunct to psychotherapy. *Journal of Psychology and Theology, 13*, 284–290.

Finney, J. R., & Malony, H. N. (1985b). Contemplative prayer and its use in psychotherapy: A theoretical model. *Journal of Psychology and Theology, 13*, 172–181.

Finney, J. R., & Malony, H. N. (1985c). Empirical studies of Christian prayer: A review of the literature. *Journal of Psychology and Theology, 13*, 104–115.

Fisher, S., & Greenberg, R. P. (1996). *Freud scientifically reappraised: Testing the theories and therapy*. New York: Wiley.

Fishman, D. B., & Franks, C. M. (1992). Evolution and differentiation within behavior therapy: A theoretical and epistemological review. In D. K. Freedheim (Ed.), *History of psychotherapy: A century of change* (pp. 159–196). Washington, DC: American Psychological Association.

Flynn, M., & Gregg, D. (1993). *Inner healing.* Downers Grove, IL: InterVarsity.

Foa, E. B., Hembree, E. A., Cahill, S. P., Ranch, S. A. M., Riggs, D. S., Feeny, N. C., & Yadin, E. (2005). Randomized trial of prolonged exposure for posttraumatic stress disorder with and without cognitive restructuring: Outcome at academic and community clinics. *Journal of Consulting and Clinical Psychology, 73,* 953–964.

Foster, R. J. (1978). *Celebration of discipline.* San Francisco: Harper & Row.

Foster, R. J. (1988). *Celebration of discipline* (Rev. ed.). San Francisco: Harper & Row.

Foster, R. J. (1992). *Prayer: Finding the heart's true home.* San Francisco: HarperSanFrancisco.

Foster, R. J. (1998). *Streams of living water: Celebrating the great traditions of Christian faith.* New York: HarperSanFrancisco.

Foster, R. J., & Beebe, G. D. (2009). *Longing for God: Seven paths of Christian devotion.* Downers Grove, IL: InterVarsity.

Frame, M. W. (2003). *Integrating religion and spirituality into counseling: A comprehensive approach.* Pacific Grove, CA: Brooks/Cole.

Frank, J. D. (1982). Therapeutic components shared by all psychotherapies. In J. H. Harvey & M. M. Parks (Eds.), *Psychotherapy research and behavior change* (Master Lecture Series, vol. 1, pp. 5–37). Washington, DC: American Psychological Association.

Frankl, V. (1963). *Man's search for meaning: An introduction to logotherapy.* Boston: Beacon.

Frankl, V. (1969). *The will to meaning: Foundations and applications of logotherapy.* New York: New American Library.

Frankl, V. (1978). *The unheard cry for meaning.* New York: Simon & Schuster.

Frankl, V. (1997). *Viktor Frankl—Recollections: An autobiography.* New York: Plenum.

Frazier, R. E., & Hansen, N. D. (2009). Religious/spiritual psychotherapy behaviors: Do we do what we believe to be important? *Professional Psychology: Research and Practice, 40,* 81–87.

Freedman, J., & Combs, G. (2002). *Narrative therapy with couples . . . and a whole lot more: A collection of papers, essays, and exercises.* Adelaide, Australia: Dulwich Centre Publications.

Freedman, J., & Combs, G. (2008). Narrative couple therapy. In A. S. Gurman (Ed.), *Clinical handbook of couple therapy* (4th ed., pp. 229–258). New York: Guilford Press.

Freeman, J., Epston, D., & Lobovits, D. (1997). *Playful approaches to serious problems: Narrative therapy with children and their families*. New York: Norton.

Freud, A. (1936). *The ego and mechanisms of defense*. New York: International Universities Press.

Freud, A. (1965). Normality and pathology in childhood: Assessments of development. In *Writings* (Vol. 6). New York: International Universities Press.

Freud, S. (1900). *The interpretation of dreams*. (Standard edition, vol. 4). London: Hogarth Press.

Freud, S. (1927). *The future of an illusion*. New York: Norton.

Freud, S., & Breuer, J. (1895). *Studies on hysteria*. London: Hogarth Press.

Friedlander, M., & Tuason, Ma. T. (2000). Processes and outcomes in couples and family therapy. In S. D. Brown & R. W. Lents (Eds.), *Handbook of counseling psychology* (3rd ed., pp. 797–824). New York: Wiley.

Friedman, E. H. (1985). *Generation to generation: Family process in church and synagogue*. New York: Guilford Press.

Frisch, M. B. (2006). *Quality of life therapy: Applying a life satisfaction approach to positive psychology and cognitive therapy*. Hoboken, NJ: Wiley.

Galatzer-Levy, R. M., Bachrach, H., Skolnikoff, A., & Waldron, S. (2000). *Does psychoanalysis work?* New Haven, CT: Yale University Press.

Garzon, F. (2005). Interventions that apply Scripture in psychotherapy. *Journal of Psychology and Theology, 33*, 113–121.

Garzon, F., & Burkett, L. (2002). Healing of memories: Models, research, future directions. *Journal of Psychology and Christianity, 21*, 42–49.

Garzon, F., & Tilley, K. A. (2009). Do lay Christian counseling approaches work? What we currently know. *Journal of Psychology and Christianity, 28*, 130–140.

Gass, S. C. (1984). Orthodox Christian values related to psychotherapy and mental health. *Journal of Psychology and Theology, 12*, 230–237.

Gawrysiak, M., Nicholas, C., & Hopko, D. R. (2009). Behavioral activation for moderately depressed university students: Randomized controlled trial. *Journal of Counseling Psychology, 56*, 468–475.

Gay, P. (1988). *Freud: A life for our time*. New York: Norton.

Gendlin, E. T. (1996). *Focusing-oriented psychotherapy: A manual of the experiential method*. New York: Guilford Press.

Germer, C. K., Siegel, R. D., & Fulton, P. R. (Eds.). (2005). *Mindfulness and psychotherapy*. New York: Guilford Press.

Getz, G. (1976). *Measure of a family*. Ventura, CA: Regal.

Giesen-Bloo, J., Van Dyck, R., Spinhoven, P., Van Tilburg, W., Dirksen, C., Van Asselt, T., et al. (2006). Outpatient psychotherapy for borderline personality disorder: Randomized trial of schema-focused therapy versus transference-focused psychotherapy. *Archives of General Psychiatry, 63*, 649–658.

Gilbert, M. G., & Brock, R. T. (Eds.). (1985). *The Holy Spirit and counseling*, Vol. 1: *Theology and theory*. Peabody, MA: Hendrickson.

Gilbert, M. G., & Brock, R. T. (Eds.). (1988). *The Holy Spirit and counseling*, Vol. 2: *Principles and practice*. Peabody, MA: Hendrickson.

Gilbert, P., & Leahy, R. L. (Eds.). (2007). *The therapeutic relationship in the cognitive behavioral therapies*. New York: Routledge.

Gilliam, A. (2004). The efficacy of William Glasser's reality/choice theory with domestic violence perpetrators: A treatment outcome study. (Doctoral dissertation.) *Dissertation Abstracts International*, Section B: *The Sciences and Engineering, 65* (1–B), 436.

Gladding, S. T. (2007). *Family therapy: History, theory, and practice* (4th ed.). Upper Saddle River, NJ: Merrill/Prentice Hall.

Glass, C. R., & Arnkoff, D. B. (1992). Behavior therapy. In D. K. Freedheim (Ed.), *History of psychotherapy: A century of change* (pp. 587–628). Washington, DC: American Psychological Association.

Glass, R. M. (2008). Psychodynamic psychotherapy and research evidence: Bambi survives Godzilla? *Journal of the American Medical Association, 300*, 1587–1589.

Glasser, N. (Ed.). (1980). *What are you doing? How people are helped through reality therapy*. New York: Harper & Row.

Glasser, N. (Ed.). (1989). *Control theory in the practice of reality therapy: Case studies*. New York: Harper & Row.

Glasser, W. (1961). *Mental health or mental illness?* New York: Harper & Row.

Glasser W. (1965). *Reality therapy: A new approach to psychiatry*. New York: Harper & Row.

Glasser, W. (1969). *Schools without failure*. New York: Harper & Row.

Glasser, W. (1976). *Positive addiction*. New York: Harper & Row.

Glasser, W. (1981). *Stations of the mind*. New York: Harper & Row.

Glasser, W. (1985). *Control theory: A new explanation of how we control our lives*. New York: Harper & Row.

Glasser, W. (1986). *Control theory in the classroom*. New York: Harper & Row.

Glasser, W. (1990). *The basic concepts of reality therapy* [chart]. Canoga Park, CA: Institute for Reality Therapy.

Glasser, W. (1998a). *Choice theory: A new psychology of personal freedom.* New York: HarperCollins.

Glasser, W. (1998b). *The quality school* (Rev. ed.). New York: Harper & Row.

Glasser, W. (2000a). *Every student can succeed.* Chatsworth, CA: William Glasser Institute.

Glasser, W. (2000b). *Reality therapy in action.* New York: HarperCollins.

Glasser, W. (2001). *Counseling with choice theory: The new reality therapy.* New York: HarperCollins.

Glasser, W. (2002). *Unhappy teenagers: A way for parents and teachers to reach them.* New York: HarperCollins.

Glasser, W. (2003). *Warning: Psychiatry can be hazardous to your mental health.* New York: HarperCollins.

Glasser, W. (2005). *Defining mental health as a public health problem: A new leadership role for the helping professions.* Chatsworth, CA: William Glasser Institute.

Glasser, W., & Glasser, C. (1999). *The language of choice theory.* New York: HarperCollins.

Glasser, W., & Glasser, C. (2000). *Getting together and staying together.* New York: HarperCollins.

Glasser, W., & Zunin, L. M. (1979). Reality therapy. In R. Corsini (Ed.), *Current psychotherapies* (2nd ed., pp. 302–339). Itasca, IL: F. E. Peacock.

Goldenberg, I., & Goldenberg, H. (2008a). Family therapy. In R. J. Corsini & S. Wedding (Eds.), *Current psychotherapies* (8th ed., pp. 402–436). Belmont, CA: Brooks/Cole.

Goldenberg, I., & Goldenberg, H. (2008b). *Family therapy: An overview* (7th ed.). Belmont, CA: Brooks/Cole.

Goldfried, M. (1971). Systematic desensitization as training in self-control. *Journal of Consulting and Clinical Psychology, 37,* 228–234.

Goldfried, M. R., & Davison, G. (1994). *Clinical behavior therapy* (Expanded ed.). New York: Wiley.

Goldfried, M. R., & Merbaum, M. (Eds.). (1973). *Behavior change through self-control.* New York: Holt, Rinehart & Winston.

Gomes-Schwartz, B. (1978). Effective ingredients in psychotherapy: Prediction of outcome from process variables. *Journal of Consulting and Clinical Psychology, 46,* 1023–1035.

Gonsiorek, J. C., Richards, P. S., Pargament, K. I., & McMinn, M. R. (2009). Ethical challenges and opportunities at the edge: Incorporating spirituality and religion into psychotherapy. *Professional Psychology: Research and Practice, 40,* 385–395.

Gonzalez, J. E., Nelson, J. R., Gutkin, T. B., Saunders, A., Galloway, A., & Shwery, C. (2004). Rational emotive therapy with children and adolescents: A meta-analysis. *Journal of Emotional and Behavioral Disorders*, 12, 222–235.

Gotham, H. J. (2006). Advancing the implementation of evidence-based practices into clinical practice: How do we get there from here? *Professional Psychology: Research and Practice*, 37, 606–613.

Gottman, J. M. (1994a). *What predicts divorce?* Hillsdale, NJ: Erlbaum.

Gottman, J. M. (1994b). *Why marriages succeed or fail*. New York: Simon & Schuster.

Gottman, J. M. (1999). *The marriage clinic: A scientifically based marital therapy*. New York: Norton.

Gottman, J. M., & Gottman, J. S. (2007). *And baby makes three*. New York: Crown.

Gottman, J. M., & Gottman, J. S. (2008). Gottman method couple therapy. In A. S. Gurman (Ed.), *Clinical handbook of couple therapy* (4th ed., pp. 138–164). New York: Guilford Press.

Gottman, J. M., & Silver, N. (1999). *The seven principles for making marriage work*. New York: Crown.

Gould, W. B. (1993). *Viktor E. Frankl: Life with meaning*. Pacific Grove, CA: Brooks/Cole.

Grawe, K., Donati, R., & Bernauer, F. (1998). *Psychotherapy in transition*. Seattle: Hogrefe & Huber.

Green, J. B. (2008). *Body, soul, and human life: The nature of humanity in the Bible*. Grand Rapids: Baker Academic.

Green, J. B., & Palmer, S. L. (Eds.). (2005). *In search of the soul: Four views of the mind-body problem*. Downers Grove, IL: InterVarsity.

Greenberg, J. R. (2001). The analyst's participation: A new look. *Journal of the American Psychoanalytic Association*, 49, 417–426.

Greenberg, J. R., & Mitchell, S. A. (1983). *Object relations in psychoanalytic theory*. Cambridge, MA: Harvard University Press.

Greenberg, L. S. (2002). *Emotion-focused therapy: Coaching clients to work through their feelings*. Washington, DC: American Psychological Association.

Greenberg, L. S., Elliott, R., & Lietaer, G. (1994). Research on experiential psychotherapy. In A. E. Bergin & S. L. Garfield (Eds.), *Handbook of psychotherapy and behavior change* (4th ed., pp. 509–539). New York: Wiley.

Greenberg, L. S., & Foerster, F. S. (1996). Task analysis exemplified: The process of resolving unfinished business. *Journal of Consulting and Clinical Psychology*, 64, 439–446.

Greenberg, L. S., & Goldman, R. N. (2008). *Emotion-focused couples therapy: The dynamics of emotion, love, and power.* Washington, DC: American Psychological Association.

Greenberg, L. S., & Johnson, S. M. (1988). *Emotionally focused therapy for couples.* New York: Guilford Press.

Greenberg, L. S., Korman, L. M., & Paivio, S. C. (2002). Emotion in humanistic psychotherapy. In D. J. Cain & J. Seeman (Eds.), *Humanistic psychotherapies: Handbook of research and practice* (pp. 499–530). Washington, DC: American Psychological Association.

Greenberg, L. S., & Malcolm, W. (2002). Resolving unfinished business: Relating process to outcome. *Journal of Consulting and Clinical Psychology, 70,* 406–416.

Greenberg, L. S., Rice, L. N., & Elliott, R. (1993). *Facilitating emotional change: The moment-by-moment process.* New York: Guilford Press.

Greenberg, L. S., & Watson, J. C. (2006). *Emotion-focused therapy for depression.* Washington, DC: American Psychological Association.

Greenberg, L. S., Watson, J. C., & Lietaer, G. (Eds.). (1998). *Handbook of experiential psychotherapy.* New York: Guilford Press.

Greenberger, D., & Padesky, C. A. (1995). *Mind over mood: Change how you feel by changing the way you think.* New York: Guilford Press.

Greggo, S. P. (2008). *Trekking toward wholeness: A resource for care group leaders.* Downers Grove, IL: IVP Academic.

Griffith, J. L., & Griffith, M. E. (2001). *Encountering the sacred in psychotherapy.* New York: Guilford Press.

Gross, B. H. (2001). Informed consent. *Annals of the American Psychotherapy Association, 4,* 24.

Grounds, V. (1976). *Emotional problems and the gospel.* Grand Rapids: Zondervan.

Grudem, W. (1994). *Systematic theology: An introduction to biblical doctrine.* Grand Rapids: Zondervan.

Gurman, A. S. (2002). Brief integrative marital therapy: A depth-behavioral approach. In A. S. Gurman and N. S. Jacobson (Eds.), *Clinical handbook of couple therapy* (3rd ed., pp. 180–220). New York: Guilford Press.

Gurman, A. S. (2003). Marital therapies. In A. S. Gurman & S. B. Messer (Eds.), *Essential psychotherapies: Theory and practice* (2nd ed., pp. 463–514). New York: Guilford Press.

Gurman, A. S. (Ed.). (2008a). *Clinical handbook of couple therapy* (4th ed.). New York: Guilford Press.

Gurman, A. S. (2008b). Integrative couple therapy: A depth-behavioral approach. In A. S. Gurman (Ed.), *Clinical handbook of couple therapy* (4th ed., pp. 383–423). New York: Guilford Press.

Gurman, A. S., & Fraenkel, P. (2002). The history of couple therapy: A millennial review. *Family Process, 41*, 199–260.

Gurman, A. S., & Jacobson, N. S. (Eds.). (2002). *Clinical handbook of couple therapy* (3rd ed.). New York: Guilford Press.

Gurman, A. S., & Kniskern, D. P. (Eds.). (1981). *Handbook of family therapy* (Vol. 1). New York: Brunner/Mazel.

Gurman, A. S., & Kniskern, D. P. (Eds.). (1991). *Handbook of family therapy* (Vol. 2). New York: Brunner/Mazel.

Gurman, A. S., Kniskern, D. P., & Pinsof, W. M. (1986). Process and outcome research in family and marital therapy. In A. E. Bergin & S. L. Garfield (Eds.), *Handbook of psychotherapy and behavior change* (3rd ed., pp. 565–624). New York: Wiley.

Gurman, A. S., & Messer, S. B. (Eds.). (2003). *Essential psychotherapies: Theory and practice.* (2nd ed.). New York: Guilford Press.

Guttmann, D. (1996). *Logotherapy for the helping professional: Meaningful social work.* New York: Springer.

Guy, J. D. (1987). *The personal life of the psychotherapist.* New York: Wiley.

Hackney, C. H. (2007). Possibilities for a Christian positive psychology. *Journal of Psychology and Theology, 35*, 211–221.

Haden, N. (1987). Qoheleth and the problem of alienation. *Christian Scholar's Review, 17*, 52–66.

Haggbloom, S. J., Warnick, R., Warnick, J. E., Jones, V. K., Yarbrough, G. L., Russell, T. M., et al. (2002). The 100 most eminent psychologists of the 20th century. *Review of General Psychology, 6*, 139–152.

Hahlweg, K., & Markman, H. J. (1988). Effectiveness of behavioral marital therapy: Empirical status of behavioral techniques in preventing and alleviating marital distress. *Journal of Consulting and Clinical Psychology, 56*, 440–447.

Haley, J. (1963). *Strategies of psychotherapy.* New York: Grune & Stratton.

Haley, J. (1973). *Uncommon therapy: The psychiatric techniques of Milton H. Erickson, M.D.* New York: Norton.

Haley, J. (1976). *Problem-solving therapy: New strategies for effective family therapy.* San Francisco: Josey-Bass.

Haley, J., & Richeport-Haley, M. (2003). *The art of strategic therapy.* New York: Brunner-Routledge.

Haley, J., & Richeport-Haley, M. (2007). *Directive family therapy.* New York: Haworth Press.

Hall, G. C. N. (2001). Psychotherapy research with ethnic minorities: Empirical, ethical, and conceptual issues. *Journal of Consulting and Clinical Psychology*, 69, 502–510.

Hall, M. E. L., & Hall, T. W. (1997). Integration in the therapy room: An overview of the literature. *Journal of Psychology and Theology*, 25, 86–101.

Halligan, F. G. (1983). Reaction depression and chronic illness: Counseling patients and their families. *The Personnel and Guidance Journal*, 61, 401–406.

Hamilton, J. C. (2000). Construct validity of the core conditions and factor structure of the Client Evaluation of Counselor Scale. *Person-Centered Journal*, 7, 40–51.

Hannah, B. (1976). *Jung: His life's work. A biographical memoir*. New York: Putnam.

Hansen, N. B., Lambert, M. J., & Forman, E. M. (2002). The psychotherapy dose-response effect and its implications for treatment delivery services. *Clinical Psychology: Science and Practice*, 9, 329–343.

Hargrave, T. D. (1994). *Families and forgiveness: Healing wounds in the intergenerational family life*. New York: Brunner/Mazel.

Hargrave, T. D., & Pfitzer, F. (2003). *The new contextual therapy: Guiding the power of give and take*. New York: Brunner-Routledge.

Harris, A. S. (1996). *Living with paradox: An introduction to Jungian psychology*. Albany, NY: Brooks/Cole.

Hart, A. D. (1995). *Adrenaline and stress* (Rev. ed.). Dallas: Word.

Hart, A. D. (1999). *The anxiety cure*. Nashville: Word.

Hart, A. D., & Hart-Weber, C. (2006). Positive psychology and strength-based therapy: A new paradigm. *Christian Counseling Today*, 14 (4), 14–18.

Hartmann, H. (1958). *Ego psychology and the problem of adaptation*. New York: International Universities Press.

Hathaway, W. L., & Ripley, J. S. (2009). Ethical concerns around spirituality and religion in clinical practice. In J. D. Aten & M. M. Leach (Eds.), *Spirituality and the therapeutic process: A comprehensive resource from intake to termination* (pp. 25–52). Washington, DC: American Psychological Association.

Hayes, S. C., Follette, V. M., & Linehan, M. M. (Eds.). (2004). *Mindfulness and acceptance: Expanding the cognitive-behavioral tradition*. New York: Guilford Press.

Hayes, S. C., Levin, M., Plumb, J., Boulanger, J., & Pistorello, J. (in press). Acceptance and commitment therapy and contextual behavioral science: Examining the progress of a distinctive model of behavioral and cognitive therapy. *Behavior Therapy*.

Hayes, S. C., Luoma, J. B., Bond, F. W., Masuda, A. L., & Lillis, J. (2006). Acceptance and commitment therapy: Model, processes, and outcomes. *Behaviour Research and Therapy*, *44*, 1–25.

Hayes, S. C., & Smith, S. (2005). *Get out of your mind and into your life: The new acceptance and commitment therapy*. Oakland, CA: New Harbinger Publications.

Hayes, S. C., & Strosahl, K. D. (Eds.). (2004). *A practical guide to acceptance and commitment therapy*. New York: Springer.

Hayes. S. C., Strosahl, K. D., & Wilson, K. G. (1999). *Acceptance and commitment therapy: An experiential approach to behavior change*. New York: Guilford Press.

Hayford, J. (2005). Spirit-formed in purity and power. *Spectrum*, *6* (2), 5–6.

Hays, P. A. (2009). Integrating evidence-based practice, cognitive-behavior therapy, and multicultural therapy: Ten steps for culturally competent practice. *Professional Psychology: Research and Practice*, *40*, 354–360.

Hays, P. A., & Iwamasa, G. Y. (Eds.). (2006). *Culturally responsive cognitive-behavioral therapy: Assessment, practice, and supervision*. Washington, DC: American Psychological Association.

Heidegger, M. (1962). *Being and time*. New York: Harper & Row.

Helgeson, V. S., Reynolds, K. A., & Tomich, P. L. (2006). A meta-analytic review of benefit finding and growth. *Journal of Consulting and Clinical Psychology*, *74*, 797–816.

Henggeler, S. W., Schoenwald, S. K., Borduin, C. M., Rowland, M. D., & Cunningham, P. B. (1998). *Multisystemic treatment of antisocial behavior in children and adolescents*. New York: Guilford Press.

Henggeler, S. W., Schoenwald, S. K., Borduin, C. M., Rowland, M. D., & Cunningham, P. B. (2009). *Multisystemic therapy for antisocial behavior in children and adolescents* (2nd ed.). New York: Guilford Press.

Hesselgrave, D. (1984). *Counseling cross-culturally*. Grand Rapids: Baker Academic.

Hettema, J., Steele, J., & Miller, W. R. (2005). Motivational interviewing. *Annual Review of Clinical Psychology*, *1*, 91–111.

Hill, K. (1987). Meta-analysis of paradoxical interventions. *Psychotherapy*, *24*, 266–270.

Hill, P. C., & Pargament, K. I. (2003). Advances in the conceptualization and measurement of religion and spirituality: Implications for physical and mental health research. *American Psychologist*, *58*, 64–74.

Hill, P. C., Pargament, K. I., Hood, R. W., Jr., McCullough, M. E., Swyers, J. P., Larson, D. B., & Zinnbauer, B. J. (2000). Conceptualizing religion and spirituality: Points of commonality, points of departure. *Journal for the Theory of Social Behavior, 30,* 51–77.

Hillmann, M. (2004). *Viktor E. Frankl's existential analysis and logotherapy.* New York: Wiley.

Hoffman, E. (1994). *The drive for self: Alfred Adler and the founding of Individual Psychology.* Reading, MA: Addison-Wesley.

Hoffman, L. W., & Strawn, B. D. (2009). Normative thoughts, normative feelings, normative actions: A Protestant, relational psychoanalytic reply to E. Christian Brugger and the faculty of IPS. *Journal of Psychology and Theology, 37,* 125–133.

Hoffman, M. (2007). From libido to love: Relational psychoanalysis and the redemption of sexuality. *Journal of Psychology and Theology, 35,* 74–82.

Hofmann, S. G., Sawyer, A. T., Witt, A. A., & Oh, D. (2010). The effect of mindfulness-based therapy on anxiety and depression: A meta-analytic review. *Journal of Consulting and Clinical Psychology, 78,* 169–183.

Hollon, S. D., & Beck, A. T. (2004). Cognitive and cognitive behavioral therapies. In M. J. Lambert (Ed.), *Bergin and Garfield's handbook of psychotherapy and behavior change* (5th ed., pp. 447–492). New York: Wiley.

Hook, J. N., Worthington, E. L., Jr., Davis, D. E., Jennings, D. J., II, Gartner, A. L., & Hook, J. P. (2010). Empirically supported religious and spiritual therapies. *Journal of Clinical Psychology, 66,* 46–72.

Houston, J. (1989). *The transforming friendship: A guide to prayer.* Oxford: Lion.

Howard, E. B. (2008). *The Brazos introduction to Christian spirituality.* Grand Rapids: Brazos.

Hoyt, M. F. (2008). Solution-focused couple therapy. In A. S. Gurman (Ed.), *Clinical handbook of couple therapy* (4th ed., pp. 259–298). New York: Guilford Press.

Hubble, M. A., Duncan, B. L., & Miller, S. D. (Eds.). (1999). *The heart and soul of change: What works in therapy.* Washington, DC: American Psychological Association.

Hull, C. (1943). *Principles of behavior.* New York: Appleton-Century-Crofts.

Humphrey, K. (1986). Laura Perls: A biographical sketch. *Gestalt Journal, 9* (1), 5–11.

Hunsinger, D. v. D. (2006). *Pray without ceasing: Revitalizing pastoral care.* Grand Rapids: Eerdmans.

Hunsley, J., & Lee, C. M. (2007). Research-informed benchmarks for psychological treatments: Efficacy studies, effectiveness studies, and beyond. *Professional Psychology: Research and Practice, 38,* 21–33.

Huppert, J. D., Bufka, L. F., Barlow, D. H., Gorman, J. M., Shear, M. K., & Woods, S. W. (2001). Therapists, therapist variables, and cognitive-behavioral therapy outcome in a multicenter trial for panic disorder. *Journal of Consulting and Clinical Psychology, 69,* 747–755.

Hurding, R. F. (1985). *The tree of healing: Psychological and biblical foundations for counseling and pastoral care.* Grand Rapids: Zondervan.

Hurding, R. F. (1992). *The Bible and counselling.* London: Hodder & Stoughton.

Hurley, J. B., & Berry, J. T. (1997a). The relation of Scripture and psychology in counseling from a pro-integration position. *Journal of Psychology and Christianity, 16,* 323–345.

Hurley, J. B., & Berry, J. T. (1997b). Response to Welch and Powlison. *Journal of Psychology and Christianity, 16,* 350–362.

Hutchison, J. C. (2005). *Thinking right when things go wrong: Biblical wisdom for surviving tough times.* Grand Rapids: Kregel.

Hycner, R., & Jacobs, L. (1995). *The healing relationship in Gestalt therapy: A dialogic self psychology approach.* Highland, NY: Gestalt Journal Press.

Ingersoll, R. E. (2005). Gestalt therapy and spirituality. In A. L. Woldt & S. M. Toman (Eds.), *Gestalt therapy: History, theory, and practice* (pp. 133–150). Thousand Oaks, CA: Sage.

Ingram, J. (1996). Psychological aspects of the filling of the Holy Spirit: A preliminary model of post-redemptive personality functioning. *Journal of Psychology and Theology, 24,* 104–113.

Jacobson, E. (1938). *Progressive relaxation.* Chicago: University of Chicago Press.

Jacobson, N. S., & Christensen, A. (1998). *Acceptance and change in couple therapy: A therapist's guide to transforming relationships.* New York: Norton.

Jacobson, N. S., & Margolin, G. (1979). *Marital therapy: Strategies based on social learning and behavior exchange principles.* New York: Brunner/Mazel.

Jeeves, M., & Brown, W. S. (2009). *Neuroscience, psychology, and religion: Illusions, delusions, and realities about human nature.* West Conshohocken, PA: Templeton Press.

Jenaro, C., Flores, N., & Arias, B. (2007). Burnout and coping in human service practitioners. *Professional Psychology: Research and Practice, 38,* 80–87.

Johnson, C. B. (1987). Religious resources in psychotherapy. In D. G. Benner (Ed.), *Psychotherapy in Christian perspective* (pp. 31–36). Grand Rapids: Baker Academic.

Johnson, E. L. (1997). Christ, the Lord of psychology. *Journal of Psychology and Theology*, *24*, 11–27.

Johnson, E. L. (2007). *Foundations for soul care: A Christian psychology proposal*. Downers Grove, IL: IVP Academic.

Johnson, E. L. (Ed.). (2010). *Psychology and Christianity: Five views*. Downers Grove: IVP Academic.

Johnson, E. L., & Jones, S. L. (Eds.). (2000). *Psychology and Christianity: Four views*. Downers Grove, IL: InterVarsity.

Johnson, R. B. (1999). Myers-Briggs Type Indicator. In D. G. Benner & P. C. Hill (Eds.), *Baker encyclopedia of psychology and counseling* (2nd ed., pp. 777–778). Grand Rapids: Baker Academic.

Johnson, S. M. (2002). *Emotionally focused couple therapy with trauma survivors*. New York: Guilford Press.

Johnson, S. M. (2004). *The practice of emotionally focused marital therapy: Creating connection* (2nd ed.). New York: Brunner-Routledge.

Johnson, S. M. (2008a). Emotionally focused couple therapy. In A. S. Gurman (Ed.), *Clinical handbook of couple therapy* (4th ed., pp. 107–137). New York: Guilford Press.

Johnson, S. M. (2008b). *Hold me tight: Seven conversations for a lifetime of love*. New York: Little, Brown.

Johnson, S. M., Bradley, B., Furrow, J., Lee, A., Palmer, G., Tilley, D., & Wooley, S. (2005). *Becoming an emotionally focused couple therapist: The workbook*. New York: Routledge.

Johnson, W. B. (2007a). The boundary waters are murky: A case for virtue. *Professional Psychology: Research and Practice*, *38*, 409–410.

Johnson, W. B. (2007b). Transformational supervision: When supervisors mentor. *Professional Psychology: Research and Practice*, *38*, 259–267.

Johnson, W. B., Elman, N. S., Forrest, L., Robiner, W. N., Rodolfa, E., & Schaffer, J. B. (2008). Addressing professional competence problems in trainees: Some ethical considerations. *Professional Psychology: Research and Practice*, *39*, 589–599.

Jones, E. (1953). *The life and work of Sigmund Freud* (Vol. 1). New York: Basic Books.

Jones, E. (1955). *The life and work of Sigmund Freud* (Vol. 2). New York: Basic Books.

Jones, E. (1957). *The life and work of Sigmund Freud* (Vol. 3). New York: Basic Books.

Jones, E. (1961). *The life and work of Sigmund Freud* (Abridged ed.). New York: Basic Books.

Jones, I. F. (2006). *The counsel of heaven on earth: Foundation for biblical Christian counseling.* Nashville: B&H.

Jones, S. L. (1994). A constructive relationship for religion with the science and profession of psychology: Perhaps the boldest model yet. *American Psychologist, 49,* 184–199.

Jones, S. L. (1996). Reflections on the nature and future of the Christian psychologies. *Journal of Psychology and Christianity, 15,* 133–142.

Jones, S. L., & Butman, R. E. (1991). *Modern psychotherapies: A comprehensive Christian appraisal.* Downers Grove, IL: InterVarsity.

Jones, S. L., Butman, R. E., Dueck, A., & Tan, S. Y. (1988, April). *Psychotherapeutic practice and the Lordship of Christ.* Symposium presented at the National Convention of the Christian Association for Psychological Studies, Denver, CO.

Jung, C. G. (1907/1960). Psychology of dementia praecox. In *The psychogenesis of mental disease* (Vol. 3 of *Collected works,* pp. 1–151). Princeton, NJ: Princeton University Press.

Jung, C. G. (1921/1971). *Psychological types* (Vol. 6 of *Collected works*). Princeton, NJ: Princeton University Press.

Jung, C. G. (1961). *Memories, dreams, reflections.* New York: Random House.

Kabat-Zinn, J. (1990). *Full catastrophe living: Using the wisdom of your body and mind to face stress, pain, and illness.* New York: Dell.

Karkkainen, V.-M. (2002). *Pneumatology: The Holy Spirit in ecumenical, international, and contextual perspective.* Grand Rapids: Baker Academic.

Kaslow, F. (Ed.). (1996). *Handbook of relational diagnosis and dysfunctional family patterns.* New York: Wiley.

Kaslow, N. J., Dausch, B. M., & Celano, M. (2003). Family therapies. In A. S. Gurman & S. B. Messer (Eds.), *Essential psychotherapies: Theory and practice* (2nd ed., pp. 400–462). New York: Guilford Press.

Kaslow, N. J., Rubin, N. J., Bebeau, M. J., Leigh, I. W., Lichtenberg, J. W., Nelson, J. D., et al. (2007). Guiding principles and recommendations for the assessment of competence. *Professional Psychology: Research and Practice, 38,* 441–451.

Kazantzis, N., Reinecke, M. A., & Freeman, A. (Eds.). (2009). *Cognitive and behavioral theories in clinical practice.* New York: Guilford Press.

Kazdin, A. E. (1973). Covert modeling and the reduction of avoidance behavior. *Journal of Abnormal Psychology, 81,* 87–95.

Kazdin, A. E. (1991). Effectiveness of psychotherapy with children and adolescents. *Journal of Consulting and Clinical Psychology, 39,* 785–798.

Kazdin, A. E. (2001). *Behavior modification in applied settings* (6th ed.). Pacific Grove, CA: Brooks/Cole.

Kazdin, A. E. (2008). Evidence-based treatment and practice: New opportunities to bridge clinical research and practice, enhance the knowledge base, and improve patient care. *American Psychologist, 63,* 146–159.

Keijsers, G. P. J., Schaap, C. P. D. R., & Hoogduin, C. A. L. (2000). The impact of interpersonal patient and therapist behavior on outcome in cognitive-behavioral therapy: A review of empirical studies. *Behavior Modification, 24,* 264–297.

Kellemen, R. W. (2005a). *Soul physicians: A theology of soul care and spiritual direction.* Taneytown, MD: RPM Books.

Kellemen, R. W. (2005b). *Spiritual friends: A methodology of soul care and spiritual direction.* Taneytown, MD: RPM Books.

Kellogg, S. H., & Young, J. E. (2006). Schema therapy for borderline personality disorder. *Journal of Clinical Psychology, 62,* 445–458.

Kellogg, S. H., & Young, J. E. (2008). Cognitive therapy. In J. L. Lebow (Ed.), *Twenty-first century psychotherapies: Contemporary approaches to theory and practice* (pp. 43–79). Hoboken, NJ: Wiley.

Kelly, G. (1955). *The psychology of personal constructs.* New York: Norton.

Kelsey, M. (1972). *Encounter with God.* London: Hodder & Stoughton.

Kendall, P. C., & Bemis, K. M. (1983). Thought and action in psychotherapy: The cognitive-behavioral approaches. In M. Hersen, A. E. Kazdin, & A. S. Bellack (Eds.), *The clinical psychology handbook* (pp. 565–592). New York: Pergamon Press.

Kendall, P. C., & Hollon, S. D. (Eds.). (1979). *Cognitive-behavioral interventions: Theory, research, and procedures.* New York: Academic Press.

Kendall, P. C., Reber, M., McLeer, S., Epps, J., & Ronan, K. R. (1990). Cognitive-behavioral treatment of conduct-disordered children. *Cognitive Therapy and Research, 14,* 279–297.

Kernberg, O. F. (1975). *Borderline conditions and pathological narcissism.* New York: Jason Aronson.

Kernberg, O. F. (1976). *Object-relations theory and clinical psychoanalysis.* New York: Jason Aronson.

Kernberg, O. F., Ellis, A., Person, E., Burns, D. D., & Norcross, J. C. (1993). *A meeting of the minds: Is integration possible?* Two-day conference sponsored by the Institute for Rational-Emotive Therapy, New York.

Kim, R. J., & Hwang, J. G. (1996). "Making the world I want"—Based on reality therapy. *Journal of Reality Therapy, 16,* 26–35.

Kirschenbaum, H. (1979). *On becoming Carl Rogers.* New York: Delacorte Press.

Kirschenbaum, H., & Jourdan, A. (2005). The current status of Carl Rogers and the person-centered approach. *Psychotherapy, 42,* 37–51.

Klein, D. N., Schwartz, J. E., Santiago, N. J., Vivian, D., Vocisano, C., Castonguay, L. G., et al. (2003). Therapeutic alliance in depression treatment: Controlling for prior change and patient characteristics. *Journal of Consulting and Clinical Psychology, 71,* 997–1006.

Klein, M. (1957). *Envy and gratitude.* New York: Basic Books.

Klein, M. (1975). *Love, guilt, and reparation and other works.* London: Hogarth Press.

Klein, M. H., Kolden, G. G., Michels, J. L., & Chisholm-Stockard, S. (2002). Congruence. In J. C. Norcross (Ed.), *Psychotherapy relationships that work* (pp. 195–215). New York: Oxford University Press.

Knapp, S., Gottlieb, M., Berman, J., & Handelsman, M. M. (2007). When laws and ethics collide: What should psychologists do? *Professional Psychology: Research and Practice, 38,* 54–59.

Knapp, S., & VandeCreek, L. (2006). *Practical ethics for psychologists: A positive approach.* Washington, DC: American Psychological Association.

Knapp, S., & VandeCreek, L. (2007). When values of different cultures conflict: Ethical decision making in a multicultural context. *Professional Psychology: Research and Practice, 38,* 660–666.

Koenig, H. G. (Ed.). (1998). *Handbook of religion and mental health.* San Diego: Academic Press.

Koenig, H. G., McCullough, M. E., & Larson, D. B. (Eds.). (2001). *Handbook of religion and health.* New York: Oxford University Press.

Kohut, H. (1971). *The analysis of the self.* New York: International Universities Press.

Kohut, H. (1977). *The restoration of the self.* New York: International Universities Press.

Kohut, H. (1984). *How does analysis cure?* Chicago: University of Chicago Press.

Kraft, C. H. (1993). *Deep wounds, deep healing.* Ann Arbor, MI: Vine Books.

Kriston, L., Holzel, L., & Harter, M. (2009). Analyzing effectiveness of long-term psychodynamic psychotherapy. *Journal of the American Medical Association, 301,* 930–931.

Kruis, J. G. (2000). *Quick Scripture reference for counseling* (3rd ed.). Grand Rapids: Baker Academic.

Kunst, J., & Tan, S. Y. (1996). Psychotherapy as "work in the Spirit": Thinking theologically about psychotherapy. *Journal of Psychology and Theology, 24,* 284–291.

Kuyken, W., Padesky, C. A., & Dudley, R. (2009). *Collaborative case conceptualization: Working effectively with clients in cognitive-behavioral therapy.* New York: Guilford Press.

Laing, R. D. (1959). *The divided self.* London: Tavistock.

Laing, R. D. (1961). *Self and others.* Harmondsworth, England: Penguin.

Lambert, M. J. (1992). Psychotherapy outcome research: Implications for integrative and eclectic therapists. In J. C. Norcross & M. R. Goldfried (Eds.), *Handbook of psychotherapy integration* (pp. 94–129). New York: Basic Books.

Lambert, M. J., & Barley, D. E. (2002). Research summary on the therapeutic relationship and psychotherapy outcome. In J. C. Norcross (Ed.), *Psychotherapy relationships that work* (pp. 17–32). New York: Oxford University Press.

Lambert, M. J., & Bergin, A. E. (1994). The effectiveness of psychotherapy. In A. E. Bergin & S. L. Garfield (Eds.), *Handbook of psychotherapy and behavior change* (4th ed., pp. 143–189). New York: Wiley.

Lambert, M. J., DeJulio, S. S., & Stein, D. M. (1978). Therapist interpersonal skills: Process, outcome, methodological considerations, and recommendations for future research. *Psychological Bulletin, 85,* 467–489.

Lambert, M. J., & Ogles, B. M. (2004). The efficacy and effectiveness of psychotherapy. In M. J. Lambert (Ed.), *Bergin and Garfield's handbook of psychotherapy and behavior change* (5th ed., pp. 139–193). New York: Wiley.

Lantz, J., & Walsh, J. (2007). *Short-term existential intervention in clinical practice.* Chicago: Lyceum Books.

Lawrence, D. H. (2004). The effects of reality therapy group counseling on the self-determination of persons with developmental disabilities. *International Journal of Reality Therapy, 23* (2), 9–15.

Lazarus, A. A. (1958). New methods in psychotherapy: A case study. *South African Medical Journal, 32,* 660–664.

Lazarus, A. A. (1966). Broad spectrum behavior therapy and the treatment of agoraphobia. *Behaviour Research and Therapy, 4,* 95–97.

Lazarus, A. A. (1971). *Behavior therapy and beyond.* New York: McGraw-Hill.

Lazarus, A. A. (1973). Multimodal behavior therapy: Treating the BASIC I.D. *Journal of Nervous and Mental Disease, 156,* 404–411.

Lazarus, A. A. (1976). *Multimodal behavior therapy.* New York: Springer.

Lazarus, A. A. (1981). *The practice of multimodal therapy.* New York: McGraw-Hill.

Lazarus, A. A. (1985). *Casebook of multimodal therapy.* New York: Guilford Press.

Lazarus, A. A. (1989). *The practice of multimodal therapy* (Updated ed.). Baltimore: Johns Hopkins University Press.

Lazarus, A. A. (1994). How certain boundaries and ethics diminish therapeutic effectiveness. *Ethics & Behavior, 4,* 255–261.

Lazarus, A. A. (1997). *Brief but comprehensive psychotherapy: The multimodal way.* New York: Springer.

Lazarus, A. A. (2007). Restrictive Draconian views must be vigorously challenged. *Professional Psychology: Research and Practice, 38,* 405–406.

Lazarus, A. A. (2008). Multimodal therapy. In R. J. Corsini & D. Wedding (Eds.), *Current psychotherapies* (8th ed., pp. 368–401). Belmont, CA: Brooks/Cole.

Lazarus, A. A., & Lazarus, C. N. (1991). *Multimodal life-history inventory.* Champaign, IL: Research Press.

Lazarus, A. A., & Zur, O. (Eds.). (2002). *Dual relationships and psychotherapy.* New York: Springer.

Leahy, R. L. (Ed.). (2004). *Contemporary cognitive therapy: Theory, research, and practice.* New York: Guilford Press.

Lebow, J. L. (1997). The integrative revolution in couple and family therapy. *Family Process, 36,* 1–17.

Lebow, J. L. (2008). Couple and family therapy. In J. L. Lebow (Ed.), *Twenty-first century psychotherapies: Contemporary approaches to theory and practice* (pp. 307–346). Hoboken, NJ: Wiley.

Lee, R. G. (Ed.). (2004). *The values of connection: A relational approach to ethics.* Cambridge, MA: Gestalt Press.

Leichsenring, F., & Rabung, S. (2008). Effectiveness of long-term psychodynamic psychotherapy: A meta-analysis. *Journal of the American Medical Association, 300,* 1551–1565.

Leichsenring, F., & Rabung, S. (2009). Analyzing effectiveness of long-term psychodynamic pyschotherapy—reply. *Journal of the American Medical Association, 301,* 932–933.

Levant, R. F. (1984). *Family therapy: A comprehensive overview.* Englewood Cliffs, NJ: Prentice Hall.

Levant, R. F., & Hasan, N. T. (2008). Evidence-based practice in psychology. *Professional Psychology: Research and Practice, 39,* 658–662.

Levicoff, S. (1991). *Christian counseling and the law.* Chicago: Moody Press.

Levy, K. N., Clarkin, J. F., Yeomans, F. E., Scott, L. N., Wasserman, R. H., & Kernberg, O. F. (2006). The mechanisms of change in the treatment of borderline personality disorder with transference focused psychotherapy. *Journal of Clinical Psychology, 62,* 481–501.

Lewinsohn, P. M. (1974). The behavioral study and treatment of depression. In K. S. Calhoun, H. E. Adams, & K. M. Mitchell (Eds.), *Innovative treatment methods in psychopathology* (pp. 157–186). New York: Wiley.

Lewis, J. M., Beavers, W. R., Gossett, J. T., & Philips, V. A. (1976). *No single thread: Psychological health in family systems.* New York: Brunner/Mazel.

Lilienfeld, S. O. (2007). Psychological treatments that cause harm. *Perspectives on Psychological Science, 2,* 53–70.

Linehan, M. M. (1993). *Cognitive-behavioral treatment of borderline personality disorder.* New York: Guilford Press.

Linehan, M. M., Comtois, K. A., Murray, A. M., Brown, M. Z., Gallop, R. J., Heard, H. L., et al. (2006). Two-year randomized trial + follow-up of dialectical behavior therapy vs. therapy by experts for suicidal behaviors and borderline personality disorder. *Archives of General Psychiatry, 63,* 757–766.

Linley, R. A., & Joseph, S. (Eds.). (2004). *Positive psychology in practice.* Hoboken, NJ: Wiley.

Linnenberg, D. (1997). Religion, spirituality and the counseling process. *Journal of Reality Therapy, 17,* 55–59.

Lints, R., Horton, M. S., & Talbot, M. R. (Eds.). (2006). *Personal identity in theological perspective.* Grand Rapids: Eerdmans.

Loeb, K. L., Wilson, G. T., Labouvie, E., Pratt, E. M., Hayaki, J., Walsh, B. T., et al. (2005). Therapeutic alliance and treatment adherence in two interventions for bulimia nervosa: A study of process and outcome. *Journal of Consulting and Clinical Psychology, 73,* 1097–1106.

Lovinger, R. J. (1984). *Working with religious issues in therapy.* New York: Jason Aronson.

Lovinger, R. J. (1990). *Religion and counseling: The psychological impact of religious belief.* New York: Continuum.

Luborsky, E. B., O'Reilly-Landry, M., & Arlow, J. A. (2008). Psychoanalysis. In R. J. Corsini & D. Wedding (Eds.), *Current psychotherapies* (8th ed., pp. 15–62). Belmont, CA: Brooks/Cole.

Luborsky, L. (1984). *Principles of psychoanalytic psychotherapy: A manual for supportive-expressive treatment.* New York: Basic Books.

Luborsky, L., & Crits-Christoph, P. (1998). *Understanding transference: The core conflictual relationship theme method* (2nd ed.). Washington, DC: American Psychological Association.

Luborsky, L., Diguer, L., Seligman, D., Rosenthal, R., Krause, E., Johnson, S., Halperin, G., Bishop, M., Berman, J., & Scheweizer, E. (1999). The researcher's own therapy allegiances: A "wild card" in comparisons of treatment efficacy. *Clinical Psychology: Science and Practice, 6,* 95–106.

Luborsky, L., Singer B., & Luborsky, L. (1975). Comparative studies of psychotherapies. *Archives of General Psychiatry, 32,* 995–1008.

Lucado, M. (2007). *3:16: The numbers of hope.* Nashville: Thomas Nelson.

Luoma, J. B., Hayes, S. C., & Walser, R. D. (2007). *Learning ACT: An acceptance & commitment therapy skills-training manual for therapists.* Oakland, CA: New Harbinger Publications.

Lyons, L. C., & Woods, P. J. (1991). The efficacy of rational-emotive therapy: A quantitative review of the outcome research. *Clinical Psychology Review, 11,* 357–369.

MacNutt, F. (1995). *Deliverance from evil spirits: A practical manual.* Grand Rapids: Chosen Books.

Madanes, C. (1981). *Strategic family therapy.* San Francisco: Jossey-Bass.

Madanes, C. (1984). *Behind the one-way mirror: Advances in the practice of strategic therapy.* San Francisco: Jossey-Bass.

Madanes, C. (1990). *Sex, love, and violence: Strategies for transformation.* New York: Norton.

Madanes, C. (2006). *The therapist as humanist, social activist, and systemic thinker: The selected papers of Cloe Madanes.* New York: Zeig & Tucker.

Magaletta, P. R., & Brawer, P. A. (1998). Prayer in psychotherapy: A model for its use, ethical considerations, and guidelines for practice. *Journal of Psychology and Theology, 26,* 322–330.

Mahler, M. (1968). *On human symbiosis and the vicissitudes of individuation.* New York: International Universities Press.

Mahler, M. (1979a). *The selected papers of Margaret S. Mahler.* Vol. 1, *Infantile psychosis and early contributions.* New York: Jason Aronson.

Mahler, M. (1979b). *The selected papers of Margaret S. Mahler.* Vol. 2, *Separation-individuation.* New York: Jason Aronson.

Mahoney, M. J. (1974). *Cognition and behavior modification.* Cambridge, MA: Ballinger.

Mahoney, M. J. (1977). Personal science: A cognitive learning therapy. In A. Ellis & R. Geiger (Eds.), *Handbook of rational-emotive therapy* (pp. 352–366). New York: Springer.

Mahoney, M. J. (1991). *Human change processes: The scientific foundations of psychotherapy.* New York: Basic Books.

Mahoney, M. J. (2003). *Constructive psychotherapy: A practical guide.* New York: Guilford Press.

Mahoney, M. J., & Arnkoff, D. B. (1978). Cognitive and self-control therapies. In S. L. Garfield & A. E. Bergin (Eds.), *Handbook of psychotherapy and behavior change* (2nd ed., pp. 689–722). New York: Wiley.

Malony, H. N. (Ed.). (1980). *A Christian existential psychology: The contribution of John G. Finch.* Washington, DC: University Press of America.

Malony, H. N. (1987). Inner healing. In D. G. Benner (Ed.), *Psychotherapy in Christian perspective* (pp. 171–179). Grand Rapids: Baker Academic.

Malony, H. N. (1988). The clinical assessment of optimal religious functioning. *Review of Religious Research, 30,* 2–17.

Malony, H. N. (1995). *Integration musings: Thoughts on being a Christian professional* (2nd ed.). Pasadena, CA: Integration Press.

Malony, H. N., & Augsburger, D. W. (2007). *Christian counseling: An introduction.* Nashville: Abingdon Press.

Marks, I. (1978). Behavioral psychotherapy of adult neurosis. In S. L. Garfield & A. E. Bergin (Eds.), *Handbook of psychotherapy and behavior change: An empirical analysis* (2nd ed., pp. 493–547). New York: Wiley.

Marra, T. (2005). *Dialectical behavior therapy in private practice: A practical and comprehensive guide.* Oakland, CA: New Harbinger Publications.

Martell, C. R., Addis, M. E., & Jacobson, N. S. (2001). *Depression in context: Strategies for guided action.* New York: Norton.

Martell, C. R., Dimidjian, S., & Herman-Dunn, R. (2010). *Behavioral activation for depression: A clinician's guide.* New York: Guilford Press.

Martinez, J. S., Smith, T. B., & Barlow, S. H. (2007). Spiritual interventions in psychotherapy: Evaluations by highly religious clients. *Journal of Clinical Psychology, 63,* 943–960.

May, R. (1950). *The meaning of anxiety.* New York: Ronald Press.

May, R. (1958). The origins and significance of the existential movement in psychology. In R. May, E. Angel, & H. Ellenberger (Eds.), *Existence: A new dimension in psychiatry and psychology* (pp. 3–36). New York: Basic Books.

May, R. (1961). *Existential psychology.* New York: Random House.

May, R. (1969). *Love and will.* New York: Norton.

May, R. (1981). *Freedom and destiny.* New York: Norton.

May, R., & Yalom, I. (2000). Existential psychotherapy. In R. J. Corsini & D. Wedding (Eds.), *Current psychotherapies* (6th ed., pp. 273–302). Itasca, IL: F. E. Peacock.

McCullough, M. E., & Larson, D. B. (1999). Prayer. In W. R. Miller (Ed.), *Integrating spirituality into treatment* (pp. 85–110). Washington, DC: American Psychological Association.

McGoldrick, M., & Hardy, K. V. (Eds.). (2008). *Re-visioning family therapy: Race, culture, and gender in clinical practice.* New York: Guilford Press.

McGoldrick, M., Giordano, J., & Garcia-Preto, N. (Eds.). (2005). *Ethnicity and family therapy* (3rd ed.). New York: Guilford Press.

McGrath, A. (1995). *Evangelicalism and the future of Christianity*. Downers Grove, IL: InterVarsity.

McHugh, R. K., & Barlow, D. H. (2010). The dissemination and implementation of evidence-based psychological treatments: A review of current efforts. *American Psychologist, 65,* 73–84.

McKnight, S. (2004). *The Jesus creed: Loving God, loving others*. Brewster, MA: Paraclete Press.

McKnight, S. (2008). *The blue parakeet: Rethinking how you read the Bible*. Grand Rapids: Zondervan.

McLemore, C. (1984). *Honest Christianity*. Philadelphia: Westminster.

McMinn, M. R. (1996). *Psychology, theology, and spirituality in Christian counseling*. Wheaton: Tyndale.

McMinn, M. R. (2008). *Sin and grace in Christian counseling: An integrative paradigm*. Downers Grove, IL: IVP Academic.

McMinn, M. R., & Campbell, C. D. (2007). *Integrative psychotherapy: Toward a comprehensive Christian approach*. Downers Grove, IL: InterVarsity.

McMinn, M. R., & McRay, B. W. (1997). Spiritual disciplines and the practice of integration: Possibilities and the challenges for Christian psychologists. *Journal of Psychology and Theology, 25,* 102–110.

McMinn, M. R., Orton, J. J., & Woods, S. W. (2008). Technology in clinical practice. *Journal of Psychology and Christianity, 27,* 56–60.

McMinn, M. R., & Phillips, T. R. (Eds.). (2001). *Care for the soul: Exploring the intersection of psychology and theology*. Downers Grove, IL: InterVarsity.

McMullin, R. E. (1999). *The new handbook of cognitive therapy techniques*. New York: Norton.

McWilliams, N. (2004). *Psychoanalytic psychotherapy: A practitioner's guide*. New York: Guilford Press.

Mearns, D. (1997a). Central dynamics in client-centered therapy training. *The Person-Centered Journal, 4,* 31–43.

Mearns, D. (1997b). *Person-centred counselling training*. London: Sage.

Mearns, D., & Thorne, B. (1999). *Person-centred counselling in action* (2nd ed.). London: Sage.

Mearns, D., & Thorne, B. (2000). *Person-centred therapy today: New frontiers in theory and practice*. London: Sage.

Meichenbaum, D. (1977). *Cognitive-behavior modification: An integrative approach*. New York: Plenum Press.

Meichenbaum, D. (1985). *Stress inoculation training*. Elmsford, NY: Pergamon Press.

Meichenbaum, D. (1993). Stress inoculation training: A 20-year update. In R. L. Woolfolk & P. M. Lehrer (Eds.), *Principles and practice of stress management* (pp. 373–406). New York: Guilford Press.

Meichenbaum, D. (1994). *Treating adults with PTSD*. Clearwater, FL: Institute Press.

Meichenbaum, D. (1997). The evolution of a cognitive-behavior therapist. In J. K. Zeig (Ed.), *The evolution of psychotherapy: The third conference* (pp. 96–104). New York: Brunner/Mazel.

Meichenbaum, D. (2002). *Treatment of individuals with anger-control problems and aggressive behaviors: A clinical handbook*. Clearwater, FL: Institute Press.

Meichenbaum, D. (2003). Stress inoculation training. In W. O'Donohue, J. E. Fisher, & S. C. Hayes (Eds.), *Cognitive behavior therapy: Applying empirically supported techniques in your practice* (pp. 407–410). Hoboken, NJ: Wiley.

Meichenbaum, D. (2005). 35 years of working with suicidal patients: Lessons learned. *Canadian Psychology, 46*, 64–72.

Meichenbaum, D. (2007). Stress inoculation training: A preventative and treatment approach. In P. M. Lehrer, R. L. Woolfolk, & W. E. Sime (Eds.), *Principles and practice of stress management* (3rd ed., pp. 497–576). New York: Guilford Press.

Meichenbaum, D., & Fitzpatrick, D. (1993). A constructivist narrative perspective on stress and coping: Stress inoculation applications. In L. Goldberger & S. Breznitz (Eds.), *Handbook of stress: Theoretical and clinical aspects* (2nd ed., pp. 706–723). New York: Free Press.

Meichenbaum, D., & Jaremko, M. D. (Eds.). (1982). *Stress prevention and management: A cognitive-behavioral approach*. New York: Plenum Press.

Meichenbaum. D., & Turk, D. C. (1987). *Facilitating treatment adherence: A practitioner's guidebook*. New York: Plenum Press.

Melnick, J., & Nevis, S. M. (2005). Gestalt therapy methodology. In A. L. Woldt & S. M. Tolman (Eds.), *Gestalt therapy: History, theory, and practice* (pp. 101–115). Thousand Oaks, CA: Sage.

Mendelowitz, E., & Schneider, K. (2008). Existential psychotherapy. In R. J. Corsini & D. Wedding (Eds.), *Current psychotherapies* (8th ed., pp. 295–327). Belmont, CA: Brooks/Cole.

Mickel, E., & Liddle-Hamilton, B. (1996). Black family therapy: Spirituality, social constructivism and choice theory. *Journal of Reality Therapy, 16*, 95–100.

Miller, G. (2003). *Incorporating spirituality in counseling and psychotherapy: Theory and technique*. Hoboken, NJ: Wiley.

Miller, J. C. (2004). *The transcendent function: Jung's model of psychological growth through dialogues with the unconscious*. Albany, NY: State University of New York Press.

Miller, P. A. (2002). *Quick Scripture reference for counseling women.* Grand Rapids: Baker Academic.

Miller, P. A., & Miller, K. R. (2006). *Quick Scripture reference for counseling youth.* Grand Rapids: Baker Academic.

Miller, W. R. (Ed.). (1999). *Integrating spirituality into treatment: Resources for practitioners.* Washington, DC: American Psychological Association.

Miller, W. R. (2000). Rediscovering fire: Small interventions, large effects. *Psychology of Addictive Behaviors, 14,* 6–18.

Miller, W. R., & C'de Baca, J. (2001). *Quantum change: When epiphanies and sudden insights transform ordinary lives.* New York: Guilford Press.

Miller, W. R., & Martin, J. E. (Eds.). (1988). *Behavior therapy and religion: Integrating spiritual and behavioral approaches to change.* Newbury Park, CA: Sage.

Miller, W. R., & Rollnick, S. (1991). *Motivational interviewing: Preparing people for change.* New York: Guilford Press.

Miller, W. R., & Rollnick, S. (2002). *Motivational interviewing: Preparing people for change* (2nd ed.). New York: Guilford Press.

Miller, W. R., & Rose, G. S. (2009). Toward a theory of motivational interviewing. *American Psychologist, 64,* 527–537.

Miller, W. R., & Thoresen, C. E. (2003). Spirituality, religion, and health: An emerging research field. *American Psychologist, 58,* 24–35.

Miller, W. R., Yahne, C. E., Moyers, T. B., Martinez, J., & Pirritano, M. (2004). A randomized trial of methods to help clinicians learn motivational interviewing. *Journal of Consulting and Clinical Psychology, 72,* 1050–1062.

Miller, W. R., Zweben, A., DiClemente, C. C., & Rychtarik, R. G. (1992). *Motivational Enhancement Therapy manual: A clinical research guide for therapists treating individuals with alcohol abuse and dependence.* Rockville, MD: National Institute on Alcohol Abuse and Alcoholism.

Miltenberger, R. G. (2008). *Behavior modification: Principles and procedures* (4th ed.). Belmont, CA: Wadsworth.

Minuchin, P., Colapinto, J., & Minuchin, S. (2007). *Working with families of the poor* (2nd ed.). New York: Guilford Press.

Minuchin, S. (1974). *Families and family therapy.* Cambridge, MA: Harvard University Press.

Minuchin, S., & Fishman, H. C. (1981). *Family therapy techniques.* Cambridge, MA: Harvard University Press.

Minuchin, S., Lee, W.-Y., & Simon, G. M. (2006). *Mastering family therapy: Journeys of growth and transformation* (2nd ed.). New York: Wiley.

Minuchin, S., Montalvo, B., Guerney, G. G., Rosman, B. L., & Schumer, F. (1967). *Families of the slums: An exploration of their structure and treatment*. New York: Basic Books.

Minuchin, S., Nichols, M. P., & Lee, W.-Y. (2007). *Assessing families and couples: From symptom to system*. Boston: Allyn & Bacon.

Minuchin, S., Rosman, B. L., & Baker, L. (1978). *Psychosomatic families: Anorexia nervosa in context*. Cambridge, MA: Harvard University Press.

Miranda, J., Bernal, G., Kohn, A., Hwang, W.-C., & La Fromboise, T. (2005). Psychosocial treatment of minority groups. In S. Nolan-Hoeksema (Ed.), *Annual review of clinical psychology* (Vol. 1, pp. 113–142). Palo Alto: Annual Reviews.

Mischel, W. (1973). Toward a cognitive social learning reconceptualization of personality. *Psychological Review, 80*, 252–283.

Mitchell, S. A. (1988). *Relational concepts in psychoanalysis: An integration*. Cambridge, MA: Harvard University Press.

Mitchell, S. A. (2000). *Relationality: From attachment to intersubjectivity*. Hillsdale, NJ: Analytic Press.

Moltmann, J. (1997). *The source of life: The Holy Spirit and the theology of life*. Minneapolis: Fortress Press.

Monk, G., Winslade, J., Crocket, K., & Epston, D. (Eds.). (1997). *Narrative therapy in practice: The archaeology of hope*. San Francisco: Jossey-Bass.

Monroe, P. G. (1997). Building bridges with biblical counselors. *Journal of Psychology and Theology, 25*, 28–37.

Monroe, P. G. (2008). Guidelines for the effective use of the Bible in counseling. *Edification: Journal of the Society for Christian Psychology, 2* (2), 53–61.

Moon, G. W., & Benner, D. G. (Eds.). (2004). *Spiritual direction and the care of souls*. Downers Grove, IL: InterVarsity.

Moon, G. W., Willis, D. E., Bailey, J. W., & Kwasny, J. C. (1993). Self-reported use of Christian spiritual guidance techniques by Christian psychotherapists, pastoral counselors, and spiritual directors. *Journal of Psychology and Christianity, 12*, 24–37.

Moon, K. (2002). Nondirective client-centered work with children. In J. C. Watson, R. N. Goldman, & M. S. Warner (Eds.), *Client-centered and experiential psychotherapy in the 21st century: Advances in theory, research, and practice* (pp. 485–492). Ross-on-Wye, England: PCCS Books.

Moriarty, G. L. (Ed.). (2010). *Integrating faith and psychology: Twelve psychologists tell their stories*. Downers Grove, IL: IVP Academic.

Morris, P. (1980). Love therapy. In G. R. Collins (Ed.), *Helping people grow: Practical approaches to Christian counseling* (pp. 223–240). Santa Ana: Vision House.

Mosak, H. H. (1985). Interrupting a depression: The push-button technique. *Individual Psychology, 41*, 210–214.

Mosak, H. H., & Dreikurs, R. (1967). The life tasks: III. The fifth life task. *Individual Psychologist, 5*, 16–22.

Mosak, H. H., & Maniacci, M. (1999). *A primer of Adlerian psychology.* Philadelphia: Brunner/Mazel.

Mosak, H. H., & Maniacci, M. (2008). Adlerian psychotherapy. In R. J. Corsini & D. Wedding (Eds.), *Current Psychotherapies* (8th ed., pp. 63–106). Belmont, CA: Brooks/Cole.

Mosher, L. (2001). Treating madness without hospitals: Soteria and its successors. In R. J. Schneider, J. F. T. Bugental, & J. F. Pierson (Eds.), *The handbook of humanistic psychology: Leading edges in theory, practice, and research* (pp. 389–402). Thousand Oaks, CA: Sage.

Moyers, T. B., & Rollnick, S. (2002). A motivational interviewing perspective on resistance in psychotherapy. *Journal of Clinical Psychology: In Session, 58*, 185–194.

Murphy, L. (1997). Efficacy of reality therapy in schools: A review of research from 1980–1995. *Journal of Reality Therapy, 16*, 12–20.

Murphy, N. (2006). Nonreductive physicalism: Philosophical challenges. In R. Lints, M. S. Horton, & M. R. Talbot (Eds.), *Personal identity in theological perspective* (pp. 95–117). Grand Rapids: Eerdmans.

Myers, D. G. (2000). A levels-of-explanation view. In E. L. Johnson & S. L. Jones (Eds.), *Psychology and Christianity: Four views* (pp. 54–83). Downers Grove, IL: InterVarsity.

Nathan, P. E., & Gorman, J. M. (Eds.). (2007). *A guide to treatments that work* (3rd ed.). New York: Oxford University Press.

Nathan, P. E., Stuart, S. P., & Dolan, S. L. (2000). Research on psychotherapy efficacy and effectiveness: Between Scylla and Charybdis? *Psychological Bulletin, 126*, 964–981.

Natiello, P. (2001). *The person-centred approach: A passionate presence.* Ross-on-Wye, England: PCCS Books.

National Institute for Clinical Excellence. (2004). *Eating disorders—Core interventions in the treatment and management of anorexia reversa, bulimia nervosa, and related eating disorders.* NICE Clinical Guideline no. 9. London: NICE. Retrieved from http://www.nice.org.uk.

Nelson, A. A., & Wilson, W. P. (1984). The ethics of sharing religious faith in psychotherapy. *Journal of Psychology and Theology, 12*, 15–23.

Nelson, J. (2009). *Psychology, religion, and spirituality.* New York: Springer.

Nelson, M. L., Barnes, K. L., Evans, A. L., & Triggiano, P. J. (2008). Working with conflict in clinical supervision: Wise supervisors' perspectives. *Journal of Counseling Psychology, 55*, 172–184.

Neuner, F., Onyut, P. L., Ertl, V., Odenwald, M., Schauer, E., and Elbert, T. (2008). Treatment of posttraumatic stress disorder by trained lay counselors in an African refugee settlement: A randomized controlled trial. *Journal of Consulting and Clinical Psychology, 76*, 686–694.

Newman, C. F., Leahy, R. L., Beck, A. T., Reilly-Harrington, N. A., & Gyulai, L. (2001). *Bipolar disorder: A cognitive therapy approach*. Washington, DC: American Psychological Association.

Nichols, M. P. (with Schwartz, R. C.). (2006). *Family therapy: Concepts and methods* (7th ed.). Boston: Allyn & Bacon.

Nielsen, S. L., Johnson, W. B., & Ellis, A. (2001). *Counseling and psychotherapy with religious persons: A rational emotive behavior therapy approach*. Mahwah, NJ: Lawrence Erlbaum Associates.

Norcross, J. C. (1990). An eclectic definition of psychotherapy. In J. K. Zeig & W. M. Munion (Eds.), *What is psychotherapy?* (pp. 218–220). San Francisco: Jossey-Bass.

Norcross, J. C. (Ed.). (2002). *Psychotherapy relationships that work*. New York: Oxford University Press.

Norcross, J. C., Beutler, L. E., & Levant, R. F. (Eds.). (2006). *Evidence-based practices in mental health: Debate and dialogue on the fundamental questions*. Washington, DC: American Psychological Association.

Norcross, J. C., & Guy, J. D. (2007). *Leaving it at the office: A guide to psychotherapist self-care*. New York: Guilford Press.

O'Donnell, D. J. (1987). History of the growth of the Institute for Reality Therapy. *Journal of Reality Therapy, 7*, 2–8.

Ohlschlager, G. W., & Clinton, T. E. (2002). The ethical helping relationship: Ethical conformation and spiritual transformation. In T. E. Clinton & G. W. Ohlschlager (Eds.), *Competent Christian counseling* (Vol. 1, pp. 244–293, 750–751). Colorado Springs: WaterBrook Press.

Ohlschlager, G. W., & Mosgofian, P. (1992). *Law for the Christian counselor*. Dallas: Word.

Oman, D., & Driskill, J. D. (2003). Holy name repetition as a spiritual exercise and therapeutic technique. *Journal of Psychology and Christianity, 22*, 5–19.

Orange, D. M., Atwood, G. E., & Stolorow, R. D. (1997). *Working intersubjectively: Contextualism in psychoanalytic practice*. Hillsdale, NJ: Analytic Press.

Orgler, H. (1963). *Alfred Adler, the man and his work: Triumph over the inferiority complex*. New York: Liveright.

Ortberg, J. (2002). *The life you've always wanted: Spiritual disciplines for ordinary people* (Expanded ed.). Grand Rapids: Zondervan.

Osborne, G. R. (2006). *The hermeneutical spiral: A comprehensive introduction to biblical interpretation* (2nd ed.). Downers Grove, IL: InterVarsity.

Ososkie, J. N., & Turpin, J. O. (1985). Reality therapy in rehabilitation counseling. *Journal of Applied Rehabilitation Counseling, 16,* 34–38.

Ost, L. G. (2008). Efficacy of the third wave of behavioral therapies: A systematic review and meta-analysis. *Behaviour Research and Therapy, 46,* 296–321.

Ouellet, M. C. (2006). *Divine likeness: Toward a trinitarian anthropology of the family.* Grand Rapids: Eerdmans.

Packer, J. I. (1973). *Knowing God.* Downers Grove, IL: InterVarsity.

Padesky, C. A. (2004). Aaron T. Beck: Mind, man, and mentor. In R. L. Leahy (Ed.), *Contemporary cognitive therapy: Theory, research, and practice* (pp. 3–24). New York: Guilford Press.

Paivio S. C., & Greenberg, L. S. (1995). Resolving "unfinished business": Efficacy of experiential therapy using empty-chair dialogue. *Journal of Consulting and Clinical Psychology, 63,* 419–425.

Palmer, R. B., White, G., & Chung, W. (2008). Deficient trainees: Gatekeeping in Christian practitioner programs. *Journal of Psychology and Christianity, 27,* 30–40.

Paloutzian, R. F., & Park, C. L. (Eds.). (2005). *Handbook of the psychology of religion and spirituality.* New York: Guilford Press.

Papadopolous, R. (Ed.). (2006). *The handbook of Jungian psychology.* New York: Routledge.

Pargament, K. I. (1997). *The psychology of religion and coping.* New York: Guilford Press.

Pargament, K. I. (2007). *Spiritually integrated psychotherapy: Understanding and addressing the sacred.* New York: Guilford Press.

Pargament, K. I., Murray-Swank, N. A., Magyar, G. M., & Ano, G. G. (2005). Spiritual struggle: A phenomenon of interest to psychology and religion. In W. R. Miller & H. D. Delaney (Eds.), *Judeo-Christian perspectives on psychology: Human nature, motivation, and change* (pp. 245–268). Washington, DC: American Psychological Association.

Park, C. L. (2010). Making sense of the meaning literature: An integrative review of meaning making and its effects on adjustment to stressful life events. *Psychological Bulletin, 136,* 257–301.

Park, C. L., & Helgeson, V. S. (2006). Introduction to the special section: Growth following highly stressful events—Current status and future directions. *Journal of Consulting and Clinical Psychology, 74,* 791–796.

Parker, S. (2008). Winnicott's object relations theory and the work of the Holy Spirit. *Journal of Psychology and Theology, 36*, 285–293.

Parloff, M. B., Waskow, I. E., & Wolfe, B. E. (1978). Research on therapist variables in relation to process and outcome. In S. L. Garfield & A. E. Bergin (Eds.), *Handbook of psychotherapy and behavior change* (2nd ed., pp. 233–282). New York: Wiley.

Parrott, L., III. (2003). *Counseling and psychotherapy* (2nd ed.). Pacific Grove, CA: Brooks/Cole.

Parrott, L., III, & Tan, S. Y. (2003). *Exercises for effective counseling and psychotherapy* (2nd ed.). Pacific Grove, CA: Brooks/Cole.

Parsons, T. D., & Rizzo, A. A. (2008). Affective outcomes of virtual reality exposure therapy for anxiety and specific phobias. *Journal of Behavior Therapy and Experimental Psychiatry, 39*, 250–261.

Patterson, C. H. (1973). *Theories of counseling and psychotherapy* (2nd ed.). New York: Harper and Row.

Patterson, C. H. (1995). A universal system of psychotherapy. *Person-Centered Journal, 2*, 54–62.

Patterson, C. H., & Watkins, C. E. (1996). *Theories of psychotherapy* (5th ed.). New York: HarperCollins.

Patterson, J., Williams, L., Edwards, T. M., Chamow, L., & Grauf-Grounds, C. (2009). *Essential skills in family therapy: From the first interview to termination* (2nd ed.). New York: Guilford Press.

Payne, I. R., Bergin, A. E., & Loftus, P. E. (1992). A review of attempts to integrate spiritual and standard psychotherapy techniques. *Journal of Psychotherapy Integration, 2*, 171–192.

Payne, L. (1991). *Restoring the Christian soul: Overcoming barriers to completion in Christ through healing prayer*. Grand Rapids: Baker Academic.

Pearlman, L. A., & MacIan, P. S. (1995). Vicarious traumatization: An empirical study of the effects of trauma work on trauma therapists. *Professional Psychology: Research and Practice, 26*, 558–565.

Peck, M. S. (1993). *Further along the road less traveled*. New York: Simon & Schuster.

Pedersen, P. (1983). Asian personality theory. In R. J. Corsini & A. J. Marsella (Eds.), *Personality theories, research, and assessment* (pp. 537–582). Itasca, IL: Peacock.

Perkins, B. R., & Rouanzoin, C. C. (2002). A critical evaluation of current views regarding eye movement desensitization and reprocessing (EMDR): Clarifying points of confusion. *Journal of Clinical Psychology, 58*, 77–97.

Perls, F. (1947/1969a). *Ego, hunger, and aggression*. New York: Vintage.

Perls, F. (1969b). *Gestalt therapy verbatim.* Moab, UT: Real People Press.

Perls, F. (1969c). *In and out of the garbage pail.* Moab, UT: Real People Press.

Perls, F. (1970). Four lectures. In J. Fagan & I. L. Shepherd (Eds.), *Gestalt therapy now* (pp. 14–38). Palo Alto, CA: Science and Behavior Books.

Perls, F. (1973). *The Gestalt approach.* Palo Alto, CA: Science and Behavior Books.

Perls, F., Hefferline, R. F., & Goodman, P. (1951/1994). *Gestalt therapy: Excitement and growth in the human personality.* New York: Julian.

Perls, L. (1990). A talk for the 25th anniversary. *Gestalt Journal, 13* (2), 15–22.

Persons, J. B. (1989). *Cognitive therapy in practice: A case formulation approach.* New York: Norton.

Persons, J. B. (2008). *The case formulation approach to cognitive-behavior therapy.* New York: Guilford Press.

Persons, J. B., Davidson, J., & Tompkins, M. A. (2001). *Essential components of cognitive-behavior therapy for depression.* Washington, DC: American Psychological Association.

Peterson, A. V., Chang, C., & Collins, P. L. (1997). The effects of reality therapy on locus of control among students in Asian universities. *Journal of Reality Therapy, 16,* 80–87.

Peterson, A. V., Chang, C., & Collins, P. L. (1998). The effects of reality therapy and choice theory training on self concept among Taiwanese university students. *International Journal for the Advancement of Counseling, 20,* 79–83.

Peterson, C., & Seligman, M. E. P. (2004). *Character strengths and virtues: A handbook and classification.* Washington, DC: American Psychological Association.

Peterson, E. H. (2005). *Christ plays in ten thousand places: A conversation in spiritual theology.* Grand Rapids: Eerdmans.

Peterson, E. H. (2006). *Eat this book: A conversation in the art of spiritual reading.* Grand Rapids: Eerdmans.

Peterson, E. H. (2007). *The Jesus way: A conversation on the ways that Jesus is the way.* Grand Rapids: Eerdmans.

Peterson, E. H. (2008). *Tell it slant: A conversation on the language of Jesus in his stories and prayers.* Grand Rapids: Eerdmans.

Peterson, E. H. (2010). *Practice resurrection: A conversation on growing up in Christ.* Grand Rapids: Eerdmans.

Petra, J. R. (2000). The effects of a choice theory and reality therapy parenting program on children's behavior. (Doctoral dissertation.) *Dissertation Abstracts International,* Section B, *61* (9–B), 5001.

Pinnock, C. (1996). *Flame of love: A theology of the Holy Spirit*. Downers Grove, IL: InterVarsity.

Pinsof, W. M., Wynne, L. C., & Hambright, A. B. (1996). The outcomes of couple and family therapy: Findings, conclusions, and recommendations. *Psychotherapy, 33*, 321–331.

Plante, T. G. (2007). Integrating spirituality and psychotherapy: Ethical issues and principles to consider. *Journal of Clinical Psychology, 63*, 891–902.

Plante, T. G. (2009). *Spiritual practices in psychotherapy: Thirteen tools for enhancing psychological health*. Washington, DC: American Psychological Association.

Plante, T. G., & Sherman, A. C. (Eds.). (2001). *Faith and health: Psychological perspectives*. New York: Guilford Press.

Plummer, R. L. (2009). Are the spiritual disciplines of "silence and solitude" really biblical? *Journal of Spiritual Formation and Soul Care, 2*, 101–112.

Poloma, M. M., & Pendleton, B. F. (1989). Exploring types of prayer and quality of life: A research note. *Review of Religious Research, 31*, 46–53.

Poloma, M. M., & Pendleton, B. F. (1991). The effects of prayer and prayer experiences on measures of general well-being. *Journal of Psychology and Theology, 19*, 71–83.

Polster, E., & Polster, M. (1973). *Gestalt therapy integrated: Contours of theory and practice*. New York: Brunner/Mazel.

Polster, M. (1987). Gestalt therapy: Evolution and application. In J. K. Zeig (Ed.), *The evolution of psychotherapy* (pp. 312–325). New York: Brunner/Mazel.

Pope, K. S., & Vasquez, M. J. T. (2007). *Ethics in psychotherapy and counseling: A practical guide* (3rd ed.). San Francisco: Jossey-Bass.

Pope, K. S., & Wedding, D. (2008). Contemporary challenges and controversies. In R. J. Corsini & D. Wedding (Eds.), *Current psychotherapies* (8th ed., pp. 512–540). Belmont, CA: Brooks/Cole.

Porter, S. L. (2010a). Theology as queen and psychology as handmaid: The authority of theology in integrative endeavors. *Journal of Psychology and Christianity, 29*, 3–14.

Porter, S. L. (2010b). A reply to the respondents of "Theology as queen and psychology as handmaid." *Journal of Psychology and Christianity, 29*, 33–40.

Pos, A. E., Greenberg, L. S., & Elliott, R. (2008). Experiential therapy. In J. L. Lebow (Ed.), *Twenty-first century psychotherapies: Contemporary approaches to theory and practice* (pp. 80–122). Hoboken, NJ: Wiley.

Poser, E. G. (1977). *Behavior therapy in clinical practice: Decision making, procedure, and outcome*. Springfield, IL: Charles C. Thomas.

Powell, L. H., Shahabi, L., & Thoresen, C. E. (2003). Religion and spirituality: Linkages to physical health. *American Psychologist, 58*, 36–52.

Powers, M. B., & Emmelkamp, P. M. (2008). Virtual reality exposure therapy for anxiety disorders: A meta-analysis. *Journal of Anxiety Disorders, 22*, 561–569.

Powers, W. T. (1973). *Behavior: The control of perception.* Hawthorne, NY: Aldine.

Powlison, D. (2000). A biblical counseling view. In E. L. Johnson & S. L. Jones (Eds.), *Psychology and Christianity: Four views* (pp. 196–225). Downers Grove, IL: InterVarsity.

Prater, J. S. (1987). Training Christian lay counselors in techniques of prevention and outreach. *Journal of Psychology and Christianity, 6* (2), 30–34.

Prochaska, J. O., & Norcross, J. C. (2010). *Systems of psychotherapy: A transtheoretical analysis* (7th ed.). Belmont, CA: Brooks/Cole.

Project MATCH Research Group. (1993). Project MATCH: Rationale and methods for a multisite clinical trial matching patients to alcoholism treatment. *Alcoholism: Clinical and Experimental Research, 17*, 1130–1145.

Project MATCH Research Group. (1997). Matching alcoholism treatments to client heterogeneity: Project MATCH posttreatment drinking outcomes. *Journal of Studies on Alcohol, 58*, 7–29.

Propst, L. R. (1980). The comparative efficacy of religious and non-religious imagery for the treatment of mild depression in religious individuals. *Cognitive Therapy and Research, 4*, 167–178.

Propst, L. R. (1988). *Psychotherapy in a religious framework: Spirituality in the emotional healing process.* New York: Human Sciences Press.

Propst, L. R., Ostrom, R., Watkins, P., Dean, T., & Mashburn, D. (1992). Comparative efficacy of religious and nonreligious cognitive-behavioral therapy for the treatment of clinical depression in religious individuals. *Journal of Consulting and Clinical Psychology, 60*, 94–103.

Puffer, K. A. (2007). Essential biblical assumptions about human nature: A modest proposal. *Journal of Psychology and Christianity, 26*, 45–56.

Pugh, J. (2008). *Christian formation counseling: The work of the Spirit in the human race.* Mustang, OK: Tate Publishing & Enterprises.

Purves, A. (2007). *The crucifixion of ministry: Surrendering our ambitions to the service of Christ.* Downers Grove, IL: InterVarsity.

Rachor, R. (1995). An evaluation of the first step PASSAGES domestic violence program. *Journal of Reality Therapy, 14*, 29–36.

Radnitz, C. L. (Ed.). (2000). *Cognitive-behavioral therapy for persons with disabilities.* Northvale, NJ: Jason Aronson.

Radtke, L., Sapp, M., & Farrell, W. (1997). Reality therapy: A meta-analysis. *International Journal of Reality Therapy, 17*, 4–9.

Rank, O. (1945). *Will therapy, truth and reality.* New York: Knopf.

Rapaport, D. (Ed. and trans.). (1951). *Organization and pathology of thought: Selected sources.* New York: Columbia University Press.

Raskin, N. J. (1992, August). *Not necessary, perhaps sufficient, definitely facilitative.* Paper presented at the 100th annual convention of the American Psychological Association, Washington, DC.

Raskin, N. J., Rogers, C. R., & Witty, M. C. (2008). Client-centered therapy. In R. J. Corsini & D. Wedding (Eds.), *Current psychotherapies* (8th ed., pp. 141–186). Belmont, CA: Brooks/Cole.

Rattner, J. (1983). *Alfred Adler.* New York: Ungar.

Ray, W. A. (2007). Jay Haley—a memorial. *Journal of Marital and Family Therapy, 33*, 291–292.

Rehm, L. P. (1977). A self-control model of depression. *Behavior Therapy, 8*, 787–804.

Reinecke, M. A., & Freeman, A. (2003). Cognitive therapy. In A. S. Gurman & S. B. Messer (Eds.), *Essential psychotherapies* (2nd ed., pp. 224–271). New York: Guilford Press.

Rennie, D. L. (1998). *Person-centered counseling: An experiential approach.* London: Sage.

Rice, L. N., & Greenberg, L. S. (1984). *Patterns of change.* New York: Guilford Press.

Richards, P. S. (2006). Theistic psychotherapy. *Psychology of Religion Newsletter, 31* (1), 1–12.

Richards, P. S., & Bergin, A. E. (1997). *A spiritual strategy for counseling and psychotherapy.* Washington, DC: American Psychological Association.

Richards, P. S., & Bergin, A. E. (Eds.). (2000). *Handbook of psychotherapy and religious diversity.* Washington, DC: American Psychological Association.

Richards, P. S., & Bergin, A. E. (Eds.). (2004). *Casebook for a spiritual strategy in counseling and psychotherapy.* Washington, DC: American Psychological Association.

Richards, P. S., & Bergin, A. E. (2005). *A spiritual strategy for counseling and psychotherapy* (2nd ed.). Washington, DC: American Psychological Association.

Richardson, R. (2005). *Experiencing healing prayer.* Downers Grove, IL: InterVarsity.

Ridley, C. R. (1986). Cross-cultural counseling in theological context. *Journal of Psychology and Theology, 14*, 288–297.

Ridley, C. R. (2005). *Overcoming unintentional racism in counseling and therapy: A practitioner's guide to intentional intervention* (2nd ed.). Thousand Oaks, CA: Sage.

Roazen, P. (2001). *The historiography of psychoanalysis.* New Brunswick, NJ: Transaction.

Roberts, R. C. (1993). *Taking the Word to heart: Self and others in an age of therapies.* Grand Rapids: Eerdmans.

Roberts, R. C. (2000). A Christian psychology view. In E. L. Johnson, & S. L. Jones (Eds.), *Psychology and Christianity: Four views* (pp. 148–177). Downers Grove, IL: InterVarsity.

Roemer, L., & Orsillo, S. M. (2009). *Mindfulness- and acceptance-based behavioral therapies in practice.* New York: Guilford Press.

Roepke, S., & Renneberg, B. (2009). Analyzing effectiveness of long-term psychodynamic psychotherapy. *Journal of the American Medical Association, 301,* 931–932.

Rogers, C. R. (1939). *The clinical treatment of the problem child.* Boston: Houghton Mifflin.

Rogers, C. R. (1942). *Counseling and psychotherapy.* Boston: Houghton Mifflin.

Rogers, C. R. (1951). *Client-centered therapy: Its current practice, implications, and theory.* Boston: Houghton Mifflin.

Rogers, C. R. (1957). The necessary and sufficient conditions of therapeutic personality change. *Journal of Consulting Psychology, 21,* 95–103.

Rogers, C. R. (1959). A theory of therapy, personality, and interpersonal relationships as developed in the client-centered framework. In S. Koch (Ed.), *Psychology: A study of science,* Vol. 3, *Formulations of the person and the social context* (pp. 184–256). New York: McGraw-Hill.

Rogers, C. R. (1961). *On becoming a person.* Boston: Houghton Mifflin.

Rogers, C. R. (1962). The interpersonal relationship: The core of guidance. *Harvard Educational Review, 32,* 416–429.

Rogers, C. R. (1967). Autobiography. In E. G. Boring & G. Lindzey (Eds.), *A history of psychology in autobiography* (Vol. 5, pp. 341–384). New York: Appleton.

Rogers, C. R. (1969). *Freedom to learn: A view of what education might become.* Columbus, OH: Charles E. Merrill.

Rogers, C. R. (1970). *Carl Rogers on encounter groups.* New York: Harper & Row.

Rogers, C. R. (1972). *Becoming partners: Marriage and its alternatives.* New York: Delacorte Press.

Rogers, C. R. (1975). Empathic: An unappreciated way of being. *Counseling Psychologist, 5,* 2–10.

Rogers, C. R. (1977). *Carl Rogers on personal power.* New York: Delacorte Press.

Rogers, C. R. (1980). *A way of being.* Boston: Houghton Mifflin.

Rogers, C. R. (1983). *Freedom to learn for the 80s.* Columbus, OH: Charles E. Merrill.

Rogers, C. R. (1986). Client-centered therapy. In I. L. Kutash & A. Wolfe (Eds.), *Psychotherapist's casebook: Therapy and technique in practice* (pp. 197–208). San Francisco: Jossey-Bass.

Rogers, C. R., Gendlin, G. T., Kiesler, D. V., & Truax, C. (Eds.). (1967). *The therapeutic relationship and its impact: A study of psychotherapy with schizophrenics.* Madison: University of Wisconsin Press.

Rogers, C. R., & Haigh, G. (1983). I walk softly through life. *Voices: The Art and Science of Psychotherapy, 18,* 6–14.

Rogers, H. E. (1965). A wife's view of Carl Rogers. *Voices: The Art and Science of Psychotherapy, 1,* 93–98.

Rogers, N. (1993). *The creative connection: Expressive arts as healing.* Palo Alto, CA: Science & Behavior Books.

Rogers, N. (1995). *Emerging woman: A decade of midlife transitions.* Manchester, England: PCCS Books.

Rogers, S. A. (2007). Where the moment meets the transcendent: Using the process as a spiritual intervention in object relations psychotherapy. *Journal of Psychology and Christianity, 26,* 151–158.

Rollnick, S., & Miller, W. R. (1995). What is motivational interviewing? *Behavioral and Cognitive Psychotherapy, 23,* 325–334.

Rollnick, S., Miller, W. R., & Butler, C. C. (2008). *Motivational interviewing in health care: Helping patients change behavior.* New York: Guilford Press.

Rose, E. M., Westefeld, J. S., & Ansley, T. N. (2001). Spiritual issues in counseling: Clients' beliefs and preferences. *Journal of Counseling Psychology, 48,* 61–71.

Rosen, G. M., & Davison, G. C. (2003). Psychology should list empirically supported principles of change (ESPs) and not credential trademarked therapies or other treatment packages. *Behavior Modification, 27,* 300–312.

Rosenfeld, E. (1978). An oral history of Gestalt therapy, Part 1: A conversation with Laura Perls. *Gestalt Journal, 1* (1), 8–31.

Rosengren, D. B. (2009). *Building motivational interviewing skills: A practitioner workbook.* New York: Guilford Press.

Rosner, R. I., Lyddon, W. J., & Freeman, A. (Eds.). (2003). *Cognitive therapy and dreams.* New York: Springer.

Roth, A., & Fonagy, P. (2005). *What works for whom? A critical review of psychotherapy research* (2nd ed.). New York: Guilford Press.

Rothbaum, B. O., & Hodges, L. F. (1999). The use of virtual reality exposure in the treatment of anxiety disorders. *Behavior Modification, 23,* 507–525.

Rupert, P. A., & Kent, J. S. (2007). Gender and work setting differences in career-sustaining behaviors and burnout among professional psychologists. *Professional Psychology: Research and Practice, 38,* 88–96.

Ryckman, R. M. (2008). *Theories of personality* (9th ed.). Belmont, CA: Wadsworth.

Safran, J. D., & Segal, Z. V. (1990). *Interpersonal process in cognitive therapy.* New York: Basic Books.

Saley, E., & Holdstock, L. (1993). Encounter group experiences of black and white South Africans in exile. In D. Brazier (Ed.), *Beyond Carl Rogers* (pp. 201–216). London: Constable.

Sandage, S. J., & Shults, F. L. (2007). Relational spirituality and transformation: A relational integration model. *Journal of Psychology and Christianity, 26,* 261–269.

Sandberg, J. G., Johnson, L. N., Dermer, S. B., Gfeller-Strouts, L. L., Seibold, J. M., Stringer-Seibold, T. A., et al. (1997). Demonstrated efficacy of models of marriage and family therapy: An update of Gurman, Kniskern, and Pinsof's chart. *American Journal of Family Therapy, 25,* 121–137.

Sandell, R., Blomberg, J., Lazar, A., Carlsson, J., Bromberg, J., & Schubert, J. (2000). Varieties of long-term outcome among patients in psychoanalysis and long-term psychotherapy. *International Journal of Psychoanalysis, 81,* 921–942.

Sanders, P. (2004a). History of client-centered therapy and the person-centered approach: Events, dates, and ideas. In P. Sanders (Ed.), *The tribes of the person-centered nation* (pp. 1–20). Ross-on-Wye, England: PCCS Books.

Sanders, P. (Ed.). (2004b). *The tribes of the person-centered nation.* Ross-on-Wye, England: PCCS Books.

Sanders, R. K. (Ed.). (1997). *Christian counseling ethics: A handbook for therapists, pastors, and counselors.* Downers Grove, IL: InterVarsity.

Sanford, J. A. (1999). Jungian analysis. In D. G. Benner & P. C. Hill (Eds.), *Baker encyclopedia of psychology and counseling* (2nd ed., pp. 658–660). Grand Rapids: Baker Academic.

Satir, V. M. (1964). *Conjoint family therapy: A guide to theory and technique.* Palo Alto, CA: Science & Behavior Books.

Satir, V. M. (1972). *Peoplemaking.* Palo Alto, CA: Science & Behavior Books.

Satir, V. M. (1983). *Conjoint family therapy: A guide to theory and technique* (3rd ed.). Palo Alto, CA: Science & Behavior Books.

Satir, V. M. (1988). *The new peoplemaking.* New York: Science & Behavior Books.

Satir, V. M., & Baldwin, M. (1983). *Satir step by step*. Palo Alto, CA: Science & Behavior Books.

Satir, V. M., Bauman, J., Gerber, J., & Gamori, M. (1991). *The Satir model: Family therapy and beyond*. Palo Alto, CA: Science & Behavior Books.

Satir, V. M., & Bitter, J. R. (2000). The therapist and family therapy: Satir's human validation process model. In A. M. Horne (Ed.), *Family counseling and therapy* (3rd ed., pp. 62–101). Itasca, IL: F. E. Peacock.

Saunders, T., Drishell, J. E., Johnson, J. H., & Salas, E. (1996). The effect of stress inoculation training on anxiety and performance. *Journal of Occupational Health Psychology, 1*, 170–186.

Scharff, D. E., & Scharff, J. S. (1987). *Object relations family therapy*. Northvale, NJ: Jason Aronson.

Scharff, D. E., & Scharff, J. S. (1991). *Object relations couple therapy*. Northvale, NJ: Jason Aronson.

Scharff, J. S., & Scharff, D. E. (2008). Object relations couple therapy. In A. S. Gurman (Ed.), *Clinical handbook of couple therapy* (4th ed., pp. 167–195). New York: Guilford Press.

Schneider, K. J. (1998). Existential processes. In L. S. Greenberg, J. C. Watson, & G. Lietaer (Eds.), *Handbook of experiential psychotherapy* (2nd ed., pp. 103–120). New York: Guilford Press.

Schneider, K. J. (2003). Existential-humanistic psychotherapies. In A. Gurman & S. Messer (Eds.), *Essential psychotherapies* (pp. 149–181). New York: Guilford Press.

Schneider, K. J. (2004). *Rediscovery of awe: Splendor, mystery and the fluid center of life*. St. Paul, MN: Paragon House.

Schneider, K. J. (2007). *Existential integrative psychotherapy: Guideposts to the core of practice*. New York: Routledge.

Scott, J., Williams, J. M. G., & Beck, A. T. (Eds.). (1989). *Cognitive therapy in clinical practice*. London: Routledge & Kegan Paul.

Seamands, D. A. (1985). *Healing of memories*. Wheaton: Victor Books. (Republished as *Redeeming the past*. Wheaton: Victor Books, 2002.)

See, J. D. (1985). Person-centered perspective. *Journal of Applied Rehabilitation Counseling, 16*, 15–20.

Seeman, T. E., Dubin, L. F., & Seeman, M. (2003). Religiosity/spirituality and health: A critical review of the evidence for biological pathways. *American Psychologist, 58*, 53–63.

Segal, Z. V., Williams, J. M. G., & Teasdale, J. D. (2002). *Mindfulness-based cognitive therapy for depression: A new approach for preventing relapse*. New York: Guilford Press.

Seligman, L. (1986). *Diagnosis and treatment planning in counseling*. New York: Human Sciences Press.

Seligman, M. E. P. (1975). *Helplessness: On depression, development, and death*. San Francisco: W. H. Freeman.

Seligman, M. E. P. (1995). The effectiveness of psychotherapy: The *Consumer Reports* study. *American Psychologist, 50*, 965–974.

Seligman, M. E. P., & Czikszentmihalyi, M. (2000). Positive psychology: An introduction. *American Psychologist, 55*, 5–14.

Seligman, M. E. P., Rashid, T., & Parks, A. C. (2006). Positive psychotherapy. *American Psychologist, 61*, 774–788.

Seligman, M. E. P., Steen, T. A., Park, N., & Peterson, C. (2005). Positive psychology progress: Empirical validation of interventions. *American Psychologist, 60*, 410–421.

Selvini, M. (Ed.). (1988). *The work of Mara Selvini Palazzoli*. Northvale, NJ: Jason Aronson.

Selvini-Palazzoli, M. (1986). Towards a general model of psychotic games. *Journal of Marital and Family Therapy, 12*, 339–349.

Selvini-Palazzoli, M., Boscolo, L., Cecchin, G. F., & Prata, G. (1978). *Paradox and counterparadox: A new model in the therapy of the family schizophrenic transaction*. New York: Jason Aronson.

Sexton, T. L., & Alexander, J. F. (1999). *Functional family therapy: Principles of clinical intervention, assessment, and implementation*. Henderson, NV: FFT.

Sexton, T. L., Alexander, J. F., & Mease, A. L. (2004). Levels of evidence for the models and mechanisms of therapeutic change in family and couple therapy. In M. J. Lambert (Ed.), *Bergin and Garfield's handbook of psychotherapy and behavior change* (5th ed., pp. 590–646). New York: Wiley.

Sexton, T. L., Weeks, G. R., & Robbins, M. S. (Eds.). (2003). *Handbook of family therapy: The science and practice of working with families and couples*. New York: Brunner-Routledge.

Shadish, W. R., & Baldwin, S. A. (2003). Meta-analysis of MFT interventions. *Journal of Marital and Family Therapy, 29*, 547–570.

Shadish, W. R., & Baldwin, S. A. (2005). Effects of behavioral marital therapy: A meta-analysis of randomized controlled trials. *Journal of Consulting and Clinical Psychology, 73*, 6–14.

Shadish, W. R., Montgomery, L. M., Wilson, P., Wilson, M. R., Bright, L., & Okwumakua, T. (1993). The effects of family and marital psychotherapies: A meta-analysis. *Journal of Consulting and Clinical Psychology, 61*, 992–1002.

Shadish, W. R., Ragsdale, K., Glaser, R. R., & Montgomery, L. M. (1995). The efficacy and effectiveness of marital and family therapy: A perspective from meta-analysis. *Journal of Marital and Family Therapy, 21*, 345–360.

Shafranske, E. P. (Ed.). (1996). *Religion and the clinical practice of psychology.* Washington, DC: American Psychological Association.

Shamdasani, S. (2003). *Jung and the making of modern psychology.* Cambridge: Cambridge University Press.

Shapiro, D. A., & Shapiro, D. (1982). Meta-analysis of comparative therapy outcome studies: A replication and refinement. *Psychological Bulletin, 92,* 581–604.

Shapiro, F. (2001). *Eye movement desensitization and reprocessing: Basic principles, protocols, and procedures* (2nd ed.). New York: Guilford Press.

Shapiro, F. (2002). *EMDR as an integrative psychotherapy approach.* Washington, DC: American Psychological Association.

Sharf, R. S. (2008). *Theories of psychotherapy and counseling: Concepts and cases* (4th ed.). Belmont, CA: Brooks/Cole.

Shedler, J. (2010). The efficacy of psychodynamic psychotherapy. *American Psychologist, 65,* 98–109.

Shepard, M. (1975). *Fritz.* Sagaponack, NY: Second Chance Press.

Shepherd, I. L. (1970). Limitations and cautions in the Gestalt approach. In J. Fagan & I. L. Shepherd (Eds.), *Gestalt therapy now* (pp. 234–238). Palo Alto, CA: Science and Behavior Books.

Shoham-Salomon, V., & Rosenthal, R. (1987). Paradoxical interventions: A meta-analysis. *Journal of Consulting and Clinical Psychology, 55,* 22–28.

Shults, F. L., & Sandage, S. J. (2006). *Transforming spirituality: Integrating theology and psychology.* Grand Rapids: Baker Academic.

Shuster, M. (1987). *Power, pathology, paradox: The dynamics of evil and good.* Grand Rapids: Zondervan.

Silverstein, L. B., & Goodrich, T. J. (Eds.). (2003). *Feminist family therapy: Empowerment in social context.* Washington, DC: American Psychological Association.

Simon, G. M. (2008). Structural couple therapy. In A. S. Gurman (Ed.), *Clinical handbook of couple therapy* (4th ed., pp. 323–349). New York: Guilford Press.

Sin, N. L., & Lyubomirsky, S. (2009). Enhancing well-being and alleviating depressive symptoms with positive psychology interventions: A practice-friendly meta-analysis. *Journal of Clinical Psychology: In Session, 65* (5), 467–487.

Skinner, B. F. (1948). *Walden Two.* New York: Macmillan.

Skinner, B. F. (1953). *Science and Human Behavior.* New York: Macmillan.

Skinner, B. F. (1971). *Beyond freedom and dignity.* New York: Knopf.

Skinner, B. F. (1990). Can psychology be a science of mind? *American Psychologist, 45,* 1206–1210.

Skinner, B. F., Solomon, H. C., & Lindsley, O. R. (1953). Studies in behavior therapy: Status report I. November 30, 1953. Unpublished report, Metropolitan State Hospital, Waltham, MA.

Skovholt, T. M. (2001). *The resilient practitioner: Burnout prevention and self-care strategies for counselors, therapists, teachers, and health professionals*. Needham Heights, MA: Allyn & Bacon.

Sloan, R. P., & Bagiella, E. (2002). Claims about religious involvement and health outcomes. *Annals of Behavioral Medicine, 24* (1), 14–21.

Smith, D. (1982). Trends in counseling and psychotherapy. *American Psychologist, 37*, 802–809.

Smith, E. M. (2002/2005). *Healing life's hurts through theophostic prayer*. Campbellsville, KY: New Creation.

Smith, M. L., & Glass, G. V. (1977). Meta-analysis of psychotherapy outcome studies. *American Psychologist, 32*, 752–760.

Smith, M. L., Glass, G. V., & Miller, T. I. (1980). *The benefits of psychotherapy*. Baltimore: Johns Hopkins University Press.

Smith, T. B., Bartz, J., & Richards, P. S. (2007). Outcomes of religious and spiritual adaptations to psychotherapy: A meta-analytic review. *Psychotherapy Research, 17*, 643–655.

Smuts, J. (1926/1996). *Holism and evolution*. New York: MacMillan.

Snyder, D. K., & Whisman, M. A. (Eds.). (2003). *Treating difficult couples: Helping clients with coexisting mental and relationship disorders*. New York: Guilford Press.

Snyder, D. K., Castellani, A. M., & Whisman, M. A. (2006). Current status and future directions in couple therapy. *Annual Review of Psychology, 57*, 317–344.

Sommers-Flanagan, J. (2007). The development and evolution of person-centered expressive art therapy: A conversation with Natalie Rogers. *Journal of Counseling and Development, 85* (1), 120–125.

Sommers-Flanagan, J., & Sommers-Flanagan, R. (2003). *Clinical interviewing* (3rd ed.). New York: Wiley.

Sommers-Flanagan, J., & Sommers-Flanagan, R. (2004). *Counseling and psychotherapy theories in context and practice: Skills, strategies, and techniques*. Hoboken, NJ: Wiley.

Sommers-Flanagan, R., & Sommers-Flanagan, J. (2007). *Becoming an ethical helping professional: Cultural and philosophical foundations*. Hoboken, NJ: Wiley.

Sorenson, R. L. (2004). *Minding spirituality*. Hillsdale, NJ: Analytic Press.

Sperry, L., & Shafranske, E. P. (Eds.). (2005). *Spiritually oriented psychotherapy*. Washington, DC: American Psychological Association.

Spiegler, M. D. (2008). Behavior therapy 1: Traditional behavior therapy. In J. Frew & M. D. Spiegler (Eds.), *Contemporary psychotherapies for a diverse world* (pp. 275–319). Boston: Lahaska Press.

Spiegler, M. D., & Guevremont, D. C. (2003). *Contemporary behavior therapy* (4th ed.). Belmont, CA: Wadsworth.

Spivack, G., Platt, J. J., & Shure, M. B. (1976). *The problem-solving approach to adjustment.* San Francisco: Jossey-Bass.

Sprenkle, D. H., & Piercy, F. P. (2005). *Research methods in family therapy* (2nd ed.). New York: Guilford Press.

Sprenkle, D. H., Davis, S. D., & Lebow, J. L. (2009). *Common factors in couple and family therapy: The overlooked foundation for effective practice.* New York: Guilford Press.

St. Clair, M., & Wigren, J. (2004). *Object relations and self psychology: An introduction* (4th ed.). Belmont, CA: Brooks/Cole.

Stampfl, T. G., & Levis, D. J. (1967). Essentials of implosive therapy: A learning-theory-based psychodynamic behavioral therapy. *Journal of Abnormal Psychology, 72,* 496–503.

Stampfl, T. G., & Levis, D. J. (1973). *Implosive therapy: Theory and technique.* Morristown, NJ: General Learning Press.

Stanton, M. D., & Shadish, W. R. (1997). Outcome, attrition, and family-couples treatment for drug abuse: A meta-analysis and review of the controlled, comparative studies. *Psychological Bulletin, 122,* 170–191.

Steering Committee. (2002). Empirically supported therapy relationships: Conclusions and recommendations of the Division 29 Task Force. In J. C. Norcross (Ed.), *Psychotherapy relationships that work* (pp. 441–443). New York: Oxford University Press.

Stein, D. M., & Lambert, M. J. (1995). Graduate training in psychotherapy: Are therapy outcomes enhanced? *Journal of Consulting and Clinical Psychology, 63,* 182–196.

Stevens, A. (1982). *Archetypes: A natural history of the self.* New York: Morrow.

Stevenson, D. H., Eck, B. E., & Hill, P. C. (Eds.). (2007). *Psychology and Christianity integration: Seminal works that shaped the movement.* Batavia, IL: Christian Association for Psychological Studies.

Stewart, R. E., & Chambless, D. L. (2009). Cognitive-behavioral therapy for adult anxiety disorders in clinical practice: A meta-analysis of effectiveness studies. *Journal of Consulting and Clinical Psychology, 77,* 595–606.

Stolorow, R. D., Atwood, G. E., & Brandchaft, B. (Eds.). (1994). *The intersubjective perspective.* Northvale, NJ: Jason Aronson.

Stolorow, R. D., Brandchaft, B., & Atwood, G. E. (1987). *Psychoanalytic treatment: An intersubjective approach*. Hillsdale, NJ: Analytic Press.

Storr, A. (1983). *The essential Jung*. Princeton, NJ: Princeton University Press.

Strawn, B. D. (2007). Slouching toward integration: Psychoanalysis and religion in dialogue. *Journal of Psychology and Theology, 35*, 3–13.

Strümpfel, U., & Courtney, M. (2004). Research on Gestalt therapy. *International Gestalt Journal, 27* (1), 9–54.

Strümpfel, U., & Goldman, R. (2002). Contacting Gestalt therapy. In D. J. Cain & J. Seeman (Eds.), *Humanistic psychotherapies: Handbook of research and practice* (pp. 189–219). Washington, DC: American Psychological Association.

Sturkie, J., & Tan, S. Y. (1992). *Peer counseling in youth groups*. Grand Rapids: Zondervan/Youth Specialties.

Sturkie, J., & Tan, S. Y. (1993). *Advanced peer counseling in youth groups*. Grand Rapids: Zondervan/Youth Specialties.

Sue, D., & Sue, D. M. (2008). *Foundations of counseling and psychotherapy: Evidence-based practices for a diverse society*. Hoboken, NJ: Wiley.

Sue, D. W., & Sue, D. (2008). *Counseling the culturally diverse: Theory and practice* (5th ed.). Hoboken, NJ: Wiley.

Sue, D. W., Capodilupo, C. M., Torino, G. G., Bucceri, J. M., Holder, A. M. B., Nadal, K. L., & Esquilin, M. (2007). Racial microaggressions in everyday life: Implications for clinical practice. *American Psychologist, 62*, 271–286.

Suinn, R. M., & Richardson, F. (1971). Anxiety Management Training: A nonspecific behavior therapy program for anxiety control. *Behavior Therapy, 2*, 498–510.

Summers, R. F., & Barber, J. P. (2009). *Psychodynamic therapy: A guide to evidence-based practice*. New York: Guilford Press.

Sweeney, T. J. (1998). *Adlerian counseling: A practitioner's approach* (4th ed.). Philadelphia: Accelerated Development.

Swindoll, C. R. (1994). Helping and the Holy Spirit. *Christian Counseling Today, 2* (1), 16–19.

Szasz, T. S. (1970). *The manufacture of madness*. New York: McGraw-Hill.

Szasz, T. S. (1971). *The myth of mental illness*. New York: Hoeber.

Takle, D. (2008). *The truth about lies and lies about truth*. Pasadena, CA: Shepherd's House.

Tan, S. Y. (1987a). Cognitive-behavior therapy: A biblical approach and critique. *Journal of Psychology and Theology, 15*, 103–112.

Tan, S. Y. (1987b). Intrapersonal integration: The servant's spirituality. *Journal of Psychology and Christianity, 6* (1), 34–39.

Tan, S. Y. (1991). *Lay counseling: Equipping Christians for a helping ministry.* Grand Rapids: Zondervan.

Tan, S. Y. (1992). The Holy Spirit and counseling ministries. *Christian Journal of Psychology and Counseling,* 7 (3), 8–11.

Tan, S. Y. (1994). Ethical considerations in religious psychotherapy: Potential pitfalls and unique resources. *Journal of Psychology and Theology,* 22, 389–394.

Tan, S. Y. (1996a). *Managing chronic pain.* Downers Grove, IL: InterVarsity.

Tan, S. Y. (1996b). Practicing the presence of God: The work of Richard J. Foster and its application to psychotherapeutic practice. *Journal of Psychology and Christianity,* 15, 17–28.

Tan, S. Y. (1996c). Religion in clinical practice: Implicit and explicit integration. In E. P. Shafranske (Ed.), *Religion and the clinical practice of psychology* (pp. 365–387). Washington DC: American Psychological Association.

Tan, S. Y. (1997a). Lay counselor training. In R. K. Sanders (Ed.), *Christian counseling ethics: A handbook for therapists, pastors, and counselors* (pp. 235–245). Downers Grove, IL: InterVarsity.

Tan, S. Y. (1997b). The role of the psychologist in paraprofessional helping. *Professional Psychology: Research and Practice,* 28, 368–372.

Tan, S. Y. (1998). The spiritual disciplines and counseling. *Christian Counseling Today,* 6 (2), 8–9, 20–21.

Tan, S. Y. (1999a). Cultural issues in Spirit-filled psychotherapy. *Journal of Psychology and Christianity,* 18, 164–176.

Tan, S. Y. (1999b). Holy Spirit: Role in counseling. In D. G. Benner & P. C. Hill (Eds.), *Baker encyclopedia of psychology and counseling* (2nd ed., pp. 568–569). Grand Rapids: Baker Academic.

Tan, S. Y. (2001a). Empirically supported treatments. *Journal of Psychology and Christianity,* 20, 282–286.

Tan, S. Y. (2001b). Integration and beyond: Principled, professional, and personal. *Journal of Psychology and Christianity,* 20, 18–28.

Tan, S. Y. (2002a). Empirically informed principles of treatment selection: Beyond empirically supported treatments. *Journal of Psychology and Christianity,* 21, 54–56.

Tan, S. Y. (2002b). Lay helping: The whole church in soul-care ministry. In T. Clinton & G. Ohlschlager (Eds.), *Competent Christian counseling* (Vol. 1, pp. 424–436, 759–762). Colorado Springs: WaterBrook Press.

Tan, S. Y. (2003a). Empirically supported therapy relationships: Psychotherapy relationships that work. *Journal of Psychology and Christianity,* 22, 64–67.

Tan, S. Y. (2003b). Inner healing prayer. *Christian Counseling Today, 11* (4), 20–22.

Tan, S. Y. (2003c). Integrating spiritual direction into psychotherapy: Ethical issues and guidelines. *Journal of Psychology and Theology, 31,* 14–23.

Tan, S. Y. (2003d). *Rest: Experiencing God's peace in a restless world.* Vancouver, BC: Regent College.

Tan, S. Y. (2004). Spiritual direction and psychotherapy: Ethical issues. In G. W. Moon & D. G. Benner (Eds.), *Spiritual direction and the care of souls* (pp. 187–204). Downers Grove, IL: InterVarsity.

Tan, S. Y. (2006a). Applied positive psychology: Putting positive psychology into practice. *Journal of Psychology and Christianity, 25,* 68–73.

Tan, S. Y. (2006b). *Full service: Moving beyond self-serve Christianity to total servanthood.* Grand Rapids: Baker Books.

Tan, S. Y. (2007a). Empirically based principles of therapeutic change: Principles of therapeutic change that work. *Journal of Psychology and Christianity, 26,* 61–64.

Tan, S. Y. (2007b). Use of prayer and Scripture in cognitive-behavioral therapy. *Journal of Psychology and Christianity, 26,* 101–111.

Tan, S. Y. (2007c). Using spiritual disciplines in clinical supervision. *Journal of Psychology and Christianity, 26,* 328–335.

Tan, S. Y. (2008a). Evangelical spirituality: An essential aspect of evangelical activism. *Theology, News & Notes, 55* (1), 28–31.

Tan, S. Y. (2008b). Faith in psychology and counseling: Being Spirit-filled servants of Jesus Christ. *Edification: Journal of the Society for Christian Psychology, 2* (1), 63–68.

Tan, S. Y. (2008c). Potentially harmful therapies: Psychological treatments that can cause harm. *Journal of Psychology and Christianity, 27,* 61–65.

Tan, S. Y. (2009a). Developing integration skills: The role of clinical supervision. *Journal of Psychology and Theology, 37,* 54–61.

Tan, S. Y. (2009b). The primacy of servanthood. In E. O. Jacobsen (Ed.), *The three tasks of leadership: Worldly wisdom for pastoral leaders* (pp. 77–90). Grand Rapids: Eerdmans.

Tan, S. Y., & Gregg, D. H. (1997). *Disciplines of the Holy Spirit.* Grand Rapids: Zondervan.

Tan, S. Y., & Johnson, W. B. (2005). Spiritually oriented cognitive-behavioral therapy. In L. Sperry & E. P. Shafranske (Eds.), *Spiritually oriented psychotherapy* (pp. 77–103). Washington, DC: American Psychological Association.

Tan, S. Y., & Ortberg, J. (2004). *Coping with depression* (Rev. ed.). Grand Rapids: Baker Books.

Tang, A. (2008). Not just for monks: Spiritual disciplines are for anyone who wants to love God and others more. *Asian Beacon*, *40* (1), 8–9.

Tashiro, T., & Mortensen, L. (2006). Translational research: How social psychology can improve psychotherapy. *American Psychologist*, *61*, 959–966.

Task Force on Promotion & Dissemination of Psychological Procedures (1995). Training in and dissemination of empirically validated psychological treatments: Report and recommendations. *Clinical Psychologist*, *48*, 3–23.

Tausch, R. (1990). The supplementation of client-centered communication therapy with other valid therapeutic methods: A client-centered necessity. In G. Lietaer, J. Rombauts, & R. Van Balen (Eds.), *Client-centered and experiential psychotherapy in the nineties* (pp. 447–455). Leuven, Belgium: Leuven University Press.

Terrell, C. J. (2007). A discussion of intentional incarnational integration in relational psychodynamic psychotherapy. *Journal of Psychology and Christianity*, *26*, 159–165.

Thomas, G. (2000a). *Sacred marriage: What if God designed marriage to make us holy more than to make as happy?* Grand Rapids: Zondervan.

Thomas, G. (2000b). *Sacred pathways: Discover your soul's path to God.* Grand Rapids: Zondervan.

Thomas, G. (2002). *Authentic faith: The power of a fire-tested life.* Grand Rapids: Zondervan.

Thomas, G. (2004). *Sacred parenting: How raising children shapes our souls.* Grand Rapids: Zondervan.

Thombs, B. D., Bassel, M., & Jewett, L. R. (2009). Analyzing effectiveness of long-term psychodynamic psychotherapy. *Journal of the American Medical Association*, *301*, 930.

Thorne, B. (2003). *Carl Rogers* (2nd ed.). London: Sage.

Thorpe, C. (2008). *The healing timeline: God's shalom for the past, present and future.* Bellevue, WA: Timeline Press.

Tillich, P. (1952). *The courage to be.* New Haven, CT: Yale University Press.

Tjeltveit, A. C. (1992). The psychotherapist as Christian ethicist: Theology applied to practice. *Journal of Psychology and Theology*, *20*, 89–98.

Tjeltveit, A. C. (1999). *Ethics and values in psychotherapy.* New York: Routledge.

Todd, J., & Bohart, A. C. (2006). *Foundations of clinical and counseling psychology* (4th ed.). Long Grove, IL: Waveland Press.

Toh, Y. M., & Tan, S. Y. (1997). The effectiveness of church-based lay counselors: A controlled outcome study. *Journal of Psychology and Christianity*, *16*, 260–267.

Tolle, E. (2005). *A new earth: Awakening to your life's purpose*. New York: Dutton.

Truax, C., & Carkhuff, R. (1967). *Toward effective counseling and psychotherapy*. Chicago: Aldine.

Truscott, D. (2010). *Becoming an effective psychotherapist: Adopting a theory of psychotherapy that's right for you and your client*. Washington, DC: American Psychological Association.

Turner, J. A., Edwards, L. M., Eicken, I. M., Yokoyama, K., Castro, J. R., Tran, A. N. T., & Haggins, K. L. (2005). Intern self-care: An exploratory study into strategy use and effectiveness. *Professional Psychology: Research and Practice, 36*, 674–680.

Tweedie, D. (1961). *Logotherapy: An evaluation of Frankl's existential approach to psychotherapy from a Christian viewpoint*. Grand Rapids: Baker Academic.

Tyler, K. (1999). Examining unconditional positive regard as the primary condition of therapeutic personality change. *Person-Centered Journal, 6*, 100–107.

Tyrell, B. J. (1982). *Christotherapy II*. New York: Paulist Press.

Ulanov, A. B., & Dueck, A. (2008). *The living God and our living psyche: What Christians can learn from Carl Jung*. Grand Rapids: Eerdmans.

Unger, M. F. (1981). *Unger's Bible dictionary* (3rd ed.). Chicago: Moody.

Uomoto, J. M. (1986). Delivering mental health services to ethnic minorities: Ethical considerations. *Journal of Psychology and Theology, 14*, 15–21.

Vaihinger, H. (1911). *The psychology of "as if."* New York: Harcourt, Brace, & World.

Van Duerzen, E. (2001). *Existential counselling and psychotherapy in practice* (2nd ed.). Thousand Oaks, CA: Sage.

Van Duerzen, E., & Kenward, R. (2005). *Dictionary of existential psychotherapy and counselling*. London: Sage.

Van Duerzen-Smith, E. (1990). *Existential therapy*. London: Society for Existential Analysis Publications.

Van Duerzen-Smith, E. (1997). *Everyday mysteries: Existential dimensions of psychotherapy*. London: Routledge.

Van Duerzen-Smith, E. (1998). *Paradox and passion in psychotherapy: An existential approach to therapy and counselling*. Chichester, England: Wiley.

Van Heusden, A., & Van den Eerenbeemt, E. (1987). *Balance in motion: Ivan Boszormenyi-Nagy and his vision of individual and family therapy*. New York: Brunner/Mazel.

Van Ingen, D. J., Freiheit, S. R., & Vye, C. S. (2009). From the lab to the clinic: Effectiveness of cognitive-behavioral treatments for anxiety disorders. *Professional Psychology: Research and Practice, 40*, 69–74.

Vande Kemp, H. (1996). Psychology and Christian spirituality: Explorations of the inner world. *Journal of Psychology and Christianity*, *15*, 161–174.

Vining, J. K. (1995a). *Pentecostal caregivers: Anointed to heal.* East Rockaway, NY: Cummings & Hathaway.

Vining J. K. (1995b). *Spirit-centered counseling: A pneumascriptive approach.* East Rockaway, NY: Cummings & Hathaway.

Vining, J. K., & Decker, E. E. (Eds.). (1996). *Soul care: A Pentecostal-charismatic perspective.* East Rockaway, NY: Cummings & Hathaway.

Vittengl, J. R., Clark, L. A., Dunn, T. W., & Jarrett, R. B. (2007). Reducing relapse and recurrence in unipolar depression: A comparative meta-analysis of cognitive-behavioral therapy's effects. *Journal of Consulting and Clinical Psychology*, *75*, 475–488.

Vitz, P. (1994). *Psychology as religion: The cult of self-worship* (2nd ed.). Grand Rapids: Eerdmans.

Voss Horrell, S. C. (2008). Effectiveness of cognitive-behavioral therapy with adult ethnic minority clients: A review. *Professional Psychology: Research and Practice*, *39*, 160–168.

Wachtel, P. L. (2008). *Relational theory and the practice of psychotherapy.* New York: Guilford Press.

Wade, N. G., Worthington, E. L., Jr., & Vogel, D. L. (2007). Effectiveness of religiously tailored interventions in Christian therapy. *Psychotherapy Research*, *17*, 91–105.

Wagner, C. P. (1994). *Your spiritual gifts can help your church grow* (Rev. ed.). Ventura, CA: Regal.

Walker, D. F., Gorsuch, R. L., & Tan, S. Y. (2005). Therapists' use of religious and spiritual interventions in Christian counseling: A preliminary report. *Counseling and Values*, *49*, 107–119.

Walker, D. F., Gorsuch, R. L., Tan, S. Y., & Otis, K. E. (2008). Use of religious and spiritual interventions by trainees in APA-accredited Christian clinical programs. *Mental Health, Religion & Culture*, *11*, 623–633.

Walker, D. F., Reese, J. B., Hughes, J. P., & Troskie, M. J. (2010). Addressing religious and spiritual issues in trauma-focused cognitive behavior therapy for children and adolescents. *Professional Psychology: Research and Practice*, *41*, 174–180.

Walker, G. (1987). Rehabilitation counseling with dual diagnosis clients. *Journal of Applied Rehabilitation Counseling*, *18*, 35–37.

Wallerstein, R. S. (1986). *Forty-two lives in treatment: A study of psychoanalysis and psychotherapy.* New York: Guilford Press.

Wallerstein, R. S. (1996). Outcomes of psychoanalysis and psychotherapy at termination and follow up. In E. Nesessian & R. G. Kopff Jr. (Eds.), *Textbook of psychoanalysis* (pp. 531–573). Washington, DC: American Psychiatric Press.

Wallerstein, R. S. (2001). The generations of psychotherapy research: An overview. *Psychoanalytic Psychology, 18,* 243–267.

Walsh, F. (Ed.). (2009). *Spiritual resources in family therapy* (2nd ed.). New York: Guilford Press.

Walsh, R. A., & McElwain, B. (2002). Existential psychotherapies. In D. J. Cain & J. Seeman (Eds.), *Humanistic psychotherapies: Handbook of research and practice* (pp. 253–278). Washington, DC: American Psychological Association.

Wampold, B. E. (2001). *The great psychotherapy debate: Models, methods, and findings.* Mahwah, NJ: Erlbaum.

Wampold, B. E., Mondin, G. W., Moody, M., Stich, F., Benson, K., & Ahn, H. N. (1997). A meta-analysis of outcome studies comparing bona fide psychotherapies: Empirically, "All must have prizes." *Psychological Bulletin, 122,* 203–215.

Wardle, T. (2001). *Healing care, healing prayer.* Orange, CA: New Leaf Books.

Watkins, C. E., Jr., & Guarnaccia, C. A. (1999). The scientific study of Adlerian theory. In R. E. Watts & J. Carlson (Eds.), *Interventions and strategies in counseling and psychotherapy* (pp. 207–230). Philadelphia: Accelerated Development.

Watson, D. L., & Tharp, R. G. (2007). *Self-directed behavior: Self-modification for personal adjustment* (9th ed.). Belmont, CA: Wadsworth.

Watson, J. C. (2002). Re-visioning empathy. In D. J. Cain & J. Seeman (Eds.), *Humanistic psychotherapies: Handbook of research and practice* (pp. 445–471). Washington, DC: American Psychological Association.

Watson, W. H. (1997). Soul and system: The integrative possibilities of family therapy. *Journal of Psychology and Theology, 25,* 123–135.

Watts, R. E. (Ed.). (2003). *Adlerian, cognitive, and constructivist therapies: An integrative dialogue.* New York: Springer.

Watts, R. E., & Holden, J. M. (1994). Why continue to use "fictional finalism"? *Individual Psychology, 50,* 161–163.

Webber, R. E. (2006). *The divine embrace: Recovering the passionate spiritual life.* Grand Rapids: Baker Academic.

Weeks, G. R., & L'Abate, L. (1982). *Paradoxical psychotherapy: Theory and practice with individuals, couples, and families.* New York: Brunner/Mazel.

Weiner, D. N. (1988). *Albert Ellis: Passionate skeptic*. New York: Praeger.

Weishaar, M. E. (1993). *Aaron T. Beck*. Thousand Oaks, CA: Sage.

Weisz, J. R., Hawley, K. M., & Doss, A. J. (2004). Empirically tested psychotherapies for youth internalizing and externalizing problems and disorders. *Child & Adolescent Psychiatric Clinics of North America, 13*, 729–815.

Weisz, J. R., Weiss, B., Alicke, M. D., & Klotz, M. L. (1987). Effectiveness of psychotherapy with children and adolescents: A meta-analysis for clinicians. *Journal of Consulting and Clinical Psychology, 55*, 542–549.

Weisz, J. R., Weiss, B., Han, S. S., Granger, D. A., & Morton, T. (1995). Effects of psychotherapy with children and adolescents revisited: A meta-analysis of treatment outcome studies. *Psychological Bulletin, 117*, 450–468.

Welch, E., & Powlison, D. (1997a). "Every common bush afire with God": The Scripture's constitutive role for counseling. *Journal of Psychology and Christianity, 16*, 303–322.

Welch, E., & Powlison, D. (1997b). Response to Hurley and Berry. *Journal of Psychology and Christianity, 16*, 346–349.

Weld, C., & Eriksen, K. (2007). Christian clients' preferences regarding prayer as a counseling intervention. *Journal of Psychology and Theology, 35*, 328–341.

Wenzel, A., Brown, G. K., & Beck, A. T. (2009). *Cognitive therapy for suicidal patients: Scientific and clinical applications*. Washington, DC: American Psychological Association.

Westen, D. (1998). The scientific legacy of Sigmund Freud: Toward a psychodynamically informed psychological science. *Psychological Bulletin, 124*, 333–371.

Westen, D., Novotny, C., & Thompson-Brenner, H. (2004). The empirical status of empirically supported psychotherapies: Assumptions, findings, and reporting in controlled clinical trials. *Psychological Bulletin, 130*, 631–663.

Whaley, A. L., & Davis, K. E. (2007). Cultural competence and evidence-based practice in mental health services: A complementary perspective. *American Psychologist, 62*, 563–574.

Whitaker, C. A. (1989). *The midnight musings of a family therapist*. New York: Norton.

Whitaker, C. A., & Bumburry, W. M. (1988). *Dancing with the family: A symbolic-experiential approach*. New York: Brunner/Mazel.

Whitaker, C. A., & Keith, D. V. (1981). Symbolic-experiential family therapy. In A. S. Gurman & D. P. Kniskern (Eds.), *Handbook of family therapy* (Vol. 1, pp. 187–225). New York: Brunner/Mazel.

Whitaker, C. A., & Malone, T. (1953). *The roots of psychotherapy*. New York: Blakiston.

White, F. J. (1987). Spiritual and religious issues in therapy. In D. G. Benner (Ed.), *Psychotherapy in Christian perspective* (pp. 37–46). Grand Rapids: Baker Academic.

White, M. (2007). *Maps of narrative practice*. New York: Norton.

White, M., & Epston, D. (1989). *Literate means to therapeutic ends*. Adelaide, Australia: Dulwich Centre Publications.

White, M., & Epston, D. (1990). *Narrative means to therapeutic ends*. New York: Norton.

Whitmont, E. C. (1991). *The symbolic quest*. Princeton, NJ: Princeton University Press.

Whitney, D. S. (1991). *Spiritual disciplines for the Christian life*. Colorado Springs: NavPress.

Whittington, B. L., & Scher, S. J. (2010). Prayer and subjective well-being: An examination of six different types of prayer. *The International Journal for the Psychology of Religion, 20*, 59–68.

Wiederhold, B. K., & Wiederhold, M. D. (2005). *Virtual reality therapy for anxiety disorders: Advances in evaluation and treatment*. Washington, DC: American Psychological Association.

Wilhoit, J. C. (2008). *Spiritual formation as if the church mattered: Growing in Christ through community*. Grand Rapids: Baker Academic.

Willard, D. (1988). *The spirit of the disciplines*. San Francisco: Harper & Row.

Willard, D. (1996). Spirituality: Going beyond the limits. *Christian Counseling Today, 4* (1), 16–20.

Willard, D. (1998). *The divine conspiracy: Rediscovering our hidden life in God*. New York: HarperSanFrancisco.

Willard, D. (2002). *Renovation of the heart: Putting on the character of Christ*. Colorado Springs: NavPress.

Willard, D. (2006). *The great omission: Reclaiming Jesus' essential teachings on discipleship*. San Francisco: HarperSanFrancisco.

Williams, J. M. G., Russell, I., & Russell, D. (2008). Mindfulness-based cognitive therapy: Further issues in current evidence and future research. *Journal of Consulting and Clinical Psychology, 76*, 524–529.

Wilson, G. T. (2008). Behavior therapy. In R. J. Corsini & D. Wedding (Eds.), *Current psychotherapies* (8th ed., pp. 223–262). Belmont, CA: Brooks/Cole.

Wilson, G. T., & Shafran, R. (2005). Eating disorders guidelines from NICE. *Lancet, 365*, 79–81.

Winnicott, D. W. (1966). *The maturational processes and the facilitating environment*. New York: International Universities Press.

Winnicott, D. W. (1971). *Playing and reality*. New York: Basic Books.

Winterowd, C., Beck, A. T., & Gruener, D. (2003). *Cognitive therapy with chronic pain patients*. New York: Springer.

Wolitzky-Taylor, K. B., Horowitz, J. D., Powers, M. B., & Telch, M. J. (2008). Psychological approaches in the treatment of specific phobias: A meta-analysis. *Clinical Psychology Review, 28*, 1021–1037.

Wolpe, J. (1958). *Psychotherapy by reciprocal inhibition*. Stanford, CA: Stanford University Press.

Wolpe, J. (1989). The derailment of behavior therapy: A tale of conceptual misdirection. *Journal of Behavior Therapy and Experimental Psychiatry, 20*, 3–15.

Wolpe, J. (1990). *The practice of behavior therapy* (4th ed.). Elmsford: NY: Pergamon Press.

Wolpe, J., & Lazarus, A. A. (1966). *Behavior therapy techniques*. New York: Pergamon Press.

Wong, P. T. P., Wong, L. C. J., McDonald, M. J., & Klaassen, D. W. (Eds.). (2007). *The positive psychology of meaning and spirituality*. Abbortsford, BC: INPM Press.

Woody, S. R., Weisz, J., & McLean, C. (2005). Empirically supported treatments: 10 years later. *Clinical Psychologist, 58*, 5–11.

Worthington, E. L., Jr. (2003). *Forgiving and reconciling: Bridges to wholeness and hope*. Downers Grove, IL: InterVarsity.

Worthington, E. L., Jr. (Ed.). (2005a). *Handbook of forgiveness*. New York: Routledge.

Worthington, E. L., Jr. (2005b). *Hope-focused marriage counseling: A guide to brief therapy* (Expanded paperback ed.). Downers Grove, IL: InterVarsity.

Worthington, E. L., Jr. (2006). Trends and needs in Christian counseling research: What you need to know even if you don't plan to conduct research. *Christian Counseling Today, 14* (4), 20–23.

Worthington, E. L., Jr. (2010). *Coming to peace with psychology: What Christians can learn from psychological science*. Downers Grove: IVP Academic.

Worthington, E. L., Jr., & Sandage, S. (2001). Religion and spirituality. *Psychotherapy, 38*, 473–478.

Worthington, E. L., Jr., Hook, J. N., Davis, D. E., & Ripley, J. S. (2008). Empirically supported Christian treatment for counseling. *Christian Counseling Today, 16* (3), 34–36.

Worthington, E. L., Jr., Hook, J. N., Davis, D. E., & McDaniel, M. A. (in press). Religion and spirituality. In J. C. Norcross (Ed.), *Psychotherapy relationships that work* (2nd ed.). New York: Oxford University Press.

Wright, J. H., Thase, M. E., Beck, A. T., & Ludgate, J. W. (Eds.). (1993). *Cognitive therapy with inpatients*. New York: Guilford Press.

Wubbolding, R. E. (1988). *Using reality therapy*. New York: Harper & Row.

Wubbolding, R. E. (1996). Professional issues: The use of questions in reality therapy. *Journal of Reality Therapy, 16*, 122–127.

Wubbolding, R. E. (2000). *Reality therapy for the 21st century*. Philadelphia: Brunner-Routledge.

Wubbolding, R. E. (2007). Reality therapy theory. In D. Capuzzi & R. D. Gross (Eds.), *Counseling and psychotherapy: Theories and interventions* (4th ed., pp. 289–312). Upper Saddle River, NJ: Merrill Prentice-Hall.

Wubbolding, R. E. (2008). Reality therapy. In J. Frew & M. D. Spiegler (Eds.), *Contemporary psychotherapies for a diverse world* (pp. 360–396). Boston: Lahaska Press.

Wubbolding, R. E., Al-Rashidi, B., Brickell, J., Kakitani, M., Kim, R. I., Lennon, B., et al. (1998). Multicultural awareness: Implications for reality therapy and choice theory. *International Journal of Reality Therapy, 17* (2), 4–6.

Wubbolding, R. E., & Brickell, J. (1998). Qualities of the reality therapist. *International Journal of Reality Therapy, 17*, 47–49.

Wubbolding, R. E., & Brickell, J. (2005). Reality therapy in recovery. *Directions in Addiction Treatment and Prevention, 9* (1), 1–10.

Wubbolding, R. E., Brickell, J., Imhof, L., In-Za Kim, R., Lojk, L., & Al-Rashidi, B. (2004). Reality therapy: A global perspective. *International Journal for the Advancement of Counseling, 26*, 219–228.

Wulff, D. (1998). Does the psychology of religion have a future? *Psychology of Religion Newsletter, 23* (4), 1–9.

Yalom, I. D. (1980). *Existential psychotherapy*. New York: Basic Books.

Yalom, I. D. (1989). *Love's executioner: And other tales of psychotherapy*. New York: Basic Books.

Yalom, I. D. (1999). *Momma and the meaning of life: Tales of psychotherapy*. New York: Basic Books.

Yalom, I. D. (2008). *Staring at the sun: Overcoming the terror of death*. San Francisco: Jossey-Bass.

Yalom, I. D., & Leszcz, M. (2005). *The theory and practice of group psychotherapy* (5th ed.). New York: Basic Books.

Yang, H. (1996). *Cross-cultural counseling: A Christ centered approach and application*. Cleveland, TN: Pathway.

Yankura, J., and Dryden, W. (1994). *Albert Ellis*. Thousand Oaks, CA: Sage.

Yarhouse, M. A., & Sells, J. N. (2008). *Family therapies: A comprehensive Christian appraisal*. Downers Grove, IL: IVP Academic.

Yarhouse, M. A., Butman, R. E., & McRay, B. W. (2005). *Modern psychopathologies: A comprehensive Christian appraisal*. Downers Grove, IL: InterVarsity.

Yontef, G., & Jacobs, L. (2008). Gestalt therapy. In R. J. Corsini & D. Wedding (Eds.), *Current psychotherapies* (8th ed., pp. 328–367). Belmont, CA: Brooks/Cole.

Young, J. (1982). The morality of reality therapy. *Journal of Reality Therapy, 1*, 8–11.

Young, J. E. (2002). *Schema therapy for borderline personality disorder: Conceptual model and overview*. New York: Guilford Press.

Young, J. E., Klosko, J. S., & Weishaar, M. E. (2003). *Schema therapy: A practitioner's guide*. New York: Guilford Press.

Zinbarg, R. E., & Griffith, J. W. (2008). Behavior therapy. In J. L. Lebow (Ed.), *Twenty-first century psychotherapies: Contemporary approaches to theory and practice* (pp. 8–42). Hoboken, NJ: Wiley.

Zinker, J. (1978). *Creative process in Gestalt therapy*. New York: Random House (Vintage).

Zinnbauer, B. J., & Pargament, K. I. (2005). Religiousness and spirituality. In R. F. Paloutzian & C. L. Park (Eds.), *Handbook of the psychology of religion and spirituality* (pp. 21–42). New York: Guilford Press.

Zur, O. (2007). *Boundaries in psychotherapy: Ethical and clinical explorations*. Washington, DC: American Psychological Association.

Name Index

473

Subject Index

About the Author

Siang-Yang Tan served as director of the PsyD (Doctor of Psychology) program in clinical psychology (1989–97) and is now professor of psychology in the Graduate School of Psychology at Fuller Theological Seminary in Pasadena, California. He is a licensed psychologist with a PhD in clinical psychology from McGill University and a Fellow of the American Psychological Association (APA). He has published articles on lay counseling and lay counselor training, intrapersonal integration and spirituality, religious psychotherapy, the use of spiritual disciplines in counseling and clinical supervision, cognitive behavior therapy, epilepsy, pain, and cross-cultural counseling with Asians and Hispanics, as well as several books, including *Lay Counseling: Equipping Christians for a Helping Ministry* (Zondervan, 1991), *Managing Chronic Pain* (InterVarsity, 1996), *Disciplines of the Holy Spirit* (with Douglas Gregg, Zondervan, 1997), *Rest: Experiencing God's Peace in a Restless World* (Regent College, 2003), *Exercises for Effective Counseling and Psychotherapy* (2nd ed., with Les Parrott III, Brooks/Cole, 2003), *Coping with Depression* (rev. ed., with John Ortberg, Baker Books, 2004), and *Full Service: Moving from Self-Serve Christianity to Total Servanthood* (Baker Books, 2006). He has received several awards, including the Distinguished Member Award from the Christian Association for Psychological Studies International, the Gary R. Collins Award for Excellence in Christian Counseling from the American Association of Christian Counselors, and the William Bier Award for outstanding and sustained contributions from Division 36 (Psychology of Religion) of APA. He is associate editor of the *Journal of Psychology and Christianity* and serves or has served on the editorial boards of the *Journal of Consulting and Clinical Psychology, Professional Psychology: Research and Practice, Journal of Psychology and Theology,* and *Journal of Spiritual Formation and Soul Care.* He was president of Division 36 (Psychology of Religion) of APA (1998–99). He also serves as senior pastor of First Evangelical Church Glendale in Glendale, California. Originally from Singapore, he now lives in Arcadia, California, with his wife, Angela. They have two grown children, Carolyn and Andrew.